Table of Contents

Acknowledgments

The Emergency Nurses Association (ENA) would like to extend its appreciation to the 2009–2012 ENPC Revision Work Group for the revision and implementation of the fourth edition of the *Emergency Nursing Pediatric Course.*

Nancy Denke, MSN, RN, FNP-C, ACNP-BC, FAEN, Chair
Trauma Nurse Practitioner
Scottsdale Healthcare Osborn-Trauma Department
Scottsdale, Arizona

Paul C. Boackle, BSN, RN, CCRN, CEN, CFRN, CPEN, CTRN
Flight Nurse
University of Mississippi Medical Center AirCare
Jackson, Mississippi

Angela M. Bowen, BSN, RN, CPEN, NREMT-P
Regional Coordinator, Emergency Medical Services for Children/
    Trauma Coordinator
East Tennessee Children's Hospital
Knoxville, Tennessee

Cam Brandt, MS, RN, CEN, CPEN, CPN
Education Coordinator, Emergency Services
Cook Children's Health Care System
Fort Worth, Texas

Julie L. Miller, RN, CEN
Emergency Services Supervisor
Mercy Regional Health Center
Manhattan, Kansas

Dianne Molsberry, MA, RN
Pediatric Outreach & PALS Coordinator, Professional Outreach
    Education
Providence Sacred Heart Medical Center & Children's Hospital
Spokane, Washington

Contributing Authors

Ruth C. Bindler, PhD, RNC
Professor, Director of PhD in Nursing Program
Washington State University College of Nursing
Spokane, Washington
Chapter 8

Angela Black, MSN, RN, CPN
Manager of Pediatrics, PICU, and Outpatient Pediatrics
Central DuPage Hospital
Winfield, Illinois
Chapter 20

Paul C. Boackle, BSN, RN, CCRN, CEN, CFRN, CPEN, CTRN
Flight Nurse
University of Mississippi Medical Center AirCare
Jackson, Mississippi
Chapter 23

Angela M. Bowen, BSN, RN, CPEN, NREMT-P
Regional Coordinator, Emergency Medical Services for
Children/Trauma Coordinator
East Tennessee Children's Hospital
Knoxville, Tennessee
Chapter 9

Cam Brandt, MS, RN, CEN, CPEN, CPN
Education Coordinator, Emergency Services
Cook Children's Health Care System
Fort Worth, Texas
Chapter 14

Maria do Céu Machado, PhD
High Commissioner for Health
Office of the High Commissioner for Health
Lisbon, Portugal
Chapter 2

Liz Cloughessy, AM, MHM, RN, FAEN
Executive Director
Australian College of Emergency Nursing Ltd
Sydney, Australia
Chapter 2

Alice Conway, PhD, CRNP, FNP-BC
Professor (retired)
Edinboro University of Pennsylvania
Edinboro, Pennsylvania
Chapter 3

Christy L. Cooper, MSN, RN, CEN, CPEN, NREMT-P
Emergency Department Nurse Manager
East Tennessee Children's Hospital
Knoxville, Tennessee
Chapter 7

Luísa Couceiro, MSc
Coordinator of the Information and Research Department
Office of the High Commissioner for Health
Lisbon, Portugal
Chapter 2

Nancy Denke, MSN, RN, FNP-C, ACNP-BC, FAEN
Trauma Nurse Practitioner
Scottsdale Healthcare Osborn-Trauma Department
Scottsdale, Arizona
Chapter 16

Margaret M. Dymond, BSN, RN
Clinical Nurse Educator, Emergency Department
University of Alberta Hospital
Edmonton, Alberta, Canada
Chapter 2

Kathleen Flarity, PhD, ARNP, CEN, CFRN, FAEN
Commander
34th Aeromedical Evacuation Squadron
Peterson Air Force Base, Colorado
Emergency Clinical Nurse Specialist
Memorial Hospital
Colorado Springs, Colorado
Chapter 19

Julie L. Gerberick, MS, RN, CEN
Emergency Department Education Nurse Specialist
Nationwide Children's Hospital
Columbus, Ohio
Chapter 13

Janelle Glasgow, RNC, CPEN
Trauma Nurse Leader
Nationwide Children's Hospital
Columbus, Ohio
Chapter 13

David Golder, BS, RN, CEN, CPEN
Clinical Manager of Trauma Service
Dell Children's Medical Center of Central Texas
Austin, Texas
Chapter 11

Beverly G. Hart, PhD, RN, PMHNP-BC
Professor, Baccalaureate and Graduate Nursing
Eastern Kentucky University
Richmond, Kentucky
Chapter 18

Susan M. Hohenhaus, MA, RN, CEN, FAEN
Executive Director
Emergency Nurses Association and ENA Foundation
Des Plaines, Illinois
Chapter 4

Patricia Kunz Howard, PhD, RN, CEN, CPEN, NE-BC, FAEN
Operations Manager, Emergency and Trauma Services
University of Kentucky Chandler Medical Center
Lexington, Kentucky
Chapter 10

Justin J. Milici, MSN, RN, CCRN, CEN, CFRN, TNS
Education Specialist, Emergency Department
Methodist Health System
Dallas, Texas
Chapter 21

DonnaMarie Miller, BSN, RN, CEN
Senior Professional Staff
Children's Hospital of Pittsburgh of UPMC
Pittsburgh, Pennsylvania
Chapter 6

Tracy Ann Pasek, MSN, RN, CCNS, CCRN, CIMI
Advanced Practice Nurse, Pain/Pediatric Intensive Care Unit
Children's Hospital of Pittsburgh of UPMC
Pittsburgh, Pennsylvania
Chapter 6

Sharon Payne, MSN, NP
Emergency Department
Hawkes Bay Hospital
Hastings, New Zealand
Chapter 2

Mary Puchalski, MS, RNC-NIC, APN, CNS, NNP-BC
Neonatal Nurse Practitioner, Instructor
Rush University Medical Center
Chicago, Illinois
Chapter 12

Nancy C. Smith, RN
Staff Nurse
Children's Hospital of Pittsburgh of UPMC
Pittsburgh, Pennsylvania
Chapter 6

Sally K. Snow, BSN, RN, CPEN, FAEN
Trauma Program Director
Cook Children's Medical Center
Fort Worth, Texas
Chapter 5

Rose Ann Gould Soloway, MSEd, BSN, RN, DABAT
Clinical Toxicologist
National Capital Poison Center
Washington, District of Columbia
Chapter 17

Nancy G. Stevens, MS, MSN, RN, APRN-BC, CEN, FAEN
Clinical Educator, Family Nurse Practitioner
Erlanger Health Systems
Chattanooga, Tennessee
Chapter 9

Tiffiny Strever, BSN, RN, CEN
Injury Prevention/Outreach Coordinator
Maricopa Integrated Health System
Phoenix, Arizona
Chapter 2

Lori A. Upton, MS, BSN, RN, CEM
Assistant Director, Emergency Management
Texas Children's Hospital
Houston, Texas
Chapter 22

Darleen A. Williams, MSN, RN, CEN, CCNS, EMT-P
Clinical Nurse Specialist for Emergency Services
Orlando Regional Medical Center
Orlando, Florida
Chapter 15

Kathy Woloshyn, BSN, RN
Nurse Educator
Children's Emergency Health Sciences Centre
Winnipeg, Manitoba, Canada
Chapter 6

ENA Board Liaisons

Deena Brecher, MSN, RN, APRN, CEN, CPEN
Clinical Nurse Specialist – Emergency/Trauma/Transport
Nemours/A. I. DuPont Hospital for Children
Wilmington, Delaware

Tiffiny Strever, BSN, RN, CEN
Injury Prevention/Outreach Coordinator
Maricopa Integrated Health System
Phoenix, Arizona

ENA Staff

Betty Mortensen, MS, BSN, RN, FACHE
Chief Nursing Officer
Emergency Nurses Association
Des Plaines, Illinois

Marlene Bokholdt, MS, RN, CPEN, CCRN
Nurse Education Editor
Emergency Nurses Association
Des Plaines, Illinois

Renée Herrmann, MA
Copy Editor
Emergency Nurses Association
Des Plaines, Illinois

Curriculum Consultant

Vicki C. Patrick, MS, RN, ACNP-BC, CEN, FAEN
Clinical Instructor/Lead Teacher
University of Texas Arlington College of Nursing
Arlington, Texas

Content Reviewers

Jason T. Nagle, RN, CEN, CPN, CPEN, FNE, EMT
Charge Nurse
Brenner Children's Emergency Department
Wake Forest Baptist Medical Center
Winston-Salem, North Carolina

Anne Renaker, DNP, RN, CNS-BC
University of Minnesota Amplatz Children's Hospital
Emergency Department
Minneapolis, Minnesota

Sally K. Snow, BSN, RN, CPEN, FAEN
Trauma Program Director
Cook Children's Medical Center
Fort Worth, Texas

Flora Tomoyasu, RN, MSN, CNS
Clinical Nurse Educator, Emergency Services
Saddleback Memorial Medical Center
San Clemente, California

Michael Vicioso, MSN, BS, RN, CPEN, CCRN
Pediatric Manager
St. Joseph Hospital
Orange, California

A special thanks to the following work group members, who made previous editions of ENPC possible.

2002–2004 ENPC Revision Work Group

Harriet Hawkins, RN, CCRN (Chair)
Beth N. Bolick, MS, RN, PCCCNP, CCRN
Nancy Denke, MSN, RN, FNP-C
Cindy Garlesky, MSN, ARNP, CEN
Pamela Williams, RN, CPN, CEN, CLNC
Kathy Woloshyn, BSN, RN

1998 Task Force

Pam Baker, BSN, RN, CCRN, CEN
Nancy Eckle, MSN, RN, CEN, CNS
Kathy Haley, BSN, RN, CEN
Harriet Hawkins, RN, CCRN
Beth Nachtsheim, MS, RN, PCCNP
Reneé Semonin-Holleran, PhD, RN, CEN, CCRN, CFRN

1992 Task Force

Lisa Bernardo, MSN, PhD, RN
Jan Fredrickson, MSN, RN, CPNP
Janice Rogers, MS, RN, CS
Reneé Semonin-Holleran, PhD, RN, CEN, CCRN, CFRN
Donna Thomas, MSN, RN, CEN
Pam Baker, BSN, RN, CCRN, CEN

While trauma is the leading cause of death in children, acute illness is also a source of unnecessary pediatric death. Emergency care visits by infants, children, and adolescents account for more than 31 million emergency department visits each year. It is estimated that one pediatric patient per second seeks care in the United States. The majority of children seeking care are seen in general emergency departments. Fortunately, severe, life-threatening illness is still relatively infrequent. However, to lessen the morbidity and mortality of children, emergency nurses must be knowledgeable about preventative strategies for injury and disease, as well as triage assessment and categories, nursing assessment, and the appropriate interventions for children requiring emergency care.

In response to requests by ENA's membership for a greater focus on the pediatric patient, the ENA Pediatric Committee was formed in 1991. One of the charges of this new committee was to assess the need for a pediatric emergency nursing course. A needs assessment done at the 1991 ENA Scientific Assembly overwhelmingly supported the need for such a course.

The first *Emergency Nursing Pediatric Course (ENPC)* was published in 1993 with the first revision completed in 1998. This fourth edition continues in the same tradition, which is to improve the care of the pediatric patient in the emergency care setting and to increase the skill and confidence of emergency nurses who care for children worldwide. First, you will notice the use of *pediatric patient* throughout the manual. This term better reflects the age continuum of the pediatric population from infants to toddlers to adolescents.

Next, many changes have been made in this revision to ensure that it reflects current pediatric emergency care. We have standardized the use of the term *caregiver,* to reflect the population and the ever-changing nature of what defines a family. New chapters, including **"Chapter 13, The Adolescent," "Chapter 19, Environmental Emergencies,"** and **"Chapter 22, Disaster,"** have been added as well. The former triage chapter is now called **"Chapter 4, Prioritization: Focused Assessment, Triage, and Decision Making"** to reflect the role emergency nurses play in establishing a plan of care for pediatric patients.

In addition, ENA has been working with other organizations who also offer pediatric life support education, such as the American Academy of Pediatrics and the American Heart Association, to ensure continuity of terms (i.e., spinal stabilization versus spinal immobilization), and information across these courses (i.e., definitions of *respiratory distress* and *failure*).

Lastly, ENPC continues to grow internationally. ENPC is offered in Australia, Canada, Sweden, The Netherlands, and Portugal.

ENPC represents the hard work, collaboration, and dedication of many people and continues to receive overwhelming support nationally and internationally.

Chapter 1 | Introduction:
Preparing for Pediatric Emergencies

It's a busy Saturday night. You scan the waiting room and notice a child in his caregiver's arms. Something about the child just doesn't look right. Is it his skin color? Is it the way he's breathing? His caregiver looks anxious. You immediately take them back to the resuscitation room. Suddenly, the child becomes obtunded. You call for help. The team arrives as you start your assessment. Do you see confidence among your team members? Do you have the right equipment? Do you have the right size equipment? Do you know the appropriate medications and correct doses? Do you and your team have the knowledge and experience to successfully resuscitate this child?

Introduction

Frequently, caregivers who bring their children to the emergency department (ED) experience anxiety as to whether their child "will live" or "will be alright." Emergency nurses perform a pivotal role in all phases of pediatric emergency care to try to answer these simple questions. They are aware that children respond differently to illness or injury and have different physical, emotional, and psychological needs than adults.

A study of 1,500 EDs in the United States, published in 2007, indicated that 89% of pediatric ED visits occur in non-children's hospitals.[1] Twenty-six percent of these visits occur in rural or remote facilities. Most (75%) of the hospital respondents reported seeing over 7,000 pediatric patients annually; however, only 6% of the EDs surveyed reported having all of the pediatric equipment and supplies recommended by the American Academy of Pediatrics (AAP) and the American College of Emergency Physicians (ACEP) (see **Appendix 1-A**).[1] Half of the ED directors and managers responding to the survey were not aware of the AAP and ACEP guidelines.[1]

The National Hospital Ambulatory Medical Care Survey reported that in 2006, there were approximately 3,833 EDs in the United States, most of which cared for patients of all ages. Of the 119 million ED visits in the United States in 2006, almost 20% were for children.[2,3]

In 2006, the Institute of Medicine described the care of pediatric patients in our EDs as uneven, noting that pediatric care among rural, community, and regional pediatric centers lacked consistency.[4] In 2009, the AAP, ACEP, and the Emergency Nurses Association (ENA) published a joint policy statement, which delineated guidelines and the resources necessary to prepare hospital EDs to serve pediatric patients.[5] A survey is in development for distribution in early 2012 to reassess for improvement in ED preparedness following the release of the 2009 joint policy statement.

ENA has a strong stance on the care of children in the ED setting and a commitment to educate emergency nurses on the *Guidelines for Care of Children in The Emergency Department* (see **Appendix 1-A**). The goal is to improve and establish consistencies among caregivers, facilities, and regions in how we care for children. With that in mind, this chapter presents a few key strategies that can be employed to help improve the consistency of care at your facility.

History of Pediatric Emergency Care

Pediatric emergency care is a relatively new emergency care paradigm in the history of emergency services. The establishment of pediatric trauma centers, pediatric-focused training, and pediatric-focused professional societies and divisions of professional societies began in the 1970s.[6] In 1984 the federal Emergency Medical Services for Children (EMSC) program was established. The first pediatric emergency care textbook was published in 1983, and the first journal devoted to pediatric emergency care was launched in 1985. In 1988, the American Heart Association (AHA) and the AAP initiated the Pediatric

Advanced Life Support (PALS) course, with the Advanced PALS course published in 1989.

The Emergency Nursing Pediatric Course (ENPC) was developed in the 1990s. In 2008, collaboration between the Pediatric Nurse Certification Board (PNCB) and the Board of Certification for Emergency Nurses (BCEN) established the Certified Pediatric Emergency Nurse (CPEN) exam. Earning a CPEN credential demonstrates that a nurse has extensive experience and the necessary knowledge and skills to provide pediatric emergency nursing care beyond basic registered nurse licensure.

How to Prepare My ED to Care for Pediatric Patients

In the *Guidelines for Care of Children in the Emergency Department*, specific recommendations are described to help the institution, department and individual prepare for pediatric emergencies.[5] A checklist, based on these recommendations, was developed to help EDs determine their ability to effectively care for pediatric patients. **Appendix 1-A** provides this resource to help you assess whether or not your ED is prepared for pediatric patients.

The ENA/AAP/ACEP joint guidelines point to the establishment of a pediatric nurse coordinator as a key element for preparing your department for pediatric emergencies. A pediatric nurse coordinator should:

- Be a registered nurse with special interest, knowledge, and skill in the emergency nursing care of children. ENA defines the standards of care for emergency nursing and the National Association of Pediatric Nurse Practice and the Society of Pediatric Nurses define the scope and standards of pediatric nursing practice.

- Complete the ENPC verification as well as attain CPEN certification, demonstrating an expertise in pediatric emergency nursing care. **Box 1-1** provides a list of ENA's resources related to standards for training, skills, and experience needed for appropriate pediatric care.

- Pursue increased knowledge and understanding for current, evidence-based practice in continuing education related to the emergency nursing care of children.

- Be recognized by the hospital to care for ill or injured children.

In addition to attaining proper credentials and knowledge, the pediatric nursing coordinator should take on the following management and educational roles:

- Serve as a liaison to in-hospital and out-of-hospital committees. Liaison relationships are important with in-hospital units, regional referral hospitals, trauma centers, and emergency medical service agencies. Primary care providers in the community should be considered a valuable resource for integrating services across the continuum of care for the pediatric patient.

- Assure that pediatric-specific elements are included in the orientation of new staff, as well as initial and ongoing competency evaluations for all staff. ENA offers an online emergency nursing orientation program that includes age-specific elements. In addition, the Emergency Nursing Triage Program includes triage considerations for the pediatric patient.

Emergency departments should develop policies and procedures for the care of pediatric patients including, but not limited to, triage; assessment and reassessment of the pediatric patient; vital signs and interventions when assessment data are not within expected parameters; caring for the victim of child maltreatment; and caring for the family during the death of a child in the ED. Emergency nurses should also serve as champions for family-centered pediatric care in their organizations and communities.

Box 1-1 ENA's Resources for Pediatric Training, Skills, and Experience

Pediatric-Specific Position Statements

Joint Policy Statement—Guidelines for Care of Children in the Emergency Department: http://aappolicy.aappublications.org/cgi/reprint/pediatrics;124/4/1233.pdf

Pediatric Procedural Pain Management: http://www.ena.org/SiteCollectionDocuments/Position%20Statements/PediatricProceduralPainManagement.pdf

Prevention and Treatment of Burns in the Pediatric Population (retired): http://www.ena.org/about/position/archive/Documents/Pediatric_Burns_-_ENA_PS.pdf

General Scopes and Standards and Advanced Practice Resources

Emergency Nurses Association. (2011). *Emergency nursing scope and standards of practice* (2011 ed.). Des Plaines, IL: Author.

Resources for Advance Practice Nursing: http://www.ena.org/IQSIP/NursingPractice/advanced/Pages/Default.aspx

---

The Role of the Emergency Nurse in Pediatric Emergencies

The emergency nurse is confronted with multiple competing priorities. Pediatric patients often present with subtle symptoms, and the ability to recognize changes from what is normal is crucial in the assessment of a pediatric patient. Managing sick children can be challenging, requiring the nurse to have a variety of resources. Children are usually accompanied by adult caregivers. Using the principles of patient- and family-centered care helps the nurse understand how and why family dynamics play a role in achieving and maintaining wellness. Pediatric emergency nurses are comfortable with including family in the care of the child. ENPC gives you the basic tools to supplement your knowledge base of how to provide teaching and promote health and safety strategies to families through the knowledge and experience gained from practicing pediatric emergency nursing in the real world.

The Emergency Nursing Pediatric Course

Purpose

ENPC was developed to educate participants how to recognize the ill or injured child and identify significant and sometimes subtle changes in the less acutely ill child. The course teaches many aspects of pediatric emergency nursing, including pediatric trauma and resuscitation. ENPC's psychomotor skill stations facilitate initial integration of these skills in a setting that simulates pediatric patient situations. It is the intent of the course to enhance the provider's ability to rapidly and accurately assess the pediatric patient. The ultimate goal of the course is to improve the care of the pediatric patient by increasing the knowledge, skill, and confidence of emergency nurses.

ENPC is the first course of its kind offered on an international level and is the only pediatric emergency nursing course written by pediatric nurse experts. It is also the only course that carries the endorsement of a major nursing specialty organization with the purpose of providing a consistent and standardized knowledge base and approach among nurses caring for the pediatric patient.

ENPC incorporates adult learning theory in the development of the curriculum and course content. Utilizing a combination of classroom lecture type format in conjunction with hands on scenario-based training, ENPC utilizes many different learning styles, including visual, auditory, and kinesthetic.

This varied approach promotes critical thinking and an organized approach to care and supports the nursing process. Learning is a continuum (i.e., a dynamic process), and it is intended that the *ENPC Provider Manual* will be a reference not only for the course but for future care of pediatric patients.

Changes to the Emergency Nursing Pediatric Course

To help healthcare providers recognize that the care of children starts at birth and extends through adolescence, the term *pediatric patient* has been used instead of child or children, when appropriate.

The concept of what makes up a family has evolved and continues to evolve. Therefore, the ENPC Work Team has decided to refer to responsible caregiver as *caregivers* to help healthcare providers recognize this changing dynamic.

For the chapters that cover the body systems, they begin with general assessment, history, and interventions based on the system involved. Then specific illnesses and injuries are discussed with additional assessment, history, and interventions indicated for the specific disorder. New chapters have been added to this revision. The first is **Chapter 13, "The Adolescent."** Adolescents are a unique population who establish patterns of behavior and make lifestyle choices that affect both their current and future health. Understanding this population will allow the emergency nurse to have the most positive impact on their health. **Chapter 19, "Environmental Emergencies,"** includes information extrapolated from the former edition's toxicology chapter in order to help the emergency nurse better understand how these factors affect the pediatric population. As disaster management has come to the forefront of emergency care, we have included **Chapter 22, "Disaster,"** to help explain how this pertains to the pediatric population.

The former triage chapter has been reworked into **Chapter 4, "Prioritization: Focused Assessment, Triage, and Decision Making"** and has been organized to direct students to consider what could go wrong for their patient and to develop an appropriate plan of action as indicated by the patient healthcare problem. Being able to identify and anticipate potential problems and then intervene to correct these problems demonstrates the development of critical thinking, which is an outcome we anticipate developing in this interactive course. This chapter no longer includes a diagnostic testing station.

Finally, information regarding children with special needs has been incorporated into each chapter rather than in a stand-alone chapter.

Summary

The delivery of emergency care to the pediatric patient requires specialized knowledge, training, equipment, and planning. ENA believes that the knowledge and psychomotor skills identified in the ENPC will assist participants to systematically assess the pediatric patient and to intervene in a manner that will improve the care and safety of all pediatric patients. Together, nurses can make an environment of care in our EDs conducive to a better approach and be better prepared to save lives.

References

1. Gausche-Hill, M., Schmitz, C., & Lewis, R.J. (2009) Pediatric preparedness of United States emergency departments: A 2003 survey. *Pediatrics, 120*(6), 1229–1237

2. McCaig, L. F., & Nawar, E. W. (2006). National Hospital Ambulatory Medical Care Survey: 2004 emergency department summary. *Advance Data, (372)*, 1–29.

3. Middleton, K. R., & Burt, C. W. (2006). Availability of pediatric services and equipment in emergency departments: United States, 2002–2003. *Advance Data,* (367), 1–16.

4. Institute of Medicine; Committee of the Future of Emergency Care in the United States Health System. (2006). *Emergency care for children: Growing pains.* Washington, DC: National Academies Press.

5. American Academy of Pediatrics, Committee on Pediatric Emergency Medicine, American College of Emergency Physicians, Pediatric Committee, & Emergency Nurses Association Pediatric Committee. (2009). Joint policy statement—Guidelines for care of children in the emergency department. *Pediatrics, 124*(4), 1233–1243.

6. Committee on Pediatric Emergency Medical Services. (1993). *Emergency medical services for children.* Washington, DC: National Academies Press.

CHECKLIST

Guidelines for Care of Children in the Emergency Department

This checklist is based on the American Academy of Pediatrics (AAP), American College of Emergency Physicians (ACEP), and Emergency Nurses Association (ENA) 2009 joint policy statement "Guidelines for Care of Children in the Emergency Department," which can be found online at http://aappolicy.aappublications.org/cgi/reprint/pediatrics;124/4/1233.pdf. Use the checklist to determine if your emergency department (ED) is prepared to care for children.

Administration and Coordination of the ED for the Care of Children

○ *Physician Coordinator for Pediatric Emergency Care.* The pediatric physician coordinator is a specialist in emergency medicine or pediatric emergency medicine; or if these specialties are not available then pediatrics or family medicine, appointed by the ED medical director, who through training, clinical experience, or focused continuing medical education demonstrates competence in the care of children in emergency settings, including resuscitation.

○ *Nursing Coordinator for Pediatric Emergency Care.* The pediatric nurse coordinator is a registered nurse (RN), appointed by the ED nursing director, who possesses special interest, knowledge, and skill in the emergency care of children.

Physicians, Nurses and Other Healthcare Providers Who Staff the ED

○ Physicians who staff the ED have the necessary skill, knowledge, and training in the emergency evaluation and treatment of children of all ages who may be brought to the ED, consistent with the services provided by the hospital.

○ Nurses and other ED health care providers have the necessary skill, knowledge, and training in providing emergency care to children of all ages who may be brought to the ED, consistent with the services offered by the hospital.

○ Baseline and periodic competency evaluations completed for all ED clinical staff, including physicians, are age specific and include evaluation of skills related to neonates, infants, children, adolescents, and children with special health care needs. (Competencies are determined by each institution's medical and nursing staff privileges policy.)

Guidelines for QI/PI in the ED

○ The QI/PI plan shall include pediatric specific indicators.

○ The pediatric patient care-review process is integrated into the ED QI/PI plan. Components of the process interface with out-of-hospital, ED, trauma, inpatient pediatric, pediatric critical care, and hospital-wide QI or PI activities.

Guidelines for Improving Pediatric Patient Safety

The delivery of pediatric care should reflect an awareness of unique pediatric patient safety concerns and are included in the following policies or practices:

○ Children are weighed in kilograms.

○ Weights are recorded in a prominent place on the medical record.

○ For children who are not weighed, a standard method for estimating weight in kilograms is used (e.g., a length-based system).

○ Infants and children have a full set of vital signs recorded (temperature, heart rate, respiratory rate) in medical record.

○ Blood pressure and pulse oximetry monitoring are available for children of all ages on the basis of illness and injury severity.

○ A process for identifying age-specific abnormal vital signs and notifying the physician of these is present.

○ Processes in place for safe medication storage, prescribing, and delivery that includes precalculated dosing guidelines for children of all ages.

○ Infection-control practices, including hand hygiene and use of personal protective equipment, are implemented and monitored.

○ Pediatric emergency services are culturally and linguistically appropriate.

○ ED environment is safe for children and supports patient- and family-centered care.

○ Patient identification policies meet Joint Commission standards.

○ Policies for the timely reporting and evaluation of patient safety events, medical errors, and unanticipated outcomes are implemented and monitored.

Guidelines for ED Policies, Procedures, and Protocols

Policies, procedures, and protocols for the emergency care of children should be developed and implemented in the areas listed below. These policies may be integrated into overall ED policies as long as pediatric specific issues are addressed.

○ Illness and injury triage.

○ Pediatric patient assessment and reassessment.

Produced by the AAP, ACEP, ENA, the EMSC National Resource Center, and Children's National Medical Center 1

Guidelines for ED Policies, Procedures, and Protocols, Cont.

○ Documentation of pediatric vital signs and actions to be taken for abnormal vital signs.
○ Immunization assessment and management of the under-immunized patient.
○ Sedation and analgesia, including medical imaging.
○ Consent, including when parent or legal guardian is not immediately available.
○ Social and mental health issues.
○ Physical or chemical restraint of patients.
○ Child maltreatment and domestic violence reporting criteria, requirements, and processes.
○ Death of the child in the ED.
○ Do not resuscitate (DNR) orders.
○ Family-centered care:
  ○ Family involvement in patient decision-making and medication safety processes;
  ○ Family presence during all aspects of emergency care;
  ○ Patient, family, and caregiver education;
  ○ Discharge planning and instruction; and
  ○ Bereavement counseling.
○ Communication with the patient's medical home or primary care provider.
○ Medical imaging, specfically policies that address pediatric age- or weight-based appropriate dosing for studies that impart radiation consistent with ALARA (as low as reasonably achievable) principles.

Policies, Procedures, and Protocols for All-Hazard Disaster Preparedness

Policies, procedures, and protocols should also be developed and implemented for all-hazard disaster-preparedness. The plan should address the following preparedness issues:

○ Availability of medications, vaccines, equipment, and trained providers for children.
○ Pediatric surge capacity for injured and non-injured children.
○ Decontamination, isolation, and quarantine of families and children.
○ Minimization of parent-child separation (includes pediatric patient tracking and timely reunification of separated children with their family).
○ Access to specific medical and mental health therapies, and social services for children.
○ Disaster drills which include a pediatric mass casualty incident drill every two years.
○ Care of children with special healthcare needs.
○ Evacuation of pediatric units and pediatric subspecialty units.

Policies, Procedures, and Protocols for Patient Transfers

○ Written pediatric inter-facility transfer procedures should be established.

Guidelines for ED Support Services

Radiology capability must meet the needs of the children in the community served. Specifically:

○ A process for referring children to appropriate facilities for radiological procedures that exceed the capability of the hospital is established.
○ A process for timely review, interpretation, and reporting of medical imaging by a qualified radiologist is established.

Laboratory capability must meet the needs of the children in the community served, including techniques for small sample sizes. Specifically:

○ A process for referring children or their specimens to appropriate facilities for laboratory studies that exceed the capability of the hospital is established.

Guidelines for Equipment, Supplies, and Medications for the Care of Pediatric Patients in the ED

○ Pediatric equipment, supplies, and medications are appropriate for children of all ages and sizes (see list below), and are easily accessible, clearly labeled, and logically organized.
○ ED staff is educated on the location of all items.
○ Daily method in place to verify the proper location and function of equipment and supplies.
○ Medication chart, length-based tape, medical software, or other systems is readily available to ensure proper sizing of resuscitation equipment and proper dosing of medications.

Medications

○ atropine
○ adenosine
○ amiodarone
○ antiemetic agents
○ calcium chloride
○ dextrose (D10W, D50W)
○ epinephrine (1:1000; 1:10 000 solutions)
○ lidocaine
○ magnesium sulfate
○ naloxone hydrochloride
○ procainamide
○ sodium bicarbonate (4.2%, 8.4%)
○ topical, oral, and parenteral analgesics
○ antimicrobial agents (parenteral and oral)
○ anticonvulsant medications
○ antidotes (common antidotes should be accessible to the ED)
○ antipyretic drugs
○ bronchodilators
○ corticosteroids
○ inotropic agents
○ neuromuscular blockers
○ sedatives
○ vaccines
○ vasopressor agents

Equipment/Supplies: General Equipment

- ○ patient warming device
- ○ intravenous blood/fluid warmer
- ○ restraint device
- ○ weight scale in kilograms (not pounds)
- ○ tool or chart that incorporates weight (in kilograms) and length to determine equipment size and correct drug dosing
- ○ age appropriate pain scale-assessment tools

Equipment/Supplies: Monitoring Equipment

- blood pressure cuffs
  - ○ neonatal
  - ○ infant
  - ○ child
  - ○ adult-arm
  - ○ adult-thigh
- ○ doppler ultrasonography devices
- ○ electrocardiography monitor/defibrillator with pediatric and adult capabilities including pads/paddles
- ○ hypothermia thermometer
- ○ pulse oximeter with pediatric and adult probes
- ○ continuous end-tidal CO_2 monitoring device

Equipment/Supplies: Vascular Access

- arm boards
  - ○ infant
  - ○ child
  - ○ adult
- catheter-over-the-needle device
  - ○ 14 gauge
  - ○ 16 gauge
  - ○ 18 gauge
  - ○ 20 gauge
  - ○ 22 gauge
  - ○ 24 gauge
- intraosseous needles or device
  - ○ pediatric
  - ○ adult
- ○ IV administration sets with calibrated chambers and extension tubing and/or infusion devices with ability to regulate rate and volume of infusate
- umbilical vein catheters
  - ○ 3.5F
  - ○ 5.0F
- central venous catheters (any two sizes)
  - ○ 4.0F
  - ○ 5.0F
  - ○ 6.0F
  - ○ 7.0F
- intravenous solutions
  - ○ normal saline
  - ○ dextrose 5% in normal saline
  - ○ dextrose 10% in water

Equipment/Supplies: Fracture-Management Devices

- extremity splints
  - ○ femur splints, pediatric sizes
  - ○ femur splints, adult sizes
- ○ spine-stabilization devices appropriate for children of all ages

Equipment/Supplies: Respiratory

- endotracheal tubes
  - ○ uncuffed 2.5 mm
  - ○ uncuffed 3.0 mm
  - ○ cuffed or uncuffed 3.5 mm
  - ○ cuffed or uncuffed 4.0 mm
  - ○ cuffed or uncuffed 4.5 mm
  - ○ cuffed or uncuffed 5.0 mm
  - ○ cuffed or uncuffed 5.5 mm
  - ○ cuffed 6.0 mm
  - ○ cuffed 6.5 mm
  - ○ cuffed 7.0 mm
  - ○ cuffed 7.5 mm
  - ○ cuffed 8.0 mm
- feeding tubes
  - ○ 5F
  - ○ 8F
- laryngoscope blades
  - ○ straight: 0
  - ○ straight: 1
  - ○ straight: 2
  - ○ straight: 3
  - ○ curved: 2
  - ○ curved: 3
- ○ laryngoscope handle
- magill forceps
  - ○ pediatric
  - ○ adult
- nasopharyngeal airways
  - ○ infant
  - ○ child
  - ○ adult
- oropharyngeal airways
  - ○ size 0
  - ○ size 1
  - ○ size 2
  - ○ size 3
  - ○ size 4
  - ○ size 5
- stylets for endotracheal tubes
  - ○ pediatric
  - ○ adult
- suction catheters
  - ○ infant
  - ○ child
  - ○ adult
- tracheostomy tubes
  - ○ 2.5 mm
  - ○ 3.0 mm
  - ○ 3.5 mm
  - ○ 4.0 mm
  - ○ 4.5 mm
  - ○ 5.0 mm
  - ○ 5.5 mm
- ○ yankauer suction tip
- bag-mask device, self inflating
  - ○ infant: 450 ml
  - ○ adult: 1000 ml
- masks to fit bag-mask device adaptor
  - ○ neonatal
  - ○ infant
  - ○ child
  - ○ adult

Produced by the AAP, ACEP, ENA, the EMSC National Resource Center, and Children's National Medical Center

3

Equipment/Supplies: Respiratory, Continued	Equipment/Supplies: Specialized Pediatric Trays or Kits

Equipment/Supplies: Respiratory, Continued

clear oxygen masks
- ○ standard infant
- ○ standard child
- ○ standard adult
- ○ partial nonrebreather infant
- ○ nonrebreather child
- ○ nonrebreather adult

nasal cannulas
- ○ infant
- ○ child
- ○ adult

nasogastric tubes
- ○ infant: 8F
- ○ child: 10F
- ○ adult: 14-18F

laryngeal mask airway
- ○ size: 1
- ○ size: 1.5
- ○ size: 2
- ○ size: 2.5
- ○ size: 3
- ○ size: 4
- ○ size: 5

Equipment/Supplies: Specialized Pediatric Trays or Kits

- ○ lumbar puncture tray (including infant/pediatric 22 gauge and adult 18-21 gauge needles)

- ○ supplies/kit for patients with difficult airway (supraglottic airways of all sizes, laryngeal mask airway, needle cricothyrotomy supplies, surgical cricothyrotomy kit)

- ○ tube thoracostomy tray

chest tubes:
- ○ infant: 10-12F
- ○ child: 16-24F
- ○ adult: 28-40F

- ○ newborn delivery kit, including equipment for resuscitation of an infant (umbilical clamp, scissors, bulb syringe, and towel)

- ○ urinary catheterization kits and urinary (indwelling) catheters (6F–22F)

American Academy of Pediatrics
DEDICATED TO THE HEALTH OF ALL CHILDREN™

EMERGENCY NURSES ASSOCIATION
SAFE PRACTICE, SAFE CARE

American College of Emergency Physicians®
ADVANCING EMERGENCY CARE

Children's
National Medical Center

4

Chapter 2 | Epidemiology

Liz Cloughessy, AM, MHM, RN, FAEN
Luisa Couceiro, MSc
Maria do Céu Machado, PhD
Margaret M. Dymond, BSN, RN
Sharon Payne, MSN, NP
Tiffiny Strever, BSN, RN, CEN

Objectives

On completion of this chapter, the learner should be able to do the following:

- Review multinational epidemiologic characteristics of pediatric illness and injury.
- Describe the common causes and characteristics of life-threatening illnesses in multinational populations of pediatric patients.
- Discuss pediatric injuries in relation to multinational morbidity and mortality data.
- Compare health promotion strategies related to illness prevention.

Introduction

Children who require emergency care have unique needs, especially when emergencies are serious or life-threatening.[1] These unique needs involve differences in anatomy, immature physiology, and developmental levels; the needs of children are definitely different from those of adults. During the past three decades, awareness of the needs of pediatric patients has increased, involving not only emergency medical services (EMS) but also hospitals. This focus has helped improve the outcomes for children. Pediatric patients should have seamless emergency care from home to hospital. The previously noted factors affect the illnesses and injuries seen in the pediatric population and clinical presentation. This chapter will discuss and describe pediatric population characteristics and the epidemiology of emergencies.

United States

Characteristics of the Pediatric Population

The factors influencing the characteristics of the pediatric population treated in emergency care settings have remained relatively the same during the past several decades. These factors include, but are not limited to, access to care (specialty or primary), community variables, and socioeconomic conditions. Of the 119 million emergency department (ED) visits in the United States in 2006, almost 20% were for children.[1] Injuries account for an estimated 9.2 million visits to the ED each year, according to a 2008 Centers for Disease Control and Prevention (CDC) report.[2] The leading cause of non-fatal injury in children ages 0–14 years is falls.

Access to Pediatric Healthcare Services

- Most pediatric patients who require emergency services in the United States receive care in a nonchildren's hospital, with 50% of EDs providing care for fewer than 10 children per day.[1]

- The presence of children's hospitals or large urban facilities affects the capabilities of the general EDs and hospitals in the area. This is the result of a lack of patient exposure and services available at the general emergency department. Half (52.9%) of hospitals admitted pediatric patients but did not have a specialized inpatient pediatric ward.[3] Only 6% of hospitals had all the recommended pediatric supplies; however, only half of the hospitals had greater than 85% of the recommended supplies.[3]

- Insurance status influences the quality, quantity, and outcomes of care for children.[4] Pediatric patients may be enrolled in health maintenance organizations, point-of-service plans, or some type of managed care plan. Having public insurance does not guarantee access to care, as shown in a study conducted at Vanderbilt University, which evaluated care denial reports and experiences with TennCare, the Medicaid managed care program.[4] Often, these plans have limitations on emergency care, access to children's hospitals, and access to pediatric specialties. To obtain the required services may mean hours of telephone calls and attainment of required permission.

Continued Use of the Emergency Department as a Primary Source of Episodic Healthcare

- From 2005 to 2006, 6.3% of children were without a primary source of healthcare.[5] More than 13 million US children are estimated to be living in families with an income of less than the poverty level. Poverty often leads to a transient lifestyle and lack of primary healthcare. In fact, in one CDC report, 14.4% of all children younger than 18 years had no healthcare visits to an office or clinic in the past 12 months.[5]

- Use of the ED for care is often related to a real or perceived lack of options. Although children may have a primary care physician, the hours of availability may be limited, thus creating a need to take a sick or mildly injured child somewhere else to be treated. Urgent care clinics with expanded hours have made some difference, but the ED still continues to be where many of these children are seen and treated.

Referral Patterns of Primary Care Providers

- Although the goal of primary care providers (PCPs) is to establish a system for children to be given consistent care by a specific provider, the system itself may prevent the attainment of this goal. From 2005 to 2006, 6% of children younger than 6 years and 14% of children aged 6 to 17 years did not have a healthcare visit to a physician's office or a clinic in the past year.[5] This can be related to lack of an available appointment or physician availability. The ratio of physician to population continues to increase slowly, but the supply is not equally distributed across the country.[5]

- Patients who do attempt to follow up with a PCP for nonurgent conditions are often triaged to the ED for care. This can be because of day of the week, time of day, or a perception by the PCP that the condition is outside his or her skill set.

Violence and Children

- More than 70% of school-aged children from low-income communities in the United States have observed domestic violence, assault, arrests, drug deals, gang violence, and shootings.[6] Children of all ages and income levels, not just low-income children, are exposed to violence in family and community environments. Violence causes physical and psychosocial harm to children,[6] thus affecting the overall health of children.

- A report published in November 2009 on violence, abuse, and crime exposure noted that 60.6% of the children and youth surveyed for the report had at least one direct or witnessed victimization in the previous year. In the previous year, 46.3% had been exposed to a physical assault, 10.2% had been exposed to some form of maltreatment by a significant adult in their life, and 6.1% had been exposed to sexual victimization.[7]

- Maltreatment continues to affect children on a daily basis. Although the untimely deaths of children as the result of illness and injuries have been closely monitored, deaths that result from physical assault or severe neglect can be more difficult to track because the perpetrators, usually parents, are less likely to be forthcoming about the circumstances.[8]

- Deaths and death rates from child maltreatment continued to increase yearly from 2004 to 2009, except for 2005, when the rate actually decreased. In 2009, there were 2.35 deaths per 100,000 children in the United States.[9] Younger children continue to be at greatest risk, with those younger than one year accounting for 45.2% of the deaths.[9] When looking at all fatalities related to maltreatment for children up to the age of four years, that percentage increases to 80.8%.[9] However, the concern still exists that maltreatment is underreported, even with mandatory reporting.

- In 2005, homicide was the second leading cause of death among children aged 15 to 19 years, accounting for 2,076 deaths, and the fourth leading cause of death among children aged 10 to 14 years, accounting for 220 deaths.[10] Although homicides have decreased, the impact of violence remains high. In 2007, 668,000 young people aged 10 to 24 years were treated in EDs for injuries sustained from violence.[11]

- Homicide is the leading cause of death for African Americans aged 10 to 24 years; it is the second leading cause of death for Hispanics and the third leading cause of death for Asians/Pacific Islanders, American Indians, and Alaskan Natives.[11]

- Violence is seen on TV, at the movies, and in many of the video games children are exposed to on a daily basis. This may increase the violence of youth. Bullying at school has become more evident, with an estimated 30% of sixth to tenth graders in the United States being a bully, the target of a bully, or both.[11]

- A 2007 survey of ninth to twelfth graders revealed these statistics:[11]

  ○ 12.4% reported being in a physical fight on school property in the 12 months preceding the survey.

- 5.5% did not go to school on one or more days in the 30 days preceding the survey because they felt unsafe at school or on their way to or from school.

- 5.9% reported carrying a weapon (gun, knife, or club) on school property on one or more days in the 30 days preceding the survey.

- Gang violence is a real and natural concern for most parents.[12] Children remain victims or active participants of gang violence. Although there has been a decrease in gang violence overall, it remains a threat to teenagers everywhere. The Office of Juvenile Justice and Delinquency Prevention in the Department of Justice offers these statistics from its National Youth Gang Survey:[12]

  - More than half of the homicides reported in Los Angeles, California, and more than half of the homicides reported in Chicago, Illinois, are related to gang violence.

  - A total of 11% of rural and 35% of suburban counties report gang activity.

  - As many as 37% of gang members are currently younger than 18 years.

  - Gun violence costs more than $100 billion a year.

- A new type of violence is more concerned with an attitude on "snitchin." This new idea is heard in music, seen on clothes, and discussed by youth. Over time, the idea of "snitchin" has evolved from those involved in a violent act not discussing it with authorities to an attitude of even witnesses not discussing the violent act.

Immunization

Vaccination is among the most cost-effective tools to decrease childhood morbidity and mortality.[13] Despite the availability of vaccines for children and a decrease in many infectious diseases, there has been an increase in some infectious diseases. From 1990 to 2006, the incidence of pertussis increased from 1.8 to 5.3 cases per 100,000 population. Pertussis may contribute to neonatal deaths when family members are not properly vaccinated. Children living in poverty were less likely to be properly vaccinated. According to the National Immunization Survey, the 2008 vaccination rate for children aged 19 to 35 months was 76%.[14] In September 2008, one report noted that vaccination rates for teenagers continued to increase; for the first time, with the *Healthy People 2010* target of 90%, coverage among adolescents aged 13 to 15 years was met for measles-mumps-rubella [vaccine] and hepatitis B.[15]

Use of Prehospital Emergency Medical Services

There are several perceived barriers to using prehospital emergency medical services (EMS), including the following: (1) lack of universal understanding/application of a definition of emergency, and (2) lack of pediatric training/experience for prehospital emergency medical services. Although many improvements have been made since 1992, most notable regarding prehospital care are the improvements in pediatric education for EMS providers and the Pediatric Education for Prehospital Professionals program.[1] Although the emphasis has been to transport children via EMS, caregivers and even physicians often opt for ill or injured children to be transported by private vehicle instead of emergency medical services. This results in children presenting without prehospital care and may mean they are more compromised.

Pediatric Illness

Caregivers bring children to the ED for a variety of illnesses, with reasons for the visit varying because of age, season, region, and time of day. Many of the common illnesses are related to respiratory, fever, and gastrointestinal issues. The pediatric patient may also be brought in by the caregiver because of a change in the symptoms of a current illness or the sudden onset of a new illness.

Challenges exist when reviewing pediatric illness and injury.

- There is not a clear definition of the pediatric patient. The American College of Surgeons considers pediatric patients as those younger than 15 years for trauma, whereas the American Academy of Pediatrics uses those aged 21 years and younger as its cutoff. That age may increase if there are developmental delays.

- Data are collected and reported in different ways. The CDC, for example, often groups late adolescents (15–19 years) and young adults (20–24 years) together in reports.

- In 2006, there were 902 million visits to a primary care physician, but only 13.6% of those visits related to pediatrics.[16]

- There remains a lack of a nationally standardized reporting system for ED and hospital discharge data across states.

Pediatric Hospitalizations as the Result of Illness

In 2006, for those children younger than 17 years, roughly 5% of the hospital stays were from pediatric emergency visits; and in 2007, there were fewer than 30 hospital stays for every 1,000 children aged one to 17 years.[17]

- Asthma continues to be the most common reason for admission to the hospital.

- Pneumonia remains in the top five reasons, but a decline occurs amongst those younger than 17 years.
- Appendicitis and mood disorders (defined as depression and bipolar diseases) are among the most common diagnoses. Both increased by 27% between 1997 and 2007.[17]

Pediatric Deaths as the Result of Illness

The infant mortality rate reflects those children that die before the age of one year. There was little progress in lowering the U.S. infant mortality rate from 2000 to 2005. In 2005, the infant mortality rate was 6.87 deaths per 1,000 live births, which is not statistically different than the rate in 2004 (6.79 deaths per 1,000 live births).[5] The causes of deaths remain unchanged.

- For neonates (from birth to the age of 28 days), the leading causes are prematurity and congenital anomalies.
- Sudden infant death syndrome (SIDS) and congenital anomalies are the leading causes of death for infants from 28 days to 11 months.
- Unintentional injury is the leading cause of death after the age of one year.
- Infant mortality is highest among non-Hispanic African American mothers.[5]
  - The rate is also high among American Indian and Alaskan Native mothers.[5]

Pediatric Trauma

Trauma affects all children and is the leading cause of death for all children older than one year. The leading causes of death from trauma in U.S. children ages 1–19 years are as follows:

- Falls, drowning, motor vehicle crashes, and violence.
- Motor vehicle crashes are the leading unintentional cause of death among 5–19 year olds.
- For those ages one through four years, drowning is the leading cause of unintentional death.[17]
- For those ages 15 through 19 years, homicide is the second leading cause of death. (For those between the ages of five and 14 years, medical reasons are second.) Additional information can be found in **Chapter 13, "Adolescents."**
- American Indians/Alaskan Natives have the highest age-adjusted rate of injury-related death, followed by African Americans.[2]

Canada

Characteristics of the Pediatric Population

- Canada is a large and varied land mass that incorporates 10 provinces and three territories; 16.6% of the population is younger than 14 years.[18]

- Canada is culturally diverse, with people of aboriginal descent encompassing 4% of the total population.[19] Children younger than 19 years represent 44% of the aboriginal population.[20]
- In 2008, Canada's immigration rate was 0.7% of the total population, with the largest portion of immigrants from Asia, the Pacific, Africa, and the Middle East. Children younger than 14 years represent 51.9% of the Asian and Pacific immigrants and 20.9% of the African and Middle East immigrants.[21]
- Cultural diversity brings challenges in caring for children and their families. Canada recognizes the special needs of children and youth in its culturally diverse nation and strives to create policies that protect the rights of children.
  - The family structure in Canada consists of the following:[22, 23]
    - 66% of children living with married parents.
    - 15% of children living with common-law parents.
    - 18.3% of children living in single-parent families.
    - Most single-parent families being headed by women.
    - A small group of children living with grandparents or other extended family members.
    - 50% of children living in single-parent families living in poverty.

The Canada Health Act

The organization of Canada's healthcare system is largely determined by the Canadian Constitution, in which roles and responsibilities are divided between the federal and the combined provincial and territorial governments. The provincial and territorial governments have most of the responsibility for delivering health and other social services. The federal government is responsible for some direct delivery of services for certain groups of people (First Nations, military personnel, and federal employees).

Basic healthcare is covered by the federal and provincial governments. Most provincial and territorial governments offer and fund supplementary benefits for certain groups (e.g., low-income residents and senior citizens), such as drugs prescribed outside hospitals, ambulance costs, and hearing, vision, and dental care that are not covered under the Canada Health Act.

Individuals and families who do not qualify for this publicly funded coverage may pay these costs directly (out-of-pocket), may be covered under an employment-based group insurance plan, or may buy private insurance.[24]

Access to Pediatric Health-care Services

Most children in Canada visit general EDs rather than those that specialize in pediatric care. Canada has 16 hospitals dedicated to the care of pediatric patients. Children with special healthcare needs or those who are critically ill or injured are transferred to these hospitals that provide pediatric specialty care.

- Most provinces and territories have developed referral patterns for the safe transfer of those children with complex needs via specialized pediatric transfer teams.

- In Canada, programs are in place to assist practitioners caring for children in rural or northern communities to be able to access timely care for the pediatric patient. Technology, in the form of telehealth or call centers (critical care lines), is available in many provinces to assist providers caring for children to manage their care and safely transfer the children to a pediatric center.

    ○ 80% of Canadian pediatricians work in cities with a population of greater than 100,000, making pediatric care a challenge.[23] The Canadian Pediatric Society (CPS) states that a commitment to a coordinated approach with family physicians, pediatricians, child and adolescent psychiatrists, nurses, and other specialists is vital to provide quality care for children.[23]

Emergency Department Visits

In 2008, the Canadian Institute for Health Information studied the characteristics of ED visits and children in Ontario. Their findings include the following:[25]

- 23% of all ED visits were for newborns to those aged 17 years, with children aged one through four years making up the most visits (30.1% of all pediatric visits were made by children in this age group).

- 31.8% of the children made two or more visits, with 25% returning within 72 hours of their previous visit.

    ○ Newborns and babies from birth to the age of one year had the highest rate of visits (802) per 1,000 children.

    ○ 51.5% waited one hour or less to be seen by a physician.

    ○ One in 10 children waited longer than five hours in an ED to be seen by a physician.

    ○ 90.3% returned home, whereas 4.1% were admitted to the hospital.

    ○ 4.6% left before their visit was completed.

    ○ The most common time of day for children to visit the ED was 7:00 p.m.

    ○ The most common day of the week for children to visit an ED was Sunday.

- Although the study is reflective of one province in Canada, similarity in patterns of pediatric ED visits can be noted in many EDs in Canada.

Child Advocacy/Child Poverty

- The CPS examined issues of health promotion and primary prevention and the long-term well-being of children and youth.

- Poor children and youth are not as healthy, have higher infant mortality, and have shorter life expectancy. Disparities in family socioeconomic status influence the health of children and youth.[23]

    ○ Poor children are at a greater risk of low birth weight and poor physical and emotional well-being as they grow older. They achieve lower levels of education, increasing the chance of lifelong poverty as adults.

    ○ Children of new immigrants and aboriginal children are at risk. One in four aboriginal children lives in a low-income family compared with one in 10 in the nonaboriginal population.

    ○ In Canada, efforts have been slow, but some gains have been achieved in pediatric health promotion and primary prevention through government initiatives. These programs include introduction of the national child tax benefit system, income security programs, labor market training, minimum wage policies, access to quality child care, and drug, dental, and vision care insurance for low-income families.[23]

Smoking[23]

- Smoking rates among teenagers decreased in 2008 to 15% among those aged 15 through 19 years. However, aboriginal youth smoke at rates three to four times the national average. Children from low-income families smoke at higher rates than the national average.

- Several provinces in Canada have recently introduced legislation against smoking in cars when children are present and banning all tobacco advertising in magazines and newspapers. The Canadian government has increased tobacco taxes and has a disincentive for children to purchase tobacco products.

Mental Health

The CPS states that approximately 70% of mental illnesses have their onset in childhood or adolescence. It is estimated that 75% of children who need specialized treatment are not able to receive it. Work is under way to develop a national mental health strategy.[23]

Immunization

The CPS and the National Advisory Committee on Immunization in Canada noted that, in addition to the routine immunizations, five additional vaccines have been recommended (at no charge): varicella, adolescent pertussis, certain forms of meningitis, pneumococcal, and human papillomavirus. Coverage of these extra recommended vaccines is not universal in Canada, and not all physicians are administering them according to the schedule recommended by CPS and the National Advisory Committee on Immunization. The list of required immunizations can be found online.[26]

- Children from low-income families are more likely to have incomplete immunizations, increasing the risk of adverse health and well-being for the child.[23]

- In 2009, H1N1 immunization was offered in Canada at no cost to the public. Children were a priority group to immunize.

Violence Against Children

In 2007, the rate of physical assault against children and youth was higher than the rate of physical assault against adults. In the same period of time, sexual assault was five times higher against children than the rate against adults.[25]

- When children or youth were assaulted by a relative, 57% of the time a parent was identified as the abuser.[25]

- Four in 10 child victims of family violence sustained physical injuries, most being minor.[25]

- Some regions in Canada have implemented a domestic violence screening program as part of the initial assessment of the patient when the patient arrives in an emergency department.[25]

Pediatric Illness and Injury

In 2004, the leading cause of hospital admissions in children younger than nine years was diseases of the respiratory system. In the 10- to 14-year-old group, unintentional injuries were the leading cause of hospital admissions. For those in the 15- to 19-year-old group, mental disorders were the leading cause of hospital admissions.[27]

- A 10-year review of trauma-related data shows that hospitalization and death rates have declined by almost 29%, partly because of bicycle helmet legislation and helmet laws in six Canadian provinces. In provinces in which bicycle helmet legislation has been enacted, injuries have been reduced by 25%.[23]

- Youth aged 15 through 19 years account for most all-terrain vehicle injuries, with 30% seen in youth younger than 16 years. One province in Canada has restricted youth younger than 14 years from operating an all-terrain vehicle and has seen a 50% reduction in related injuries.[23]

- Motor vehicle crashes are the leading cause of injury-related death among Canadian children. Child passenger restraints have been shown to reduce this risk by 40% to 60%. In a collision, young children secured with a seat belt, instead of a booster seat, are three and a half times more likely to sustain a serious injury and four times more likely to sustain a head injury. The CPS is recommending that Canadian provinces and territories amend their legislation to require that children who weigh 18 to 36 kg be properly secured in booster seats.[23]

Trends in the Health of Canada's Youth

- During the past 25 years, the percentage of Canadian children who are overweight has increased considerably. The largest increase is among 12- to 17-year-old children whose rate of obesity has tripled to 9% in the past 20 years.[28] A significantly high percentage of young aboriginal people (off reserve) were obese (20%), two and a half times the national average. Type II diabetes mellitus, related to childhood obesity, has been reported in children as young as eight years in aboriginal communities.[28] Fitness levels of children and youth have declined in more than three decades, resulting in the development of chronic disease and higher health costs.

- In 2007, a Canadian study found that children and adolescents had less favorable fitness scores and increased body mass indices when compared with 1981 data.

- The likelihood of being overweight increased as screen time increased (i.e., watching TV, playing video games, or using a computer).[29]

- The Canadian Diabetes Association recommends children have a healthy diet with more selection of fruits and vegetables, less screen time, and more activity to reduce the trend of obesity and the onset of chronic disease.

- Bullying is a concern in Canada's youth. The many Canadian students who report bullying or being bullied confirm that this represents an important social problem for Canada. There have been tragic cases of Canadian children who have died or have been seriously impaired by bullying.[30]

  o The Canadian Initiative to Prevent Bullying (2003-2006) is funded by Canada's National Crime Prevention Program. The aim of the Canadian Initiative to Prevent Bullying is to develop a national framework for addressing problems of bullying in Canada through partnerships among government, national organizations, businesses, community groups, and individuals, with the view that bullying is a community problem, not just a school problem, and one that operates across the life span.

Substance Abuse

- Alcohol is by far the most common substance used by youth. A recent national school survey of students in grades seven to nine found that about two-thirds had already consumed alcohol.

- Another national survey of Canadian youth aged 15 through 24 years showed that 83% were current (or past-year) drinkers; the most common pattern of alcohol use reported by drinkers was "light-infrequent."

- Cannabis (marijuana) is the second most commonly used substance.
  - Lifetime cannabis use is reported by 17% of students in grades seven to nine. Approximately 29% of 15- to 17-year-old individuals and almost half of 18- to 19-year-old individuals report past-year cannabis use.

- Hallucinogenic drugs, such as psilocybin (magic mushrooms) and mescaline, are the next most popular illicit drugs after cannabis, with approximately 10% of junior high and high school students reporting use.

- Past-year use of other illicit drugs, such as ecstasy or cocaine, is less than 10% among adolescents.[31]

Australia

Characteristics of the Pediatric Population

In June 2006, there were four million children younger than 15 years in Australia, representing one-fifth (20%) of the total population.[32] With improved living conditions, education, medical care, and vaccinations, one might reasonably expect that this generation of children would be the healthiest ever. There are, however, emerging concerns related to rapid social change and associated new morbidities, such as increasing levels of behavioral, developmental, mental health, and social problems.[33] There are high risks of mental health problems among children and adolescents living in low-income step-blended families (i.e., families that are merged because of divorce or separation) and single-parent families.

Access to Pediatric Healthcare Services

As seen all across the world, pediatric patients are often limited in access to healthcare for a variety of reasons: lack of resources available, distance to those resources, and time of day that resources are available.

Emergency Department Visits

The same issues that affect healthcare services ultimately affect the use of the ED as the primary source of care.

Issues may include a real or perceived lack of primary care practitioners' office or clinic hours, which are limited, and lack of available appointments.

Trends in Health of Australia's Children

- From 2004 to 2005, 41% of children younger than 15 years had a long-term health condition, with boys (44%) more likely than girls (38%) to have such a condition. Health outcomes for indigenous babies remain significantly poorer than those experienced by the general Australian population.

- Many indigenous mothers and children are socioeconomically disadvantaged; this has adverse impacts on their health and well-being.
  - The proportion of low–birth-weight babies born to indigenous mothers is double the rate for nonindigenous mothers.
  - There are more indigenous than nonindigenous prenatal deaths.

- Between 1985 and 2005, deaths from SIDS declined by 83%, from 523 deaths in 1985 to 87 deaths in 2005. This decline was attributed to raising awareness of risk factors associated with sudden infant death and the importance of safer practices, such as placing babies to sleep on their backs.

- Breastfeeding has a positive impact on the health, growth, and development of an infant. From 2004 to 2005, 67% of infants up to the age of three months and 52% of infants aged four to six months were being fully or partially breastfed.[32]

- From 2004 to 2005, 7% of children younger than 15 years had some form of mental or behavioral problem as a long-term health condition, with higher rates among children aged 10 to 14 years.[34] Childhood obesity has emerged as a major lifestyle risk factor for Australian children. In New South Wales in 2004, 26% of boys and 24% of girls aged five to 16 years were overweight or obese compared with 11% of all children aged seven to 16 years in 1985.[35]

- Respiratory disease (25%) and injury (12%) were the main causes of hospitalization of children aged one to 14 years.[33]

- Death rates for both infants (< 1 year) and children (aged 1–14 years) have decreased in recent decades and continue to decrease.[33]

- Most childhood deaths (68% in 2004) occurred in the first year of life, with 15% for those aged one through four years and the remaining 17% for those aged five through 14 years.[33]

Immunization

There has been a trend of increasing age-appropriate immunization coverage for children aged one, two, and six years, per the National Immunization Programme Schedule. However, the rates of increase did slow from 2005 to 2006, especially for children aged one and two years. In 2006, vaccination coverage was 91% at the age of one year, 92% at the age of two years, and 84% at the age of six years.[33]

Pediatric Injury

- Approximately one in five people admitted to a hospital because of injury from 2001 to 2002 were children, in line with the proportion of children in Australia's population.

- The special vulnerability of toddlers to injury is indicated by the prominence of submersion injury and pedestrian injuries in this age group. "Home" is the most commonly recorded place of occurrence of injuries in this age group.

- For older children (43%), the prominence of injuries is related to bicycling and falls.[36]

Pediatric Trauma

Safety requires both passive measures, which automatically reduce risk, and education and behavior change of children and adults. Preventable injuries remain higher in children compared with all other age groups. More than one-third of all deaths for those aged one through 14 years are from injury. The most common injury types are as follows:

- Submersion injury (especially toddlers)
- Transport injuries (especially as pedestrians)
- Interpersonal violence (especially in infancy)
- Assault (physical assault by another individual), which tends to result in relatively long hospital stays.
- Poisoning which is a common cause of admissions for those from birth to the age of four years, although hospitalization is usually brief.

New Zealand

Characteristics of the Pediatric Population

New Zealand has a population of approximately 4,300,000 people, of whom 24% are younger than 15 years. Although most New Zealand children enjoy good health, some groups experience a disproportionate burden of morbidity and mortality as the result of long-term health conditions or injuries. In New Zealand, all births are assigned a domicile code, based on the residential address of the mother at her baby's birth registration. This allows births to be linked to the New Zealand Deprivation (NZDep) Index, a small area index of deprivation, which assigns each domicile in New Zealand a decile ranking ranging from one (the least deprived 10% of areas) to 10 (the most deprived 10% of areas). In 2006, 7.7% and 14.3% of all babies were born into deciles one and 10, respectively. Overall in 2006, 39.1% of all births were born into NZDep deciles eight through 10.

- On average, Pacific and Māori babies were born into more deprived areas than European and other babies.

- More than 60% of Pacific and 40% of Māori children and young people live in crowded housing.

Access to Pediatric Healthcare Services

- Most EDs are general departments that may have separate areas for children but are still within the confines of the general department. Pediatric patients account for 25% of the patient presentations.

- New Zealand has a significant rural population, and access to health services for this group can be delayed. Rural services are limited; many areas lack medical staff but have specially trained nurses who provide these much-needed services.

  ○ Ambulance and helicopter retrieval services are used frequently to access these patients.

- Within New Zealand, there is one pediatric tertiary hospital, although other hospitals have significant pediatric specialty units. However, the tertiary facility provides treatment for cancer and organ transplantation in addition to caring for critically ill and injured patients. Children from all over New Zealand are seen at this facility.

Access to Healthcare

General practice services are open to all children, and all families are encouraged to register with a general practice physician. Visits for children younger than six years with their registered primary healthcare provider are free, and prescriptions are well subsidized, with many medications free to this population. Older children also have subsidized healthcare, with special provisions for those in lower-income families using a community services card and multiple facilities that provide care for Māori and Pacific Island children. Access to a 24-hour primary healthcare service is available but not in rural or smaller urban areas. After-hours services vary from area to area, and the ED remains the only option.

Referral Patterns of Primary Healthcare Providers

According to the Ministry of Health, primary healthcare is essential. It can be defined as healthcare based on practical, scientifically sound, culturally appropriate, and socially acceptable methods that are universally acceptable to people in their communities. Access to high-quality primary healthcare is associated with better health outcomes, improved preventive care, and reduction in hospitalizations.[37] The goal is that everyone be enrolled in a primary health organization. The primary health organizations are composed of general practitioners, primary care nurses, and other health professionals, such as Māori health providers. Survey data on general practice use suggest that people with low incomes or living in deprived areas are more likely to be frequent users of general practitioners.[37] These same surveys suggest that there are barriers to accessing general practitioner care, with more Māori and Pacific peoples and people residing in deprived areas having cost and transportation issues and problems obtaining an appointment. In 2006, 98% of children and 93% of young people were enrolled in a primary health organization.[37]

Violence Against Children

- From 1990 to 2001, New Zealand saw a decline in mortality as a result of assaults, neglect, or maltreatment; however, the rates from 2001 to 2004 were much more variable.

- Hospital admissions for injuries related to assault, neglect, and maltreatment were highest among children younger than two years and older than 11 years.

- The highest admission rates to hospitals were among males, Māori and Pacific children, and those in the most deprived areas.

- The highest mortality was seen in those younger than one year.

Immunization

New Zealand, like many countries, has a vaccination schedule. The vaccination rates are often an indicator of access to care and effectiveness of healthcare received in the communities. In 2005, the immunization rate for children younger than two years was 77%. There is an overall vaccination rate of 90% to 95%, with certain populations having lower rates. New Zealand's vaccination schedule is available online.[38]

Pediatric Hospitalizations

In New Zealand, from 2003 to 2007, gastroenteritis, asthma, and acute upper respiratory infections made the greatest contribution to admission rates in children from birth to the age of four years. There was a shift from 1990 to 2007 that resulted in a reduction in ambulatory-sensitive hospital admission rates. From 2003 to 2007, ambulatory-sensitive hospital admission rates were significantly higher for Pacific and Māori children, males, and those in urban or more deprived areas.

Pediatric Mortality

- From 1988 to 2005, SIDS declined, but there were increases in death from suffocation/strangulation in bed or unspecified causes. (This may be explained by sudden unexplained death incidences not being noted as sudden infant death syndrome.)

- From 1996 to 2005, although sudden unexplained death incidences declined for all ethnic groups, Māori infants had the highest rate, followed by Pacific and European infants. The most suffocation/strangulation in bed deaths occurred in those younger than 20 weeks. Sudden unexplained death incidences were also significantly higher for Māori infants, followed by Pacific, European, and Asian infants and those in the most deprived areas.

Pediatric Trauma

- From 2003 to 2007, falls, followed by inanimate mechanical forces, were the leading causes of injury admission for children. In contrast, from 2001 to 2005, "unintentional threats to breathing" were the leading cause of injury-related mortality in children, although most deaths were in infants, raising the possibility of diagnostic crossover with sudden infant death syndrome. Vehicle occupant injuries, followed by intentional self-harm, were the leading causes of mortality in young people.

- From 1990 to 2005, unintentional nontransport injury deaths in children gradually declined. From 2003 to 2007, admissions for unintentional nontransport injuries were significantly higher for Pacific children, followed by Māori, European, and Asian children; males; and children living in more deprived or urban areas.

- From 1990 to 2005, land transport mortality declined in children. From 2003 to 2007, land transport injury admissions were significantly higher for Māori children, then European, Pacific, and Asian children; males; and those living in more deprived or rural areas.

Portugal

Characteristics of the Pediatric Population

Under Article One of the Convention on the Rights of the Child (ratified by Portugal in 1990), "A child means every human being below the age of 18 years." According to the Law for the Protection of Children and Young People at Risk, a child or young person is defined as someone younger than 18 or 21 years, who requires extension of the care provided, which started before he or she reached the age of 18 years.[39]

The cutoff for the definition of pediatric age is 14 years 364 days, although according to the guidelines of the National Commission for the Health of Children and Adolescents,[40] all pediatric services should provide care to everyone younger than 18 years (17 years 364 days). In Portugal, there is no homogeneity in the maximum age for care provided (appointments, hospital stays, and emergency services) in pediatric services, thus statistical analysis is compromised. Another similar constraint relates to the fact that information systems in emergency care and appointments do not disaggregate the information per age and diagnosis.

Between 1991 and 2008, the ratio of young people from birth to the age of 17 years (i.e., < 18 years) in relation to the total residents in Portugal decreased from 24.2% to 18.3%. This decrease was more noticeable in the 15- to 17-year-old group than in the birth to 14-year-old group. However, the population of children and young people is not evenly distributed throughout the whole territory. The ratios vary between 19% in the northern region and 15.7% in the Alentejo.

Access to Pediatric Healthcare Services

The interaction between PCPs and hospital providers is one of the greatest priorities of the National Commission for the Health of Children and Adolescents (CNSCA); thus, promoting continuity and communication between these components is essential in the care of pediatric patients. The cooperation between the different levels of care provided is boosted as follows:

- Promotion of interaction between the different functional coordinating units.

- Creation of the role of consultant pediatricians in health center groups, who shall discuss clinical cases, refer patients, and organize ongoing training.

- Upgrade training in general pediatrics for undergraduates and interns in general practice.

The CNSCA pursues other priorities at the level of pediatric healthcare (i.e., the promotion of pediatric day hospitals, the recording of all medical acts in the Child Health Card, and the incorporation of specialist nurses in Child and Pediatric Health). In 2008, 1,314 of these specialists were registered at the Nurses Professional Association in Healthcare teams.

Primary Healthcare

According to the National Health Service in Portugal, there were 346 health centers and 1,620 health poles (National Health Service), with family physicians and nurses playing an extremely important role in child surveillance. These health centers employed 43 pediatricians and 145 specialist nurses in child and pediatric healthcare.[41] Following the CNSCA guidelines, some health centers are retaining pediatricians and nurses before replacing them with consultant pediatricians. The number of appointments in child and youth healthcare/pediatrics has been irregular in the past years, showing opposite trends in numbers. In 2008, according to the National Institute of Statistics, there were 2,858,655 medical appointments in pediatric care in Portuguese health centers. The number of private appointments in pediatric care is unknown, although it is estimated as quite high, mainly in the cities.

Hospital Admissions

- In Portugal, there are four maternities, three pediatric hospitals, 65 hospitals with pediatric services, and 38 hospitals with pediatric emergency services (National Health Service).

  ○ These employ approximately 857 pediatricians and 412 specialist nurses in child and pediatric healthcare.[41]

- In these settings, the total number of outpatient pediatric appointments increased more than 50% between 2000 and 2008.

  ○ One of the measures to assess improvement in ambulatory healthcare is the analysis of the first appointments to total appointments ratio. In 2008, first appointments in pediatric services were at 24.1% of the total number of appointments in this specialty, lower than all other specialties.

  ○ In 2008, Portuguese public hospitals registered a total of 1,251,052 emergency pediatric consultations.

Emergency Department Visits

- Children who do not attend primary healthcare services are more prone to using emergency services.

- The low attendance of primary healthcare is often related to economic factors, although the National Health Service is mainly providing free-of-charge healthcare. According to the Survey on Life Quality and Income, approximately 21% of children younger than 18 years in Portugal lived at risk of poverty.[42]

- In Portugal, similar to many other countries, the Ministry for Health promotes scheduled consultations in primary healthcare settings and hospitals (instead of unjustified attendance of emergency services).

The integrated healthcare model notes that surveillance of child health should start with the family physician and that only the more serious, complex, and less frequent diseases or those requiring hospital stays should be referred to pediatric services. Although the number of pediatric appointments in health centers is high, there is still overattendance at hospital emergency services.

Violence Against Children

The Units for Protection of Children and Young People at Risk,[43] part of the National Commission for the Protection of Children and Young People at Risk[44] located in the health centers and hospitals, are paramount in supporting health professionals who, in first-level care, work in the prevention of abuse and deal directly with these cases, within the scope of their medical interventions.[41]

- In 2008, the Comissão Nacional de Protecção das Crianças e Jovens em Risco started 29,279 proceedings and noted considerable growth in the past years in abuse cases. This may be because of a better case reporting network.

- The generic profile of the families in which these children live is as follows:
  ○ Most of the children live with their biological families (85.9%).
  ○ The parents' average age is 25 to 44 years.
  ○ The families have low schooling, have alcohol abuse patterns, and live in underprivileged social settings.

- The largest age group affected is children aged 11 to 14 years (27.6%), followed by those aged six to 10 years (25.3%).

- In all age groups, there is a prevalence of males (53.1%) in detriment to females (46.9%).

The main causes for reporting cases to Comissão Nacional de Protecção das Crianças e Jovens em Risco are as follows:

- Neglect (36.5%)

- Exposure to deviant behaviors (16.8%)

- School dropout (14.6%)

- Emotional abuse (12.9%)

- Physical abuse (7.4%)

In 2008, Portuguese public hospitals reported that 76 hospital stays were because of child abuse. Two age groups, five to nine and 10 to 14 years, rank higher in hospital admissions caused by child abuse, in relation to the total number of cases.

Immunization

In 1965, the National Vaccination Program[39] was started, providing universal and free-of-charge vaccines to all.[42] In the years after the initiation of this program, there was a considerable decrease in morbidity and mortality rates caused by infectious diseases, which are now covered by the vaccination program.[39]

Currently, the vaccine coverage for tuberculosis, diphtheria, tetanus, pertussis, measles, poliomyelitis, and hepatitis B, diseases caused by type b *Haemophilus influenzae*, rubella, and mumps, is greater than 96%.[45] Once the high coverage rates have been achieved, it is a priority of the vaccination program to then look at the geographical differences regarding protection levels provided by vaccination and to treat appropriately.[39]

In 2008, the National Vaccination Program incorporated the vaccine for cervical cancer (human papillomavirus). During the first year, girls born in 1995 (after completing 13 years) were offered the vaccine, with the vaccination coverage reaching 75%.

Pediatric Illness

In 2009, the status of pediatric illness changed. Infectious diseases are largely controlled, and the mortality rate caused by injuries remains at the same level. There are new pathologies, such as obesity, child depression, and at-risk cases (e.g., physical abuse, cancer, children with chronic diseases, and children with special needs).

One of the most effective ways of estimating the incidence and prevalence of the disease in pediatric patients is through emergency cases, both in primary healthcare, as in hospitals, or through hospital admissions. In Portugal, the information services at EDs do not include diagnosis or age group–related data; thus, it is impossible to determine information at the national level. However, several studies indicate that the most frequent causes are trauma, gastrointestinal disorders, respiratory diseases, and fever without a focus.

Pediatric Hospitalizations

In 2008, in mainland Portugal, there were 109,371 hospital admissions (including at day hospitals) of children younger than 18 years. Among the admitted patients, the one- to four-year-old group (26.3%) is the most significant, with the 15- to 17-year-old group being the least significant (12.9%).

The top two main diagnoses causing hospital stays in those younger than 18 years include respiratory diseases (21.4%) and diseases of the digestive system (12.6%).[40]

Causes vary with different age groups:

- In the first years of life (< 10 years), respiratory diseases are the most frequent.

- In those 10 years and older, diseases of the digestive system are the most frequent.

- Diseases of the circulatory system (1.94%), oncological diseases (1.65%), and prenatal diseases (1.63%) are the most frequent causes of hospital mortality.

- Technological and scientific discoveries have shortened hospital stays. In only five years (2003–2008), the average hospital stay of people younger than 18 years decreased by almost half, from 17.7 to 9.4 days.

Pediatric Epidemiology

According to the World Health Organization, Portugal ranks sixth, among the top 80 countries with more than 10 million inhabitants, for a child to be born in that country. In the past 30 years, there have been significant and consistent improvements in mortality decreases in several age groups, with a special focus on the child mortality rate that has reached its minimum of 3.3% in 2008 (relative decrease of 89% between 1978 and 2008). This decrease in mortality is essentially for the following reasons:

- Better social and economic conditions of the population

- Global health reforms

- Political actions mainly in the areas of maternal and child health[42]

Both in the neonatal period (< 28 days old), and in infants younger than one year, the most important causes for death are related to congenital anomalies and disorders related to the duration of the pregnancy and fetal growth.

- Infant mortality accounts for approximately 79% of the deaths of children younger than five years. From the ages of one to four years, the main causes of death are congenital malformation and diseases of the circulatory system.

- For children older than five years, external causes and malignant tumors rank first among the most frequent causes of death.

Pediatric Trauma

External causes, including injuries and poisonings, rank high in the morbidity and mortality of children and young people. The most common causes in hospital admissions as the result of pediatric trauma are as follows:

- Fractures (46.8%)

- Open wounds (7.7%)

- Burns (6.3%)

However, there are other external causes (including physical abuse), internal thoracic and abdominal injuries, trauma complications, and nonspecified injuries that account for greater mortality in hospitals.

- These causes include motor vehicle crashes, injuries of unknown origin, self-inflicted injuries, and aggressions. For all of these causes, male mortality is much higher than female mortality, reported at greater than 70%.

- In all age groups, more than 50% of mortality is caused by road motor vehicle crashes. Children and young passengers of vehicles, pedestrians, or cyclists show a high risk of injuries.

- According to data from the National Authority for Road Safety,[46] in 2008, 6,522 people younger than 20 years were victims of motor vehicle crashes (including deaths and injuries), most of them as passengers in light or heavy vehicles (57.4%).

Summary

Pediatric patients compose a large part of the global population. Worldwide, the issues affecting children are similar. Access to healthcare, disparity in care among the poorer populations, lack of immunization, and injury affect pediatric patients across the world. Improvements are being made to provide healthcare access, decrease the disparities, and educate parents on the benefits of immunizations and injury prevention worldwide. However, more education and resources are needed to ensure the health and safety of children around the world.

References

Please note that the international references are as complete as possible.

1. American Academy of Pediatrics. (2009). Joint policy statement guidelines for care of children in the emergency department. *Pediatrics, 124,* 1233–1243.

2. Sleet, D. A., & Moffett, D. B. (2009) Framing the problem injuries and public health. *Family Community Health, 32,* 88–97.

3. Middleton, K. R., & Burt, C. W. (2006). Availability of pediatric services and equipment in emergency departments: United States, 2002-03. *Advance Data From Vital and Health Statistics, 367,* 1–16.

4. Fry-Johnson, Y. W., Daniels, E. C., Levine, R., & Rust, G. (2005). Being uninsured: Impact on children's healthcare and health. *Current Opinion in Pediatrics, 17,* 753–758.

5. Centers for Disease Control and Prevention. (2008). *Health, United States, 2008, with a special feature on the health of young adults.* Retrieved from http://www.cdc.gov/nchs/data/hus/hus08.pdf#091

6. Skybo, T., & Polivka, B. (2006). Health promotion model for childhood violence prevention and exposure. *Journal of Clinical Nursing, 16,* 35–38.

7. Finkelhor, D., Turner, H., Ormrod, R., & Hamby, S. (2009). Violence, abuse, and crime exposure in a national sample of children and youth. *Pediatrics, 124,* 1411–1423.

8. Child Welfare Gateway. (2008). *Child abuse and neglect fatalities: Statistics and interventions.* Retrieved from http://www.childwelfare.gov/pubs/factsheets/fatality.cfm

9. US Department of Health and Human Services, Administration on Children, Youth and Families. (2009). *Child maltreatment 2009.* Retrieved from http://www.acf.hhs.gov/programs/cb/stats_research/index.htm#can.

10. Centers for Disease Control and Prevention. (2005). *Youth violence: National statistics fact sheets.* Retrieved from http://www.cdc.gov/violenceprevention/youthviolence/stats_at-a_glance/national_stats.html

11. Centers for Disease Control and Prevention. (2009). *Youth violence facts at a glance.* Retrieved from http://www.cdc.gov/violenceprevention/pdf/YV_DataSheet_Summer2009-a.pdf

12. Teen Violence Statistics. (2009). *Gang violence.* Retrieved from http://www.teenviolencestatisitcs.com/content/gang-violence.html

13. Miranda, W. M. M., & Nascimento-Carvalho, C. M. (2007). Letter to the editor: Accessing vaccination rates at an emergency room. *American Journal of Infection Control, 35,* 286–287

14. Centers for Disease Control and Prevention. (2009). National, state, and local area vaccination coverage among children aged 19-35 months: United States, 2008. *Morbidity and Mortality Weekly Report (MMWR), 58,* 921–926. Retrieved from http://www.cdc.gov/mmwr

15. Centers for Disease Control and Prevention. (2009). National, state, and local area vaccination coverage among adolescents aged 13-17 years: United States, 2008. *Morbidity and Mortality Weekly Report (MMWR), 58,* 997–1001. Retrieved from http://www.cdc.gov/mmwr

16. Cherry, D. K., Hing, E., Woodwell, D.A., & Rechtsteiner, E. A. (2008). *National Ambulatory Medical Care Survey: 2006 summary in National Health Statistics report number 3.* Retrieved from http://www.cdc.gov/nchs/data/nhsr/nhsr003.pdf

17. Centers for Disease Control and Prevention. (2009). Ten leading causes of death by age group. Retrieved from http://www.cdc.gov/injury/wisqars/leadingcause.html

18. Statistics Canada. (2009). *Population estimates, age distribution, and median age as of July 1, 2009.* Retrieved from http://www.statcan.gc.ca/daily-quotidien/091127/dq091127b-eng.htm

19. Statistics Canada. (2006). *2006 census.* Retrieved from http://www.12.statcan.ca/english/census06/analysis/aboriginal/charts/chart1.htm

20. Health Canada. (2005). *A statistical profile on the health of first nations in Canada: Population projections of registered Indians.* Retrieved from http://www.hc-sc.gc.ca/fniah-spnia/pubs/aborig-autoch/2009-stats-profil-vol3/index-eng.php#fig1

21. Citizenship and Immigration Canada. (2008). *Immigration overview: Permanent and temporary residents.* Retrieved from http://www.cic.gc.ca/english/resources/statistics/facts2008/index.asp

22. Statistics Canada. (2007). *Children and youth.* Retrieved from http://www.41.statcan.ca/2008/20000/ceb20000_000_e.htm

23. Canadian Pediatric Society. (2009). *Are we doing enough: A status report on Canadian public policy and child and youth health.* Ottawa, ON: Author.

24. Health Canada. (2006, June 7). *Canada's healthcare system.* Retrieved from http://www.hc-sc.gc.ca/hcs-sss/pubs/system-regime/2005-hcs-sss/role-eng.php

25. Canadian Institute for Health Information. (2008). *Analysis in brief: Emergency departments and children in Ontario.* Retrieved from http://secure.cihi.ca/cihiweb/dispPage.jsp?cw_page=AR_2089_E&cw_topic=2089

26. Public Health Agency of Canada. (2010). *Immunization schedule.* Retrieved from http://www.phac-aspc.gc.ca/im/is-cv/index-eng.php#a

References *continued*

27. Smartrisk. (2009). *The economic burden of injury in Canada: SMARTRISK, Toronto, Ontario.* Retrieved from http://www.smartrisk.ca/downloads/research/publications/burden/EBI-Eng-ExecSumm.pdf

28. Shield, M. (2006). Overweight and obesity among children and youth. *Health Reports, 17,* 27–42.

29. Tremblay, M. S., Shield, M., Laviolette, M., Craig, C. L., Janssen, I., & Gorber, S.C. (2010). Fitness of Canadian children and youth: Results from the 2007-2009 Canadian Health Measures Survey. *Health Reports, 21,* 7–20.

30. Prevnet. (2010). *Promoting relationship and eliminating violence.* Retrieved from http://www.prevnet.ca/Bullying/BullyingStatistics/tabid/122/language/en-US/Default.aspx

31. Canadian Centre on Substance Abuse. (2007). *Substance abuse in Canada: Youth in focus.* Ottawa, ON: Author.

32. Australian Bureau of Statistics. (2006). *Population by age and sex, Australian states and territories, cat. No. 3201.0.* Canberra, Australia: Author.

33. Australian Institute of Health and Welfare. (2006). *Australia's health 2006, AIHW cat. No AUS 73.* Canberra, Australia: Author.

34. Sawyer, M., Arney F., Bughrust, P., Clark, J. J., Graetz, B. W., Kosky, R. J., ... Zubrik, S. R. (2000). *The mental health of young people in Australia.* Canberra, Australia: Mental Health and Special Programs Branch, Commonwealth Department of Health and Aged Care.

35. NSW Centre for Overweight and Obesity. (2006). *NSW schools physical activity and nutrition survey (SPANS) 2004 full report.* Sydney, Australia: Author.

36. National Public Health Partnership. (2004). *The National Injury Prevention and Safety Promotion Plan: 2004–2014.* Canberra, Australia: Author.

37. Taylor, B., Dickson, N., & Phillips, A. (2008). *NZPSU annual reports.* Retrieved from http://dnmeds.otago.ac.nz/departments/womens/paediatrics/research/nzpsu/pdf/2008_report.pdf

38. World Health Organization. (2010). *Immunization surveillance assessment and monitoring.* Retrieved from http://www.who.int/immunization_monitoring/en/globalsummary/ScheduleResult.cfm

39. Direcção Geral de Saúde. (2005). *Programa Nacional de Vacinação 2006.* Lisbon, Portugal: Orientações Técnicas.

40. Alto Comissariado da Saúde/Comissão Nacional de Saúde da Criança e do Adolescente e Missão para os Cuidados de Saúde Primários [National Commission for Child and Adolescent]. (2008). Pediatras nos Agrupamentos dos Centros de Saúde. Pediatra Consultor [Pediatrics Pools Health Centers–Consultant Paediatrician]. Retrieved from http://translate.google.com/

41. Direcção Geral de Saúde. (2007). Centros de Saúde e Hospitais. Recursos Humanos e Produção do SNS. Lisbon, Portugal. Retrieved from http://www.dgs.pt/

42. Alto Comissariado da Saúde [High Commissioner of Health]. (2009). *Comissão Nacional de Saúde da Criança e do Adolescente 2004–2008 [National Commission for Child and Adolescent 2004-2008].* Lisbon, Portugal. Retrieved from http://www.acs.min-saude.pt/2009/06/09/cnsca/

43. Burned, M., Silva, M., & Teresa, E. M. (2008). *Supporting children and youth at risk by the NACJR.* Evora, Portugal: Health Centre of Evora.

44. *Comissão Nacional de Protecção das Crianças e Jovens em Risco.* (n.d.). Retrieved from http://www.cnpcjr.pt/

45. *WHO European Health for All Database.* (2009). Retrieved from http://www.euro.who.int/en/what-we-do/data-and-evidence/databases/european-health-for-all-database-hfa-db2

46. Autoridade Nacional para a Segurança Rodoviária. (2008). *Relatório Anual de Sinistralidade Rodoviária 2008.* Lisbon, Portugal.

Chapter 3 | From the Start

Alice Conway, PhD, CRNP, FNP-BC

Objectives

On completion of this chapter, the learner should be able to do the following:

- Compare anatomical, physiological, and developmental characteristics of pediatric patients that may affect responses to illness and injury.
- Determine key growth and development characteristics of infants, toddlers, preschoolers, school-aged children, and adolescents that modify the assessment and intervention process.
- Indicate health promotion strategies for all developmental levels.

Vignette One: You are called to a room to assist with a four-year-old boy who was brought to the emergency department (ED) via prehospital providers after falling from a second-story window. His cervical spine is stabilized, and he is immobilized on a backboard. The Pediatric Assessment Triangle reveals that he appears to be in no respiratory distress, his color is pale, he is quietly crying, he does not respond to verbal commands, and his eyes are tightly closed. Prehospital providers stated that he was verbal en route until he saw bleeding from lacerations and abrasions on his arms and legs.

What can you do to facilitate the assessment of this preschooler? Preschoolers have intense body integrity concerns and believe their insides are held in by their skin. Thus, breaks in the skin are serious and bandages are important. The nurse tells the child that she will be cleaning the cuts and putting bandages on them. She wants the boy to help by holding a bandage and helping to decide what kind of bandages he wants (if there are options); this gives him some control.

Vignette Two: Emily, aged 15 months, is being seen for the second time in your ED for sticking a pin in an electrical outlet and receiving a significant shock. She is assessed as being stable, but her caregivers ask you, "Is something wrong with Emily? Why doesn't she learn? This is the second time she's done this!"

Based on your knowledge of this age group, how do you respond? Cognitively, children of this age cannot transfer knowledge from one situation to another. Each time they do something, it is new. The child is not delayed or impaired; instead, she is age appropriate. The caregivers need education in putting on outlet covers and keeping the child entertained with other activities.

Introduction

A variety of health issues and injuries lead pediatric patients and their families to seek care in the ED. These include medical conditions, such as respiratory and gastrointestinal infections, diabetes, and asthma, as well as traumatic injuries. More than 20% of all ED visits are from children younger than 18 years, with the largest group younger than 6 years old. Knowledge of age-appropriate assessment techniques and strategies to help children cope with their ED experience is critical for safe and effective care.

Pediatric patients with special healthcare needs are also presenting more frequently to EDs as the technologies to assist them increase and allow them a better quality of life and a longer life. They present to the ED for treatment of their underlying health conditions and for the usual childhood illnesses and injuries. In a 2005 to 2006 national survey of children with special healthcare needs, almost 25% of children with special healthcare needs had four or more functional difficulties. These patients include those with complex visible disabilities (e.g., congenital anomalies) and those who are technology dependent, as well as those with less visible conditions (e.g., asthma, diabetes mellitus, and learning disabilities). With one in five households having at least one child with a chronic or disabling condition, it is important for EDs not only to have necessary equipment, written policies, and procedures but also that the personnel have disability awareness.[2] See **Box 3-1** for guidelines related to disability awareness. This may be difficult to remember, when the situation is emergent, but is important for establishing a positive relationship with the child and family.

Childhood is a dynamic state of change. It is the change that brings joy and challenge to every caregiver but also brings fear and anxiety into the hearts of many healthcare providers. Healthcare providers caring for children need to understand basic growth and development to provide age-appropriate assessments and plans of care required to treat the pediatric patient.

Each stage of childhood brings about unique changes in anatomical, physiological, and developmental characteristics that will affect assessments and interventions. Each stage necessitates a different approach. Healthcare providers must recognize the unique characteristics when caring for children with special healthcare needs. The purpose of this chapter is to highlight pediatric developmental changes and describe specific approaches to pediatric patients that will facilitate their effective assessment.[3, 4] This chapter also provides many web-based resources for providers. Web addresses change frequently; if you are experiencing difficulty accessing a specific address, access the primary website and then look for the desired details.

The Child and the Family

The family plays an integral role in the growth and development of children. First, we must define a family. Over the years, family has been defined differently in terms of roles and responsibilities, structure and function, and biological and genetic relationships, just to name a few. Most significantly, when referring to children, families comprise a group of individuals (at least one adult) living in the same house or nearby who take care of each other and provide support and direction for the children.[5] However the family is defined (i.e., single, blended, foster, adopted, or extended families), all have common concerns regarding their ill or injured child. The identification of Mom and Dad may be extended to individuals within the family unit who function in the role.

The parents and other caregivers play an essential role in a child's healthcare experience.[6] This factor alone differentiates caring for pediatric patients, compared with adults. The child, the identified patient, is not the only individual who requires attention. The family unit must be considered during every interaction with a child, especially if the child is seriously ill or injured. Communicating effectively with the caregivers is critically important when obtaining the medical history and consent for treatment.[6] The family's response to a child's illness or injury will directly influence how the child responds. The child's and the family's responses may be influenced by many of the factors listed in **Box 3-2** and **Box 3-3**.[5–7] Natural parental

---

Box 3-1 Guidelines for Disability Awareness*

Use the word *disability* instead of the word *handicap*.

Refer first to the person and then to the particular disability. (i.e., a child with autism, not an autistic child)

Avoid calling a person wheelchair bound or saying that the person is confined to a wheelchair. In reality, people with disabilities are made more mobile by using a wheelchair.

Avoid using negative descriptions of people with disabilities, such as invalid, mongoloid, epileptic, suffers from, and afflicted with. Avoid referring to seizures as fits.

Do not use the "N" word (normal) when describing people without disabilities. Instead use typical or people without disabilities.

Avoid making reference to a person's disability unless it is relevant.

*Data are from: Coalition From Tennesseans with Disabilities. (1993). *Talking about disabilities: A guide to using appropriate language.* Nashville, TN: Author.

Box 3-2 Factors That Influence Child's and Family's Responses to Illness and Injury*

The child's age and developmental stage.

The actual and perceived severity of the situation.

The severity of the physical pain.

Any previous experiences with the healthcare system.

Previously developed coping skills.

Their cultural beliefs and practices regarding health, illness, pain, and death.

Presence of language barriers.

The presence or availability of support systems.

The current events within the family unit.

The suddenness or expectedness of the situation.

*Data taken from Barrera and Hockenberry[6] and Conway.[7] Other sources are as follows: DiMaggio, T.J., Clark, L.M., & Czarnecki, M.L. (2010). Pediatric pain management. In B. St Marie (Ed.), *Core curriculum for pain management nurses* (2nd ed.) (pp.481–550). Dubuque, IA: American Society for Pain Management Nursing–Kendall Hunt Publishing. Jacob, E. (2007). Pain assessment and management in children. In M.J. Hockenberry & D. Wilson (Eds.), *Wong's nursing care of infants and children* (8th ed.) (pp.205–256). St. Louis, MO: Mosby/Elsevier.

instincts sometimes evoke strong emotional responses to situations involving the children. Parental responses are affected by a number of emotional factors, including guilt, fear, disbelief, anger, and loss of control.[6] A caregiver's own anxiety and reaction may negatively affect his or her ability to comfort the child, to understand information communicated to the child, to participate in decision making regarding the child's care, and to recall information required for discharge.[5]

Cultural and religious traditions and values influence family function, healthcare beliefs and practices, and the family's and child's response to an illness or injury. Health-related cultural perceptions and the perceived meaning of health and illness affect approaches to treatment and help-seeking behaviors.[8] During the assessment period, it is helpful to elicit information regarding the child's

birth country, the length of time the child has lived in this country, the language spoken at home, and information regarding the use of home remedies (i.e., over-the-counter and prescription medications and herbal and natural supplements) and healthcare practices. Healthcare providers must be aware of cultural differences that can create communication barriers. These cultural differences include eye contact, personal space, and the use of touch and conversation style.[6] Because of the diversity of society, the healthcare provider is often confronted not only by an ill or injured child but also by a range of diverse beliefs related to health and healing practices. Performing a cultural assessment is an approach that healthcare providers can use to facilitate understanding of the family's lifestyle, beliefs, and decision-making processes. Failure to recognize how culture influences health and illness can contribute to ineffective and culturally biased care.[9] Six key elements facilitate the process of becoming culturally competent **Box 3-4**.[9]

Box 3-5 provides some additional resources that can increase cultural awareness. When caring for children and

---

Box 3-3 Common Fears and Emotions in the Emergency Department Setting*

Infants (aged 1 month to 1 year): pain and discomfort, unfamiliarity with the environment, loud sounds, being handled by strangers, separation from caregiver, and disruptions in feeding and sleeping.

Toddlers (aged 1 to 3 years): pain and discomfort, separation from caregiver, being handled by strangers, darkness, sudden or loud noises, loss of control, and loss of mobility.

Preschoolers (aged 3 to 5 years): pain and discomfort are often misinterpreted, fear of injury and insides leaking out, and unfamiliar environment increases imagination and fear of monsters, ghosts, and the dark.

School-aged children (aged 5 to 11 years): pain and discomfort, feel guilty and responsible for event, fear of darkness, especially in unfamiliar environment, staying alone, and appearing physically different from friends.

Adolescents (aged 11 to 18 years): extreme self-consciousness, loss of autonomy, change in body image, feeling of hopelessness (with chronic illness), anger, separation from peer group and social isolation, and appearing physically different from friends.

*Data taken from Barrera and Hockenberry[6] and Conway.[7]

Box 3-4 Key Elements to Facilitate Becoming Culturally Competent*

Actively work on changing your view of the world and reframe thinking about groups with different thoughts and beliefs.

Increase knowledge about the cultural groups within your community.

Identify core cultural issues with these cultural groups (e.g., style of communication, personal space, and family relationships).

Identify core cultural issues within these cultural groups related to health, healthcare practices, and illness beliefs.

Develop a trusting relationship with empathy, understanding, and respect.

Discuss and adapt interventions that are culturally acceptable to the family and medically beneficial (not harmful) to the patient.

*Data taken from Dunn.[10]

Box 3-5 Cultural Competency (Web Resources)

American College of Emergency Physicians
http://www.acep.org/practres.aspx?id=29158

This website contains a policy statement regarding the care of culturally diverse patients in the emergency department. In addition, it contains specific guidelines for cultural and competent care of patients.

Children's National Medical Center
http://www.childrensnational.org/EMSC/PubRes/OldToolboxPages/CulturalCompetency.aspx

This website contains healthcare provider resources, databases, and example practices to assist healthcare providers in working effectively with culturally diverse patients.

American Academy of Pediatrics
http://practice.aap.org/content.aspx?aid=2992
http://www.aap.org/sections/adolescenthealth/pdfs/Assessing%20Cultural%20Competence.pdf

This website contains links to additional websites that assist healthcare providers in developing cultural competent practices with children. It includes a community tool box cultural competency tool kit.

University of California Center for Health Professions
http://depts.washington.edu/ccph/pdf_files/Brochure.pdf

This website gives information about a workshop that was designed to prepare clinicians to teach the knowledge and communication skills needed for providing culturally competent healthcare.

Georgetown University National Center for Cultural Competence
http://www11.georgetown.edu/research/gucchd/nccc/

This website provides information on how to design, implement, and deliver a culturally competent healthcare system. It provides conceptual models, definitions, tools, and processes to assist providers in assessing their cultural competency.

Table 3-1 Diversity Practice Model*

Definition	Application to Assessment
Assumptions: the act of taking for granted or supposing that a thought or idea is true.	Assumptions are often based on limited experience, bias, or generalizations. What are my assumptions, and what are they based on?
Beliefs and behaviors: beliefs are shared ideas about how a group operates, and behaviors are the ways a group conducts itself.	All patients must be treated with the same respect and dignity, regardless of their diversity. How do your assumptions compare with what you believe about certain groups?
Communication: the two-way sharing of information that results in an understanding between the receiver and the sender.	An early assessment must be made regarding the patient's ability to comprehend what is being said. As communication begins, the emergency care provider's body language must be one of acceptance and respect.
Diversity: the way in which people differ and the effect that differences have on the response to healthcare.	There is a wide variety of symptom management among diverse groups. How does the patient's diversity affect his or her response to health/illness or the emergency care provider's response to the patient?
Education and ethics: gaining knowledge about a cultural group and recognizing that ethical issues may be viewed differently by different culturally diverse groups.	The development of a cultural reference manual or a collection of reference materials on cultural practices and health beliefs is indispensable in the emergency department. Criteria for evaluation of staff competency must be developed with periodic evaluation.

*Data taken from Hooke.[9]

families from various cultural backgrounds, it is important to identify healthcare patterns and beliefs that may be a factor in treatment interventions or discharge planning.[10] The information obtained from the cultural assessment is essential in the provision of culturally competent care. Assessment of the views and beliefs of the child and family facilitates treatment and discharge planning, incorporation of cultural practices, and negotiation of culturally acceptable modifications to the discharge plan.[8, 9] If the family's approach or practices may be harmful to the child, the healthcare providers can approach these issues and provide the family with information concerning the implications of those customs. The nurse needs to inform the caregivers that these practices, if continued, may be harmful and considered maltreatment. The detail and depth of the cultural assessment will be dependent on the situation and the needs of the child and family. **Table 3-1** provides a practice model for assisting emergency care providers in their approach to cultural diversity and cultural assessment.[8, 9] **Box 3-6** contains a series of questions that may assist the emergency nurse in identifying religious and cultural beliefs related to a child's illness and the family's usual healthcare routines, including folk-healing practices.[8–10]

Sensitivity to the issues of culture and religion is essential in the emergency care of the pediatric patient. It is impossible for the emergency care team to have knowledge of all types of cultural and religious diversity. Therefore, the use of a diversity model approach is an integral part of the nursing process.

Family-Centered Care

The family is a constant in the child's life and must be able to provide comfort and support to the pediatric patient during emergency care. The development of a family-supportive environment is an important component of providing family-centered care. In the ED, family-centered care incorporates supporting and encouraging family participation and presence during all phases of care.[6] Family participation and involvement in the child's healthcare promotes collaborative relationships among the healthcare professional, the patient, and the family. Most families want to be present for all aspects of their child's care and be involved in all medical decision making. Families who are provided with patient and family-centered care are more satisfied with their care.[11, 12] Facilitating family presence during invasive procedures or resuscitation situations is a core component of family-centered care practices.[13, 14]

Core components in family-centered care include the following:

- Treating the patients and families with dignity and consideration.
- Communicating information without bias.
- Encouraging family participation that enhances control and autonomy.

Family members of critically ill patients have identified that their most important needs include the following:

- Being present with the patient.

- Being helpful to the patient.
- Being informed and updated about the patient's condition.
- Being comforted and supported by family members and healthcare providers.
- Feeling that the patient received the best care possible.[14]

Family Presence

The Emergency Nurses Association,[15] the American Association of Critical-Care Nurses, and numerous physician groups support the option of family presence during invasive procedures and resuscitation. The practice of allowing family presence during invasive procedures and resuscitation is a component of family-centered care. However, barriers do exist to family presence, at least for some healthcare providers. These may include stress over repeated intravenous access attempts, anxiety over possible or perceived mistakes, and concerns regarding how family members may react to invasive procedures such as incision and airway management.

Research results support allowing family presence during invasive procedures and resuscitation. In one study involving pediatricians, findings indicated that those with more frequent contact with seriously ill children were more likely to accept parental presence during cardiopulmonary resuscitation and that the exposure to parental presence during resuscitation increased the probability of allowing parental presence in future resuscitations.[16] In a study from the United Kingdom, 100% of pediatric critical care nurses and 68% of pediatric critical care physicians indicated that parental presence during resuscitation should be a choice.[14] A recent study surveying American Association of Critical-Care Nurses and Emergency Nurses Association members revealed that nearly half of the participants indicated that their departments permitted the option of family presence during invasive procedures or resuscitation, even though few institutions have written policies or guidelines regarding family presence.[17]

Before a family member is offered the option to be present during the invasive procedure or resuscitation, a healthcare provider must assess if the family can cope with the situation. If a family member exhibits distractive behavior that impedes the healthcare professional in providing adequate care to the pediatric patient, it may not be advisable to offer the opportunity for family presence. A consistent designated member of the staff who functions to support the family and serve as a patient and parent advocate should remain with the family independent of their decision to be present with the child. This designated staff member can also explain what is happening to the child at any point.[18]

The option to remain present during invasive or resuscitation procedures must be the choice of the caregiver.[19] If the caregiver chooses not to stay with the child, that decision should be respected and appropriate support and explanations should continue to be provided.[14] If the caregiver chooses to remain with the child, the healthcare team must ensure that the caregiver is provided with the following:

- Clear explanations of the procedure(s) and the child's expected responses.
- Clear instructions about where to stand and touch the child so that the child can hear his or her voice.
- Instruction on strategies to use to facilitate the child's coping with the procedure, as appropriate.
- Assessment in relation to his or her support needs.
- Emotional support and ongoing explanations by designated staff during resuscitation measures.
- Support by staff, as needed, during other invasive procedures.

Before escorting family members into the room of a child being resuscitated, the healthcare provider supporting the family must prepare them for what they will hear, see, and smell.[14] The family should be informed of where they should remain while in the room and, if possible, should have the opportunity to touch the child. The healthcare provider supporting the family should offer an ongoing narration of activities in a soft, calm, and directive voice. The child's responses and changes in condition should be the focus. Should the resuscitation efforts not result in positive changes in the child's condition, the healthcare provider supporting the family must remember that his or her role is to support family presence and to avoid being drawn into the "doing" role that emergency providers are accustomed to during critical situations and resuscitation. In many smaller EDs, other qualified staff (e.g., clergy or social workers) may be used as the support person if an ED staff member is not available. However, these individuals would need to receive education regarding their role during a resuscitation.

Historically, family members have been excluded from participation and presence during invasive procedures or resuscitation has not been allowed,[17] so encouraging family presence during these events is controversial for some healthcare providers. Many are concerned that family presence will hinder caring for the patient, that it will be distracting to the members of the team providing care, and that it will increase stress among the team.[17] Contrary to this belief, studies that have been published to date have not reported such findings.[13]

The Process of Growth and Development

Although growth and development occur simultaneously, they are distinct and separate processes. Patterns of growth and development are predictable, directional, and sequential. They are multifaceted processes that involve and are affected by genetic, nutritional, and environmental factors. Disturbances in these factors may alter the process of growth and development in a child. The sequential nature of growth and development remains the same in normally developing children.[20] Factors that affect growth and development include heredity, neuroendocrine processes, sex, chronic diseases, environmental hazards, prenatal influences, nutrition, socioeconomic status, and relationships with significant others.[7]

The term growth refers to the increase in weight and the body mass index. Growth and anatomical and physiological features of children are similar in all cultures, but key differences in race, ethnicity, and sex can be identified.[7] These changes can be plotted on growth charts specific for boys and girls and age range (including head circumference, height and weight, and body mass index). **Table 3-2** reviews the anatomical and physiological features of children.

Development refers to the gradual and successive increase in abilities or skills along a predetermined path (often referred to as developmental milestones or tasks).[7] Development is generally age specific and reflects neurological, emotional, and social maturation. Although there is cross-cultural similarity in the sequence and timing of developmental milestones, culture exerts a pervasive influence on the developing child.[8]

General Approach to the Pediatric Patient

Remembering these basic caveats will assist all healthcare providers in working with pediatric patients and their families.

- Establish a child-friendly environment using bright colors, paintings, mobiles, and cartoons.
- Allow the caregiver to remain with the child whenever possible.
- Address the pediatric patient by his or her name or nickname. Ask the patient or caregiver what name to use, when addressing them.
- Communicate with the family using nonmedical terminology, especially when talking about planned interventions, treatments, and findings.
- Observe the level of consciousness, activity (interaction with environment and caregiver), position of comfort, skin color, respiratory rate and effort, and degree of discomfort before touching the child.
- Provide privacy.
- Keep neonates and infants warm.
- Compare assessment findings with the caregiver's description of his or her child's usual behavior (e.g., eating and sleeping habits, activity level, and level of consciousness).
- Be honest with the child and caregiver. Provide explanations at the child's developmental level.
- Speak in a calm, empathetic, and directive tone.
- Provide reassurance and explanations of the situation and the anticipated plan of treatment to caregivers.
- Acknowledge positive behavior, encourage the child during the procedure, and praise the child afterward.
  - Provide rewards, such as stars, stickers, and bandages.
- Allow the child to make simple age-appropriate choices and to participate in his or her care.
  - Examples include asking the child which arm to measure his or her muscle (blood pressure) and then

Table 3-2 Anatomical and Physiological Features of Children with Clinical Implications*

Assessment	Pediatric Features	Clinical Implications
Airway	Large tongue relative to size of oropharynx	Common cause of airway obstruction; resolved with repositioning of airway.
	Obligate nose breathers	Infants younger than four months can develop respiratory distress from nasal congestion; resolved by keeping nasal passages clear of secretions.
	Smaller airway diameter	Small amounts of blood, mucus, or edema or small foreign objects can easily obstruct the airway and increase resistance to airflow.
	Cricoid cartilage narrowest area	Provides an anatomical seal for uncuffed or cuffless endotracheal tubes in children younger than eight years.
	Larynx more anterior and cephalad	Increased risk for aspiration causing airway obstruction.
	Cartilaginous larynx	Increased risk for compression of airway with hyperflexion or hyperextension, resulting in airway obstruction.
	Short neck and short trachea	Easily dislodged endotracheal tube of intubated patient with head movement; also increases risk to right main stem intubation.
Breathing	Compensatory mechanisms less effective	Although children in respiratory distress may initially increase both their work of breathing and respiratory rate, they tire easily, resulting in rapid decompensation.
	Higher metabolic rate	Results in a more rapid respiratory rate and less efficient use of oxygen and glucose. In addition, other symptoms, such as fever and anxiety, may further increase metabolic rate.
	Respiratory rate varies with age	The normal respiratory rate is inversely related to age; rates are higher in infants and decrease with age. Children with sustained respiratory rates of greater than 60 breaths/minute are at risk for respiratory arrest. A slow or irregular respiratory rate in an acutely ill infant or child is an ominous sign.*
	Thin chest wall	Breath sounds are easily transmitted (e.g., breath sounds may be auscultated over a pneumothorax).
	Cartilaginous sternum and ribs and resultant compliant chest wall	Children in respiratory distress often display retractions; if severe, they can result in the inability to generate adequate tidal volume.
	Poorly developed intercostal muscles	Children rely on the diaphragm for respirations; resolved by maintaining a sitting position to promote diaphragmatic excursion.
	Diaphragm positioned flat	Anything that impinges on movement of the diaphragm from above (e.g., asthma) or below (e.g., abdominal distention) impedes diaphragm function and respirations.
	Ribs horizontally oriented	Prevents increasing tidal volume when stressed; therefore, respiratory rate is increased.
	Fewer smaller alveoli	Fewer alveoli, thus less surface area for gas exchange.
Circulation	Increased circulating blood volume: infant, 90 mL/kg; child, 80 mL/kg; and adult, 70 mL/kg	Small amounts of blood loss can lead to circulatory compromise.
	Rapid heart rate (HR)	Normal ranges vary with age.
	Myocardium less compliant with less contractile mass and limited stroke volume (SV)	Cardiac output (CO) is maintained by increasing HR rather than SV: $CO = HR \times SV$. The CO decreases quickly with the HR (> 200 beats per minute or bradycardia). Tachycardia is an early sign of shock.
	Infants have higher CO than adults	This provides for increased oxygen demand but depletes CO reserve; times of increased stress, such as hypothermia or sepsis, may lead to rapid deterioration.
	Strong compensatory mechanisms maintain CO for long periods. Rapid deterioration occurs when compensatory mechanisms are exhausted.	Compensatory mechanisms will shunt blood to vital organs and away from the periphery. Skin temperature, skin color, and capillary refill will be affected. Hypotension is a late sign of circulatory compromise because children may remain noromotensive until 25% of the volume is lost.*

Assessment	Pediatric Features	Clinical Implications
Circulation *continued*	Higher percentage body water for body weight	Can become dehydrated more rapidly.
	Immature renal function in infants	Dehydration can occur rapidly in infants as the result of their inability to concentrate urine. Need to monitor output closely. Normal urine output is 1–2 mL/kg per hour.
	Neonates have a poorly developed sympathetic nervous system	Neonates are sensitive to parasympathetic stimulation, such as suctioning and defecating, and may have a bradycardic response.
Disability (neurological)	Immature reflexes present at birth	Babinski and Moro reflexes are normal findings.
	Anterior fontanel closes between the ages of 12 and 18 months	Gradual increases in intracranial pressure can be accommodated by increasing skull size.
	Level of consciousness is more difficult to determine	Greatly affected by adequate ventilation and oxygenation.
	Babinski reflex normal until child begins to walk	Presence of Babinski in walking child is an abnormal finding.
	Flexion is the normal body posture of an infant	Useful assessment finding, indicating normal neurological function.
	Infants have an immature autonomic nervous system	Body temperature control in response to environmental changes is limited.
Exposure	Infants younger than three months are unable to produce heat through shivering and must burn brown fat for thermogenesis (known as nonshivering thermogenesis)	This process increases metabolic rate and use of oxygen and glucose.
	Infants and children have a higher body surface area to weight ratio. Significant heat loss occurs from the skin on the infant's large head.	Ill and injured infants and children are at increased risk for hypothermia. Hypothermia may result in respiratory depression, impaired peripheral oxygen delivery, heart irritability, metabolic acidosis, hypoglycemia, coagulopathy, and alteration in the level of consciousness.
Additional differences	Body weight changes with age. Updated formulas for estimation of weight are being developed in evidence-based studies. Suggested formulas include: weight (in kg) = (3 x age in years) + 7.[†]	Accurate estimates necessary for administration of fluids and medications. When possible, all pediatric patients should be weighed on admission. If weight is not available, use standardized length-based resuscitation tapes that estimate weight based on length.
	High metabolic rate with limited glycogen stores	Increases use of glucose/glycogen storage and increases risk for hypoglycemia.
	Greater insensible fluid loss	Insensible fluid losses occur through respiration and skin losses. Children have a greater maintenance fluid requirement, which is calculated per kilogram and adjusted to their condition.
	Incomplete bone calcification	Absence of fractures (even in long bones) does not rule out injury to other structures.
	Medications are metabolized differently in children	All medications are based on kilogram weight.
	Children have a proportionally larger and heavier head compared with body size, which contributes to a higher center of gravity	Children are at high risk for head injury. They tend to fall head first.
	Infants have weak neck muscles combined with a large and heavy head	Infants and toddlers should remain in a rear-facing car seat until they reach the maximum height and weight recommended by the car seat manufacturer, at least to the age of 1 year and weight of 9 kg.

*Data taken from American Heart Association. (2006). Recognition of respiratory failure and shock. In *PALS provider manual* (pp. 23–42). Dallas, TX: Author.

[†]Luscombe, M. D., Owens, B. D., & Burke, D. (2010). Weight estimation in paediatrics: A comparison of the APLS formula and the formula "weight = 3(age) + 7." *Emergency Medicine Journal*. Advance online publication. doi:10.1136/emj.2009.087288

providing directions to inflate the blood pressure cuff. The child can also hold tape or bandages.

- Encourage play.
  ○ Use diversion and distraction. Encourage children to blow bubbles and blow the hurt away, to sing their favorite songs (and sing with them), to picture their favorite place, and to describe in detail with their senses.
- Give children permission to express their feelings. Tell them it is okay to cry. Empathy and sympathy are essential.
- Assess for pain using age-appropriate assessment tools and guidelines.
  ○ Identify the child's typical response to pain. Most pain states are characterized by a global pattern of physiological arousal, which can result in increased heart rate, blood pressure, and respiratory rate and depth. However, if pain has persisted for several hours or days, these responses are often modified and cardiovascular and respiratory measurements may be normal.
- Be cautious about what you say in the presence of any child, including an apparently unconscious child.
- Health promotion teaching must be tailored to the child's potential risks and needs associated with the child's current developmental level and upcoming developmental changes.
  ○ Anticipatory guidance should also be provided and should include well care and injury and illness prevention.
  ○ Health promotion education and anticipatory guidance applicable to all age groups may include the following points:
    - The importance of establishing and maintaining a medical home with a primary care provider (PCP) for the child. For children without a PCP, provide information for referrals to PCPs or provide information on how to obtain healthcare.
    - Reviewing the immunization status of the child, identifying community resources for obtaining low- or no-cost immunizations, and referring to the current Childhood Immunization Schedule (available at http://www.cdc.gov/vaccines/recs/schedule//default.htm).
    - Acknowledging the health risks associated with the child's exposure to secondhand smoke, particularly if the child has any allergies, frequent upper respiratory problems, or hyperactive airway disease.
    - The use of hand washing to prevent the spread of infections and the need to reduce contacts when a viral or bacterial infection is present.

    - Injury prevention focused on risks associated with the child's developmental level, including home safety, the use of appropriate child restraints for cars, seat belts, helmets, and other protective equipment. Convey to caregivers that preventable injuries are the leading cause of death and disability in children.
    - Following tips for choosing age-appropriate toys. Suggest the use of the choke tube or toilet paper roll to judge the size of toys that are too small for children younger than three years.
    - Providing the National Poison Center contact number (1-800-222-1222). Telephone stickers and information are available by calling the toll-free number.
    - Knowing about child abuse prevention and community domestic violence resources.
    - Having parenting information and community resources, including The National Safe Kids Campaign, Safe Kids Worldwide, and cardiopulmonary resuscitation courses.
- Communicating with children takes knowledge, thoughtfulness, and practice. In any healthcare setting and particularly in the emergency setting, children are often frightened by the surroundings, the strangers, and the reason why they are there (**Box 3-7**). The initial interaction with the pediatric patient needs to acknowledge psychosocial characteristics of the child's developmental level, particularly common fears and emotions. Understanding these characteristics will promote more effective interactions and accurate assessment of the child (**Appendix 3-A**).[7, 21]

Neonates (Birth to the Age of 28 Days)

Psychosocial Development

After birth, neonates may sleep for the next two to three days to recover from the trauma of birth.

- They like to be swaddled.
- Neonates will indiscriminately visually follow anyone meeting their basic needs.[6]
- The parent uses stimulation to play with the neonate (e.g., looking at the neonate at close proximity, talking and singing, and cradling and rocking the neonate).
- Pleasure is demonstrated by a quieting attitude.[22–24]
- Crying is the primary language to express need or displeasure.
- Behavior is reflexive (e.g., sucking, swallowing, rooting, grasping, and crying).[22–24]

Anatomical and Physiological Characteristics

- The neonate loses between 5% and 10% of his or her birth weight by the third or fourth day of life. Most neonates will return to their birth weight by the tenth day of life.

- The preterm infant is considered a neonate until the expected due date is reached plus 28 days.

- Neonatal reflexes should be symmetrical. Arm and leg recoil to a state of complete flexion is symmetrical. Primary reflexes present at birth include the sucking, rooting, grasping, startle, Moro, and Babinski reflexes.[22–24]

- Flexion is the normal posture, with the extremities pulled close to the chest and abdomen.

- Most neonates are awake and crying for one to four hours a day. The other hours of the day comprise varying sleep patterns and alert inactivity.[25]

- The breasts of neonates, in both sexes, may be enlarged with white liquid (witch's milk) for up to two weeks as the result of maternal estrogen. Female neonates may have some vaginal discharge.

- The body surface area to weight ratio is three times that of the adult; therefore, heat loss is of great concern.

- Neonates are vulnerable to hypoglycemia because of their limited glycogen stores.

Approaching Neonates

- The neonate should be observed for general appearance and condition, skin color, and work of breathing before he or she is touched. Neonates will usually cry when disturbed.

- Assessment should progress from the toe-to-head direction.

- Neonates are unconcerned about strangers and respond to soothing voices and warm gentle hands.

Infants (Aged One Month to 12 Months)[23, 25]

Psychosocial Development

- Infancy is a period of rapid physical and psychosocial growth and development. Infants are dependent on caregivers to meet their needs.

- Infants understand and experience the world through their bodies. Being held, cuddled, rocked, or comforted with familiar touch and smells soothes infants and develops their sense of trust.[23]

- Common fears, especially for older infants, include separation anxiety and stranger anxiety. Infants' relationship with primary caregivers is crucial for their sense of well-being.

- Infants explore objects by sucking, chewing, and biting. The more mobile older infant has an increased risk for injury by poisoning, foreign body aspiration, falls, and drowning.

Anatomical and Physiological Characteristics

- The fiftieth percentile weight is 3.5 to 10 kg.

- Infants are obligate nose breathers for the first four to six months of life. Blocked or partially blocked nasal passages may cause respiratory distress.

- Infants breathe predominantly using abdominal muscles. Any pressure on the diaphragm from above or below can impede respiratory effort.

- The metabolic rate in infants is approximately two times the adult rate. This results in an increased need for oxygen and glucose (calories).

- The infant's circulating blood volume is 90 mL/kg. Volume losses that may be perceived as insignificant can cause circulatory compromise.

  ○ Volume losses occur primarily because of inadequate intake, vomiting and diarrhea, increased insensible losses, or hemorrhaging.

- In the first few months of life, infants have immature renal function. The kidneys cannot efficiently concentrate the urine to conserve water. Normal urine output is 1–2 mL/kg per hour.

- In infants, the autonomic nervous system is not fully developed. The ability to control body temperature in response to environmental changes is limited.

- Although the central nervous system remains immature, by six to eight weeks, infants can fix on and follow objects placed in front of them.

Approaching Infants

- Approach the infant slowly, gently, and calmly. Loud voices and rapid movements may frighten the infant.

- Assess the infant while he or she is held by the caregiver, whenever possible, to decrease separation anxiety.

- Provide comfort by rocking, swaying, swaddling, and singing to infants. Up to approximately the age of seven months, infants can be comforted by strangers as long as their basic needs are met. Stranger anxiety varies among infants and is dependent on the variety of caregivers in the infant's life and individual temperament.

- Vary the sequence of the assessment with the infant's activity level. If the infant is calm and quiet, obtain the respiratory rate and auscultate the lungs at the beginning of the assessment.[25]

- Complete the most distressing (touching) components of the examination last. When examining the infant, warmed hands and stethoscope are less distressing.

- Provide the opportunity for self-comforting measures by encouraging access to a hand for sucking and using pacifiers.[6] Avoid insertion of intravenous lines into the infants' favored extremities whenever possible because they may want to suck their finger(s), thumb, or hand.

- Provide distraction and diversion during treatments and procedures.

- Explain to the caregivers that the infant will cry once the procedure is initiated. Unlike other age groups, young infants make no link between approaching stimulus and pain.

Anticipatory Guidance and Health Promotion for Neonates and Infants

- Encourage caregivers to lessen the risk for injury within the home by shortening window shade cords and covering electrical outlets.

- Place infants on their backs to sleep.

- If using pacifiers, purchase those with a one-piece construction and a looped handle.

- Provide age-appropriate injury prevention pamphlets, such as those given by The National Safe Kids Campaign, the Emergency Nurses Association, and the American Academy of Pediatrics.

- Instruct caregivers to transport infants safely when traveling in motor vehicles and by aircraft. The only safe location for the infant car seat is rear facing in the rear seat. Provide air bag information, including injury risk associated with air bag deployment and car seats. Remind caregivers that the infant should be strapped in the infant car seat whenever and wherever the car seat is used. The car seat should be used only for transportation. The infant should not be left in the car seat for sleeping, playing, or other activities.

- Encourage caregivers with older infants and toddlers to select shopping carts with seat belts attached to the seat section and to avoid children riding in the basket or standing.

- Discourage caregivers from using baby walkers. Walker use increases mobility and access to dangerous objects. This places infants at risk for injury because of falls and the ability to reach potentially dangerous items on tables, counters, and stove tops. Encourage caregivers to use stationary play stations, such as playpens and highchairs.[23]

- Provide poison center information, and encourage caregivers to survey the home for potential hazards and to remove them before the infant becomes mobile.

- Review the recommended routine immunizations with the family.[7] If the infant's immunization record is available and the infant is behind schedule, administer needed immunizations and document them on the immunization record. Provide appropriate vaccine information. Be prepared to discuss the risks and benefits, contraindications, and possible reactions.

- Infants explore with their mouths, which places them at greater risk for foreign body airway obstruction. Encourage caregivers to keep small objects from infants. Educate the family on the use of a choke tube or toilet paper roll to safely measure toys and objects that are too small for the young child to handle and play with. The choke tube is a commercially available safety measure that is intended to simulate the size of a child's airway in relationship to the size of object that a small child can handle safely.

Toddlers (Aged One Year to Three Years)[24, 26]

Psychosocial Development

- Toddlers are in a stage of rapid physical and psychological growth and development. By approximately the age of 18 months, toddlers are able to run, grasp, and manipulate objects; feed themselves; play with toys; and communicate with others.

- Toddlers are curious: with their improved mobility, they have no sense of danger, thus making them vulnerable to serious injury.
- Toddlers may have erratic eating patterns compared with infants and older children.
- Cognitively, a toddler's thinking is concrete, and he or she interprets words literally. Toddlers have an increased ability to problem solve through trial and error.
  - Toddlers are able to communicate verbally. Their negativism and insistence express an increasing need for autonomy.[24]
  - They strive for independence and are strong willed, with their favorite word being "NO."
- Common fears include separation from the caregiver and loss of control. They delight in the ability to control themselves and others. The toddler tends to cling to a caregiver when apprehensive.
- Physiological and psychological readiness for toilet training usually occurs between 18 and 24 months of age. Some toddlers are not ready until 36 months or later.[26]
- Toddlers' experiences are still strongly sensory based; seeing is believing.
- Toddlers imitate the health behaviors of primary caregivers.

Anatomical and Physiological Characteristics

- The fiftieth percentile weight is 10 to 12 kg.
- Normal urinary output is 1 mL/kg per hour.
- A Babinski reflex is normally present until the toddler starts walking. After the age of two years, the child should have a plantar reflex.
- The toddler continues to use abdominal muscles for breathing.
- The toddler has improved thermoregulatory ability but may still develop cold stress when critically ill or injured and exposed for extended periods.
- In toddlers, the head is larger than the rest of the body, making it more vulnerable to injury until approximately the age of six to eight years.

Approaching Toddlers

- Approach the toddler gradually. Keep physical contact minimal until the toddler is acquainted with you. Use a quiet and soothing voice.
- Incorporate play while assessing the toddler (e.g., "Show me your belly button"). If the child becomes upset or apprehensive, complete the assessment as expeditiously as possible.
- Encourage caregivers to hold and comfort their children during assessments and interventions.
- Introduce and use equipment gradually. Allow the child to handle minor equipment, such as a stethoscope.
- Provide the toddler with limited choices, such as "Do you want me to measure your muscle in your right arm or left arm?" This provides the toddler with a sense of control.
- Prepare the child immediately before a procedure, using simple, concrete, age-appropriate terms. Throughout the procedure, provide reassurance.
- Tell the child when the assessment or procedure is completed.
- Provide the toddler with positive reinforcement after procedures and praise his or her assistance, regardless of the toddler's reaction.[6]

Anticipatory Guidance and Health Promotion for Toddlers

The toddler has become more mobile, requiring closer supervision. Minimize home hazards for injury, such as placing household products and medications in secure locations, keeping handles from cooking utensils pointed away from the edge of the stove, and eliminating clutter around stairways to lessen risk for stairway falls.

Child safety restraint devices in motor vehicles are required. Best practice indicates that the safest position for the toddler's car seat is in the rear seat. References for caregivers include the car owner's manual, car seat packaging information, and local car seat experts (i.e., The National Safe Kids Campaign, police, and emergency medical services). A toddler should remain in a rear-facing position until he or she reaches the upper weight and height limit of the particular infant car seat. When the infant car seat is outgrown, the toddler can travel in a forward facing seat. Review information regarding risk of injury with air bag deployment and inappropriate installation of child safety seats.

Caregivers should practice toy safety by choosing toys according to the child's age and development, not according to the child's desires.

Children of this age are extremely malleable and observant, and their health behaviors reflect those of their primary caregivers.

Preschoolers (Aged Three to Five Years)[26, 27]

Psychosocial Development

- Preschoolers are magical and illogical thinkers. They often confuse coincidence with causation, have difficulty distinguishing fantasy from reality, and have many misconceptions about illness, injury, and body functions (e.g., if they have a cut, they fear that their insides will leak out).

- ○ Preschoolers' thinking has been described as magical; they often have imaginary playmates.[26]

- Preschoolers often take words and phrases literally. **Table 3-3** reviews words and phrases that are often confusing to this aged child.

- Preschoolers ask many questions and are more independent.

- Common fears include body mutilation, especially genitalia, loss of control, death, darkness, and being left alone; therefore, the preschooler needs much reassurance and simple explanations.

- Health practices are seen as tasks that must be mastered, such as brushing teeth. They have no concept of cause and effect; illness is often seen as punishment.

Anatomical and Physiological Characteristics

- The fiftieth percentile weight is 14 to 18 kg.

- Normal urinary output is 1 mL/kg per hour.

- The preschooler continues to use abdominal muscles for breathing.

Approaching the Preschooler

- Allow the child to handle equipment (or similar play equipment), such as a stethoscope.

- Immediately before the procedure, prepare the child by using simple concrete terms. Explain in terms of the sensory experience (e.g., hearing, feeling, and seeing). Delays in proceeding with the procedure after preparation can lead to increased anxiety and increased imagination of fearful things. The time lag should be less than two minutes.[6]

- Set limits on behavior but offer choices whenever possible to enhance feelings of control.

- Enlist the child's help (e.g., tell children to hold still but give them permission to cry). Do not link "good" behavior with stoic behavior. Avoid the use of the word "bad" because children tend to link it with themselves being bad.

- Assess the child's level of understanding and correct erroneous or unclear ideas because adult vocabulary may be misleading.

- Consider age-related language in explaining procedures to children.

- Use games to gain cooperation.

- Use dressings freely to promote preschoolers' feelings of body integrity.

Anticipatory Guidance and Health Promotion for Preschoolers

Motor vehicle safety restraint devices are still required for all children in this age group. Be aware of laws affecting child restraints in your state or country. Many child restraint devices are designed for children up to 45 kg. Preschoolers learn through example and will begin noticing if caregivers are not using safety restraints themselves.

Children of this age are extremely malleable and observant. By this age, children are able to understand the need for injury prevention and the reason for it. Riding toys are beginning to be used. Remind caregivers that safety helmets must be correctly fitted and worn. Instruct caregivers to place beds away from windows because this age group is at risk of falls from windows.

Provide safety information on "stranger danger."

School-Aged Children (Aged Five to 11 Years)[27, 28]

Psychosocial Development

- School-aged children are developing a sense of accomplishment and mastery of new skills. Successes contribute to positive self-esteem and a sense of control.

- Although the ability for logical thought processes is beginning, misinterpretation of words and phrases is common. Avoid using technical words and phrases.

  - ○ By the age of nine years, children can understand simple explanations about their anatomy and body functions. They believe that people can be part healthy and part unhealthy.

- Their concept of time is improved; awareness of possible long-term consequences of illness is present.

- Provide specific instructions to children about their behavior (e.g., "It's okay to cry as long as you hold your arm still"). Setting limits provides the child with a sense of control and a sense of accomplishment once the procedure is completed.

- Older school-aged children tend to hide their thoughts and feelings.

- Common fears include separation from friends, loss of control, and physical disability. Risk-taking behavior is emerging and is most concerning if present by the age of six years.

  - ○ School-aged children develop a general knowledge of medical intervention, often based on media reports, TV shows, and nightmarish fantasies.

  - ○ They are more likely to want to participate in their care.[28]

Table 3-3 Considerations When Communicating With Children: Are They Hearing What You Are Saying?*

Words that have more than one meaning are especially confusing to children, especially the older toddler and the preschool-aged child. At that age, the child is unable to interpret the abstract meaning of words and interprets them literally. If the use of medical terminology is unavoidable, it is imperative to explain these words at the age-appropriate level to the child. It is ideal to hold discussions with parents out of the hearing range of the child to avoid the child misinterpreting words or phrases.

Words or Terms to AVOID	Interpretation	Suggested Substitutions
Take ... as in I'm going to take your temperature.	Are you going to take something away from me?	Instead state: "I'm going to measure your temperature."
Dressing change	Why are they going to undress me? I don't want to change my clothes.	Instead state: "I'm going to put a clean bandage on you."
Urine	You're in. You're in what?	Instead use child's familiar term such as "pee," "your water," or "number one."
Stool	A chair.	Instead use child's familiar terms such as "BM," "poop," "do dee," "ca-ca," or "number two."
Computed tomography (CT) scan (CAT scan)	Can my cat do it? I'm allergic to cats. I'm afraid of cats.	Instead state: "We're going to take you to get a special picture of your insides."
Shot (also avoid use of the word bee sting)	With a gun? Are you going to hurt me?	Instead state: "I am going to give you some medicine with a little needle or medicine under the skin." Or use descriptions, such as pinch and a little owie.
IV (intravenously)	Ivy? I don't like plants. Are you going to plant me in the yard?	Instead describe in simple terms, such as, "I am going to put a straw in your skin and give your body a drink." Show if possible and allow touching.
Move you to the floor	Why are you going to take my bed away?	Instead try "Move you to a new bed."
ICU (intensive care unit)	Was I invisible before?	Instead try "Move you to a special room."
I'm going to stick you.	With what? I got poked with a stick before.	Instead state "I'm going to make a little pinch in your arm so we can give you some medicine."
Dye	Am I gonna die?	Instead tell them you are giving them a special medicine.
Put to sleep	They put my dog to sleep. Mommy said my fish was sleeping and she flushed him.	Instead tell them you are going to give them some medicine to give them a special sleep, and "When you wake up ..."
We're going to fix your cut.	With scissors? Will it hurt?	Instead state: "We're going to make your boo-boo better."
A stretcher's coming to get you.	A monster? A machine that will stretch my body?	Instead tell them "a special bed on wheels."
We are going to conduct some tests.	What if I fail? I don't like tests; I'm not good at them.	Instead state: "We are going to find out why you are feeling sick."

*Data taken from Hockenberry and Barrera[8] and Deering and Cody.[33]

Anatomical and Physiological Characteristics

- The fiftieth percentile weight is 20 to 32 kg.
- By approximately the age of eight years, the child's respiratory anatomy and physiology approximates that of an adult. The child's circulatory blood volume is 80 mL/kg.
- Normal urinary output is 1 mL/kg per hour.

Approaching School-Aged Children

- Provide the older school-aged child the choice of having the caregiver present during assessment.
  - Provide privacy. Privacy needs are changing, and some children may not want caregivers in the room when they undress. They are really modest.
- Allow them to participate in their care. Examples of this include opening a bandage and removing a blood pressure cuff.
- Explain procedures simply, and allow time for questions. The school-aged child may be reluctant to ask questions or to admit not knowing something that he or she perceives that he or she is expected to know.
  - Be honest, explain procedures, and describe how the child can be involved in his or her own care.
  - Provide reassuring comments with positive reinforcement after procedures, and praise their assistance regardless of the children's reaction.
- Reassure the child that he or she did nothing wrong. The procedure, illness, or injury discomfort is not punishment and is unrelated to his or her actions.

Anticipatory Guidance and Health Promotion for School-Aged Children

- Because of their desire for social acceptance, school-aged children may exhibit risk-taking behaviors to prove themselves worthy of acceptance. Because they have limited understanding of causal relationships between events, they may not think through the consequences of their actions.[29]
- Remind the caregivers and the child that bicycle helmets must be worn. Helmets must be replaced every three years or sooner, depending on the child's head growth, if cracks or chips develop in the helmet material, or if damage is sustained after a significant crash.
- Remind the caregiver and the child that safety pads for knees, elbows, and wrists must also be worn when in-line skating or skateboarding.

- Caregivers need to ensure safe transportation of children in motor vehicles through appropriate use of car safety restraints, including car seats and seat belts. The safest place in a motor vehicle for all children younger than 13 years is in the rear seat. Provide information regarding injury risks associated with air bag deployment.
- Provide safety information on the avoidance of strangers and saying no to the use of alcohol and drugs.

Adolescents (Aged 11–18 Years)[10, 30]

Psychosocial Development

- Adolescence is a period of experimentation and risk-taking activity.
- Adolescents are acutely aware of their body appearance. Anything that differentiates them from their peers is perceived as a major problem.
- Psychosomatic complaints are common.
- The adolescent's quest for independence from his or her family often leads to family dissension.
- Peer relationships are the most important relationships and provide psychological support and social development. Sexual interests are common.
- Adolescents may experience mood swings, depression, eating disorders, and violent behavior. These behaviors should be further evaluated as an emerging or developing mental health concern versus normal adolescent behavior.
- Common fears include changes in appearance, dependency, and loss of control.
- Beliefs may be influenced by the peer group in terms of acceptance and rejection.
- To seek comfort, adolescents may regress to earlier stages of development when stressed, ill, or in pain.[31]
- Adolescents progress from concrete to formal operational cognitive development but still lack the conceptual thinking skills of the adult. They need concrete explanations.[31]
- Health is perceived as feeling good and in control.

Anatomical and Physiological Characteristics

- Weights range from 36 kg to adult weight.
  - This weight is out of the range for length-based resuscitation tapes.
- Adolescence is characterized by rapid growth and heightened emotions, usually associated with hormonal changes.[10]
  - Puberty begins between the ages of eight and 14 years in females (median age of menarche, 12.5 years) and between the ages of nine and 16 years in males.[10]

Approaching Adolescents

- Provide adolescents with concrete information about their illness or injury, normal body functions, and plan of care, treatments, and diagnostic procedures.

- Respect privacy and confidentiality unless the information divulged is harmful to the adolescent or others (e.g., suicidal ideation or threat of harm of others).

  - Issues such as sexual activity, sexually transmitted infections, and pregnancy must be communicated in a private setting without the presence of the primary caregiver. In many states, procedures for any of these issues or concerns can be done without parental consent; however, it is not commonly the initial reason for seeking emergency care.

  - Offer the opportunity for adolescents to choose a support person during assessments and interventions, thus allowing them autonomy and decision making.

- Treat adolescents as adults. They expect it, but give them much reassurance.

- When talking with adolescents, avoid interruptions and distractions. Encourage adolescents to ask questions and participate in their own healthcare. Address their concerns first and then those of the caregivers.[7]

  - Be attentive to nonverbal cues.

  - Be honest and nonjudgmental. Avoid talking down to the adolescent, and avoid the use of slang terms. Use terms the adolescent can understand.

- Provide feedback about the adolescents' health status. When appropriate, emphasize the normalcy of physical findings.

  - Clearly explain how their body will be affected by the illness or procedure.

- Include a screening for health risk behaviors when obtaining the medical history.

  - The rate of suicide, exposure to violence, and substance abuse is high.

Anticipatory Guidance and Health Promotion for Adolescents

- Promote recreational safety and the use of safety equipment, including helmets and other safety equipment.

- Promote proper seat belt use and motor vehicle safety.

  - Always use a seat belt/shoulder harness in all vehicles, front and back seats.

  - Provide injury awareness and prevention literature about driving safely and the hazards of driving, or riding in a car when another driver is under the influence of drugs or alcohol, and distractions such as texting.

- Provide counseling related to reducing the risk of sexually transmitted infections, the use of birth control, safe sexual practices, and responsible sexual behavior.[10]

- Use resources available through agencies such as the American Academy of Pediatrics and the Emergency Nurses Association.

- Promote and provide health guidance information regarding the following[10]:

  - Parenting

    - Development

    - Diet and physical activity

    - Healthy lifestyles (including safe sexual behavior and avoiding substance use)

    - Injury prevention

  - Promote annual visits for preventive services with the PCP.[10] The preventive services visit facilitates early recognition of potential and actual health problems and the early establishment of health promotion practices.

Children, Adolescents, and Young Adults with Special Healthcare Needs

As a result of tremendous improvements in healthcare delivery and technology, children with a congenital condition or life-threatening illnesses and injuries survive longer. Children and youth with special healthcare needs present to the ED for treatment related to their underlying health condition and for the usual childhood illnesses and injuries.[32] This special population should have a written emergency care plan that is kept in easily accessible places in the children's home or other location, where they frequently spend time.[33] Consideration needs to be included and communicated with families and their children with special healthcare needs. **Table 3-4** describes selected healthcare conditions commonly seen in pediatric patients.

To facilitate the emergency care of these children, it is recommended that a mechanism be available to identify the child or youth with special healthcare needs when that child presents to the ED.[34] A standardized information form is available to prepare caregivers and healthcare professionals for emergencies involved with children and youth with special healthcare needs. It can be downloaded (http://www.aap.org/advocacy/eif.doc). In addition, a discharge-planning guide that begins with the initial ED visit is available to assist in planning for children and youth with special healthcare needs. These guidelines are available from the Emergency Medical Services for Children National Resource Center (http://www.childrensnational.org/EMSC). **Box 3-8** lists additional websites.

Table 3-4 Descriptions of Selected Special Healthcare Conditions

Body System	Description
Respiratory	Congenital: Laryngeal malacia; underdeveloped lungs; cystic fibrosis
	Acquired: Pulmonary neoplasms; asthma; chronic bronchitis; bronchopulmonary dysplasia
Cardiovascular	Congenital: Heart disease
	Acquired: Heart disease
Neurological	Congenital: Spina bifida; Arnold-Chiari malformation; chromosomal anomalies; Dandy-Walker malformation; hydrocephalus
	Perinatal: Infections; anoxic encephalopathy; birth trauma; cerebral palsy
	Postnatal: Head and spinal cord trauma; neoplasms
	Seizure disorders: Infantile spasms; Lennox-Gastaudt syndrome; epilepsy
Immunological	Congenital: Immune disorders
	Acquired: Human immunodeficiency virus; hepatitis; carcinomas
	Induced: Immunosuppression following solid organ or bone marrow transplants and chemotherapy for cancer treatment
Cognitive delay/ Intellectual disability	Physical appearance: Well-proportioned physical features or characteristic features such as low-set ears, soft neurological signs (e.g., microcephaly), poor fine and/or gross motor coordination
	Cognitive function: Educable or needing assistance or total care
Other	Physical: Limb deformities; craniofacial malformations; paralysis
	Sensory: Alterations in hearing, vision, or tactile perceptabilities
	Cognitive: Alterations in thinking abilities

Adapted from Wertz, E. (2001). The patient with special needs. In N. E. McSwaine (Ed.), *The basic EMT—comprehensive prehospital patient care* (2nd ed., p. 770). St. Louis, MO: Mosby–Year Book.

Box 3-8 Children with Special Healthcare Needs in the Emergency Department (Web Resources)

American Academy of Pediatrics

http://www.aap.org/advocacy/emergprep.htm

This website includes information on emergency preparedness for children with special healthcare needs. It includes a program overview, policy statements, and sample emergency information forms. It also includes some special case forms for specific special needs and links to additional resources.

American College of Emergency Physicians

http://www.acep.org/pressroom.aspx?id=26128

Included in this website is a fact sheet that discusses main points, questions, and answers regarding the care of special needs pediatric patients in the emergency department.

Family Voices

http://www.familyvoices.org/index.php

Family Voices aims to achieve family-centered care for all children and youth with special healthcare needs and/or disabilities. Through their national network, they provide families the tools to make informed decisions, advocate for improved public and private policies, build partnerships among professionals and families, and serve as a trusted resource on healthcare.

Tennessee Disability Coalition

http://www.tndisability.org/disability_links

This website includes a multitude of links to information on people with disabilities. It includes disability etiquette and ways to talk about disability that are appropriate.

Americans with Disabilities Act

http://www.ada.gov/

This website contains complete information on the Americans With Disabilities Act. It includes the law surrounding the act and links to other federal agencies with Americans With Disabilities responsibilities, including healthcare. It includes information on specific special needs and the law and requirements associated with the disability or special need.

National Dissemination Center for Children With Disabilities

http://www.nichcy.org/FamiliesAndCommunity/Pages/Default.aspx

This website includes information on specific disorders and disabilities, state resources, and resources for providers and families. It includes links to state agencies and information on understanding the laws surrounding special needs and disabilities issues.

Specific Health Promotion: Childhood Obesity: The New Childhood Morbidity

The increasing number of obese children and youth throughout the United States is a critical public health issue. These young people are at increased risk for serious medical and psychosocial threats. Emergency nurses can assist in tracking a child's weight and measuring and recording the body mass index in children and youth. Offering relevant evidence-based materials and guidance about childhood obesity and partnering with other professional organizations and healthcare providers to support prevention efforts are ways to be involved in decreasing this epidemic.[35] **Box 3-9** and **Box 3-10** provide additional information on obesity.

Role of Play

Through play, children learn about themselves and the world in which they live. Play functions to develop sensorimotor, intellectual, and socialization skills and to foster self-awareness, creativity, and values. Play reflects children's development and awareness of their environ-

---

Box 3-9 Childhood Obesity Prevention (Web Resources)

Office of the Surgeon General

http://www.surgeongeneral.gov/obesityprevention/

This website provides statistics on the numbers of children who are overweight and what we must do to ensure a healthy future for America's children.

Mayo Clinic

http://www.mayoclinic.com/health/childhood-obesity/DS00698/DSECTION=prevention

This website offers advice for those who are overweight and those who are at risk of becoming overweight. It offers suggestions about how to take protective measures to get or keep things on the right track.

American Academy of Pediatrics

http://www.aap.org/obesity/index.html

http://aappolicy.aappublications.org/cgi/content/full/pediatrics;112/2/424

This website provides information on what you can do to help your family live an active and healthy life and support a healthy and active community. It also provides advice about what health professionals can do and how to partner with the community.

Box 3-10 Childhood Obesity (Web Resources)

Center for Disease Control and Prevention

http://www.cdc.gov/obesity/childhood/index.html

This website provides information about childhood overweight and obesity, including how overweight and obesity are defined for children, the prevalence of obesity, the factors associated with obesity, and the related health consequences.

Mayo Clinic

http://www.mayoclinic.com/health/childhood-obesity/DS00698

This website provides the definition of childhood obesity, as well as the causes, risk factors, and advice about when to seek help and information on treatment and drugs.

The Obesity Society

http://www.obesity.org/information/childhood_overweight.asp

This website talks about the prevalence of childhood obesity and the consequences of childhood obesity and contributing factors. It also provides advice on how to measure childhood obesity.

National Center of Chronic Disease Prevention and Health Promotion

http://www.cdc.gov/HealthyYouth/obesity/

This website talks about the ways to make a difference at your school and with the use of the body mass indices. In addition, it gives policy guidance and information on local, national, and state programs.

American Academy of Pediatrics

http://www.aap.org/obesity/whitehouse/index.html

This website gives information on the American Academy of Pediatrics' initiative with the White House and the U.S. Department of Health and Human Services to reduce rates of overweight and obesity in our nation's children.

---

ment,[20, 36] as outlined in **Table 3-5**. Patterns of play begin with the most simple and become increasingly complex, reflecting the child's stage of development. Play allows children to practice skills they have already attained and to continually learn and gain new skills.[21] It also helps them cope with stressful situations.

Spontaneous play is child initiated. Therapeutic play is provider initiated and often used to reduce stress related to illness, injury, or medical procedures to explore relationships with significant members of the child's life.[36]

In any setting, including the ED, play is a useful assessment tool in children. For example, the assessment of a five-year-old asthmatic child after an aerosol treatment reveals a pale child with intercostal retractions, sitting cross-legged, actively engaged in coloring a picture. Reassessment of the child 30 minutes later reveals a pale child with intercostal retractions, leaning back against the bed and holding a crayon, but no longer coloring. In this example, the differences in play activity may be subtle indications of changes in the child's status and the dynamic process of the child's illness or injury.

General Safety in the Emergency Environment

The healthcare setting may not always be a safe environment for the child. This is particularly true of the ED setting, with high volume and rapid turnover of patients, transportation of patients and equipment to other areas via wheelchair and stretchers, multiple routes of access and egress, and the normal risks for children related to injury. Children must always be supervised; therefore, ED staff should instruct caregivers to keep side rails on the child's hospital bed in the up and locked position, to avoid leaving their child unattended, and to discourage children from running in the hallways. Consider child safety and injury prevention when purchasing furniture, room decorations, and toys for waiting areas, play stations, and patient rooms. **Box 3-11** lists specific resources for pediatric emergency departments.

Health Promotion

In addition to providing specific discharge information regarding the reason for the ED visit, additional age-specific health promotion and injury prevention information can be provided. Resources such as Bright Futures (2008) and *Instructions for Pediatric Patients*[37] have tear-out pages that can be duplicated without copyright concerns once the book is purchased. A web-based resource useful for discharge planning is http://www.kidshealth.org. These and other resources can provide the emergency nurse with excellent methods of assisting children and their families to learn from their ED experience and to learn more about their health promotion. **Box 3-12** provides resources for health promotion in pediatrics.

Table 3-5 Developmental Relationship of Play*	
Stage of Developmental Play Exhibited	**Activities**
Infants: Infants seek pleasure through social play by exhibiting social behaviors (i.e., smiling) that elicit positive attention from caregivers. They may be attracted (and distracted) with lights and moving brightly colored objects. In this exploratory stage, they explore their world through the touch of objects.	Speak to infants in a soft singsong rhythm. Allow them to hold and touch items you are using (stethoscope or tape roll). Use distraction, such as a flashlight, room light, bubbles, singing, playing peek-a-boo, and clapping.
Toddlers: Toddlers participate in parallel play; they play alongside, not with, others. Less complex pretend play often imitates parental roles (i.e., mowing the yard or pushing a grocery cart). They enjoy push-pull toys, blocks, and large balls.	Provide toys that are lifelike (e.g., telephones and tools). Allow them to keep and hold any item they might bring (e.g., stuffed animal, dolls, or cars).
Early childhood: Cooperative play with sharing can be seen in the preschooler. Imaginary friends develop with pretend play. Through pretend play, children act out the activities of daily life (i.e., acting like a teacher, policeperson, or postperson).	Provide coloring books, books, videos, toys, and games that encourage imagination.
School-aged children: Play becomes more competitive and complex. Interest in games, hobbies, and sports. Rules and rituals are important aspects of games and play.	Provide playing cards, puzzles, books, crafts, and board and video games.
Adolescents: Competition serves as a motivation for play.	Facilitate private space. Provide radio or other music device and video or computer games. Provide telephone access.

*Data taken from Hockenberry and Barrera.[8]

Box 3-11 Emergency Department Web Resources for Pediatric Patients

Society of Pediatric Nurses

https://www.pedsnurses.org/

This website contains many resources for pediatric care providers.

American Society for Pain Management Nursing

http://www.aspmn.org/

This website represents the American Society for Pain Management Nursing and includes broad information on the delivery of optimal nursing care to patients affected by pain.

American Academy of Pediatrics

http://www.aap.org/

This website is dedicated to the health of all children and includes many resources for pediatric care providers, including policy statements and pediatric guidelines.

National Emergency Medicine Association

http://www.nemahealth.org/

This website includes information on the prevention of illness by addressing health and social issues through applied research, technology, and equipment.

American College of Emergency Physicians

http://www.acep.org/practres.aspx?id=31364

This website includes pediatric policy statements, including guidelines for the care of children in the emergency department.

Children's National Medical Center

http://www.childrensnational.org/EMSC/

This website provides information on the Emergency Medical Services for Children National Resource Center, which was established to help improve the pediatric emergency care infrastructure throughout the United States and its territories.

Emergency Nurses Association

http://www.ena.org/

The Emergency Nurses Association website includes information on courses and education, injury prevention, research, and many more resources to assist pediatric emergency healthcare providers.

Box 3-12 Health Promotion (Web Resources)

Pediatrics in Practice

http://www.pediatricsinpractice.org/about_site_curriculum.asp (Video)

This website contains health promotion curricula that address six core concepts: partnership, communication, health promotion/illness prevention, time management, education, and advocacy (intended to facilitate effective patient interaction and care).

American Academy of Pediatrics

http://brightfutures.aap.org/clinical_practice.html

This website has a tool and resource kit, including sample forms for infants through adolescence. It also includes Bright Futures training on the value of using Bright Futures in primary care.

National Institutes of Health

http://www.nlm.nih.gov/medlineplus/childrenshealth.html#cat11

This website covers the various aspects of children's health, including physical, mental, and social well-being. In addition, it includes many resources on how to keep children healthy from all of these vantages.

Healthy Children

http://healthychildren.org

This website is sponsored by the American Academy of Pediatrics, specifically for parents. There is a monthly newsletter and short segments on season-related children's issues, injury prevention, and national children's concerns.

Childhood Immunization

http://www.cdc.gov/vaccines/recs/schedule//default.htm. This website provides the current recommendations and vaccine schedule according to the child's age, including downloadable tools for caregivers.

Summary

Providing healthcare to pediatric patients requires an understanding of the characteristics of growth and development. It is essential to use these facts during your assessment and interventions to obtain accurate information and the most effective treatment possible. The child exists within the context of a family. Even children who have been neglected or maltreated refer to their caregivers for support.

Crying is an infant's and young child's way of communication. Instead of crying being perceived as noise, consider crying as an assessment component to indicate adequate strength and possibly improved status. However, a cry that cannot be alleviated needs further assessment. Different-pitched cries and tones have different meanings; encourage the caregivers to help understand the source.

Play is a child's work. Use it as a part of assessment: a child who is able to stay engaged in play has a relatively intact mental status, whereas a child who is no longer interested in play has a changing or decreasing mental status.

Always consider the developmental stage of the child before entering a room to perform an intervention or assessment. There are more similarities than differences between adults and children. Approach the family as you do the child (i.e., with the same care and concern). An organized approach will help ensure confidence and consistent patient care.

Anticipatory guidance is the best preventive measure when dealing with children and families. Every interaction with a child and family should include appropriate teaching to deal with a situation before it becomes a problem. In the ED setting, the most beneficial anticipatory guidance involves injury prevention and home safety.

Appendix 3-A Childhood Development

Physical and Motor Development	Intellectual or Psychosocial Development	Language Development	Pain	Death
Infant Development (Aged One Month to One Year)				
Growth: period of most rapid growth; infant weight gain, one ounce per day; weight doubles by the age of six months and triples by the age of one year	Trust versus mistrust (Erikson): when physical needs are consistently met, infants learn to trust self and environment; common fears (after the age of six months) include separation and strangers	Sensorimotor period: infants learn by the use of their senses and activities	Infants do experience pain; the degree of pain perceived is unknown	Infants do not understand the meaning of death; the developing sense of separation serves as a basis for a beginning understanding of the meaning of death
Toddler Development (Aged One to Three Years)				
Growth: rate significantly slows down, accompanied by a tremendous decrease in appetite; usually are approximately half adult height by the age of two years general appearance is potbellied, exaggerated lumbar curve, wide-based gait, increased mobility, and hallmark of physical development in the toddler	Autonomy versus shame and doubt (Erikson): increasing independence and self-care activities; expanding the world with which the toddler interacts; need to experience joy of exploring and exerting some control over body functions and activity while maintaining support of "anchor" (i.e., primary caregiver); common fears include separation, loss of control, altered rituals, and pain	Sensorimotor period: cognition and language not yet sophisticated enough for children to learn through thought processes and communication	No formal concept of pain due to immature thought process and poorly developed body image; react as intensely to painless procedures as to those that hurt, especially when restrained; intrusive procedures, such as taking a temperature, are distressing; react to pain with physical resistance, aggression, negativism, and regression; rare for toddlers to fake pain; verbal responses concerning pain are unreliable	Understanding of death still limited; belief that loss of significant others is temporary; reinforced by developing sense of object permanence (i.e., objects continue to exist even if they cannot be seen); repeated experiences of separations and reunions; magical thinking; and TV shows (e.g., cartoon characters)
Preschool Development (Aged Three to Five Years)				
Growth: weight gain of two kilograms/year; height gain of six to eight centimeters per year; general appearance of "baby fat" and protuberant abdomen disappear	Initiative versus guilt (Erikson): greater autonomy and independence; still intense need for caregivers when under stress; initiate activities, rather than just imitating others; age of discovery, curiosity, and development of social behavior; sense of self as individual; common fears include mutilation, loss of control, death, dark, and ghosts	Preoperational (Piaget): time of trial-and-error learning; egocentric (experiences from own perspective); understand explanations only in terms of real events or what their senses tell them; no logical or abstract thought; coincidence confused with causation; magical thinking continues; difficulty distinguishing between reality and fantasy; may see illness or injury as punishment for "bad" thoughts or behavior; imaginary friends; fascination with superheroes and monsters	Pain perceived as punishment for bad thoughts or behavior; difficulty understanding that painful procedures help them get well; cannot differentiate between "good" pain (resulting from treatment) and bad pain (resulting from injury or illness); react to painful procedures with aggression and verbal reprimands (e.g., "I hate you" and "You're mean")	Incomplete understanding of death fosters anxiety because of fear of death; death is seen as an altered state of consciousness in which a person cannot perform normal activities, such as eating or walking; perceive immobility, sleep, and other alterations in consciousness as deathlike states; associate words and phrases (e.g., "put to sleep") with death; death is seen as reversible (reinforced by TV and cartoons); unable to perceive inevitability of death as the result of limited time concept; view death as punishment

Physical and Motor Development	Intellectual or Psychosocial Development	Language Development	Pain	Death
School-Aged Children (Aged 5 to 11 Years)				
Growth: relatively latent period	Industry versus inferiority (Erikson): age of accomplishment, increasing competence, and mastery of new skills; successes contribute to positive self-esteem and a sense of control; need parental support in time of stress (may be unwilling or unable to ask); common fears include separation from friends, loss of control, and physical disability	Concrete operations (Piaget): beginning of logical thought; deductive reasoning develops; improved concept of time; awareness of possible long-term consequences of illness; more sophisticated understanding of causality; still interpret phrases and idioms at face value	Reaction to pain affected by past experiences, parental response, and the meaning attached to it; better able to localize and describe pain accurately; pain can be exaggerated because of heightened fears of bodily injury, pain, and death	Concept of death more logically based; understand death as the irreversible cessation of life; view death as a tragedy that happens to others, not themselves; when death is an actual threat, may feel responsible for death and experience guilt
Adolescent Development (Aged 11 to 18 Years)				
Growth: for females, growth spurt begins at the age of nine and a half years; for males, growth spurt begins at the age of 10.5 years; at puberty, secondary sex characteristics begin to develop between the ages of eight and 13 years for females and between the ages of 10 and 14 years for males	Identity versus role confusion (Erikson): transition from childhood to adulthood; quest for independence often leads to family dissension; major concerns: establishing identity and developing mature sexual orientation; risk-taking behaviors include feeling that nothing bad can happen to them; common fears include changes in appearance or functioning, dependency, and loss of control	Concrete to formal operations (Piaget): memory fully developed; concept of time well understood; adolescents can project to the future and imagine potential consequences of actions and illnesses; some adolescents do not achieve formal operations	Can locate and quantify pain accurately and thoroughly; often hyperresponsive to pain; reacts to fear of changes in appearance or function; in general, highly controlled in responding to pain and painful procedures	Understanding of death similar to that of adults; intellectually believe that death can happen to them but avoid realistic thoughts of death; many adolescents defy the possibility of death through reckless behavior, substance abuse, or daring sports activities

References

1. Heron, M., Sutton, P. D., Xu, J., Ventura, S. J., Strobino, D. M., & Guyer, B. (2010). Annual summary of vital statistics: 2007. *Pediatrics,125,* 4–15.

2. Looman, W., O'Connor-Von, S., & Lindeke, L. (2008). Caring for children with special healthcare needs and their families: What advanced practice nurses need to know. *Journal of Nurse Practitioners, 4,* 512–517.

3. Swartz, M.H. (2009). *Textbook of physical diagnosis: History and examination* (6th ed., pp. 583–639). Philadelphia, PA: Saunders/Elsevier.

4. Algren, C. L., & Arnow, D. (2007). Pediatric variations of nursing intervention. In M. J. Hockenberry & D. Wilson (Eds.), *Wong's nursing care of infants and children* (8th ed., pp. 1083–1139). St. Louis, MO: Mosby/Elsevier.

5. Barrera, P., & Hockenberry, M. J. (2007). Family influences on child health promotion. In M. J. Hockenberry & D. Wilson (Eds.), *Wong's nursing care of infants and children* (8th ed., pp. 56–91). St. Louis, MO: Mosby/Elsevier.

6. Conway, A. E. (2009). Developmental and psychosocial considerations. In D. O. Thomas, L. M. Bernardo, & B. Herman (Eds.), *Core curriculum for pediatric emergency nursing* (2nd ed., pp. 29–44). Des Plaines, IL: Emergency Nurses Association.

7. Hockenberry, M. E., & Barrera, P. (2007). Communication and physical and developmental assessment of the child. In M. J. Hockenberry & D. Wilson (Eds.), *Wong's nursing care of infants and children* (8th ed., pp. 141–204). St. Louis, MO: Mosby/Elsevier.

8. Hooke, M.C. (2007). Social, cultural and religious influences on child health. In M. J. Hockenberry & D. Wilson (Eds.), *Wong's nursing care of infants and children* (8th ed., pp. 28–54). St. Louis, MO: Mosby/Elsevier.

9. Dunn, A. M. (2002). Culture competence and the primary provider. *Journal of Pediatric Health, 16,* 105–111.

10. Dunn, A. M. (2009). Developmental management of adolescents. In C. E. Burns, A. M. Dunn, M. A. Brady, N. B. Starr, & C. G. Blosser (Eds.), *Pediatric primary care* (4th ed., pp. 132–152). St. Louis, MO: Saunders/Elsevier.

11. Brown, K., Mace, S. E., Dietrich, A. M., Knazik, S., & Schamban, N. E. (2008). Patient and family-centered care for pediatric patients in the emergency department. *Canadian Journal of Medicine, 10,* 38–43.

12. Hemmelgran, A. L., Glisson, C., & Dukes, D. (2001). Emergency room culture and the emotional support component of family-centered care. *Children's Healthcare, 30,* 93–110.

13. Dudley, N. C., Hansen, K. W., Furnival, R.A., Donaldson, A.E., van Wagenen, K.L., & Scaife, E.R. (2009). The effect of family presence on the efficiency of pediatric trauma resuscitation. *Annals of Emergency Medicine, 53,* 777–784.

14. Dingeman, R.S., Mitchell, E.A., Meyer, E.C., & Curly, M. A. Q. (2007). Parent presence during complex invasive procedures and cardiopulmonary resuscitation: A systematic review of the literature. *Pediatrics, 120,* 842–854.

15. Emergency Nurses Association. (2005). *Family presence at the bedside during invasive procedures and resuscitation* [position statement]. Des Plaines, IL: Author.

16. O'Brien, M. M., Creamer, K. M., Hill, E. E., & Welham, J. (2002). Tolerance of family presence during pediatric cardiopulmonary resuscitation: A snapshot of military and civilian pediatricians, nurses, and residents. *Pediatric Emergency Care, 18,* 409–413.

17. Maclean, S. L., Guzzetta, C. E., White, C., Fontaine, D., Eichorn, D. J., Meyers, T. A., & Désy, P. (2003). Family presence during cardiopulmonary resuscitation and invasive procedures: Practice of critical care and emergency nurses. *Journal of Emergency Nursing, 29,* 208–221.

18. Bernardo, L. M., & Schenkel, K. (2003). Pediatric trauma. In L. Newberry (Ed.), *Sheehy's emergency nursing: Principles and practice* (5th ed., pp. 379–400). St. Louis, MO: Mosby.

19. Boudreaux, E. D., Francis, J. L., & Layacano, T. (2002). Family presence during invasive procedures and resuscitations in the emergency department: A critical review and suggestions for future research. *Annals of Emergency Medicine, 40,* 193–205.

20. Wertz Evans, E. M. (2009). Children and youth with special healthcare needs. In D. O. Thomas & L. Bernardo (Eds.), *Core curriculum for pediatric emergency nursing* (2nd ed., pp. 77–82). Des Plaines, IL: Emergency Nurses Association.

21. Algren, C. L. (2007). Family-centered care of the child during illness and hospitalization. In M. J. Hockenberry & D. Wilson (Eds.), *Wong's nursing care of infants and children* (8th ed., pp. 1047–1082). St. Louis, MO: Mosby/Elsevier.

22. Wheeler, B., & Berry, A. (2007). Health promotion of the newborn and family. In M. J. Hockenberry & D. Wilson (Eds.), *Wong's nursing care of infants and children* (8th ed., pp. 257–309). St. Louis, MO: Mosby/Elsevier.

23. Wilson, D. (2007). Health promotion of the infant and family. In M. J. Hockenberry & D. Wilson (Eds.), *Wong's nursing care of infants and children* (8th ed., pp. 499–565). St. Louis, MO: Mosby/Elsevier.

24. Wilson, D. (2007). Health promotion of the toddler and family. In M. J. Hockenberry & D. Wilson (Eds.), *Wong's nursing care of infants and children* (8th ed., pp. 607–642). St. Louis, MO: Mosby/Elsevier.

25. Deloian, B. J., & Berry, A. (2009). Developmental management of infants. In C. E. Burns, A. M. Dunn, M. A. Brady, N. B. Starr, & C. G. Blosser (Eds.), *Pediatric primary care* (4th ed., pp. 71–90). St. Louis, MO: Saunders/Elsevier.

References *continued*

26. Murphy, M. A., & Berry, A. (2009). Developmental management of toddlers and preschoolers. In C. E. Burns, M. A. Brady, N. B. Starr, & C. G. Blosser (Eds.), *Pediatric primary care* (4th ed., pp. 91–104). St. Louis, MO: Saunders/Elsevier.

27. Monroe, R. A. (2007). Health promotion of the preschooler and family. In M. J. Hockenberry & D. Wilson (Eds.), *Wong's nursing care of infants and children* (8th ed., pp. 643–662). St. Louis, MO: Mosby/Elsevier.

28. Gance-Cleveland, B., & Yousey, Y. (2009). Developmental management of school-age children. In C. E. Burns, M. A. Brady, N. B. Starr, & C. G. Blosser (Eds.), *Pediatric primary care* (4th ed., pp. 109–131). St. Louis, MO: Saunders/Elsevier.

29. Rogers, C. C. (2007). Health promotion of the school-age child. In M. J. Hockenberry & D. Wilson (Eds.), *Wong's nursing care of infants and children* (8th ed., pp. 712–751). St. Louis, MO: Mosby/Elsevier.

30. Saewyc, E. M. (2007). Health promotion of the adolescent and family. In M. J. Hockenberry & D. Wilson (Eds.), *Wong's nursing care of infants and children* (8th ed., pp. 811–848). St. Louis, MO: Mosby/Elsevier.

31. Deering, C. G., & Cody, D. J. (2002). Communicating with children and adolescents. *American Journal of Nursing, 102,* 34–41.

32. Wertz, E. M. (2009). Children and youth with special healthcare needs. In D. O. Thomas & L. M. Bernardo (Eds.), *Core curriculum for pediatric emergency nursing* (2nd ed.). Des Plaines, IL: Emergency Nurses Association.

33. Committee on Pediatric Emergency Medicine. Emergency preparedness for children with special healthcare needs. *Pediatrics, 104,* e53.

34. American Academy of Pediatrics. (2010). AAP policy statement emergency information forms and emergency preparedness for children with special healthcare needs. *Pediatrics, 125,* 829–837.

35. Hohenhaus, S. M. (2009). Health promotion and prevention of illness and injury. In D. O. Thomas & L.M. Bernardo (Eds.), *Core curriculum for pediatric emergency nursing* (2nd ed., pp. 45–54). Des Plaines, IL: Emergency Nurses Association.

36. Byrant, R. (2007). Family-centered care of the child with chronic illness or disability. In M. J. Hockenberry & D. Wilson (Eds.), *Wong's nursing care of infants and children* (8th ed., pp. 921–956). St. Louis, MO: Mosby/Elsevier.

37. Schmitt, B. D. (1999). *Instructions for pediatric patients* (2nd ed.). Philadelphia, PA: W. B. Saunders.

Internet Resources

U.S. Consumer Product Safety Commission (http://www.cpsc.gov)

National Safe Kids Organization (http://www.safekids.org/)

American College of Emergency Physicians (http://www.acep.org)

American Academy of Pediatrics (http://www.aap.org)

Centers for Disease Control and Prevention (http://www.cdc.gov)

National Emergency Medical Services for Children (http://www.ems-c.org)

National Association of Children's Hospitals and Related Institutions (http://www.childrenshospitals.net/nachri)

Chapter 4 | Prioritization:
Focused Assessment, Triage, and Decision Making

Susan M. Hohenhaus, MA, RN, CEN, FAEN

Objectives

On completion of this chapter, the learner should be able to do the following:

- Explain the components of the pediatric prioritization process.
- Describe interventions for life- and limb-threatening illnesses and injuries.
- Discuss the red flags of clinical and administrative pediatric prioritization.
- Analyze case-based scenarios to determine prioritization process priorities.

Case Scenario A

A six-year-old girl arrives at the emergency department (ED), walking with her mother. The child smiles at you, she has unlabored respirations and her color is pink.

Case Scenario B

A six-month-old infant arrives at the ED, carried by his mother. The infant does not react to his mother's voice, he has mild intercostal retractions and nasal flaring and his color is pink.

Case Scenario C

An ambulatory 12-year-old girl arrives at the ED with her father. She is quietly talking to her father, has unlabored respirations, and her skin appears pale and slightly diaphoretic.

According to the pediatric assessment triangle (PAT), which of the preceding patients is "sick, sicker, and sickest"?

Please see answers at the end of the chapter.

Introduction

The process of prioritization of the pediatric patient occurs in a variety of locations where children and their families present for emergency care. This includes EDs, inpatient units, urgent care and clinic settings, schools, and other out-of-hospital settings. Accurate prioritization must also occur during intrafacility and interfacility transport, disaster management and mass casualty incidents (MCIs), search-and-rescue events, and in-theater events encountered by members of the armed services. Ongoing assessment and reevaluation are also important in these settings.

The traditional method of *triage* (the sorting of patients according to the urgency of their need for care) has its roots in battlefield and disaster medicine incidents, during which the allocation of resources and responses was used to increase the number of survivors. This traditional triage method has evolved into the need for an updated practice that reflects the safe, effective, and appropriate provision of care for children. This practice includes the assessment of the needs and urgency of each individual patient based on limited data acquisition; it also considers resource availability. A review of triage decision-making research emphasized the experience level of the nurse, identification of critical thinking, use of intuition, and various cognitive factors that influence decisions made in emergency situations.[1]

Patient Safety and the Prioritization of Pediatric Emergency Care

Because pediatric patients often present with subtle signs and symptoms of illness and injury, the pediatric prioritization process is critically important and may even warrant recognition as a specialty within emergency nursing.[2] The systematic approach to prioritization of the pediatric patient begins even before the arrival of a patient. This preparation process should include formal pediatric-specific education and training programs that include a focus on acuity and prioritization of care. This training should be supplemented with periodic simulation of pediatric emergency presentation scenarios. In addition, institutional and unit-based performance and quality improvement measures should include scheduled standardized review of the accuracy and appropriateness of pediatric prioritization decisions. The Emergency Nurses Association and others recommend that only experienced nurses be assigned to the role of providing the initial assessment and emergency intervention for pediatric patients.[2-6]

Prioritization and Acuity Rating Systems

Although no one standard system for prioritization and acuity rating exists, the Emergency Nurses Association and the American College of Emergency Physicians have recommended that clinicians use a valid, reliable, five-level acuity system.[7] Five-level acuity rating systems that are both reliable and valid are as follows: the Emergency Severity Index; the Canadian Triage and Acuity Scale,[7-12] recommended by the Canadian Association of Emergency Physicians and the National Emergency Nurses Affiliation; the Australasian Triage Scale[13]; the Manchester Triage System[14]; and the French Emergency Nurses Classification in Hospital scale.[15] **Table 4-1** lists the different prioritization systems.

Disaster and Mass Casualty Prioritization

It is difficult to imagine a more challenging situation than when a disaster or MCI involves pediatric patients. Prioritizing injured children requires specific modifications to traditional MCI systems. Disaster and MCI triage systems adhere to the principle that conventional standards of medical care cannot be delivered to all victims when the system is overwhelmed. These events can occur in both field situations and hospital settings, including the emergency department. One pediatric MCI triage system that is beginning to gain general acceptance is JumpSTART. Developed in 1995 as a pediatric modification of the adult focused

Simple Triage and Rapid Treatment system, it is the first objective tool designed specifically for the triage of children during a mass casualty incident. JumpSTART's objectives are as follows: (1) to optimize the primary triage of injured children in the MCI setting, (2) to enhance the effectiveness of resource allocation for *all* MCI victims, and (3) to reduce the emotional burden on triage personnel who may have to make rapid life-or-death decisions about injured children in chaotic circumstances.[16]

Prioritizing Pediatric Emergency Care

In the ED, the role of the intake nurse is important. This is the first place that a child and family or caregivers make contact with healthcare providers when seeking emergency care. While accurately and safely prioritizing patients, the nurse must also acknowledge that there are an increasing number of patients presenting for care with a dwindling market of limited resources. Although there are also patient satisfaction issues that sometimes drive many decisions in the emergency care setting,[17] the emphasis on safety during the prioritization process should remain the focus for care. The overall goals of prioritization are the same for children as for adults: to rapidly assess the patients presenting for emergency care and to determine the severity of illness or injury and the corresponding need for emergency care. The challenge in assessing a pediatric patient and assigning an acuity rating is that assessment requires understanding the effects of the developmental and physiological characteristics of children.

There are four components in the prioritization of pediatric emergency care. These components include the PAT, the focused assessment (objective information), the focused pediatric history (subjective information), and the assignment of an acuity rating decision. Although the PAT is most commonly the initial component and the assignment of an acuity rating is last, it is recognized that the four components to prioritization are often performed simultaneously.

Unlike the prioritization of adult patients, pediatric patients generally require additional assessment and history taking to arrive at the acuity rating decision. The rationale for additional assessment includes the following:

- The significance of the developmental stage of each child, comparing current with typical behavior.

- The awareness of illnesses and injuries that are common with different developmental stages.

- The identification of risk factors for child maltreatment.

Table 4-1 Prioritization Systems*

Acuity Rating Decision Systems	Categories	Comments
Australasian Triage Scale Implementation Guidelines (http://www.acem.org.au/media/policies_and_guidelines/G24_Implementation__ATS.pdf) and Educational Guidelines (http://www.health.vic.gov.au/emergency/bgdocs/edupack.pdf)	**1,** Immediately life threatening; **2,** immediately life-threatening or important time critical treatment; **3,** potentially life-threatening or situational urgency; **4,** potentially serious or situational urgency or significant complexity or severity; and **5,** less urgent or clinic-administrative problems.	Includes options for reevaluation and retriage; states that pediatric patients are triaged using all five categories and "fast-tracking" should have no impact on the acuity rating decision. Most urgent/high-risk clinical features determine the category; specific identifiers for pediatric patients are listed in clinical descriptors.
Canadian Triage Acuity Scale Implementation Guidelines (http://www.cjem-online.ca/v3/n4/PaedCTAS)	**I,** Resuscitation conditions that threaten life or limb (or imminent risk of deterioration), requiring immediate aggressive intervention; **II,** emergent conditions that are a potential threat to life, limb, or function, requiring rapid medical intervention or delegated acts; **III,** urgent conditions that could potentially progress to a serious problem requiring an emergency intervention; **IV,** less urgent/semiurgent conditions that would benefit from intervention or reassurance within one to two hours as the result of the patient's age, distress, or potential for deterioration or complications; and **V,** nonurgent conditions that may be acute but nonurgent or part of a chronic problem with or without evidence of deterioration (some could be referred elsewhere).	Extensive implementation guidelines for use in pediatric patient populations.
Emergency Severity Index Implementation Handbook (http://www.ahrq.gov/research/esi/)	**1,** Requires immediate life-saving intervention, resource intensive; **2,** patient should not wait; high-risk situation, confused, lethargic, disoriented, or severe pain or distress, resource intensive; **3,** two or more resources required for care; **4,** one resource required for care; and **5,** no resources required for care.	Accounts for the patient's acuity, plus the number and extent of the hospital's resources needed for patient care. Handbook includes a poster and a pocket card, both containing the algorithm, and reproducible practice and competency case work sheets that can be used in teaching situations. Danger vital signs and fever considerations for pediatric patients included.
French Emergency Nurses Classification in Hospital Scale (http://www.triage-urgence.com/downloads/Triage%20FRENCH%20EJEM%202009.pdf)	**1,** Immediately life threatening; **2,** marked impairment of a vital organ or imminently life-threatening or functionally disabling traumatic lesion; **3,** functional impairment or organic lesions likely to deteriorate within 24 hours or complex medical situation justifying the use of several hospital resources; **4,** stable and noncomplex functional impairment or organic lesions, justifying the urgent use of at least one hospital resource; and **5,** no functional impairment or organic lesion justifying the use of hospital resources.	Accounts for the complexity of the patient; resource consumption, descriptions include both nursing and medicine definitions.
Manchester Triage System	**Red,** Emergent, needs instantaneous evaluation; **orange,** very urgent, needs evaluation within 10 minutes; **yellow,** urgent, within 60 minutes; **green,** standard, within 120 minutes; and **blue,** nonurgent, can wait for up to 240 minutes.	Most widely used triage system in Europe and Australia; specifically validated in pediatric emergency care.

*Data are taken from Grouse et al.[15]

- The extent of the compensatory mechanisms of children that may mask serious illness or injury.
- The risk for rapid deterioration once compensatory mechanisms fail.

Similarly, the rationale for additional history taking includes the following:

- The communication with the family or primary caregiver about parental concerns and perceptions. This is especially important for medically fragile children or children with special healthcare needs.
- The consideration for the absence of mature communication skills in most children.
- The portability of children with caregivers who often ignore the use of emergency medical services and delay definitive care.
- Any treatments provided before arrival, including the use of cultural and home treatments and their effects.
- The presence or lack of primary healthcare and preventive care.

Age-specific recommendations to the approach on physical assessment of a pediatric patient can be found in **Table 4-2**.

First Impressions: Using the Pediatric Assessment Triangle

The PAT provides a physiological assessment from an across-the-room perspective.[18–20] There are three components to the PAT: general appearance, work of breathing, and circulation to the skin.[18–20] The PAT can also be used to provide a quick reevaluation of pediatric patients to identify changes in condition and response to interventions. It allows for a rapid assessment of the pediatric patient's overall physiological stability and the development of an overall general impression (i.e., looks good versus looks bad).[18]

Appearance

The child's general appearance is the most important thing to consider when determining how severe the illness or injury is and the need for treatment. It reflects the adequacy of ventilation, oxygenation, brain perfusion, and central nervous system function. From across the room, the child should be assessed for tone, interactiveness, consolability, look/gaze, and speech/cry.[19]

Work of Breathing

A child's work of breathing is a more accurate indicator of oxygenation and ventilation than respiratory rate or the auscultation of chest sounds. Look and listen for abnormal airway sounds, abnormal positioning, retractions, and nasal flaring.[19]

Circulation to the Skin

Observing the child's skin allows the assessment of the adequacy of cardiac output and core perfusion or perfusion of vital organs. Inspect the skin for color in central areas, the lips, and the mucous membranes. Look for pallor, mottling, and cyanosis. **Figure 4-1** lists the components of the PAT.

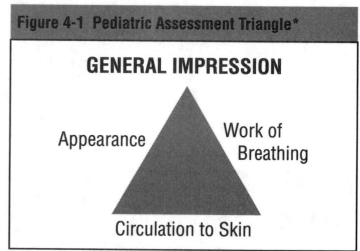

Figure 4-1 Pediatric Assessment Triangle*

GENERAL IMPRESSION

Appearance

Work of Breathing

Circulation to Skin

*Data are taken from the American Academy of Pediatrics.[20]

Sick, Sicker, Sickest

In general, pediatric patients with a normal appearance, work of breathing, and color are stable enough to warrant a more focused assessment and acuity rating decision. Yet, even if the child appears well, it is prudent to consider the child sick simply based on the fact that the caregiver was concerned enough to bring the child to the emergency department. Although the child will likely be assigned a lower acuity rating, the child should be considered sick until proved otherwise by conducting the more focused assessment. If there is acute disruption in any one component of the PAT, the child may be considered to be sicker and may require a higher acuity rating decision and the initiation of a focused treatment intervention. If there is acute disruption in two or more of the components of the PAT, this child should be considered sickest, with a high acuity rating decision and rapid resuscitation treatment interventions (**Table 4-3**).

Table 4-2 Age-Specific Approaches to Pediatric Physical Assessment*

Age	Position	Sequence	Preparation
Young infant	**Infant too young to sit unsupported:** seat the infant on the caregiver's lap or against the caregiver's shoulder.	If the infant is quiet or sleeping, auscultate the heart, lungs, and abdomen; and then palpate these areas as needed.	Undress to diaper but keep wrapped in a blanket; use distraction techniques (bright objects, rattles, or soft talking) to gain cooperation; smile and use a soft and gentle voice.
	Infant aged four to six months: place the infant on the caregiver's lap or examination table.	Proceed using a systematic method: assess skin, cardiovascular system, thorax, and lungs; proceed with abdomen, genitalia, and lower extremities; and finish with the head. Elicit Moro (startle) reflex last.	Pacify with a feeding (if permitted) or a pacifier; ask the parent to assist with assessment if he or she is able to do so. For example, have the caregiver palpate the affected area or perform passive range-of-motion exercises to elicit tenderness.
Older infant	**Infant able to sit unsupported:** place the infant on the caregiver's lap whenever possible; if the infant is positioned on the examination table, keep caregivers in full view.	Perform the most intrusive aspects of the assessment last. Elicit reflexes as the body part is examined.	Avoid quick movements or prolonged eye contact (older infants) to prevent surprises and promote trust.
Toddler	Position sitting or standing on or by caregiver or sitting upright on caregiver's lap.	Inspect body areas through play (count fingers and tickle toes); use minimal contact initially; introduce equipment slowly; discuss the child's fears with the parent and order the examination sequence accordingly; auscultate, percuss, and palpate when the child is quiet; perform the most intrusive aspects of the assessment last.	Have the caregiver remove outer clothing; remove the underpants when that body area is examined; encourage inspection of equipment; allow the child to hold a transitional object or toy during the assessment; demonstrate the assessment on a toy, the parent, or self; create a story about the assessment; speak to the child in terms that a toddler can understand; keep the caregiver's face in the child's view; perform the assessment quickly and efficiently if the child is uncooperative; praise and reward cooperative behavior; elicit the caregiver's assistance if he or she is able to do so, as described in the "Infant" section.
Preschooler	Position sitting, lying, or standing; may cooperate when prone or supine; prefers caregivers nearby.	If cooperative, proceed in head-to-toe fashion; if uncooperative, proceed as with toddler; perform the most intrusive aspects of the assessment last.	Request self-undressing; permit underpants to be worn and ensure privacy; offer equipment for inspection; demonstrate on the caregiver or a doll; create a story about the procedure (e.g., "Let's see how strong your muscles are."); offer choices when appropriate; expect cooperation; elicit the child's help whenever possible ("Point to where it hurts."); educate the child about his or her body ("I am going to listen to your heart; can you point to your heart?").
School-aged child	Prefers sitting; cooperates when placed in most positions; younger school-aged child usually prefers caregiver presence; older school-aged child may want privacy.	Proceed in head-to-toe examination; examine genitalia last (may be deferred).	Request self-undressing; allow wearing of underpants and ensure privacy; explain purpose of equipment and significance of procedure in terms the child can understand; teach about body functioning and healthy habits; tell the child it is permissible to cry; offer choices when appropriate.
Adolescent	Prefers sitting; offer parental or peer presence for support; speak with the adolescent first before talking with the caregiver.	Proceed in head-to-toe examination; examine genitalia last (usually deferred).	Maintain a sense of control and privacy by permitting adolescents to undress unattended; expose only the body area to be examined; explain assessment findings; maintain objectivity and professional demeanor when addressing sexual development and sexual history; emphasize normalcy; examine genitalia if warranted; approach examination as any other body part; may leave until the end; consider using a mirror during the genital examination to allow the adolescent to view the genital area.

*Data are taken from the following sources. (1) Hockenberry, M. (2005). *Wong's essentials of pediatric nursing* (7th ed.). St Louis, MO: Mosby. (2) Wong, D. (1999). Physical and developmental assessment of the child. In D. Wong (Ed.), *Whaley and Wong's nursing care of infants and children* (6th ed., pp. 217–283). St Louis, MO: Mosby–Year Book.

Table 4-3 Sick, Sicker, and Sickest

Category	PAT Assessment	Intervention
Sick	Normal appearance, work of breathing, and circulation to the skin.	Consider lower-acuity rating decision; observe for any change in PAT; provide comfort measures and reassurance to child and caregiver.
Sicker	Acute disruption in one component of the PAT.	Consider higher-acuity rating decision; provide focused clinical intervention (i.e., oxygen for respiratory distress).
Sickest	Acute disruption in two or more components of the PAT.	Immediate transport to treatment area; pediatric team activated and called to bedside; resuscitation efforts to support oxygenation, ventilation, and circulation.

Note: PAT indicates pediatric assessment triangle.

Case Scenario D

A nine-year-old child arrives to the ED in a wheelchair pushed by her mother. The child's head is floppy and bounces with the movement of the wheelchair, her eyes are not tracking movement, and she does not interact with her surroundings. She is slightly tachypneic; her color is pale. Her mother is frantic and crying.

1. Based on the PAT, does this child require a more focused assessment to establish an acuity rating?

   This child's general appearance is abnormal, and circulation to skin is abnormal. Based on the PAT, this child is sickest. Further assessment, including focused assessment and medical history, should be conducted in the treatment area.

2. Would you take vital signs on this patient before making an acuity rating decision?

   This child has a significantly abnormal PAT result, and the acuity rating should be considered life-threatening in any of the five-level acuity categorization systems. Obtaining vital signs would not change this categorization.

3. How rapidly should this child be treated?

   This child requires immediate admission to the ED treatment area for resuscitation.

Focused Assessment

Performing a focused assessment means that critical thinking is required. Understanding the possible disease processes and the pediatric normal is important. Asking standardized open-ended questions may also assist in gathering pertinent data. Consider your previous experiences and observations in conjunction with cues found in sensory factors, such as sight, smell, hearing, and touch. These may each assist you in formulating and validating your assessment. For example, if a child is doubled over, grimacing, sweating, and moaning, the organization of your previous experiences and observations infer that the child is in pain. These data create a foundational basis from which to inquire further regarding the source of pain.

After assessment of the child using the PAT, and the provision of appropriate interventions to address immediate life-threatening disturbances, a focused assessment is performed. The focused assessment follows the A-to-I standardized approach, as described in **Chapter 5, "Initial Assessment."** In addition, vital signs and medical history play a role in assigning an acuity rating.

Vital Signs and the Acuity Rating Decision

During the past several years, there have been many discussions and debates regarding the need for vital sign measurement in the setting of prioritization of care. The use of various prioritization systems can help to guide the process of what vital signs to obtain and when to obtain them. For example, the Emergency Severity Index supports raising the acuity rating decision from level three to level two based on fever status. The Canadian Triage and Acuity Scale lists vital signs as "first-order modifiers" that, by using objective criteria, may change the acuity rating. Intake nurses should adhere to the principles of the acuity rating system that is used by their institution. If the institution is using a system not recommended or endorsed by professional emergency organizations, nurses can join together to advocate for and plan the implementation of an appropriate five-level acuity rating system.

Vital signs are measurements of physiological parameters. Heart rate, respiratory rate, oxygen saturation, blood pressure, and pain assessment are the traditional measures obtained from patients in the ED setting. The best-practice method for obtaining vital signs in pediatric patients includes tactile and auscultatory procedures, especially to determine heart and respiratory rates.[2] When there is an unusual reading or the nurse is concerned, manual measurements should be attempted to verify electronic recording; however, caution should be used to not become distracted from visual clinical signs and symptoms to obtain these readings, especially blood pressure.

Because changes in physiological status may be exhibited by subtle changes in young children, heart rate, respiratory rate, oxygen saturation, and temperature are required points of initial vital sign measurement in children younger than three years. Trauma patients should be assessed for the following: PAT, neurological status using an appropriate Glasgow Coma Score, pain assessment, and determination if trauma system activation is necessary.

Temperature Measurement

Rectal temperatures are the most dependable means of obtaining a temperature when an accurate temperature is needed to make an acuity rating decision.[21] Avoid obtaining rectal temperatures in children with any potential or actual immunocompromise, children who have undergone rectal surgery, or children who have a chronic illness (e.g., sickle cell anemia) because this procedure may allow for the entrance of bacteria through an abrased rectal mucosal wall. Axillary temperatures may be considered for neonates presenting for well-baby checks or issues such as bilirubin checks because this is the practice used in most newborn nurseries, including neonatal intensive care units. Rectal temperatures in neonates should be considered individually and in consultation with the emergency or pediatric provider.

Measuring Weight in Pediatric Patients

A pediatric patient's weight is important information because it is often used to calculate the appropriate medication dose. When medication errors arise as the result of inaccurate or unknown patient weights, the dose of a prescribed medication could be significantly different from what is appropriate. Strategies to address these problems include having the necessary equipment, both scales that weigh pediatric patients **ONLY** in kilograms AND a method of length-based calculation of weight ONLY in kilograms when the child is too critically ill to allow for an exact weight measurement.[22] This is a critical element of safe and effective pediatric emergency care that should be accomplished at intake.

The Crying Child

One of the most challenging aspects of caring for children in the ED is safely and accurately assessing a crying child, especially a child younger than two years. Crying and fussiness are vague symptoms. Because of the child's inability to communicate and to localize complaints, these symptoms can indicate a wide range of illnesses and injuries. The overall appearance and stability of the pediatric patient should guide the triage process. In most children presenting with crying and irritability, the general appearance and ability of the child to be consoled may be the best indication of the child's status.

Fever, Pain, and Skin Rash

Other challenging aspects of pediatric acuity decision making involve whether the pediatric patient has a fever, is in pain, or has a skin rash. The intake nurse should use sound clinical judgment in making the final acuity rating decision and accounting for both the clinical picture and the child's age. For example, a neonate with a fever will likely be assigned a higher acuity rating than a three-year-old with the same temperature reading.

There are several validated pediatric pain scores and scales. For example, the Face Legs Activity Cry Consolability[23] score for infants and nonverbal children and the FACES score[24] for children three years of age and older are both validated and easy-to-use scoring systems. A validated pediatric pain scale should be available and used correctly and consistently. A discussion of pediatric pain systems should be part of the pediatric assessment training process.

Rashes can be confounding to even the most skilled clinician. The most important assessment tool to use when determining if a rash is life threatening is whether the result of the PAT is normal or abnormal. If the child has a rash and the result of the PAT is abnormal, the child should be considered seriously ill until proved otherwise. This also helps to quickly isolate children from the rest of the ED population and from potentially contagious diseases associated with a skin rash.

Immunization Status and Children in the Emergency Department

Families with children often use the ED as their primary source of healthcare. Many of these children are at risk for preventable diseases and are not properly immunized. In addition, children present to the ED with diseases that may have been prevented by vaccines. At an appropriate time during the child's visit to the ED, questions should be asked about immunizations previously received by that child and a comparison should be made with current recommendations of immunizations for that child's age group. Vaccination guidelines should be reviewed, updated frequently, and posted in a location that is easily accessible to frontline clinical staff.

Awareness of Child Maltreatment

When there is suspicion or concern that a child presenting to the ED has been abused or assaulted, the priorities of the clinician are to identify injuries and to provide appropriate stabilization. Accurately document the history described by the child and/or caregiver. If necessary, initiate the investigative process by reporting to child protective services and/or law enforcement agencies and preserve forensic evidence when appropriate. Never assume that someone else will initiate this report. During transition of care of the patient, be sure that reporting procedures are discussed and notification responsibilities are clear and documented.

Reevaluation of Waiting Children

Many children are unable to report signs and symptoms of illness and injury directly, thus the waiting area of an ED can be one of great vulnerability. Reassessment should be performed and documented at regular intervals. The PAT is an excellent method that can be used as the reassessment tool.

The Canadian Triage and Acuity Scale system has clear guidelines that represent best-practice recommendations for the reevaluation of waiting patients.[5] The recommended reassessment intervals are as follows:

- Level 1 patients should receive continuous nursing care
- Level 2 patients should receive care every 15 minutes
- Level 3 patients should receive care every 30 minutes
- Level 4 patients should receive care every 60 minutes
- Level 5 patients should receive care every 120 minutes

Handoffs and Transitions in Care

During the handoff of duties in the intake area where children are waiting for emergency care or transitions in care between intake and treatment areas, a verbal briefing is required between clinicians, off going and oncoming. The PAT status of waiting children or those entering the treatment area should be briefly discussed and documented. The Situation-Background-Assessment-Recommendation (SBAR) method is ideal for a structured approach.[22]

Pediatric Patient History

The pediatric patient history assessment is an important source of information between the clinical team and a variety of sources, including prehospital professionals, the family or caregiver, and/or the child. The goal in obtaining a history is to elicit accurate information regarding the problem or chief complaint and specific information regarding the illness or injury to help determine the urgency of need for emergency care.

Language or communication barriers can complicate the history-taking process. The accuracy of the pediatric patient's history may be diminished if barriers exist and may affect the accuracy of the acuity rating decision. The use of translators should be obtained as quickly as possible from resources within the facility or by using a professional language service. Discourage the use of friends and family members to translate because of the information you are requesting and the confidentiality of the discussion that is to be translated. Errors in translation are less likely to occur when professional translators are used.[25]

Communication barriers, such as hearing or verbally impaired, must also be identified. Alternative communication methods include writing, signing, or using a Teletype machine or a computer.[26]

Specific pediatric historical factors place children at risk for certain patterns of illness and injury. These factors include the following:

- Biological factors such as age and sex
- Behavioral factors such as poor nutritional intake and substance use
- Sociocultural factors such as cultural health practices
- Environmental factors such as seasonal changes or inner-city living
- Developmental factors such as prematurity or developmental delay[27]

A standardized and consistent method must be used to obtain a pediatric assessment history. There are a variety of formats used to elicit information in the emergency setting, including the widely accepted CIAMPEDS,[2] which is described in **Chapter 5, "Initial Assessment."**

Case Scenario E

A five-year-old girl presents to the ED with her babysitter. The child is quiet and hides behind the babysitter at the registration desk; she is breathing normally. You note the skin on her face to be reddened with a raised rash, but otherwise, her color is pink.

1. Based on the PAT, is this child sick, sicker, or sickest?

   This child is behaving in a developmentally appropriate manner; shyness is normal at this age. Her general appearance is normal despite the presence of the rash. A rash is evaluated after the PAT is complete. A normal PAT indicates a rash that is not life-threatening. An abnormal PAT means the rash should be considered life-threatening and isolation precautions should be instituted until the rash is identified. Her breathing is unlabored; normal. Her circulation to the skin is normal; pink. Based on no abnormal components of the PAT, this child should be considered sick.

2. What aspects of the focused medical history can assist you in making the acuity rating decision for this child?

   The A-to-I process can help identify any other areas of concern, such as wheezing and additional areas of rash.

3. What aspects of the CIAMPEDS history tool can assist you in making the acuity rating decision for this child?

   In the CIAMPEDS history tool, the I section (for immunizations and exposure to illness) and the "Diet" section (for exploring food allergens) may assist in making the decision and deciding about isolation processes.

Making the Acuity Rating Decision

The final step in the prioritization process is the intake nurse's interpretation of the child's assessment, resulting in an acuity rating decision. The determination of the acuity rating decision provides conclusion for the urgency and order for care. Additional assessments can and should be documented over time, and new ratings may be assigned based on these changes; however, the initial triage acuity score should not be changed. In one observational study, this was a significant issue and caused confusion in acuity ratings, potentially leading to misacuitization.[2] Careful adherence to established, evidence-based, standardized guidelines for prioritization, regardless of which system is used, is important. This includes the ability of the initial contact nurse to make the acuity decision. Other red flag administrative issues that may affect the assignment of an accurate acuity rating are listed in **Table 4-4**.

There are also clinical red flags to be aware of when making acuity rating decisions in pediatric patients (**Table 4-5**). These should be considered when assessing children because they affect the acuity rating decisions differently in various developmental stages and ages.

Table 4-4 Administrative Red Flags

Red Flag	Possible Solutions
Deviation from standardized evidence-based guidelines for assigning acuity rating	Acuity ratings should be used according to the principles that have been studied and validated.
Inadequate equipment for accurate assessment of children at intake	Ready availability of accurate pediatric scales and length-based measuring devices that measure only in kilograms; availability of accurate, up-to-date pediatric equipment; report pediatric patient's weight to others, including caregivers, only in kilograms; do not reuse single-use items, such as pulse-oximetry probes.
Lack of awareness of pediatric normal vital signs and baseline values	Formal education and training regarding normal and abnormal pediatric vital sign values; evidence-based medical records posted in intake areas.
Limited use or poor accuracy of evidence-based pain scores	Need further studies of implementation of pain scores used in pediatric prioritization decision-making.
Multiple children from same family being assessed together	Children should be assessed and interviewed one at a time.
Language barriers	Establish patient's language and assist in obtaining a qualified interpreter.
Improper reevaluation of waiting children	Adherence or development of standardized method for reassessing waiting children.
Lack of standardized data collection	Consider standardized computer support systems to aid in acuity rating decisions.

Answers to Case Scenarios A, B, and C

Case Scenario A

A six-year-old girl arrives at the ED, walking with her mother. The child smiles at you, she has unlabored respirations and her color is pink.

Case Scenario B

A six-month-old infant arrives at the ED, carried by his mother. The infant does not react to his mother's voice, he has mild intercostal retractions with nasal flaring and his color is pink.

Case Scenario C

An ambulatory 12-year-old girl arrives at the ED with her father. She is quietly talking to her father, has unlabored respirations, and her skin appears pale and slightly diaphoretic.

According to the PAT, which of the preceding patients is sick, sicker, and sickest?

Child A has no abnormal findings on the PAT. She is smiling, has unlabored breathing, and pink skin color. This means she should be considered "sick" and a focused assessment and focused history should be performed for further triage acuity designation. Child B has abnormal findings in two of the three components of the PAT. He does not respond to his mother's voice, demonstrating a possible altered level of consciousness, has mild retractions with nasal flaring. His normal finding is circulation to the skin.* Child C has one abnormal finding. She is interacting with her father and has normal respiratory effort, but appears pale and diaphoretic.**

Child A is sick, Child C is sicker, and Child B is sickest.

* *Child B should be considered "sickest" and needs an immediate primary survey and indicated interventions.*

** *Child C should be considered "sicker" and may need a focused intervention and high priority treatment.*

Table 4-5 Red Flags of Pediatric Triage*

Airway	Apnea, choking, drooling, audible airway sounds, and positions
Breathing	Grunting, sternal retractions, increased work of breathing, irregular respiratory patterns, respiratory rate of > 60 or < 20 breaths per minute for children younger than six years, absence of breath sounds, and cyanosis
Circulation	Cool or clammy skin, tachycardia, bradycardia, heart rate of > 200 beats per minute, heart rate of < 60 beats per minute, hypotension, diminished or absent peripheral pulses, decreased tearing, and sunken eyes
Disability	Altered level of consciousness, inconsolability, and sunken or bulging fontanel
Exposure	Petechia, purpura, and signs and symptoms of abuse
Full set of vital signs	Hypothermia, fever in an infant younger than three months (>38°C or 100.4° F), temperature of greater than 40°C to 40.6°C (104°F to 105°F) at any age
Give comfort	Severe pain
History	History of a chronic illness or a family crisis and return visit to the emergency department within 24 hours

*Data are taken from Romig.[19] Additional data are taken from the following sources: (1) Mecham, N. (2009). Triage. In D.O. Thomas & L. M. Bernardo (Eds.), *Core curriculum for pediatric emergency nursing* (2nd ed.) (pp. 71–76). Des Plaines, IL: Emergency Nurses Association. (2) Thomas, D. O. (2002). Special considerations for pediatric triage in the emergency department. *Nursing Clinics of North America, 37,* 145–159. (3) American Academy of Pediatrics (Eds.). (2005). *Pediatric education for prehospital professionals* (2nd ed.). Boston, MA: Jones & Bartlett. (4) American Heart Association. (2007). *PALS provider manual.* Dallas, TX: Author. (5) Andreoni, C. P., & Klinkhammer, B. (2000). *Quick reference for pediatric emergency nursing.* Philadelphia, PA: Saunders.

Summary

Children and their families deserve a professional healthcare provider who is educated, comfortable, and confident in making the right decision, which provides recognition for the urgency of the situation and the order in which pediatric patients should be treated. This prioritization involves the use of a standardized, evidence-based, systematic process that recognizes life-threatening conditions, identifies injuries, and determines priorities of care. This systematic approach consists of four components: the PAT, the focused assessment, collection of the CIAMPEDS history, and the acuity rating decision. It is the responsibility of the intake/triage nurse to identify abnormal assessment findings to provide safe and effective pediatric emergency care. Nurses who are responsible for making acuity rating decisions should have ongoing access to education that is specific to the physiological, developmental, and psychological needs of children.

References

1. Smith, A., & Cone, K. J. (2010). Triage decision-making skills: A necessity for all nurses. *Journal for Nurses in Staff Development, 26,* E14–E19.

2. Hohenhaus, S. M., Travers, D., & Mecham, N. (2008). Pediatric triage: A review of emergency education literature. *Journal of Emergency Nursing, 34,* 308–313.

3. Gilboy, N., Tanabe, P., Travers, D., Rosenau, A., & Eitel, D. (2005). *Emergency severity index version 4: Implementation handbook.* Rockville, MD: Agency for Healthcare Research and Quality.

4. Murray, M., Bullard, M., & Grafstein, E. (2004) Revisions to the Canadian Emergency Department Triage and Acuity Scale implementation guidelines. *Canadian Journal of Emergency Medicine, 6,* 421–427.

5. Warren, D., Jarvis, A., LeBlanc, L., Gravel, J., & CTAS Working Group. (2008). *Revisions to the Canadian Triage and Acuity Scale Paediatric Guidelines.* Retrieved from http://www.cjem-online.ca/sites/default/files/CJEM_Vol_10,_No_3,_p224.pdf

6. Emergency Nurses Association. (2011, February). *Triage qualifications* [position statement]. Retrieved from http://www.ena.org/SiteCollectionDocuments/Position%20Statements/TriageQualifications.pdf

7. Fernandes, C. M., Tanabe, P., Gilboy, N., Johnson, L. A., McNair, R. S., Rosenau, A. M., ... Suter, R.E. (2005). Five-level triage: A report from the ACEP/ENA Five-level Triage Task Force. *Journal of Emergency Nursing, 31,* 39–50.

8. Travers, D. A., Waller, A. E., Bowling, J. M., Flowers, D., & Tintinalli, J. (2002). Five-level triage system more effective than three-level in a tertiary emergency department. *Journal of Emergency Nursing, 28,* 395–400.

9. Manos, D., Petrie, D. A., Beveridge, R. C., Walter, S., & Ducharme, J. (2002). Inter-observer agreement using the Canadian Emergency Department Triage and Acuity Scale. *Canadian Journal of Emergency Medicine, 4,* 16–22.

10. Beveridge, R., Ducharme, J., Janes, L., Beaulieu, S., & Walter, S. (1999). Reliability of the Canadian Emergency Department Triage and Acuity Scale: Inter-observer agreement. *Annals of Emergency Medicine, 34,* 155–159.

11. Worster, A., Gilboy, N., Fernandes, C. M., Eitel, D., Eva, K., Geisler, R., Tanabe, P. (2004). Assessment of inter-observer reliability of two five-level triage and acuity scales: A randomized controlled trial. *Canadian Journal of Emergency Medicine, 6,* 240–245.

12. Stenstrom, R., Grafstein, E., Innes, G., & Christenson, J. (2003). Real-time predictive validity of the Canadian Triage and Acuity Scale (CTAS). *Academic Emergency Medicine, 10,* 512.

13. Wuerz, R.C., Milne, L. W., Eitel, D. R., Travers, D., & Gilboy, N. G. (2000). Reliability and validity of a new five-level triage instrument. *Academic Emergency Medicine, 7,* 236–242.

14. Grouse, A. I., Bishop, R. O., Bannon, A. M. (2009). The Manchester Triage System provides good reliability in an Australian emergency department. *Emergency Medicine Journal, 26,* 484–486.

15. Taboulet, P., Moreira, V., Haas, L., Porcher, R., Braganca, A., Fontaine, J., & Poncet, M. (2009). Triage with the French Emergency Nurses Classification in Hospital scale: Reliability and validity. *European Journal of Emergency Medicine, 16,* 61–67.

16. Romig, L. (2002). Pediatric triage: A system to JumpSTART your triage of young patients at MCIs. *Journal of Emergency Medical Services, 27,* 52–58, 60–63.

17. Fry, M., & Burr, G. (2001). Current triage practice and influences affecting clinical decision-making in emergency departments in NSW, Australia. *Accident and Emergency Nursing, 9,* 227–234.

18. Romig, L. E. (2001). PREP for peds—patient physiology, rescuer responses, equipment, protocols: Size-up & approach tips for pediatric calls. *Journal of Emergency Medical Services, 26,* 24–33.

19. American Academy of Pediatrics (Eds.). (2006). *Pediatric education for prehospital professionals* (PEPP) (2nd ed). Boston, MA: Jones & Bartlett.

20. Ralstonl, M., Hazinski, M., Zaritsky, A., Schexnayder, S., & Kleinman, M. (2006). *Textbook of pediatric advanced life support.* Chicago, IL: American Academy of Pediatrics and American Heart Association.

21. Pennsylvania Patient Safety Authority. (2009). Medication errors: Significance of accurate patient weights. *Pennsylvania Patient Safety Advisor, 6,* 10–15.

22. Hohenhaus, S., Powell, S., & Hohenhaus, J. T. (2006). Enhancing patient safety during hand-offs: standardized communication and teamwork using the "SBAR" method. *American Journal of Nursing, 106,* 72A–72B.

23. Merkel, S. I., Voepel-Lewis, T., Shayevitz, J. R., & Malviya, S. (1996). The FLACC: A behavioral scale for scoring postoperative pain in young children. *Pediatric Nursing, 23,* 293–297.

24. Bieri, D., Reeve, R. A., Champion, G. D., Addicoat, L., & Ziegler, J. B. (1990). The Faces Pain Scale for the self-assessment of the severity of pain experienced by children: Development, initial validation, and preliminary investigation for ratio scale properties. *Pain, 41,* 139–150.

25. Flores, G., Laws, M. B., Mayo, S. J., Zuckerman, B., Abreu, M., Medina, L., & Hardt, E. J. (2003). Errors in medical interpretation and their potential clinical consequences in pediatric encounters. *Pediatrics, 111,* 6–14.

26. Zimmermann, P. G. (2002). Guiding principles at triage: Advice for new triage nurses. *Journal of Emergency Nursing, 28,* 24–33.

27. Muscari, M. E. (2001). *Advanced pediatric clinical assessment: skills and procedures.* Philadelphia, PA: Lippincott Williams & Wilkins.

Chapter 5 | Initial Assessment

Sally K. Snow, BSN, RN, CPEN, FAEN

Objectives

On completion of this chapter the learner should be able to do the following:

- Incorporate anatomical, physiological, and developmental characteristics of pediatric patients into the initial assessment process.
- Demonstrate the initial assessment process.
- Demonstrate common interventions utilized during the initial assessment process.
- Employ health promotion strategies related to illness prevention.

Introduction

A systematic process for the initial assessment of every ill or injured pediatric patient is necessary for recognizing life-threatening conditions, identifying indicators of illness and injury, and determining priorities of care based on the assessment findings.[1] Although most children present with nonemergent illnesses or injuries, it is essential to remember that cardiopulmonary failure in children is rarely a sudden event. Rather, arrest is the end result of a progressively deteriorating respiratory or circulatory function.[2] Emergency care providers should be prepared to identify signs and symptoms of a life-threatening illness or injury and be able to rapidly provide the child with the appropriate interventions, spinal immobilization, and evaluation.[3] Using an organized and systems approach when assessing each child helps ensure that signs of physiological compromise, no matter how subtle, will not be missed. The initial assessment is divided into two phases: primary and secondary assessments. Both phases can be completed within minutes unless resuscitative measures are required.

A Guide to Initial Assessment

The materials presented in this chapter represent comprehensive primary and secondary assessments.

The following mnemonic describes the components of the initial assessment of the pediatric patient.

Primary Assessment

A = Airway with simultaneous cervical spine immobilization for any injured child whose mechanism of injury, symptoms, or physical findings suggest spinal trauma or whose medical history is incongruent with the pediatric patient's physical condition.

B = Breathing

C = Circulation

D = Disability or neurological status

E = Exposure and environmental control to prevent heat loss

Secondary Assessment

F = Full set of vital signs, including weight; family presence; and focused adjuncts

G = Give comfort measures

H = History and head-to-toe assessment

I = Inspect posterior surfaces

Assessing the Child with Special Health Care Needs

Assessing the child with special healthcare needs follows the same priorities as with all pediatric patients, with a few exceptions. Latex-free gloves and supplies should be available to the staff caring for children with special healthcare needs because some children are prone to latex allergy.

Primary Assessment

The primary assessment consists of assessment of the airway with cervical spine immobilization or maintenance of spinal immobilization when trauma is suspected, breathing, circulation, disability or neurological status, and exposure with environmental control. Interventions to correct any life-threatening conditions must be performed before further assessment is continued. The interventions are listed in order of priority.

A—Airway Assessment

Inspect the pediatric patient's airway for the following factors:

- Vocalization: Can the pediatric patient talk or cry?

- Tongue obstruction: In an unresponsive pediatric patient, the most common cause of airway obstruction is the tongue.

- Other causes of airway obstruction include the following:

  ○ Loose teeth or foreign objects, such as food, hard candy, or small toys, in the oropharynx or hypopharynx.

  ○ Vomitus, bleeding, or other secretions in the mouth.

  ○ Edema of the lips and/or tissues of the mouth.

- Preferred posture (e.g., the tripod position is characterized by the pediatric patient sitting up and leaning forward, with the head extended and tilted up in an effort to maximize the airway)

- Drooling and inability to handle secretions (in children other than teething infants)

- Dysphagia (i.e., difficulty swallowing, which indicates airway edema)

- Abnormal airway sounds, such as stridor, snoring, or gurgling

  ○ Inspiratory sounds are characteristic of extrathoracic or upper airway causes of obstruction.

  ○ Expiratory sounds are characteristic of intrathoracic or lower respiratory tract causes of obstruction.

Interventions

Airway Is Patent

For any pediatric patient whose mechanism of injury, symptoms, or physical findings suggest a possible cervical spine injury, manually stabilize the cervical spine. Maintain spinal immobilization, if completed in the prehospital environment, after checking that the devices are placed appropriately. All airway maneuvers for these children must be performed with the cervical spine in a neutral position to prevent possible secondary injury to the spinal cord/column. Any child with an unexplained alteration in mental status should create a high index of suspicion for intentional trauma. Immobilization of the cervical spine may avoid further injury to a child with no history of trauma, but who may, in fact, be a victim of physical abuse.

If a pediatric patient is awake and breathing, he or she may have assumed a position that maximizes his or her ability to maintain a spontaneously open airway. Allow the patient to maintain this position or a position of comfort until the appropriate personnel and equipment can be assembled if the need should arise for taking over the patient's airway.

Airway Partially or Totally Obstructed

If the pediatric patient is unresponsive and/or unable to maintain a spontaneously open airway, position the pediatric patient in a sniffing position and manually open the airway.

Techniques to open or clear an obstructed airway during the primary assessment include the following:

- Head tilt chin lift (difficult to perform in the younger child). NEVER use this technique if trauma is suspected or if there is any index of suspicion for intentional trauma. Jaw thrust is the maneuver of choice when in doubt.

  ○ Infants and young children have a large occiput; positioning them supine on a bed or backboard may cause their cervical vertebrae to flex anteriorly. Flexion may contribute to airway compromise or may decrease the effectiveness of the jaw thrust or chin lift maneuvers.

  ○ To provide neutral alignment of the cervical spine and a neutral position for the child's airway, place padding under the younger child's upper torso to bring the shoulders into horizontal alignment with the external auditory meatus. A disposable diaper is often the right size and may be immediately available.

- Suction the oropharynx with a rigid tonsil suction device to remove debris. Vomitus or secretions should be removed immediately by using suctioning to prevent aspiration. Suctioning or other interventions must be performed in a manner to prevent stimulation of the child's gag reflex, which may cause subsequent vomiting or aspiration and bradycardia.

- Suction the nose of the young infant with nasal secretions with a bulb syringe or suction catheter.
- Follow pediatric basic life support guidelines to relieve foreign body airway obstructions.[2]
- If the pediatric patient is unable to maintain a patent airway after proper positioning, perform the following procedures:
  - Insert an appropriately sized nasopharyngeal airway if the pediatric patient is conscious and if there is no evidence of facial trauma or basilar skull fracture, such as rhinorrhea, Battle sign, or raccoon eyes. Small nasopharyngeal tubes (for infants) may be easily obstructed by secretions.
  - Insert an oropharyngeal airway if the pediatric patient is unconscious or does not have a gag reflex. Proper positioning of the head and jaw must be maintained even in the presence of a patent airway. If the patient requires assistance to maintain the airway, the nurse must anticipate the need for further intervention.
- Prepare for endotracheal intubation.

Assessing the Airway of a Child with Special Healthcare Needs

Children with special healthcare needs may have abnormal airways that occur at any level of the airway from the oral cavity to the bronchial tree. Children with certain syndromes have exceptionally large tongues that predispose them to airway obstruction. Minor decreases in level of consciousness exacerbate this risk. Children with special healthcare needs may also be prone to an inability to handle secretions and require suctioning or other methods to help them maintain their airways. Syndromes resulting in facial bone anomalies can produce abnormally small airways, as is the case in Pierre Robin syndrome. Tracheal abnormalities that result in the softening of the trachea, the narrowing of the trachea, an opening between the esophagus and the trachea, or the incomplete formation of the trachea predispose a child with special healthcare needs to airway obstruction. These conditions place the child at particular risk of obstruction by a foreign body, increased risk for aspiration, and increased risk of morbidity from common childhood illnesses, such as bronchiolitis and croup.

B—Breathing

Once a patent airway has been established, assess for the following symptoms:

- Level of consciousness compared with baseline
- Spontaneous respirations

- Rate and depth of respirations
- Symmetrical chest rise and fall
- Skin color: pale, dusky, and pallor of nail beds or lip margin (cyanosis is first noted in the mucous membranes of the mouth and is a late sign of respiratory compromise)
- Presence and quality of bilateral breath sounds in anterior/lateral lung fields, along with the axilla
  - The chest wall of infants and young children is thin: breath sounds may be transmitted from one side to the opposite side, leading to seemingly equal breath sounds, even in the presence of a pneumothorax. An appropriately sized stethoscope will reduce the transmitted sounds in the chest of these patients.
- Presence of indicators of increased work of breathing
  - Nasal flaring, especially in infants
  - Substernal, subcostal, intercostal, supraclavicular, or suprasternal retractions
  - Head bobbing
  - Expiratory grunting
  - Accessory muscle use
- Jugular vein distention; it is difficult to assess in infants and young children because of their short fat necks
- Paradoxical respirations as the result of a flail segment or interruption of chest wall integrity
- Soft tissue integrity
- Measurement of oxygen saturation by a pulse oximeter, if readily available
  - A pulse oximetry reading of less than 92% at sea level is indicative of respiratory compromise; exceptions include children with uncorrected congenital heart defects.

Assessing Breathing in the Child with Special Healthcare Needs

Disorders of the airway, neurological system, or immunological system or decreased activity levels may place a child with special needs at risk for disruption in the delivery of oxygen to the tissues. There may be an alteration in the pulmonary-alveolar interface itself, resulting in the inability of oxygen to cross over from the lungs to the bloodstream; or a limited ability for respiratory excursion from an external element, resulting in decreased tidal volume and respiratory compromise. Knowledge of the baseline status of the child with special healthcare needs as described by the caregiver, will help the nurse determine changes that are significant.

Interventions

Breathing is present and effective

- Position the pediatric patient to facilitate respiratory effectiveness and comfort; respiratory mechanics are better with the pediatric patient in an upright position and the caregiver present to relieve anxiety.

- In the spontaneously breathing pediatric patient, deliver supplemental oxygen using the most appropriate method the child will tolerate, as indicated by the pediatric patient's clinical condition. This may begin with blow-by oxygen. Blow-by oxygen does not deliver a consistent concentration of oxygen and should be a temporary measure or a last resort for those children who will not tolerate a contact method of oxygen delivery.

- All seriously ill or injured patients should have oxygen administered at the highest concentration in a manner that the pediatric patient will tolerate. Allowing the patient to stay with the caregiver will decrease anxiety and, therefore, decrease oxygen demand.

- Consider using a nonrebreather mask at a flow rate sufficient to keep the reservoir bag inflated during inspiration, usually requiring 12 to 15 L/minute.

Breathing is ineffective

- Assist ventilation with 100% oxygen via a bag-mask device for apnea or hypoventilation.

  ○ Avoid overventilating the patient during resuscitation, causing increased intrathoracic pressure, air trapping, and barotrauma. Deliver only the volume needed to make the chest rise.[2]

- Assess the effectiveness of assisted ventilation by observing chest rise and fall and auscultating for the presence of breath sounds. When assistance is needed, the nurse should always anticipate the next step.

- Prepare for endotracheal intubation.

  ○ Indications for intubation are as follows:

    - Inadequate central nervous system control of ventilation, resulting in apnea or inadequate respiratory effort (e.g., severe head injury with decreasing level of consciousness or Pediatric Coma Scale or Glasgow Coma Scale [GCS] score of eight or less)

    - Loss of protective airway reflexes

    - Functional or anatomical airway obstruction

    - Excessive work of breathing, leading to fatigue

    - Need for high peak inspiratory pressures or positive end expiratory pressures to maintain effective alveolar gas exchange

    - Permitting paralysis or sedation for diagnostic studies while ensuring protection of the airway and control of ventilation.

  ○ Assemble the following equipment for intubation:

    - Suction device (e.g., tonsil-tipped or large-caliber catheter and suction catheter to fit into the endotracheal tube [ETT])

    - Bag-mask device with oxygen source

    - Appropriately sized stylet, laryngoscope blade, and handle

    - Endotracheal tubes (recommend three different ETTs: one tube of the estimated required size and tubes half a millimeter smaller and half a millimeter larger)

      » Tube size can be estimated using various strategies (**Table 5-1**).

    - Tape or commercially marketed tube holder device

    - Exhaled carbon dioxide (CO_2) detector or colorimetric device

    - Medications to facilitate intubation as ordered (if a neuromuscular blocking agent is used, a sedative must also be given)

      » Monitoring devices and resuscitative equipment must be in use at the bedside before the administration of any neuromuscular blocking agent.

- The routine use of cricoid pressure during intubation is no longer recommended. There is no research in the pediatric population demonstrating its use in preventing aspiration. Any laryngeal manipulation can adversely affect the ability to visualize or intubate the trachea and should be used with caution. Be prepared to monitor the pediatric patient's condition and immediately discontinue, at any sign of impaired ventilation.

- Confirm ETT placement at insertion and each time the child is moved.

  ○ Initial (primary) confirmation consists of the following variables:[5]

    - Direct visualization of the cords

    - Observe chest rise and fall

    - Listen for breath sounds bilaterally (anterior/lateral chest wall and the axilla)

    - Listen over the stomach for the absence of gurgling; in infants and young children, referred sounds may be heard over the stomach; any sounds heard over the stomach should always be fainter than those heard in the axillary areas.

    - Position the depth marker at the vocal cord level to prevent endobronchial intubation and unintentional extubation.[6]

Table 5-1 Estimating Tracheal Tube Size*

Uncuffed Tube Size[†] = (Age in Years/4) + 4

Cuffed Tube Size[†] = (Age in Years/4) + 3.5

These formulas allow for estimation of proper endotracheal tube size for children aged 1–10 years, based on the child's age. Endotracheal tube size is more reliably based on the child's body length. Use of a length-based resuscitation tape, such as the Broselow tape, is helpful for children up to approximately 35 kilograms.

*Data are taken from the American Heart Association.[2]
[†]Tube size is in millimeters of internal diameter.

- Look for water vapor in the tube during expiration; this finding is not conclusive because ETT misting can occur even with an esophageal intubation.[7]

○ Secondary confirmation involves evaluation of exhaled CO_2 and oxygenation.

- Assessment of exhaled CO_2 can be performed using the following methods:

» Use a colorimetric device (i.e., a pediatric device for those patients < 15 kg), after ventilating the patient six times to clear any retained CO_2 after bag-mask ventilation, mouth-to-mouth resuscitation, or the use of carbonated beverages. (The device may not register CO_2 in circumstances in which not enough CO_2 is delivered to the lungs or exhaled because of conditions such as cardiopulmonary arrest, status asthmaticus, and pulmonary edema).

In children who weigh less than 2 kg, CO_2 monitors may not be accurate. Establishing the presence of bilateral breath sounds along with direct visualization of ETT placement in conjunction with other clinical signs is essential in addition to the use of the end-tidal carbon dioxide dectector.[8]

» Continuous capnography can be used.

• Capnography may be used in all settings to confirm endotracheal intubation in pediatric patients with a perfusing rhythm.

• Capnometry detects exhaled CO_2 in intubated infants and children.

• During cardiopulmonary arrest, if exhaled CO_2 is not detected, the tube position should be confirmed using direct laryngoscopy.

» The esophageal detector may be considered for confirmation of tracheal tube placement in children weighing more than 20 kg.[9] It is unreliable in children younger than one year.

» Oxygen saturation can be assessed by pulse oximeter.

» Changes or improvement of skin and mucous membrane color can be assessed.

- Secure the tube, maintaining the child's head in a neutral position.

- Document ETT size, cuffed versus uncuffed tube, and depth by assessing location of the tube at the lip, gum, or tooth line.

- The appropriate depth of insertion can be estimated by the following formula: Depth of Insertion (in centimeters) = Internal Tube Diameter (in millimeters) × 3. Studies show that use of the length-based resuscitation tape to determine depth of the ETT is the most accurate method.[10]

- Obtain a chest radiograph.

- Decompress the stomach with a gastric tube to minimize the risk of aspiration. (Patients who have undergone bag-mask ventilation are prone to gastric distention. Gastric distention may impede adequate ventilation by limiting downward movement of the diaphragm.)

- Decompress tension pneumothorax via needle thoracentesis, as needed. This may be indicated if the patient is in severe respiratory distress or is intubated and not improving with other interventions.

C—Circulation

Once adequate breathing is established or verified, assess for the following variables:

• Central and peripheral pulse rate and quality (volume/strength).

○ Palpate a brachial pulse as the central pulse in the infant; palpate a carotid pulse in children older than one year.[1] The femoral pulse may also be used as a central pulse in any patient, regardless of age. The presence of central pulses with absent or weak peripheral pulses is a sign of poor tissue perfusion.

• Skin color (pale, mottled, dusky, or pallor of nail beds or lip margin), temperature, and moisture.

• Capillary refill. Blanch the nail bed or the skin over the torso, palms, or soles of feet with sustained pressure for a few seconds and then release pressure. The time it takes for the nail bed to return to its original color is the capillary refill time. Normal capillary refill is two seconds or less in a warm ambient environment. Factors that may affect capillary refill, not related to an alteration in general tissue perfusion, include a cool ambient temperature and injury with vascular compromise.

- Uncontrolled external bleeding.

Assessing the Circulation of the Child with Special Healthcare Needs

Children with special healthcare needs may have circulatory abnormalities that occur in any of the anatomical structures of the circulatory system. Congenital heart anomalies can be relatively minor to severe and complex. Children with rhythm disturbances may have implanted devices and should have their presenting condition compared with their baseline rather than the standard norms. Anomalies of the peripheral vasculature may also have implications for vascular access.

Interventions

The following may be used when circulation is ineffective:

- Control any uncontrolled external bleeding by applying direct pressure over the bleeding site(s).
- Obtain vascular access by inserting the largest-caliber catheter that the vessel can accommodate and initiating an intravenous infusion, as indicated by the pediatric patient's illness or injury.
  - Administer a rapid 20 mL/kg fluid bolus of a warmed isotonic crystalloid solution (e.g., 0.9% normal saline or lactated Ringer's/Hartmann solution), as indicated by the pediatric patient's perfusion status.
  - In the unconscious pediatric patient of any age, if peripheral access cannot be rapidly achieved, intraosseous access should be immediately considered.[2]
  - If the child presents in cardiogenic shock, fluids must then be administered at 10 mL/kg over 30 minutes.
  - In the pediatric patient with a severe volume deficit, the bolus should be infused within five to 10 minutes (depending on the caliber of the catheter that has been inserted).
  - Repeat the bolus, if reassessment findings indicate inadequate tissue perfusion. Boluses should be repeated until systemic perfusion improves.[2] If symptoms of shock persist, the pediatric patient may need blood. If hemorrhagic loss is suspected after two fluid boluses have been administered, the need for blood should be considered; colloid solutions may be necessary with evidence of septic shock, or vasopressors should be considered with evidence of septic/neurogenic shock.
    - If the decision is to administer blood, then the recommended administration volume is 10 mL/kg.

- Initiate medication therapy as indicated by the illness or injury and perfusion status.
- Initiate synchronized cardioversion or defibrillation, as indicated by dysrhythmias.
- Initiate cardiac compressions if the pulse rate is less than 60 beats per minute and perfusion is ineffective.

D—Disability: Brief Neurological Assessment

After the assessment and correction of any life-threatening conditions involving the ABCs of the pediatric patient, conduct a brief neurological evaluation to determine the degree of disability. Disability is determined by measuring the pediatric patient's level of consciousness. The findings must be based on the pediatric patient's age and developmental level.

Assessment

Determine the pediatric patient's level of consciousness by assessing the patient's response to verbal and/or painful stimuli. The AVPU mnemonic is a quick method for assessing level of consciousness, but the pediatric patient's pupils should also be assessed. Pupil assessment should include size, shape, equality, and reactivity to light.

A = Awake and alert

V = Responsive to verbal stimuli

P = Responsive only to painful stimuli

U = Completely unresponsive

Assessing the Neurological Status of the Child with Special Healthcare Needs

In children with chronic neurological impairment, assess responsiveness in relation to their normal or baseline status; ask the caregiver what the typical level of responsiveness for the child would be.

Interventions

- If the assessment indicates a decreased level of consciousness, conduct further investigations during the secondary assessment to identify the cause.
- Initiate pharmacological therapy as prescribed (e.g., naloxone [Narcan], glucose, or mannitol).
- Consider the need for endotracheal intubation to maintain airway patency and/or ensure adequate ventilation and oxygenation. A GCS of 8 or less may necessitate intubation to protect the airway.

E—Exposure and Environmental Control

Assessment

Undress the pediatric patient to examine and identify any underlying injury or additional signs of illness. Infants and children have a larger body surface area to body weight ratio and are at a greater risk of rapidly losing body heat when left exposed. Initiate methods to maintain a normothermic state or warm the patient, if hypothermic. Cold stress in critically ill or injured infants can increase metabolic demands, exacerbate the effects of hypoxia and hypoglycemia, and affect responses to resuscitative efforts. Coagulopathy is a common sequelae of hypothermia. Pay attention to the need for privacy for children, including those with special healthcare needs, when possible.

Interventions

Provide the following measures to maintain normal body temperature or warm the patient:

- Warm blankets, especially around the head
- Overhead warming lights or another warming device
- Warm and ambient environment, increasing the room temperature as needed
- Warm intravenous fluids via a fluid warmer when bolus volumes of intravenous fluids are administered (a variety of commercially available fluid warmers specifically designed for intravenous fluids are available).

For pediatric patients with fever, provide measures to cool the patients (metabolic demand increases depletion of nutrients and water).

- Measures should be initiated to restore hydration and create a comfortable environment by adjusting the amount of the pediatric patient's activity and clothing. Steps should be taken to avoid shivering because shivering not only increases metabolic and oxygen demand but also increases temperature.
  - Remove excessive clothing or blankets.
  - Administer antipyretics per protocol.
  - In the febrile pediatric patient, consider administering intravenous fluids at normal body temperature.

Consider the Need for Transfer

Not all hospitals are capable of providing definitive emergency care to critically ill or injured children. During the primary assessment, enough information should be collected to determine the pediatric patient's need for a higher level of care. The earlier the patient transfer is initiated, the sooner that the patient can be transported to a hospital capable of providing tertiary care. The need for pediatric critical care, surgical, or pediatric specialists not available at the initial hospital necessitates the need for transfer. **Chapter 23, "Stabilization and Transfer,"** provides more information.

Secondary Assessment

F—Full Set of Vital Signs

Assessment

Vital signs (**Table 5-2** and **Table 5-3**) may be obtained before the secondary assessment phase, especially when a team of providers is simultaneously involved in providing care to a seriously ill or injured pediatric patient. A complete set of vital signs should be obtained, if not done so already. Recognizing subtle and significant alterations in vital signs is an important part of analyzing the assessment data.

Table 5-2 Normal Respiratory and Heart Rates by Age Group

Age Group	Normal Respiratory Rate, Breaths per Minute	Normal Heart Rate, Beats per Minute
Infant (1–12 months)	30–60	100–160
Toddler (1–3 years)	24–40	90–150
Preschooler (3–5 years)	22–34	80–140
School-aged child (5–11 years)	18–30	70–120
Adolescent (11–18 years)	12–16	60–100

Table 5-3 Lowest Acceptable Systolic Blood Pressure Ranges by Age Group*

Age Group	Normal Blood Pressure, mm Hg
Term neonate (from birth to 28 days)	> 60 (or strong central pulse)
Infant (1–24 months)	> 70 (or strong central pulse)
Child (2–10 years)	> 70 + (2 × age in years)
Child (> 10 years)	> 90

*Data are from Aehlert, B. (2006). *Mosby's comprehensive pediatric emergency care.* Sudbury, MA: Elsevier.

The following vital signs should be assessed in all pediatric patients:

- Respirations: Assess the rate, rhythm, and depth of respirations, with special attention to increased work of breathing.

- Heart rate: Auscultate an apical pulse for a full minute, as a baseline rate in infants and younger children and in any critically ill or injured infant, child, or adolescent.

  ○ Compare central and peripheral pulses bilaterally for strength and equality. When evaluating central and peripheral perfusion, palpate the peripheral pulse on an uninjured extremity. Compare distal pulses in all extremities for strength and equality.

- Pulse oximetry: Pulse oximetry measures saturation of hemoglobin with oxygen. It does not measure ventilation.

  ○ It should be applied to a warm extremity with an adequate pulse for a proper reading.

  ○ Note that hypovolemic shock, anemia, and exposure to carbon monoxide can result in unreliable information regarding the child's oxygenation.

- Blood pressure (BP): Measure the BP by auscultation, palpation, ultrasonic flow meter, or noninvasive BP monitor.

  ○ Blood pressure cuff size can affect the accuracy of readings. An appropriately sized BP cuff bladder covers one-half to two-thirds of the pediatric patient's upper arm, upper, or lower leg.

  ○ Auscultate the initial BP in infants, children, and adolescents with signs of poor perfusion.

  ○ Noninvasive automated BP monitors should be used with caution on critically ill or injured pediatric patients. Some models are not accurate for extremely high or low BP readings. Abnormal readings or significant changes in readings should be validated by auscultation or another manual method.

  ○ The BP in a pediatric patient may be within normal limits for the pediatric patient's age despite significant fluid/blood loss; pediatric patients can compensate for greater than 25% volume loss before their systolic BP decreases.[12]

    - The typical systolic pressure in children two years or older is calculated as follows: Normal Systolic BP (mm Hg) = 90 + (2 × Age [Years]).

    - The lowest acceptable limit of systolic pressure in children two years or older is calculated as follows: Lower Limit of Normal Systolic BP (mm Hg) = 70 + (2 × Age [Years]).

- Temperature: Obtain temperature via an appropriate route (e.g., oral, rectal, axillary, tympanic, or temporal artery) considering the pediatric patient's age and condition.

  ○ Avoid rectal temperatures in immunocompromised patients. **Appendix 5-A** provides a conversion table for Celsius and Fahrenheit temperatures.

- Weight: The pediatric patient's weight (in kilograms) is needed for calculating medication doses and intravenous fluid amounts. A pediatric patient should ALWAYS be weighed in kilograms. All scales used for pediatric patients should be adjusted to weigh only in kilograms.

  ○ Obtain a measured weight whenever possible. If circumstances do not permit a measured weight, the weight may be estimated. Validated evidence-based strategies for estimating pediatric weights can include the following:

    - Asking the caregiver the pediatric patient's last measured weight.[13] This method may be the least reliable based on caregiver memory and time since last weight.

    - Using formulas

      » The advanced pediatric life support for weight estimation is weight (in kilograms) = 2 × (age in years + 4). Recently, several studies on this formula tested its validity and have found it to significantly underestimate a child's weight.[13]

      » A new formula has been developed, and its validity has been proven to accurately provide an estimated weight for children ages 1 to puberty. The formula is **weight (in kilograms) = (3 x age in years) + 7**.[13]

      » A common method for estimating a child's weight includes use of a length-based resuscitation tape, such as the Broselow tape. Recent studies indicate that estimates of weight determined by length-based tapes may underestimate a child's weight because of the increase in the prevalence of childhood obesity.[14]

Abnormal Vital Signs

- Factors affecting heart and respiratory rates are listed in **Table 5-4**.

- Serial BP measurements are useful for identifying subtle changes.

  ○ A widening pulse pressure (systolic pressure minus diastolic pressure) may occur secondary to increased intracranial pressure and early septic shock; a narrowing pulse pressure may be seen in early hypovolemic shock.

  ○ Hypotension is defined by age and can occur secondary to significant fluid or blood losses, sepsis, and certain medications. Hypotension is a late sign of shock in the pediatric patient.

  ○ Hypertension is defined as BP at or higher than the ninety-fifth percentile for age.

- Temperature variations that may indicate a serious condition include the following:

  ○ Rectal temperature greater than 38.0°C (100.4°F) with no localized sign of infection.[12]

Table 5-4 Factors Affecting Heart Rate and Respiratory Rate

Increased Heart Rate and Respiratory Rate	Decreased Respiratory Rate	Decreased Heart Rate
Medications	Medications	Medications
Hypothermia (early)	Hypothermia (late)	Hypothermia (late)
Hypoxia (early)	Hypoxia (late)	Hypoxia (late)
Shock (early)	Increased intracranial pressure	Shock (late)
Hypovolemia	Respiratory muscle fatigue	Increased intracranial pressure
Fear, anxiety, and agitation		Vagal stimulation
Pain		Cardiac pathology
Crying		
Fever		

○ Rectal temperature less than 36.0°C (96.8°F).[12]

F—Family Presence

The family is the pediatric patient's primary support system and, therefore, the patient and family should be treated as a unit. The Emergency Nurses Association recognizes the role of the family in the health and well-being of the patient and supports facilitating family presence for invasive and resuscitative procedures.[15] Collaboration among other healthcare providers is needed to develop multidisciplinary guidelines that will provide consistent, safe, and caring practices for the patients, families, and providers. Facilitation of family presence must be guided by the assessment of patient/family needs and the institutional protocols.[15]

These guidelines must address the following variables:

- Assigned staff members to provide family support and explanations about procedures.

- Cultural variances should be considered based on the communities' population.

- Resources should be provided for families with specific religious affiliations and contact information. The role of the emergency nurse is as an advocate and facilitator to support the family's involvement in the pediatric patient's care.

F—Focused Adjuncts

The need for continuous physiological monitoring is determined by the pediatric patient's condition, risk for deterioration, or need to evaluate physiological responses to treatment. A combination of cardiac monitor, pulse oximeter, and noninvasive BP monitoring may be indicated. Invasive BP and exhaled CO_2 monitoring are valuable adjuncts for the care of the critically ill or injured pediatric patient.

Evaluate the need for the following procedures:

- Infants and toddlers with serious illness or injury should have blood glucose measured (bedside glucose testing or serum glucose level) because of their increased risk for hypoglycemia when physiologically stressed.

- A urinary catheter and gastric tube if they have not yet been placed.

  ○ If the patient requires a urinary catheter, the collected urine should be measured and documented. A urine monitor should be placed on the collection bag and monitored for hourly output. This will provide the information necessary to determine the effectiveness of fluid resuscitation.

    - Normal hourly urine output varies with the size and age of the child: infant, 2 mL/kg per hour; child, 1 to 2 mL/kg per hour; and adolescent, 0.5 to 1 mL/kg per hour.

    - In infants and young children, the decision may be made to weigh diapers rather than insert a urinary catheter (one gram increase in diaper weight equals 1 mL of urine).

- If fluid resuscitation is necessary, consult a chart or length-based resuscitation tape to determine the correct tube size.

- Be sure that appropriate laboratory specimens have been initiated.

G—Give Comfort Measures

- Children perceive, interpret, and respond to pain differently than adults. Factors that contribute to the nature of pain have psychological, biological, and sociological components.[12]

Assess the pediatric patient's pain score using an age-appropriate pain scale. (**Chapter 6, "Pain"** provides more information.)

- Consider and initiate nonpharmacological comfort measures based on the pediatric patient's chief complaint and injuries. Examples are listed in **Table 5-5**.
- Inform the physician of the patient's level of pain, and be prepared to administer analgesics as ordered. Children with special healthcare needs may have an increased need for pain management based on history.

Table 5-5 Nonpharmacological Comfort Measures

Evaluate for the presence of pain. Pain can be assessed using self-report, behavioral observation, or physiological measures, depending on the age of the pediatric patient and his or her communication capabilities. A self-report should be the primary source of pain intensity estimates whenever possible.

Stabilize suspected fractures, including the joints above and below the injury.

Apply cold to injury sites while considering the risk for hypothermia.

Dress open wounds after noting details for documenting a description.

Provide a wheelchair or stretcher as indicated by the pediatric patient's condition and chief complaint.

Consider nonpharmacological and developmentally appropriate techniques to reduce pain, such as distraction and massage.

H—History

The history is obtained from the caregiver of the pediatric patient or from both the caregiver and the older child or adolescent. The history is an important piece of the initial data that assists the healthcare provider in analyzing assessment findings. The MIVT (i.e., Mechanism of injury, Injuries sustained, Vital signs, and Treatment before arrival) mnemonic can be used to elicit a history from prehospital providers for pediatric patients who have sustained a trauma, injury, or illness. The Emergency Nurses Association recommends following the CIAMPEDS (see **Table 5-6**) mnemonic. Children with special healthcare needs require additional history collection, but the type of history necessary is dependent on their underlying illness or condition. The use of an Emergency Information Form (**Appendix 5-B**) is extremely helpful in obtaining critical information about the pediatric patient. Emergency contact information, names and doses of medications, names and telephone numbers of specialists, allergies, and a list of medical issues can usually be found on this valuable form. Efforts to improve access to this information through the Internet are being developed. In addition, it is important to obtain information about assistive devices at home, sibling responses to the pediatric patient, and the pediatric patient's normal daily activities. Additional information, including social and family histories, may also be needed.[16]

Table 5-6 CIAMPEDS

	Definition	Description
C	Chief complaint	Reason for the pediatric patient's ED visit and duration of complaint (e.g., fever for past two days)
I	Immunizations	Evaluation of the pediatric patient's current immunization status.
		The completion of all scheduled immunizations for the child's age should be evaluated.
		If the pediatric patient has not received immunizations because of religious or cultural beliefs, document this information.
I	Isolation	Evaluation of the pediatric patient's exposure to communicable diseases (e.g., meningitis, chickenpox, shingles, whooping cough, and tuberculosis).
		A pediatric patient with active disease or who is potentially infectious must be placed in respiratory isolation on arrival to the ED.
		Other exposures that may be evaluated include exposure to meningitis and scabies.
A	Allergies	Evaluation of the pediatric patient's previous allergic or hypersensitivity reactions.
		Document reactions to medications, foods, products (e.g., latex), and environmental allergens. The type of reaction must also be documented.
M	Medications	Evaluation of the pediatric patient's current medication regimen, including prescription medications, over-the-counter medications, and herbal and dietary supplements, including: Dose administered Time of last dose Duration of use

Table 5-6 CIAMPEDS *continued*

	Definition	Description
P	**Past medical history**	A review of the pediatric patient's health status, including prior illnesses, injuries, hospitalizations, surgical procedures, and chronic physical and psychiatric illnesses. Use of alcohol, tobacco, drugs, or other substances of abuse should be evaluated as appropriate.
		The medical history of the neonate should include the prenatal and birth history: Maternal complications during pregnancy or delivery Infant's gestational age and birth weight Number of days infant remained in the hospital after birth The medical history of the menarche female should include the date and description of her last menstrual period
		The medical history for sexually active patients should include the following: Type of birth control used Barrier protection Prior treatment for sexually transmitted infections Gravida (pregnancies) and para (births, miscarriages, abortions, and living children)
P	**Caregiver's impression of the pediatric patient's condition**	Evaluation of the caregiver's concerns and observations of the patient's condition.
		These factors are especially significant when evaluating the pediatric patient with special needs
		Consider cultural differences that may affect the caregiver's impressions
E	**Events surrounding the illness or injury**	Evaluation of the onset of the illness or circumstances and mechanism of injury.
		Time and date injury occurred M: Mechanism of injury, including the use of protective devices (seat belts and helmets) I: Injuries suspected V: Vital signs in the prehospital environment T: Treatment by prehospital providers
		Description of circumstance leading to injury
		Witnessed or unwitnessed
		Illness Length of illness, including date and day of onset and sequence of symptoms Treatment provided before the ED visit
D	**Diet**	Assessment of the pediatric patient's recent oral intake and changes in eating patterns related to the illness or injury.
		Time of last meal and last fluid intake
		Changes in eating patterns or fluid intake
		Usual diet: Breast milk, type of formula, solid foods, diet for age and developmental level, and cultural differences
		Special diet or dietary restrictions
D	**Diapers**	Assessment of the patient's urine and stool output: Frequency of urination during the past 24 hours and changes in frequency Time of last void Changes in odor or color of urine Last bowel movement and color and consistency of stool Change in the frequency of bowel movements
S	**Symptoms associated with the illness or injury**	Identification of symptoms and progression of symptoms since the onset of the illness or injury event.

Note: ED indicates emergency department.

H—Head-to-Toe Assessment

Information from the head-to toe assessment is collected through inspection, palpation, and auscultation. The order and type of information collected in the secondary assessment will vary based on the pediatric patient's developmental level, chief complaint, and clinical appearance. The pediatric patient with special healthcare needs should be assessed in the same head-to-toe manner as with other pediatric patients. When the assessment reveals an abnormality, compare it with the pediatric patient's baseline. The caregiver will be the most likely historian for that information.

General Appearance

The Pediatric Assessment Triangle (PAT) is an observational assessment that provides physiological information in three areas to rapidly identify how sick the pediatric patient is and to determine how quickly treatment is required.[17] The three areas addressed by the PAT include the following: assessments of the patient's general appearance, work of breathing, and circulation to the skin. **Chapter 4, "Prioritization: Focused Assessment, Triage, and Decision Making,"** provides more information on the PAT.

The general appearance of the pediatric patient can assist the nurse in discerning problems that need further investigation. The pediatric patient's activity level, interaction with the environment, outward appearance (i.e., cleanliness, appropriateness of clothing for the season, and general nutritional status), and reactions to caregivers are important factors in the overall assessment of the patient. Body position and alignment, guarding or self-protective movements, muscle tone, and unusual odors (e.g., gasoline, chemicals, urine, and feces) may be identified during the secondary assessment.

Head, Ears, Eyes, Nose, and Throat

During the secondary assessment, a more complete neurological assessment is performed.

- A Pediatric Coma Scale or a GCS score may be determined (**Table 5-7**).
- The Full Outline of UnResponsiveness (FOUR) Score is a new coma scale that was recently developed and validated in adults as an alternative to the GCS. Although further validation of its use in pediatrics is needed, preliminary studies indicate that the FOUR Score is a reliable and valid tool for use in a wide variety of neuroscience patients.[18]
- The FOUR Score assesses eye response, motor response, brainstem reflexes, and respirations. Its

advantage over the GCS is its usefulness in patients who cannot speak (**Figure 5-1**).

Inspect for:

- Surface trauma (i.e., lacerations, abrasions, ecchymosis, rashes, asymmetry, edema, petechiae, or subconjunctival hemorrhage)
- Loose teeth or foreign material in the mouth
- Bony deformities or angulation
- Symmetry of facial expressions
- Eye and eyelid position and ear position
  - Color of the sclera and conjunctiva
  - Subconjunctival hemorrhage
  - Hyphema (which may be difficult in a supine patient [because blood in the anterior chamber of the eye is gravity dependent] or in a patient who has dark sclera)
  - Ptosis (drooping of the upper eyelid)
  - Periorbital ecchymosis or raccoon eyes (suggestive of anterior basilar skull fracture with bleeding into the anterior fossa)
  - Postauricular ecchymosis or the Battle sign, which is bleeding into the tissue behind the ears (suggestive of a posterior basilar skull fracture with bleeding into the posterior fossa)
    - Battle sign and raccoon eyes are late signs occurring approximately eight hours after injury.
  - Eyeglasses or contact lenses
  - Pupils, including size, shape, equality, reactivity to light, and opacity
  - Extraocular eye movements
    - Observe the child's ability to follow your finger in all six directions.
    - Observe the infant's or toddler's tracking of an object in all six directions.

Palpate for:

- Anterior and posterior fontanels in infants for fullness, bulging, or depression
  - To provide meaningful information, fontanels should be palpated while the child is upright and calm. The anterior fontanel closes by approximately the age of 18 months, and the posterior fontanel closes by approximately the age of 8 weeks.[12]
- Periorbital tenderness or pain
- Auricular tenderness or pain
- Nasal tenderness or pain

Table 5-7 Pediatric Glasgow Coma Scale*

Eye Opening	≥ 1 Year	0–1 Year	
	4: Spontaneously 3: To verbal command 2: To pain 1: No response	4: Spontaneously 3: To verbal command 2: To pain 1: No response	
Best Motor Response	**≥ 1 Year**	**0–1 Year**	
	6: Obeys 5: Localizes pain 4: Flexion–withdrawal 3: Flexion–abnormal (decorticate rigidity) 2: Extension (decerebrate rigidity) 1: No response	6: Spontaneous or purposeful movement 5: Localizes pain 4: Flexion–withdrawal 3: Flexion–abnormal (decorticate rigidity) 2: Extension (decerebrate rigidity) 1: No response	
Best Verbal Response	**0–2 Years**	**2–5 Years**	**> 5 Years**
	5: Cries appropriately, smiles, and coos 4: Cries 3: Inappropriate crying/screaming 2: Grunts 1: No response	5: Appropriate words and phrases 4: Inappropriate words 3: Cries/screams 2: Grunts 1: No response	5: Oriented and converses 4: Disoriented and converses 3: Inappropriate words 2: Incomprehensible sounds 1: No response

Note: Score is the sum of the individual scores from eye opening, best motor response, and best verbal response, using age-specific criteria.
    A score of 13 to 15 indicates mild head injury; 9 to 12, moderate head injury; and 8 or less, severe head injury.

*Data are taken from Barkin, R. M., & Rosen, P. (2003). *Emergency pediatrics: A guide to ambulatory care* (6th ed.). St. Louis, MO: Mosby.
    Used with permission.

Figure 5-1 The Full Outline of UnResponsiveness Score Pocket Card

Eye Response (E)

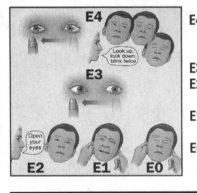

E4 Eyelids open or opened, tracking or blinking to command
E3 Eyelids open but not tracking
E2 Eyelids closed, opens to loud voice, not tracking
E1 Eyelids closed, opens to pain, not tracking
E0 Eyelids remain closed with pain

Motor Response (M)

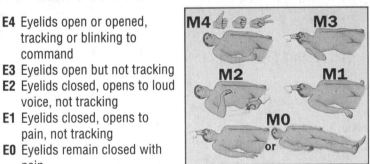

M4 Thumbs up, fist, or peace sign to command
M3 Localizing to pain
M2 Flexion response to pain
M1 Extensor posturing
M0 No response to pain or generalized myoclonus status epilepticus

Brainstem Reflexes (B)

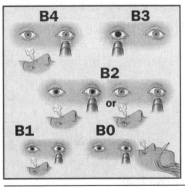

B4 Pupil and corneal reflexes present
B3 One pupil wide and fixed
B2 Pupil or corneal reflexes absent
B1 Pupil and corneal reflexes absent
B0 Absent pupil, corneal, and cough flex

Respiratory Response (R)

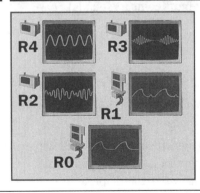

R4 Not intubated, regular breathing pattern
R3 Not intubated, Cheyne-Stokes breathing pattern
R2 Not intubated, irregular breathing pattern
R1 Breathes above ventilator rate
R0 Breathes at ventilator rate or apnea

- Tracheal position
- Bony depressions/crepitus
- Foreign bodies

Neck

Inspect for:

- Lacerations, abrasions, or edema
- Ecchymosis or bruising
- Jugular vein distention

Palpate for:

- Cervical (bony) tenderness or step offs
- Foreign bodies

Chest

Inspect for:

- Respiratory rate and depth, work of breathing, retractions, use of accessory muscles, abdominal breathing, and paradoxical chest wall movement.
- Symmetry of chest wall movements.
- Lacerations, abrasions, contusions, lesions/rashes, puncture wounds, impaled objects, ecchymosis, swelling, scars, or the presence of central venous access devices. Impaled objects should be stabilized in place. These objects should not be removed until the appropriate equipment and personnel are assembled. This will typically be performed by a physician in a controlled setting, such as the operating room.
- Scars from healed chest tube sites, central lines, surgical incisions, or penetrating wounds.

Auscultate for:

- Equality of breath sounds. Listening over lateral, anterior, axilla, and, if possible, posterior lung fields.
- Adventitious sounds, such as wheezes, crackles, and friction rubs.
- Heart sounds for rate and rhythm and adventitious sounds (e.g., murmurs or distant or muffled heart sounds).

Palpate for:

- Chest wall tenderness
- Palpation of one side at a time will identify the location of tenderness
- Bony deformities
- Crepitus/subcutaneous emphysema can be detected when the nurse places the diaphragm of a stethoscope on the chest. Crackling will be heard when the diaphragm is pushed into the chest wall. Palpation of subcutaneous emphysema resembles the feel of popping bubble wrap.

Abdomen

Inspect for:

- Use of abdominal muscles for breathing.
- Lacerations, abrasions, contusions, rashes, impaled objects, or ecchymosis.
- Observe for seat belt marks in pediatric patients involved in motor vehicle crashes and handlebar marks in pediatric patients involved in bicycle crashes.
  - Information regarding restraint devices will facilitate the index of suspicion for injury.
- Distention, feeding tubes, or gastrostomy buttons.
- Penetrating wounds or scars from healed surgical incisions.

Auscultate for:

- Bowel sounds in all quadrants.

Palpate for:

- The abdomen should be palpated in all four quadrants for rigidity, rebound tenderness, and guarding (peritoneal signs). In the infant or young child who is crying, evaluation for firmness or rigidity is more difficult. Palpating the abdomen on inspiration allows for palpation when the abdominal muscles are relaxed. Allowing the pediatric patient to remain with the caregiver and providing some distraction can facilitate calming the pediatric patient, which leads to a more relaxed abdomen.

Pelvis and Genitalia

Inspect for:

- Lacerations, abrasions, rashes, or edema
- Drainage from the meatus or vagina
- Scrotal bleeding or edema
- Priapism (indicative of pathological features, such as sickle cell crisis or spinal cord injury)

Palpate for:

- Pelvic stability using gentle downward pressure over the iliac crest
  - Do NOT rock the pelvis
- Anal sphincter tone (may be assessed by observing for a "wink" response to perianal stimulation while assessing a rectal temperature)
- Femoral pulses compared bilaterally

Extremities

Inspect for:

- Angulation, deformity, open wounds with evidence of protruding bone fragments, puncture wounds, edema, ecchymosis, rashes, purpura, or petechiae
- Color (dusky or mottled)
  - With injury to an extremity, it is important to compare the injured extremity with the uninjured extremity.
- Abnormal movement/positioning
- Scars or venous access devices
- Signs of congenital anomalies, such as a club foot, length discrepancies, or clubbing of digits

Palpate for:

- Skin temperature (with injuries, compare the injured extremity with the uninjured extremity)
- Symmetry, quality of distal pulses, and capillary refill (compare bilateral peripheral pulses for strength and equality)
- Bony crepitus
- Muscle strength and range of motion
- Sensation (with injuries, compare the injured extremity with the uninjured extremity)

I—Inspect Posterior Surfaces

Log roll your patient as a unit, maintaining full spinal immobilization if indicated.

Inspect for:

- Bleeding, abrasions, wounds, impaled objects, hematomas, or ecchymosis
- Rashes, petechiae, edema, or purpura
- Patterned injuries or injuries in various stages of healing (suggestive of intentional trauma)
- Foreign bodies

Palpate for:

- Tenderness and deformity of the spine
- Costovertebral angle tenderness and/or flank hematoma

Diagnostic Procedures

The necessity of laboratory and radiographic studies is determined by the pediatric patient's clinical presentation, pattern of injury, history, and specific institutional protocols.

Planning and Implementation

Interventions for life-threatening conditions are performed as soon as the condition is recognized. Corresponding interventions have been listed with each component of the primary assessment. Additional interventions may be identified during or after the secondary assessment. These interventions may include the following:

- Prepare for admission or transfer to a pediatric tertiary care center, as indicated by the pediatric patient's clinical condition.
- Initiate the administration of maintenance fluids or medication(s). The administration of maintenance intravenous fluids may be required to replace insensible losses (skin and respiratory tract) and ongoing losses (vomiting and diarrhea).
  - The rate and type of fluid are tailored to the specific needs of the pediatric patient. The appropriate fluid is based on the pediatric patient's glucose, sodium, and potassium needs.
  - Solutions commonly used include the following:
    - Lactated Ringer's solution, a combination of 5% dextrose and 0.2% saline, or 0.45% normal saline (United States); and 4% dextrose in one-fourth or one-fifth normal saline (Australia).
  - Fluid requirements are calculated based on the pediatric patient's weight (in kilograms) (**Table 5-8**). In some circumstances, maintenance fluids may be restricted (i.e., in patients with an increased intracranial pressure or a pulmonary contusion).
    - Restricted rates are calculated by the following method: Maintenance volume per hour multiplied by the desired degree of restriction (e.g., for a 15 kg patient who is given two-thirds maintenance, the hourly rate is as follows: 50 mL/hour [maintenance] multiplied by two-thirds [restricted] = 33 mL/hour).[19]
    - Determine the need to keep the pediatric patient without food or drink.
- Monitor the pediatric patient's intake and output, as indicated by condition.
- Administer medications (e.g., antibiotics, vaccines, and pain medications), as prescribed.
- Initiate appropriate isolation measures.

Table 5-8 Maintenance Fluid Calculations*

4 mL/kg per hour for the first 10 kilograms of body weight
+ 2 mL/kg per hour for the second 10 kilograms of body weight
+ 1 mL/kg per hour for each additional kilogram over 20 kilograms

Example: The hourly maintenance fluid needed for a 15-kilogram child would be as follows:

$$4 \text{ milliliters} \times 10 \text{ kilograms} = 40 \text{ mL/hour}$$
$$\underline{+ 2 \text{ milliliters} \times \quad 5 \text{ kilograms} = 10 \text{ mL/hour}}$$
$$15 \text{ kilograms} = 50 \text{ mL/hour}$$

Example: The hourly maintenance fluid needed for a 25-kilogram child would be as follows:

$$4 \text{ milliliters} \times 10 \text{ kilograms} = 40 \text{ mL/hour}$$
$$+ 2 \text{ milliliters} \times 10 \text{ kilograms} = 20 \text{ mL/hour}$$
$$\underline{+ 1 \text{ milliliter} \quad \times \quad 5 \text{ kilograms} = \quad 5 \text{ mL/hour}}$$
$$25 \text{ kilograms} = 65 \text{ mL/hour}$$

*Data are taken from Greenbaum.[19]

- Facilitate family presence in the treatment area, as guided by the assessment of family needs and institutional protocols.
  - Provide timely and clear explanations of procedures and treatment plans.
  - Assign a healthcare professional to provide ongoing explanation and support.

- Provide psychosocial support to help the pediatric patient cope with fear of treatment procedures.
- Evaluate for indicators of intentional trauma.

Evaluation and Ongoing Assessment

The evaluation phase of the nursing process occurs when the nurse evaluates the patient's responses to the interventions and continued effects of the illness or injury event. The achievement of expected outcomes is evaluated, and the treatment or intervention plan is adjusted as needed to attain unmet outcomes. If the pediatric patient's condition deteriorates, the primary assessment must be repeated. General evaluation of the pediatric patient's progress includes ongoing assessment of the following variables:

- Airway patency
- Breathing effectiveness
- Circulation and end-organ perfusion
- Skin temperature and color and color of the mucous membranes
- Central and peripheral pulse rate and quality
- Level of consciousness and activity level (deviations from baseline)
- Intake and output
- Vital signs, pulse oximetry monitoring, and cardiac monitor (as the pediatric patient's condition indicates)
- Pain and discomfort with initiation of nonpharmacological and pharmacological pain control measures, as indicated
- Body systems, as appropriate, based on assessment findings and desired outcomes

Summary

The initial assessment of ill or injured pediatric patients requires a systematic process that recognizes life-threatening conditions, identifies injuries, and determines priorities of care based on the assessment. The recognition of life-threatening conditions requires knowledge of normal growth and development of the anatomical and physiological characteristics unique to infants, children, and adolescents. The key to a successful outcome is early recognition of the prearrest state with the goal to prevent arrest with the appropriate treatment. The nurse must strive to be proactive when caring for the pediatric patient and maintaining a high index of suspicion.

Appendix 5-A Temperature Conversion*

Celsius	Fahrenheit	Celsius	Fahrenheit
34.2	93.6	38.6	101.4
34.6	94.3	39.0	102.2
35.0	95.0	39.4	102.9
35.4	95.7	39.8	103.6
35.8	96.4	40.2	104.3
36.2	97.1	40.6	105.1
36.6	97.8	41.0	105.8
37.0	98.6	41.4	106.5
37.4	99.3	41.8	107.2
37.8	100.0	42.2	108.0
38.2	100.7	42.6	108.7

*To convert Celsius to Fahrenheit: (9/5 × Temperature) + 32 = Degrees Fahrenheit or (Temperature × 1.8) + 32 = Degrees Fahrenheit. To convert Fahrenheit to Celsius: (Temperature − 32) × 5/9 = Degrees Celsius or (Temperature − 32)/1.8 = Degrees Celsius.

Emergency Information Form for Children With Special Needs

Last name:

American College of Emergency Physicians®

American Academy of Pediatrics

Date form completed	Revised	Initials
By Whom	Revised	Initials

Name:	Birth date:	Nickname:

Home Address:	Home/Work Phone:
Parent/Guardian:	Emergency Contact Names & Relationship:
Signature/Consent*:	
Primary Language:	Phone Number(s):

Physicians:

Primary care physician:	Emergency Phone:
	Fax:
Current Specialty physician: Specialty:	Emergency Phone:
	Fax:
Current Specialty physician: Specialty:	Emergency Phone:
	Fax:
Anticipated Primary ED:	Pharmacy:
Anticipated Tertiary Care Center:	

Diagnoses/Past Procedures/Physical Exam:

1.

2.

3.

4.

Synopsis:

Baseline physical findings:

Baseline vital signs:

Baseline neurological status:

*Consent for release of this form to health care providers

Last name:

Diagnoses/Past Procedures/Physical Exam continued:

Medications:

1.

2.

3.

4.

5.

6.

Significant baseline ancillary findings (lab, x-ray, ECG):

Prostheses/Appliances/Advanced Technology Devices:

Management Data:

Allergies: Medications/Foods to be avoided   **and why:**

1.

2.

3.

Procedures to be avoided   **and why:**

1.

2.

3.

Immunizations

Dates						Dates					
DPT						Hep B					
OPV						Varicella					
MMR						TB status					
HIB						Other					

Antibiotic prophylaxis: Indication: Medication and dose:

Common Presenting Problems/Findings With Specific Suggested Managements

Problem   Suggested Diagnostic Studies   Treatment Considerations

Comments on child, family, or other specific medical issues:

Physician/Provider Signature: **Print Name:**

References

1. Proehl, J. A. (2007). Initial assessment and resuscitation. In K. S. Hoyt & J. Selfridge-Thomas (Eds.), *Emergency nursing core curriculum* (6th ed., p. 1–25). St. Louis, MO: Saunders/Elsevier.

2. American Heart Association. (2010). Pediatric basic and advanced life support: 2010 international consensus on cardiopulmonary resuscitation and emergency cardiovascular care science with treatment recommendations. *Circulation, 122,* S466–S515.

3. Emergency Nurses Association. (2007). *Care of the pediatric patient in the emergency setting* [position statement]. Des Plaines, IL: Author.

4. Ellis, D. Y., Harris, T., & Zideman, D. (2007). Cricoid pressure in emergency department rapid sequence tracheal intubations: A risk-benefit analysis. *Annals of Emergency Medicine, 50,* 653–665.

5. Donald, M. J., & Paterson, B. (2006). End tidal carbon dioxide monitoring in prehospital and retrieval medicine: A review. *Emergency Medicine Journal, 23,* 728–730.

6. Yoo, S. Y., Kim, J. H., Hee Han, S., & Oh, A. (2007). A comparative study of endotracheal tube positioning methods in children: Safety from neck. *Anesthesia and Analgesia, 105,* 620–625.

7. DeBoer, S., Seaver, M., & Arndt, K. (2003). Verification of endotracheal tube placement: A comparison of confirmation techniques and devices. *Journal of Emergency Nursing, 29,* 444–450.

8. Molloy, E. F., & Deakins, K. (2006). Are carbon dioxide detectors useful in neonates? *Archives of Disease in Childhood: Fetal Neonatal Edition, 91,* F295–F298.

9. American Heart Association. (2010). *2010 International consensus on cardiopulmonary resuscitation (CPR) and emergency cardiovascular care (ECC) science with treatment recommendations.* Retrieved from: http://www.americanheart.org/presenter.jhtml?identifier=3060115#Airway

10. Phipps, L. M., Thomas, N. J., Gilmore, R. K., Raymond, J. A., Bittner, T. R., Orr, R. A., & Robertson, C. L. (2005). Prospective assessment of guidelines for determining appropriate depth of endotracheal tube placement in children. *Pediatric Critical Care Medicine, 6,* 519–522.

11. American Academy of Pediatrics (AAP), American College of Emergency Physicians (ACEP), Emergency Nurses Association (ENA) 2009 joint policy statement. (2009). *Guidelines for care of children in the emergency department.* Retrieved from http://aappolicy. aappublications.org/cgi/reprint/pediatrics;124/4/1233/pdf

12. Emergency Nurses Association. (2009). In D. Thomas & L. M. Bernardo (Eds.), *Core curriculum for pediatric emergency nursing* (2nd ed.). Des Plaines, IL: Author.

13. Luscombe, M. D., Owens, B. D., & Burke, D. (2010). Weight estimation in paediatrics: a comparison of the APLS formula and the formula "weight=3(age)+7." *Emergency Medicine Journal.* Advance online publication. doi:10.1136/emj.2009.087288

14. Nieman, C. T., Manacii, C. F., Super, D. M., Mancuso, C., Fallon Jr, W. F. (2006). Use of Broselow tape may result in the underresuscitation of children. *Academic Emergency Medicine, 13,* 1011–1019.

15. Emergency Nurses Association. (2005). *Family presence at the bedside during invasive procedures and cardiopulmonary resuscitation* [Position statement]. Des Plaines, IL: Author.

16. American Academy of Pediatrics; Committee on Pediatric Emergency Medicine and Council on Clinical Information Technology; American College of Emergency Physicians; Pediatric Emergency Medicine Committee. (2010). Policy statement: Emergency information forms and emergency preparedness for children with special healthcare needs. *Pediatrics, 125,* 829–837.

17. American Academy of Pediatrics. (2009). In J. M. Callahan (Ed.), *Pediatric education for prehospital professionals: Provider manual.* Sudbury, MA: Jones & Bartlett.

18. Cohen, J. (2009). Interrater reliability and predictive validity of the FOUR score coma scale in a pediatric population. *Journal of Neuroscience Nursing, 41,* 261–267.

19. Greenbaum, L. A. (2004). Pathophysiology of body fluids and fluid therapy. In R. E. Behrman, R. M. Kleigman, & H. B. Jenson (Eds.), *Nelson textbook of pediatrics* (p. 310). Philadelphia, PA: Saunders.

Chapter 6 | Pain

DonnaMarie Miller, BSN, RN, CEN
Tracy Ann Pasek, MSN, RN, CCNS, CCRN, CIMI
Nancy, C. Smith, RN
Kathy Woloshyn, BSN, RN

Objectives

On completion of this chapter, the learner should be able to do the following:

- Identify misconceptions regarding the assessment and treatment of pain in pediatric patients in the emergency department (ED).
- Summarize pathophysiological and behavioral indicators of pain in pediatric patients.
- Discuss selection of pediatric pain assessment tools according to developmental and behavioral characteristics.
- Compare opioid analgesic and non-opioid pharmacological analgesic alternatives for procedural pain management.
- Discuss nonpharmacological nursing interventions commonly selected for procedural pain management.

Introduction

Pediatric patients experience pain as a result of illness, injury, and emergency intervention as part of diagnosis and treatment. Up to 78% of patients who are evaluated in a pediatric ED report pain as a symptom.[1] Despite advances in understanding pain, children's pain in EDs is poorly managed.[2–4] The initial and ongoing assessment and treatment of pain in a fast-paced setting such as the ED can be challenging. Several history-related factors influence a child's experience with pain, including:

- Underlying medical condition
- Previous painful events
- Coping strategies
- Cultural influences
- Meaning of the pain for the pediatric patient and family
- Developmental level of the patient

Immediate pain assessment and management considerations for the pediatric patient in pain, include:

- Location of the pain
- Factors that relieve or exacerbate the pain
- Emotional distress
- Threat of and preparation for a procedure

- Previous interventions pharmacological and nonpharmacological
- Familial influences
- Environmental factors

The treatment of pain can be particularly difficult in the pediatric population. Children may be unable (e.g., pre-verbal) or unwilling (e.g., fearful) to express or describe characteristics of the pain they are experiencing. Emergency nurses must advocate for thorough pain assessment and appropriate interventions for these vulnerable patients.

Pain is highly individualized and should be treated via a multimodal and multisystem approach.[5] Emotions, such as fear and anger, can increase a child's perception of pain.[5, 6] Because pain is influenced by many psychological and behavioral factors, it is important to include nonpharmacological pain management techniques as part of pediatric ED pain standards and protocols.[4]

Table 6-1 discusses fallacies and facts about pediatric pain. Despite advances in neonatal and pediatric pain research, the development of pain policies, and position papers by professional societies, myths and prejudices about pediatric pain persist in the clinical setting. These myths and prejudices significantly contribute to pediatric patients being undermedicated and undertreated for pain. The tendency toward undermedication is far more

Table 6-1 Fallacies and Facts About Children and Pain*

Fallacy	Fact
Infants and children do not feel pain.	Myelination varies depending on the age of the child. Infants demonstrate delayed physical pain responses. It takes longer for a noxious stimulus to reach the brain because of incomplete myelination. This is balanced by the shorter distance pain impulses must travel in infants' smaller bodies. A delayed reaction to pain does not mean that pain is less intense for a baby. Pain is no less significant for babies than it is for older children or adults. Uncontrolled pain has multiple long-term implications.
Analgesic administration makes pain evaluation more difficult and negatively affects assessment and diagnostic accuracy.	There is no evidence that pain management masks symptoms or clouds mental status, preventing adequate assessment and diagnosis.
Children cannot tell you where they hurt.	By the age of 4 years, children can accurately point to the body area or mark the painful site on a drawing; children as young as three years can use pain scales, such as the FACES Scale.
Children always tell the truth about pain.	Children may not admit to having pain to avoid an injection. If children have persistent pain, they may not realize how much they are hurting. Children may believe that others know how they are feeling and not ask for analgesia.
Children become accustomed to pain or painful procedures. Children can also exaggerate their pain.	Children may demonstrate increased behavioral signs of discomfort with repeated painful procedures.
Behavioral manifestations reflect pain intensity. A child cannot be in pain when playing in the waiting room.	Children's developmental level, coping abilities, and temperament and history with pain are factors that may influence pain behavior. Children with more active resisting behaviors may rate pain lower than children with passive accepting behaviors.
The administration of an opioid to a child will induce respiratory depression.	Reports of respiratory depression in children are also uncommon. By the age of 3–6 months, healthy infants can metabolize opioids like other children. However, emergency nurses must take into account that patients may be opioid naive.
Children will become addicted to narcotics.	Concerns about children who are in pain becoming addicted to opioids are unfounded.

*Data are taken from LeMay et al,[2] Pasek et al,[9] Hockenberry et al,[13] and Zempsky et al.[23] Data are also taken from the following sources:
(1) Helms, J. E., & Barone, C. P. (2008). Physiology and treatment of pain. *Critical Care Nurse, 28,* 38–49. (2) Connelly, M., & Schanberg, L. (2006). Opioid therapy for the treatment of refractory pain in children with juvenile rheumatoid arthritis. *Nature Clinical Practice Rheumatology, 2,* 636–637.

pronounced in children than in adults. Studies reveal that children receive much less post-operative analgesia than adults who have the same diagnoses and have undergone the same procedures. Children younger than two years of age are less likely to be treated than are older children. The emergency nurse must be equipped with facts to refute these myths when they are encountered.

Types of Pain

The International Association for the Study of Pain defines *pain* as "an unpleasant sensory and emotional experience associated with actual or potential tissue damage, or described in terms of such damage."[7] The inability to communicate verbally does not negate the possibility that an individual is experiencing pain and is in need of appropriate pain-relieving treatment. Pain is always subjective. Each individual learns the application of the word through experiences related to injury in early life. Biologists recognize that those stimuli that cause pain are liable to damage tissue. Accordingly, pain is the experi-

ence we associate with actual or potential tissue damage. It is unquestionably a sensation in a part or parts of the body, but it is also always unpleasant and, therefore, an emotional experience.[5] Children in the ED may experience acute pain (e.g., fracture or procedural pain), persistent pain (e.g., cancer), or recurrent pain (e.g., migraine).[7]

Pain Physiology

Bradykinins, prostaglandin E, and histamine are mediators that are released when pain occurs with tissue damage. These mediators stimulate peripheral afferent nerve endings or nociceptors. Nociceptors are located in the skin, subcutaneous tissues, periosteum, joint surfaces, arterial walls, fascia, muscles, and viscera.[8, 9]

After nociceptor stimulation, a pain stimulus is transmitted to the spinal cord via A-delta or C-fiber afferents.[9, 10] A-delta fibers are fine moderately myelinated fibers that rapidly conduct a pain stimulus.[8, 9] Sharp sensations from mechanical stimuli are transmitted by these fibers, and they produce the pain that is associated with acute conditions.[8, 9] C-fibers are smaller, unmyelinated, and polymodal. These fibers produce the pain that is associated with chronic conditions.[9, 10] Children who are developmentally able to describe pain transmitted by C-fibers do so using words such as "dull," "aching," or "burning."[9, 10]

In the dorsal horn of the spinal cord, these pain signals are modified and sent through the spinal pathway for transmission to the cerebral cortex. The somatosensory cortex is where the pain is perceived and the severity is recorded.[11]

Pain Assessment

Pain should be assessed using scales that are consistent with a child's age and developmental ability. A pain history obtained by the caregiver provides for a more clear understanding of the patient's pain and coping strategies. Some questions you may want to ask the caregiver are as follows:

- Is there anything special you would like me to know about your child and pain?
- How does your child express pain?
- How does your child usually respond to pain?
- What do you do when your child is hurting?
- What works best for pain relief for your child?

Emergency nurses should have self-report and behavioral pain assessment tools at their disposal. Pain assessment tools should be validated and reliable for their intended populations. Moreover, they should be user friendly and readily accessible to nurses and patients.

Physical Responses

Most pain states are characterized by a global pattern of physiological arousal related to catecholamine release that can result in tachycardia, hypertension, increased respiratory rate, pupil dilation, pallor, and diaphoresis. Infants experience diaphoresis in their palms, which is sometimes referred to as palmar water loss. If pain has persisted for several hours or days, these autonomic nervous system responses are often modified and vital signs, for example, may be normal and no longer reflect pain or stress. This is why assessing physiological responses alone should only be done when other factors that contribute to a thorough pain assessment are limited or nonexisting (e.g., verbal self-report from a child with severe traumatic injuries).

Behavioral Responses

Table 6-2 presents behavioral responses to pain by children at different developmental stages. The emergency

Table 6-2 Pediatric Responses to Painful Stimuli/Indicators of Pain*

Neonates (from birth to 28 days)

Weak ability to localize pain

Exhibits generalized body movements, facial grimacing, chin quivering, tightly closed fists and eyes, poor feeding, crying, vital sign and oxygenation changes, vagal tone, and palmar sweating

Infants (from birth to 12 months)

Improved ability to localize pain

Exhibits reflex withdrawal to stimulus with increasing age; facial grimacing; irritability; physical resistance; high-pitched, tense, or irregular cry; and lacrimation

Toddlers (1–3 years)

Able to localize pain with a limited vocabulary to describe pain

Exhibits localized withdrawal, resistance, pushing away, clinging to parent, and reluctance to move injured or painful body part

Preschoolers (3–5 years)

May associate pain with unrelated events (i.e., pain is a punishment for misbehavior)

Limited vocabulary

Able to point to where it hurts; expressive responses may include crying, screaming, and verbal reprimands to caregivers, such as "I hate you!"

Exhibits active physical resistance, such as thrashing, guarding, and reluctance to move body parts

Developing the ability to quantify and use self-report pain assessment scales

Fear is exacerbated if preparation for a procedure takes place too far in advance

School-aged Children (5–11 years)

May cooperate as the result of mastery and achievement characteristics of this developmental phase, organized by rules; and responds well to rituals

Able to describe pain characteristics in detail

May suppress typical overt pain behaviors to "behave" (e.g., teeth and fist clenching or body rigidity)

May try to appear brave

Early adolescents (commonly referred to as "tweens") **and Adolescents** (11–18 years)

Abstract and critical thinking; capable of "if-then" relationships

Refined ability to identify pain characteristics (type, onset, duration, and exacerbating factors)

May vacillate between "typical" child and adult behaviors

Mood swings, increased independence, and regression affect pain responses

May attempt to appear stoic in the presence of peers

*Data are taken from Mullen and Pate[12] and Hockenberry et al.[13]

nurse should consider these responses within the context of a normal healthy child, with the understanding that they may change in the presence of illness, injury, or alterations in cognitive and physical development.

Verbal Report

Self-report is the most reliable indicator of pain; however, not all pediatric patients are capable or willing to verbalize their discomfort.[12] Therefore, exploring past pain experiences with the caregiver will help identify the child's typical response to pain and identify methods that have previously provided comfort or facilitated coping. This is of particular importance for children with special healthcare needs or atypical development. Caregivers can provide helpful information about facial expressions, cry pitch, and behavior patterns that are indicative of pain because they know the child best.

Obtaining a pain history and performing a pain assessment can be involved, especially for children with a complex medical history. Use of the mnemonic PQRST helps provide a more thorough assessment of pain.
- Precipitating and palliating factors
  - What makes the pain worse? What alleviates it?
- Quality
  - Sharp or dull? Aching or burning?
- Radiation
  - Does is spread or radiate from where it started?
- Severity, symptoms, and site
  - Are there other symptoms, such as nausea?
  - Generalized or local? What is the location?
- Time or triggering factors
  - When did it begin?
  - Is there an identified cause?
  - Is it continuous or intermittent?

Pain Assessment Scales

Pain assessment scales measure different dimensions of a child's pain. They should be validated, reliable, user friendly, and readily available to the caregiver. Families should also have access to a basic pain assessment scale (e.g., posted on the wall in an examination room) so that they can participate in assessing their child's pain. Selection of a pain assessment tool should be based on age, cognitive level, and the child's ability to self report. **Table 6-3** summarizes observational (behavioral) pain assessment tools suitable for use in the emergency department.

Self-report is the gold standard for pain assessment. These scales are popular and easy to use and are available in many language translations. Some are useful in assessing procedural-, disease-, and trauma-related pain. **Figure 6-1** is a reproduction of the FACES Pain Rating Scale.[13] **Figure 6-2** portrays the Faces Pain Scale—Revised.[19–21] **Figure 6-3** is a reproduction of the Color Analog Scale.[9, 14–18] The simple question, "How would you rate your pain on a scale of one to 10?" works in a fast-paced situation, but children must be able to quantify or understand rank and order to do this effectively without something to view. While there is some variability in opinion regarding the age at

Table 6-3 Summary of Observational Pain Assessment Tools for Infants and Preverbal Children*

PAT	Signs and Symptoms	PAT	Signs and Symptoms
N-PASS	Cry/irritability (-2 to +2)	**FLACC/Revised FLACC**	Facial expression
Neonatal Pain, Agitation, and Sedation Scale (infants)	Behavior/state (-2 to +2)	Face, Legs, Activity, Cry, Consolability (preverbal children and critically ill children/ cognitively impaired children [Revised FLACC])	Leg movement
	Facial expression (-2 to +2)		Activity
	Extremities/tone (-2 to +2)		Cry
	Vital signs: HR, RR, BP, SaO$_2$ (-2 to +2)		Consolability
	Scoring Range		**Scoring Range**
	pain score, 0 to 10 (0, no pain; 10, intense pain);		pain score, 0 to 10 (0, no pain; 10, intense pain)
	sedation score, 0 to 10 (0, no sedation; 10, deep sedation)		For use with infants through adults. Behaviors need to be considered within the context of the child's physiological status, cognitive level, and environmental factors.

Note: BP indicates blood pressure; HR, heart rate; PAT, Pain Assessment Tool; RR, respiratory rate; SaO$_2$, arterial oxygen saturation.

*Data are taken from Pasek et al.[9] Data are also taken from the following sources: (1) Manworren, R. C., & Hynan, L. S. (2003). Clinical validation of FLACC: Preverbal patient pain scale. *Pediatric Nursing, 29,* 140–146. (2) Merkel, S. I., Voepel-Lewis, T., Shayevitz, J. R., & Malviya, S. (1997). The FLACC: A behavioral scale for scoring postoperative pain in young children. *Pediatric Nursing, 23,* 293–297. (3) Voepel-Lewis, T., Zanoti, J., Dammeyer, J. A., & Merkel, S. (2010). Reliability and validity of the Face, Legs, Activity, Cry, Consolability behavioral tool in assessing acute pain in critically ill patients. *American Journal of Critical Care, 19,* 55–61. (4) Hummel, P., Puchalski, M., Creech, S., & Weiss, M. (2008). Clinical reliability and validity of the N-PASS: Neonatal Pain, Agitation, and Sedation Scale. *Journal of Perinatology, 28,* 55–60. (5) Malviya, S., Voepel-Lewis, T., Burke, C., Merkel, S., & Tait, A. R. (2006). The revised FLACC observational pain tool: Improved reliability and validity for pain assessment in children with cognitive impairment. *Paediatric Anesthesia, 16*(3), 258–265.

which children are able to utilize this scale, recent research indicates that most developmentally normal children are able to do this by approximately three years of age.[22]

Table 6-4 summarizes self-report pain assessment scales. Transcultural literature supports using some of the pain assessment scales with children from a variety of cultures. For example, the FACES scale is available in several translations and the FACES Pain Scale—Revised is available in more than 30 translations.[18]

Pain Management Interventions

Nonpharmacological Interventions

Nonpharmacological pain management has been recognized as an effective method for the reduction of pain, anxiety, fear, and distress in children. Key principles regarding the use of this method of pain control revolve around early introduction of these methods and their use in addition to, and not as a replacement for, pharmacological management. Interventions must be based on the child's age, the child's developmental level, and the desired outcome or task at hand. Nothing will guarantee that a child will not cry during invasive treatments and painful procedures, but nonpharmacological interven-

tions can reduce the intensity of these experiences.[23–26] It is prudent to seek the advice of a child life specialist or pain clinical nurse specialist to choose or develop nonpharmacological interventions. Family should always be included as partners in pain management. General strategies to consider are listed in **Table 6-5**.

Distraction

Distraction or refocusing is a good way to keep a pediatric patient's mind from pain. The use of distraction requires little patient or caregiver preparation. The distraction techniques selected should be developmentally and age appropriate. The caregiver's participation with distraction techniques should be encouraged. General refocusing approaches include the following:

- Music therapy: playing soothing music, children's songs, and stories
- Playing cartoons, videotapes, video games, or a hospital-based imagery channel on the television
- Looking through a kaleidoscope
- Using soap bubbles, glitter wands, or puppets
- Asking the caregiver to read or tell the child a story

Figure 6-1 FACES Pain Rating Scale*

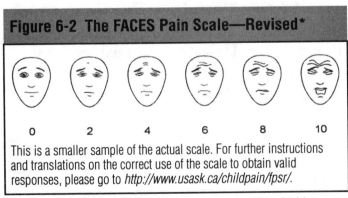

O	2	4	6	8	10
NO HURT	HURTS LITTLE BIT	HURTS LITTLE MORE	HURTS EVEN MORE	HURTS WHOLE LOT	HURTS WORST

This rating scale is recommended for people three years and older. Brief word instructions: Point to each face using the words to describe the pain intensity. Ask the child to choose the face that best describes his or her pain and record the appropriate number.

*Data are taken from Pasek et al.[9] and Hockenberry et al.[13]

Figure 6-2 The FACES Pain Scale—Revised*

0	2	4	6	8	10

This is a smaller sample of the actual scale. For further instructions and translations on the correct use of the scale to obtain valid responses, please go to *http://www.usask.ca/childpain/fpsr/*.

*Data from Hicks et al.[20] This figure has been reproduced with permission of the International Association for the Study of Pain® (IASP®). The figure may not be reproduced for any other purpose without permission.

Figure 6-3 The Color Analog Scale (5 years of age and older)*

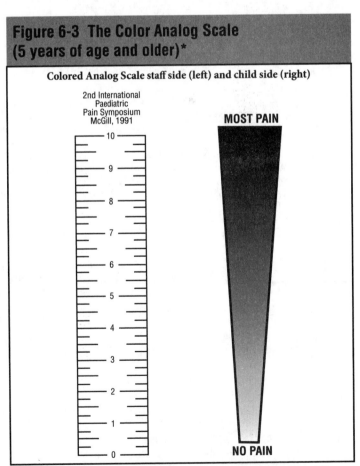

Colored Analog Scale staff side (left) and child side (right)

2nd International Paediatric Pain Symposium McGill, 1991

MOST PAIN

NO PAIN

*Data are taken from Pasek et al.[9], Stinson et al.[14], McGrath et al.[15], McConahay et al.[16], McConahay et al.[17], and Bulloch and Tenenbein.[18]

Table 6-4 Self-Report Pain Assessment Scales for Children*

Rating Scale	Overview
The Oucher Scale (approximately 3–12 years)	This tool uses six pictures of an actual child's face, representing "no hurt" to "biggest hurt ever." Faces are combined with a vertical numeric scale (0 to 10) to use with older children. The child is asked to choose the face or number that best describes the pain. This scale can be used for preschoolers through early adolescents. The numeric portion of the scale can be used with children who know how to count and quantify (e.g., understand that five is more pain than three).
Poker Chip Tool (also referred to as Pieces of Pain) (preschool through school-aged children)	This tool uses four red poker chips placed in front of the child. The chips are placed horizontally, and the child is told that "these are pieces of hurt." Once the child understands that the poker chips are pieces of hurt, the nurse asks, "How many pieces of hurt do you have right now?" This tool is for use with preschoolers and older children. Children should be supervised to prevent a child from placing the game pieces in the mouth.
FACES Pain Rating Scale (approximately 3 years and older)	This tool consists of what are intended to be "neutral" face drawings that range from a smiling "no pain" face to a tearful face for "worst pain." A script accompanies this scale. The child should be asked, "Which face looks like the pain you are having?" This scale can be used with preschoolers and older children. A common misconception is that a patient's face is compared with a face drawing. This is not an objective pain scale. It requires patient self-report for proper use.
Numeric scale (older school-aged children and adolescents)	A numeric scale typically uses a straight line with end points or anchors labeled as "no pain" and "worst pain." Divisions with corresponding numbers from 0–10 are marked along the line, similar to a ruler. The child is asked to point to the line that best represents the pain. Numeric scales are often verbalized without showing a patient an actual scale (e.g., "What is your pain on a scale of 0–10?") This may work for older school-aged children and adolescents but is too conceptual for preschool- and young school-aged children. Ideally, the child should be able to look at the scale.
Visual Analog Scale (school-aged children and adolescents)	Visual analog scales are similar to numeric scales in structure, but the end points or anchors can include words and faces. They may not be marked with lines and may require measurement. Visual analog scales may be components of elaborate pain inventories for children with complex pain histories. These may not be ideal for younger children because they tend to be fairly conceptual.
Word-Graphic Rating Scale (school-aged children and adolescents)	These pain assessment scales use pain descriptors to describe varying pain intensity levels (e.g., "no pain," "medium pain," and "worst possible pain"). The child selects the words that best describe the pain. These may require measurement. Children must be able to read to use these types of scales.

*Data are taken from Pasek et al.,[9] Hockenberry et al.,[13] and Beyer et al.[21] Data are also taken from the following sources: (1) Yeh, C. H. (2005). Development and validation of the Asian version of the Oucher: A pain intensity scale for children. *Journal of Pain, 6,* 526–534. (2) Jennings, P. A., Cameron, P., & Bernard, S. (2009). Measuring acute pain in the prehospital setting. *Emergency Medical Journal, 2,* 552–555. (3) Beyers, J. E., Villarreal, A. M., & Denyes, M. J. (2010). *OUCHER!* Retrieved from http://www.oucher.org. (4) Hester, N., Foster, R., & Kristensen K. (1990). Measurement of pain in children: Generalizability and validity of the pain ladder and the poker chip tool. In D. C. Tyler & E. J. Krane (Eds.), *Advances in pain research therapy* (Vol. 15, pp. 79–84). New York, NY: Raven. (5) Gharaibeh, M., & Abu-Saad, H. (2002). Cultural validation of pediatric pain assessment tools: Jordanian perspective. *Journal of Transcultural Nursing, 13,* 12–18. (6) Suraseranivongse, S., Montapaneewat, T., Monon, J., Chainhop, P., Petcharatana, S., & Kraiprasit, K. (2005). Cross-validation of a self-report scale for postoperative pain in school-aged children. *Journal of Medical Association of Thailand, 88,* 412–418. (7) Cohen, L. L., Lemanek, K., Blount, R., Dahlquist, L. M., Lim, C. S., Palermo, T. M., … Weiss, K. (2008). Evidence-based assessment of pediatric pain. *Journal of Pediatric Psychology, 33,* 939–955.

Table 6-5 General Strategies for Nonpharmacological Pain Management*

Form a trusting relationship with the child and family. Express concern regarding their reports of pain. Take an active role in seeking effective pain management strategies.

Be honest with the child and family. Use pain descriptors that other children commonly use (e.g., "Some children say this feels like a poke").

Avoid judging the child's pain responses.

Encourage the parent or primary caregiver to stay with his or her child during a procedure.

Teach the child and family about pain through all phases of the emergency department admission (e.g., before a procedure or at discharge). Education should include information about what to expect (e.g., the quality of pain and exacerbating factors), interventions (e.g., analgesic adverse effects and availability of prescription and over-the-counter analgesics), when to call the physician about pain, and referral if indicated.

*Data are taken from Zempsky et al,[23] McGrath and Finley,[24] Petrack et al,[25] and Anderson and Weisman.[26]

- Asking the child to sing a song or count aloud

Other distraction or coping techniques require teaching the pediatric patient the strategy and providing an opportunity for rehearsal of the techniques. Older children and adolescents may use breathing and relaxation techniques that include the following:

- Deep breathing
  - The child is coached in deep breathing, focusing on the inhalation and exhalation phases of each breath.
- Relaxation
  - Tactile stimulation (massage) or kinesthetics (gentle rocking) can be relaxing when done in combination with softly spoken soothing words (e.g., "Mommy's here"). Children may be asked if they prefer to open or close their eyes.
- Blowing away the pain
  - It is suggested to the child that blowing away the pain may be helpful. Pretending to blow out candles on a birthday cake or having the child use bubbles or pinwheels works with this technique.
  - A penlight, which the nurse turns off as the child blows slowly, may also be used.
- Imagery
  - A pediatric patient is talked or sung through a pleasant or enjoyable scenario. The nurse, child life specialist, or parent can partner with a child to describe details (e.g., "feel the cool breeze," "see the beautiful colors," or "tell me what you hear").
- Positive self-talk
  - The child is coached to say positive statements, such as "I can do it" or "I'm doing great."

Sucrose Analgesia

Sucrose analgesia has a role in pain management for infants in the emergency department. When breast milk or breastfeeding are not options, 24% oral sucrose solution provides safe, effective, nonpharmacological analgesia to infants undergoing minor procedural pain.[9, 27–29] Sucrose analgesia is an adjunct to analgesics and nonpharmacological interventions, such as nonnutritive sucking (e.g., a pacifier) and swaddling.[9] For optimal effect, sucrose should be given two minutes before the painful procedure, some immediately on beginning and some halfway through if the procedure lasts longer than 10 minutes.[30, 31] Oral sucrose may relieve pain as manifested by decreased crying episodes and cry duration. Sucrose analgesia may be used for neonates up to the age of one month, or longer for premature infants.[9, 27–29] Effectiveness with older infants is possible, although the effects are less clear. Interpretation of the oral sucrose literature specific to the administration for immunization pain at two, four, and six months has led experts to conclude that there is a diminished analgesic effect at four months.[32–35] Sucrose volumes ranging from 0.5 to 2 mL per dose have provided analgesia for infants.[32–34, 36] The volume of solution is less important than the baby's detection of the sucrose on the tongue, unlike other oral medications that may be given in the cheeks or toward the back of the throat. Evidence reveals that 0.05 to 0.5 mL of 24% to 25% sucrose or glucose provides sufficient analgesia.[32, 36] Oral sucrose is not a first-line pain intervention for moderate, severe, or chronic infant pain. Pain assessment should be ongoing to determine if sucrose analgesia interventions are adequate.

The use of sucrose may include, but not be limited to, the following emergency procedures:

- Venous access (intravenous or capillary puncture)
- Intramuscular or subcutaneous injections
- Dressing or tape removal
- Lumbar puncture
- Suturing or suture removal
- Urinary catheterization

Physical Comfort Measures

Basic comfort measures are considered components of nonpharmacological pain management. Comfort measures can minimize pain, prevent pain exacerbations, and relieve fear and other emotions associated with pain. Comfort measures include, but are not limited to, the following:

- Simple rhythmic tactile stimulation (e.g., rubbing or a massage by parents)
- Facilitation of an infant sucking on a pacifier, bottle, or breast
- Swaddling (infants)
- Application of splints or immobilization devices to suspected fractures and extremity injuries
- Application of ice, cold packs, or hot packs to an injury site or painful sites from disease
- Elevation of an injured extremity
- Facilitation of positioning with pillows, bed linens, stuffed toys, and the parent
- Protection of wounds with dressings to prevent nerve stimulation from air flow
- Transportation of patients by wheelchair or stretcher to eliminate pain with ambulation

Pharmacological Interventions

The World Health Organization (WHO) Pain Relief Ladder promotes the following three concepts: (1) analgesics should be administered on a scheduled basis, (2) analgesics should be administered by the least invasive route, and (3) analgesics should be tailored to the individual child's circumstance and needs (**Figure 6-4**).[37] WHO's Pain Relief Ladder is a multistep approach to treating pain and is a guide for initiating analgesics and dosages of analgesics that correspond to the patient's reported level of pain.[37] Originally intended to guide cancer pain therapy, some of the principles may apply to patients in the emergency department. The ladder begins with nonopioid oral medications for mild pain and progresses to strong opioids, adjuvants, and invasive therapies for severe and/or intractable pain. The key to pain management is providing the appropriate analgesic to meet the specific needs of the patient. For example, if a child reports severe pain with traumatic injury, a potent opioid (e.g., morphine sulfate) should be considered. It would be inappropriate to begin acetaminophen therapy in a child with severe pain and then progress up the ladder from that point. Moreover, subjective pain intensity scores are one measure of pain. Administering an opioid analgesic based solely on a self-reported pain intensity score (as with a pain management algorithm that links intensity scores with specific opioids and opioid doses) may be dangerous with regard to decreased level of consciousness and respiratory depression.[38] Psychological and emotional components of pain are not measured by a one-dimensional score; these components are poorly treated by opioids.[38]

Nonopioids

Nonopioids, such as acetaminophen and nonsteroidal anti-inflammatory medications (e.g., ibuprofen or ketorolac), are used to control acute pain of mild to moderate intensity. They also have a role in chronic pain management. These medications have a ceiling effect, and once maximal dosages are reached and pain persists, the change to or addition of an opioid should be considered.[39] Emergency nurses should assess if acetaminophen or over-the-counter combination medications that contain acetaminophen were administered for pain before admission to prevent the risk of toxicity.[40]

Opioids

Opioids bind with certain receptors in the central nervous system and peripheral tissues to provide analgesic effects. The administration of opioids by the oral route can be as effective as the parenteral route when an equianalgesic dose is administered (i.e., one that achieves the same effect despite the change in route).[39, 41] Moderate pain is most commonly managed with the use of oral opioids, such as codeine, morphine, or fentanyl. Acute pain of a moderate to severe nature may be managed effectively with intravenous administration of an opioid analgesic. Commonly used analgesics in the ED include morphine sulfate, fentanyl citrate, and ketamine (for procedural pain).

The route of administration is determined by the pediatric patient's condition, developmental level, intake status, and intravenous access. Pain medication should be administered as soon as an assessment is performed and the patient is stabilized. It should never be delayed while diagnostic procedures or noncritical interventions are completed. Common routes of analgesic administration in the ED are listed in **Table 6-6**. **Table 6-7** lists options for topical local anesthetics for procedural pain. **Table 6-8** summarizes common procedures that pediatric patients undergo in the ED, requiring sedation, analgesia, or both. **Table 6-9** outlines medications used for children in the ED who require sedation and/or analgesia. Indications, routes, nursing implications for administration, and risk factors are included in this table.

Adjuvant Medications

Adjuvant medications are compounds that alone have undesirable adverse effects or low potency; however, in combination with opioids, these medications permit a reduction in opioid dosing.[42] Anticonvulsants have a low

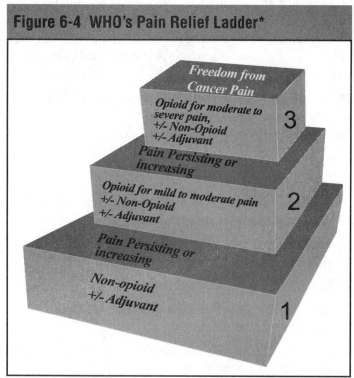

Figure 6-4 WHO's Pain Relief Ladder*

Freedom from Cancer Pain

3 — Opioid for moderate to severe pain, +/- Non-Opioid +/- Adjuvant

Pain Persisting or increasing

2 — Opioid for mild to moderate pain +/- Non-Opioid +/- Adjuvant

Pain Persisting or increasing

1 — Non-opioid +/- Adjuvant

*Data are taken from the World Health Organization.[37] Data are also taken from World Health Organization. (n.d.). *WHO's pain ladder.* Retrieved from http://www.who.int/cancer/palliative/painladder/en/.

potency for acute pain; however, in combination with opioids, they may contribute to improved analgesia. Other examples of adjuvants that may augment analgesia include corticosteroids, *N*-methyl-D-aspartate antagonists, such as methadone or tramadol, and acetylcholine esterase inhibitors, such as physostigmine or neostigmine. Adjuvants may also help manage the negative adverse effects of opioid therapy and may include laxatives and antiemetics.

Discharge Education

Discharge education should include information about pain management concerns once a pediatric patient is home after the ED admission. Children and families should be taught about what to expect regarding pain (e.g., improvement). Information about analgesics and adjuvants should be provided by the emergency nurse (e.g., adverse effects and medication compatibilities). Often, the term *narcotic* results in parental fear of addiction. This fear should be addressed. Changing the terminology and using the term *opioid* or *pain medicine* as opposed to narcotic may lessen parental fear of addiction. There should also be

a clear plan outlining follow-up with the child's primary care provider. If pain is not resolved or worsens, the family should feel supported to return to the ED if necessary. Referral to a pain evaluation and treatment center may be recommended for a child with complex pain problems. Written materials are helpful to families provided that health literacy, cultural factors, and language are taken into account. Nurses should document that patient and family education occurred.

Table 6-6 Common Routes of Analgesia Administration in the Emergency Department*

Route of Analgesia Administration	Description
Oral	Preferred for mild to moderate pain if child is not NPO; oral doses are usually higher than parenteral doses to achieve equianalgesia
Sublingual/buccal/oral transmucosal	More rapid onset than oral; few analgesics are available in this form
Topical or transdermal	May be used in a variety of preparations to provide both local anesthesia and systemic analgesia; examples of topical anesthetics include LMX4 and LET; examples of transdermal analgesics include the fentanyl transdermal patch (this is not recommended for acute pain); patients may present to the ED with transdermal analgesia in place
Intranasal	Midazolam and fentanyl citrate are examples of medications that can be administered via the intranasal route; administration may be frightening and overwhelming for young children; absorption is variable; some describe a sensation of "stinging" or "burning" with this route
Intravenous	The most reliable and controllable method of pain relief; continuous infusions have fewer "peaks and valleys"
Inhalation	Administration of a gas; hospital-specific procedural sedation guidelines should clearly define equipment, monitoring parameters, documentation requirements, and a validated sedation scale; there is growing evidence to support using concentrations greater than 50% safely in children aged one to three years

Note: ED indicates emergency department; LET, lidocaine hydrochloride, epinephrine bitartrate, and tetracaine hydrochloride, prepared in a KY jelly base; LMX4, 4% lidocaine cream; NPO, nothing by mouth.

*Data are taken from McGhee et al.[39] and Babl et al.[40]

Table 6-7 Examples of Topical Anesthetics*

Topical Anesthetic	Description
4% Lidocaine cream (LMX4)	Nonmucosal skin; intravenous cannulation, venipuncture, implantable venous device access, subcutaneous catheter insertion, lumbar puncture, abscess drainage, and joint aspiration
	20- to 30-minute onset of action; effectiveness may depend on duration of application
	Cleanse sites with soap and water
	Apply to a minimum of two sites in preparation for intravenous insertion; no more than two for neonates and infants who may have systemic absorption of the lidocaine through thinner skin.
	Protect cream with a transparent dressing, particularly if there is risk for ingestion by the patient
	Allergy to amide anesthetics is a contraindication

Topical Anesthetic	Description
Lidocaine hydrochloride, epinephrine bitartrate, and tetracaine hydrochloride, prepared in a KY jelly base (LET)	Nonmucosal skin lacerations up to five centimeters in length; because of epinephrine content, avoid on fingers, toes, penis, nose, or ear cartilage
	Apply to sterile cotton or gauze, insert into the wound, cover, and apply constant pressure for 30 minutes
	Suturing must be done immediately after effectiveness is achieved because analgesia dissipates in 15–30 minutes
	20- to 30-minute onset of action is effective for scalp and face lacerations; less effective on extremities
	Avoid on grossly contaminated wounds
	Allergy to amide anesthetics is a contraindication

Topical Anesthetic	Description
4% Ametop gel	Effective topical local anesthetic containing tetracaine (amethocaine)
	It has a minimum 30-minute onset of action and should be applied under an occlusive dressing
	Safe for use in the newborn population and cannot be used on open wounds
	May be associated with a local allergic reaction

Topical Anesthetic	Description
Vapocoolant sprays	Transient anesthesia via evaporation-induced skin cooling
	Instantly effective for short periods
	Risk of frostbite and tissue damage with inappropriate use by overspraying or spraying too closely to the skin

*Data are taken from McGhee et al.[39] Data are also taken from the following sources: (1) Bhargava, R., & Young, K. D. (2007). Procedural pain management patterns in academic pediatric emergency departments. *Academic Emergency Medicine, 14,* 479–482. (2) Pasek, T., Thomas, D., Khimji, I., Schmitt, C., Spencer, A., & Hanni, R. (2007). Implementation of a nurse-driven topical analgesic protocol: Two steps forward, one step back. *Pediatric Pain Letter, 9,* 25–31. (3) Farion, K. J., Splinter, K. L., Newhook, K., Gaboury, I., & Splinter, W. M. (2008). The effect of vapocoolant spray on pain due to intravenous cannulation in children: a randomized controlled trial. *Canadian Medical Association Journal, 179,* 31–36.

Table 6-8 Common Emergency Department Procedures That May Require Sedation and/or Analgesia

Sedation Alone	Analgesia Alone	Sedation/Analgesia
Neuroimaging	Wound care	Placement of a central line
Thoracentesis	Abscess drainage	Lumbar puncture
Chest tube placement	Fracture reduction	Fracture reduction
Sexual assault examination		Dislocation reduction
Endotracheal intubation		Removal of a deep foreign body
Removal of a superficial foreign body		Joint aspiration
		Hernia reduction
		Cardioversion
		Burn care
		Thoracentesis
		Chest tube placement

Table 6-9 Medications Used for Sedation in Pediatric Patients*

Sedatives

Diazepam (Valium)	Benzodiazepine sedatives may be administered IV, IM, PO, or rectally
	Long duration of action (two to six hours); half-life of 20–40 hours; results in lengthy monitoring
	Flumazenil (Romazicon) will reverse effects, but observe carefully for resedation; antidote has shorter half-life
Midazolam (Versed)	Most frequently used benzodiazepine; may be administered IV, PO, sublingually, intranasally, or rectally
	Rapid acting; short half-life
	Higher doses per kilogram may be required for infants and toddlers to achieve the desired effect
	Flumazenil will reverse effects, but observe carefully for resedation; antidote has shorter half-life
Pentobarbital sodium (Nembutal)	Barbiturate may be administered IV or PO
	Does not have analgesic properties; for painful procedures, also administer an analgesic
	Rapid onset of action; duration of action is 20–60 minutes
	Prolonged recovery when combined with other sedative or analgesic medications
Chloral hydrate	Most effective for children younger than 4 years
	Delayed sedative effects can be seen up to 20 hours after administration
	Deaths from respiratory depression have been reported. These have been the result of a delayed effect of chloral hydrate with the administration of a second dose or a successive dose of an opioid.

General Anesthetic

Ketamine (Ketalar)	May be administered IV, IM, or PO; onset of action depends on route having the most immediate response
	Should be used under the direct supervision of physicians experienced in administering general aesthetics and maintaining an airway
	Resuscitative equipment should be available for use
	May be used for short procedures, as a supplement to nitrous oxide, and for dressing changes

Opioids (provide analgesia and sedative effects)

Morphine sulfate	May be administered IV, IM, SC, rectally, or PO; onset of action depends on route, with IV having the most immediate response
	Duration of action is 3–5 hours; results in lengthy monitoring; suitable for longer procedures
	Naloxone (Narcan) will reverse effects, but observe carefully for resedation; antidote has a shorter half-life
Fentanyl citrate (Sublimaze)	May be administered IV, IM, or intranasally
	Rapid onset and short acting; suitable for brief procedures
	Rapid administration may result in respiratory depression and chest wall rigidity
	Duration of action is 30–120 minutes
	Naloxone (Narcan) will reverse effects, but observe carefully for resedation; antidote has a shorter half-life
Hydromorphone (Dilaudid)	May be administered IV, IM, SC, or PO
	Analgesic effects within 15–30 minutes after oral administration; peak effects within 30 to 90 minutes, persisting for four to five hours
	Naloxone (Narcan) will reverse effects, but observe carefully for resedation; antidote has a shorter half-life

Note: IM indicates intramuscular; IV, intravenous; PO, oral; SC, subcutaneous.

Height, weight, body mass index, and body surface area vary. Pediatric formulas commonly use weight or body surface area to determine medication dosages. This means that medications are ordered in milligrams/kilograms (weight) or milligrams/meter-squared (body surface area). *These methods are more accurate than extrapolating doses from those used for adults; doses intended for adults should not simply be decreased to determine pediatric doses.* Generally, IM injections should be avoided in the pediatric population. Administering an injection to relieve pain contradicts pain management principles. However, IM injections may be necessary in situations when venous access or other routes of administration are unavailable or inferior.

*Data are taken from McGhee et al.[39]

Summary

Emergency nurses play a crucial role in the recognition, assessment, and management of pain in pediatric patients. Early recognition of the physiological and behavioral responses that children have to pain is paramount to timely intervention. Appreciation of the emotional and physical link in the response to pain is vital to integrating both nonpharmacological and pharmacological pain therapies for optimal pain management.

References

1. Drendel, A. M., Brousseau, D. C., & Gorelick, M. H. (2006). Pain assessment for pediatric patients in the emergency department. *Pediatrics, 117,* 1511–1518.

2. LeMay, S., Johnston, C. C., Choiniere, M., Fortin, C., Kudirka, D., Muarray, L., & Chalut, D. (2009). Pain management practices in a pediatric emergency room (PAMPER) study: Interventions with nurses. *Pediatric Emergency Care, 25,* 498–503.

3. *Pain clinical updates.* (2005). Retrieved from http://www.iasp-pain.org/AM/AMTemplate.cfm?Section=Home&TEMPLATE=/CM/ContentDisplay.cfm&CONTENTID=7638

4. Buaman, B. H., & McManus, J. G. (2005). Pediatric pain management in the emergency department. *Emergency Medical Clinics of North America, 23,* 393–413.

5. Khan, K. A., & Weisman, S. M. (2007). Nonpharmacologic pain management strategies in the pediatric emergency department. *Clinical Pediatric Emergency Medicine, 8,* 240–247.

6. McGrath, P. A. (1994). Psychological aspects of pain perception. *Archives of Oral Biology, 39* (suppl), 55–62.

7. The International Association for the Study of Pain. (n.d.). *IASP pain terminology.* Retrieved from http://www.iasp-pain.org/AM/Template.cfm?Section=Pain_Definitions&Template=/CM/HTMLDisplay.cfm&ContentID=1728#Pain

8. Caterina, M. J., Gold, M. S., & Myer, R. A. (2005). Molecular biology of nociceptors. In S. Hunt & M. Klotzenburg (Eds.), *The neurobiology of pain* (pp. 1–34). Oxford, England: Oxford University Press.

9. Pasek, T. A., Wright, E. K., & Campese, C. E. (2009). Pain assessment and management. In D. O. Thomas & L. M. Bernardo (Eds.), *Core curriculum for pediatric emergency nursing* (2nd ed., pp. 119–137). Des Plaines, IL: Emergency Nurses Association.

10. Edwards, A. D. (2002). Physiology of pain. In B. St. Marie (Ed.), *American Society of Pain Management Nurses core curriculum for pain management nursing* (pp. 121–145). Philadelphia, PA: Saunders.

11. Bennet, R. (2002). *Understanding pain.* Retrieved from http://www.myalgia.com/Pain_amplification/Overview.htm

12. Mullen, J. E., & Pate, M. F. D. (2006). Caring for critically ill children and their families. In M. Slota (Ed.), *Core curriculum for pediatric critical care nursing* (p. 1039). St. Louis, MO: Saunders Elsevier.

13. Hockenberry, M. J., & Wilson, D. (2011). *Wong's nursing care of infants and children (9th ed.).* St. Louis, MO: Elsevier Mosby.

14. Stinson, J. N., Kavanagh, T., Yamad, J., Gill, N., & Stevens, B. (2006). Systematic review of the psychometric properties, interpretability and feasibility of self-report pain intensity measures for use in clinical trials in children and adolescents. *Pain, 125,* 143–157.

15. McGrath, P. A., Seifer, C. E., & Speechley, K. N. (1996). A new analogue scale for assessing children's pain: An initial validation study. *Pain, 64,* 435–443.

16. McConahay, T., Bryson, M., & Bulloch, B. (2006). Defining mild, moderate, and severe pain by using the color analog scale with children presenting to pediatric emergency department. *Academic Emergency Medicine, 13,* 341–344.

17. McConahay, T., Bryson, M., & Bulloch, B. (2007). Clinically significant changes in acute pain in a pediatric ED using the Color Analog Scale. *American Journal of Emergency Medicine, 25,* 739–742.

18. Bulloch, B., & Tenenbein, M. (2002). Validation of 2 pain scales for use in the emergency department. *Pediatrics, 110,* e33.

19. Bieri, D., Reeve, R. A., Champion, G. D., Addicoat, L., & Ziegler, J. (1990). The Faces Pain Scale for the self-assessment of the severity of pain experienced by children: Development, initial validation, and preliminary investigation for the ratio scale properties. *Pain, 41,* 139–150.

20. Hicks, C. L., von Baeyer, C. L., Spafford, P., van Korlaar, I., & Goodenough, B. (2001). The Faces Pain Scale—Revised: Toward a common metric in pediatric pain measurement. *Pain, 93,* 173–183.

21. Beyer, J. E., Turner, S. B., Jones, L., Young, L., Onikul, R., & Bohaty, B. (2005). The alternate forms reliability of the Oucher Pain Scale. *Pain Management Nursing, 6,* 10–17.

22. von Baeyer, C. L., Spagrud, L. J., McCormick, J. C., Choo, E., Neville, K., & Connelly, M. A. (2009). Three new datasets supporting use of the Numerical Rating Scale (NRS-11) for children's self-reports of pain intensity. *Pain, 143(3),* 223–227.

23. Zempsky, W. T., Craver, J. P., & American Academy of Pediatrics Committee on Pediatric Emergency Medicine and Section on Anesthesiology and Pain Medicine. (2004). Relief of pain and anxiety in pediatric patients in emergency medical systems. *Pediatrics, 114,* 1348–1356.

24. McGrath, P. J., & Finley, G. A. (1999). Pediatric pain sourcebook of protocols, policies, and pamphlets. Retrieved from http://www.painsourcebook.ca

25. Petrack, E., Perry, L. S., & Vehar, K. (2008). Integration of pharmacologic and non-pharmacologic techniques to enhance pediatric minor procedures. *Journal of Urgent Care Medicine, 2,* 11–16.

26. Anderson, K., & Weisman, S. J. (2007). Nonpharmacologic pain management strategies in the pediatric emergency department. *Clinical Pediatric Emergency Medicine, 8,* 240–247.

27. Anand, K. J., & International Evidence-Based Group for Neonatal Pain. (2001). Consensus statement for the prevention and management of pain in the newborn. *Archives of Pediatric and Adolescent Medicine, 155,* 173–180.

References *continued*

28. Thompson, D. G. (2005) Utilizing an oral sucrose solution to minimize neonatal pain. *Journal for Specialists in Pediatric Nursing, 10,* 3–10.

29. Rogers, A. J., Greenwald, M. H., Degusman, M. A., Kelley, M. E., & Simon H. K. (2006). A randomized controlled trial of sucrose analgesia in infants younger than 90 days of age who require bladder catheterization in the pediatric emergency department. *Academic Emergency Medicine, 13,* 617–622.

30. Eriksson, M., & Finnstrom, O. (2004). Can daily repeated doses of orally administered glucose induce tolerance when given for neonatal pain? *Acta Paediatrica, 93,* 2246–2249.

31. Tsao, J. C. I., Evans, .S, Meldrum, M., Altma, T., Zeltzer, L. K. (2008). A review of CAM for procedural pain in infancy: Part 1: Sucrose and non-nutritive sucking. *Evidence-based Complementary and Alternative Medicine, 5,* 317–381.

32. Lefrak, L., Burch, K., Caravantes, R., Knoerlein, K., DeNolf, N., Duncan, J., ... Toczylowski, K. (2006). Sucrose analgesia: Identifying better practices. *Pediatrics, 118,* S197–S202.

33. Curtis, S. J., Jou, H., Ali, S., Vandermeer, B., Klassen, T. (2007). A randomized control trial of sucrose and/or pacifier for infants receiving venipuncture in the emergency department. *Biomed Central Pediatrics, 7,* 27.

34. Dunbar, A. E., Sharek, P. J., Mickas, N. A., Coker, K. L., Duncan, J., McLendon, D., ... Johnston, C. C. (2006). Implementation and case-study results of potentially better practices to improve pain management of neonates. *Pediatrics, 118,* S87–S94.

35. Barr, R. G., Young, S. N., Wright, J. H., Cassidy, K. L., Hendricks, L., Bedard, Y., ... Treherne, S. (1995). "Sucrose analgesia" and diphtheria-tetanus-pertussis immunizations at 2 and 4 months. *Journal of Developmental and Behavioral Pediatrics, 16,* 220–225.

36. Batton, D. G., Barrington, K. J., & Wallman, C. (2006). Prevention and management of pain in the neonate: an update. *Pediatrics, 118,* 2231–2241.

37. US Department of Health and Human Services, Agency for Healthcare Policy and Research Clinical Practice Guidelines. (1994). *World Health Organization pain relief ladder.* Retrieved from http://www1.va.gov/Pain_Management/page.cfm?pg=22

38. Vila, H., Smith, R. A., Augustyniak, M. J., Nagi, P. A., Soto, R. G., Ross, T. W., ... Miguel, R. V. (2005). The efficacy and safety of pain management before and after implementation of hospital-wide pain management standards: Is patient safety compromised by treatment based solely on numerical pain ratings? *Anesthesia Analgesia, 101,* 474–480.

39. McGhee, B., Howrie, D., Schmitt, C., Nguyen, P., Berry, D., Sandy, J., ... Khimji, I. (2007). *Pediatric drug therapy handbook & formulary* (5th ed.). Hudson, OH: Lexi-Comp.

40. American Academy of Pediatrics Committee on Drugs. (2009). Acetaminophen in children. *Pediatrics, 108,* 1020–1024.

41. Babl, F. E., Oakley, E., Seaman, C., Barnett, P., & Sharwood, L. N. (2008). High concentration nitrous oxide for procedural sedation in children: Adverse events and depth of sedation. *Pediatrics, 121,* e528–e532.

42. Buvanendran, A., & Kroin, J. S. (2007). Useful adjuvants for postoperative pain management. Best Practice & Research. *Clinical Anaesthesiology, 21,* 31–49.

Chapter 7 | Common Procedures and Sedation

Christy L. Cooper, MSN, RN, CEN, CPEN, NREMT-P

Objectives

On completion of this chapter, the learner should be able to do the following:

* Plan procedural preparation according to anatomical and physiological characteristics of the pediatric patient.
* Describe positioning techniques and equipment selected for procedural preparation.
* Utilize specialized nursing techniques to facilitate successful outcomes in selected emergent pediatric procedures.
* Recognize the importance of family presence and caregiver assistance during therapeutic and diagnostic procedures.
* Discuss pre-, intra-, and post-procedure responsibilities of the nurse during procedural sedation.

Introduction

Every day, thousands of pediatric patients and their caregivers visit emergency departments, seeking care or treatment for an illness or injury. Many of these patients will require therapeutic and diagnostic procedures during their visits. These procedures can produce extreme anxiety in both the patient and their caregivers. Careful and clear explanations of procedures, and the use of techniques such as music, distraction, and other nonpharmacological interventions, can often relieve many fears. However, not all procedures are appropriate for nonpharmacological intervention. Some procedures will require the use of sedative agents to ensure the comfort and safety of the pediatric patient. This chapter will explore the concepts of procedural preparation and sedation in the pediatric patient.

A Child Life Specialist, if available, is an invaluable member of the pediatric healthcare team. Child Life Specialists are trained to ease a pediatric patient's fears and anxiety with therapeutic play activities. They foster understanding and cooperation by providing non-medical preparation for children undergoing medical procedures. They promote an environment that includes emotional support of the child and the child's family.

Procedural Preparation

Preparing a pediatric patient for a therapeutic or diagnostic procedure can be both challenging and rewarding. Items to consider before preparing the child and family include the following:

* The age and developmental level of the child: The nurse should recognize that every child grows and develops differently based on his or her temperament, family environment, and past experiences.[1]

* The patient's previous experiences with the healthcare environment: Today, many children have experiences in the healthcare setting at an early age. Some children experience no more than routine primary care and the occasional sick visit; however, other children have special healthcare needs and may have experiences in the healthcare system that include not only routine care, but inpatient admissions, surgical procedures, painful procedures, and emergency visits. Obtaining information from the caregiver about these experiences, no matter how routine or emergent, will allow the emergency nurse to anticipate the unique needs of the child during the current illness or injury.

* The culture of the family: Cultural variances affect the patient's perception of illness and injury and guide the

treatment plan of the patient. Language barriers and cultural differences in child-rearing practices are potential barriers in the procedural preparation process.[1]

After assessing the patient and making an individualized plan for the patient's experience, the procedure needs to be communicated and explained to the patient and family. Items to consider include the following:

- Provide age-appropriate communication of the procedure to the child. Describe the procedure in words and terms that the child can understand. Offer choices to the child if available and age appropriate.

- Give explanations about sounds, smells, and sensations that the patient may experience. Be truthful and use developmentally appropriate language and descriptions.

  ○ Do not forget to talk to both the patient and the family about any monitor alarms or alerts that they may hear and what the alarm may mean. Also, discuss with them any actions that the nurse may take if an alarm sounds.

- Be realistic about the time the procedure will take. Remember that young children understand time in terms of daily tasks and activities.

- Assess patient and caregiver understanding of the communicated information. Encourage family members to ask questions and validate concerns.

- Discuss the role of the caregiver during the procedure. Offer caregivers the option of being present for the procedure, but also offer them reassurance that it is acceptable to step away if they feel they will not be able to be supportive or tolerate observation of the procedure.

  ○ Ensure that your hospital has a policy on family presence during procedures.[2]

  ○ Ensure the comfort of the rest of the care team with the caregiver's presence and role.[2]

  ○ Remind the caregiver that the patient is the staff's primary concern during the procedure.

During the procedure or diagnostic test, items to consider include the following:

- Offer reassurance to both the patient and the caregiver.

- Communicate in soothing tones. Keep the environment calm. Only one person should speak at a time, in a low calm voice.[3]

- Let the patient and caregiver know at regular intervals how much longer the procedure will last.

- If caregivers appear uncomfortable or are about to faint, offer to let them step out of the procedure area or ensure they are sitting instead of standing.

- At the end of the procedure, praise the child for his or her cooperation during the procedure.

Techniques to Facilitate Coping During the Procedure

No single approach to relieving anxiety and stress during a procedure typically works for all pediatric patients. Although every child deserves the appropriate psychological preparation previously described, many pediatric patients will require a combination of psychological preparation and other techniques, such as distraction, positioning, pharmacological therapy to relieve pain, and possibly sedation to alleviate fear and anxiety. The following section will discuss appropriate positioning during procedures and the use of restrictive devices. **Chapter 6, "Pain,"** provides pain management information; sedation will be covered in a later section of this chapter.

Positioning for Comfort During Procedures

To facilitate the ease of examination and ensure the comfort of pediatric patients during procedures, a technique called *therapeutic hugging,* or positioning for comfort, should be used whenever possible.[4] These techniques decrease anxiety and stress on the patient and promote safety during the examination or procedure.

The following techniques foster comfort and ease of the examination in a number of ways:[5]

- Allow the child to sit up or recline in an upright position. After children have learned to sit upright, forcing them to lay down causes them to feel a loss of control. This loss of control may be displayed by resistance, crying, and struggling. Continued efforts to force them to lie supine will increase their resistance and will significantly increase their stress and anxiety during the procedure.

- Comforting positions, such as swaddling, hugging, and cuddling, reinforce the support of the caregiver and allow the child to feel some sensations of normalcy during an anxiety-provoking procedure. These techniques also allow the caregiver to participate in the child's care in a positive manner, rather than in a negative restraining manner.

- Ensure effective immobilization of the desired body area. This promotes the safety of the patient during the procedure.

- Attempt to complete the procedure using fewer people, thus decreasing the child's fear and anxiety with an overwhelming number of strangers present.

- Decrease separation from caregivers. This will enhance cooperation and lessen anxiety.

Examples of appropriate positioning are shown in **Figure 7-1, Figure 7-2,** and **Figure 7-3.**

Figure 7-1 Securing a Child for a Blood Draw*

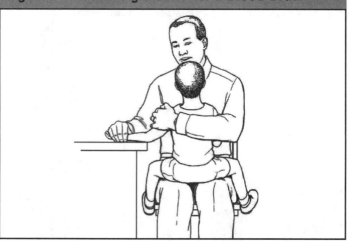

*Reprinted with permission from: Wilson, D., Hockenberry, M. J., & Wong, D.L. (2008). *Wong's clinical manual of pediatric nursing* (7th ed.) St. Louis, MO: Mosby Elsevier.

Figure 7-2 Securing a Child for Extremity Intravenous Line Placement*

*Reprinted with permission from: Hockenberry, M. J. (2005). *Instructor's resource to accompany Wong's essentials of pediatric nursing* (7th ed.). St. Louis, MO: Elsevier Mosby.

Figure 7-3 Therapeutic Hugging for a Procedure Involving the Neck or Face*

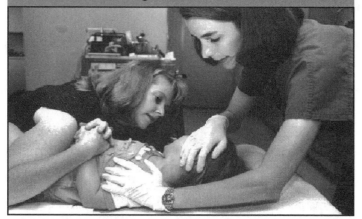

*Reprinted with permission from: Hockenberry, M. J. (2005). *Instructor's resource to accompany Wong's essentials of pediatric nursing* (7th ed.). St. Louis, MO: Elsevier Mosby.

Tips to Remember During Positioning

- The use of positioning and hugging does not remove the need for appropriate psychological preparation of both the patient and the caregiver.

- Remove the child's shoes before positioning to prevent painful kicks.

- When holding the child's legs, appropriate control is best gained by positioning the holder's hands directly over the knees.

- Make sure the caregiver is appropriately prepared if he or she is going to participate by holding during the procedure.

- Make sure that the hold is secure before beginning the procedure to prevent injury to the child, caregiver, and staff.

- Keep the caregiver in the child's line of sight.

- Provide reassurance throughout the procedure in a quiet and calm voice.

- Monitor the patient for deterioration during the procedure.

Use of Restrictive Devices During Procedures

The use of restrictive devices during pediatric procedures should be rare and limited to times during which other means of procedural positioning are impossible or pose a risk of harm to the child, caregiver, or staff. Most children with adequate psychological preparation, positioning, and pain management will cooperate and tolerate procedures better without the use of restrictive devices.[4] If restrictive devices must be used, consider the following items:

- Age and developmental level of the child

- Prior experiences with procedures and need for restrictive device use

    ○ Any history of child maltreatment and how the child may respond to being restrained should be considered.

- Type of procedure to be performed

- Type of restrictive device needed

    ○ The least restrictive device that will allow the procedure to be completed safely and efficiently should be used.

- Length of time the restrictive device will need to be in place

- Use of both pharmacological and nonpharmacological means of preparation and their effectiveness

- Medical indications for the use of the restraint device

    ○ The device must be initiated to promote patient safety and enhance the effectiveness of the procedure.

- Be familiar with your hospital's policy regarding the use of procedural restraints and document appropriately.

- Patient and caregiver perceptions of the need for restrictive device use.

  - Careful explanations about the need for the restrictive device's use and the type of device that will be used should be communicated to both the patient and caregiver.

  - Ensure that the caregiver is still allowed to participate in the patient's care.

    - Keep the caregiver in the room and in the line of sight of the patient.

    - Position the device so that the caregiver can hold the child's hand or have a place to maintain physical contact with the child.

If a restrictive device must be used, the list below covers some of the more common means of restriction and restrictive devices.

- If restriction of the child's arms or hands is required, some minimally restrictive means of restraint are as follows:

  - Have the patient place his or her hands beneath his or her buttocks, so that the patient is sitting or lying on his or her hands. This will help remind the patient not to reach or grab.

  - Place the patient's hands and arms in a pillowcase and pull it up to his or her shoulders from behind. Lie the child down on the pillowcase. This will restrict the movement of the patient's arms. Make the application of the pillowcase fun for the child by calling it a cape, using a favorite superhero as an example.

- If restriction of the entire body is required, some options are as follows:

  - Use a sheet or baby blanket and wrap the child like a mummy. Position the patient on the sheet and wrap one side around, tucking it under the patient. Repeat the same measure on the opposite side. The patient's weight on the tucked sheet will restrict the movement of both arms and legs.

  - A child restraint board or papoose can also be used to control the pediatric patient's movement. Most children find the board more intimidating than the use of sheets and other devices. Position the patient on the board. Secure the wraps with the provided Velcro to keep the patient in place, using the least number of the three provided wraps possible to control patient movement and provide a secure hold (**Figure 7-4**).

Figure 7-4 Papoose Board™

*Image courtesy of Natus Medical Incorporated.

Positioning for Common Procedures

Lumbar Puncture

The term *lumbar puncture* refers to a procedure during which a needle is placed into the lower back between the spinal processes to access the subarachnoid space and the cerebrospinal fluid located there.[6] In the emergency department setting, the most common goal of this procedure is diagnosis of a central nervous system infection, such as meningitis. The lumbar puncture is a routine portion of the septic workup of neonatal and pediatric patients.[6] In the pediatric patient, two different positions are possible to gain access to the lumbar area and subarachnoid space. Correct positioning is a vital factor to ensure a successful and safe outcome from this procedure.[7]

- The lateral decubitis or side-lying position

  - Have the patient lie on their side near the edge of the stretcher. An assistant helps position patients with their knees pulled toward the chest and their head and neck flexed in a downward position. It may also help to have the patient tuck their arms between their legs to help keep them from moving and grabbing during the procedure (**Figure 7-5**). The assistant helps control the position of the patient by placing one arm under their knees and the other arm around the back of their shoulders.[8]

Figure 7-5 Lateral Decubitus Position for Lumbar Puncture*

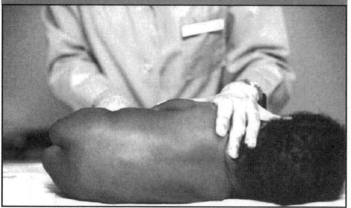

*Reprinted with permission from Hockenberry, M. J. (2005). *Instructor's resource to accompany Wong's essentials of pediatric nursing* (7th ed.) St. Louis, MO: Mosby/Elsevier.

Figure 7-6 Upright Position for Lumbar Puncture*

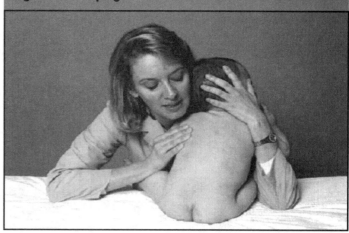

*Reprinted with permission from Hockenberry, M. J. (2005). *Instructor's resource to accompany Wong's essentials of pediatric nursing* (7th ed.) St. Louis, MO: Mosby/Elsevier.

○ If a patient is old enough and cooperative, he or she can be asked to stretch his or her back like a cat. This arching position fully opens up the lumbar spaces, allowing easier placement of the needle into the subarachnoid space.[8]

○ Ensure the child's airway is maintained at all times. Adequate airway and breathing is continually assessed while the child is in this position. Supplemental oxygen is recommended.

• The upright or sitting position

○ This position is commonly used in the infant population and may be an alternative to the side-lying position for the cooperative older child.[6] This position may be preferred for patients in respiratory distress or when access to the lumbar region has proven difficult in a side-lying position.[8]

○ For the infant, place the patient in a knee to abdomen position and flex the neck forward. The assistant should grasp the infant around each leg and arm, using one hand on each side of the patient (**Figure 7-6**).

○ The older child should be positioned with his or her legs dangling over the stretcher, bending forward at the waist. To assist with optimal positioning of the patient, a rolled blanket or pillow may be placed under the child's arms to facilitate the curved spine position. The assistant should stand and position himself or herself in a hugging-type position. Sometimes having the child's legs wrapped around the assistant will help encourage the older child to hold still.

Clinical Tips

• Needle selection for lumbar puncture:[8]

○ Neonates to the age of two years: 22 gauge by 1.5 inches in length

○ Children aged two to 12 years: 22 gauge by 2.5 inches in length

○ Children older than 12 years: 20 or 22 gauge by 3.5 inches in length

• Allow adequate time for topical anesthesia to work. Some patients may require additional medications for pain and anxiety control, or they may require sedation during the procedure.

• If a urine specimen is required from the patient, place a bag to collect the specimen or plan to catheterize the patient before the procedure; this may be particularly important in the infant or child who has not mastered toilet training.

• Avoid hyperflexion of the neck and vigorous holding of infants. Hyperflexion may lead to airway compromise.[6]

• Be alert to changes in clinical condition. This procedure is often performed on critically ill patients who may decompensate during the procedure. Pulse oximetry monitoring is recommended during the procedure to monitor respiratory status because of the risk of respiratory compromise in neonates and infants is caused by improper positioning.

• After the procedure, older children and teenagers should lie flat to decrease the risk of a headache after lumbar puncture. Adequate hydration and intake of caffeine-containing fluids also help decrease the risk of a headache after lumbar puncture.[8]

Gastric Tube Insertion

In the pediatric population, gastric tubes are placed in the emergency department for a number of reasons. The primary reason is decompression of the stomach to maximize lung expansion in the intubated patient. It is also done to perform gastric lavage, instill medications, and administer fluids and nutrition.

Two routes of gastric tube placement are available in the pediatric patient and are indicated for different reasons.

- The oral route
  - This route is commonly used in infants younger than six weeks who are obligate nasal breathers. It is also recommended for use when the ability to perform gastric lavage is indicated and in any patient who has a head injury and requires a gastric tube.
  - Larger gastric tubes (22–36 French) may be passed when using the oral route. Larger tubes facilitate the ease of gastric lavage.
  - Appropriate measurement of an orogastric tube for placement is accomplished as follows: measure from the corner of the mouth to the earlobe and from the earlobe to the area between the tip of the xiphoid process and the umbilicus. This length should be marked on the tube with either permanent marker or tape.
  - Once placed, secure the tube to the child's cheek with tape and a clear occlusive dressing.
- The nasal route
  - The nasogastric route is commonly used when a pediatric patient requires the temporary administration of fluids and nutrition via a gastric tube. Nasogastric tubes are also used to facilitate gastric decompression.
  - To ease the insertion of a nasogastric tube, place 2% lidocaine jelly in each nare a few minutes before insertion. Use a water-soluble lubricant on the tube itself to ease the passage of the tube.
  - To appropriately measure the nasogastric tube for depth of placement, measure from the tip of the nose to the earlobe, then from the earlobe to the area between the tip of the xiphoid process and the umbillicus. Mark this length on the tube with either permanent marker or tape.
  - Once placed, secure the tube with tape to the bridge of the nose or upper lip and cover with a clear occlusive dressing (**Figure 7-7**).

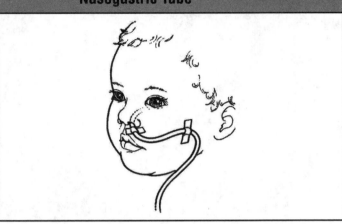

Figure 7-7 Proper Method for Taping a Nasogastric Tube*

*Reprinted with permission from Hockenberry, M. J. (2005). *Instructor's resource to accompany Wong's essentials of pediatric nursing* (7th ed.) St. Louis, MO: Mosby/Elsevier.

Clinical Tips

- Appropriate tube sizes:
  - Infants: 8 French
  - Toddlers to preschoolers: 10 French
  - School-aged children: 12 French
  - Adolescents: 14 to 16 French
- During the insertion of a gastric tube, the nurse should have suction with a rigid tonsil tip on and ready for use. It is also a good idea to have additional appropriately sized tubes readily available.
- **Never** force the tube if resistance or obstruction is met.
  - If the patient develops signs of respiratory distress or color change or is unable to cry or speak, remove the tube immediately.
  - Talking or crying during the procedure is a good indicator that the tube has not been placed in the trachea and is in the gastric system.
- Patient positioning and preparation: Several types of positioning are helpful when placing a gastric tube. The nurse should always attempt to insert the gastric tube in the least threatening and most comfortable manner for the patient.
  - Explain the procedure using age-appropriate and developmentally appropriate psychological preparation. The use of distraction and relaxation techniques may help facilitate tube placement.
  - Infants may be swaddled in a blanket and held upright in the caregiver's arms, with a second staff member present to help control the infant's head. If possible,

have the infant suck on a pacifier to assist with swallowing the tube. Blowing into the infant's face may help with tube placement by causing reflex swallowing.

- In toddlers and younger children, the caregiver may assist with the procedure by positioning them in a hugging hold. This provides the child a comforting position and allows the caregiver to help keep the patient's hands from grabbing during the procedure. If not contraindicated, the patient should sip water during the procedure to help facilitate swallowing of the tube.

- Older children and teenagers may be positioned in a high Fowler's position with the head slightly flexed. Older children and teenagers may also need assistance with holding still and not grabbing at the tube because of the uncomfortable nature of the procedure.

- If the patient is unconscious, gastric tube insertion can be facilitated by placing the patient on his or her left side, then lowering the head of the bed in a Trendelenburg position. If endotracheal intubation is indicated, it should be performed before insertion of the gastric tube to prevent aspiration.

- After the tube is in position, it may be necessary to control the patient's hands with mittens or soft restraints to keep the tube in place. Refer to your institution's protocol for use of restraints to protect medical devices.

- Tube placement
  - The best way to confirm gastric tube placement has undergone much debate in the past several years. Incidents of improper placements and adverse outcomes have caused the standard method of auscultation to undergo much scrutiny.[9]

  - Many institutions have policies and procedures in place for verifying initial placement with a radiograph before using a gastric tube. Subsequent use of the tube then requires placement to be verified by testing the pH of gastric aspirate before instilling feedings or medications. **Figure 7-8** shows a typical algorithm for verifying tube placement in infants and children.[10]

- A nasal gastric tube may increase the risk of sinus infections if used long-term.

Gastrostomy Tube Placement and Complications

Gastrostomy tubes (G-tubes) are often placed in order to provide nutrition and medication to pediatric patients who have difficulty with oral ingestion. Patients with dislodged G-tubes often present to the emergency department in order to have their tube replaced. A G-tube should be replaced as quickly as possible in the emergency depart-

ment, unless the tube was recently placed. A feeding tube tract can narrow or close within hours of tube displacement. A simple G-tube may require up to two weeks to form a mature tract.[11] If the tract appears recently placed, immediately contact the provider who placed the tube prior to emergency department replacement, as operative or fluoroscopic replacement may be required. Replacing a G-tube that has not formed a tract can lead to misplacement in the peritoneal cavity. Replacement should not be performed if any evidence of infection—such as erythema, exudate, or warmth—is found at the G-tube site. G-tube replacement generally requires no anesthesia, but if the skin site is sore, use of a topical numbing agent may decrease discomfort associated with tube replacement.

When the patient arrives in the emergency department with a dislodged G-tube, it should be replaced with the same tube or same type of tube. The fact that the G-tube was dislodged can indicate a malfunction with that particular tube (such as balloon rupture); thus, a new tube should be used. When information on the tube type is not available or known to the patient, a dedicated feeding tube suffices. If no feeding tube is accessible, a Foley catheter can be used temporarily until a dedicated feeding tube can be placed.[12] Certain tubes require specialized plugs, connectors, and clamps. In addition, some tubes necessitate the use of a guidewire or other support to assist tube passage.

The G-tube occasionally is only partially dislodged. In such cases, the tube must be removed prior to replacement. Most G-tubes can be removed with simple traction after deflating the balloon (if one exists). Refer to institutional policy and procedures regarding the emergency nurse's role in G-tube removal.

Secure the tube and ensure orders for confirmation studies are completed (e.g., pH, abdominal radiograph with contrast) per institutional protocol prior to use.[13]

Urinary Catheterization

Urinary catheterization is performed to collect a sterile urine sample, to monitor urine output, or to relieve urinary retention in the pediatric patient. With current attention on catheter-acquired urinary tract infections, assess for definitive need of a catheter before insertion. A urine sample obtained via catheterization is a standard part of the septic workup in neonatal patients and may be performed on older children who are unable or unwilling to collect a clean catch specimen for diagnostic procedures. The procedure for obtaining a urine specimen via catheterization is the same for both intermittent and indwelling catheters.

- Ensure adequate lighting and privacy for the examination.

Decision tree for nasogastric tube placement checks in CHILDREN and INFANTS (NOT NEONATES)

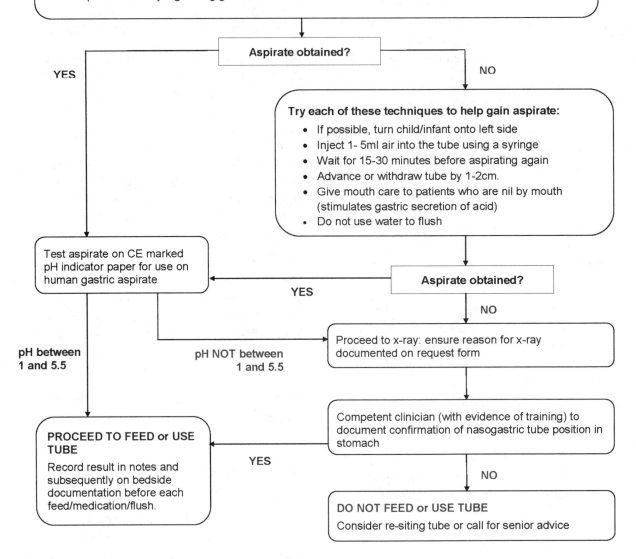

- Estimate NEX measurement (Place exit port of tube at tip of nose. Extend tube to earlobe, and then to xiphisternum)
- Insert fully radio-opaque nasogastric tube for feeding (follow manufacturer's instructions for insertion)
- Confirm and document secured NEX measurement
- Aspirate with a syringe using gentle suction

Aspirate obtained?

YES NO

Try each of these techniques to help gain aspirate:
- If possible, turn child/infant onto left side
- Inject 1-5ml air into the tube using a syringe
- Wait for 15-30 minutes before aspirating again
- Advance or withdraw tube by 1-2cm.
- Give mouth care to patients who are nil by mouth (stimulates gastric secretion of acid)
- Do not use water to flush

Test aspirate on CE marked pH indicator paper for use on human gastric aspirate

Aspirate obtained?

YES NO

pH between 1 and 5.5

pH NOT between 1 and 5.5

Proceed to x-ray: ensure reason for x-ray documented on request form

Competent clinician (with evidence of training) to document confirmation of nasogastric tube position in stomach

PROCEED TO FEED or USE TUBE

Record result in notes and subsequently on bedside documentation before each feed/medication/flush.

YES NO

DO NOT FEED or USE TUBE

Consider re-siting tube or call for senior advice

A pH of between 1 and 5.5 is reliable confirmation that the tube is not in the lung, however it does not confirm gastric placement as there is a small chance the tube tip may sit in the oesophagus where it carries a higher risk of aspiration. If this is any concern, the patient should proceed to x-ray in order to confirm tube position.

Where pH readings fall between 5 and 6 it is recommended that a second competent person checks the reading or retests.

www.npsa.nhs.uk/alerts

*Reprinted with permission from National Patient Safety Agency.[10]
NEX, nose to ear to xyphoid (midway between xyphoid and umbilicus) process.

- Older children and teenagers may be uncomfortable with having their caregivers in the room for the procedure.

- Position the patient supine on the stretcher or examination table.

  ◦ Female patients should be placed in the frog-leg position to facilitate ease of access to the urinary meatus.

    - To aid in the visualization of the urinary meatus, use the nondominant hand to pull up on and spread the labia minora.

  ◦ Male patients should be supine with the penis held perpendicular to the patient's body.

    - For uncircumcised male patients, carefully retract the foreskin enough to reveal the urethral opening.

    - Replace the foreskin after the procedure.

    - If the foreskin is tight and cannot be retracted, aim for the center of the glans. Do not force the foreskin back.

- After cleansing, use sterile technique, generously lubricate and slowly insert the catheter. 2% Lidocaine jelly may be applied to the urinary meatus before catheter insertion. This may help with the burning and discomfort of catheter insertion.[4]

- Never force the catheter. If you meet resistance, ask the patient to take a deep breath, or wait for the crying infant to take a deep breath, to help relax the sphincter. Slowly advance the catheter to the hub. Ensure the catheter is inserted into the bladder (urine return) before inflating the balloon to avoid urethral injury. Once there is urine return, you may inflate the balloon and obtain your sample.

- If the catheter is inadvertently placed in the vagina, leave it in place temporarily. Obtain a new catheter and reattempt the procedure. The original catheter will help with the identification of the vaginal opening and eliminate it as a site for placement.

- Tape the indwelling catheter to the thigh to help secure it in place.

  ◦ Promptly remove iodine solution from the skin with warm saline or water.

Clinical Tips

- Catheter selection:[4]

  ◦ Term neonate: 5–6 French

  ◦ Infant to the age of three years: 5–8 French

  ◦ Children aged four to eight years: 8 French

  ◦ Children aged eight years to prepubertal children, 10–12 French for girls and 8–10 French for boys

  ◦ Pubertal children, 12–14 French

- The insertion of a urinary catheter is contraindicated if there is blood at, or other noted trauma of, the perineal area or at the urethral meatus.

- Parents may have questions about the need for the procedure to be performed and its effects on the child's virginity. This cultural misunderstanding can be corrected with education about genitourinary anatomy and reassurance that the procedure will have no effect on the child's virginity.[4]

- The procedure should be explained using age-appropriate terms. Distraction and relaxation techniques may help ease the placement of the catheter. Older children and teenagers may be embarrassed by the need to have a catheter placed.

- Remember to ask about allergies to latex before any catheter insertion. Use latex-free materials for all children if possible.

Sedation

Although many procedures can be accomplished in the emergency department setting with appropriate psychological preparation, positioning for comfort, and minor pain or anxiety control, some patients will require the use of sedation to attain a safe and optimum outcome during even seemingly minor procedures.

A vast array of literature has been published during the past decade about the safe and effective management of sedation. This is in direct correlation to the expanding use of sedation in the outpatient and emergency department setting. Many of these articles focus on the use of sedation in the pediatric population and are geared toward providing the most safe, positive, and pain-free experience to children. Many of the guidelines and studies have been used to develop the charts and other information about sedation offered in this chapter.

The use of sedation in the pediatric population differs from its routine use in adults. Although some of the concepts are common, many of the medications, indications, and complications are unique to the pediatric population. Pediatric patients more often require sedation for common procedures because of their inability to cooperate. This inability is dependent on the child's growth and developmental level, the procedure to be performed, and the patient's prior experiences with the healthcare system. These factors are most commonly recognized in children younger than six years and in children with neurodevelopmental delays.[14]

Sedation is not without risks. Because of the high-risk nature of the procedure, standards have been established in the United States by The Joint Commission. These standards are in place to help ensure safe practice and safe patient outcomes when any type of sedation or anesthesia is used. These standards, which are incorporated throughout this section, apply across the age continuum. They are applicable in any setting in which a patient receives, by any route and for any reason, moderate or deep sedation, as well as general, spinal, or regional anesthesia.[15]

Sedation Goals

The goals of sedation use in the pediatric population for diagnostic and therapeutic procedures include the following:[14]

- Ensuring the patient's safety and welfare

- Promoting patient and family comfort

- Minimizing the patient's physical discomfort and pain

- Controlling anxiety

- Minimizing psychological trauma and enhancing the potential for amnesia

- Controlling behavior and movement to allow the safe completion of the procedure

- Returning the patient to the presedation level of consciousness

Common Procedures Requiring Sedation

Table 7-1 provides a brief overview of some of the common procedures performed in the emergency departments that require sedation.

This chart is only a list of common procedures. Some pediatric patients will require sedation for minor laceration repair, whereas others may be able to tolerate an entire magnetic resonance imaging procedure without intervention. This broad spectrum of patient reactions is why an appropriate assessment of the patient before a procedure is so important. Also, strategies for pain control must be considered in combination with the use of sedation. Studies have shown that pain control and other environmental modifications can enhance the effectiveness of sedation.[16] Some of these recommendations include the following:

- Procedural preparation and play

- Distraction

- Reduction of noise and stimulation

- Adjunctive pain relief strategies
  - Acetaminophen (Tylenol) or Ibuprofen (Motrin)
  - Hydrocodone and acetaminophen (Lortab) or other oral pain relievers
  - LMX or other topical numbing agents
  - Buffered lidocaine for injection
  - Vapocoolant sprays

Levels of Sedation

Procedural sedation, as defined by the American Society of Anesthesiologists (ASA), occurs on a continuum, ranging from minimal to general.[14] In the pediatric patient, this continuum is a narrow window that requires the provider and the nurse to balance the need for sedation with the ability to manage the patient's hemodynamic status during the procedure.[17] The level of sedation produced can be assessed by looking at the patient's level of consciousness. **Table 7-2** addresses the differences between the levels of consciousness. The level of sedation is related to the amount and type of medication administered, and it is impossible to predict for a given patient what level of sedation the medication will produce because of individual variances in response. The dosing parameters are guidelines that give the healthcare provider an idea about the depth of sedation to expect and are specifically designed to induce a level of sedation that does not cause loss of protective airway reflexes.[18]

Other factors to consider and address before a sedation procedure include the following:[16]

- The pediatric patient's hemodynamic stability and neurological status

- The presence of high-risk criteria (use of ASA status provides a physical class status for anesthesia and is recommended before any sedation administration); ASA status is outlined in **Table 7-3**

- Last oral intake or nothing-by-mouth status

- Amount of pain and/or anxiety the patient is experiencing

- Depth of sedation required and length of the planned procedure

- Informed consent from caregiver or legal guardian

- Availability of equipment and sedation-trained staff

- Comfort level of the sedation provider

- Impact of increased length of stay in the emergency department

Sedation Procedure

Before sedation is administered to a pediatric patient, the following items should be addressed and documented by the healthcare provider or sedation-qualified nurse. These standards are a reflection of the main concepts identified in current literature and are not a substitute for, but should be included in, your institution's policy and procedure on procedural sedation.

Table 7-1 Common Emergency Department Procedures That Require Sedation*

Minor Trauma	Medical Treatments	Diagnostic Procedures	Diagnostic Imaging
Laceration repair	Incision and drainage	Lumbar puncture	CT scans
Fracture reductions	Chest tube placement	Slit-lamp examination	MRI
Dental trauma	Cardioversion	Sexual assault examination	Barium enema
Dislocations	Foreign body removal	Joint aspiration	
Burn care	Central line placement		
	Endotracheal intubation		

Note: CT indicates computed tomography; MRI, magnetic resonance imaging.

*Data are adapted from Krauss, B., & Green, S. (2006). Procedural sedation and analgesia in children. *Lancet, 367*, 766–780.

Table 7-2 Levels of Sedation*

Level	Description
Minimal sedation (anxiolysis)	Medication-induced state in which patients respond normally to verbal commands. Although cognitive function may be impaired, respiratory and cardiovascular functions are unaffected.
Moderate sedation/analgesia	Medication-induced state of depressed consciousness in which patients respond purposefully to verbal commands, either alone or in conjunction with light tactile stimulation. No interventions are required to maintain a patent airway or spontaneous respirations; cardiovascular function is usually maintained. This term replaces *conscious sedation*.
Deep sedation/analgesia	Medication-induced depression of consciousness in which patients cannot be easily aroused but respond purposefully after repeated or painful stimuli. Patients may require assistance to maintain a patent airway, and ventilatory efforts may be inadequate. Cardiovascular function is usually maintained. According to the American Academy of Pediatrics, the American Society of Anesthesiologists, and The Joint Commission, deep sedation is inseparable from general anesthesia.
Anesthesia (general, spinal, or major regional anesthesia [not including local anesthesia])	General anesthesia is defined as a medication-induced loss of consciousness during which patients are not arousable, even by painful stimuli. Patients often require assistance in maintaining a patent airway, positive pressure ventilation may be required, and cardiovascular function may be impaired.

*Data are adapted from the American Academy of Pediatrics and American Academy of Pediatric Dentistry[14] and the Joint Commission on Accreditation of Healthcare Organizations.[15] Data are also adapted from the following source: American Academy of Pediatrics Committee on Drugs. (2002). *Guidelines for monitoring and management of pediatric patients during and after sedation for diagnostic and therapeutic procedures: addendum [Policy statement]*. Retrieved from http://aappolicy.aappublications.org/cgi/content/full/pediatrics;110/4/836

Table 7-3 ASA Physical Status Classification*

ASA Class	Examples	Suitability for Sedation
1: Healthy patient	No significant medical history	Excellent
2: Patient with mild systemic disease (no functional limitations)	Mild controlled asthma, seizure disorder with adequate seizure control, and controlled diabetes mellitus	Generally good
3: Patient with severe systemic disease (definite functional limitation)	Moderate to severe asthma, pneumonia, moderate obesity, and poorly controlled seizures or diabetes	Intermediate to poor: weigh risks versus benefits
4: Patient with severe systemic disease that is a constant threat to life	Severe bronchopulmonary dysplasia; and advanced pulmonary, cardiac, hepatic, renal, or endocrine disease	Poor: benefits rarely outweigh risks
5: Moribund patient who is not expected to survive without the procedure	Severe trauma, septic shock, and multisystem failure	Extremely poor

Note: ASA indicates American Society of Anesthesiologists.

*Data are adapted from American Society of Anesthesiologists.[17] Data are also adapted from Krauss, B., & Green, S. (2006). Procedural sedation and analgesia in children. *Lancet, 367*, 766–780.

- Preprocedural assessment and evaluation
  - The pediatric patient should have a health history and physical assessment, including ASA status documented before the procedure.
    - Typically, patients receiving ASA classes of 1 and 2 are suitable for procedural sedation in the emergency department.
  - Airway assessment, vital signs, and a procedural risk assessment should also be documented.
- Nothing by mouth status
  - Ideally, the pediatric patient should have had nothing by mouth for several hours before the procedure.
  - However, in the emergency department setting, the need to complete the procedure for a therapeutic outcome outweighs the risks of performing the procedure on a full stomach.
    - If the procedure is performed on a full stomach, this risk-benefit assessment should be documented and all members of the sedation team should be on high alert for the potential for aspiration and airway compromise during the procedure.
- Informed consent
  - A caregiver or legal guardian must consent to the sedation procedure. Risks, benefits, and alternative options must be presented to the family. Questions and concerns must be answered before obtaining informed consent.
- Monitoring
  - All pediatric patients receiving sedation should be continuously monitored by a healthcare provider capable of recognizing adverse sedation events.[16] Specifically, these providers should be skilled at recognizing airway problems, maintaining airway patency, and assisting ventilation if indicated.
  - All sedated patients must undergo continuous monitoring of their cardiorespiratory status throughout the procedure. The minimal acceptable form of monitoring is pulse oximetry.[14]
    - Patients who are sedated must be continuously assessed, and vital signs must be obtained and documented every five minutes.
- Equipment
  - Appropriate equipment (**Table 7-4**) must be available and in working order at the bedside.
  - A common acronym that may be useful in the assembly of equipment and planning for sedation is SOAP ME:[19]
    - **S**uction: size-appropriate flexible catheters, rigid tonsil-tip catheters, and a suction apparatus, checked and in working order
    - **O**xygen: appropriate masks and delivery devices and an adequate oxygen supply
    - **A**irway: size-appropriate airway equipment, including a bag-mask device, a laryngoscope, blades, and endotracheal tubes
    - **P**harmacy: all medications needed for the procedure, including antagonist medications, and readily accessible emergency medications in appropriate pediatric dosages and routes
    - **M**onitors: functioning monitors, appropriate for the age and size of the child, including pulse oximetry, cardiorespiratory, noninvasive blood pressure, and exhaled CO_2 monitors
    - **E**quipment: any special additional equipment needed for the procedure or patient condition
  - Reversal agents must be readily available in the event that hemodynamic compromise occurs.
- Discharge criteria
  - All patients must meet a minimum set of criteria for discharge (**Table 7-5**). These criteria should be objective and standardized within the institutional policy for ease of assessment and prevention of complications.

Table 7-4 Equipment for Sedation*

Minimum equipment at the bedside (checked and in working order):

Bag-mask device with appropriately sized face mask

Supplemental oxygen source, such as a nonrebreather mask

Suction with a tonsil tip

Pulse oximetry

Cardiorespiratory monitor

Capnography

Noninvasive blood pressure capability

Equipment that should be readily available:

Reversal agents for sedative medication being administered

Appropriately sized intubation equipment

Emergency equipment/resuscitation cart

*Data are adapted from: American Academy of Pediatrics and American Academy of Pediatric Dentistry[14] and the Joint Commission on Accreditation of Healthcare Organizations.[15] Data are also adapted from Doyle, L., & Colletti, J. (2006). Pediatric procedural sedation and analgesia. *Pediatric Clinics of North America, 53,* 279–292.

° The emergency nurse should ensure that the pediatric patient undergoing sedation receives discharge teaching about after-sedation care. Some of the items to cover with families include the need for a safe and protective environment for several hours after the procedure until residual medication effects have disappeared.

Role of the Nurse in Sedation

The nursing role during procedural sedation is vital. Nurses are responsible for patient safety throughout the procedure. Nurses are essential for their ability to assess the patient's need for sedation and how the patient will cope if sedation is not used. Nurses are the patient's advocate during the procedure, when decisions are made, and when caregivers have questions. Nurses are also vital during the actual procedure for their skill in monitoring the patient's hemodynamic parameters and their ability to intervene appropriately during times of crisis.[14] After the procedure, nurses are responsible for ensuring that caregivers are capable of following postsedation and home care instructions. **Table 7-6** addresses some of the nursing roles and responsibilities in pediatric sedation.

Nurses who provide sedation care and monitoring should be familiar with their hospital's policy on procedural sedation and the many standards and regulations that surround the use of procedural sedation. Nurses must also be knowledgeable about their state nurse practice act and understand how it affects their ability to monitor or administer certain sedation levels and medications.

Medications Used for Sedation in Pediatric Patients

In the emergency department, several classes of medications are used for procedural sedation. The most common medications are discussed in **Table 7-7**. These medications are in one of the following classes: analgesics, benzodiazepines, sedatives, and dissociative agents.[20]

Prevention and Management of Complications

The best way to prevent complications during procedural sedation is to anticipate their occurrence and to be vigilant in the assessment and monitoring of the patient during the procedure. Complications can occur anytime during the procedure but are most common immediately after medication administration. Nurses administering sedation medications should be familiar with the medications being used and any unusual or adverse effects that should be anticipated. Patients receiving intravenous medications are at a higher risk for complications. Intravenous medications should be administered slowly and titrated to effect in pediatric patients, with the goal of providing the least amount of medication to attain the desired level of sedation.

In general, the most common complications from procedural sedation include the following:[21]

- Vomiting
- Respiratory depression, apnea, and hypoventilation
- Loss of airway patency
- Laryngospasm
- Cardiovascular collapse, bradycardia, and hypotension
- Emergence reactions to ketamine (Ketalar) are increased with the following:
  ° Rapid intravenous administration
  ° Children older than 10 years
  ° Females
  ° Excessive environmental stimulation during recovery
- Allergic or anaphylactic reactions
- Hypothermia

Table 7-5 Sedation Discharge Criteria*

Must exhibit stable cardiovascular and respiratory status and vital signs that are returning to baseline levels.

Must be able to talk, sit up unaided, control his or her head and extremities, and follow commands; must be alert and orientated for age; and must have returned to presedation state.

Must be able to maintain hydration status.

Must be returned to presedation baseline regarding communication, mobility, and level of alertness.

Note: Specific discharge criteria for infants younger than four weeks and premature infants with a postconceptual age of younger than 50 weeks should also be established.

*Data are adapted from the American Academy of Pediatrics and American Academy of Pediatric Dentistry.[14] Data are also adapted from the following sources: (1) American Academy of Pediatrics Committee on Drugs. (2002). *Guidelines for monitoring and management of pediatric patients during and after sedation for diagnostic and therapeutic procedures: Addendum (Policy statement).* Retrieved from http://aappolicy.aappublications.org/cgi/content/full/pediatrics;110/4/836 and (2) Doyle, L., & Colletti, J. (2006). Pediatric procedural sedation and analgesia. *Pediatric Clinics of North America, 53,* 279–292.

Table 7-6 Nursing Roles and Responsibilities in Pediatric Sedation*

Phases of Sedation	Behavioral Interventions	Monitoring Interventions	Pharmacological Interventions
Before the procedure	Create a nonthreatening environment.	Set up monitoring equipment and set alarms.	Calculate medication doses according to weight.
	Speak in a quiet, calm, and confident manner.	Set up an appropriately sized face mask and a bag-mask device; ensure working order.	Verify orders.
	Encourage family participation.	Set up and check the working order of tonsil-tip suction.	Prepare medication doses and saline flushes.
	Explain the sedation procedure to the family and patient at the age-appropriate level.	Ensure the availability and location of emergency equipment/crash cart.	Label all syringes after medications or flush solutions have been drawn up.
	Answer questions and provide information as requested.	Plan the patient's body position to promote airway patency and effective ventilation.	Calculate doses of reversal agents and have them readily accessible.
	If possible, offer the opportunity for a caregiver to remain in the room during the procedure.	Document preparation on the medical record (sedation record, if available).	Establish and secure IV access.
	Ensure that the consent form is signed.	Observe time out procedures to confirm "right patient, right site, right procedure."	
During the procedure	Use distraction.	The primary responsibility is to continuously monitor the patient.	Assess the patency of the IV line.
	Allow the child to hold a familiar object.	Continuously monitor vital signs and O_2 saturation and document every five minutes (including HR and RR).[†]	Administer O_2
	Direct the family to a location where they can wait during the procedure if family presence is not an option.	Initiate interventions to prevent heat loss.	Administer medication, titrating to effect.
	Involve caregivers.	Communicate concerns to physician performing sedation regarding patient status and response.	
	Explain progress or procedure and the patient's responses.	Document assessments on the medical record (sedation record, if available).	
After the procedure	Maintain a quiet and calm environment.	Assess the patient for discharge.	Depending on the sedative used, administer IV fluids.
	Encourage caregivers to talk or sing soothingly to the child.	Monitor for development of deeper levels of sedation, especially after completion of the procedure and diminished stimulation.	Discontinue IV access once the patient is taking oral fluids well.
	Reassure caregivers if behavior is not normal for the child.	Document assessments on the medical record (sedation record, if available)	
	Provide caregivers with individualized discharge instructions, including diet, activity, sleep, when to call the physician, and when to return to the ED.	Document discharge criteria and discharge score.	

Note: ED indicates emergency department; HR, heart rate; IV, intravenous; O_2, oxygen; RR, respiratory rate.

*Data are adapted from: Ruddle.[19] Data are also adapted from Damian, F., & Smith, M. F. (1999). Nursing principles in the management of sedated patients. In B. Krauss & R. M. Brustowicz (Eds.), *Pediatric procedural sedation and analgesia* (pp. 108–114) Philadelphia, PA: Lippincott Williams & Wilkins.

[†]If a patient is deeply sedated, the patient must have continuous monitoring that includes: electrocardiogram, O_2 saturation level, HR and RR (with precordial stethoscope if available), capnogram if available, blood pressure every five minutes, visual assessment of skin color, and airway patency.

Table 7-7 Medications Used in the Procedural Sedation of Pediatric Patients*

Medication	Medication Class	Route of Administration	Onset/Duration, in Minutes	Administration Recommendations and Antagonist
Morphine sulfate	Opioid	IV, IM, SC, PR, or PO	Onset, depends on route, with IV being the most rapid/duration, 180–240	Naloxone (Narcan)
Fentanyl citrate (Sublimaze)	Opioid	IV, IM, intranasal or transmucosal	Onset, rapid, 1–3 (IV)/duration, 30–60	Rapid administration may result in respiratory depression and chest wall rigidity; naloxone (Narcan)
Diazepam (Valium)	Benzodiazepine	IV, IM, PR, or PO	Onset, depends on route, with IV being the most rapid/duration, 120–360	Flumazenil (Romazicon)
Midazolam (Versed)	Benzodiazepine	IV, PR, PO, SL, or intranasal	Onset, rapid, usually < 15 for IM and 2–3 for IV/duration, 45–120	Flumazenil (Romazicon)
Pentobarbital sodium (Nembutal)	Barbiturate	IV or PO	Onset, 3–5 (IV) or 15–30 (PO)/ duration, 20–60	None
Chloral hydrate		PO or PR	Onset, 15–30/duration, 60–120	Use in children younger than three years
Ketamine (Ketalar)	Dissociative	IV or IM	Onset, rapid, < 5/duration, 30–60	Emergence phenomena possible; excess secretions can be controlled with the administration of atropine or glycopyrrolate (Robinul) before the procedure
Etomidate	Hypnotic	IV	Onset, 2/duration, 5–15	Can cause adrenal insufficiency in a patient with impaired function or with repeat doses.
Propofol (Diprivan)	General anesthetic	IV	Onset, < 1/duration, 5–15	Contraindicated in patients with egg or soy allergies
Nitrous oxide	Inhaled anesthetic	Inhalation	Onset, < 5/duration, < 5 after discontinuation of flow	100% oxygen inhaled for several minutes will counteract effects

Note: IM indicates intramuscular; IV indicates intravenous; PO, oral; PR, per rectum; SC, subcutaneous; SL, sublingual.

*Data are adapted from the following sources: (1) Doyle, L., & Colletti, J. (2006). Pediatric procedural sedation and analgesia. *Pediatric Clinics of North America, 53,* 279–292. (2) Krauss, B., & Green, S. (2006). Procedural sedation and analgesia in children. *Lancet, 367,* 766–780.

Clinical Tips

- Sedation is a continuum. Patients may rapidly move from one level to another.
  - There is no ideal medication dose or combination. Each patient will react differently to the medications administered. Thus, the ability to monitor, assess, and intervene in a rapid fashion is the best way to provide safe sedation.
  - When noxious stimulation decreases (i.e., the procedure is complete), an increased level of sedation may occur.
- Intravenous administration is the preferred route of delivery in the pediatric patient.
  - Infants metabolize medications differently than older children because of decreased liver metabolism and renal excretion. Delayed onset of the medication and delayed adverse reactions may occur.
  - Infants should be monitored for extended periods to ensure that they return to a presedation baseline.
  - Avoid pushing the entire dose at one time. Titrate and monitor the patient's response.
    - Slower administration may actually allow the sedation to occur at a lower dose of medication and may decrease recovery time and minimize the potential for complications.
- If administration of antagonist medications is required, the patient should be monitored for at least two hours afterward to detect possible resedation.
  - Use caution with the administration of antagonists in patients who may be chemically dependent on opioids or in those taking benzodiazepines for seizures.

Summary

Every day, thousands of pediatric patients undergo therapeutic and diagnostic procedures in emergency departments. Appropriate psychological preparation and positioning for comfort, with family involvement, significantly reduces the stress and anxiety experienced during procedures. Although nonpharmacological interventions, such as distraction and guided imagery, work for some children, others will require the administration of procedural sedation. Procedural sedation in the emergency department has significantly affected the way care is provided to thousands of pediatric patients each year. These pediatric patients are able to undergo painful or difficult procedures with little pain and sometimes experience amnesia for the entire event, thus making their healthcare experience more positive.

References

1. Conway, A. E. (2009). Developmental and psychosocial considerations. In D. O. Bernardo (Ed.), *Core curriculum for pediatric emergency nursing* (2nd ed., pp. 29–44). Des Plaines, IL: Emergency Nurses Association.

2. Emergency Nurses Association. (2005). *Position statements*. (2010, September). *Family presence during invasive procedures and resuscitation in the emergency department* [position statement]. Retrieved from http://www.ena.org/SiteCollectionDocuments/Position%20Statements/FamilyPresence.pdf

3. Leahy, S., Kennedy, R. M., Hesselgrave, J., Gurwitch, K., Barkey, M., & Millar, T. F. (2008). On the front lines: lessons learned in implementing multidisciplinary peripheral venous access pain-management programs in pediatric hospitals. *Pediatrics, 122,* S161–S167.

4. Algren, C., & Arnow, D. (2005). Pediatric variations of nursing interventions. In M. J. Hockenberry (Ed.), *Wong's essentials of pediatric nursing* (pp. 706–786). St. Louis, MO: Elsevier Mosby.

5. Stephen, B., & Barkey, M. (1994). *Positioning for comfort.* Mt. Royal, NJ: Association for the Care of Children's Health.

6. Hough, A., & Gekas, J. (2008). Caring for the child requiring lumbar puncture. In J. Kelsey & G. McEwing (Eds.), *Clinical skills in child health practice* (1st ed., pp. 350–357). Edinburgh, Scotland: Sauders Elsevier.

7. Gough, L. (2006). Lumbar puncture. In E. Trigg & T. Mohammed (Eds.), *Practices in children's nursing: Guidelines for hospital and community.* Edinburgh, Scotland: Churchill Livingstone.

8. Cronan, K. M., & Wiley, J. F. (2008). Lumbar puncture. In C. King & F. M. Henretig (Eds.), *Textbook of pediatric emergency procedures* (2nd ed., pp. 505–514). Philadelphia, PA: Lippincott Williams & Wilkins.

9. Kelsey, J., & McEwing, G. (2008). Nasogastric tube insertion and feeding. In J. Kelsey & G. McEwing (Eds.), *Clinical skills in child health practice* (pp. 139–153). Edinburgh, Scotland: Churchill Livingstone.

10. National Patient Saftey Agency. (2005). *How to confirm the correct position of nasogastric feeding tubes in infants, children, and adults.* Retrieved from http://www.npsa.nhs.uk/advice

11. Tkacz Browne, N., Flanigan, L. M., McComiskey, C. A., & Pieper, P. (2007). *Nursing care of the pediatric surgical patient* (2nd ed.). Boston, MA: Jones & Bartlett.

12. Samuels, L. E., Roberts, J. R., & Hedges, R. J. (2004). Nasogastric and feeding tube placement. In *Clinical procedures in emergency medicine* (4th ed., p. 41). Philadelphia, PA: WB Saunders.

13. Burke D. T., El Shami A., Heinle E., & Pina, B. D. (2006). Comparison of gastrostomy tube replacement verification using air insufflation versus gastrograffin. *Archives of Physical Medicine & Rehabilitation, 87*(11), 1530–1533.

14. American Academy of Pediatrics and American Academy of Pediatric Dentistry. (2006).Guidelines for monitoring and management of pediatric patients during and after sedation for diagnostic and therapeutic procedures: An update. *Pediatrics, 118,* 2587–2602.

15. Joint Commission on Accreditation of Healthcare Organizations. (2009). *2010 Hospital accreditation standards.* Oakbrook Terrace, IL: Author.

16. Nelson, D. (1999). Procedural sedation in the emergency department. In B. Krauss & R. Brustowicz (Eds.), *Pediatric procedural sedation and analgesia* (pp. 161–168). Philadelphia, PA: Lippincott Williams & Wilkins.

17. American Society of Anesthesiologists. (2002). Practice guidelines for sedation and analgesia by non-anesthesiologists: An updated report by the American Society of Anesthesiologists Task Force on Sedation and Analgesia by Non-Anesthesiologists. *Anesthesiology, 86,* 1004–1017.

18. American College of Emergency Physicians. (1998). Clinical policy for procedural sedation and analgesia in the emergency department. *Annals of Emergency Medicine , 31,* 663–677.

19. Ruddle, T. (2003). Sedation: An overview. *Paediatric Nursing, 15,* 38–41.

20. American College of Emergency Physicians. (2004). Clinical policy: Evidence-based approach to pharmacologic agents used in pediatric sedation and analgesia in the emergency department. *Annals of Emergency Medicine, 44,* 342–377.

21. Vance, C. (1999). Management of complications. In B. Krauss & R. Brustowicz (Eds.), *Pediatric procedural sedation and analgesia* (pp. 151–159). Philadelphia, PA: Lippencott Williams & Wilkins.

Chapter 8 | Medication Administration

Ruth C. Bindler, PhD, RNC

Objectives

On completion of this chapter, the learner should be able to do the following:

- Incorporate anatomical, physiological, and developmental characteristics into safe medication administration practice.
- Determine focused assessment parameters required before and after medication administration.
- Describe correct techniques for administering medications via various routes to pediatric patients.
- Compare common routes of medication administration for pediatric patients.
- Plan medication administration discharge teaching and instructions for pediatric patients and families.
- Perform sample medication calculations.

Introduction

Medication administration is an integral component of the emergency nurse's role. Many pediatric patients are already taking medications, ranging from prescription to over-the-counter to herbal or other alternative treatments. Therefore, the medication history should assess the full range of possible agents. Medication administration is complex in pediatric patients: organs are immature and dosages are different from those of adults; and the cognitive, emotional, and developmental needs of children demand individualized and supportive approaches in both administration routes and techniques. In addition, pediatric patients present unique risk factors that can contribute to medication errors, and reducing or managing these risk factors is important.[1] The Joint Commission determined that a pediatric formulary of medications should be available in all health systems treating children, to specify selection, use, and evaluation of pediatric medications.[2] Resources, such as standardized reference books and computerized formulas and calculations, should be readily available in the patient care area. Healthcare providers should work with the pharmacy to develop institutional best practices, including standardizing medication concentrations. Some of the key components of pharmacokinetics, administration principles, and developmental approaches are discussed in this chapter.

Anatomy and Physiology

Pharmacokinetics, the absorption, distribution, and excretion of medication, presents a need for unique knowledge by the nurse.[3, 4]

- Height, weight, body mass index, and body surface area vary. Pediatric formulas commonly use weight or body surface area to determine medication dosages. This means that medications are ordered in milligrams per kilograms (weight) or milligrams per meter squared (body surface area). These methods are more accurate than extrapolating doses from those used for adults; doses intended for adults should not simply be decreased to determine child doses.
- Muscle mass contributes less to the total body weight in young children than it does in older children or adults, leading to fewer muscular injection sites.
- A young child's body weight contains a higher proportion of fat, so lipid-soluble medications may be stored in the young child's fatty tissue. Blood levels of lipid-soluble medications increase only after the available sites in fatty tissue are saturated with the medication. This also contributes to lipid-soluble medications staying in the system for a longer period of time.

- Much of the body weight of premature babies, infants, and young children is composed of water. Because of the relatively high daily turnover of water, especially in the extracellular tissue, water-soluble medications may be more quickly excreted.

- The liver and kidney function of young children (< two years) is immature as the result of decreased enzyme production and lower glomerular filtration. Therefore, the excretion of some medications that are metabolized in the liver and kidneys may be delayed.

- Young children have more skin surface and a thin dermis and epidermis, leading to faster and more complete absorption of both toxins and medications through the skin.

- Infant and child variations in the gastrointestinal system (i.e., longer gastric emptying time), the cardiovascular system (i.e., faster pulse and lower blood pressure), and the respiratory system (i.e., more rapid respirations) may also influence the absorption and distribution of medications.

Developmental Review

The age and developmental stage of the pediatric patient are essential to consider whenever administering medications. Not only will age influence medication absorption, distribution, and excretion, but the child's age will often determine the best route for administration and appropriate developmental approaches.[5]

- Sedation for painful procedures, and adequate holding to limit movement, are essential.

- Infants should be approached in a calm and comforting manner. Caregivers often can assist with administering an oral medication safely and with little stress for the child.

- Toddlers often cooperate with medication administration when caregivers are present. Explanations before performing painful administration are essential.

- Preschoolers understand simple explanations and can be engaged in the process of taking medications when there is adequate time. Constant clarification of procedures and how the preschooler feels will help decrease the fears of the preschooler in the emergency situation. Providing books, pictures, and toy boxes with play medical equipment is a technique that can decrease fear and stress.

- Providing privacy and explanations to school-aged children allows them to better understand why medications are given and why the route of administration has been chosen. Comfort measures, such as family presence or a stuffed animal, are still valued at this age.

- Adolescents may have limited experience with healthcare, even though they understand procedures explained to them. Their level of fear can be high, interfering with their understanding. The presence of a parent or other supportive person is essential in stressful emergency situations.

Focused Assessment

An accurate and thorough assessment is vital to successful medication treatment. Medication administration to children in emergency situations is challenging because of the limitations in patient data that may be collected. Baseline assessment data are crucial in recognizing the effects of medications and determining the best medications, dosages, and approaches for the pediatric patient. Important information to be gathered quickly and efficiently includes the following.

- Medical history: acute and chronic diseases and conditions, recent exposure to disease, home medications or other treatments, allergies, and injuries

- Body measurement: accurate height and weight in kilograms (needed for accurate dosing)

- General observations: skin color and temperature, symmetry of movement, level of consciousness and engagement, and interactions with caregivers and the environment

- Cardiovascular: pulse, blood pressure, oxygen saturation, and general perfusion

- Respiratory: respiratory rate, rhythm, and depth; and work of breathing

- Metabolic, hepatic, and renal: laboratory studies

- Gastrointestinal: presence of nausea, vomiting, diarrhea, abdominal distention, and dehydration

- Urinary: amount and characteristics of urinary output

Planning and Implementation of Medication Administration

The major principle related to medication administration is providing the right patient with the right medication in the right dose, in the right concentration, by the right route at the right time.

- Before medications are administered, the pediatric patient's identification should be verified by at least two methods. Commonly, an electronic scan of the name band and the medical record with the ordered medication is performed. An alternate method is for the caregivers or other care providers (when available), and the pediatric patient (if possible), to state the name, date of birth, and any allergies of the child.

- Check for potential medication interactions with reported prescription, over-the-counter, or herbal remedies that the pediatric patient may have been given.

- Confirm that assessments relative to prescribed medications have been completed.

- **Table 8-1** provides an overview of common routes of administration and tips to facilitate administration.

Administering an Injection

Apply the knowledge gained from your assessment in planning medication administration by injection to the pediatric patient. Plan for adequate and appropriate positioning, and prepare the caregiver and patient (if old enough to understand) for the procedure. When convenient, the caregiver may hold the child on his or her lap for injections into the leg or arm. Generally, if the child is unable to be placed in the caregiver's lap, the patient must be placed supine on a stretcher or bed. In this situation, the caregiver may be at the patient's head to provide comfort. Be certain that the caregiver understands any restraint that must be used and have additional adequate assistance available to hold the patient's extremity firmly so that the injection can be administered safely and quickly, with minimum stress to the patient.

Procedures common to all types of medication administration include the following:

- Perform hand hygiene. Prepare the injection out of the patient's sight. Verify the order, route, and amount. Many facilities endorse the practice of independent verification of all injectable medications for pediatric patients by two registered nurses.

- After the medication is drawn into the syringe, consider changing the needle before administration to ensure a sharp needle with no residual medication that can track through the dermal tissues on skin entry.

- Provide developmentally appropriate explanations as needed for the patient and family.

- Position and secure the patient.

- Clean the site, administer the injection, and dispose of the equipment in approved containers.

- After the injection, comfort the child. Provide verbal praise or a small reward, such as a sticker or ice pop.

- Document the medication, site, route, and other observations.

Intramuscular Injections

- When selecting the injection site, consider the pediatric patient's age, weight, and muscle mass; and the medication volume and viscosity. **Table 8-2** lists the recommended intramuscular injection sites, solution volume, and recommended needle lengths. Consider the use of dermal anesthetic to the site before injection.

Subcutaneous Medication Administration

- Sites used for the administration of subcutaneous medication include the upper lateral arm, the anterior thigh, and the anterior abdominal wall.

- The volume of medication administered should be limited to 0.5 to 1 mL, depending on the age of the child and the site of the injection.

- The needle should be inserted at a 45° to 60° angle in the thin child with little subcutaneous tissue or at a 90° angle for the child with generous amounts of subcutaneous fat.

- Needle size: for an infant or thin child, use a 25- to 30-gauge needle (length, 3/8 or 4/8 of an inch); and for a larger child, use a 25-gauge needle (length, 5/8 of an inch).

Intravenous Medication Administration

- Use needleless systems whenever available.

- Medications may be given by intravenous bolus, constant infusion, or intermittent infusion. Administration times and preparation vary.

- Prepare the medication and plan for administration following the guidelines for dilution and infusion of the specific medication.

- A syringe or infusion pump should be used to deliver continuous or intermittent medication infusions. These devices help to ensure accurate and timely delivery of medications. After medication administration, flush the intravenous tubing with normal saline to clear any residual medication from the line. Syringe pumps with low-volume tubing are available to minimize the amount of flush solution needed. This is important in premature infants or children with cardiac or renal conditions and fluid restriction.

- Medications such as antibiotics may be administered using a volume chamber. After the infusion, a 20 mL flush should be infused to flush the remainder of the medication from the chamber. Label the chamber device when administering medications so that other healthcare providers are aware that medication is infusing.

Table 8-1 Pediatric Medication Administration Considerations*

Route	Considerations
Nasal	Have the caregiver hold the child across his or her lap in a supine position with the child's head down. Place the child's arm that is the closest to the caregiver around the caregiver's back. Firmly hug the child's other arm and hand with the caregiver's arm; snuggle the head between the caregiver's body and arm.
Eye	Explain the procedure; tell the child the medication will feel cool. Prepare the child if the medication will sting.
	Have the child lie on his or her back with hands tucked under the buttocks.
	Alternatively, have the smaller child sit on the caregiver's lap and have the caregiver hug the child while securing the arms.
	Have the child look up, retract the lower eyelid, and instill medication.
	Provide distractions.
Oral	Consider the child's age when determining the medication preparation (liquid, chewable, sprinkle, or junior-sized pills).
	Ask the caregiver how the child usually takes oral medicine.
	Use an oral syringe or calibrated cup for liquids to ensure correct dosage.
	To prevent aspiration, administer oral medication while the child's head is raised or the child is in a sitting position.
	For infants, liquid medication may be administered through a nipple, followed by 5 mL of water.
	When administering medication with an oral syringe, place the syringe between the gum and cheek. Administer slowly, no more than 0.5 mL at a time.
	Do not administer chewable tablets to children without teeth; give children something to drink after the chewable tablet.
	Do not crush enteric-coated tablets or caplets.
	Do not open capsules if medication is sustained release; check with a pharmacist before opening any capsule for administration.
	Avoid mixing medication with formula because the infant may refuse formula thereafter.
	When mixing medication with food or liquids, use as little diluent as possible. Masking the taste with food or fluid is often helpful; however, if the quantity is large, the child may not finish the entire amount and the full dose will not be ingested.
Rectal	Consult a pharmacist before cutting a suppository because the medication is not necessarily distributed evenly through the suppository (e.g., some suppositories must be divided lengthwise but not widthwise).
	Place the child in the knee-chest position on his or her side.
	Lubricate the suppository with water-soluble lubricant before insertion.
	Hold the buttock cheeks together until the urge to expel has passed. Consider eliciting the assistance of the caregiver.
	Commercially available adult enemas and/or tap-water enemas should be avoided. Isotonic solutions should be used when enemas are needed.
Inhaled	Commercially available spacer devices are available with or without masks for metered-dose inhalers.
	Nebulized medication may need to be given with a face mask adapter.
	Use distractions and stickers as rewards to facilitate cooperation.
Dermal	Pastes absorb moisture. Medications in pastes are released slower than medications that are in creams or ointment bases.
	Bath treatments are helpful in widespread dermatitis, but NEVER leave a child alone in a tub. Avoid rubbing the skin dry; pat instead.
	Soaks can be helpful for the child who cannot cooperate with wet dressing techniques.
	Cover the ointment or medication as indicated.

*Data taken from Bindler, R.C., Ball, J.W., London, M.L., & Ladewig, P.W. (2010). *Clinical skills manual for maternal & child nursing care* (3rd ed.). Upper Saddle River, NJ: Pearson Education.

- Caution should be used when administering infusions so that the total volume of medication and flushes does not exceed the recommended volumes for the pediatric patient's weight. The amount of medications and flushes should be added to the intake calculation.

- Bolus doses should be administered by carefully titrating the infusion to meet the requirements for infusion time and dilution. Constant assessment may be warranted, such as during administration of narcotics for pain management.

Table 8-2 Pediatric Intramuscular Injection Sites*

Site	Recommended Age
Vastus lateralis	Infant
	Can be used at any age and is the preferred site in children younger than 3 years
	Considerations
	Large muscle mass, free of important nerves and blood vessels
	Acceptable injection volumes: Infants, 0.5–1 mL; Older children, up to 2 mL
	Use a 22- to 25-gauge needle (length, 5/8 to 1 inch)
Site	**Recommended Age**
Ventrogluteal	Child
	Consider for children older than 3 years
	Considerations
	Large muscle mass, free of important nerves and blood vessels
	Easily accessible site
	Injection volume for a child: up to 2 mL
	Use a 20- to 25-gauge needle (length, 1 to 1.5 inches)
Site	**Recommended Age**
Deltoid	Child
	Considerations
	Small muscle mass, easily accessible, with a rapid absorption rate
	Danger of radial nerve injury in young children
	Injection volumes for a child: 0.5–1 mL
	Use a 22- to 25-gauge needle (length, 1/2 to 1 inch)

*Data taken from Bindler and Howry.[3]

In addition to medications, intravenous fluids may need to be administered. To administer an intravenous fluid bolus rapidly, the most accurate and efficient method is to use a stopcock with a 20 mL syringe and push the number of times equal to the weight in kilograms. For adolescents, a pressure bag may be used, but they are not accurate enough for children. Infusion pumps are accurate, but slower as most have an upper limit of 999 mL/hour. For rapid administration a large-bore catheter should be used. For nonemergent infusions, use the smallest bore needed for the infusion.

Nasal Administration

- Nasal medication administration may be used to treat respiratory conditions or induce anesthesia. In the latter case, ongoing cardiopulmonary monitoring is essential.

- Nasal medications are best administered with the head slightly hyperextended. This can be achieved by having the infant or toddler sit on the caregiver's lap, with his or her head hyperextended. The older child may be positioned with pillows under the shoulders to create hyperextension of the head.

- Drops should be slowly administered to avoid choking. Ensure that the child remains in position for several minutes to enhance absorption.

- Document the medication, site, route, and other observations.

Inhalation Administration

Nebulized pharmacological agents and metered-dose inhalers (MDIs) are inhalation medications that may be given to pediatric patients.

- The caregiver may hold the patient during delivery, if desired.

- Monitor vital signs, including respiratory status and oxygen saturation, before, during, and after administration.

- A face mask, instead of a mouthpiece, may be used for infants and children.

- Commercial pediatric nebulizer sets are available using a variety of pediatric-friendly characters.

- Consider making administration a game. For example, have the patient take a deep breath in, before pretending to blow out candles, or use distraction techniques, such as watching the vapor go in and out.

- For effective medication delivery, a spacer should be used with MDIs if the patient cannot hold his or her breath or close his or her mouth over the mouthpiece. Allow several breaths between delivery puffs.

Dermal Administration

Topical therapies include gel, paste, cream, lotion, and liquid.

- Gloves must be used to protect both the pediatric patient and the healthcare provider.

- Make sure the area of application is clean before administration. Cleanse if needed.

- Apply a thin layer of medication to the skin, spreading in the direction of hair growth. Room temperature medications are the most comfortable.

- Prevent the pediatric patient from scratching by trimming the patient's nails or covering the patient's hands with socks or mittens.

- When an anesthetic cream with an occlusive dressing is applied to the hand to facilitate pain control during an intravenous start, use the patient's nondominant hand. This way it is less likely that the patient will put the hand with medication on it into his or her mouth. A caregiver can hold and help distract the child for the 30 to 60 minutes that the medication and dressing are in place.

- When dermal patches are used to deliver medication, they should be applied in a body area out of reach of the young child (i.e., the back or buttocks), as long as this is consistent with the patch directions.

Evaluation

An evaluation includes immediate and ongoing observations of the child. Vital signs, oxygen saturation, level of consciousness, and pain control are relevant. Consider the expected action time for the medication, and return to complete and document assessment of pertinent areas. The patient's understanding of, and comfort with, the medication experience is also important to observe and record. Document administration of medication immediately after it is given, and complete ongoing documentation of the patient's condition.

Discharge Education

Caregivers and pediatric patients (when age appropriate) should be provided with information about any medications that are sent home with them. This includes the medication name, route of administration, action, dosage, and potential adverse effects. In addition, if there will be ongoing effects of the medications that were administered in the emergency department, this should be explained as well.

Adequate discharge instructions promote safe and accurate administration of medication at home. The following information should be included in the instructions:

- Time of day the medication should be given

- Duration of medication therapy

- Medication administration techniques needed for various routes, including methods of measuring and administering liquid medications and application of dermal medications.

- Arrange for a return demonstration by the caregiver when possible, and provide diagrams and other written material.

- Demonstrate methods for proper administration of MDIs and be sure the patient and family have adequate time to practice.

- Address cleaning and maintenance issues related to nebulizers and spacers and cleaning of the skin before dermal applications.

- Educate caregivers about potential adverse effects of the medications. These may include skin changes as a result of topical medications, respiratory symptoms, or changes in behavior or level of consciousness. Emphasize the serious adverse effects that should be reported immediately.

- Teach the family when to seek additional medical care, such as when symptoms do not resolve or worsen or if an error in dose or medication has occurred. Provide telephone numbers and other resources.

- Instruct the family to check with the healthcare provider before taking any other medications. These include over-the-counter or herbal products that may interact with the newly prescribed medication.

- Instruct the family about the next recommended healthcare visit and the importance of bringing medications and information to the visit.

Sample Medication Calculation Problems

1. A single dose of morphine sulfate (Morphine) of 0.1 mg/kg is ordered to be given intramuscularly to a 10-year-old child. The child's weight was 30 kilograms.

   a. What is the dosage appropriate for the child?

   b. Morphine sulfate is available in 2 mg/mL solution. How many milliliters should be administered?

   c. Considering the answer to b (above), and the child's age, what site(s) are acceptable for the intramuscular injection?

2. Furosemide (Lasix), 1 mg/kg, is ordered for a child who weighs 25 kg.

   a. What dose should the child receive?

3. Phenobarbital, 300 mg, is prescribed for a child and is to be administered intravenously over 30 minutes.

   a. The medication comes in 60 mg/mL vials. What is the volume to draw up?

   b. Phenobarbital should be administered in 50 mL of intravenous fluid over 30 minutes. What rate should the infusion pump be set at to administer the proper dose in the desired time?

Sample Medication Calculation Answers

1. a. 3 mg
   b. 1.5 mL
   c. vastus lateralis and ventrogluteal

2. a. 25 mg

3. a. 5 mL
   b. 100 mL/hour

Summary

Safe medication administration for any patient can be daunting. When considering administering medications to pediatric patients, it is important for nurses to understand the developmental considerations of pediatric patients and how they relate to safe medication administration. It is also important to remember that the pediatric patient's caregivers need to be included and supported through the administration process. Since medication administration is such an integral part of emergency nursing, it is important for emergency nurses to advocate and promote medication administration practices that reduce and eliminate the potential for medication errors.

References

1. Skapik, J. L., Pronovost, P. J., Miller, M. R., Thompson, D. A., & Wu, A. W. (2009). Pediatric safety incidents from an intensive care reporting system. *Journal of Patient Safety, 5,* 95–101.

2. Joint Commission Sentinel Event Alert. (2008). *Preventing pediatric medication errors.* Retrieved from http://www.jointcommission.org

3. Bindler, R., & Howry, L. (2005). *Pediatric drug guide.* Upper Saddle River, NJ: Pearson Education.

4. Gal, P., & Reed, M. D. (2007). Principles of drug therapy. In R. M. Kliegman, R. E. Behrman, H. B. Jenson, & B. F. Stanton (Eds.). *Nelson textbook of pediatrics* (18th ed.) (pp. 331–339). Philadelphia, PA: Saunders Elsevier.

5. Novak, E., & Allen, P. J. (2007). Prescribing medications in pediatrics: Concerns regarding FDA approval and pharmacokinetics. *Pediatric Nursing, 33,* 64–70.

Chapter 9 | Vascular Access

Angela M. Bowen, BSN, RN, CPEN, NREMT-P
Nancy G. Stevens, MS, MSN, RN, APRN-BC, CEN, FAEN

Objectives

On completion of this chapter, the learner should be able to do the following:

- Identify anatomical and physiological considerations when identifying vascular access sites and routes.
- Compare preparation techniques for selected vascular access sites.
- Describe techniques to evaluate patency of vascular access routes or sites.

Introduction

Vascular access is commonly required in an emergency care setting for fluid and/or intravenous medication administration. Access routes include peripheral intravenous, intraosseous (IO), central venous, and subcutaneous.

Based on the pediatric patient's presenting complaint, the initial assessment of the pediatric patient should include the evaluation of dehydration status and the determination of the need for vascular access. In general, dehydration may be classified as mild (5% fluid deficit), moderate (10% fluid deficit), and severe ($\geq$ 15% fluid deficit). In a study by Gorelick et al,[1] it was determined that dehydration could be assessed by using four basic clinical indicators: general appearance, capillary refill greater than two seconds, dry mucous membranes, and absence of tears. Of these findings, the presence of any two indicates a fluid deficit of 5% or greater. The presence of three or more findings indicates a deficit of 10% or greater.

Preparation

Preparation of the pediatric patient and the caregiver before any vascular access procedure is imperative. The initiation of any type of vascular access can be painful or uncomfortable, and information about what to expect should be presented to the pediatric patient in age-appropriate language. Caregivers can provide information about their child's medical history that may be essential

to successfully establishing vascular access. Caregivers will feel more confident about the care provided if they are included in that care and are presented with a thorough explanation of any procedures that must take place. Be a careful listener, and allow time for questions.

Standard precautions, including hand washing and wearing personal protective equipment, should be used during all vascular access procedures. Depending on the type of access and institutional protocol, a time out (or interdisciplinary discussion) focused on ensuring that key procedural details have been addressed may need to be taken immediately before the procedure.

A Child Life Specialist can be instrumental in preparing the patient for intravenous access. See **Chapter 7, "Common Procedures and Sedation,"** for more information.

Children with Special Healthcare Needs

Children with special healthcare needs present a unique challenge when establishing vascular access. Some of these children have central venous lines in place, and these will be reviewed in a subsequent section. For those children with special healthcare needs who do not already have vascular access, seek input from the patient and/or the caregiver before proceeding. They can provide invaluable information regarding an appropriate site and catheter size. Depending on the child's underlying diagnosis, vessels may be fragile or scarred from repeated use for vascular access. At times, smaller catheters may need to be used on fragile vessels, and care should be taken when advancing the catheter. Occasionally, nontraditional access sites may be selected.

Peripheral Vascular Access

Gaining peripheral intravenous access on a pediatric patient can be difficult. Peripheral intravenous sites commonly used in infants and children include the hands, feet, and antecubital fossa. Superficial scalp veins may also be used in infants. Ideally, the sites to avoid for vascular access include injured extremities and any area that is edematous or burned.

When caring for a seriously ill or injured pediatric patient, the healthcare provider should use the largest catheter possible to facilitate rapid fluid administration and/or resuscitation medications. Over-the-needle catheters are preferred because of their stability. Butterfly and metal needles are rarely used in pediatric patients, except during phlebotomy procedures. In nonemergent situations, distal sites should be attempted first. In emergent situations, the antecubital and greater saphenous veins are often preferred sites because they are larger veins and can be accessed readily without disruption of resuscitative efforts. In a resuscitation situation, the healthcare provider should consider IO access early if there is difficulty with cannulation of a peripheral vein.

The age and developmental level of the patient will help determine preparatory techniques. If a treatment room is unavailable, prepare equipment before the procedure, out of sight of the pediatric patient. Remember to give explanations in a manner that the pediatric patient will understand. Use of verbiage that has a positive connotation, including an explanation of the steps in the procedure and the reason for the procedure, does appear to lessen not only the patient's anxiety but the caregiver's anxiety as well. The use of phrases such as "This will feel like a bee sting" and "Hold real still and it will not hurt as bad" does not lessen the pain and may actually increase the anticipation, resulting in greater pain and anxiety.[2]

Pediatric patients are almost always less anxious if their caregiver is in the room with them. The younger the child is, the more likely the healthcare provider will need to use restraint techniques during insertion. Allow the caregivers to stay in the room but do not ask them to hold the patient (doing so may create distrust between the patient and caregiver and can be stressful for both). Engage the caregiver in providing comfort measures, such as touch, talking, or singing to the child. In addition, distraction and other nonpharmacological techniques can alleviate pain and anxiety.[3] These techniques include the use of imagery and distraction tools or toys. During insertion, allow the child to have calming items close by, such as a special blanket or a stuffed animal. Based on institutional protocol, topical analgesia can be used to decrease the pain associated with intravenous access. There are several analgesic products readily available, ranging from creams to topical sprays. **Chapter 6, "Pain,"** contains more information.

Positioning the pediatric patient appropriately and securing the selected extremity and insertion site are important to maintaining catheter placement during and after the procedure. The decision to use a tourniquet should be based on the healthcare provider's judgment and institutional protocol; tourniquets may increase the pressure in a small vein to the point of being detrimental. When inserting a small-gauge catheter, pause once the skin has been pierced to allow for possible movement of the extremity (the pediatric patient may jerk when the needle penetrates the skin). Advance the needle and catheter slowly into the vein because blood return may be delayed for a few seconds because of the small diameter of the needle. Visualizing a flashback of blood may be facilitated by inserting the catheter bevel side down in children with a compromised vasculature. To prevent shearing of the catheter, never reintroduce the needle into the catheter once it has been withdrawn. Do not repeatedly invade the tissue with the needle; nerve, tendon, ligament, and joint damage may occur.

Once the catheter is in place, blood samples may be obtained before initiating fluid therapy. (Always follow institutional protocol regarding blood sampling from an intravenous catheter.) Insert a vacuum adapter directly into the catheter hub or use a T-connector (short extension connector) and syringe. If a smaller-gauge intravenous needle is used, the suction from a vacuum adaptor may collapse the vessel. Manipulation at the site may also dislodge the newly placed catheter. If a T-connector and syringe are to be used, withdraw the blood sample before flushing the T-connector with normal saline. If blood samples are not to be drawn, attach a T-connector flushed with normal saline to the hub of the catheter as soon as the stylet is removed. The T-connector provides an access port at the closest point to the site and allows easier manipulation of the site should it need to be retaped or redressed at a later time.

Secure the catheter with a transparent dressing or tape and gauze. Secure the catheter while maintaining visualization of the site. When taping, use caution not to bend the hub of the catheter. Small catheters have memory, and bends or kinks can permanently damage the catheter and render it useless. Use tape to secure the extremity to an appropriately sized arm board. Position the pediatric patient's fingers to grasp the arm board in an anatomically correct position rather than leaving the fingers outstretched. Use gauze rolls as necessary to support the pediatric patient's extremity in a functional position.

Loop the intravenous tubing away from the catheter and secure with tape, taking any tension off the tubing; consequently, if the intravenous tubing is caught or pulled on, it should not displace the catheter. Label the site and tubing per institutional protocol. To further protect the catheter and intravenous site, use a nonrestrictive covering that allows for visualization of the site. Commercially prepared devices are available. If the patient is unable to visualize or access the catheter, he or she will be less likely to dislodge it. Routinely evaluate the site per institutional protocol. Observe for signs of infiltration, determine whether the dressing is intact, and check any connections for leakage.

Tell the pediatric patient and the caregiver when the procedure is complete. This will keep the patient and the caregiver from anticipating any further painful vascular interventions. Offer rewards, such as stickers, and praise positive behavior.

Upper-Extremity Vein Cannulation

Upper-extremity veins include the cephalic, median, and basilic veins; and the venous network found on the dorsum of the hand. Opt for the nondominant hand if possible. When attempting to locate veins on the dorsum of the hand, it may be helpful to close the patient's hand tightly and flex the wrist to better visualize the vein. In non-Caucasian infants, a povidone solution may make

it easier to visualize veins. In thin infants, ultrasound, a transilluminator or light source under the hand may help in locating veins (**Figure 9-1**).

Lower-Extremity Vein Cannulation

Lower-extremity veins include the saphenous vein and veins in the dorsal venous plexus. The saphenous vein is located anterior to the medial malleolus and runs toward the popliteal fossa. It is a large vein and is often accessible when vasoconstriction has made the smaller veins harder to find. If the child is ambulatory, lower-extremity vascular insertions should be avoided (**Figure 9-2**).

Scalp Vein Cannulation

Superficial scalp veins that may be used for intravenous access in the infant include the following:

- Frontal
- Superficial temporal
- Posterior auricular
- Supraorbital
- Occipital
- Posterior facial veins

When starting a scalp intravenous line, remember that the catheter should be inserted in the direction of the blood flow (caudally if the vein is more vertical and dorsally if the vein is more horizontal). A tabbed rubber band can be used as a tourniquet, if necessary. If used, be watchful that it does not slip into the infant's eyes (**Figure 9-3**).

Figure 9-1 Veins of the Hand and Forearm*

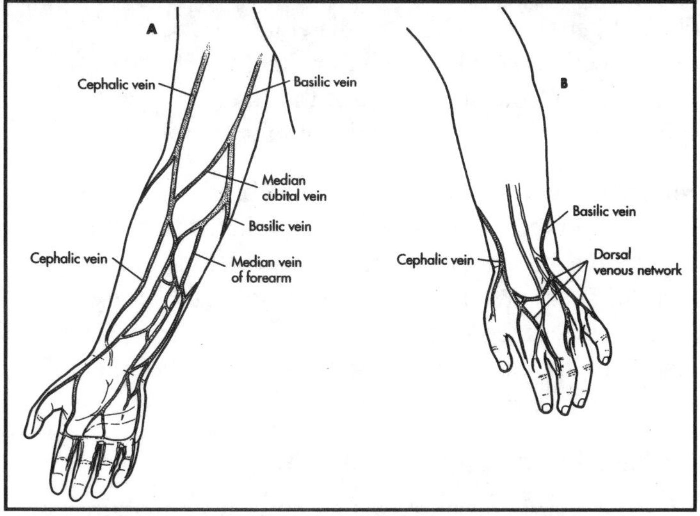

*Reprinted with permission from Webster, P.A., & Salassi-Scooter, M.R. (1997). Vascular access and hemodynamic monitoring. In R.A. Dieckmann, D.H. Fiser, & S.M. Selbst (Eds.), *Pediatric emergency and critical care procedures* (pp. 187–195). St. Louis, MO: Mosby.

Figure 9-2 Veins of the Lower Extremity*

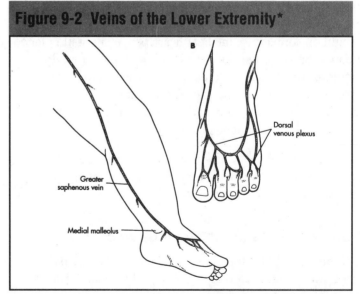

*Reprinted with permission from Webster, P.A., & Salassi-Scooter, M.R. (1997). Vascular access and hemodynamic monitoring. In R.A. Dieckmann, D.H. Fiser, & S.M. Selbst (Eds.), *Pediatric emergency and critical care procedures* (pp. 187–195). St. Louis, MO: Mosby.

Figure 9-3 Superficial Scalp Vein

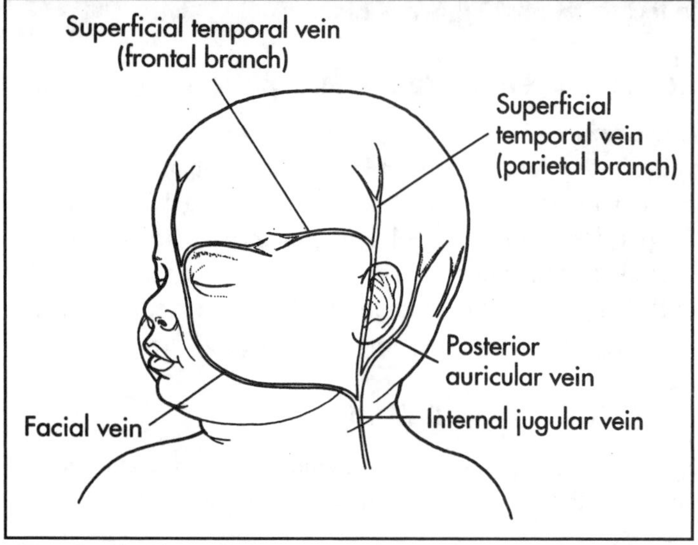

Superficial temporal vein (frontal branch)

Superficial temporal vein (parietal branch)

Posterior auricular vein

Internal jugular vein

Facial vein

*Reprinted with permission from Webster, P.A., & Salassi-Scooter, M.R. (1997). Vascular access and hemodynamic monitoring. In R.A. Dieckmann, D.H. Fiser, & S.M. Selbst (Eds.), *Pediatric emergency and critical care procedures* (pp. 187–195). St. Louis, MO: Mosby.

The healthcare provider may need to clip the hair in the area around the catheter, as well as areas that tape will cover to avoid pulling hair out by the root when removing the catheter. If this is done, consider saving the hair and offering it to the caregiver as a first hair cut. Avoid shaving the head to prevent microabrasions, which may introduce bacteria. Once a site is located, palpate the vein for the absence of a pulse before accessing, as arteries run next to veins on the scalp.

When securing a scalp intravenous line, a skin adherent (e.g., tincture of benzoin) may be useful in helping an occlusive dressing and tape stick to the scalp. If the positioning of the hub of the cannula is such that it may become caught on something, the healthcare provider should place a cotton ball or other dressing between it and the scalp to increase surface contact area. Burn netting may also be used to help stabilize the site. Tension at the site can be avoided by looping the intravenous tubing and taping it in the middle of the patient's back.

Contraindications to scalp vein insertion include age older than 12 months, hydrocephalus, ventricular shunt, anencephaly, and skull fracture.

Complications of Intravenous Access

Complications of intravenous cannulation include pain, infiltration/extravasation, phlebitis, and venous thrombosis. Compartment syndrome from extravasation has been reported. Signs of infiltration of an intravenous site include the following:

- Pain at or near the insertion site
- Taut and rigid skin around the insertion site
- Swelling proximal or distal to the insertion site
- Puffiness of the dependent part of the limb or body
- Blanching and coolness of the skin close to the insertion site
- Damp or wet dressing at the site
- Slowed transfusion rate or occlusion of the flow of fluid

If infiltration is suspected, fluids and medications should be stopped immediately. Further intervention should be per institutional protocol but may include discontinuing the intravenous line and applying a warm compress to the site.

Intraosseous Access

Intraosseous access (IO) is indicated as an emergency intervention that may be used when vascular access cannot be readily obtained by more conventional means. This route is a safe and rapid method of accessing the circulatory system for fluid and medication administration and is associated with a low complication rate.[4] Any medication that can be given via a peripheral intravenous line may be given via an IO line. The absorption rate of fluids and medications from an IO line into the central circulation has been shown to be similar to that of a peripheral intravenous line. Intraosseous access may be used in any age patient.

The initiation of IO access is accomplished by insertion of a rigid needle into the medullary cavity of a bone, providing access to a noncollapsible space. The preferred placement site in pediatric patients is 2 cm below the tibial tuberosity on the medial aspect of the proximal tibia. Other sites, such as the distal femur, the distal tibia directly above the medial malleolus, the proximal metaphysis of the humerus, and the anterior superior iliac spine, may be used based on institutional protocol.

Numerous types of devices are available for IO access. There are several brands of manually inserted devices that are placed using a simultaneous twisting and pushing motion. There are also drill-type devices and spring-loaded devices, both of which are often easier to use in older children in whom the bone matrix has become more calcified (**Figure 9-4**).

For intraosseous insertion at the proximal tibia:

- Use standard precautions at all times, wearing gloves and disposing of sharps in designated locations.
- Position the patient supine with the knee flexed.

Figure 9-4 Intraosseous Placement*

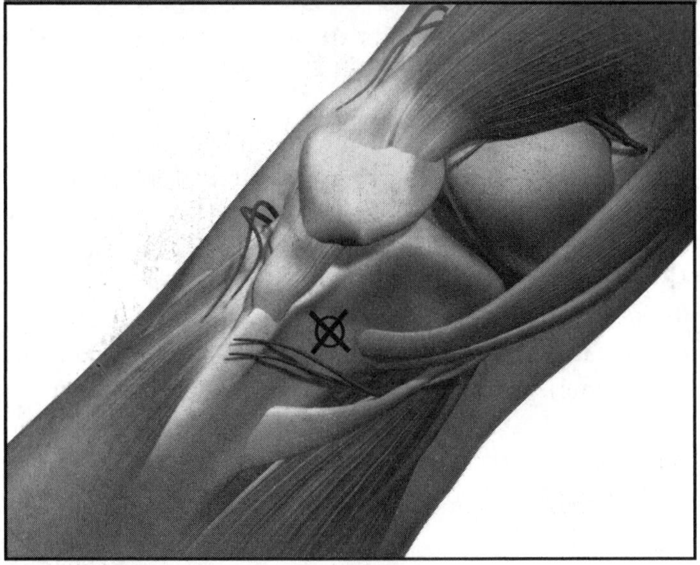

*Reprinted with permission from Vidacare.

- Support the leg on a rolled blanket or firm surface.

- Stabilize the lower leg by placing one hand firmly distal to the knee for support. The healthcare provider should not place his or her hand underneath the knee (popliteal fossa area) during the needle insertion. This is a safety precaution to prevent possible lacerations and through-and-through penetration during insertion.

- Prepare the puncture site with a topical antiseptic (e.g., povidone iodine or chlorhexidine gluconate).

- Hold the needle at a 90° angle to the bone and tilt it caudally to avoid puncturing the epiphysis.

- Advance until the needle gives a sudden loss of resistance. Advancing beyond this point can penetrate the bone on the opposite wall, causing an infiltration. When correctly placed, the needle will stand erect without support.

- Remove the stylet (if present) and attach a syringe, with or without extension tubing. Attempt to aspirate bone marrow at this point. Although the presence of bone marrow is an indication the needle is correctly placed, it is not always possible to aspirate bone marrow; therefore, its absence does not indicate incorrect placement. Many diagnostic studies may be processed from bone marrow. Label blood tubes according to the source. Bone marrow aspirate may also be used to obtain a bed-side glucose reading. Laboratory studies that may not be comparable to serum studies include the following:

  ○ Complete blood cell count
  ○ Coagulation profiles
  ○ Arterial blood gases

- Attach intravenous tubing to the hub or to the extension tubing and infuse fluid. Fluid administered through an IO needle may not run by gravity; application of a pressure bag or an infusion pump is usually required. Fluids may also be pushed manually.

- Secure the line firmly. An acceptable technique is to apply tape to either side of the plastic skirt or to crisscross tape over the plastic hub. Additional stability may be achieved by placing a small cup with a hole for the intravenous tubing over the device as an additional layer of protection. Many commercially produced stabilization devices are also available. Loop tubing and secure it as with a peripheral intravenous line to prevent dislodgement with traction.

- After insertion of the IO needle, ongoing inspection of the surrounding tissue (particularly the posterior surface) should be routinely performed for signs of infiltration/extravasation.

Intraosseous insertion is contraindicated if there is a fracture of the bone selected or if previous IO access has been recently attempted in that bone. Relative contraindications for IO access include cellulitis, burns, or other soft tissue injury at the chosen site; or a history of osteogenesis imperfecta/osteoporosis or other bone disease processes. Complications of IO placement, which are rare, include fracture at the site, compartment syndrome, skin necrosis, and air, fat, or bone embolus.

Once a peripheral or central line is established, the healthcare provider may choose to discontinue IO access. Most IO devices are removed by simple in-line pressure, pulling the device in the opposite direction from which it was inserted. Attaching an empty syringe to the hub of the IO device may provide additional leverage if needed. When the IO needle is removed, apply manual pressure to the site for several minutes, then apply a dressing and label it as a discontinued IO site.

Central Venous Access

Central venous devices allow for more secure access to the central circulation and provide the ability to deliver medications that may result in vessel or tissue damage if administered peripherally. In addition, central venous access devices allow for central venous pressure to be monitored, if needed.

Central venous access may be obtained in the femoral, subclavian, or internal jugular veins. The internal jugular site is often difficult to access in children with short necks. Central venous access should only be attempted by clinicians experienced with the technique and familiar with the unique anatomical features of the pediatric central venous system (**Figure 9-5**).

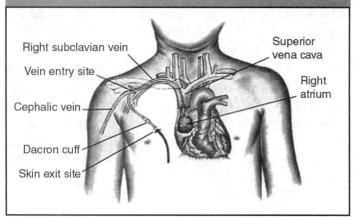
Long-term central venous access devices are often used when prolonged or frequent venous access is needed and/or peripheral access is not obtainable. The pediatric patient may present to the emergency department with a long-term central venous access device in place. Products vary and include subcutaneous venous ports (port-a-caths), tunneled central venous catheters (e.g., Broviac and Hickman), and peripherally inserted central catheters. Consult with the primary caregiver regarding the care of the child's particular device, and follow appropriate institutional protocols when accessing these devices. Use a sterile technique during any access procedures and during central venous catheter dressing changes. After the collection of blood specimens, or on completion of an infusion, central venous catheters should be flushed with normal saline and heparin solution to maintain patency. The pediatric patient's weight, the catheter or device size and type, and institutional protocol will influence the amount of saline, and the concentration and amount of heparin that is used.

Subcutaneous Venous Ports

Subcutaneous venous ports are surgically implanted beneath the skin and are generally located in the chest region. The right side of the chest is often chosen because the right brachiocephalic vein (versus the left brachiocephalic vein) curves down more directly to the superior vena cava. Another site used for placement is in the abdominal cavity, with the tip of the catheter tunneled into the inferior vena cava. Subcutaneous venous ports are often preferred over other central access devices in pediatric patients because there are no external components to break. This is especially important in active children and adolescents. Subcutaneous venous ports are also often used in patients with body image concerns (i.e.,

the patient's body image is not threatened by external catheters), as is often seen in the adolescent population.

Subcutaneous venous ports are accessed percutaneously via a self-sealing compressed silicone septum using a special noncoring needle (e.g., Huber). Standard hypodermic needles are not recommended because they may damage the septum, requiring the patient to return to surgery for replacement of the device. Many patients and caregivers have been taught to apply topical anesthetic cream (e.g., EMLA, ELA-Max, or LMX) before going to the hospital to eliminate the pain of needle insertion during access. Several commercially made subcutaneous venous ports are available in single- or double-lumen designs. Access needle gauge and length should be chosen based on the patient's size and information obtained from the patient and/or caregiver.

Tunneled Central Venous Catheters

Tunneled central venous catheters are surgically inserted. The catheter tunnels under the skin and enters the vein some distance away. Passing the catheter under the skin helps to prevent infection and provides stability. In addition to suturing, several brands of central venous catheters are held in place by a cuff that sits just beneath the skin; this cuff serves to further reduce infection risk and maintain stability. The catheter exit site is typically located in the chest, making the access ports visible at that location.

Most often, the exposed catheter access ports are covered by a sterile dressing taped to the skin. Dependent on its use, a central venous catheter can have one or multiple lumens. Clamping of the catheter is dependent on the type of central venous access device that is in place. The Hickman and Broviac catheters must be clamped when accessed; the Groshong catheter should not be clamped because it contains a two-way valve that opens as fluid is withdrawn or infused (and remains closed when not in use).

Peripherally Inserted Central Catheters

Peripherally inserted central catheters are placed in a peripheral vein, such as the cephalic or basilic veins, and then advanced through increasingly larger veins toward the heart until the tip rests in the distal superior vena cava or cavoatrial junction. Peripherally inserted central catheter insertion is a sterile procedure; however, it does not require the use of an operating room. In some patients, peripherally inserted central catheter lines are an alternative to other central venous catheters that have potentially higher rates of infection and other complications.

Subcutaneous Rehydration

For those pediatric patients who have sustained mild to moderate dehydration, subcutaneous rehydration offers an alternative fluid delivery method. Subcutaneous infusions can be administered easily and quickly. This method is relatively painless, and many sites are suitable for use.

The subcutaneous needle insertion site should be chosen based on the comfort of the pediatric patient and the likelihood that the patient will pull on the line. If the latter is a possibility, the healthcare provider should choose an out-of-sight/out-of-reach placement site. The preferred sites for the pediatric patient are the upper back between the scapula and the back of the upper arm, although any tissue-dense subcutaneous site may be used. Subcutaneous needles should not be placed in an infected or acutely inflamed area because of the danger of spreading a localized infection.

A small-gauge needle, either an over-the-needle catheter or a metal butterfly needle, is inserted into the subcutaneous tissue using an aseptic technique and is then covered by a transparent disposable dressing. During the initial fluid bolus, there may be a collection of fluid in the subcutaneous space, which should dissipate within 30 minutes. Subcutaneous fluid boluses should be based on a milliliter/kilogram calculation, just as with any other fluid administration. The rate and volume of subcutaneous fluid administration should not exceed those used for intravenous infusions. Medications that can be administered through subcutaneous lines are limited, and few have U.S. Food and Drug Administration approval, except in special situations such as the administration of antiemetics and pain medications in patients undergoing chemotherapy.[5]

Subcutaneous tissue resistance at the infusion site and subsequent slow administration of fluids are main concerns when considering hydration via this route. There are medications available that increase tissue perfusion and enhance fluid absorption at the site, thus allowing fluids to be administered rapidly. Recombinant hyaluronidase is one of the most current medications available for this purpose. The U.S. Food and Drug Administration has not approved the administration of any medications with recombinant hyaluronidase in children.

Summary

Vascular access procedures can be frightening and painful to the pediatric patient. The healthcare provider should explain all procedures to the pediatric patient in an age-appropriate manner and include the caregiver in all aspects of treatment. Allow time for questions, listen carefully, and consider all information the patient and caregiver have to share about the patient's medical history and previous experiences with vascular access. Evaluate all potential intravenous sites before attempting access. If possible, avoid placing vascular access devices in the patient's dominant hand or the hand the patient uses for self-comforting measures (e.g., thumb sucking). Avoid prolonged use of tourniquets and access over bony prominences. The healthcare provider should obtain assistance if unable to gain access within several attempts or based on guidelines set forth by his or her particular institution.

Always maintain standard precautions when performing any procedure. Help may be needed to secure and comfort the pediatric patient during vascular access. Avoid using caregivers to secure the pediatric patient. Pharmacological and/or nonpharmacological pain management techniques should always be used to decrease the pain of vascular access procedures and to facilitate coping mechanisms. The pediatric patient should be rewarded and comforted after the completion of the procedure. If mild to moderate dehydration is present, and vascular access is to be used only for hydration purposes, consider subcutaneous infusion. In emergent situations, consider IO access early. Monitor all vascular access sites for signs of infiltration and infection at least hourly when administering fluid boluses or medications.

References

1. Gorelick, M. H., Shaw, K. N., & Murphy, K. O. (1997). Validity and reliability of clinical signs in the diagnosis of dehydration in children. *Pediatrics, 99,* E6.

2. Lang, E. V., Hatsiopoulou, O., Koch, T., Berbaum, K., Lutgendorf, S., Kettenmann, E., … Kaptchuk, T. J. (2005). Can words hurt? Patient-provider interactions during invasive procedures. *Pain, 114,* 303–309.

3. MacLaren, J. E., & Cohen, L. L. (2005). A comparison of distraction strategies for venipuncture distress in children. *Journal of Pediatric Psychology, 30,* 387–396.

4. Leidel, B. A., Kirchhoff, C., Bogner, V., Stegmaier, J., Mutschler, W., Kanz, K. G., & Braunstein, V. (2009). Is the intraosseous access route fast and efficacious compared to conventional central venous catheterization in adult patients under resuscitation in the emergency department? A prospective observational pilot study. *Patient Safety in Surgery, 3,* 24.

5. Allen, C. H., Etzwiler, L. S., Miller, M. K., Maher, G., Mace, S., Hostetler, M. A., … Harb, G.; Increased Flow Utilizing Subcutaneously-Enabled Pediatric Rehydration Study Collaborative Research Group. (2009). Recombinant human hyaluronidase-enabled subcutaneous pediatric rehydration. *Pediatrics, 124,* e858–e867.

Chapter 10 | Respiratory Emergencies

Patricia Kunz Howard, PhD, RN, CEN, CPEN, NE-BC, FAEN

Objectives

On completion of this chapter, the learner should be able to do the following:
- Determine anatomical, physiological, and developmental characteristics of pediatric patients as basis for signs and symptoms of respiratory distress and failure
- Describe common causes and characteristics associated with respiratory distress or failure in pediatric patients.
- Plan appropriate interventions for pediatric patients with respiratory distress or failure.
- Indicate health promotion strategies related to decreasing respiratory distress and failure occurrence.

Introduction

Respiratory disorders remain a major cause of illness and hospitalization in the pediatric population.[1] Pediatric patients are unique in their responses to respiratory problems because of their anatomical, physiological, and developmental characteristics. Respiratory compromise in pediatric patients can be caused by upper and lower respiratory tract infections and obstructive disorders, sedating medications, central nervous system disorders, musculoskeletal deformities, or congenital anomalies and disorders.

Respiratory distress is part of a continuum that, if left untreated, results in respiratory failure. Respiratory failure is the most common pathway to cardiopulmonary arrest in pediatric patients. The survival to discharge rates for pediatric patients after cardiopulmonary arrest are better than those for adults: 8% for out-of-hospital cardiopulmonary arrest and 27% for in-hospital cardiopulmonary arrest in the pediatric population.[2] Although these rates are improving, they are still low and, thus, early recognition and treatment of the pediatric patient in respiratory distress are critical.

Anatomical, Physiological, and Developmental Characteristics as a Basis for Signs and Symptoms

Central Control of Respiration

The respiratory center is located in the brainstem and controls the rate of ventilation by responding to changes in arterial partial pressure of carbon dioxide ($PaCO_2$), and hydrogen ion (H^+) concentrations. An excess of either substance causes a direct excitatory effect on the respiratory center, resulting in an increased rate of ventilation.

$$\uparrow PaCO_2 \text{ or } \uparrow H^+ = \uparrow \text{Respiratory Rate}$$

Oxygen does not have a significant effect on the respiratory center; instead, it acts on chemical receptors (chemoreceptors) located in the carotid and aortic bodies. Chemoreceptors indirectly control the rate of ventilation by sending signals to the respiratory center through afferent nerves. Although chemoreceptors are sensitive to $PaCO_2$ and H^+ levels, they are most strongly stimulated when the

Table 10-1 Key Anatomical Characteristics*

Characteristics	Clinical Significance
Nares have little supporting cartilage.	Nasal flaring is an early sign of distress.
Infants younger than four months are obligate nasal breathers.	Nasopharyngeal secretions or nasogastric tubes can cause airway obstruction.
Head is large in proportion to body, with weak supporting musculature and occipital prominence.	Flexion of the airway can cause obstruction when the pediatric patient is supine; head bobbing occurs when the patient is distressed.
Tongue is large in proportion to oropharynx.	Tongue can easily occlude airway when supine.
Epiglottis is "U" shaped, higher, and more anterior in the airway.	Epiglottis is more prone to infection and trauma.
Larynx is positioned more anteriorly and cephalad.	Position of larynx increases risk for aspiration.
Cricoid cartilage is the narrowest part of the airway, and the trachea is funnel shaped.	Provides an anatomical cuff for endotracheal tubes and a frequent site of foreign body obstruction.
Airway diameter in the infant and child is smaller and shorter than in an adult.* The infant's tracheal diameter approximates the diameter of the little finger.	Airway obstruction can quickly develop in infants and young children. A small amount of edema or secretions can markedly increase airway resistance and result in partial or complete airway obstruction.
Tracheal length is proportional to the child's size. The length for an infant is approximately 7 cm.	Correct depth of endotracheal tube insertion varies with the size of the child. Right main stem intubation occurs when the endotracheal tube is inserted beyond the tracheal length.
Tracheal and bronchial cartilaginous support rings are "C" rather than "O" shaped.	Allow airway collapse that can be exacerbated during illness or when the neck is hyperextended or flexed.
Alveoli increase until middle childhood to nine times as many as were present at birth.[†] Alveoli have less elastic recoil and less supportive elastic tissue.	Less alveolar surface is for gas exchange in infants and young children. A child requires faster respiratory rates for normal function; respiratory rate increases with distress. Alveoli are more prone to collapse at the end of expiration.
Lung (tidal) volume is approximately 10 mL/kg (e.g., 100 mL in a 10-kg child) vs 50 mL/kg (e.g., 2500 mL in a 50-kg adult).	Results in low residual capacity and oxygen reserve. Variation in tidal volume must be considered when bag-mask ventilation is performed to avoid overinflation or underinflation.
Metabolic rate is twice that of adults, with twice the oxygen consumption.	Hypoxia occurs more rapidly when the child is in respiratory distress. Other factors that increase metabolic rate (e.g., fever) contribute to respiratory demands.
Rib orientation is more horizontal than vertical.	Chest diameter is maximally expanded at baseline and cannot be increased with distress (barrel chested).
Ribs are cartilaginous, and intercostal muscles are immature.	Allows chest wall collapse rather than expansion during distress, causing retractions.
Chest wall is thin, and thorax is small (with organs in close proximity).	Allow transmitted breath sounds. Breath sounds from one area are heard in other areas of the chest and are not easily differentiated.
Diaphragm is the major muscle of breathing.	Ventilation is directly affected when diaphragmatic excursion is impeded by pressure from above, such as with the hyperexpansion seen in asthma; or from below, such as with abdominal distension from gastric insufflation. Abdominal breathing is common.
Hemoglobin concentrations vary by age. A low value (9.5 g/100 mL) occurs at 3 months, and volume increases until adult values are reached at puberty.[‡]	Cyanosis develops when 5g of hemoglobin are desaturated or when as much as 50% of the child's blood is deoxygenated. Therefore, cyanosis is a late sign of distress.

*Data are taken from Mecham, N. L. (2010). Pediatric emergencies. In P. K. Howard & R. A. Steinman (Eds.), *Sheehy's emergency nursing practices and principles* (6th ed., p. 631). St. Louis, MO: Mosby–Year Book.

[†]Data are taken from Askin, D. F., & Wilson, D. (2007). The high-risk newborn and family. In M. J. Hockenberry & D. Wilson (Eds.), *Wong's nursing care of infants and children* (8th ed., pp. 378–379). St. Louis, MO: Mosby–Year Book.

[‡]Data are taken from Hockenberry, M. J., & Wilson, D. (2007). *Wong's nursing care of infants and children* (8th ed., p. 1869). St. Louis, MO: Mosby–Year Book.

partial pressure of oxygen, arterial (PaO_2), decreases to less than 60 mmHg.[3]

$$\downarrow PaO_2 = \uparrow \text{Respiratory Rate (Early Sign) and}$$
$$\downarrow \text{Respiratory Rate (Late Sign)}$$

In the infant, the central nervous system and the peripheral nerves are not well developed, and there are fewer peripheral chemoreceptors. Although healthy infants and children will compensate for hypercarbia, hypoxia, and acidosis with hyperventilation, younger infants are less able to compensate for these stressors. Premature infants, rather than responding with hyperventilation, may initially respond with tachypnea, followed by bradypnea and apnea.[4]

The pediatric patient's respiratory system is in a constant state of growth and development until approximately the age of seven to eight years, when it is similar to that of the adult. **Table 10-1** summarizes key anatomical characteristics and their clinical significance to respiratory distress and failure.

Definition of Respiratory Distress and Failure

Respiratory distress is a clinical state characterized by signs of increased respiratory rate and increased respiratory effort; these signs include tachypnea, nasal flaring, use of accessory muscles, and retractions.[5] Respiratory failure is characterized by inadequate oxygenation, ventilation, or both.[5] Therefore, respiratory distress and failure represent the two ends of a continuum of ventilatory dysfunction. The clinical manifestations of progression in this continuum can be subtle and are often not recognized early.

Respiratory failure. Fatigue from excessive work of breathing is often a precipitating factor. Work of breathing and an evaluation of ventilatory effectiveness may be more helpful in determining the pediatric patient's potential for respiratory failure than blood gas results alone. Ventilatory assistance or intervention must never be delayed while awaiting blood gas results because rapid deterioration and respiratory arrest may occur.

Causes of Respiratory Distress and Failure

In the pediatric patient, the most common causes of respiratory distress and failure are upper or lower airway obstructive disorders (**Table 10-2**). Other causes of respiratory failure include central nervous system depression, musculoskeletal disorders, and thoracic disorders. It is not always necessary to identify the cause of the distress immediately. It is more important to recognize that respiratory distress exists and to initiate the proper interventions to prevent the deterioration to respiratory failure or arrest.

Table 10-2 Causes of Respiratory Distress and Failure

Upper Airway	
Anaphylaxis	Sleep apnea
Bacterial tracheitis	Smoke inhalation
Croup	Subglottic stenosis
Epiglottis	Tracheomalacia
Foreign body aspiration	Trauma
Retropharyngeal abscess	

Lower Airway	
Acute respiratory distress syndrome	Pleural effusions
Aspiration	Pneumothorax/hemothorax
Asthma	Pneumonia
Atelectasis	Pulmonary contusion
Bronchiolitis	Pulmonary edema
Bronchomalacia	Smoke inhalation
Foreign bodies	Trauma
Pertussis	

Nursing Care of the Child With Respiratory Distress or Failure

The pediatric patient who is in respiratory distress or failure requires simultaneous assessment and the initiation of critical interventions. **Chapter 5, "Initial Assessment,"** provides a review of a comprehensive primary and secondary assessment. Additional or specific history data important to the evaluation of respiratory distress are listed later. Assessment findings that may indicate respiratory distress or failure are listed in the "Signs and Symptoms" section.

Additional History

- Time of onset
- Characteristic of onset (rapid or gradual)
- Previous episodes of respiratory distress

Signs and Symptoms

- Altered level of consciousness. Any alteration in the level of consciousness must be considered a result of cerebral hypoxia until proven otherwise.

- Inability to recognize caregivers
- Decreased interaction with the environment
- Restlessness/agitation
- Anxiety
- Confusion
- Inability to be consoled
- Increased work of breathing
  - Nasal flaring (an attempt to decrease airway resistance)
  - Retractions (**Figure 10-1**).
  - Head bobbing: the neck muscles extend forward during inhalation and relax during exhalation in an attempt to increase inspiratory pressure.
  - Grunting: created by premature closure of the glottis in an attempt to increase the physiological positive end expiratory pressure. It is a compensatory mechanism to relieve collapsing alveoli.
  - Abdominal breathing (normal in young infants but worsens as respiratory distress progresses to failure).
- Tripod position: leaning forward while sitting up allows the tongue to remain forward and open the airway.
  - The child who is refusing to lie down is attempting to maintain an airway.
- Paradoxical respirations, often called seesaw breathing, represent increased dependence on the diaphragm and are a sign of impending respiratory failure. This is an ineffective form of breathing, and the child can fatigue quickly.
- Pallor

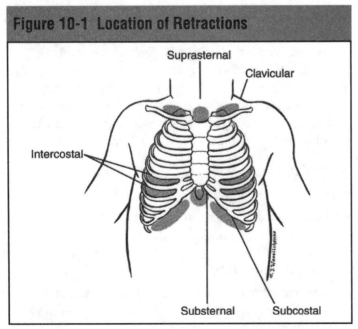

Figure 10-1 Location of Retractions

Suprasternal
Clavicular
Intercostal
Substernal
Subcostal

*Reprinted with permission from Wilson, D., & Hockenberry, M. J. (2008). *Wong's clinical manual of pediatric nursing* (7th ed.). St. Louis, MO: Mosby.

- Cyanosis (late sign; represents significant hypoxia)
- Unusual drooling: inability to swallow may indicate pharyngeal obstruction.
- Decreased gag reflex (may be from decreased level of consciousness or muscle tone).
- Altered respiratory rate
  - Tachypnea
  - Bradypnea or a sudden decrease in respiratory rate (late sign; represents fatigue and impending arrest).
  - Apnea: usually considered pauses in breathing of more than 20 seconds. Periodic breathing that occurs in neonates is irregular breathing with pauses of less than 15 seconds.
- Altered heart rate
  - Tachycardia
  - Bradycardia (late sign; related to hypoxia; represents impending arrest)
- Snoring (represents partial obstruction of the nasopharyngeal space)
- Stridor (inspiratory sound representing partial obstruction, inflammation, or collapse of the trachea)
- Adventitious breath sounds. Wheezing and crackles are common in reactive airway disease, asthma, bronchiolitis, pneumonia, and pulmonary edema.
- Decreased, absent, or unequal breath sounds. Physical examination findings may vary over time as the result of secretions, bronchoconstriction, fluid shifts, or airway collapse.

Diagnostic Procedures

A variety of radiographic, imaging, and laboratory studies may be performed based on the suspected etiology of the pediatric patient's condition. Definitive diagnostic procedures are completed while the resuscitation efforts are in progress or after the pediatric patient has been stabilized.

Monitors

- Pulse oximetry
  - Poor perfusion may impede the monitor's ability to obtain an accurate reading.
  - A normal reading does not negate the pediatric patient's need for supplemental oxygen.
  - Probe placement for infants: consider forehead, large toe, top or bottom of the foot, or sides of the ankle.
- Cardiac monitor, as indicted.
- Capnography, as indicated.

Radiographic Studies

- Chest radiograph to determine the presence of cardiomegaly, foreign body, pulmonary infection, pulmonary edema, hyperexpansion, pneumothorax, or hemothorax; and for definitive placement of an endotracheal tube (ETT), when indicated.

- Lateral radiograph of the neck or thorax to evaluate the presence of a foreign body, pleural effusions, or soft tissue swelling.

- Other radiographic and imaging studies may be indicated based on the clinical presentation of respiratory compromise.

Laboratory Studies

- Arterial or capillary blood gas measurement may be obtained, depending on the pediatric patient's condition and clinical concern. Capillary blood gas may be used to evaluate pH and CO_2 levels. A decreasing pH indicates a worsening of the cellular oxygen debt as metabolic acidosis develops because of anaerobic metabolism and lactic acid production. An elevated $PaCO_2$ indicates respiratory acidosis and impaired ventilation of the alveoli. A low PaO_2 indicates hypoxia.

- Increasing CO_2 retention represents hypoventilation. This can be measured with blood gases and monitored or trended with the use of capnography.

- Other laboratory studies, including cultures, may be indicated based on the pediatric patient's condition and treatment plan.

Planning/Implementation

Chapter 5, "Initial Assessment," describes the general nursing interventions for the pediatric patient. After a patent airway, breathing, and circulation are ensured, the following interventions are initiated, as appropriate, for the pediatric patient's condition.

Additional Interventions

- Position the pediatric patient to facilitate respiratory effectiveness and comfort.
  - Have the patient sit on the caregiver's lap.
  - Raise the head of the bed to the most comfortable angle.
  - Try to avoid invasive procedures or actions that may upset the pediatric patient until the airway is secured (e.g., patients with partial airway obstruction from a foreign body or epiglottis).

- If the patient is unresponsive, position the head in a neutral position, using caution to not overextend the neck.

- Suction as needed. Use a rigid suction tip, suction catheter, or bulb syringe as indicated.

- Administer supplemental oxygen by the most appropriate method, delivering the highest concentration of oxygen for the pediatric patient's condition.

- Give nothing by mouth, as appropriate.
  - Pediatric patients with extreme tachypnea, severe respiratory distress, or impending failure must receive nothing by mouth because of the risk of aspiration and the potential need for intubation.
  - Feeding may also compound the respiratory problem in infants because it increases metabolic demand and oxygen requirements.

For those with mild distress, encourage oral intake because tachypnea can lead to increased insensible fluid losses. Milk other than breast milk should be avoided if oral fluids are permitted. Breastfeeding may increase mild respiratory distress, and oxygen saturation should be monitored. If the child is to receive nothing by mouth for a significant period, subcutaneous or intravenous fluids are required.

- Relieve any conditions that are impeding diaphragmatic excursion.

- Insert a gastric tube to reduce gastric distention. Air in the stomach from swallowing air or bag-mask ventilation will result in gastric distention, which can impede ventilatory efforts.
  - If a gastrostomy tube is in place for feeding, decompression via the gastrostomy tube may be needed.

- Prepare and administer medications, per protocol.

- Airway adjuncts: oral and nasal airway.
  - Anticipate the need and prepare for assisted ventilation, intubation, and other advanced support measures, as appropriate.

- Assess ETT placement.
  - Observe for symmetrical chest rise.
  - Auscultate for breath sounds over the epigastrium, then bilaterally at the anterior chest fields and at the midaxillary areas. Compare pitch, intensity, and location of the sounds. Caution should be exercised because breath sounds can be transmitted to other areas in the pediatric patient.
  - An exhaled CO_2 detector and/or an esophageal aspirator device can be used to confirm tube placement.

○ Confirm ETT positioning with a chest radiograph.

○ Record the position of the ETT at the level of the gum, lip, or teeth.

○ Use of cuffed ETTs has become more common in the pediatric population. The previous disadvantage of assumed soft tissue injury has been questioned in recent studies. Cuffed and uncuffed ETTs should be available in appropriate sizes. Cuffed ETT size can be calculated from the following equation: (16 + age [in years]) / 3.5, or a half size smaller than the calculated uncuffed ETT diameter.[6]

- Capnography is a reliable method of monitoring ETT placement as well as trending respiratory status.

- Rapid-sequence induction for intubation may be required for the pediatric patient in impending and actual respiratory failure.

- Prepare for alternate airway and breathing support measures, if indicated.

○ A laryngeal mask airway may be indicated for the unresponsive pediatric patient.

○ A needle cricothyrotomy is indicated only in cases of complete upper airway obstruction when all other interventions have failed to produce an adequate airway. (Surgical cricothyrotomy is not recommended for children < 12 years. It may cause damage to the cricoid cartilage).[7]

○ An emergency tracheostomy is rarely indicated in children and must be performed only by physicians with demonstrated competence in this procedure.

- Prepare for needle decompression of tension pneumothorax.

Evaluation and Ongoing Assessment

Pediatric patients with respiratory emergencies require meticulous and frequent reassessment of airway patency, breathing effectiveness, perfusion, and mental status. The etiologies of respiratory distress and failure encompass a broad range of disorders. Initial improvements may not be sustained, and additional interventions may be required. The pediatric patient's response to interventions and trending of the pediatric patient's condition must be closely monitored for achievement of desired outcomes. To evaluate the pediatric patient's respiratory progress, monitor the following:

- Airway patency

- Level of consciousness and interaction with the environment

- Work of breathing

- Breath sounds and quality of air exchange

- Peak flow measurements

- Oxygen saturation and exhaled CO_2, as indicated

- Vital signs

Selected Emergencies

Upper Airway

Respiratory distress and failure can result when structures of the upper airway are occluded by edema, secretions, foreign bodies, or anatomical defects. Examples of these include croup, epiglottitis, bacterial tracheitis, foreign-body obstruction, obstructive sleep apnea, and tracheomalacia or vascular rings. Croup, epiglottitis, and foreign body obstruction are further compared in **Table 10-3**.

Lower Airway

Respiratory distress and failure can also result when edema, bronchoconstriction, secretions, foreign bodies, weak muscle walls, or anatomical defects occlude structures of the lower airway. Examples of these include asthma, bronchiolitis, pertussis, pneumonia, foreign-body obstruction, bronchomalacia, muscular dystrophy, and scoliosis or kyphosis.

Asthma

Asthma is the most common chronic illness in children, affecting 9.3% of children in the United States alone.[8] Asthma is defined as a chronic inflammatory disorder of the airways.[9] The disease is characterized by hyperreactiveness of the airway, widespread inflammatory changes, bronchospasm, and mucous plugging. Recurrent episodes may include any of the following common symptoms: wheezing, breathlessness, chest tightness, and coughing. Seasonal and environmental allergies, exercise, infections, medications, irritants, weather changes, smoking, exposure to secondhand smoke, and emotions often precipitate asthmatic exacerbations.

Confirmation of the diagnosis of asthma is usually delayed until the child has had repeated episodes and is older than one year. Diagnosing asthma in infants is often difficult. Failure to recognize asthma and undertreatment are common problems in this age group. Treatment is best directed toward long-term control rather than episodic emergency care.[9]

Table 10-3 Common Causes of Upper Airway Emergencies*

Croup	Epiglottitis	Foreign Body Aspiration
Insidious inflammation that results in partial airway obstruction as the result of tracheal narrowing.	Abrupt inflammation of the epiglottis that results in a subglottic obstruction and acute airway emergency.	Size of object determines severity of upper or lower airway partial or complete obstruction.
Viral illness caused by parainfluenza virus, rhinovirus, influenza A, or respiratory syncytial virus.	Bacterial illness with a decreased incidence as the result of availability of the *Haemophilus influenzae* type B vaccine; may also be caused by *Streptococcus pneumoniae* and *Staphylococcus*.	Most often caused by food items, especially hot dogs, round candy, and peanuts, but may also be plastic or glass beads, buttons, coins, and disc batteries; frequently follows history of gagging.
Occurs most commonly in children aged 6–36 months. Boys have a slightly higher prevalence than girls.	Occurs most in children who do not have current vaccinations and those children too young to have received the vaccine.	Occurs most commonly in children younger than 3 years but may occur in any age group.
Peak incidence in cooler months.	No seasonal preference.	No seasonal preference.
Presents with the gradual onset of cold symptoms, a barking cough that is worse at night, a hoarse voice, and low-grade fever. Tachypnea, tachycardia, retractions, and inspiratory stridor are common; expiratory wheezing may be present. A soft tissue neck radiograph may indicate tracheal narrowing, referred to as the steeple sign.	Presents acutely with high fever, sore throat, difficulty swallowing, and muffled voice, which leads quickly to respiratory distress. Drooling may be present, and tripod positioning may be used to maintain airway patency. Stridor is present as the airway narrows, but there are no adventitious sounds heard on auscultation. The pediatric patient may appear anxious and ill. A lateral neck radiograph may indicate epiglottic and aryepiglottic swelling, referred to as the thumb sign and the posterior triangle. Most blood cultures are positive for the causative agent.	Presentation varies depending on the following: (1) when the aspiration occurred and (2) the location and degree of obstruction. Signs and symptoms may include drooling, stridor, wheezing or unequal breath sounds, or chest pain. Chest radiograph anterior/posterior, lateral, and decubitus views may reveal radiopaque or obstructing items. Partially obstructing nonradiopaque items can be difficult to evaluate by radiograph. Direct visualization by deep laryngoscopy or bronchoscopy may be required for definitive diagnosis.

Interventions	Interventions	Interventions
Relieve anxiety	Remain in a position of comfort, and do not separate from the caregiver.	Initiate pediatric basic life support techniques to relieve choking as appropriate.
Provide supplemental oxygen, cool mist, or humidified air as tolerated	No invasive procedures until airway is stabilized, including throat examination, rectal temperature, and blood work or intravenous access. Examination of the throat or visualization of the pharynx can precipitate gagging and coughing which can produce complete obstruction.	Remain in position of comfort, and do not separate from caregiver
Monitor oxygen saturation	Provide blow-by oxygen as tolerated.	No invasive procedures until airway is stabilized, including throat examination, rectal temperature, and blood work or intravenous access.
Encourage fluids	Anticipate controlled endotracheal intubation.	Provide blow-by oxygen, as tolerated.
Administer medications as ordered: nebulized racemic epinephrine, 0.25 mL in 3–5 mL of normal saline. Children should be monitored for two to three hours because the medication effect may not be sustained (the rebound effect). Steroids are often given.	Complete intravenous access, radiographs, laboratory work, and antibiotics after the airway is secured.	Complete intravenous access and radiographs once the airway is stabilized.
Discharge teaching: Teach caregivers to take child into cool air, open the freezer, or run the the shower for steam and sit with the child in the bathroom. This change in temperature or humidity can decrease inflammation in the upper airway.		

*Data are taken from Hueckel and Wilson.[14]

Additional History

- Frequent coughing, especially at night
- Recurrent wheezing
- Recurrent breathlessness
- Recurrent chest tightness
- Fatigue
- Known triggers or exposure to any of the following before this illness:
  - Indoor allergens (i.e., cockroaches, dust mites, and rodents)
  - Animal allergens
  - Indoor fungi (mold)
  - Outdoor allergens (i.e., trees, grass, weed pollen, and seasonal mold spores)
  - Irritants (i.e., tobacco smoke, wood smoke, sprays, or odors)
  - Exposure to occupational chemicals
  - Exercise
  - Cold air
  - Weather changes
  - Environmental changes
  - Strong emotional expression, such as laughing or crying hard
  - Stress and anxiety
  - Foods
  - Viral or upper respiratory tract infections
  - Medications, such as salicylates or nonsteroidal anti-inflammatory medications
- Atopic dermatitis or eczema
- Previous history of reactive airway disease, asthma, or wheezing episodes
  - Frequency of symptoms
  - Number of school days missed
  - Present medications, including dose, route, and frequency
  - Morning baseline peak flow volumes
  - Number of emergency department visits per year
  - Number of hospitalizations and date of the last hospitalization
  - Number of critical care unit admissions and date of the last admission to the critical care unit
  - Number of endotracheal intubations and date of last intubation
- Increased use of inhaled short-acting ß$_2$-agonists (decreased responsiveness/effectiveness to their use)
- Deterioration in peak flow measurements
- Management by primary care provider, pulmonologist, or allergy specialist

Signs and Symptoms

- Wheezing on inspiration or expiration
- Prolonged expiratory phase
- Decreased or unequal breath sounds
- Tachypnea
- Retractions
- Coughing, especially at night and in the early morning

Diagnostic Procedures

Laboratory Studies

Arterial blood gas is measured in cases of severe exacerbations. A PaCO$_2$ level of greater than 42 mm Hg or a PaO$_2$ level of less than 90 mm Hg, with signs of muscle fatigue or a declining level of consciousness, despite maximal therapy, may indicate impending respiratory failure and the need for endotracheal intubation.[9]

Additional Interventions

Deliver supplemental oxygen per protocol. Monitor oxygen saturation until a clear response to bronchodilator therapy has occurred.[9]

- Obtain a peak expiratory flow or forced expiratory volume measurement. Record percentage of predicted best measurement.
- Administer medications as ordered. **Table 10-4** describes medications and recommended doses.
  - Short-acting ß$_2$-agonists should be used, with the addition of ipratropium bromide (Atrovent) in severe exacerbations.[10] These treatments may be delivered as a nebulized aerosol or a metered-dose inhaler.
  - Nebulizers are usually administered every 20 minutes to a total of three treatments or may be administered continuously, depending on patient condition.
  - Anticholinergic agents may potentiate the bronchodilatory effect of ß$_2$-agonists.
  - Systemic corticosteroids should be used in individuals who do not respond to short-acting ß$_2$-agonists. Oral administration of prednisone has had effects equivalent to those of intravenous methylprednisolone sodium succinate (Solu-medrol).[9] Adjunct therapies (i.e., magnesium or heliox) should be considered in individuals who are not responsive to the previously mentioned therapies.[10]

Table 10-4 Usual Dosage for Quick-Relief Medications in Children*

Medication	Dosage Form	From Birth to 4 Years	Aged 5–11 Years	Comments
Inhaled Short-Acting ß₂-Agonists				
Albuterol CFC	MDI: 90 mcg/puff, 200 puffs/canister	1–2 puffs 5 minutes before exercise	2 puffs 5 minutes before exercise	Differences in potencies exist, but all products are essentially comparable on a per-puff basis.
Albuterol HFA	MDI: 90 mcg/puff, 200 puffs/canister	2 puffs every 4–6 hours, as needed	2 puffs every 4–6 hours, as needed	An increasing use or lack of expected effect indicates diminished control of asthma. Not recommended for long-term daily treatment. Regular use exceeding two days per week for symptom control (not prevention of EIB) indicates the need for additional long-term control therapy. May double the usual dose for mild exacerbations.
Levalbuterol HFA	MDI: 45 mcg/puff, 200 puffs/canister	Safety and efficacy not established in children younger than 4 years	2 puffs every 4–6 hours, as needed	Should prime the inhaler by releasing four actuations before use. Periodically clean the HFA actuator because the medication may plug the orifice.
Pirbuterol CFC auto-haler	MDI: 200 mcg/puff canister	Safety and efficacy not established	Safety and efficacy not established	Children younger than 4 years may not generate sufficient inspiratory flow to activate an autoinhaler. Nonselective agents (i.e., epinephrine, isoproterenol, and metaproterenol) are not recommended because of their potential for excessive cardiac stimulation, especially in high doses.
Albuterol	Nebulizer solution: 0.63, 1.25, and 2.5 mg/3 mL; and 5 mg/mL (0.5%)	0.63–2.5 mg in 3 mL of saline every 4–6 hours, as needed	1.25–5.00 mg in 3 mL of saline every 4–8 hours, as needed	May mix with cromolyn solution, budesonide inhalant suspension, or ipratropium solution for nebulization. May double dose for severe exacerbations.
Levalbuterol (R-albuterol)	Nebulizer solution: 0.31, 0.63, and 1.25 mg/3 mL; and 1.25 mg/0.5 mL	0.31–1.25 mg in 3 mL every 4–6 hours, as needed	0.31–0.63 mg, every 8 hours, as needed	Does not have FDA-approved labeling for children younger than 6 years. The product is a sterile-filled preservative-free unit dose vial. Compatible with budesonide inhalant suspension.
Anticholinergic Agents				
Ipratropium HFA	MDI: 17 mcg/puff, 200 puffs/canister	Safety and efficacy not established	Safety and efficacy not established	Evidence is lacking for anticholinergics producing added benefit to ß₂-agonists in long-term control asthma therapy.
	Nebulizer solution: 0.25 mg/mL (0.025%)	Safety and efficacy not established	Safety and efficacy not established	
Systemic Corticosteroids				
Methyl-prednisolone	2, 4, 6, 8, 16, and 32 mg tablets	Short-course burst: 1–2 mg/kg per day; maximum, 60 mg/day, for 3–10 days	Short-course burst: 1–2 mg/kg per day; maximum, 60 mg/day, for 3–10 days	Short courses or bursts are effective for establishing control when initiating therapy or during a period of gradual deterioration. The burst should be continued until the patient achieves 80% PEF personal best or symptoms resolve. This usually requires 3–10 days but may require a longer time. There is no evidence that tapering the dose after improvement prevents relapse.

Table 10-4 Usual Dosage for Quick-Relief Medications in Children* *continued*

Medication	Dosage Form	From Birth to 4 Years	Aged 5–11 Years	Comments
Systemic Corticosteroids				
Prednisolone	5 mg tablets, 5 mg/5 mL, and 15 mg/mL	See guidelines for **methyl-prednisolone**.		
Prednisone	1, 2.5, 5, 10, 20, and 50 mg tablets; 5 mg/mL	See guidelines for **methyl-prednisolone**.		
Methyl-prednisolone acetate	Injection: 40 and 80 mg/mL	7.5 mg/kg IM once	240 mg IM once	May be used in place of a short burst of oral steroids in patients who are vomiting or if adherence is a problem.

Note: CFC indicates chloroflurocarbon; EIB, exercise-induced bronchospasm; FDA, Food and Drug Administration; HFA, hydrofluroalkane; IM, intramuscular; MDI, metered-dose inhaler; PEF, peak expiratory flow.

*Dosages are provided for those products that have been approved by the U.S. FDA or have sufficient clinical trial safety and efficacy data in the appropriate age ranges to support their use. Data are taken from National Heart, Lung, and Blood Institute. (2007). *Guidelines for the diagnosis and management of asthma: National Asthma Education Program, Expert Panel Report 3* (p. 37). Washington, DC: U.S. Dept of Health and Human Services, National Institutes of Health. (This document can be retrieved at http://www.nhlbi.nih.gov/guidelines/asthma/08_sec4_lt_0-11.pdf).

- Reassess patients after a dose of inhaled bronchodilator and at least every 60 minutes thereafter. More frequent assessment may be required for severe exacerbations.

- Classify the severity of the asthma exacerbation (**Figure 10-2**).

- Prepare for hospital admission or transfer if the patient's condition does not improve.[9]

Prepare for discharge if the patient's condition has improved and desired outcomes are achieved (peak expiratory flow ≥ 70%, response sustained for 60 minutes after last treatment, no distress, and healthy physical examination findings).[9]

- Review understanding of asthma exacerbations and home management of asthma with caregivers.
  - Medications
  - Dose, frequency, and purpose
  - Have the pediatric patient or caregiver demonstrate the proper use of the nebulizer or metered-dose inhaler and spacer.

- Review measurement of peak expiratory flow.
  - Have the pediatric patient or caregiver demonstrate use of the peak flow meter to ensure proper technique, and review indications for change in the patient's treatment.
  - At home, peak expiratory flow is usually obtained in the morning before bronchodilator therapy and is used to guide the home therapy plan.[9]

- Discuss trigger avoidance with the patient and caregiver.

- Emphasize the need for regular care in an outpatient setting. Refer the patient to a primary care provider.

- Consider the initiation of inhaled corticosteroids.

- Discharge instructions and home teaching should include the following: information about long-term maintenance medications and short-term (rescue) medications and how to complete personal assessment of current asthma status.

- Recommend a follow-up appointment (in one to four weeks) with a primary care provider or asthma specialist.

Respiratory Syncytial Virus and Bronchiolitis

Bronchiolitis is an acute viral infection involving the lower respiratory tract and is most commonly caused by the respiratory syncytial virus (RSV). Infants' symptoms generally worsen for the first three to five days and then gradually improve. The infectious process causes destruction of the lining of the bronchioles, resulting in bronchoconstriction and mucous plugging. Edema and secretions of the lower respiratory tract cause lower airway obstruction gradually. Extensive mucous plugging may progress to atelectasis and pneumonia. It occurs more often in the winter and early spring and usually in pediatric patients younger than one year. Pediatric patients with a history of prematurity and cardiac and pulmonary diseases are at greater risk for severe life-threatening manifestations of the virus. Apnea is one of the most concerning complications of bronchiolitis in young infants.

Additional History

- Symptoms of upper respiratory tract infection.

- Possible known exposure/direct contact with other infants infected with respiratory syncytial virus.

- History of vomiting and poor fluid or food intake.

Figure 10-2 Classifying the Severity of Asthma Exacerbations in the Urgent or Emergency Care Setting*

Note: Patients are instructed to use quick-relief medications if symptoms occur or if PEF drops below 80% predicted or personal best. If PEF is 50–79%, the patient should monitor response to quick-relief medication carefully and consider contacting a clinician. If PEF is below 50%, immediate medical care is usually required. In the urgent or emergency care setting, the following parameters describe the severity and likely clinical course of an exacerbation.

	Symptoms and Signs	Initial PEF (or FEV$_1$)	Clinical Course
Mild	Dyspnea only with activity (assess tachypnea in young children)	PEF ≥ 70% predicted or personal best	• Usually cared for at home • Prompt relief with inhaled SABA • Possible short course of oral systemic corticosteroids
Moderate	Dyspnea interferes with or limits usual activity	PEF 40–69% predicted or personal best	• Usually requires office or ED visit • Relief from frequent inhaled SABA • Oral systemic corticosteroids; some symptoms last for 1–2 days after treatment is begun
Severe	Dyspnea at rest; interferes with conversation	PEF < 40% predicted or personal best	• Usually requires ED visit and likely hospitalization • Partial relief from frequent inhaled SABA • Oral systemic corticosteroids; some symptoms last for > 3 days after treatment is begun • Adjunctive therapies are helpful
Subset: Life-threatening	Too dyspneic to speak; perspiring	PEF < 25% predicted or personal best	• Requires ED/hospitalization; possible ICU • Minimal or no relief from frequent inhaled SABA • Intravenous corticosteroids • Adjunctive therapies are helpful

Note: ED indicates emergency department; FEV$_1$, forced expiratory volume in 1 second; ICU, intensive care unit; PEF, peak expiratory flow; SABA, short-acting ß$_2$-agonist.

*Data are taken from National Heart, Lung, and Blood Institute. (2007). *Guidelines for the diagnosis and management of asthma: National Asthma Education Program, Expert Panel Report 3*. Washington, DC: U.S. Dept of Health and Human Services, National Institutes of Health.

• Preexisting conditions, such as chronic pulmonary insufficiency, congenital heart disease, or pulmonary hypertension.

Signs and Symptoms
• Rhinorrhea
• Pharyngitis
• Coughing/sneezing
• Tachypnea
• Retractions
• Wheezing and a prolonged expiratory phase
• Decreased air entry or exchange
• Volume depletion secondary to decreased oral intake
• Apnea spells
• Low-grade fever common in early infection

Additional Interventions
• Suction nose to clear secretions and open the airway for infants who are obligate nose breathers.

• Place in enhanced contact isolation, to include use of masks, gowns, and goggles.

• May obtain a nasopharyngeal swab or aspirate specimen for RSV testing if concerned about isolation and sharing rooms on admission. Otherwise, diagnosis is made by clinical exam, based on presence of signs and symptoms.

• Administer medications as ordered. Respiratory syncytial virus management is usually directed toward symptoms and supportive care. The routine use of bronchodilators or corticosteroids is controversial and is not recommended. Nebulized hypertonic saline may reduce the length of inpatient hospitalizations.[11] Current evidence does not support the use of ribavirin, an antiviral agent with limited efficacy and has been associated with adverse effects for both patient and provider. Palivizumab, an immunization for RSV, has been effective for high-risk infants or young children with chronic lung or heart disease or prematurity.[12]

Pertussis

Pertussis, commonly referred to as whooping cough, is a highly contagious acute bacterial infection caused by *Bordetella pertussis*. Before the availability of the pertussis vaccine in the 1940s, more than 200,000 cases were reported annually in the United States. The incidence of pertussis has been gradually increasing since the 1980s, with 10,454 cases reported in 2007, which included 10 pediatric deaths.[13] This disease has an incubation period of seven to 10 days and is characterized by three phases: the catarrhal stage, the paroxysmal stage, and the convalescent stage. An insidious onset of nasal secretions, low-grade fever, and mild occasional cough characterizes the catarrhal stage. The cough becomes more severe over one to two weeks, and the paroxysmal stage begins. This stage of the disease is when pertussis is usually first suspected and is characterized by the following symptoms (which all occur more frequently at night):

- Paroxysms of numerous rapid coughs secondary to thick mucus in the tracheobronchial tree

- Long inspiratory effort with high-pitched whoop

- Cyanosis (which may occur during a paroxysm)

- Vomiting and fatigue after each episode

The paroxysmal stage usually lasts one to six weeks, followed by gradual recovery or the convalescent stage, which occurs over two to three weeks. Complications associated with pertussis that occur most frequently in infants and young children include the following: pneumonia, hypoxia, apnea, seizures, encephalopathy, and malnutrition.

Additional History

- Nonimmunized or underimmunized status

- Recent upper respiratory tract infection symptoms

Signs and Symptoms

- Paroxysmal spasms of coughing

- Ill and distressed appearance when coughing

- Appears normal when not coughing

- Infants younger than six months may not exhibit the whoop, but paroxysms of coughing are present.[14]

Additional Interventions

- Droplet precautions

- Supportive care. Include oxygen and fluids as needed.

- Administer medications as ordered. Erythromycin is the antibiotic of choice and may be given to all close contacts.[15]

- Counsel caregivers about the need to obtain a booster or begin immunizations for others in the home, especially when a newborn is in the home.

Pneumonia

Pneumonia is a lower respiratory tract infection caused by a viral, bacterial, parasitic, or fungal organism.[16] Most pneumonias in pediatric patients are viral. Pneumonia can occur in any age group and can vary in etiology and severity, depending on the child's age and immune status. It may be a primary condition or may result secondary to other respiratory problems, such as asthma or bronchiolitis. It presents as an acute inflammatory reaction in the lung tissue. As fluid and cellular debris accumulate in the areas of infection, compliance and vital capacity decrease and work of breathing increases.

Additional History

- Worsening of symptoms of upper respiratory tract infection

- Abrupt onset of fever and chills with bacterial pneumonia

- History of vomiting and poor fluid or food intake

- Preexisting conditions, such as chronic pulmonary insufficiency, congenital heart disease, or pulmonary hypertension

Signs and Symptoms

- Cough

- Tachypnea

- Grunting

- Unequal breath sounds

- Crackles

- Wheezes

- Retractions

- Chest pain

- Apnea spells

- Fever

- Abdominal pain is more common in children with lower lobe pneumonia and may include abdominal distension and tenderness.

Additional Interventions

Administer antimicrobial medications as ordered.

Home Equipment

Tracheostomy Tubes

A tracheostomy is a surgical opening into the trachea at the level of the cricoid cartilage. Indications for tracheostomy in the pediatric patient may be for a chronic condition such as tracheomalacia, Pierre Robin syndrome, or long-term ventilatory support. Emergent conditions that may require a tracheostomy are an upper airway obstruction, epiglottitis, or trauma. **Table 10-5** delineates some of the tracheostomy tubes commonly used in pediatrics. **Figure 10-3** and **Figure 10-4** show some of these tubes and an example of the Passy-Muir speaking valve, respectively.

Tracheostomy tubes may be metal, plastic, or silicone and may be cuffed, uncuffed, or fenestrated.[16] Metal tubes are used infrequently and have a removable inner cannula. Plastic tubes are more commonly used in pediatrics and usually do not have an inner cannula. Plastic tracheostomy tubes may be equipped with an adaptor for easy connection to standard bag-mask devices. Most pediatric tracheostomy tubes are uncuffed. Fenestrated tracheostomy tubes have openings in the tube that allow the patient to be able to talk when the distal opening of the tube is occluded. Infants and older children may have a Passy-Muir valve or other speaking valves that redirect air flow and allow the patient to vocalize or speak.

The size of the tracheostomy tube is usually marked on both the package and the flanges of each tube. The size refers to the inner diameter of the tube. In addition, tubes are marked as neonatal, pediatric, or adult. This designation

Figure 10-3 Disposable Cuffless Tracheostomy and Fenestrated Tracheostomy Tube

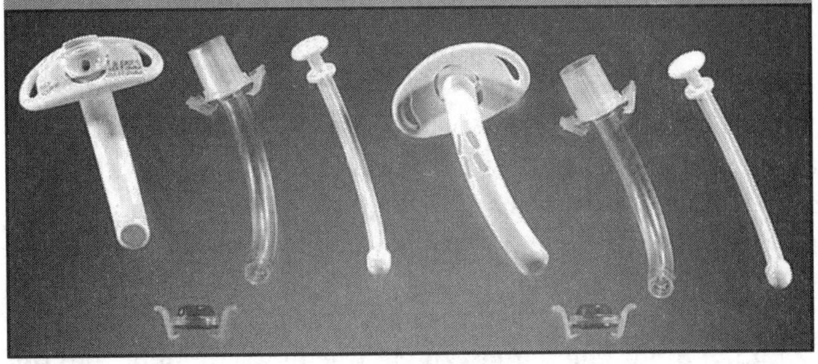

Reprinted with permission from Nellcor Puritan Bennett, Inc.

Figure 10-4 Passy-Muir Speaking Valves

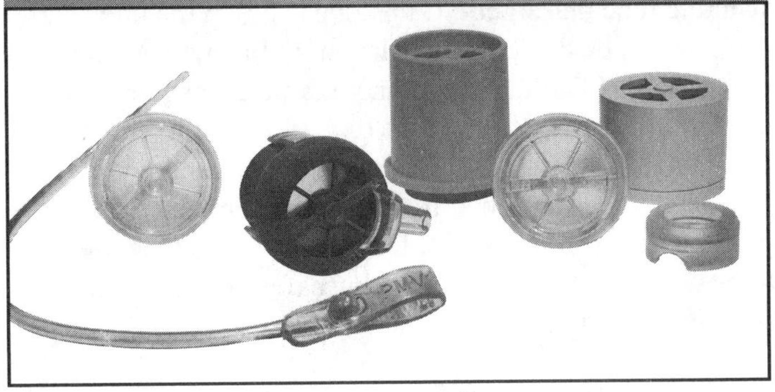

Reprinted with permission from Passy-Muir, Inc.

Table 10-5 Tracheostomy Tubes Commonly Used in Pediatrics*

	Tube Manufacturer	Tube Features	Age: Preterm (Birth Minus One Month)		1–6 Months	6–18 Months	18 Months to 3 Years	3–6 Years	6–9 Years	9–12 Years	12–14 Years
		Trachea diameter, mm		5	5–6	6–7	7–8	8–9	9–10	10–13	13
Plastic	Shiley († cuffed tube available)	Size		3.0	3.5	4.0	4.5	5.0	5.5	6.0	6.5
Plastic	Shiley	Length (mm) Neonatal		30	32	34	36				
Plastic	Shiley	Pediatric		39	40	41†	42†	44†	46†		
Plastic	Portex	Size		2.5	3.0	3.5	4.0	4.5	5.0	5.5	
Plastic	Portex	Length Neonatal		30	32	34	36				
Plastic	Portex	Pediatric		30	36	40	44	48	50	52	
Plastic	Bivona (all sizes available with a cuff)	Size	2.5	3.0	3.5	4.0	4.5	5.0	5.0		
Plastic	Bivona	Length Neonatal	30	32	34	36					
Plastic	Bivona	Pediatric	38	39	40	41	42	44	46		
Metal	Chevailer Jackson	French gauge		14	16	18	20	22	24	26	28
Metal	Sheffield	French gauge		12–14	16	18	20	22	24	26	
Metal	Sheffield	Internal diameter, mm		2.9 –3.6	4.2	4.9	6.0	6.3	7.0	7.6	

*Data are taken from Tweedie, D. J., Skilbeck, C. J., Cochrane, L. A., Cooke, J., Wyatt, M. E. (2008). Choosing a pediatric tracheostomy tube: An update on current practice. *The Journal of Laryngology and Otology, 122,* 161–169.

refers to the length of the tube. Thus, a size 3.5 mm neonatal tube has the same inner diameter as a size 3.5 mm pediatric tube, but the neonatal tube is shorter. In pediatric patients who breathe spontaneously, tracheostomy tubes may have special attachments designed to protect the patient's airway. A tracheostomy "nose" is a filtration device that keeps particulate matter out of the airway and also supplies humidification as the tracheostomy bypasses the usual humidification function of the nose.

Displacement of the tube may be assessed first by visualizing the tube. The flanges of the tracheostomy tube should be at skin level; any tubing additional to that which is external to the stoma indicates a displaced tube. An exhaled CO_2 detector may also be used as one method to assess for accurate tube placement. If the tube is not in the trachea, no CO_2 will be detected on exhalation. In an emergency, a standard ETT of the same inner diameter may be used instead of a tracheostomy tube (e.g., for a child with a size 4 French tracheal tube, use a size 4 mm ETT, although it will need to be shortened from the distal end once proper placement is confirmed.[17] If the tracheostomy tube needs to be replaced, the size the child usually uses, and one size smaller, should be readily available.

Replacement of the Tracheostomy Tube

Extend the child's neck or place a rolled towel under the child's shoulders to expose the stoma. Insert the tube using a downward forward motion to follow the normal curve of the trachea.[14] If the tube does not pass easily, attempt passage with a tube one size smaller. Assess placement with at least two confirmatory measures: auscultation (equal rise and fall of the chest) and/or verification of placement via use of an exhaled CO_2 detector. When the tube is properly placed, there should be minimal bleeding and no signs of subcutaneous emphysema.

Obstruction of the tube should be suspected when a child with a tracheostomy tube presents with fever, cough, and thick secretions; decreased breath sounds bilaterally; or decreased chest rise and fall. Attempts to ventilate a pediatric patient with an obstructed tube will yield minimal to no chest rise and fall, absent breath sounds, and resistance to manual ventilation. Once an obstruction is suspected, immediately remove the patient from the ventilator and attempt manual ventilation. To evaluate for tube obstruction, extend the patient's neck for easy access and visualization of the stoma/tube insertion site. Ventilate the patient using a bag-mask device with supplemental oxygen if complete obstruction is not present. Suction the tube using a prop-

erly sized suction catheter to remove secretions that may be causing an obstruction. Thick mucous plugs may not be able to be cleared with suction, and the tracheostomy tube will need to be replaced after the procedure previously described. Prolonged suctioning may lead to hypoxia and bradycardia, which may be prevented with supplemental breaths using a bag-mask device with supplemental oxygen.

Once airway patency has been confirmed, ventilations may need to be assisted until such time as the patient's breathing pattern and oxygenation returns to baseline. Caregivers should have received appropriate teaching before this event; however, confirmation of their knowledge needs to occur before discharge.

Apnea Monitors

The use of home apnea monitoring continues to be a source of investigation by clinicians.[18] To our knowledge, there are no studies that document a decrease in mortality as the result of sudden infant death syndrome (with use of these monitors).[19] Home apnea monitoring may be prescribed for infants who are deemed at risk for apnea of prematurity, apnea of infancy, and infants who have experienced an apparent life threatening event. Apnea is defined as cessation of breathing for 20 seconds or more.[20] Although there are many different types of home apnea monitors, most are designed to evaluate respiratory and cardiac rhythms and to sound an alarm at predetermined levels, usually for apnea or bradycardia. Hypoxia is the most common cause of bradycardia in pediatric patients. Diminished oxygen delivery results in slowing of the cardiac conduction system and subsequent bradycardia. Stimulation of the infant may increase respiratory effort; however, some infants may require supplemental oxygen and ventilation to reduce the bradycardic event.

Pediatric patients using home apnea monitors may present to the emergency department after a monitor alarm. Home apnea monitors use conventional impedance monitoring, which is subject to false alarms because of shallow breathing or normal cardiac variability. Caregivers may experience stress when these alarms are activated at times that they are not in the room with the child and they are unsure about exactly what occurred. Although there are false alarms with these monitors, when used, they are intended to detect an apneic or bradycardic episode. Each alarm should result in an assessment of the infant's status; when the infant does appear in distress, an evaluation by a healthcare professional should be performed.

Ventilators

Home ventilation is most commonly used for patients who have a stable cardiopulmonary status but are unable to provide adequate ventilatory effort on their own. It is most commonly required in pediatric patients with chronic lung disease, neuromuscular disorders, head and spinal cord injuries, and conditions that cause chronic respiratory failure. The most common type of home ventilator is a positive-pressure ventilator.

Any patient who develops acute respiratory distress while on a ventilator should be removed from the ventilator and have ventilations assisted via a bag-mask device while an assessment about the cause of the distress ensues and reversible causes are addressed. These settings can vary based on age, weight, and condition.

Health Promotion

- Provide anticipatory guidance on childproofing the environment to avoid aspiration of small objects.
- Encourage caregivers to obtain training in basic pediatric life support techniques.

- Instruct caregivers to protect young children from foods or objects that commonly cause airway obstruction.
- Provide caregivers with information on childhood immunizations, especially pertussis and *Haemophilus influenzae* vaccines, and the importance of keeping the pediatric patient up-to-date. Provide referral and resources for immunizations, as appropriate.
- For pediatric patients with asthma, provide information regarding precipitating triggers to avoid, such as allergens of all types.
- Instruct caregivers to administer medication to their children as ordered by their primary care provider.
- Use standardized asthma teaching sheets with information about long-term versus rescue bronchodilator therapies, use of spacers, and peak flow devices.
- Provide referral or information on obtaining a primary care provider if one is not already established.
- Ensure that caregivers have home resources to include basic supplies for technology-dependent pediatric patients, such as suction catheters for patients using home ventilators.

Summary

This chapter has outlined the pediatric patient's unique responses to respiratory problems because of specific anatomical, physiological, and developmental characteristics. Respiratory compromise in pediatric patients can occur during upper and lower respiratory tract infections, when they receive sedation for procedures, from musculoskeletal deformities, or even from congenital anomalies. Selective respiratory emergencies, including croup, epiglottitis, foreign body aspiration, asthma, bronchiolitis and RSV, pertussis, and pneumonia, have been reviewed. An overview of assistive technology for the child receiving chronic respiratory care needs has been provided.

Respiratory distress is part of a continuum that results in respiratory failure if left untreated, and respiratory failure is the most common pathway to cardiopulmonary arrest in pediatric patients. Further interventions for the pediatric patient with respiratory compromise have been delineated in this section. In addition, suggestions for health promotion strategies directed at altering the adverse outcomes of respiratory distress and failure have been offered. A collaborative systematic approach to care reduces fragmentation and enhances the opportunity to improve outcome. Caregiver education and health promotion are essential strategies to ensure optimal outcomes for the pediatric patient.

References

1. Health Resource and Service Administration's Maternal and Child Health Bureau. (2009). *Child health USA 2008-2009.* Retrieved from http://mchb.hrsa.gov/chusa08/hsfu/pages/309edu.html

2. Topjian, A. A., Nadkarni, V. M., Berg, R.A. (2009). Cardiopulmonary resuscitation in children. *Current Opinion in Critical Care, 15,* 203–208.

3. Hansen, M. (1998). *Pathophysiology foundations of disease and clinical intervention* (pp. 454–456). Philadelphia, PA: WB Saunders Co.

4. Hueckel, R., & Wilson, D. (2007). The child with disturbance of oxygen and carbon dioxide exchange. In M. J. Hockenberry & D. Wilson (Eds.), *Wong's nursing care of infants and children* (8th ed.). St. Louis, MO: Mosby–Year Book.

5. Ralston, M., Hazinski, M. F., Zaritsky, A. L., Schexnayder, S. M., & Kleinman, M. E. (Eds.). (2006). *Textbook of pediatric advanced life support* (pp. 40–41). Dallas, TX: American Heart Association.

6. Newth, C. J., Rachman, B., Patel, N., Hammer, J. (2004). The use of cuffed versus uncuffed endotracheal tubes in pediatric intensive care. *Journal of Pediatrics, 144,* 333–337.

7. Advanced Trauma Life Support. (2004). *Extremes of age: Pediatric trauma: Student manual* (7th ed.). Chicago, IL: American College of Surgeons' Committee on Trauma.

8. Centers for Disease Control and Prevention. (2009). *Beyond 20/20 Web data server: Public reports: Health conditions: Asthma and chronic obstructive pulmonary disease.* Retrieved from http://205.207.175.93/HDI/ReportFolders/reportFolders.aspx

9. U.S. Department of Health and Human Services. (2007). *Guidelines for the diagnosis and management of asthma: National Asthma Education Program, Expert Panel Report 3* (pp. 99–405). Washington, DC: National Institutes of Health.

10. National Heart, Lung, and Blood Institute (NHLBI). (2007). *Expert Panel Report 3 (EPR3): Guidelines for the diagnosis and management of asthma.* Retrieved from http://www.nhlbi.nih.gov/guidelines/asthma/asthgdln.htm

11. Zorc, J. J, & Breese Hall, C. (2010). Bronchiolitis: recent evidence on diagnosis and management. *Pediatrics, 125,* 342–349.

12. American Academy of Pediatrics. (2006). Diagnosis and management of bronchiolitis. *Pediatrics, 118,* 1774–1793.

13. Centers for Disease Control and Prevention. (n.d.). *Pertussis.* Retrieved from http://www.cdc.gov/ncidod/dbmd/diseaseinfo/pertussis_t.htm

14. Hueckel, R., & Wilson, D. (2007). The child with respiratory dysfunction. In M. J. Hockenberry & D. Wilson (Eds.), *Wong's nursing care of infants and children* (8th ed.). St. Louis, MO: Mosby–Year Book.

15. Hockenberry, M. J., & Creamer, L. (2011). Health problems of early childhood. In M. J. Hockenberry & D. Wilson (Eds.), *Wong's nursing care of infants and children* (9th ed., pp. 607–643). St. Louis, MO: Elsevier Mosby.

16. Hansen, M. (1998). *Pathophysiology foundations of disease and clinical intervention* (pp. 499–501). Philadelphia, PA: WB Saunders Co.

17. Bissel, C. (2004). *Types of tracheostomy tubes.* Retrieved from http://www.tracheostomy.com/faq/types.htm

18. Silvestri, J. M. (2009). Indications for home apnea monitoring (or not). *Clinics in Perinatology, 36,* 87–99.

19. American Academy of Pediatrics. (2003). Apnea, sudden infant death syndrome and home monitoring. *Pediatrics, 111,* 914–917.

20. Wilson, D. (2007). Health problems during infancy. In M. J. Hockenberry & D. Wilson (Eds.), *Wong's nursing care of infants and children* (8th ed., p. 602). St. Louis, MO: Mosby–Year Book.

Chapter 11 | Childhood Illness

David Golder, BS, RN, CEN, CPEN

Objectives

On completion of this chapter, the learner should be able to do the following:

- Determine anatomical, physiological, and developmental characteristics of pediatric patients as a basis for assessment of childhood illness signs and symptoms.
- Describe common causes and characteristics associated with childhood illnesses.
- Plan appropriate interventions for pediatric patients with selected childhood illnesses.
- Indicate health promotion strategies related to illness prevention.

Introduction

Pediatric patients who seek care at emergency departments have a variety of chief complaints that can be broadly classified as medical. Fever, ear pain, vomiting, sore throat, and rashes are just a few of the common presenting complaints. Although it is true that most of these symptoms are minor and self-limiting, they may be part of a more complex medical issue that, if left untreated, may affect morbidity and even mortality. For children younger than three years, illness-related symptoms are the most common reason for emergency department visits in the United States.

Focused Assessment

Chapter 5, "Initial Assessment," provides a detailed review of the initial assessment of the pediatric patient. Additional assessment data, signs and symptoms, and additional interventions are discussed with each selected emergency.

Planning and Implementation

- Diagnostic procedures
  - Radiographic studies
    - Radiographs and selected imaging studies may be indicated based on the child's clinical status and evaluation. Specific diagnostic studies and additional interventions are discussed for each selected emergency, as appropriate.
  - Laboratory studies
    - Specific laboratory studies should be performed depending on the appearance of the pediatric patient, the patient's medical history and signs and symptoms, and the absence of an identified source of infection. Specific laboratory studies are discussed for each selected emergency.

Interventions

- Monitor vital signs, including temperature.
  - Avoid rectal temperatures and rectal suppositories in a child who is immunocompromised, who has a history of any disorder of coagulation, or for whom there is concern for sexual assault.
- Ensure universal precautions.
- Initiate appropriate isolation measures.
- Administer antipyretics as indicated and ordered.
- Anticipate the need for fluid volume restoration, medications, and blood products.

Analysis and Expected Outcomes

The results of the medical history, physical examination, and diagnostic procedures will assist with the development of a management plan for each specific patient. The pediatric patient with a serious or life-threatening illness requires frequent reassessment and evaluation for clinical improvement or deterioration. The potential for deterioration of airway, breathing, circulation, and neurological status is real, warranting early recognition and intervention. To evaluate the patient's response to interventions, monitor the following variables:

- Airway patency
- Breathing effectiveness
- Presence of pulse, pulse quality, and capillary refill
- Level of consciousness and interaction with the caregiver
- Urinary output
- Presence and level of pain
- Cardiac rhythm
- Oxygen saturation

Selected Emergencies

Fever

Fever is the single most common complaint of pediatric patients presenting to the emergency department, accounting for up to 30% of all pediatric outpatient visits.[1] Fever represents a normal physiological response that plays a role in defending the body from infectious pathogens.

Both the evaluation and management of the febrile pediatric patient have changed dramatically during the past decade for the following reasons: (a) increasing evidence-based knowledge, (b) introduction of the *Haemophilus influenzae type b* vaccine, and (c) introduction of the *Streptococcus pneumoniae* vaccine. Although the true impact of the introduction of these vaccines is not yet known, it is hypothesized that the incidence of significant bacterial infections in children will diminish.

Fever is defined as a body temperature higher than the usual range of normal, typically thought of as higher than 38°C or 100.4°F when measured rectally, although differences in institutional definitions may exist. The duration and severity of the fever may provide clues to the cause, but the degree of fever does not reflect the severity of illness. In addition, many seriously ill infants and children are normothermic or hypothermic, rather than febrile.

Institutional policy and clinical judgment must be considered when choosing the most appropriate route for temperature measurement. In some instances, the least invasive route may be chosen. In other instances, a more accurate measure will be required. In most emergency departments, the options for temperature measurement include the following: auditory canal (tympanic), axillary, oral, rectal, or temporal artery probe. In general, the rectal route most accurately measures core body temperature. However, in children with diminished immunity, diarrhea, or suspected bleeding disorders, rectal temperatures should be avoided.

The presence of fever on presentation, or fever reported at home, may influence triage and treatment decisions in pediatric patients who are at increased risk for sepsis or other serious illness. This includes infants younger than 90 days, immunocompromised patients, patients with a chronic illness, and children younger than two years without a readily identified source of infection.

Although fever itself is not an emergency, the febrile state does affect physiological function. Fever will contribute to increased basal metabolic rate, glucose use, oxygen use, insensible fluid loss, heart rate, and respiratory rate. Reducing fever through cooling measures and antipyretics frequently contributes to increased comfort and reduced physiological demands in the seriously ill pediatric patient and increases the validity of physiological measures in diagnostic interpretation.

Specific Diagnostic Studies

- Laboratory studies
  - Complete blood cell count (CBC) with differential
  - Electrolyte levels
  - Blood glucose level
  - Urinalysis with culture
  - Blood and throat cultures
  - Cerebrospinal fluid (CSF) culture
- Radiographic studies
  - Chest

Additional Interventions

- Administration of antipyretic therapy, as ordered and indicated.
- A possible septic workup for the febrile infant younger than 90 days.
- Administration of fluids (oral, subcutaneous, or intravenous) based on the patient's need.

Dehydration

Dehydration results from fluid loss in excess of intake. The most common cause of dehydration in the pediatric patient is gastrointestinal, such as vomiting and diarrhea.

Other causes may include diabetes mellitus, starvation, or third spacing of fluids.

There are a number of unique characteristics of the pediatric patient that increase susceptibility to dehydration. These include the following:

- Relatively more total body water than an adult.

  ○ The young infant has an increased volume of interstitial fluid, leading to total body water accounting for approximately 75% of body weight. This trend persists until the child is approximately aged three years. In comparison, the average adult has approximately 60% to 70% of his or her total body weight accounted for by total body water. Most of this extra body water in the young is contained within the interstitial fluid and provides a larger reserve. However, the increased body surface area and basal metabolic rate in young children hasten fluid depletion.

- Relatively higher basal metabolic rate than an adult.

  ○ Infants and young children have a relatively high basal metabolic rate and large body surface area to volume ratio, which produces more heat and leads to increased insensible fluid loss.

  ○ In the very young, renal filtration rates are low, leading to a proportionate increase in urine production to excrete waste products. The net result of these factors is that the daily turnover of body water in an infant is approximately five times that of an adult.

  ○ The pediatric patient with dehydration may present with a variety of symptoms based on the severity of fluid loss, associated electrolyte abnormalities, and causative agent. The degree of dehydration in pediatric patients is often expressed as mild, moderate, and severe. Mild dehydration is considered as less than 5% of body weight loss; moderate dehydration, 5% to 10% of body weight loss; and severe dehydration, 10% to 15% of body weight loss. **Table 11-1** correlates the degree of dehydration with associated signs and symptoms.

Specific Diagnostic Studies

- Laboratory studies may include the following: blood glucose and electrolyte levels, CBC with differential, stool for culture and sensitivity assays, ova and parasite analyses, and a gram stain

- Electrocardiogram (EKG) to monitor for dysrhythmias

Additional Interventions

- Initiate oral rehydration therapy by providing a solution that contains glucose and sodium (e.g., Pedialyte or Infalyte) in small (5 mL) volumes every two to five minutes.

- In more severe cases, or when oral rehydration therapy fails, subcutaneous or intravascular fluid replacement therapy may be required. **Chapter 9, "Vascular Access,"** provides more information.

- Monitor fluid intake, urinary output, and the patient's body weight in relation to recent actual weight as indicators of hydration status.

- Anticipate the need for electrolyte replacement.

- Monitor the patient's neurological status.

- Consider hospital admission if rehydration attempts fail or if a severe electrolyte abnormality is present.

Table 11-1 Clinical Findings by Degree of Dehydration*

Symptoms	Degree of Dehydration		
	Mild	**Moderate**	**Severe**
Weight loss (infant and young), %	1–5	5–10	10–15
Eyes	Normal	Sunken	Sunken and dry
Mucous membranes	Moist	Dry	Very dry
Skin color	Normal	Normal to pale	Pale and mottled
Skin turgor	Normal	Decreased	Tenting
Pulse	Normal	Rapid	Rapid
Systolic blood pressure	Normal	Normal to low	Low
Urine output	Normal	Decreased	Decreased to anuric
Mentation	Normal	Normal to lethargic	Lethargic to unresponsive
Fontanel	Normal	Sunken	Sunken

*Data are taken from Soud, T. E., & Rogers, J. S. (1998). *Manual of pediatric emergency nursing* (p. 316). St Louis, MO: Mosby–Year Book.

Dermatological Disorders

Rashes are common complaints seen in the pediatric patient presenting to the emergency department. A comprehensive medical history and physical examination are often needed to identify skin disorders. Assessment includes a thorough inspection of the skin and accurate description of the location, size, shape, color, and distribution of the lesions. The appropriate terminology for documentation is in **Table 11-2**.

Rashes are often associated with a systemic illness **(Table 11-3)**. Although the incidence of some of these diseases has dropped with immunization, many cases are still reported annually. Any nonblanching skin rash requires immediate attention.

Specific Diagnostic Studies
- CBC with differential
- Serological analyses
- Coagulation studies (prothrombin time or international normalized ratio and partial thromboplastin time)
- Titers if a child has been immunized
- Blood cultures and lumbar puncture if indicated

Additional Interventions
- Institute appropriate isolation (contact, droplet, or respiratory) precautions.

Table 11-2 Type of Lesion and Description*

Type of Lesion	Description (Diameter in Centimeters)
Macule	Flat and discolored skin lesion (< 1)
Papule	Elevated and discolored skin lesion (< 1)
Wheal	Flat-topped and discolored lesion (> 1)
Cyst	Elevated and thick-walled lesion, containing fluid
Vesicle	Elevated skin lesion, containing serous fluid (< 1)
Pustule	Elevated lesion, containing purulent fluid
Petechiae	Dark red or purplish discolorations that do not blanch when pressed (< 1)
Purpura	Petechiae (> 1)
Ulcer	Concave lesion characterized by loss of epidermis and dermis
Excoriation	Superficial abrasion

*Data are adapted from the following sources: (1) Brady, W., Perron, A., & Martin, M. (2004). Disorders of the skin. In J. E. Tintanelli, G. Kelen, & S. Stapczynski (Eds.), *Emergency medicine: A comprehensive study guide* (6th ed.) (pp. 1507–1536). New York, NY: McGraw-Hill. (2) Soud, T. E., & Rogers, J. S. (1998). *Manual of pediatric emergency nursing* (p. 420). St Louis, MO: Mosby–Year Book.

Table 11-3 Common Rashes and Their Infectious Source*

Disease	Causative Agent/ Incubation Days	Prodromal Period	Clinical Presentation
Roseola	Human herpesvirus 6/ 9 to 10	Two or three days of fever	Faint, pink papular rash with rhinorrhea; cervical lymphadenopathy; cough
Erythema Infectiosum (fifth disease)	Human parvovirus B19/ 13 to 18	Low grade fever, malaise	Red or "slapped-cheek" appearance to face; diffuse, lacy pink rash begins on extremities, then chest and abdomen; symmetric arthritis of hands, wrists, and knees
Scarlet fever	Streptococcus group A/ 2 to 4	Streptococcal pharyngitis and lymphadenopathy	Sudden onset of sore throat, fever, nausea, vomiting, headache; scarletina rash with sandpaper appearance and feel, first in the creases, then becomes generalized; may develop petechiae and strawberry tongue; skin on fingers and toes peels as rash disappears
Rubeola (measles)	Paramyxovirus/ 10 to 14	Three to four days of high fever, URI symptoms, and Koplik spots	Reddened macular popular rash, begins on face and progresses downward; lesions often become confluent; high fever; photophobia; cough
Rubella (German measles)	RNA virus and Rubivirus/ 14 to 21	No fever to low-grade fever, malaise, sore throat, and URI symptoms	Pink maculopapular rash with downward progression from the face, usually resolving in three days
Varicella (chickenpox)	Varicella zoster/ 14 to 21	Slight fever and malaise for 24 hours	Pruritic rash, progressing from macules to papules to vesicles that break and form crusts; lesion in all stages present; begins centrally, spreads to face and extremities; fever; lymphadenopathy
Hand-foot-and-mouth disease	Coxsackie virus/ 3 to 6	One to two days of low-grade fever, malaise, sore throat, and vomiting	Small oval vesicles on hands, feet, and mucous membranes of the mouth

Note: RNA indicates ribonucleic acid; URI, upper respiratory tract infection.
*Data are taken from Soud, T. E., & Rogers, J. S. (1998). *Manual of pediatric emergency nursing* (pp. 425–427). St Louis, MO: Mosby–Year Book.

- Provide comfort measures.
- Prevent complications through early diagnosis and appropriate intervention.
- Provide family and patient education.

Infectious Disorders

Gastroenteritis

Vomiting and diarrhea are common complaints in the pediatric population and may be symptoms of many conditions. One of the most common causes of these complaints is a viral infection. Typical pathogens include rotavirus, adenovirus, Norwalk virus, and enterovirus; all of these are transmitted via direct contact. Children who live in crowded and impoverished or less hygienic conditions have an increased risk of contracting these diseases. Typical signs and symptoms of gastroenteritis include fever, nausea, vomiting, and diarrhea. Based on the severity and duration of the symptoms, the patient may demonstrate signs of dehydration and/or electrolyte imbalance.

Specific Diagnostic Studies

- Electrolyte studies
- Stool culture and sensitivity for pathogen identification

Additional Interventions

- Antiemetic medication
- Rehydration based on clinical presentation

Caregiver Education

- Good hand washing

Meningitis

Meningitis is an inflammation of the membranes that cover the brain and spinal cord. It is typically caused by viral or bacterial pathogens. The most common organisms involved vary with the age of the pediatric patient. In the newborn, a *Streptococcus agalactiae* (group B streptococcus) prevails. In the older child, *Neisseria meningitidis* and *H. influenzae* predominate. The number of cases has dropped with the introduction of the *Haemophilus influenzae* type B (HIB) vaccine.

Viral meningitis is often referred to as aseptic meningitis, with a relatively low rate of morbidity and mortality. Bacterial meningitis is potentially life threatening and is associated with a high mortality rate if untreated.

Acute complications of meningitis include seizures and a syndrome of inappropriate antidiuretic hormone release (SIADH). Long-term sequelae most often result from damage to the central nervous system, manifesting in hearing loss, epilepsy, hydrocephalus, and learning and behavioral difficulties.

Signs and symptoms of meningitis in pediatric patients are variable, based on age and infecting organism. Overall, younger children exhibit less specific symptoms. **Table 11-4** summarizes key physical findings suggestive of meningitis by age.

Specific Diagnostic Studies

- Laboratory studies
  - CBC with differential
  - Serum glucose and electrolyte levels
  - Blood culture
  - Urine for urinalysis and culture

Table 11-4 Signs and Symptoms of Meningitis by Age*

Age < 90 Days	Age 90 Days to 2 Years	Age > 2 Years
Seizures	Seizures	Seizures
Petechiae and purpura	Petechiae and purpura	Petechiae and purpura
Vomiting	Vomiting	Fever
Bulging fontanel	Bulging fontanel	Stiff neck
Altered level of consciousness	Altered mental status	Altered mental status
Apnea and cyanosis	Stiff neck	Headache
Temperature instability	Fever	
History of decreased feeding	Ataxia	
Irritability		

*Data are adapted from Mellis, P. (2004). Bacteremia, sepsis and meningitis. In J. E. Tintanelli, G. Kelen, & S. Stapczynski (Eds.), *Emergency medicine: A comprehensive study guide* (6th ed.) (pp. 735–741). New York, NY: McGraw-Hill.

○ CSF for cell count, culture, protein, glucose, and gram stain

- Radiographic imaging

○ There is a potential need for radiographic imaging if there is a concern of elevated intracranial pressure (ICP).

Additional Interventions

- Initiate appropriate isolation precautions.
- Obtain vascular access early.
- Anticipate the need for fluid administration.
- Anticipate early administration of antibiotics.

If a prompt lumbar puncture cannot be performed, the administration of an appropriate antibiotic should be initiated without the diagnostic procedure.

Meningococcemia

Meningococcemia is a potentially life-threatening condition, caused by *N. meningitidis* entering the bloodstream. The clinical manifestations of meningococcemia are quite varied and may occur with or without meningitis. The primary presentation is with a nonblanching, petechial rash with fever, along with any or all of the signs of meningitis. Meningococcemia may be fulminating, with a rapid onset of symptoms and death within hours, if untreated, from progressive shock. The ultimate prognosis and outcome depend on the patient's immunological status, splenic function, severity of infection, and promptness of appropriate medical care. Complications may include disseminated intravascular coagulation, arthritis, pleurisy, vasculitis, septic shock, and pericarditis.[2]

Specific Diagnostic Studies

- Blood cultures
- Cerebrospinal fluid (CSF) for culture, gram stain, cell count, and protein and glucose levels
- Coagulation studies
- Fibrinogen split products/D-dimer

Additional Interventions

- Initiate appropriate isolation precautions.
- Start antibiotics early.
- Manage the shock state early.
- Initiate cardiopulmonary monitoring.
- Monitor for signs of disseminated intravascular coagulopathy, and anticipate the potential need for clotting factor replacement.
- Anticipate the potential need for inotropic and/or vasopressor agents for blood pressure support.

- Make an appropriate incidence report to local and state health departments, as defined by your institution's policy.

Neurological Disorders

Seizures

Seizures are the most common pediatric neurological problem encountered in the emergency department. Seizures are symptomatic of central nervous system or systemic dysfunction and may be representative of an acute or chronic condition. Febrile seizures are convulsions in infants and children induced by fever, which is the most common cause of seizures in the pediatric population. Although the exact mechanism by which fever causes a seizure is not well-known, most children with febrile seizures have rectal temperatures higher than 38.9°C (102°F).

However, other causes of seizures include metabolic disturbances, toxin exposure, and trauma. Approximately 5% of all children will experience a seizure during childhood. The clinical manifestations of a seizure vary widely, depending on the location of cortical irritability, the amount and duration of electrical discharge, and the age of the child. **Table 11-5** provides a comparison of the types of seizures and symptoms.

Most childhood seizures are single, generalized, tonic-clonic events lasting only a few minutes. A seizure lasting longer than 15 minutes is considered prolonged. *Status epilepticus* is defined as continuous seizure activity or recurrent seizures without a period of recovery, lasting longer than 30 minutes. Prolonged seizure activity may result in airway obstruction, hypoxia, acidosis, elevated ICP, hypoglycemia, and hyperthermia. If the seizure is not terminated, respiratory and cardiovascular collapse can ensue.[3]

Specific Diagnostic Studies

- Laboratory studies

○ Electrolyte levels, including bedside glucose level

○ CBC

○ Lumbar puncture (LP)

○ Toxicology studies

○ Prescription medication levels for seizure prevention

- Radiographic or other studies

○ Radiographic imaging of the brain to evaluate for organic seizure causes

○ Electroencephalography (EEG)

Additional Interventions

- Provide a safe environment for the pediatric patient, and initiate seizure precautions.

- Ensure a patent airway, and have suction readily available.
- Provide supplemental oxygen.
- Initiate vascular access.
- Initiate cardiopulmonary monitoring.
- Anticipate the administration of medications.
  - Initial treatment includes benzodiazepines, such as intravenous lorazepam (Ativan).
  - Diazepam (Valium) per rectum may be considered as a second choice if there is no intravenous access.
  - Once the seizures have stopped or if the child does not respond to initial treatment prepare to administer fosphenytoin (Cerebyx) or phenobarbital.
  - Antipyretics

Table 11-5 Types of Seizures and Symptoms*

Generalized Seizures

Absence	brief lapses in awareness and staring
Myoclonic	sudden brief muscle jerks occur unilaterally or bilaterally
Tonic	muscles become tense or stiff
Clonic	rapid rhythmic jerking or flexion of extremities
Atonic	abrupt loss of muscle tone, usually causing the pediatric patient to collapse

All are associated with a loss of consciousness and may be convulsive (tonic-clonic) or nonconvulsive (absence)

Partial Seizures (Focal and Local)

Simple	associated with motor, sensory, or autonomic symptoms; consciousness is not impaired
Complex	associated with impaired consciousness

Partial seizures can progress to generalized seizures

Unclassified Seizures

Febrile seizures	with tonic-clonic movements lasting less than 15 minutes; most are benign and self-limiting; normally, they do not lead to neurological sequelae or seizure disorders; the peak incidence is at the age of 8–20 months, and most resolve by the age of five years; there is a reported 30% chance of recurrence
Neonatal seizures	resulting from metabolic, toxic, infectious, congenital, or maternal electrolyte disturbances; they include subtle behavior changes, such as rhythmic eye, arm, and leg movements; chewing; swimming; and bicycling; they occur because of the immature neonatal cortex, and they may be unilateral or bilateral

*Data are adapted from Vernon-Levett, P. (2001). Neurologic critical care problems. In M. A. Curley & P. A. Moloney-Harmon (Eds.), *Critical care nursing of infants and children* (2nd ed., pp. 695–720). Philadelphia, PA: Saunders.

Hydrocephalus

Hydrocephalus is a clinical condition that results from abnormal production, absorption, or drainage of CSF. Hydrocephalus may be communicating or noncommunicating. In communicating hydrocephalus, CSF production exceeds absorption. This may occur in association with trauma, leukemia, or meningitis. In noncommunicating hydrocephalus, the flow of CSF through the ventricles is obstructed. This is usually the result of structural abnormalities, such as arteriovenous or Chiari malformation.

Hydrocephalus is typically treated with the surgical implantation of a valve-regulated shunt system. This system diverts the CSF from the central nervous system to another part of the body, where it can be absorbed as part of the normal circulatory process. One example is a ventriculoperitoneal shunt, in which the proximal catheter is placed in the lateral ventricle and the distal end is placed in the peritoneum.

The most common complications of the valve-regulated shunt system are obstruction and disconnection. When this occurs, signs and symptoms of increased ICP will develop. Another common complication is shunt infection. The pediatric patient may present with signs and symptoms of local or systemic infection. Regardless of the cause, pediatric patients with increased ICP must be treated emergently through early identification of symptoms and prompt interventions (**Table 11-6**).[4]

Specific Diagnostic Studies

- Laboratory studies
  - CSF analysis, if suspicion of infection

Table 11-6 Clinical Manifestations of Hydrocephalus in the Infant and Child*

Infant	Child
Seizures	Seizures
Increased head circumference	Nausea and vomiting
"Setting sun" eyes	Headache
Widening sutures	Altered level of consciousness
Dilated scalp veins	Papilledema
Irritability, lethargy, poor feeding, and high-pitched cry	Diplopia

*Data are taken from Vernon-Levett, P. (2001). Neurologic critical care problems. In M. A. Curley & P. A. Moloney-Harmon (Eds.), *Critical care nursing of infants and children* (2nd ed., p. 713). Philadelphia, PA: Saunders.

- CBC
- Blood culture
- Urine culture
- Radiographic studies
  - Computed tomography (CT) or magnetic resonance imaging (MRI) of the head/brain
  - Radiographic shunt series

Additional Interventions

- Anticipate the need for temporary removal of CSF from the shunt reservoir (usually performed by a neurosurgeon), and prepare for surgical intervention.
- Anticipate early administration of antibiotics if infection is suspected.
- Frequently evaluate the patient's neurological status.
- Measure the frontal-occipital head circumference in infants.

Gastrointestinal Disorders

Gastrointestinal (GI) complaints are among the most frequent causes of pediatric emergency department visits, and caregiver concern about bowel function is common.[5]

Constipation

Constipation is generally defined as infrequent or painful defecation. In most cases, caregivers are worried that their child's stools are too large, too hard, not frequent enough, or painful to pass.

Most children with constipation have no underlying medical condition. In most cases, childhood constipation develops when the child begins to associate pain with defecation. Once pain is associated with the passage of bowel movements, the child begins to withhold stools in an attempt to avoid discomfort. As stool withholding continues, the rectum gradually accommodates, and the normal urge to defecate gradually disappears. The infrequent passage of very large and hard stools reinforces the child's association of pain with defecation, resulting in worsening stool retention.[5]

Constipation occurs in all pediatric age groups from infancy to young adulthood. Typically, childhood constipation develops during three stages of childhood. In young infants, constipation often begins at the time of a dietary transition (e.g., from breast milk to formula, the addition of solid foods into the diet, and from formula to whole milk). In toddlers, constipation often develops near the time of toilet training. In older children, constipation often develops at the time of school entry, because they refuse to defecate while at school. Before puberty, constipation appears to be equally common among girls and boys. After puberty, females are more likely to develop constipation than males.[6]

Asking the caregiver about specific symptoms of their child's constipation is important. The emergency care provider should inquire about the onset and duration of symptoms, whether the passage of bowel movements appears to be painful and whether any bleeding has been associated with defecation. Common withholding behaviors include squatting, crossing the ankles, stiffening of the body, flushing, sweating, crying, holding onto furniture or the caregiver, and hiding during defecation.[7]

Specific Diagnostic Studies

Constipation is recognized and diagnosed by most healthcare providers based on the child's clinical presentation (e.g., a patient has difficulty passing stool or has not passed stool in several days). Radiological studies may be done to confirm the presence of stool and to rule out other GI disorders, such as Hirschsprung disease. Laboratory studies are generally unnecessary unless an underlying condition is suspected to be the cause.

Additional Interventions

Childhood constipation is treated in many ways. The basic tenets of therapy include evacuation of the colon, elimination of pain with defecation, and establishment of regular bowel habits.

ED-specific interventions usually involve the administration of an enema. Additionally, it is important to educate the family about necessary dietary changes, such as increasing the amount of fiber, fluid, and complex carbohydrates (such as those found in fruit juices) in the child's diet, and that using laxatives may be necessary. This is particularly true in toddlers, because many months may pass before the association between fear of pain and defecation is extinguished. Inform the family that relapses are common and are associated with changes in the child's daily routine (e.g., vacations) or during times of stress.

Appendicitis

Acute appendicitis is an inflammation and infection of the vermiform appendix. Acute appendicitis is one of the most common causes of abdominal pain and is the most frequent condition leading to emergent abdominal surgery in children.[8]

Common symptoms of acute appendicitis include constant abdominal pain, fever, and vomiting.[8] Virtually all patients with appendicitis have abdominal pain and many have anorexia.[8] A child who states that the ride to the hospital was painful when the vehicle hit bumps in the road may have peritoneal irritation. Vague periumbilical pain, followed by migration of pain to the right lower quadrant (RLQ) is a classic sign. If the appendix perforates, an interval of pain relief is usually followed by development of generalized abdominal pain and peritonitis. High fever is not a common presenting feature unless perforation has occurred.[8]

Overall, 7% of people in the United States have their appendix removed during their lifetime. Appendicitis occurs in all age groups but is rare in infants. Appendicitis is most common in the second decade of life (ages 10–19 years). The male-to-female ratio is approximately 2:1. Appendicitis is much more common in developed countries. Although the reason for this discrepancy is unknown, potential risk factors include a diet low in fiber and high in sugar, family history, and infection.[9]

Specific Diagnostic Studies

Appendicitis is a clinical diagnosis, with radiographic imaging used to confirm questionable cases. Radiographic imaging studies include ultrasonography or abdominal CT. Laboratory studies may include CBC and urinalysis.

Additional Interventions

The definitive treatment for appendicitis is appendectomy. Treatment plans should include:

- Relief of the patient's pain and discomfort.
- Communication with the patient and family about the treatment plan.
- Plan for admission of the patient for observation if a firm diagnosis is not made.
- Administration of antibiotics as ordered.

Pyloric Stenosis

Pyloric stenosis is a narrowing of the pylorus, the opening from the stomach into the small intestine. Pyloric stenosis occurs secondary to hypertrophy and hyperplasia of the muscular layers of the pylorus, causing a functional gastric outlet obstruction. The cause of this muscular thickening is unknown, although genetic factors may play a role. Children of parents who had pyloric stenosis themselves are more likely to have this problem.[10]

Pyloric stenosis is a common cause of intestinal obstruction in infancy. The typical patient is a male infant with a previously normal feeding history who presents with nonbilious, projectile emesis. Palpation may reveal an olive-shaped mass in the right upper quadrant. Patients with pyloric stenosis are usually between the ages of 2 and 8 weeks. With delayed diagnosis, the infant may show signs of dehydration, lethargy, and a hypochloremic alkalosis due to loss of stomach acid.[11]

As noted, vomiting is the first symptom in most children. Vomiting may occur after every feeding or only after some feedings and is usually forceful or projectile. After vomiting, the infant is often hungry and wants to feed again. Other symptoms may include abdominal pain, belching, constant hunger, dehydration, weight loss or failure to gain weight, and a wave-like motion of the abdomen shortly after feeding and just before vomiting occurs.[11]

Specific Diagnostic Studies

In addition to a thorough physical exam, diagnostic tests may include:

- Ultrasound of the abdomen
- Barium radiograph
- Blood chemistry panel, CBC

Additional Interventions

The treatment for pyloric stenosis is a surgical pyloromyotomy to split the overdeveloped muscles. Balloon dilation is not thought to work as well as surgery but may be considered for infants when the risk of general anesthesia is high.[12] The healthcare provider should discuss with the caregiver what to expect after surgery. The patient will need intravenous fluids and can usually tolerate small, frequent feedings several hours after surgery. There may be vomiting after surgery, which is quite common and generally improves with time.[13]

Intussusception

Intussusception is the telescoping or prolapse of a segment of bowel into an adjacent segment. The classic presentation includes abdominal pain, currant-jelly stool, and a palpable abdominal mass. Currant-jelly stools, which is the mixing of blood leaking from venous engorgement at the affected site with fecal material is generally considered a late sign and although classic, is not often seen if the diagnosis is made early. Lethargy and drawing up of the legs are the most commonly reported signs. However, because the severe pain is episodic, some patients may be pain-free when they arrive at the emergency department.[14]

Intussusception is most common in male infants aged 3 to 12 months, with an average age of seven to eight months.

Two thirds of the cases occur before the patient's first birthday. Intussusception occurrence is rare in patients younger than three months, and it becomes even less common in patients older than 36 months.[14]

Specific Diagnostic Studies

A range of diagnostic tests may be required to make an intussusception diagnosis. In addition to a thorough physical evaluation and history, these include:

- Radiographs of the abdomen
- CT scan of the abdomen
- When intussusception is suspected, an air or barium enema can often help correct the problem by pushing the telescoped section of bowel into its proper position.
- An upper and lower GI series

Additional Interventions

Cases unresponsive to this technique may require surgical repair and the surgeon should be readily available because of the associated risk of perforation. The caregiver should be informed that the intussusception may re-manifest; this recurrence happens more often with intussusceptions that were reduced with contrast enema. After treatment, the patient will be kept in the hospital and given intravenous fluids until able to eat and have normal bowel function. Some infants may be given antibiotics to prevent infection. Most infants who are treated within the first 24 hours recover completely with no problems. Further delay increases the risk of complications, which include irreversible tissue damage, perforation of the bowel, infection, and death.[15]

Volvulus/Malrotation

A volvulus is a bowel obstruction in which a loop of bowel has abnormally twisted on itself. Such twisting can occur at various sites of the GI tract, including the stomach, small intestine, cecum, transverse colon, and sigmoid colon. Midgut volvulus is the most common type of volvulus in infants and children and refers to a twisting of the entire midgut around the axis of the superior mesenteric artery. A birth defect called intestinal malrotation can make infants more likely to develop a volvulus. However, a volvulus can occur without malrotation.[16]

Regardless of cause, volvulus causes symptoms by two mechanisms. One is bowel obstruction, manifested as abdominal distension and vomiting. The other is loss of blood flow and ischemia to the affected portion of intestine. Volvulus causes severe pain and progressive injury to the intestinal wall, with accumulation of gas and fluid in the portion of the bowel obstructed. Ultimately, this can result in necrosis of the affected intestinal wall and, eventually, death.[16]

The presenting symptoms depend on the degree of twisting and the rapidity of onset. Symptoms include pain, tenderness and distention of the abdomen; bloody or dark red stools; bilious emesis; and constipation. The older the child, the more atypical the symptoms; the teenager with chronic abdominal pain or malabsorption may be suffering from recurrent bouts of volvulus and devolvulus.[17]

Specific Diagnostic Studies

Studies include:
- Upper GI series
- Radiographs of the abdomen
- CT scan of the abdomen
- Barium enema
- Stool guaiac
- Blood chemistry panel, CBC

Additional Interventions

Volvulus requires immediate surgical intervention to untwist the affected segment of bowel and possibly resect any unsalvageable portion. Occasionally a colostomy or ileostomy is necessary.[18] The healthcare provider should provide caregivers with information regarding what to expect after surgery. Antibiotics should be administered as ordered to minimize complications such as peritonitis.

Endocrine Disorders

Diabetes Mellitus

Diabetes is a group of conditions characterized by inadequate insulin secretion, insulin resistance in the tissues, or a combination of both. The disease is a chronic condition affecting approximately 175,500 individuals 20 years or younger in the United States. **Table 11-7** compares type I with type II diabetes.

Diabetic Ketoacidosis

Diabetic ketoacidosis (DKA) is a condition caused by absolute or relative insulin deficiency, with varying degrees of insulin resistance, resulting in the following conditions:

- Hyperglycemia
- Mobilization of fatty acids
- Excess counterregulatory hormones that cause gluconeogenesis.

When this occurs, body lipids and proteins are broken down and used for energy. The mobilization of fatty acids and the production of lactic acids and ketoacids result in ketoacidosis. Osmotic diuresis from profound hyperglycemia results in hyponatremia, potassium shifts, and potential dysrhythmias related to electrolyte imbalances. Diabetic ketoacidosis can be life threatening and is the most common cause of death in diabetic pediatric patients. Of children with new-onset diabetes, 40% present to the emergency department with diabetic ketoacidosis.[19]

Diabetic ketoacidosis is characterized by the following factors:

- Hyperglycemia (the glucose level is usually elevated to > 300 mg/dL; however, in approximately 18% of patients, the blood glucose level is < 300 mg/dL[20])
- Dehydration
- Metabolic acidosis/acidemia
- Ketonemia or ketonuria
- Glycosuria

Additional History

- Frequent urination
- Excessive thirst
- Fatigue
- Weight loss
- History of diabetes and/or viral illness

Signs and Symptoms

- Abdominal pain
- Nausea and vomiting (related to electrolyte imbalances, acidosis, and underlying factors)
- Kussmaul breathing (hyperventilation is an effort to eliminate excess carbon dioxide caused by metabolic acidosis)
- Mental status changes (related to fluid shifts, with correction of dehydration and degree of acidosis)
- Dehydration (related to osmotic diuresis)
- Electrolyte imbalances (related to fluid shifts and osmotic diuresis)
- Cardiac dysrhythmias (related to electrolyte imbalances)
- Acetone or fruity odor on the patient's breath (related to excessive buildup of ketones)

Specific Diagnostic Studies

- Arterial blood gas (ABG) measurement, reflecting metabolic acidosis, with an anion gap
- Serum or whole blood glucose test, reflecting an elevated glucose level
- CBC count to evaluate for underlying infection and the degree of hemoconcentration. Leukocytosis reflects the degree of ketosis rather than the presence of infection. Only the elevation of band neutrophils has been determined to indicate the presence of infection, with a sensitivity of 100% and a specificity of 80%.
- Levels of electrolytes, blood urea nitrogen, and creatinine and osmolality. Acidosis and the hyperosmolality induced by hyperglycemia shift potassium, magnesium, and phosphorus from the intracellular to the extracellular space.
- Hemoglobin A1C per hospital protocols to detect the blood glucose level during the past three months. This test is used to show glucose control.
- Urine for urinalysis and measurement of ketones and glucose.[20]

Additional Interventions

Correct dehydration

Table 11-7 Comparison of Type I and Type II Diabetes Mellitus*

Variable	Type I Diabetes	Type II Diabetes
Age at onset	Two peaks: aged 5 and 15 years	Teenaged years
Predominant ethnic groups affected	Caucasian	Native American, Hispanic, and African American
Obesity	Same as general population	Greater than 90%
Hypertension	Uncommon	Common
Acanthosis nigracans	Rare	Common
Ketosis and diabetic ketoacidosis	Common	Uncommon
Islet autoimmunity	Present	Absent

*Data are adapted from Burns, C. E., Dunn, A. M., Brady, M. A., Starr, N. B., & Blosser, C. G. (Eds.). (2009). *Pediatric primary care* (4th ed.) (pp. 595–601). St. Louis, MO: Saunders Elsevier.

- Administer a 10 to 20 mL/kg bolus of 0.9% normal saline over one to two hours. Repeat the bolus as necessary, and give the bolus slowly to prevent cerebral edema.

- Continue to replace the fluid deficit per an institution-specific protocol, adding glucose to the solution once hyperglycemia is corrected.

- Obtain serial laboratory specimens to include glucose level, arterial blood gases, and electrolytes per institutional protocol based on the degree of illness.

- Correct acidosis by administrating a continuous intravenous infusion of regular insulin per institutional protocol.

- Replace potassium losses along with intravenous fluids once urine output is established.

- Evaluate neurological status and vital signs, watching closely for signs of cerebral edema.

- Monitor fluid intake and output.

- Monitor electrocardiogram for dysrhythmias related to hyperkalemia or hypokalemia.

Table 11-8 discusses how to manage diabetic ketoacidosis.

Diabetes Insipidus

Diabetes insipidus (DI) occurs when the secretion of antidiuretic hormone (ADH) or vasopressin drops below normal levels. Because urinary output is controlled by ADH, the kidneys lose the ability to concentrate urine by preventing the reabsorption of water and this produces massive diuresis and hyperosmolar dehydration. The underlying cause of DI can be either primary, which is usually idiopathic but with familial links, or secondary, which is associated with insult to the brain. This can be in the form of traumatic injury, surgery, infections, tumors or vascular injuries.[14]

Additional History

Pediatric patients with DI generally present with polyuria and polydipsia. If dehydration becomes severe enough, it may result in enuresis, especially in children too young to respond to their own thirst needs. Infants may show signs of continued hunger after milk but may seem satisfied with feedings of water. Older children can often drink enough to prevent circulatory collapse but may suffer from electrolyte disturbances and azotemia or increased levels of urea. Creatinine and glucose levels remain normal.[14,21]

Signs and Symptoms

- Polydipsia
  - May get up in the middle of the night to get a drink
  - May drink from unusual places, such as puddles or toilets
- Polyuria
  - May get up to urinate frequently at night
  - May regress to bedwetting
- Dehydration
  - Because the dehydration is hyperosmolar in nature, the signs and symptoms of dehydration may be less than the degree of severity
- Hyperthermia

Specific Diagnostic Studies

- Water deprivation test

Table 11-8 Management of Diabetic Ketoacidosis*

Variable	Interventions
Airway, breathing, and circulation	Provide 100% oxygen if shock is present, assist ventilation if needed, and establish two peripheral intravenous lines.
Peripheral perfusion not normal	Treat shock with a 10–20 mL/kg bolus of 0.9% normal saline or lactated Ringer's solution. If more than 20 mL/kg is needed, consider 5% albumin in 5–10 mL/kg boluses.
Peripheral perfusion normal	Use 0.9% normal saline or lactated Ringer's solution at 5 mL/kg per hour, pending laboratory results.
Measure glucose, blood gases, serum electrolytes, urea nitrogen, and creatinine; obtain the complete blood cell count; and perform a urinalysis	Estimate the degree of dehydration.
Weigh the patient	Emaciated patients younger than 2 years follow more closely.
Insulin dosing	By the end of the first hour of care, start regular insulin (0.1 units/kg per hour) by continuous infusion. Use *actual* body weight for all calculations.

*Data are adapted from Perkin et al (pp. 529–533).[5]

- Restriction of fluids and observation of urine volume and concentration
  - May only be done on patients not compromised by dehydration
  - Body weights and frequent serial weights to monitor changes
- Serum electrolytes, blood urea nitrogen
- Strict intake and output
- Urine specific gravity
- Diagnosis may take some time and may not be completed in the emergency setting
- Priority is stabilization of fluid and electrolyte balance
- It is important to rule out other conditions with similar signs and symptoms, specifically diabetes mellitus and primary kidney disorders, such as tumors.
- CT of the head will identify causes including tumors or aneurysms
- Blood cultures and lumbar puncture will identify infectious causes such as meningitis.

Additional Interventions

- Treatment of confirmed DI includes administration of intravenous vasopressin (Pitressin), a synthetic form of ADH, which can alleviate symptoms.
- An increase in urine osmolality after administration of vasopressin (Pitressin) confirms the diagnosis.
- Idiopathic DI is often a lifelong condition and the treatment of nasally administered vasopressin (Pitressin) can provide temporary treatment of symptoms. These patients must be constantly cognizant of changes in thirst and intake and output. Caregivers and patients need to monitor changes in signs and symptoms as well as notify school nurses and utilize medical alert identification.[14]

Syndrome of Inappropriate Antidiuretic Hormone

Syndrome of inappropriate antidiuretic hormone (SIADH) produces the opposite effect to that of DI and results from an oversecretion of ADH. Secretion of ADH is stimulated when the blood becomes hypotonic, indicating the need for excretion of excess water and retaining sodium. The result is hypotonicity, decreased serum osmolality and serum sodium levels, and fluid retention. The causes of SIADH can be idiopathic or associated with infections, such as meningitis and Rocky Mountain spotted fever, head trauma, or brain tumors.[14]

Additional History

Pediatric patients with SIADH generally present with decreased urine output or concentrated urine. Because of the hypotonic state, there is no generalized edema and no signs of dehydration. Cerebral edema may be the first indication of illness. Cerebral edema and hyponatremia can lead to mental status changes, deteriorating to seizures and coma.[14,21]

Signs and Symptoms

- Anorexia
- Abdominal pain
- Headache
- Nausea and vomiting
- Irritability, disorientation, weakness, which advances to seizures and coma as the sodium level drops

Specific Diagnostic Studies

- Serum electrolytes and osmolality
  - Low sodium
  - Low blood urea nitrogen
- Urine electrolytes and osmolality
  - High urine osmolality
  - High urine sodium
  - Low urine potassium
- Urine specific gravity
- Diagnosis may take some time and may not be completed in the emergency setting
- Priority is stabilization of fluid and electrolyte balance

Additional Interventions

- Fluid restriction
- Correction of electrolyte imbalances
- Hypertonic (3%) saline will correct hypotonicity and stop or prevent seizures
- Furosemide (Lasix) may be useful
- Ongoing monitoring of fluid status, weight trending, and electrolyte balance
- Strict intake and output (I&O) monitoring
- Seizure precautions
- Patients should be admitted for continuing stabilization

Hematological Disorders

Sickle Cell Disease

Sickle cell disease (SCD) is an inherited disorder characterized by the presence of an abnormal type of hemoglobin (hemoglobin S) in the red blood cells. Sickle cell disease occurs in approximately one in 600 African Americans and, to a lesser extent, in other ethnic groups from the Mediterranean, the Caribbean, and India.[22] In SCD, red blood cells that are normally round assume an irregular sickle shape when deoxygenated. Once sickled, the cells become fragile, clump together, and cannot easily flow through the capillaries. This leads to an increase in blood viscosity, which results in stasis, sludging, and further deoxygenation. The occlusion of small vessels causes tissue ischemia and infarctions, resulting in a painful sickle cell crisis. The sites most commonly involved in sickle cell crisis are the bones (joints), mesenteric vessels, liver, spleen, brain, lungs, and penis. Sickle cell crisis is considered a medical emergency in pediatric patients.

Children with SCD normally have an elevated cardiac output. This allows blood to travel between the capillaries and lungs more rapidly so that sickling does not occur. Any process that interferes with this compensatory mechanism can promote sickling. Common factors that interfere are hypoxia, acidosis, hypotension, vasoconstriction, and increased hematocrit. Therefore, sickle cell crisis may be precipitated by infection, dehydration, fatigue, and exposure to cold, emotional stress, or change in altitude.

The most common manifestations of SCD are vaso-occlusive, aplastic, and sequestration crises. Vaso-occlusive crisis, the most common form, is an acute painful episode produced by stasis of red blood cells in small capillaries, leading to tissue ischemia and infarction. The joints and extremities are the areas most often affected. Aplastic crisis normally follows a viral infection and presents with erythropoietic failure in the bone marrow, resulting in bone marrow suppression and anemia. Splenic sequestration crisis occurs with the pooling of red blood cells in the spleen, resulting in splenomegaly (enlargement of the spleen), severe anemia, and shock. If left untreated, organ failure and death can occur.

Pediatric patients with SCD are at higher risk for serious bacterial infections (e.g., meningitis, pneumonia, and sepsis) secondary to functional asplenia and immunosuppression. Infection remains the leading cause of death in early childhood for these patients. Causative agents include *S. pneumoniae, H. influenzae,* and *N. meningitidis.*

Other complications of SCD include cerebral vascular accidents, abdominal crisis, bony crisis, and acute chest syndrome (a painful crisis resulting from sickling in the pulmonary vasculature). It presents similarly to pneumonia, with pleuritic chest pain, cough, dyspnea, fever, tachypnea, hypoxia, leukocytosis, and pleural effusions.

Symptoms of Sickle Cell Anemia/Crisis

- Pain
- Weakness, dysarthria, and slurred speech
- Priapism
- Splenic infarction and sequestration
- Aplastic crisis
- Nutritional deficiencies, including folic acid, zinc, and low caloric intake
- Pneumococcal disease and sepsis
- Placental insufficiency

Complications of SCD can occur at any age. However, certain events tend to occur in different age groups. The most common SCD-related clinical events in the first 10 years of life are painful episodes, acute chest syndrome, and stroke. Delayed growth and sexual development become major issues of concern to the adolescent, but sexual maturation is eventually achieved. Psychosocial problems are common in adolescents with SCD and frequently include issues of pain management and peer separation because of inpatient stays.[22]

Additional History

- Known presence of SCD or trait
- Family members with sickle cell anemia
- Frequent infections, failure to thrive, jaundice, or anemia
- Pain, swelling, or warmth of joints or extremities
- Dactylitis or hand-foot syndrome (painful inflammation of the fingers or toes) in infants and toddlers
- Current medications
- Prophylactic antibiotics (e.g., penicillin)
- Immunizations (pneumococcal, *H. influenzae* type B, and meningococcal)
- Folic acid
- Home pain regimens

Signs and Symptoms

- Weakness, fatigue, and pallor (anemia)
- Joint or extremity soft tissue swelling and pain (vaso-occlusive crisis)

- Acute left upper quadrant pain, abdominal distention, and vomiting (splenic sequestration)
- Nausea or vomiting, abdominal pain, fever, and malaise (abdominal crisis)
- Headache and visual disturbances (stroke)
- Chest pain, dyspnea, and fever (acute chest syndrome)
- Priapism (vaso-occlusive crisis)

Specific Diagnostic Studies

- CBC count, including a reticulocyte count to evaluate for aplastic crisis
- Type and cross match, when the need for transfusion is identified
- Arterial blood gas measurement
- Cultures of blood, urine, and CSF, if infection is suspected
- Chest radiograph for suspected pneumonia or acute chest syndrome
- Head CT, if a stroke is suspected

Additional Interventions

- Promote rest to minimize oxygen expenditure.
- Administer oxygen if evidence of hypoxia is present and to help with pain.
- Promote hydration for hemodilution through oral or intravenous therapy.
- Anticipate the need for transfusion in severe anemia. An exchange transfusion may be required in severe cases.
- Consider the need for early urinary catheterization but evaluate the risk for infection before insertion.
- Administer medications
  - Analgesics (e.g., morphine sulfate)
  - Antipyretics
  - Antibiotics

Disorders of Coagulation

The most prevalent bleeding disorders are hemophilia, von Willebrand disease, and idiopathic thrombocytopenic purpura. **Table 11-9** summarizes these disorders.

Genitourinary Disorders

Urinary Tract Infection

Urinary tract infection (UTI) is one of the most common infections of childhood.[23] It distresses the child, concerns the caregivers, and may cause permanent kidney damage.

The two broad clinical categories of UTI are pyelonephritis (upper UTI) and cystitis (lower UTI). Most episodes of UTI during the first year of life are classified as pyelonephritis. Febrile infants younger than three months may present with a fever without a localizing source. Examination of these infants should always include evaluation for UTI. Older children with UTIs who have voiding symptoms or dysuria, little or no fever, and no systemic symptoms, usually have cystitis.[24]

The history and clinical course of a UTI vary with the patient's age and the specific diagnosis. Combinations of findings, including a prior history of UTI, should be taken into account. In all age groups, fever and vomiting may be present. Neonates with UTI may exhibit jaundice, failure to thrive, poor feeding, and irritability. Infants with a UTI may exhibit strong-smelling urine, abdominal pain, poor feeding, and irritability. Pre-schoolers and school age children may have strong-smelling urine, abdominal pain, and urinary symptoms such as dysuria, urgency, frequency, and enuresis. Adolescents are more likely to present with typical urinary symptoms. Adolescent girls are more likely to have vaginitis than a UTI.[25]

Specific Diagnostic Studies

- The diagnosis of a UTI is based on urinalysis and urine culture. A midstream, clean-catch specimen may be obtained from children who have urinary control. In the infant or child unable to void on request, the specimen for culture should be obtained by means of urethral catheterization.
- The American Academy of Pediatrics recommends that all infants and young children (aged two months to two years) with a first UTI undergo urinary tract ultrasonography. A voiding cystourethrogram may be indicated for recurrent or unresponsive UTI.[26]

Additional Interventions

- Administer antibiotics as ordered.
- Some patients must be aggressively treated with intravenous fluids and parenteral antibiotics.
- Educate caregivers and patients about avoidance of unnecessary use, and misuse, of antibiotics. Antibiotics can alter periurethral flora and compromise natural defenses against colonization by pathogenic agents.
- Agents with topical anesthetic and analgesic effects, such as phenazopyridine, may be used. Educate patients and caregivers that agents of this sort often cause a color change in the urine and that it only provides pain relief. The antibiotics are still needed to treat the infection.

Table 11-9 Comparison of Coagulation Disorders*

Disorder	Cause
Hemophilia	Genetic disorder characterized by a deficiency or absence on one of the clotting proteins in the plasma
	Deficiencies in factor VIII (hemophilia A) or factor IX (Christmas disease) are most common
	X-linked recessive disorder affecting mostly males; the incidence is one in 7,500 male births; inheritance is sex linked recessive; up to 33% of cases occur through spontaneous gene mutation
	Classified mild to severe according to level of circulating factor: 60%–70% considered severe
	Signs and Symptoms
	General: hemorrhage, easy bruising, and prolonged bleeding
	CNS: headache, vomiting, altered level of consciousness, and seizures related to intracranial bleeding
	Neck: paralysis, weakness, and back pain related to spinal cord bleed
	GI: hematemesis, melena, abdominal pain, palpable mass, and rigidity
	GU: scrotal bleeding, pain, and hematuria
	Joint: common bleeds, hemarthrosis, pain, swelling, and limited range of motion
	Muscle: warmth, pain, and swelling
	Treatment
	Replace missing clotting factors according to protocol with AHF VIII or coagulation factor IX concentrate
	Aminocaproic acid (Amicar) or tranexamic acid (Cyklolapron) may be useful to control oral bleeding
	Immobilization of affected joints
	Analgesia
	Minimize invasive procedures (intramuscular injections, venipunctures, and catheters)
	Avoid medications that prolong bleeding time (i.e., acetylsalicylic acid or ibuprofen)
Disorder	**Cause**
von Willebrand disease	Most common hereditary bleeding disorder
	Deficiency or defect in the von Willebrand factor, which is bound to factor VIII
	Affects both males and females
	Signs and Symptoms
	Superficial bruising, epistaxis, prolonged menses, gum bleeding, and prolonged bleeding after surgery
	Treatment
	Desmopressin acetate or plasma-derived product depending on type
Disorder	**Cause**
Idiopathic thrombocytopenic purpura	Destruction of antibody-sensitized platelets (usually by spleen)
	Often self-limiting (4–6 weeks); may be chronic
	Signs and Symptoms
	Petechiae, purpura, bruising, thrombocytopenia, and spontaneous bleeding of skin and mucous membranes (oral and GI)
	Treatment
	Depends on severity
	May range from IgG and steroid therapy to treatment of shock and replacement of RBCs

Note: AHF indicates antihemophilic factor; CNS, central nervous system; GI, gastrointestinal; GU, genitourinary; Ig, immunoglobulin; RBC, red blood cell.

*Data are adapted from the following sources: (1) Nursing Group of Hemophilia Region VI. (1998). In K. Wulff, S. Zappa, & M. Womack (Eds.). *Emergency care for patients with hemophilia: An instructional manual for medical professionals* (2nd ed.). Retrieved from http://www.hemophiliaemergencycare.com. (2) Manley, L., & Bechtel, N. M. (1998). Hematologic and immune systems. In T. E. Soud & J. S. Rogers (Eds.), *Manual of pediatric emergency nursing* (pp. 390–416). St Louis, MO: Mosby. (3) Hemphill, R. (2004). Hematologic and oncologic emergencies. In J. E. Tintanelli, G. Kelen, & S. Stapczynski. *Emergency medicine: A comprehensive study guide* (6th ed.) (pp. 1319–1368). New York, NY: McGraw-Hill.

- One study investigated the effect of daily cranberry juice in female children with recurrent UTIs and concluded that daily consumption of concentrated cranberry juice can significantly prevent the recurrence of symptomatic UTIs.[27] Caregivers must be cautioned that much of the commercially available cranberry juice is in the form of cranberry juice cocktail and contains large amounts of sugar, which should be used in moderation. Concentrated juice, without sugar, can be found through the careful reading of labels.

- Studies have shown that uncircumcised males are at a higher risk for developing UTI than circumcised males.[28–30] As this is a choice for many, the emergency nurse must be respectful and understanding, while emphasizing the need for meticulous hygiene. Teaching the child to perform his own hygiene is a vital part of normal growth and development, but as with any new developmental task, children should be monitored to ensure it is done properly.

Ovarian Cyst

An ovarian cyst is a fluid-filled sac in an ovary. Cysts can develop from the neonatal period throughout the life span. Most ovarian cysts occur during infancy and adolescence, which are hormonally active periods of development.[31] Most resolve with minimal treatment. However, when ovarian cysts are large, persistent, or painful, surgery may be required, sometimes resulting in removal of the ovary.

Ovarian cysts can result in pain, dysmenorrhea, pelvic discomfort, and abdominal distention. Some cysts are complicated by torsion, rupture, or hemorrhage. Cyst rupture is characterized by sudden, unilateral, sharp pelvic pain.[32] Hemorrhage due to cyst rupture may lead to shock.

Specific Diagnostic Studies

- Ultrasonography is the favored imaging technique to assess ovarian cysts.

- CT scanning is preferred in imaging hemorrhagic ovarian cysts or hemoperitoneum due to cyst rupture.

- A urine pregnancy test should be performed in the female patient of childbearing age.

- A CBC count should be obtained. Hematocrit and hemoglobin levels will help evaluate for anemia caused by acute bleeding. The white blood cell (WBC) count may be elevated in complications of ovarian cyst, especially torsion.

- A urinalysis should be obtained to rule out other possible causes of abdominal or pelvic pain, such as urinary tract infections or kidney stone.

Additional Interventions

- Evaluate for signs of hemorrhagic shock and provide oxygen and intravenous fluid resuscitation as needed.

- Provide pain relief as ordered.

- Prepare the patient for surgical intervention as necessary.

Acute Scrotal Pain

The diagnosis of acute scrotal pain can be difficult. The most common causes include torsion of a testicular appendage, epididymitis, testicular torsion, and trauma. Each of the causes of scrotal pain may be clinically indistinguishable because their signs and symptoms overlap. **Table 11-10** provides a way to help differentiate the potential cause. Testicular torsion must be considered in any patient who complains of acute scrotal pain and swelling. It is a surgical emergency! The cause of acute scrotal pain is established based on a careful medical history, a thorough physical examination, and appropriate diagnostic procedures. The physical examination must concentrate on the following assessment procedures:

- Assess the size, location, and tenderness of both testes

- Inspect for tender, firm, and high-riding testes, with or without surrounding fluid

- Assess for lack of transillumination

- Assess the scrotum for edema and erythematosis

- Determine whether the cremasteric reflex is absent

The determination of the onset, character, and severity of symptoms is vital.

Testicular Torsion

Testicular torsion is a urological emergency. Testicular torsion refers to twisting of the spermatic cord structures, either in the inguinal canal or just below the inguinal canal, causing disruption of the gonadal blood supply with subsequent testicular necrosis and atrophy. The clinical presentation differs between neonates and those who are older, with the older pediatric patient presenting with sharp and unilateral testicular pain with an abrupt onset that is consistent and severe. Emergent treatment is of utmost importance, with the likelihood of testicular salvage decreasing as the duration of torsion increases. The nurse must remember that there is a four- to eight-hour window from the onset of torsion symptoms until surgical

Table 11-10 Potential Clues for the Differential Diagnoses of Acute Nontraumatic Scrotal Pain*

Clue	Testicular Torsion	Appendage Torsion	Epididymitis
Young age	+	+	+/–
Intermittent signs and symptoms	+/–	–	–
Woke at night with pain	+/–	–	–
History of genital trauma	+/–	–	+/–
Nausea and vomiting	+/–	–	+/–
Fever	+/–	–	+/–
Pain beginning with physical exertion	+/–	–	–
Cremasteric reflex intact	+/–	+	+
Pain radiating to other areas	+/–	–	+/–
Testicle is diffusely tender	+	–	–
Difficulty ambulating	+/–	–	–
Blue-dot sign	–	+/–	–
Gradual pain/insidious onset	–	+	+
Scrotal erythema/edema	+/–	–	+/–
Prehn sign	+/–	–	+/–
Symptoms of UTI/dysuria	+/–	–	+/–

Note: UTI indicates urinary tract infection, +, present; –, absent.
*Data are taken from Cole and Vogler.[36]

intervention is required to save the affected testis.[33] Delays in care may necessitate orchiectomy, which has been associated with reduced fertility.[34]

Testicular torsion most often is observed in males aged 12 to 18 years, with the peak age being 14 years and a smaller peak also occurring during the first year of life.[35]

Clinical Presentation

- Sudden onset of severe unilateral pain (more often on the left)
- Past history of similar pain in 50% of the patients

Physical Examination

- Scrotal swelling with unilateral elevation of the scrotum
- Pain severe enough that the adolescent is unable to ambulate
- Nausea and vomiting
- Abdominal pain
- Fever
- Scrotal erythema
- Cremasteric reflex absent (muscle contraction moving the scrotum and testis upward when stroked)
- Prehn sign (Negative: elevation of the testes does not relieve pain)
- Horizontal lie of the testicle
- Some may be twisted 360°, 720°, or 1440°

Specific Diagnostic Studies

- Urinalysis result, normal
- If certain of diagnosis, emergent surgery
- If uncertain of diagnosis:
  - Two-dimensional color Doppler ultrasonography, documents arterial blood flow to the testicle while providing information about scrotal anatomy and other testicular disorders.

Treatment

- Refer emergently
  - Less than six hours, 90% salvage
  - Longer than 24 hours, 100% loss and atrophy
  - Surgical repair with an orchiopexy

Appendage Testicular Torsion

This process is seen in the prepubescent male between the ages of three and 13 years, with a peak at the age of nine to 13 years; it is rarely seen after puberty. Appendage testicular torsion is caused by hormonal changes seen with puberty, when the testicular appendage enlarges, causing it to strangulate.

Clinical Presentation

- Gradual unilateral pain, which is moderately severe
- Testis is not hard and is of a normal size and position
- Scrotal erythema and a boggy epididymis

Physical Examination

- The cremasteric reflex is present
- Scrotal erythema and a boggy epididymis
- "Blue dot sign" (scrotal skin with a blue discoloration) seen early, indicating an infarcted appendix
- Ensure an early examination before swelling makes any further examination suspect!

Specific Diagnostic Studies

- Color Doppler ultrasonography, will show a normal or increased blood flow

Treatment

- Treat symptomatically
  - Rest
  - Scrotal elevation
  - Scrotal support
  - Pain control (which is usually relieved within one week)
  - Urology consultation if pain lasts longer than one week
- If diagnosis is in question, surgical exploration may be indicated

Epididymitis

The ductus epididymidis forms a structure on the posterior surface of each testicle and transports maturing sperm through the vas deferens to the seminal vesicles, which reside on the underside of the prostate gland. This route serves as a descending pathway for pathogens, resulting in epididymitis.[36] The organisms involved in epididymitis vary depending on age. *Escherichia coli* is the most frequently identified organism in males before puberty.

Clinical Presentation

- Gradual onset of pain (develops over a period of hours to a day)
- Pain ranges from dull to intense, with pain that may be referred to the ipsilateral lower abdomen and flank
- Fever
- Dysuria

Physical Examination

- Erythema and edema of the genitals and scrotum
- Tenderness of the epididymis
- Prehn sign (Positive: pain relief when the testicles are elevated) may occur
- Cremasteric reflex typically intact
- Digital examination of the inguinal canal to exclude a hernia

Specific Diagnostic Studies

- Milk the penis (urethra) for discharge PRIOR to obtaining a urine specimen (especially if you suspect an STI).
- The urine specimen result is positive for leukocytes and nitrates on a dipstick, with microscopic evidence indicating the white blood cell count and organisms. If you suspect an STI, a DNA probe must be obtained for *Chlamydia trachomatis* and *Neisseria gonorrhoeae.*
- Two-dimensional color Doppler ultrasonography should be used to evaluate blood flow to **confirm that torsion of the testis does not exist**.

Treatment

- Scrotal elevation
- Bed rest
- Anti-inflammatory agents
- Antibiotic therapy (usually trimethoprim and sulfa-methoxazole [Bactrim] or cephalexin [Keflex])
- Treat STIs per the Centers for Disease Control and Prevention's guidelines.
- Educate the patient that the pain will improve in seven to 10 days, with relief of fever and discomfort in 24 to 48 hours.
- To exclude a tumor, follow up with a primary care provider or a urologist once the inflammation has resided.
- Refer patients for persistence of pain/swelling

Testicular Trauma

Most cases occur by blunt trauma but may also occur with penetration, which requires surgical repair and early exploration (< 72 hours). A urethral injury should be suspected if the patient presents with voiding symptoms.

Specific Diagnostic Studies

- Blunt etiology
  - Ultrasonography, sensitive for testicular tunical disruption
  - Exploration within 72 hours if required
- Penetrating etiology

- ○ Ultrasonography, not particularly informative
- ○ Exploration, local repair in the ED versus debridement in the main operating room

Immunological Disorders

Human Immunodeficiency Virus/Acquired Immunodeficiency Syndrome

The human immunodeficiency virus (HIV) causes a continuum of infections to occur. The end stage of this disease process is acquired immunodeficiency syndrome (AIDS), which ultimately results in death. Acquired immunodeficiency syndrome is a progressively debilitating, multisystem, viral infection that most commonly attacks the immune and nervous systems. The etiological agent is the retrovirus HIV, which selectively invades white blood cells, particularly T-helper lymphocytes. Because the pathology of the disease involves the immune system, children are at high risk for developing bacterial, viral, parasitic, and fungal infections, many of which lead to death. Pneumonia from *Pneumocystis carinii* is the most common acquired infection. The incubation period and disease course are shorter for pediatric patients than adults.

Between 1978 and 1985, many children were infected with HIV from contaminated blood and blood products, tissues, and factor concentrates. The occurrence of HIV infection was estimated to be as high as 95% in patients receiving contaminated products at that time. Few new cases of infection have been reported since the mid-1980s because of safeguards instituted in blood and tissue collection.[37]

A few children become infected with HIV as a result of sexual abuse. Practitioners caring for children who have experienced abuse must include HIV infection in the differential diagnosis of sexually transmitted diseases. HIV has also rarely been transmitted through blood exposure within household settings (e.g., via sharing razor blades or toothbrushes); to our knowledge, no cases of transmission within day-care or school settings have been reported.[38]

In 2004, 35 states that tracked HIV infections reported that adolescents and young adults, ages 13 through 19 years, composed 13% of all new HIV infections.[38] Adolescent girls between the ages of 13 and 19 years accounted for 43% of all AIDS cases reported through 2005. Because the average time from HIV infection to the development of AIDS is approximately 11 years, most young adults were infected as teenagers. Teenaged behaviors that increase the risk for exposure to HIV include unprotected sexual activity and injection substance abuse (**Table 11-11**).[37]

Additional History

- If HIV is acquired during the prenatal period, the medical history may include failure to thrive, recurrent infections, and lymphadenopathy
- Frequent or recurrent infections
- Progressive regression from developmental achievements
- Persistent weight loss
- Mother is HIV positive or has developed AIDS
- Pediatric patient is sexually active or has been sexually abused
- History of substance abuse or shared needles
- Maternal history of blood transfusion before 1985
- Current medication regimen

Signs and Symptoms

- Chronic diarrhea, vomiting, anorexia, and failure to thrive
- Recurrent fever or infection
- Generalized lymphadenopathy and hepatosplenomegaly
- Chronic encephalopathy (look for generalized weakness or ataxia)
- Other signs and symptoms may vary and are associated with opportunistic infections and organ system–related diseases

Table 11-11 Reported AIDS Cases in Children Younger Than 13 Years by Transmission Category, US and Dependent Areas*,**

Transmission Category	2006		Cumulative	
	No. of Cases	% of Cases	No. of Cases	% of Cases
Perinatally acquired	74	86	8,738	92
Transfusion associated	1	1	387	4
Hemophilia	0	0	229	2
Undetermined/not reported	11	13	168	2
Total	86	100	9,522	100

Note: AIDS indicates acquired immunodeficiency syndrome.
*Dependent areas include American Samoa, Guam, the Northern Mariana Islands, Puerto Rico, and the US Virgin Islands.
**Data are taken from Centers for Disease Control and Prevention. (2008). *HIV/AIDS surveillance report, year-end 2006* (Vol. 18, pp. 1–55). Atlanta, GA: Centers for Disease Control and Prevention, US Dept of Health and Human Services.

Specific Diagnostic Studies

- CBC
- Electrolyte levels
- Cultures of blood, wounds, and urine
- Chest radiograph
- CD4 cell count and viral load

Additional Interventions

- Initiate protective or reverse isolation measures to protect the pediatric patient from exposure to other pathogens in the emergency department.
- Administer antiretroviral therapy.
- Provide psychological support to the family and the patient.
- Provide consultation or teaching regarding nutrition.

Neutropenia

Severe neutropenia is defined as an absolute neutrophil count of less than 500/mm^3. This may occur because of either decreased production of neutrophils in the bone marrow or abnormal production of granulocytes that do not participate in phagocytosis. Pediatric patients who receive chemotherapeutic agents or radiation therapy or who have undergone transplantations typically become both neutropenic and thrombocytopenic during the disease or treatment. Infections, drugs, and chemical toxins may also cause neutropenia. Febrile neutropenia can rapidly progress to septic shock, hypotension, and cardiovascular collapse. Neutropenic pediatric patients with fever require early identification and emergent intervention to prevent further complications associated with sepsis.

Additional History

- Immune deficiency disorder or immunosuppression
- Fever
- Signs and symptoms of infection, including irritability, lethargy, pallor, chills, and/or myalgia
- Presence of a central line
- Obvious infection source, such as a lesion or open wound

Specific Diagnostic Studies

- CBC
- Cultures of blood, wound, invasive lines, and urine

Additional Interventions

- Wash hands and use an aseptic technique when performing procedures.
- Initiate protective or reverse isolation to prevent exposure to other ill patients in the waiting area.

- Calculate absolute neutrophil count: ([% neutrophils + % bands] × white blood cells) / 100
- Initiate intravenous fluid therapy.
- Administer antibiotics and antipyretics as ordered.
- Do not give ibuprofen to children with neutropenia.
- Avoid rectal temperatures and examinations, urinary catheterizations, enemas, and suppositories.

Apparent Life-Threatening Events

An *apparent life-threatening event* (ALTE) is defined as an episode in which an infant, usually younger than 3 months of age, experiences a combination of apnea (centrally or occasionally obstructive), color change, marked change in muscle tone, choking, or gagging. The observer may fear that the infant has died.[39] While most cases are idiopathic, an ALTE is often a symptom of an underlying illness or injury.

Additional History

Obtain a thorough history of events from the witness. This is the most valuable part of the evaluation. Assume the witness's perceptions are valid. Ascertain the following information:

- If the incident occurred during an awake or an asleep state
- Appearance
- Color changes
- Muscle tone changes
- Length of the event
- Association with feeding
- Position and sleep surface
- Interventions and recovery time
- Patient history: premature birth, gastroesophageal reflux disease (GERD), previous ALTE, who the child sleeps with (if anyone), breathing abnormalities, chronic and acute illnesses, and medications
- Family history: GERD, previous early deaths or ALTEs, seizures, obstructive sleep apnea, asthma, hypothyroidism, premature birth, and medications

Specific Diagnostic Studies

- Infections: CBC, blood and urine cultures, respiratory syncytial virus antigen, viral cultures, chest radiograph, and lumbar puncture
- GERD: esophageal pH monitoring or barium swallow procedure
- Seizures: EEG

- Cardiac: electrocardiogram and echocardiogram
- Pulmonary: ABG measurement, pulse oximetry, exhaled carbon dioxide monitoring, chest radiograph, sleep study, lateral airway films, and plethysmography
- Metabolic: CBC, electrolytes, glucose, calcium, phosphorus, serum ammonia, magnesium, and urine toxicology
- Neuromuscular: electromyogram, computed tomography scan, magnetic resonance imaging, and hemolytic uremic syndrome
- Child abuse: computed tomography scan, skeletal survey, head ultrasound, and video monitoring

Health Promotion

The following prevention measures can have a significant impact on medical illnesses in the pediatric population:

- Caregiver knowledge of disease processes and primary prevention strategies, including measurement of temperature, fever control, and immunization recommendations.
- Safe practices and safe sex strategies to reduce the risk of sexually transmitted infections, including human immunodeficiency virus.
- Appropriate referrals to available support groups for children with chronic medical conditions (e.g., hemophilia, HIV, AIDS, and diabetes).
- Caregiver involvement, focusing on continuity of care.
- Provision of appropriate referrals to facilitate patient follow-up.
- Age-specific prevention resources, including immunization schedules and healthy lifestyle benefits.

Summary

Childhood illnesses encompass a vast array of disorders. Knowledge of the unique characteristics of the pediatric patient is essential for the interpretation of assessment findings, the formulation of nursing diagnoses, and the provision of appropriate interventions. The timely recognition of respiratory and/or circulatory compromise and neurological alterations are fundamental to identification and prompt intervention in childhood illnesses and medical emergencies. The nurse's ability to rapidly recognize signs of distress, and to intervene appropriately, is central to optimal patient outcomes.

References

1. Tintanelli, J. E., Kelen, G., & Stapczynski, S. (2004). *Emergency medicine: A comprehensive study guide* (6th ed.). New York, NY: McGraw-Hill.

2. American Academy of Pediatrics. Meningococcal infections. (2009). In L. K. Pickering, C. J. Baker, D. W. Kimberlin, S. S. Long, (Eds.). *2009 red book* (28th ed.) (pp. 455–463). Elk Grove Village, IL: Author.

3. Barata I. (2005). Pediatric seizures. *Critical Decisions in Emergency Medicine, 19,* 1–10.

4. Kestle, J. R. (2003). Pediatric hydrocephalus: current management. *Neurological Clinics, 4,* 883–895.

5. van den Berg, M. M., Benninga, M. A., & Di Lorenzo C. (2006). Epidemiology of childhood constipation: A systematic review. *American Journal of Gastroenterology, 101*(10), 2401–2409.

6. Saps, M., Sztainberg, M., & Di Lorenzo, C. (2006). A prospective community-based study of gastroenterological symptoms in school-age children. *Journal of Pediatric Gastroenterology and Nutrition, 43*(4), 477–482.

7. Borowitz, S. M., Cox, D. J., Tam, A., Ritterband, L. M., Sutphen, J. L., & Penberthy, J. K. (2003). Precipitants of constipation during early childhood. *Journal of the American Board of Family Practice, 16*(3), 213–218.

8. Rothrock S. G., & Pagane, J. (2000). Acute appendicitis in children: Emergency department diagnosis and management. *Annals of Emergency Medicine, 36*(1), 39–51.

9. Wolfson, A. B., Hendey, G. W., Ling, L. J., Rosen, C. L., Schaider, J., & Sharieff, G. Q. (Eds.). (2010). Harwood-Nuss' clinical practice of emergency medicine (5th ed.). Philadelphia, PA: Lippincott Williams & Wilkins.

10. Krogh, C., Fischer, T. K., Skotte, L., Biggar, R. J., Oyen, N., Skytthe, A., . . . Melbye, M. (2010). Familial aggregation and heritability of pyloric stenosis. *Journal of the American Medical Association, 303*(23), 2393–2399.

11. Cincinnati Children's Hospital Medical Center. (2007). *Evidence based clinical practice guideline for hypertrophic pyloric stenosis.* Cincinnati, OH: Author.

12. Leclair M. D., Plattner V., Mirallie E., Lejus C., Nguyen J. M., Podevin G., & Heloury, Y. (2007). Laparoscopic pyloromyotomy for hypertrophic pyloric stenosis: A prospective, randomized controlled trial. *Journal of Pediatric Surgery, 42*(4), 692–698.

13. Adibe O. O., Nichol P. F., Lim F.Y., & Mattei P. (2007). Ad libitum feeds after laparoscopic pyloromyotomy: A retrospective comparison with a standardized feeding regimen in 227 infants. *Journal of Laparoendoscopic and Advanced Surgical Techniques Part A, 17*(2), 235–237.

14. Hockenberry, M. J., & Wilson, D. (2008). *Wong's essentials of pediatric nursing* (8th ed.). St. Louis, MO: Mosby.

15. Weihmiller, S. N., Buonomo, C., & Bachur, R. (2011). Risk stratification of children being evaluated for intussusception. *Pediatrics, 127*(2), e296–e303.

16. Cribbs, R. K., Gow, K.W., & Wulkan, M. L. (2008). Gastric volvulus in infants and children. *Pediatrics, 122*(3), e752–e762.

17. Chau, B., & Dufel, S. (2007). Gastric volvulus. *Emergency Medicine Journal, 24*(6), 446–447.

18. El-Gohary, Y., Alagtal, M., & Gillick, J. (2010). Long-term complications following operative intervention for intestinal malrotation: A 10-year review. *Pediatric Surgery International, 26*(2), 203–206.

19. Perkin, R. M., Swift, J. D., Newton, D. A., & Anas, N. G. (Eds.). (2008). *Pediatric hospital medicine: Textbook of inpatient management* (2nd ed.). Philadelphia, PA: Lippincott, Williams & Wilkins.

20. Marx, J. A. (Ed.). (2010). *Rosen's emergency medicine: concepts and clinical practice* (Vol. 2, 7th ed., pp. 1640–1641). Philadelphia, PA: Mosby.

21. Fleisher, G. R., & Ludwig, S. (Eds.). (2010). *Textbook of pediatric emergency medicine* (6th ed.). Philadelphia, PA: Lippincott Williams & Wilkins.

22. Steinburg, M. (2007). Sickle cell disease and associated hemoglobinopathies. In L. Goldman & D. A. Ausiello (Eds.), *Cecil medicine* (23rd ed.) (pp. 1217–1225). Philadelphia, PA: Saunders Elsevier.

23. Zorc, J. J., Levine, D. A., Platt, S. L., Dayan, P. S., Macias, C. G., Krief, W., . . . Kuppermann, N. (2005). Clinical and demographic factors associated with urinary tract infection in young febrile infants. *Pediatrics, 116*(3), 644–648.

24. Quigley, R. (2009). Diagnosis urinary tract infections in children. *Current Opinions in Pediatrics, 21*(2), 194–198.

25. Shaikh, N., Morone, N. E., Lopez, J., Chianese, J. Sangvai, S., D'Amico, F., . . . Wald, E. R. (2007). Does this child have a urinary tract infection? *Journal of the American Medical Association, 298*(24), 2895–2904.

26. Subcommittee on Urinary Tract Infection, Steering Committee on Quality Improvement and Management. (2011). Urinary tract infection: Clinical practice guidelines for the diagnosis and management of the initial UTI in febrile infants and children 2 to 24 months. *Pediatrics, 128,* 595–610.

27. Ferrara, P., Romaniello, L., Vitelli, O., Gatto, A., Serva, M., & Cataldi, L. (2009). Cranberry juice for the prevention of recurrent urinary tract infections: A randomized controlled trial in children. *Scandinavian Journal of Urology and Nephrology, 43*(5), 369–372.

28. Shaikh, N., Morone, N. E., Bost, J. E., & Farrell, M. H. (2008). Prevalence of urinary tract infection in childhood: A meta-analysis. *Pediatric Infectious Diseases Journal, 27*(4), 302–308.

References continued

29. Mukherjee, S., Joshi, A., Carroll, D., Chandran, H., Parashar, K., & McCarthy, L. (2009). What is the effect of circumcision on risk of urinary tract infection in boys with posterior urethral valves? *Journal of Pediatric Surgery, 44*(2), 421–471.

30. Singh-Grewal, D., Macdessi, J., & Craig, J. (2005). Circumcision for the prevention of urinary tract infection in boys: A systemic review of randomised trials and observational studies. *Archives of Disease in Childhood, 90*(8), 853–858.

31. Stany, M. P., & Hamilton, C. A. (2008). Benign disorders of the ovary. *Obstetrics and Gynecology Clinics of North America, 35*(2), 271–284, ix.

32. Katz, V. L., Lentz, G., Lobo, R. A., & Gershenson, D. (2007). *Comprehensive gynecology* (5th ed.). St. Louis, MO: Mosby.

33. Schneck, F. X., & Bellinger, M. F. (2002). Abnormalities of the testes and scrotum and their surgical management. In P. Walsh, A. Retik, E. Vaughan, & A. Wein (Eds.), *Campbell's urology* (8th ed., p. 2379). Philadelphia, PA: WB Saunders Co.

34. Mansbach, J., Forbes, P., & Peter, C. (2005) Testicular torsion and risk factors for orchiectomy. *Archives of Pediatric and Adolescent Medicine, 159,* 1167–1171.

35. Ringdahl, E., & Teague, L. (2006). Testicular torsion. *American Family Physician, 74,* 1739–1743.

36. Cole, F. L., & Vogler, R. (2004). The acute, nontraumatic scrotum: assessment, diagnosis, and management. *Journal of the American Academy of Nurse Practitioners, 16,* 54–60.

37. Fahrner R. & Romano S. (2009). HIV infection and AIDS. In P. Jackson Allen, J. A. Vessey, & N. Schapiro, *Primary Care of the Child with a Chronic Condition* (5th ed., pp. 527–545). St Louis, MO: Mosby.

38. Centers for Disease Control and Prevention (2009). *Cases of HIV infection and AIDS in the United States and dependent areas, 2007. In HIV/AIDS Surveillance Report* (Vol. 19). Retrieved from http://www.cdc.gov/hiv/surveillance/resources/reports/2007report.

39. Burns, C. E., Dunn, A. M., Brady, M. A., Starr, N. B., & Blosser, C. G. (Eds.). (2009). *Pediatric primary care* (4th ed.). St. Louis, MO: Saunders Elsevier.

Chapter 12 | The Neonate

Mary Puchalski, MS, RNC-NIC, APN, CNS, NNP-BC

Objectives

On completion of this chapter, the learner should be able to do the following:

- Determine anatomical, physiological, and developmental characteristics of neonates as a basis for assessment.
- Describe common emergent conditions associated with neonates.
- Plan appropriate interventions for neonates with emergent conditions.
- Indicate health promotion strategies related to neonatal care and illness prevention.

Introduction

The first year of life is a time of tremendous growth and development (physically, neurologically, and developmentally). It is also a period of great vulnerability. According to the most recent statistics (2006), the infant death rate in the United States was 6.69 per 1,000 live births, only a slight decrease from the previous year (6.8 per 1,000 live births).[1] Although the most common causes (37.4%) of deaths are congenital/chromosomal birth defects and prematurity/low birth weight, sudden infant death syndrome remains the third leading cause of death in infancy. Of the infants who die in the first year of life, more than 60% die in the neonatal period.[2]

The neonate may be brought to the emergency department (ED) for a variety of reasons. Health issues may arise from either congenital or acquired conditions. Common concerns include irritability or increased crying, poor feeding, fever, perceived constipation, vomiting, diarrhea, and jaundice. More severe concerns include decreased responsiveness, episodes of apnea, respiratory distress or tachypnea, and seizures.[3] The evaluation of the ill neonate will be reviewed in this chapter. Transitional physiology, birth history, and signs of illness or injury will be described to enable identification of necessary interventions and outcomes specific to the neonate. **Table 12-1** provides definitions and terminology related to the neonate.

Table 12-1 Terminology and Definitions*

Term	Definition
Infant	First year of life
Neonate	First 28 days of life
Newborn	First 7 days of life
Term infant	Born between 37 and 41 completed weeks of gestation
Preterm infant	Born before 37 weeks of gestation
Late preterm infant	Born between 34 and 36 completed weeks of gestation
Postterm infant	Born after 42 weeks of gestation
Corrected gestational age	Age in weeks at birth plus postnatal weeks
Appropriate for gestational age	Birth weight between the 10th and 90th percentile for gestational age
Small for gestational age	Birth weight lower than the 10th percentile for gestational age
Large for gestational age	Birth weight higher than the 90th percentile for gestational age
Low birth weight	Birth weight < 2,500 grams
Very low birth weight	Birth weight < 1,500 grams
Extremely low birth weight	Birth weight < 1,000 grams

*Data are taken from Engle, W. A. (2006). A recommendation for the definition of "late preterm" (near-term) and the birth weight–gestational age classification system. *Seminars in Perinatology, 30,* 2–7.

Overview of Systems and Risk for Disease in Neonates

Transitional Physiology

The transition from intrauterine to extrauterine life begins when the umbilical cord is cut. In fetal life, the partial pressure of oxygen, arterial (PaO_2) is approximately 30% to 35%. This relatively hypoxic environment facilitates diffusion of oxygen from the maternal circulation into the fetal circulation; it also results in vasoconstriction of the pulmonary vascular bed and high pulmonary vascular resistance (PVR). **Figure 12-1** illustrates the transitional physiology of the neonate.

The most critical factors in enabling normal transition are lung expansion and adequate oxygenation. Approximately 90% of neonates begin breathing spontaneously at birth and make the transition with minimal assistance: clearing the airway, drying, warming, and stimulating. When intervention is required, neonates usually respond to positive-pressure ventilation (PPV) with a bag-mask device. Of the 10% of infants requiring assistance, only approximately 1% require extensive resuscitative efforts.[4]

Neonates rarely experience primary cardiopulmonary arrest. Cardiopulmonary arrest in neonates generally follows a sequence of events beginning with respiratory distress and progressing to respiratory failure, respiratory arrest, and, finally, cardiopulmonary arrest. If the neonate is unable to elevate the PaO_2 to appropriate levels, the pulmonary vascular bed may fail to vasodilate, resulting in continued right to left shunting of blood through the ductus arteriosus (DA) and foramen ovale (FO). This condition, termed *persistent pulmonary hypertension of the newborn,* can lead to respiratory failure and death if it is not recognized and appropriate interventions are not implemented.

Thermoregulation

Neonates are highly susceptible to becoming hypothermic, both from increased heat loss and from a diminished ability to produce heat. The newborn's proportionally large head, increased body surface area to weight ratio, and minimal subcutaneous fat allow for rapid heat loss with environmental exposure. This risk is exacerbated in the preterm infant. Heat losses occur in a cool ambient environment through radiation, being in contact with a cool surface through conduction, having a draft blowing across the body through convection, or being wet through evaporation. Older children and adults produce heat through shivering, but infants younger than six months are unable to shiver and are dependent on nonshivering thermogenesis to produce heat. When neonates become cold, their metabolic rate increases, further increasing oxygen and glucose consumption. The ill neonate has a limited ability to compensate for these additional physiological demands, thus hypothermia can lead to hypoxia or accentuate existing hypoxia. Apnea, hypoglycemia, metabolic acidosis, and pulmonary vasoconstriction may also occur, worsening any existing cardiovascular dysfunction, leading to shock and cardiopulmonary failure. Furthermore, the presence of hypothermia can impede the infant's ability to respond to resuscitative efforts.

To prevent the deleterious effects of hypothermia, a neutral thermal environment that keeps the neonate's core temperature within normal range with minimal physiological demand must be provided. The use of an over-the-bed radiant warmer, which optimally has a servo control mechanism (modulating heat output by sensing the infant's body temperature), is critical for the neonate who is already hypothermic or requires significant body exposure for resuscitation or other procedures.[5]

The neonate also has a limited ability to dissipate heat. Elevations in body temperature may result from infection, alteration in heat production, exposure to extreme heat, or overbundling in combination with a warm or hot ambient environment. Fever, defined as a rectal temperature greater than 100.4°F (38°C), increases the physiological demands related to a resultant increase in the heart, respiratory, and metabolic rates. An infant who is delivered from a mother with a fever will present with an elevated temperature, which may or may not indicate illness in the infant.

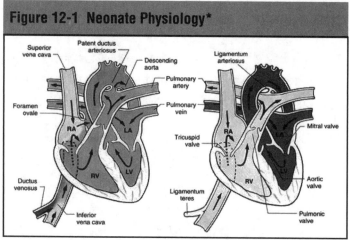

Figure 12-1 Neonate Physiology*

Note: The left-hand illustration shows prenatal circulation. The right-hand illustration shows postnatal circulation. *Arrows* indicate direction of blood flow.
*Reprinted with permission from Hockenberry, M. & Wilson, D. (2011).*Wong's nursing care of infants and children* (9th ed.). St. Louis, MO: Mosby.

Both warming of the hypothermic infant and cooling of the overwarm infant should be performed in a closely monitored environment. No studies evaluate the best method for warming or cooling, but preventing rapid temperature changes and resulting blood flow changes may represent the best approach. Continual monitoring of breathing, heart rate, and blood pressure and frequent blood glucose evaluation should be used.[6]

Respiratory System

The anatomical and physiological characteristics of the infant's pulmonary system are described in **Chapter 10, "Respiratory Emergencies."** The neonate's normally higher respiratory rate (40–60 breaths per minute) fluctuates with crying (increases) and sleep (decreases). Neonates will often exhibit periodic breathing (i.e., a period of rapid unlabored respirations followed by a pause of < 20 seconds). Periodic breathing reflects immature pulmonary control; therefore, it does not place the infant at risk for respiratory failure. However, premature and ill infants are especially at risk for apnea. *Neonatal apnea* is defined as an episode of nonbreathing for 20 seconds or more (fewer if accompanied by cyanosis or bradycardia). Apnea in any infant can lead to a life-threatening event.[7]

The small and immature pulmonary system affects the neonate's ability to respond to increased physiological demands. Increased oxygen consumption quickly leads to hypoxia in the ill neonate. Because of limited respiratory reserves, increased respiratory demands may precipitate rapid progression from respiratory distress to respiratory failure. Apneic episodes may occur as the neonate in respiratory distress fatigues. In a neonate, gasping is a sign of impending respiratory failure.[4]

Cardiovascular System

The neonate has a less compliant myocardium, a smaller contractile muscle mass, and a small stroke volume (1.5 mL/kg) compared with the older child. Neonates are limited to only increasing their heart rate when they need to increase their cardiac output.[8] The neonate's resting functional heart rate is higher than that of the older child and will vary with crying (increases) and sleep (decreases). *Transient bradycardia,* defined as a heart rate of less than 80 beats per minute, may occur with sleep or vagal stimulation during suctioning or defecation; however, sustained bradycardia is most commonly the result of hypoxemia or acidosis. In the initial minutes after birth, PPV is indicated whenever the infant's heart rate is less than 100 beats per minute.[5]

A blood pressure measurement should be obtained in the ill neonate, although auscultation of the blood pressure may be difficult because of the lower systolic blood pressure. Using an appropriately sized neonatal cuff is critical, whether done by palpation, Doppler ultrasonography, or oscillometry (i.e., electronic recording). The preferred site for blood pressure measurement is the right arm; however, other sites (e.g., the forearm, calf, or thigh) may be used as long as the cuff width is 40% of the circumference of the limb that the cuff is placed on.[9] Blood pressure measurements in all four extremities should be obtained in any infant who appears hemodynamically unstable. A difference of more than 20 mm Hg between the upper and the lower systolic pressure may indicate a ductal-dependent lesion (i.e., coarctation of the aorta). Normal vital signs for neonates are listed in **Table 12-2.**

Assessing the color of a newborn's skin provides important information about his or her cardiovascular health. Central color, assessed in the lips, mucous membranes, tongue, earlobes, and scrotum (in male infants), should be pink. Cyanosis becomes visible when five grams of hemoglobin per 100 mL of blood is not bound to oxygen (approximately 70% measured oxygen saturation). The newborn commonly has vasomotor instability and sluggish peripheral circulation, which may result in a bluish discoloration of the palms of the hands and soles of the feet, termed *acrocyanosis.* This is a benign finding that may persist for 24 to 48 hours after birth. An infant with *polycythemia* (defined as a venous hematocrit > 65%) may appear cyanotic, especially with crying, but will not be hypoxic. This is because cyanosis is apparent with only 5 g of desaturated hemoglobin, but the remaining 15 g or more of hemoglobin may be saturated with oxygen; thus, the oxygen content in the blood is adequate. Persistent

Table 12-2 Normal Vital Signs for Full-Term Neonates*

Vital Sign	Description
Temperature	Axillary: 97.7°F to 99.1°F (36.5°C–37.3°C)
	Rectal: 97.7°F to 99.8°F (36.5°C–37.7°C)
	Skin: 95.9°F to 97.7°F (35.5°C–36.5°C)
Heart rate	100 to 160 beats per minute
Respiratory rate	40 to 60 breaths per minute
Systolic blood pressure	65 to 75 mm Hg (mean should equal gestational age in weeks)

*Data are taken from Blackburn.[8]

central cyanosis that does not respond to 100% oxygen and adequate ventilation may be the result of a cardiac cause or persistent pulmonary hypertension of the newborn.[6]

The femoral and brachial pulses should be assessed (most easily performed when the infant is quiet). Comparing the rate and rhythm of pulses with the apical rate will facilitate identification of an ectopic rhythm. The strength of the right brachial pulse should be compared with that of the left brachial pulse and one femoral pulse. Because the right subclavian is located preductally, absent or weak pulses in either femoral or left brachial artery compared with the right brachial may indicate decreased aortic blood flow as the result of a closing DA in a ductal-dependent left outflow tract obstructive lesion, such as coarctation, an interrupted aortic arch, aortic stenosis/atresia, and hypoplastic left heart syndrome.[10]

The capillary filling time provides valuable information about the adequacy of cardiac output. Capillary refill should be less than three seconds in the neonate and should be evaluated by pressing a finger against the skin, holding for a count of three, and then releasing and evaluating the speed of color return. This should be performed in both a peripheral (i.e., a knee) and a central (i.e., the chest) location. A refill time of three seconds or longer may indicate an inadequate vascular volume and compromised perfusion.[6]

Integumentary System

The epidermis and dermis are thin with loose cohesion, making the epidermis more prone to injury from friction and shearing forces, such as occur with tape removal. Melanin levels are low at birth so that, regardless of race, skin color may be light pink. This also makes infants more prone to ultraviolet damage. Their skin pH is higher, making them more susceptible to superficial bacterial infections. Mottling is a normal response to a cool environment, reflecting the neonate's vasomotor instability; mottling should resolve with rewarming. Pallor is a sign of anemia, hypoxia, or poor peripheral perfusion; the cause should be investigated. A ruddy appearance may be related to a high hematocrit. Infants have a larger surface area to body mass ratio, placing them at increased risk for heat and insensible fluid loss with resultant dehydration.

The most common rash in the newborn (i.e., erythema toxicum) occurs within five days of birth as small white or pale yellow pustules surrounded by an erythematous base, similar to a mosquito bite. The cause of this benign self-resolving rash, often called newborn rash, is unknown; the rash frequently disappears and reappears on another region of the newborn's body.[10]

Dark-skinned neonates may have large hyperpigmented gray or blue-green lesions over their buttocks, flanks, or shoulders, although they may appear on any part of the body, including hands, arms, and feet. Termed *congenital dermal melanocytosis* (formerly known as Mongolian spots), these benign lesions are easily mistaken for bruises because of their color and location, leading to unnecessary and unfounded investigations of child abuse.[10]

The umbilicus should be assessed for signs of infection. The umbilical cord stump should completely separate in seven to 14 days, and the cord base should be healed by the end of the first month. Although historically alcohol has been used for daily cord care, research does not support this practice.[11] Until the umbilicus is completely healed, the umbilical vessels are a potential site of entry for infection. The umbilical cord stump should be kept clean and dry, cleansing as needed with mild pH-neutral soap and water, and drying thoroughly. Abnormal findings include redness, swelling, drainage, and foul odor; and an evaluation for cellulitis should be performed.

Gastrointestinal System

Immature innervation of the intestine results in irregular and disorganized peristalsis and increases the newborn's tendency for abdominal distention when ill. The newborn's first stool, meconium, is tarlike and should be passed within 24 hours of birth in the term infant. Nonbilious regurgitation is common because of delayed gastric emptying and a relaxed lower esophageal sphincter. Bilious vomiting and abdominal distension are always abnormal and should be rapidly evaluated. They may signal a surgical emergency, such as intestinal obstruction or malrotation with or without midgut volvulus.[3] Any history of *polyhydramnios* (a high level of amniotic fluid) should be noted because this may indicate intestinal obstruction in the neonate.

The newborn's first stool is thick and sticky and appears dark green/black. After the first three days of life, stools appear yellow and may also appear loose and seedy, especially in the breastfeeding infant. Bloody stools may indicate enteritis or infection. Stools without color (white or gray) may indicate intestinal atresia.[10]

Necrotizing enterocolitis is an inflammatory disorder of the intestine that often presents as feeding intolerance, abdominal distention, bilious gastric fluid, bloody stools, tachycardia, apnea, lethargy, and temperature instability (usually cool). Most common in the preterm infant, it can occur at any gestational age, especially after feedings have begun. The intestinal system of the preterm or ill infant is predisposed to bacterial overgrowth, complicated by slow motility and further complicated by ischemia (e.g., from an asphyxial event), leading to inflammation and mucosal damage. Gas-producing bacteria are then able to invade the bowel wall, causing intramural gas, pneumotosis intestinalis, the hallmark radiological sign of necrotizing enterocolitis. Bacteria can be translocated from the lumen of the intestine into the bloodstream, causing septicemia, even if bowel perforation does not occur.[6]

Genitourinary System

Kidney function is immature at birth. Urine output normally commences within 24 hours of birth. The urine is colorless and odorless, with a normal volume of 2 mL/kg per hour and a specific gravity of 1.008 to 1.012. Although neonates can readily secrete urine, they have a decreased ability to concentrate urine to conserve body water because of the limited reabsorptive capability of the ascending nephron tubule.[8] Increased losses of sodium, glucose, and other solutes in the urine make the infant susceptible to electrolyte abnormalities.

Hypernatremic dehydration can result from inadequate breastfeeding or feeding an infant overly concentrated formula. Hyponatremia and overhydration can occur if neonates are given a fluid volume exceeding their level of renal capacity (e.g., fed overly diluted formula or given an inappropriate intravenous infusion of sterile water).

Genitalia should appear normal and pink. In the uncircumcised male infant, the foreskin normally covers the entire head of the penis and phimosis is a normal finding as the result of adhesions to the glans. The foreskin should not be fully retracted for the first few years of life. The urethral meatus should be at the central tip of the penis, visualized by gentle traction of the foreskin. It should accommodate a 5 French catheter. A location on the ventral surface of the glans or shaft of the penis is called *hypospadias*. A location on the dorsal aspect of the glans or shaft of the penis is called *epispadias*. Either location may result in abnormalities in voiding.[10]

A small penis (average stretched length, three and one-half centimeters), an enlarged clitoris, or a hyperpigmented scrotum may indicate congenital adrenal hyperplasia, an inherited disorder of the adrenal gland preventing production of cortisol and aldosterone. A dark or bluish scrotum can indicate testicular torsion, a medical emergency that requires immediate surgical intervention.[10]

The circumcision site should be inspected for signs of infection. Expected findings include the development of a yellowish white scab by the second day after the procedure. If the Plastibell procedure was used, the plastic ring remains on the penis until it separates in approximately five to eight days. Abnormal findings include bleeding, swelling, exudate, foul odor, and erythema extending down the shaft of the penis.[12]

Musculoskeletal System

The newborn's skeleton is composed more of cartilage than ossified bone, rendering it soft and flexible, with joints that are elastic (enabling passage through the birth canal). Extremities should appear symmetrical in size and length, flexed with abduction at the hips. Their position and appearance often reflect intrauterine positioning, with external bowing and rotation being normal findings. Tight flexion of all four extremities is an expected finding in the term infant. Preterm infants will normally have less flexion, with the smallest preterm infants unable to spontaneously flex. Hands are often fisted. Neonates stressed by an acute disease process and preterm infants will be hypotonic, with outstretched and limp extremities.[10]

All skin folds should be symmetrical. The skull bones are soft, with sutures that are mobile. The spine should be intact, covered by skin, with a normal convex curvature and without tufts of hair, masses, or dimples.

Hemopoietic System

The circulating blood volume of the term infant is approximately 85 mL/kg; and of the preterm infant, 90 to 105 mL/kg. Newborn infants have a predominance of fetal hemoglobin that has a higher affinity for oxygen and a slower release to tissues than adult hemoglobin. This results in a shift to the left on the oxygen dissociation curve and a lower PaO_2 for corresponding oxygen saturation.

Normal hemoglobin and hematocrit values vary with gestational age and can be influenced by the volume of blood transfused from the placenta at delivery (e.g., if the infant is held below the level of the uterus, blood will continue to flow into the infant until the umbilical cord is clamped). In the neonate older than 34 weeks' gestation, a normal venous hemoglobin is 14 to 20 g/dL. The venous hemoglobin peaks at the age of two to four hours, with a normal venous value of approximately 50% in the term infant. Capillary blood samples may show higher levels because of peripheral vasoconstriction and should be confirmed with a central (venous or arterial) blood sample if 65% or greater. A hematocrit greater than 65%, especially if the infant is symptomatic with poor perfusion and signs of cardiac failure, may require treatment with a reduction transfusion during which a small amount of blood is withdrawn from the infant and replaced with normal saline.

Hemoglobin and hematocrit values decline at approximately 8 to 12 weeks of life in healthy term infants. This physiological anemia of infancy has a low point of approximately 9 to 11 g/dL of hemoglobin.[6, 13]

Neurological System

The healthy term infant's response to tactile and noxious stimuli should be brisk. Normal reflexes are summarized in **Table 12-3**. Movements are often uncoordinated and may include coarse tremors and quivering of the chin. Neonates stressed by an acute disease process, and preterm infants, may have little to no response to painful or noxious stimuli.[10]

Measurement of head circumference and assessment of the anterior fontanel are performed on all infants. Head circumference is measured by placing a tape measure 1 cm above the eyes and around the back of the head.

The average term infant's head circumference is 32.6 to 37.2 cm and increases by approximately 0.5 cm per week. The anterior fontanel is best assessed with the quiet infant in an upright (sitting) position. It should be open, soft, and flat, measuring approximately 3 to 4 cm long and 1 to 3 cm wide. A sunken fontanel may indicate dehydration. A bulging fontanel may indicate increased intracranial pressure.[10, 13]

Fluid and Electrolytes

The newborn has a high ratio of extracellular water that sharply increases after birth because of placental transfusion, reabsorption of fetal lung fluid, and other fluid shifts. This extracellular water is lost primarily through diuresis, which begins on day two to five of life and is reflected in the expected weight loss in the first week of life. On the first day of life, a term newborn requires 40 to 60 mL/kg per day of fluids to maintain homeostasis. This requirement increases by 20 mL/kg per day until 150 to 175 mL/kg per day is achieved. Preterm infants have higher requirements related to increased insensible and other fluid losses because of immature skin and renal functioning.[6]

After birth, the neonate must transition from a constant supply of glucose from the maternal bloodstream, transported across the placenta to use exogenous sources (breast milk or formula). Glycogen is stored in the liver during the last trimester of fetal life. These stores of glycogen are rapidly depleted in times of stress and fasting, making the neonate especially prone to hypoglycemia. Furthermore, the preterm infant has not had the opportunity to lay down these stores and is at high risk for hypoglycemia. A glucose level of less than 40 mg/dL is commonly considered to be hypoglycemia in the newborn of all gestations. Some researchers recom-

Table 12-3 Neonatal Reflexes*

Reflex	Response	Duration in Months
Sucking	Touching or gently stroking the lips causes the mouth to open and sucking movements to begin.	12
Rooting	When cheek is touched or stroked along the side of the mouth, the infant turns his or her head toward that side and begins to suck.	3–4
Grasp	Digits flex when the palm of the hand or sole of the foot is touched.	2
Startle ("Moro")	With loud noise or sudden movement, arms extend and abduct with open hands, followed by flexion of arms, fisting, and crying.	6
Babinski	When the sole of the foot is firmly stroked at the lateral side from the toes to the heel, the great toe dorsal flexes with extension of other toes.	12

*Data are taken from Kenner and Lott.[30]

mend keeping the glucose level at 50 mg/dL or greater in sick infants.[14] The normal glucose use rate in the term newborn is 4 to 7 mg/kg per minute, which is much higher than that of adults. This reflects the infant's comparatively larger brain, which is entirely dependent on glucose available in the bloodstream for metabolism. Providing the infant who is not able to be orally fed with 10% dextrose intravenously at 80 mL/kg per day will produce a glucose infusion rate of 5.6 mg/kg per minute, adequately meeting a newborn infant's basic metabolic requirements.[8]

Infants at highest risk for hypoglycemia are as follows:

- Infants who are large for gestational age and infants of diabetic mothers (with diabetes being the result of hyperinsulinemia).

- Preterm infants and infants who are small for gestational age as the result of inadequate glycogen stores.

- Septic and ill infants as the result of increased use of glucose.

- Infants who are unable to be fed because of lack of glucose supply.

All newly born infants, and ill infants, should have their glucose levels evaluated. Infants who cannot take oral feedings should be provided with an exogenous source of glucose, administered either intravenously (10% dextrose) or by nasogastric tube (infant formula or breast milk). Symptoms of hypoglycemia include jitteriness, irritability, hypotonia, lethargy, high-pitched or weak cry, hypothermia, poor suck/coordination, tachypnea, cyanosis, apnea, and seizures.

Hypoglycemia should be treated as soon as it is detected. If bedside glucose monitoring is used, treatment should begin while the glucose value is being verified by a serum blood sample. Depending on the severity of hypoglycemia, the stable neonate older than 34 weeks' gestation without respiratory distress or another sign of illness can usually be fed 30 mL of a 20-cal/oz infant formula. An infant should not be fed 5% or 10% glucose water, and the formula should not be diluted with glucose water because this will provide inadequate glucose to support metabolic requirements. However, if the neonate is experiencing respiratory distress, has a decreased level of consciousness, or has a glucose level of less than 35 mg/dL, an intravenous glucose bolus and infusion are usually indicated to correct the hypoglycemia.

- Administer a minibolus of 2 mL/kg of $D_{10}W$ intravenously over one minute, followed by a constant infusion of $D_{10}W$.

- **Do not administer a bolus with a concentration greater than $D_{10}W$** because higher concentrations can be damaging to peripheral veins.

- Reassess the serum glucose level 15 to 20 minutes after the dextrose bolus and hourly until the glucose level is stable. Maintain the serum glucose level between 55 and 110 mg/dL (a euglycemic state).[15]

Pain Assessment

Neonates do feel pain as acutely as adults; however, the quantification of pain is limited to behavioral and physiological cues. Behavioral indicators include facial activity, body movements, and crying. The *cry face* (**Figure 12-2**) is a strong indicator of pain. Physiological indicators include heart rate, respiratory rate, blood pressure, and oxygen saturation. A high index of suspicion for pain should exist when assessing the infant. Pain scales appropriate for the neonate include the following: CRIES,[16] Premature Infant Pain Profile,[17] NIPS,[18] and N-PASS.[19] **Chapter 6, "Pain,"** provides further information on the use of pain assessment tools.

Growth

Body weight and length are important indicators of well-being and should be measured and compared with gestational age-appropriate norms.[20] Accurate measurement is important for prescribing fluids and medications.

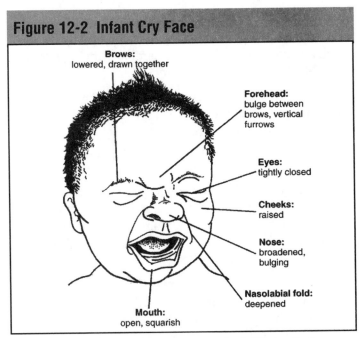

Figure 12-2 Infant Cry Face

Brows: lowered, drawn together

Forehead: bulge between brows, vertical furrows

Eyes: tightly closed

Cheeks: raised

Nose: broadened, bulging

Nasolabial fold: deepened

Mouth: open, squarish

Reprinted with permission from Wong, D. L., & Whaley, L. F. (1997). *Whaley & Wong's essentials of pediatric nursing* (5th ed.). St. Louis, MO: Mosby.

The average-term newborn weighs between 2.7 to 4 kg (6–8.5 lbs.).

Weight loss up to 10% of birth weight during the first week of life is a normal finding, with breastfed neonates often losing slightly more weight than bottle-fed neonates because of the time it takes for the mother's milk supply to fully mature. Most neonates stop losing weight by day five and will regain their birth weight by day 10. Normal neonatal weight gain is approximately 30 g per day in the first three months of life. Failure to gain weight always requires investigation for nutritional issues (e.g., under-feeding or malabsorption) or other health issues.

Body length is measured from the crown of the head to the heel. The term newborn's length varies greatly, from 48 to 53 cm (19–21 inches). To facilitate accurate measurement, with the infant in a recumbent position, mark the crown of the head on the bed, straighten the infant's leg, marking the location of the heel, and then measure the distance between the two marks.

Assessment of the Neonate

The initial assessment of the neonate is similar to that of any other pediatric patient. **Chapter 5, "Initial Assessment,"** provides a review of a comprehensive primary and secondary assessment. However, the unique developmental characteristics of the neonatal period dictate some adjustments in the approach to the assessment and the incorporation of some additional components during the secondary assessment.

- Observe the neonate before touching if possible. When disturbed, the neonate's normal reaction is to be startled and cry, thus changing the assessment of baseline respiratory and heart rates.

- Keep the neonate warm and protect against heat loss during the examination. Undress only the part of the infant being examined and redress or perform the examination under a radiant warmer.

- Handle the infant gently to facilitate cooperation.

- Perform the most intrusive aspects of the assessment last (rectal temperatures, abdominal palpation). Use the toe-to-head approach.

- Observe the general condition of the neonate, including nutritional status, quality of cry, behaviors, and responses to comforting measures. Also observe the caregiver interaction.

- Assess the neonate's color for clues of pathological features.

- Listen to the lungs, heart, and abdomen in a quiet environment.

- Palpate the femoral pulses first because they are more difficult to assess in a crying infant.

- Use sensorimotor and tactile comfort measures to calm and soothe the neonate (e.g., swaddling, rocking, or speaking with a calm and soothing voice) before and during the examination. Allow the neonate to use a pacifier; sucking is believed to modulate the perception of discomfort through the endogenous nonopioid system.

Table 12-4 details the elements that should be collected in assessing the neonate's history. Data collection should include information about the pregnancy and delivery.[3, 10]

Table 12-5 provides a mnemonic for differential diagnosis in neonates.

Table 12-6 summarizes various assessment findings that are specific to the neonate. Pain assessment of the neonate can be found in **Chapter 6, "Pain."**

Diagnostic Procedures

A variety of radiographic and laboratory studies may be indicated based on the suspected etiology of the neonate's condition.

Radiographic Studies

- A chest radiograph should be performed for any neonate with a history of respiratory or cardiac symptoms or in any febrile neonate.

- An abdominal radiograph should be performed for the neonate with gastrointestinal symptoms or a concerning abdominal examination result.

- A combined chest and abdominal radiograph, encompassing the torso from the neck to the pelvis, should be performed for the neonate with obvious abdominal distention. This particular film allows the practitioner to evaluate the effect of the abdominal distention on the lungs. In some institutions, this film may be referred to as a babygram.

- To obtain a good film, the neonate is held on the radiograph plate, head midline, clavicles straight, arms laying relaxed at the sides (not stretched over the head), and hips flat to the plate, without rotation. A pacifier may help to calm the neonate during the procedure.

Table 12-4 Neonatal History

Prenatal history	Mother's age, gravida, and parity (number of pregnancies, abortions, stillbirths, and living children).
	Estimated due date for the neonate.
	Prenatal care (started during which week of pregnancy and how many visits).
	Medical complications or high-risk pregnancy factors, treatments, and monitoring.
	Medications taken during pregnancy (over-the-counter, herbal, prescription, and illicit drug use).
	Tobacco and alcohol use during pregnancy.
	Maternal blood type and Rh, antibody screen, serology, VDRL test and status, rubella immunity, sexually transmitted infections during pregnancy, group B streptococcus screening, hepatitis B surface antigen screening, and HIV status.
	Mother's health before and during pregnancy (inquire about chronic health problems, diseases, or disorders).
	Singleton birth versus multiple gestation (e.g., twin or triplet). If multiple gestation, health status of sibling(s).
	Ages and health of other children in the family. If any child is deceased, obtain age, date, and cause of death.
	Family medical history: chronic disorders, disabilities, or known hereditary diseases.
	Social history: mother's marital status, support system, financial and housing system, and health of those living with the mother/infant.
Delivery history	Type of delivery (vaginal or cesarean section). If cesarean section, determine if emergent or planned.
	Problems associated with labor (e.g., induced, length of labor, forceps or vacuum use, bleeding, fever, or hypertension).
	Time and duration of rupture of membranes and amount and color of amniotic fluid.
	Problems with infant at birth: Apgar scores or resuscitative measures (oxygen delivery and intubation).
	Birth weight.
	Gestational age at birth.
	Length of hospital stay for both mother and infant. Ask, *"Did your baby come home from the hospital with you?"* (If the answer is "no," then question the mother about why the infant stayed longer in the hospital.)
	Problems or interventions during the hospital stay. In particular, ask about jaundice, low blood glucose level, and admission to neonatal intensive care or special care nursery.
Diet	Breastfed.
	Bottle fed.
	Formula: what type (name), which form (premixed, liquid concentrate, or powder), and how it is mixed (e.g., number of scoops of powder to ounces of water).
Feeding patterns	Length of time the neonate nurses at each feeding or amount taken per feeding.
	Typical time required to complete feeding.
	Interval between feedings.
	Awakens self for feedings. Neonates should awaken to feed every 2–3 hours. Infants generally do not sleep through the night until the age of 2–6 months.
	Quality of suck.
	Eagerness to feed.
	Does the neonate finish each feeding without prompting (or does the neonate fall asleep partway through and need repeated stimulation to finish feeding)?
	Color change with feeding.
	Changes in feeding behavior.
Sleep patterns	Has the caregiver noted any changes in sleep patterns?
	How do caregivers place the neonate for sleeping? Infants should always be placed supine, with blankets tucked below their armpits.
Urine	Last wet diaper and number of wet diapers in the previous 24 hours. Infants should have a wet diaper with every feeding, approximately 6–8 times per day.
	Changes noted (e.g., appearance or odor of urine).
Stool	Usual number of bowel movements per day. Breast milk-fed infants typically have more bowel movements per day than formula-fed infants. Color, consistency, and odor changes are noted.

Note: HIV indicates human immunodeficiency virus; VDRL, Venereal Disease Research Laboratory.

Table 12-5 Potential Neonatal Emergencies

	Differential diagnosis	Symptoms	Assessment/initial interventions (after assessment of ABCs and appropriate interventions)
N	**iNborn** errors of metabolism (metabolic acidosis, hypoglycemia, hyperammonemia)	Usually occurs 2–7 days of age, poor feeding D/T poor suck, irritability, vomiting, failure to thrive, hepatosplenomegaly, jaundice, abnormal odors	Assess electrolytes, especially glucose; obtain family history for metabolic diseases. Place NPO, correct acid-base and electrolyte abnormalities, and consult metabolic or genetic specialist
E	**Electrolyte** abnormalities (hyponatremia, hypernatremia, hypokalemia, hyperkalemia, hypocalcemia, hypoglycemia)	Related to type of abnormality, including lethargy or irritability, seizures, ECG changes, history of polyuria or oliguria	Obtain careful history, including birth weight; assess for dehydration, obtain electrolyte studies including BUN and creatinine
O	**Overdose** (toxin, poison such as ethyl alcohol, herbal remedies, maternal ingestions)	Symptoms related to type of toxin; consider alcohol poisoning if giving alcohol baths for fever or using alcohol to cleanse umbilical stump	Careful history to include dermal exposure, ingestion of contaminated breast milk, use of herbal remedies for colic
S	**Seizures**	Lip smacking, bicycling movements of legs, tongue thrusting, apnea, staring spells, jack-knifing	Initiate testing to rule out AHT, electrolyte abnormalities, metabolic emergencies, Obtain history to include maternal use of drugs. Obtain IV access and prepare for use of antiepileptic medication
E	**Endocrine** crisis (hypoglycemia, hypocalcemia, less common: congenital adrenal hyperplasia [CAH], thyrotoxicosis)	Symptoms similar to electrolyte abnormalities. CAH: Assess for presence of ambiguous genitalia in females and hyperpigmented scrotum in males. Thyrotoxicosis: tachycardia, tremors, sweating, irritability	Obtain history including birth weight; large for gestational age and small for gestational age are at additional risk. Thyrotoxicosis: maternal history of Graves disease
C	**Cardiac** abnormalities (ductal dependent lesions: left-sided obstructive, right-sided obstructive lesions)	Left-sided: severe systemic hypoperfusion including pallor, mottling, decreased or absent pulses, severe metabolic acidosis and cardiomegaly and pulmonary congestion noted on chest radiograph. Right-sided: severe cyanosis, metabolic acidosis, decreased perfusion of the lung fields or abnormally shaped heart noted on chest radiograph	Initiate oxygen at 40%–60% FiO_2, monitoring, prepare for PGE1 administration if indicated, obtain cardiology consult
R	**Recipe** (incorrect mixing of formula, addition of herbs or other additives)	Signs of hypernatremia or water intoxication (including seizures, change in activity level)	Careful history including formula preparation, use of home remedies, addition of probiotics to formula
E	**Enteric** emergencies (malrotation with or without midgut volvulus, Hirschsprung disease, necrotizing enterocolitis, pyloric stenosis, jaundice)	Feeding intolerance or bilious emesis; tender, distended abdomen, with discoloration of overlying skin, failure to pass meconium or infrequent stools	Obtain history including gestational age, feeding habits, elimination habits (premature babies, history of surgical closure of an abdominal wall defect or infant of cocaine-using mother raises increased suspicion of necrotizing enterocolitis; failure to pass meconium is suspicious of Hirschsprung disease).
T	**Trauma** (accidental and nonaccidental)	Lethargy/irritability (AHT), circulatory collapse (solid organ injury), decreased use of extremities (musculoskeletal trauma), respiratory distress (rib, solid- or hollow organ injuries)	Careful history and assessment; monitor for change in status; laboratory (including CBC, PT/PTT, LFTs) and radiologic procedures as indicated, careful documentation of assessment and caregiver conversations.
S	**Sepsis**	Lethargy/irritability, temperature instability, hemodynamic instability	History to include feeding/elimination, fever or hypothermia; careful monitoring, initiate laboratory studies including CBC, UA, CSF, blood cultures. Anticipate order for IV antibiotics.

Note: AHT indicates abusive head trauma; CBC, complete blood count; CSF, cerebrospinal fluid; ECG, electrocardiogram; FiO2, fraction of inspired oxygen; IV, intravenous; LFT, liver function test; NPO, nothing by mouth; PGE1, prostaglandin E1; PT/PTT, partial thromboplastin time/prothrombin time; UA, urinalysis.

*Adapted from Steinhorn[33] and the following: Kim, U. O., Brousseau, D. C., & Konduri, G. G. (2008). Evaluation and management of the critically ill neonate in the emergency department. *Clinical Pediatric Emergency Medicine, 9*, 140–148.

Table 12-6 Abnormal Neonatal Assessment Findings and Potential Causes

Assessment Findings	Potential Causes	
Cyanosis (mucous membranes or trunk)	Hypoxia Respiratory distress or failure Congenital heart disease or congestive heart failure causing impaired alveolar ventilation Right-to-left shunting through fetal shunts (DA and FO) Infection/sepsis	Poor perfusion and shock Acidosis Polycythemia Methemoglobinemia Central nervous system injury, malformation, or disease causing a diminished respiratory drive
Mottling of skin	Hypothermia/cold stress (vascular instability) Poor perfusion from hypovolemia Infection/sepsis	Hypoxia Congenital heart disease
Pallor	Poor perfusion Poor oxygenation Low hemoglobin (anemia) Infection/sepsis	Hypothermia Shock Hypoxia Congenital heart disease
Jaundice	Hyperbilirubinemia Blood group ABO/Rh blood group incompatibility Physiological jaundice Breast milk-associated jaundice Primary liver disease	Extrahepatic obstruction, such as biliary atresia Infection/sepsis Hemolysis reaction secondary to bruising during delivery Genetic and metabolic disorders
Lethargy, hypotonia (decreased muscle tone), poor feeding or lack of interest in feeding, difficult to arouse or elicit a response to stimuli, increased sleeping times, and decreased reflexes (e.g., suck, grasp, startle, and root)	Sepsis Hypoxia Respiratory distress or failure Dehydration	Shock Hypoglycemia Kernicterus
Irritability (increased activity level), poor sleep patterns or decreased sleeping times, and inconsolability	Infection Pain or discomfort Colic Withdrawal from maternal substance abuse Hypoglycemia	Kernicterus Feeding intolerance Overstimulation Neurological injury or dysfunction
Hypertonia: arms and hands tightly flexed, arching of back and neck, legs stiff and extended, and startles easily	Meningitis Neurological injury or dysfunction	Kernicterus
Seizures: lip smacking, eye fluttering or repeated eye movements, bicycling, movements of legs, shaking of one or more extremities, and rhythmic movement of one or more extremity	Hypoglycemia Hypocalcemia Hydrocephalus Neurologic injury or dysfunction Increased intracranial pressure	Sepsis or meningitis Seizure disorder
Hypothermia: axillary temperature lower than 97.9°F (36.5°C) and rectal temperature lower than 96.9°F (36°C)	Sepsis Cold ambient environment Electrolyte disturbance (secondary to diarrhea and vomiting or to error in formula preparation)	Meningitis
Hyperthermia: axillary temperature higher than 99.5°F (37.5°C) and rectal temperature higher than 100.4°F (38°C)	Sepsis Warm ambient environment	Bundled heavily in clothing and blankets in a warm environment

Table 12-6 Abnormal Neonatal Assessment Findings and Potential Causes *continued*

Assessment Findings	Potential Causes	
Apnea	Airway obstruction (congenital deformity, swelling, secretions, and positioning) Sepsis Respiratory infection Gastroesophageal reflux	Hypoglycemia Seizures Anemia Toxin exposure Munchausen syndrome by proxy
Bradypnea	Respiratory failure Cardiopulmonary failure	Neurological compromise
Tachypnea (respiratory rate > 60 breaths per minute after the age of 2 hours)	Respiratory infection or pneumonia Hypoxia Sepsis Hyperthermia Congenital heart disease or congestive heart failure	Hypoglycemia Acidosis Dehydration Shock Pain or discomfort
Bradycardia (heart rate < 80 beats per minute)	Late response to hypoxia Late response to shock Apnea	Sepsis Hypothermia Neurological compromise
Tachycardia (heart rate > 160 beats per minute)	Dehydration Shock Hypotension Acidosis Sepsis	Respiratory distress Hypoxia Congenital heart disease Hyperthermia Crying
Depressed or sunken anterior fontanel	Dehydration	
Bulging anterior fontanel (assessed with infant in an upright position and quiet)	Hydrocephalus Increased intracranial pressure Meningitis	
Diarrhea (increase in the number of stools with an increased water content)	Viral infection Bacterial infection	Toxic reaction to food or other poison Formula intolerance, including addition of probiotics Antibiotic therapy, adverse effect
Constipation (infrequent passage of stool), may be accompanied by abdominal distention and discomfort; and stool may be hard and blood streaked	Formula incompatibility (change of formula) Meconium plug Meconium ileus (early sign of cystic fibrosis)	Congenital intestinal obstruction, atresia, or stenosis Malrotation Hirschsprung disease
Vomiting (a forceful ejection of the gastric contents) may be present with abdominal distention	Infection Pyloric stenosis Bowel obstruction, atresia, or stenosis	Malrotation Gastroesophageal reflux Necrotizing enterocolitis
Hypoglycemia (blood glucose level < 40 mg/dL)	Increased glucose use (asphyxia or hypothermia) Sepsis Prolonged seizures	Elevated insulin levels (infant of diabetic mother) Inadequate substrate supply (premature infant, intrauterine growth retardation, or SGA) or congenital defects or syndromes

Note: DA indicates ductus arteriosus; FO, foramen ovale; SGA, small for gestational age.

Figure 12-3 Example of Heel Lancet	Figure 12-4 Heel Blood Collection Sites

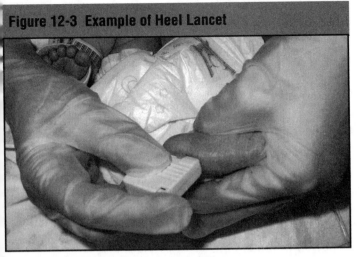

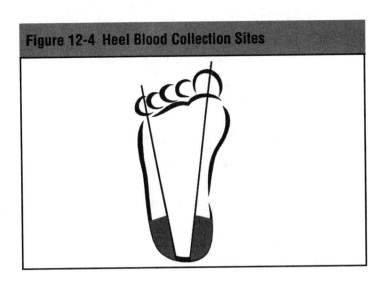

Photograph courtesy of Mary L. Puchalski

Laboratory Studies

Blood draws for the neonate can be performed as a venipuncture or from a heel stick. Often, a venipuncture can be more difficult and the need to obtain blood for a laboratory evaluation is emergent. Drawing blood with intravenous catheter insertion can result in hemolysis and loss of patency of the catheter. When performing capillary blood collection by heel stick, warming the heel for three to five minutes may help dilate capillaries and facilitate perfusion, especially if the skin is cool. Warming should be performed with commercially available heel warmers to prevent thermal injury from uncontrolled heating (e.g., a washcloth with hot water). Specially designed spring-loaded lancets that puncture no deeper than two millimeters should be used because they have a lower possibility of injury from the process (**Figure 12-3**). Puncture of the heel should only be done on the medial and lateral areas of the plantar surface, where the tissue is thickest (shaded area on **Figure 12-4**). The center of the heel should be avoided because injury to the calcaneus, nerves, and artery is possible. Avoid squeezing the heel to collect blood because this will cause bruising and hemolysis.

The following laboratory studies are commonly evaluated in ill newborns:

- Blood gas. Puncture of the radial or posttibial arteries is appropriate if oxygenation is a concern. Brachial and femoral arterial puncture should not be performed on the neonate because there is increased risk of excessive blood loss. If ventilation is the primary issue to be evaluated (pulse oximetry provides useful information about oxygenation noninvasively), then a capillary (heel stick) or venous sample is appropriate. Normal arterial

blood values for the term infant are as follows: pH, 7.32 to 7.38; partial pressure of carbon dioxide, arterial, 35 to 45 mm Hg; PaO_2, 80 to 95 mm Hg; bicarbonate, 24 to 26 mEq/L; base excess/deficit, positive or negative 3. For both venous and capillary blood gas values, the PaO_2 is of no value; pH values are slightly lower, and carbon dioxide values are generally slightly higher.[6]

- Glucose. A whole blood (bedside test) and/or serum glucose test must be performed on all ill neonates. Serial glucose testing is needed when the neonate requires correction of hypoglycemia and in any newborn who has not been feeding well or has not been fed for longer than six hours. Infants who are not feeding or with hypoglycemia should have their blood glucose measured hourly.

- Total and direct serum bilirubin. Bilirubin levels should be evaluated in all newborn infants. Jaundice is common and is not easily appreciated in dark-skinned infants (on page 193, the section on hyperbilirubinemia contains more information). Infants who present to the ED may be initially screened with transcutaneous bilirubinometry while waiting for serum results.

- CBC count with manual differential. Evaluate for signs of sepsis and anemia. An immature to total neutrophil ratio greater than 0.25 is indicative of a high risk for sepsis in the first few days of life. An absolute to total neutrophil count ratio of less than 1,800 is also indicative of a high risk for sepsis.

- Electrolytes with blood urea nitrogen, creatinine, calcium, magnesium, and phosphorus.

- Blood ammonia, lactate, and pyruvate. These values should be evaluated if an inborn error of metabolism is suspected; although testing through state laboratories is performed routinely to identify these disorders, some can present acutely in the newborn period before laboratory results are available. Most are the result of single gene defects that result in an enzyme deficiency. Problems arise because of the accumulation of substances that are toxic or interfere with normal function or if there is reduced ability to synthesize essential compounds. Another clue to the possibility of these problems is a family history of unexplained neonatal deaths. Examples include glycogen storage diseases, maple syrup urine disease, fatty acid oxidation defects, and organic acidurias.

- Blood type and screening.

Planning/Implementation

Specific Interventions for the Neonate

- Assess the need for inpatient admission. Prepare for admission or transfer to a neonatal intensive care unit, pediatric intensive care unit, or pediatric floor equipped to care for neonates.

- Prevent heat loss/correct hypothermia. Use a commercial radiant warmer or heat lamps for neonates requiring invasive procedures, resuscitation, or exposure for close observation. Cover the neonate's head and wrap in a blanket when exposure is not required for procedures or observation. Monitor temperature frequently.

- Obtain weight. Completely undress (including diaper) the infant.

- Keep the base of the umbilical stump dry and exposed to air. The diaper should be folded down so that the umbilical stump is exposed.

- Provide circumcision care. Apply petroleum jelly on a gauze dressing over the circumcision site and apply the diaper loosely to prevent friction against the penis.

- Offer the option of family presence. Encourage caregivers to remain with the neonate and to hold and comfort the neonate. Promote sensory soothing interventions (e.g., rocking, stroking skin, or sucking on a pacifier).

- Support the breastfeeding mother. The neonate may be unable to nurse during the assessment and initial treatment period. Provide the mother access to a breast pump with disposable fittings and privacy as needed.

- Treat hypoglycemia.

- If the neonate is receiving nothing by mouth, deliver glucose-containing maintenance intravenous fluids as indicated by patient condition. An infusion pump should always be used to administer fluids and intravenous medications to the neonate.

  - Sodium, potassium, and calcium may be added once serum electrolyte values have been obtained and voiding is established. Sodium requirements are 3 to 4 mEq/kg per day; potassium, approximately 2 mEq/kg per day; and calcium, approximately 400 mg/kg per day. After the first 24 hours of life, fluids commonly used are $D_{10}/0.2$ sodium chloride.

- Assess for and treat pain. Consider sucrose solution on a pacifier for painful procedures such as venipuncture, intravenous catheter placement, heel stick, and nasogastric tube insertion. (**Chapter 6, "Pain,"** provides specific information.)

Evaluation and Ongoing Assessment

- Neonates present at times with nonspecific and subtle signs of illness, and they require frequent reassessment because deterioration may occur.

- Ongoing evaluation of airway patency, breathing effectiveness, circulation, temperature, and urine output is essential in evaluating progress toward expected outcomes.

- Radiant warmers should be set to skin servo control. If heat lamps are used, meticulous reassessment of temperature should be performed to evaluate for overheating.

- Intravenous sites should be inspected hourly for signs of infiltrate or infection.

Selected Emergencies

Delivery of a Neonate in the Emergency Department

Although the obstetrical suite is the ideal location for delivery, many births will occur either in the ED or before arrival at the hospital. The ED staff must be prepared to care for both the mother and the neonate and have an understanding of the neonate's special needs in the first few minutes of life. Any neonate born before arrival in the ED must receive the same serial assessment and care as outlined for the neonate born in the hospital.

The assessment and resuscitation of the newly born infant should occur simultaneously.

There are many conditions that place the neonate at risk for complications at or immediately after delivery. Examples of these conditions are described in **Table 12-7**.

Table 12-7 Conditions Placing the Neonate at Risk for Complications*

Maternal Factors	Environmental Factors	Fetal Factors
Maternal age younger than 16 or older than 35 years	Poverty (related to poor nutrition and healthcare)	Decreased movement in utero
Prepregnancy weight less than 100 pounds (45.5 kilograms)	Maternal drug use (alcohol, cocaine, or narcotics)	Anemia or isoimmunization
Maternal obesity (prepregnancy BMI > 30)	Exposure to environmental toxins	Multiple gestation
Anemia	Narcotics administered to mother within 4 hours of delivery	Nonreassuring fetal heart rate patterns (decelerations)
Bleeding during second or third trimester or labor		Bradycardia
Placental abruption		Meconium-stained amniotic fluid
Placenta previa		Prematurity
Diabetes mellitus: primary or gestational		Postterm gestation
Hypertension: chronic or pregnancy induced		Macrosomia
Infection or chorioamnionitis		Poor fetal growth (intrauterine growth restriction)
Cephalopelvic disproportion		Prolapsed umbilical cord
Premature labor		Malformation or anomalies
Prolonged labor (> 24 hours)		Low Birth Weight (LBW)
Prolonged second stage of labor (longer than 2 hours)		
Premature rupture of membranes (before labor has started)		
Prolonged rupture of membranes (> 18 hours before delivery)		
Precipitous labor		
Medication therapy (e.g., magnesium or adrenergic blocking agents)		
No prenatal care		
Maternal nutritional deficiencies		
Chronic disease: cardiac, renal, pulmonary, thyroid, or neurological		
Previous fetal or neonatal death		
Sexually Transmitted Infections		

Note: BMI indicates body mass index (calculated as weight in kilograms divided by height in meters squared).
*Data are taken from Kattwinkel et al[5] and Tappero and Honeyfield.[10]

Should a delivery be necessary in the ED, asking the following questions will aid in preparing for the birth:

- *"What color was your water when it broke?"* An assessment should be made for the presence of meconium in the amniotic fluid. Meconium-stained infants who are not vigorous (breathing and crying) at delivery will need immediate intubation and tracheal suctioning.

- *"When is your baby due?"* Knowing the gestational age of the fetus will help in preparing for the level of support the newborn may require. Premature infants require ventilatory support more frequently than term infants.

- *"How many babies are there?"* A multiple birth will require more personnel and equipment at delivery.

- *"Have there been any problems with your pregnancy?"* Knowing what complications of pregnancy exist will assist in preparing for complications that may arise during delivery (e.g., hypertension of pregnancy, placement of cerclage, or placenta previa).

- *"Have you taken any medications or drugs in the last day?"* The use of some illegal drugs may cause premature labor and/or placental abruption. A history of narcotic use in the four hours before delivery may result in a neonate with a depressed respiratory effort. However, naloxone (Narcan) should never be administered to infants of mothers who have abused narcotics because it can lead to rapid withdrawal and seizures in the newborn.

- *"Are you HIV positive?"* The identification of human immunodeficiency virus (HIV) during pregnancy or within 48 hours of delivery enables interventions to prevent HIV transmission to the fetus/newborn. Antiretroviral prophylaxis administered during labor (zidovudine and nevirapine or lamivudine, depending on the mother's regimen) or within the first 12 hours after birth reduces the risk of mother-to-child transmission from 25% to 9%. It also has no adverse long-term safety effects for women and infants who are not infected, so it can be safely administered while waiting for confirmatory testing results. When a woman who has not been tested for HIV presents in labor, rapid testing should be used to screen the mother or infant for HIV

Table 12-8 Equipment Needed to Facilitate a Delivery in the Emergency Department*

Personal protective items, such as gloves, gowns, and masks with an eye shield

OB kit: usually contains items for a normal uncomplicated delivery, such as towels, cord clamps, scalpel, bulb syringe, footprint and thumbprint kit, and identification bands

Radiant warmer or heat lamps (if heat lamps are used, extreme caution must be taken to avoid hyperthermia in the newborn)

Warmed linens

Chemically activated warming pad (never use latex gloves filled with hot water to warm an infant)

Zipper-lock food-grade large polyethylene bag/wrap (gallon size) (to be placed over the infant's trunk to reduce heat loss if the infant is premature)

Bulb syringe

Mechanical suction with tubing

Suction catheters: sizes 5 or 6, 8, and 10 French

Meconium aspirator

Oxygen with flow meter (flow rate ≤ 10 mL/minute) and tubing

Resuscitation bag capable of delivering 90%–100% oxygen and capable of avoiding excessive pressures: 200–750 mL bag (the smaller bag is for preterm infants). A 450–500 mL bag will work for most neonates, regardless of gestational age.

Resuscitation masks: sizes for premature to term infants

Laryngoscope handle and blades: sizes zero and one

Endotracheal tubes: sizes 2.5, 3, 3.5, and 4 mm with stylets

CO_2 detector (optional): infants use up to 15 kilograms

Tape or ET tube-securing device

Pectin-based skin preparation (approved for infants), cut to be placed on cheeks under tape securing ET tube; NEVER apply benzoin to a newborn's skin!

Gastric tube: 8 or 10 French

Medications: epinephrine (1:10,000); isotonic crystalloid (normal saline or Ringer's lactate); 4.2% sodium bicarbonate, 0.5 mEq/mL; naloxone hydrochloride, 0.4 mg/mL; 10% dextrose; and normal saline for flushes

Umbilical vessel catheterization supplies (3.5 French for infants weighing < 1.5 kg and 5 French for heavier infants)

Cardiorespiratory monitor and infant leads

Pulse oximeter and infant probe

Infant stethoscope

Clock with second hand (timer)

Note: CO_2 indicates carbon dioxide; ET, endotracheal; OB, obstetrician.
*Data are taken from Verklan et al.[13]

antibodies and begin intravenous prophylaxis with zidovudine.[21]

Table 12-8 provides a list of the equipment needed to facilitate a delivery in the emergency department.

Delivery

In preparation for a delivery, it is important to remember that approximately 90% of neonates are able to make the transition from intrauterine to extrauterine life with little or no assistance in establishing effective ventilation. **Figure 12-5** illustrates the neonatal resuscitation algorithm, beginning with the birth of the neonate. Based on assessment of the newborn, resuscitation, if necessary, proceeds from one step to the next.

During and after the clamping and cutting of the umbilical cord, the initial assessment is made. The following questions enable a rapid assessment of risk:

1. Is the infant term gestation?

2. Is the amniotic fluid clear?

3. Is the infant breathing or crying?

4. Does the infant have good muscle tone?

If the answer to these four questions is "yes," the newly born infant will most likely need little intervention other than warming, drying, and facilitating airway clearance. If the answer to any of these four questions is no, the steps of resuscitation should be provided.

Steps in Neonatal Resuscitation[4]

1. Dry and warm the neonate.

   a. Place the neonate in a prewarmed area (a radiant warmer, heat lamps, or an examination light may be used as a heat source). Care should be taken not to overheat the infant.

   b. Dry the infant thoroughly with warm towels or blankets. Briskly drying the infant provides tactile stimulation and helps prevent evaporative heat loss.

   c. Remove wet towels and wrap the neonate with prewarmed towels or blankets; cover the neonate's head with a blanket or hat.

   d. If the infant is stable, maintain temperature by placing the infant skin to skin with the mother and increasing the environmental temperature.

2. Maintain airway patency.

   a. Position the neonate neutrally. A rolled washcloth or cloth diaper may be used under the shoulders to facilitate maintenance of correct airway position (**Figure 12-6**).

   b. Correct positioning of the newborn will bring the posterior pharynx, larynx, and trachea in line, which will facilitate unrestricted air entry.

   c. Care should be taken to prevent hyperextension or flexion of the neck because either may decrease air entry.

   d. Using a bulb syringe, suction the mouth and then the nose. Always suction the mouth first because nasal suctioning may cause gasping or crying, resulting in the aspiration of oral secretions. (A way to remember this is "m" comes before "n" in the alphabet, so suction the mouth before the nose.) The bulb syringe is usually adequate; however, an 8 or 10 French suction catheter connected to mechanical suction may be used (negative pressure must not exceed 100 mm Hg).

   e. Repeated suctioning of the mouth may be performed as necessary. Avoid deep suctioning the pharynx because this can produce a vagal response that causes severe bradycardia or apnea.

   f. Gastric suction is unnecessary and invasive.

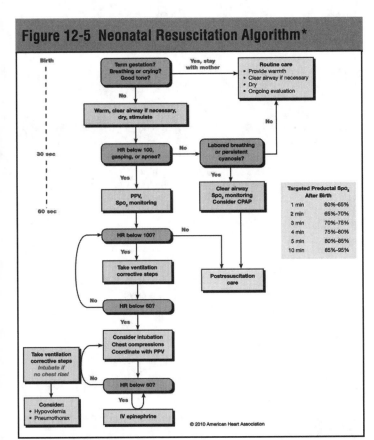

Figure 12-5 Neonatal Resuscitation Algorithm*

Note: HR indicates heart rate; sec, second.

*From Kattwinkel, J., Perlman, J. M., Aziz, K., Colby, C., Fairchild, K., . . . Zaichkin, J. (2010). Neonatal resuscitation: 2010 American Heart Association guidelines for cardiopulmonary resuscitation and emergency cardiovascular care. *Pediatrics, 126,* e1400–e1413.

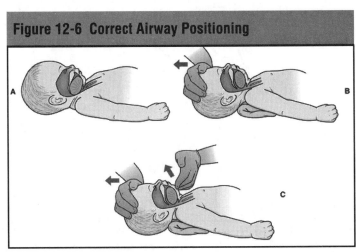

Figure 12-6 Correct Airway Positioning

Reproduced with permission from Sorrentino, S. A. (2007). *Mosby's textbook for nursing assistants* (7th ed.). St. Louis, MO: Mosby.

3. Maintain breathing effectiveness.

   a. Assess the respiratory rate, effort, and effectiveness of breathing. Most neonates will begin effective respirations in response to the stimulation provided with drying and suctioning. Newborns are commonly cyanotic at delivery but should rapidly become pink with the establishment of effective respirations (**Table 12-9**).

   b. Safe and effective methods of tactile stimulations to encourage adequate respiration include slapping or flicking the soles of the feet and gently rubbing the back, trunk, or extremities. Overly vigorous stimulation is not helpful and can cause serious injury. Potentially hazardous methods of stimulation include slapping the back or buttocks, squeezing the rib cage, forcing the thighs onto the abdomen, dilating the anal sphincter, applying hot or cold compresses or baths, and shaking.

   c. Deliver blended free flow oxygen and air if the newborn remains centrally cyanotic with effective respirations and an adequate heart rate (100 beats per minute). If after 90 seconds there is no improvement, use 100% oxygen. A simple face mask held firmly on the face is the preferred method. An alternate method is to cup your hand over the mouth and nose of the newborn and place standard oxygen tubing through your fingers so that your hand becomes a reservoir for oxygen buildup. With either method, the oxygen flow rate should be 5 L/minute. Self-inflating resuscitation bags should not be used to deliver free flow oxygen.

   d. Once the newborn's color is pink, gradually withdraw the oxygen, continually assessing the color. If at any time the newborn again becomes cyanotic, resume supplemental oxygen delivery. Oxygen should be heated and humidified if given for longer than a few minutes.

   e. Positive-pressure ventilation (PPV) at a rate of 40 to 60 breaths per minute with 100% oxygen is required if the neonate is not able to establish effective respirations after these interventions or if the heart rate is less than 100 beats per minute. **Table 12-10** lists the interventions for improving the efficacy of positive-pressure ventilation.

   f. Intubation may be required and is indicated if meconium is present and the newborn is not vigorous; to improve the efficacy of ventilation after several minutes of bag-mask ventilation; if there is ineffective bag-mask ventilation; to facilitate coordination of chest compressions and ventilation; to administer endotracheal epinephrine while intravenous access is being established, in cases of

Table 12-9 Evaluation of the Need for Further Resuscitation

Respirations: good chest movement with adequate rate and depth of respirations (gasping is ineffective).

Heart rate: should be greater than 100 beats per minute. Beats should be counted in six seconds (e.g., seven beats), multiply by 10 (equal to 70 beats per minute), and announce the actual heart rate.

Color: pink lips and pink trunk (central cyanosis indicates hypoxemia).

Table 12-10 Possible Causes of Infant Not Improving and Chest Not Adequately Expanding with Positive-Pressure Ventilation

Seal is inadequate. You may hear or feel air escaping from around the mask. Reapply the mask to the face and try to form a better seal while using a little more pressure on the rim of the mask.

Airway is blocked. Check the newborn's position and extend the neck a bit farther. Check the mouth or oropharynx and nose for secretions and suction if necessary. Try ventilating with the newborn's mouth slightly open.

Not enough pressure given. If you are not providing enough pressure to move the lungs, increase the pressure. If using a resuscitation device with a pressure gauge, the pressure limit may have to be increased. If using a bag with a pressure-release valve, increase the pressure until the valve actuates.

Malfunctioning equipment, including a torn bag, a faulty flow-control valve, or an improper connection, also may be the cause of inadequate chest expansion.

Figure 12-7 Technique for Giving Chest Compressions

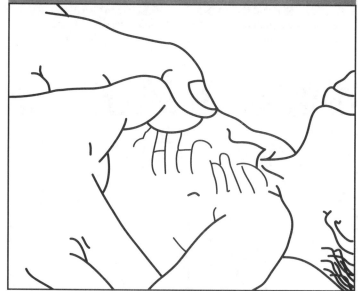

Reprinted with permission from Weil, M. H. (2009). *Cardiopulmonary resuscitation (CPR). The Merck manuals for healthcare professionals online.* Retrieved from http://www.merckmanuals.com/professional/sec06/ch064/ch064b.html?qt=chest compression&alt=sh.

Table 12-11 Recommended Size of Endotracheal Tubes for Newborns*

Tube Size in Millimeters (Inside Diameter)	Weight in Grams	Gestational Age in Weeks
2.5	< 1,000	< 28
3.0	1,000–2,000	28–34
3.5	2,000–3,000	34–38
3.5–4.0	> 3,000	> 38

*Data are taken from Kattwinkel.[4]

extreme prematurity; or if a diaphragmatic hernia is suspected. **Table 12-11** provides the recommended size of endotracheal tubes for newborns.

   g. Intubation attempts should be limited to 20 seconds and accompanied by free flow oxygen.

4. Maintain adequate circulation.

   a. Palpate a central pulse (brachial or feel at the base of the umbilicus for the aortic pulsation). The heart rate should be greater than 100 beats per minute.

   b. If the newborn's heart rate is less than 100 beats per minute, initiate PPV with blended oxygen and air increasing to 100% oxygen if there is no improvement after 90 seconds.

   c. When the heart rate stabilizes to greater than 100 beats per minute, reduce the rate and pressure of assisted ventilation until you see effective spontaneous respirations.

   d. Begin cardiac compressions if the heart rate is less than 60 beats per minute after 30 seconds of PPV with 100% oxygen. Use two fingers or two thumbs placed one finger breadth below the nipple line to provide compressions at a ratio of three compressions to one ventilation (approximately 120 beats per minute). Reevaluate the heart rate after 30 seconds of chest compressions, and stop compressions when the heart rate is 80 beats per minute or greater but continue ventilation until the heart rate is greater than 100 beats per minute (**Figure 12-7**).

5. Obtain vascular access.

   a. The umbilical vein is the most common and accessible route for administering medications and fluids in the newly born neonate. Umbilical catheter insertion is performed only by trained individuals.

   b. Veins in the scalp and extremities can be used for vascular access; however, these sites can be difficult to cannulate in the neonate with poor perfusion. Also, they are impractical if large volumes of fluid or emergent medication boluses are necessary because they cannot accommodate fast infusion rates.

   c. The intraosseous (IO) route can also be used in the neonate.

   d. Volume expanders should be given when there is evidence of hypovolemia, such as profound pallor, weak pulses with a good or rapid heart rate, a poor response to resuscitation, or a known blood loss. Administer 10 mL/kg of a 0.9% normal saline (preferred) or other isotonic crystalloid solution, such as lactated Ringer's solution, over approximately 10 minutes. If there is concern regarding blood loss, O-negative blood cross matched with the mother can be administered over 15 to 30 minutes.

6. Administer medications.

   a. If the heart rate remains less than 60 beats per minute after 30 seconds of chest compressions accompanied by PPV with 100% oxygen, epinephrine should be administered. It is indicated only after 30 seconds of adequate ventilation with PPVs accompanied by 30 seconds of chest compressions.

   b. Epinephrine, a cardiac stimulant, is the medication of choice for bradycardia or asystole. The recommended concentration is 1:10,000, and the preferred route is intravenous, (peripheral or umbilical vein), but it can be given via endotracheal tube if venous access is not established. It is the only medication in neonatal resuscitation that can be administered by the endotracheal route. The intraosseous route is also acceptable. Care should be taken not to use high-dose epinephrine (1:1,000) in the neonate.

7. If PPV fails to establish adequate ventilation, consider if any of the following may be present:

   a. A mechanical blockage of the airway from meconium or a mucous plug, choanal atresia (a condition in which the nasal passages are blocked by bone or a membrane), airway obstruction by the tongue (e.g., Pierre Robin syndrome, a condition in which the jaw is small), or other rare conditions.

   b. Fluid, air, or other collections preventing lung inflation (e.g., pneumothorax, pleural effusion, or pneumonia).

   c. The presence of a diaphragmatic hernia, a condition in which a defect in the diaphragm has allowed abdominal contents to herniate into the chest.

Infants with this condition present with a scaphoid abdomen and a barrel chest.

d. Inadequate pulmonary development (e.g., pulmonary hypoplasia or extreme prematurity).

e. Brain injury (e.g., hypoxic ischemic encephalopathy).

f. Congenital neuromuscular disorder.

g. Severe acidosis. Sodium bicarbonate 4.2% solution can be administered if severe metabolic acidosis is documented (arterial pH < 7.15), effective ventilation along with chest compressions have been performed, and the infant is not improving. Because of the risk of intraventricular hemorrhage if given too rapidly, administration of sodium bicarbonate over 10 to 30 minutes is recommended.

h. Sedation secondary to maternal drugs or medications. If PPV has restored a good heart rate and color, but the newborn continues to have poor respiratory effort and there is a history of maternal narcotic administration within the past four hours, consider the administration of naloxone (Narcan) to the neonate. Do not give naloxone (Narcan) to the newborn of a mother who is suspected to be addicted to narcotics or is receiving methadone maintenance because this may result in seizures in the newborn.

8. If an infant continues to be hypotensive after resuscitation and vascular volume expansion, dopamine can be considered for inotropic support of myocardial function, titrating until blood pressure and perfusion have improved.

Delivery of a Neonate with Meconium-Stained Amniotic Fluid

Meconium is the first stool passed by the newborn. If passed by the fetus before delivery, the amniotic fluid will appear greenish to brown and may even have particulate stool in it. If the neonate gasps in utero (e.g., resulting from hypoxia), meconium can be aspirated. In the lungs, meconium causes chemical pneumonitis and interferes with the normal expansion of the alveoli, blocking the airways. Meconium aspiration can precipitate a cascade of events that interfere with the normal transition from intrauterine to extrauterine ventilation and circulation.

If there is meconium in the amnionic fluid, assess the infant for vigor immediately after delivery. The vigorous infant will have strong respiratory efforts, good muscle tone, and a heart rate greater than 100 beats per minute. If the infant is vigorous, proceed with the initial steps of resuscitation, as previously outlined.

If the infant is not vigorous, using a meconium aspirator and an appropriately sized endotracheal tube, intubate the trachea and suction any meconium present in the lower airway as the endotracheal tube is being removed, using the endotracheal tube as a suction catheter. Reintubation and repeated suctioning may be necessary if much meconium was obtained and the heart rate is greater than 100 beats per minute. Positive pressure ventilation is indicated if the infant's heart rate decreases to less than 100 beats per minute.

Postresuscitation Care[13]

- Assess oxygenation, ventilation, and acid-base balance.
- Evaluate a chest and abdomen radiograph for lung fields, heart size, bowel gas, tubes, and line positions.
- Monitor body temperature and treat hypothermia.
- Monitor blood glucose level and treat hypoglycemia.
- Monitor electrolyte levels.
- Monitor vital signs and oxygen saturation.
- Screen for infection.
- Support the family.

Table 12-12 Apgar Score			
Sign	**Score**		
	0	**1**	**2**
Appearance (color)	Cyanotic	Pink body with blue extremities (acrocyanosis)	No cyanosis and body and extremities pink
Pulse (heart rate)	Less than 60 beats per minute	Less than 100 beats per minute	Greater than 100 beats per minute
Grimace (reflex irritability)	No response to stimulation	Grimace and feeble cry when stimulated	Cough, sneeze, and pulls away when stimulated
Activity (muscle tone)	Limp	Some flexion	Active movement
Respirations	Absent	Weak or irregular	Strong

Apgar Score

The Apgar score is a standardized rating system of five factors that reflect the infant's ability to adjust to extrauterine life (**Table 12-12**). The Apgar score is not used to determine the need for resuscitation; it provides retrospective information about the newborn's response to the initial steps of resuscitation at birth. The Apgar score is assigned at the ages of one and five minutes. When the five-minute Apgar score is less than 7, additional scores should be assigned every 5 minutes for 20 minutes, until the score is 7 or higher.

Considerations in the Assessment and Care of the Premature Infant in the Emergency Department

Preterm infants or those born small for their gestational age (SGA) are at greatest risk for complications after birth. *Prematurity* is defined as the birth of an infant born at less than 37 weeks' gestation. Premature infants generally weigh less than 2,500 grams at birth. They constituted approximately 12.8% of all births in 2006.[2] Premature infants will generally be discharged to home when the following criteria are met:[6,22] (1) the ability to maintain body temperature fully clothed in an open crib, (2) a consistent pattern of weight gain, (3) ability to take all feedings by bottle or breast without respiratory compromise or difficulty, (4) stable cardiovascular and respiratory control, (5) able to sit in a car seat without desaturations or respiratory distress,[23] (6) not receiving medications that require hospital management, and (7) no recent major changes in medications or oxygen administration.

Delays in all areas of development may be seen in the premature infant. The delays may be secondary to the prematurity itself, to complications of prematurity, or to the infant's acuity of illness and hospital course. Growth parameters should be assessed using the corrected gestational age for the first two years of life, when preterm infants generally have caught up to their full-term counterparts. Using a corrected age helps prevent concerns in the premature infant who is not developing according to the standard charts for age.[24]

The largest and most rapidly growing segment of the premature infant population is the late preterm. These infants, born at 34 to 36 6/7 weeks' gestation, often appear to be full term and are often treated in newborn nurseries as normal newborns; however, they have a three times greater risk of mortality. Although they are less likely to have long-term disabilities, as seen in the small preterm infant, they have significantly high risks for morbidity and hospital readmission during the first month of life than the term infant.[25]

The premature infant, including the late preterm infant, is more susceptible to the following:

- Respiratory distress
- Apnea and bradycardia
- Anemia
- Infection
- Hypovolemic and/or septic shock
- Intraventricular hemorrhage
- Hypothermia and cold stress
- Hypoglycemia
- Bruising (fragile skin and capillaries)
- Hyperbilirubinemia
- Feeding difficulties
- Less able to tolerate periods without fluids and nutrients

Neonatal Sepsis

Neonatal sepsis is the eighth leading cause of death in the newborn.[1] The neonate is at risk for infection and sepsis because of an immature immune system, impaired neutrophil phagocytosis, and decreased complement levels. Other contributing factors include exposure to infectious agents in the birth canal and environmental exposures. The premature infant is at highest risk. Common sites of infection include the blood, lungs, urinary tract, and cerebrospinal fluid (CSF). Sepsis is classified based on the infant's age at presentation, with early onset presenting before the sixth day of life and late onset presenting after the sixth day of life. In addition, during the winter months, infants are at increased risk for pneumonia secondary to viral pathogens. **Table 12-13** lists the most common organisms in neonatal sepsis.

The neonate may present with symptoms that are vague and generalized or may present in a prearrest state. Symptoms of neonatal sepsis include feeding intolerance, lethargy, temperature instability (fever or low temperature), and apnea. **Table 12-14** provides a comprehensive description of the signs and symptoms that a neonate with sepsis may exhibit. Low body temperature is the most common presentation of bacterial sepsis in the newborn.[6] Interventions must be used to support airway, breathing, and circulation (ABCs), as previously listed in **Chapter 5, "Initial Assessment."** It is important to differentiate septic shock from cardiogenic shock resulting from a closing/closed ductus in patients with congenital heart disease and a ductal-dependent lesion. If the infant has signs of shock

Table 12-13 Common Organisms in Neonatal Sepsis

Early-Onset Sepsis	Late-Onset Sepsis	Viral Organisms
Group B *Streptococcus*	Coagulase-negative staphylococci	Herpes simplex
Escherichia coli	*Staphylococcus aureus*	Enterovirus
Coagulase-negative *Staphylococcus Haemophilus influenzae*	*Escherichia coli*	During winter months: respiratory syncytial virus
Listeria monocytogenes	*Klebsiella*	Influenza A
	Pseudomonas	Adenovirus
	Enterobacter	
	Candida	
	Group B streptococcus	
	Serratia	
	Acinetobacter	
	Anaerobes	

Table 12-14 Signs and Symptoms of Neonatal Sepsis*

Type of Symptom	Description	
General appearance and behavior	Change in behavior pattern ("not acting right") Increased crying	Increased sleeping and not awakening for feeding Temperature instability (increased or decreased core temperature)
Respiratory	Episodes of apnea Cyanosis Tachypnea	Retractions Grunting Nasal flaring
Circulatory	Central cyanosis or pallor Tachycardia or bradycardia Mottled extremities despite warming measures	Prolonged capillary refill Hypotension (systolic blood pressure < 65 mm Hg in first week of life or < 75 mm Hg from one week to one month of age in the term infant)*
Central nervous system	Seizure activity (e.g., smacking of lips, eye deviation and fluttering, and bicycling) Decreased or altered level of consciousness Inability to focus, track objects, or maintain eye contact Decreased muscle tone (decreased resistance to extension of extremities)	Posture: extremities extended (may be limp or flaccid rather than flexed) Weak or absent reflexes Inconsolable and paradoxical irritability Decreased or no response to procedures
Gastrointestinal	Poor feeding (lack of interest in feeding) Feeding intolerance (gastric distention or vomiting)	Hemoglobin-positive stools
Hematopoietic	Jaundice	Petechiae
Integumentary	Rash Pallor	Mottling Cool extremities

*Data are taken from Goldstein, B., Giroir, B., & Randolph, A. (2005). International pediatric sepsis consensus conference: Definitions for sepsis and organ dysfunction in pediatrics. *Pediatric Critical Care Medicine, 6,* 2–8.

accompanied by hepatomegaly, heart murmur, differential upper and lower extremity blood pressures or pulses, a prostaglandin (PG) infusion should be started until congenital heart disease is ruled out by echocardiography.[26]

Septic shock should be promptly recognized and treated, with the goal of restoring circulation quickly. Crystalloid volume expansion with boluses to a maximum of 60 mL/kg should be given, and hypoglycemia and hypocalcemia should be corrected.[26,27]

After the initial assessment is performed and the ABCs are supported, the key intervention is the prompt initiation of antibiotic therapy. Before antibiotic therapy is implemented, laboratory work should be drawn, including blood cultures. Vascular access should be rapidly established, and maintenance intravenous fluid should be started. Usually, it is necessary to withhold enteral feedings (by mouth or gastric tube), especially if there is any respiratory distress or cardiovascular instability or if the neurological status is depressed. The lumbar puncture for CSF culture should be deferred until the infant is stabilized.

Broad-spectrum antibiotic therapy is generally started while awaiting culture results. A blood culture volume of 1 to 2 mL is acceptable for neonates. Antibiotic therapy usually includes ampicillin and gentamicin. Ampicillin is an important antimicrobial agent, effective against *Listeria* infection. If herpes infection is suspected, acyclovir should be administered after appropriate viral cultures are obtained (generally from conjunctiva, throat, feces, urine, and nasopharynx); surface cultures are not indicated and reflect exposure to the virus versus the infection.

Evaluate the complete blood cell count for an elevated white blood cell count (> 30,000 cells/mm^3) in the first 24 hours of life, a low absolute neutrophil count (< 1,800 cells/mm^3), or an immature to total neutrophil count greater than 25% (all immature neutrophils [bands, metamyelocytes, and myelocytes] divided by total neutrophil count).[6]

Additional diagnostic procedures that may be ordered as part of a sepsis workup include the following:

- C-reactive protein
- Electrolytes
- Serum blood glucose and bedside whole blood glucose levels
- Total and direct serum bilirubin (use nomogram for age to determine risk level)
- Arterial or capillary blood gas
- Lactic acid

- Prothrombin time and partial thromboplastin time (if bleeding suspected)
- Urine culture and urinalysis (sterile catheterized specimen or suprapubic bladder tap only)
- Culture from any obvious infected or draining site
- Nasal aspirate for respiratory viral panel (respiratory syncytial virus, adenovirus, or influenza) if respiratory symptoms are present
- Cerebrospinal fluid analysis, culture, and gram stain (normal range for neonatal CSF, 0–32 cells/mm^3; 20–170 mg/dL of protein; and 34–119 mg/dL of glucose)[6]
- Chest radiograph if respiratory symptoms or fever is present

Hyperbilirubinemia

Hyperbilirubinemia, commonly termed *jaundice*, is the most common diagnosis requiring medical intervention in the neonate.[28] Immature liver function results in elevated serum bilirubin levels when the liver's ability to excrete bilirubin from red cell hemolysis is exceeded. It appears in 50% to 70% of newborn infants.[29] Common causes of elevated bilirubin levels include hemolytic disease, infection, sepsis, hemorrhage, and polycythemia. Red blood cell hemolysis can result from maternal/infant blood group and Rh incompatibilities. If the mother is Rh negative and the infant is Rh positive, or the mother is blood type O positive and the infant is blood type A or B, maternal antibodies cross into the infant's bloodstream and lyse the infant's red blood cells. Hemolysis can also occur related to bruising or trauma from the birth process (e.g., subdural hematoma or cephalohematoma). Infants with these injuries are at higher risk for hyperbilirubinemia. Another cause of prolonged elevated bilirubin levels in the newborn is glucose-6-phosphate dehydrogenase deficiency, an X-linked hereditary disease that is the most common human enzyme defect. Breastfeeding is also associated with jaundice in the newborn, especially if the mother's milk volume is inadequate.

Jaundice, the yellow/orange color of the skin, is visible when total serum bilirubin (TSB) levels reach 5 mg/dL; however, visual judgment of bilirubin levels is highly inaccurate. It progresses in a cephalocaudal manner, peaking in full-term infants within two to four days of life, and returns to normal by the sixth day of life. In the preterm infant and late preterm infant, TSB peaks later in the first week of life. If jaundice, which is visible at birth, persists beyond the first three days of life; or with a TSB of 12 mg/dL or greater, it requires immediate intervention. Laboratory values should be compared with the nomogram published by the American Academy of Pediatrics to evaluate risk for sequela and the need for treatment with phototherapy or, in severe cases, an exchange blood transfusion in which the infant's blood is withdrawn in small aliquots and replaced with O-negative blood, cross matched with the mother's and infant's blood (**Figure 12-8** and **Figure 12-9**).[6,30]

In addition to the skin color appearing yellow or orange, the newborn may be lethargic, with mild hypotonia, decreased

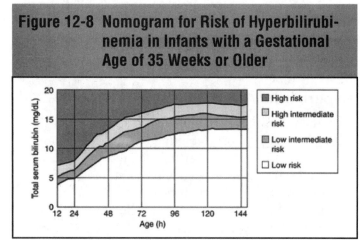

Figure 12-8 Nomogram for Risk of Hyperbilirubinemia in Infants with a Gestational Age of 35 Weeks or Older

Reprinted with permission from Jospe, N. (2009, December). *Neonatal hyperbilirubinemia. The Merck Manual for Healthcare Professionals Online.* Retrieved from http://www.merckmanuals.com/professional/sec19/ch274/ch274b.html.

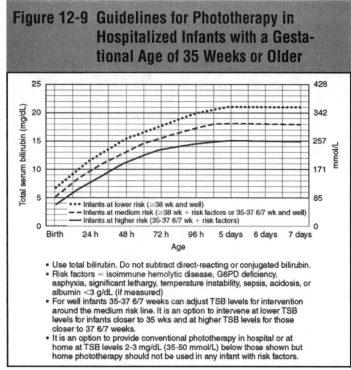

Figure 12-9 Guidelines for Phototherapy in Hospitalized Infants with a Gestational Age of 35 Weeks or Older

- Use total bilirubin. Do not subtract direct-reacting or conjugated bilirubin.
- Risk factors = isoimmune hemolytic disease, G6PD deficiency, asphyxia, significant lethargy, temperature instability, sepsis, acidosis, or albumin <3 g/dL (if measured)
- For well infants 35-37 6/7 weeks can adjust TSB levels for intervention around the medium risk line. It is an option to intervene at lower TSB levels for infants closer to 35 wks and at higher TSB levels for those closer to 37 6/7 weeks.
- It is an option to provide conventional phototherapy in hospital or at home at TSB levels 2-3 mg/dL (35-50 mmol/L) below those shown but home phototherapy should not be used in any infant with risk factors.

Reprinted with permission from the American Academy of Pediatrics Subcommittee on Hyperbilirubinemia.[30]

activity, poor sucking, and a high-pitched cry. Neurological injury occurs if unbound bilirubin crosses the blood-brain barrier. In general, TSB levels greater than 24 mg/dL are considered a medical emergency. However, the neurotoxic effects of bilirubin can occur at lower levels when the blood-brain barrier is compromised, including ill, septic, or asphyxiated infants. Emergency treatment is imperative to prevent crossing of bilirubin through the blood-brain barrier and causing bilirubin encephalopathy and irreversible neurological damage (kernicterus). This includes treatment of dehydration, intensive phototherapy, and exchange blood transfusion.

Placing the infant under special lights (i.e., phototherapy) is the first-line treatment for the reduction of elevated bilirubin levels. Phototherapy uses a specific blue light wavelength to convert bilirubin into a photoisomer that does not require liver conjugation and allows bilirubin to be excreted directed into the stool and urine. Recommendations are for this light to be delivered and applied to as much of the infant's body as possible. There are several commercial devices and delivery methods for phototherapy for use at both the hospital and home. Blue lights can be complemented with white halogen lights to cover a wider surface area; avoid shadows created with multiple lights. This therapy should be implemented as soon as jaundice is recognized; it is important to implement while still in the ED awaiting admission.[30] If levels become extremely high, or if the infant has signs of neurological compromise, an exchange blood transfusion should be considered.

When a neonate is brought to the ED and has skin that appears yellow/orange, especially if the neonate is lethargic or has a high-pitched cry, the following procedure should be implemented:

- Admit the infant as soon as possible (the longer the delay, the greater the risk of irreversible neurological injury).

- Arrange for direct admittance to the pediatric or neonatal intensive care unit if TSB levels are at or near the level at which exchange transfusion is indicated (**Figure 12-10**). If not available locally, initiate arrangements for transport.

- Carefully document the infant's neurological status at admission.

- Weigh the infant. Do not assume that if the infant's weight has not changed significantly from birth that no weight loss has occurred. Different scales have been known to weigh infants differently.

- Begin phototherapy immediately, exposing as much body surface area as possible. The goal for initiation of phototherapy should be about one hour.[28]

- Do not wait until someone can start an intravenous line or perform a venipuncture to send a serum bilirubin level to the lab. Perform a heel stick to collect capillary blood, and send for the total and direct bilirubin level immediately. Turn off the phototherapy lights during the blood collection.

- Keep the neonate under the lights until the TSB level is known. If the mother is breastfeeding, facilitate access to a breast pump and bottle feed the expressed milk while the neonate is under the lights.

- The first repeat TSB level should be checked within 2 to 4 hours of initiation of therapy to document a substantial response in TSB level. If satisfactory response is not achieved, exchange transfusion or pharmacological options should be considered.

Congenital Heart Disease

Congenital heart disease occurs in eight per 1,000 live births and ranges from a minor anomaly to a severe and life-threatening condition.[31] Heart defects may be a single structural anomaly or a combination of anomalies. They can be part of a syndrome, the result of genetic factors or environmental toxins, or because of complications of maternal disease. Symptoms may be present at birth or may not present for days, weeks, or months. When newborns are symptomatic in the first week of life, cyanosis is generally the presenting symptom. An oxygen challenge test

may be performed when trying to differentiate a cardiac or pulmonary origin for cyanosis in the neonate. Although not a specific test, cardiac causes of cyanosis can be differentiated from respiratory disease with a *hyperoxia* test, in which 100% oxygen is administered to the neonate. In cyanotic congenital heart disease, the preductal PaO_2 will remain lower than 100 mm Hg, whereas with respiratory disease, the preductal PaO_2 will increase to higher than 100 mm Hg.[13] It is often useful to obtain simultaneous measurements from the right hand and a foot to determine flow patterns through the ductus arteriosis. As the left subclavian artery may have a preductal or postductal origin from the aorta, it is best not to use the left hand for pulse oximetry monitoring.

Due to potential risks associated with hyperoxia and the effects on lung parenchyma, vascular function, and the effect on ductal-dependent lesions, initiating oxygen therapy with 40% to 60% oxygen will allow the caregiver to provide support and assess for improvement, thus guiding future interventions.[32] However, the PaO_2 may remain low even with 100% oxygen administration in persistent pulmonary hypertension of the newborn. Other common symptoms include tachypnea, fatigue, and poor perfusion. A murmur may or may not be present.

Congenital heart defects are classified in broad terms as either cyanotic or acyanotic, then further classified based on hemodynamics using the ratio of pulmonary to systemic blood flow and the direction of blood flow through the lesion as a descriptor. **Table 12-15** provides a summary of the major congenital cardiac defects using these classifications.

Defects that produce left-to-right shunts, where blood is shunted from the left (systemic) side of the heart to the right (pulmonary) side, result in increased pulmonary blood flow. This may lead to congestive heart failure, if significant. These defects are also termed *acyanotic*. Cyanotic defects, or right-to-left shunts, are those in which blood is shunted from the right side of the heart to the left side of the heart (e.g., through a septal defect, a patent Foramen Ovale (FO) or a patent Ductus Arteriosis (DA)), bypassing the pulmonary circulation and mixing with blood being pumped to the systemic circulation. Obstructive defects may occur on either side of the heart; when combined with other anomalies, shunting of blood may occur. Some obstructive and right-to-left shunt congenital heart defects would not be compatible with life except for the presence of other anomalies (e.g., a patent DA or a patent FO that allow mixing of oxygenated with deoxygenated blood).

Figure 12-10 Guidelines for Exchange Transfusion in Infants with a Gestational Age of 35 Weeks or Older

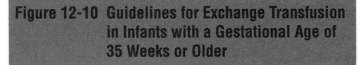

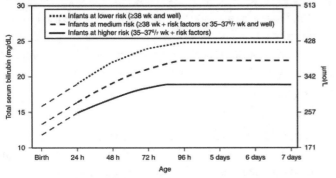

- The dashed lines for the first 24 hours indicate uncertainty due to a wide range of clinical circumstances and a range of responses to phototherapy.
- Immediate exchange transfusion is recommended if infant shows signs of acute bilirubin encephalopathy (hypertonia, arching, retrocollis, opisthotonos, fever, high pitched cry) or if TSB is 25 mg/dL, (85 μmol/L) above these lines.
- Risk factors—isoimmune hemolytic disease, G6PD deficiency, asphyxia, significant lethargy, temperature instability, sepsis, acidosis.
- Measure serum albumin and calculate bilirubin/albumin (B/A) ratio (See legend).
- Use total bilirubin. Do not subtract direct reacting or conjugated bilirubin.
- If infant is well and 35-37⁶/₇ wk (median risk) can individualize TSB levels for exchange based on actual gestational age.

Reprinted with permission from the American Academy of Pediatrics Subcommittee on Hyperbilirubinemia.[30]

Neonates with congenital heart disease may have a delayed closure of the DA, in part because of a lower partial pressure of oxygen, arterial. Neonates with defects dependent on a PDA to maintain systemic oxygenation will exhibit symptoms of profound deterioration and shock within the first weeks of life as the DA begins to close. The intravenous infusion of alprostadil (Prostaglandin E_1 or Prostin VR) has a direct dilatory effect on the ductus and is used to reestablish the patency of the ductus arteriosus.[13]

Infants with right-to-left shunting will exhibit a lower PaO_2 and oxygen saturation in their lower extremities versus their right arm (the left arm may or may not be preductal). To evaluate for right-to-left shunting, a pulse oximeter should be placed on the right hand and a second pulse oximeter should be placed on a foot. Concurrent readings will enable the identification of differential oxygenation.

Table 12-15 Major Congenital Cardiac Defects*

Severe cyanosis with separate circulations

Transposition of the great arteries

Severe cyanosis with restricted pulmonary blood flow

Tetralogy of Fallot

Tricuspid atresia

Pulmonary atresia

Pulmonary stenosis

Mild cyanosis with normal or increased pulmonary blood flow

Total anomalous pulmonary venous return

Truncus arteriosus

Systemic hypoperfusion and congestive heart failure with mild or no cyanosis

Aortic stenosis

Coarctation of the aorta and aortic arch interruption

Hypoplastic left heart syndrome

Acyanosis with no or mild respiratory distress

Patent ductus arteriosus

Ventricular septal defect

Atrial septal defect

Endocardial cushion defect (atrioventricular canal)

*Data are taken from Fanaroff, A. A., Martin, R. J., & Walsh, M. C. (2006). *Fanaroff and Martin's neonatal-perinatal medicine: Diseases of the fetus and infant* (8th ed.). Philadelphia, PA: Mosby Elsevier.

Neonates with congenital heart disease may exhibit any or all of the signs and symptoms listed in **Table 12-16**. Because the caregivers may not recognize all of these as a problem, specific behavioral information must be elicited.

Neonates with congenital heart disease typically present to the ED in severe distress, shock, or a prearrest state. In addition to supporting the ABCs, the following interventions should be initiated:

- Administer oxygen cautiously in the face of certain cardiac lesions. When neonates are dependent on the DA for systemic blood flow, as is the case with severe coarctation or hypoplastic left heart syndrome, hyperoxia can also promote ductal closure, which further compromises systemic perfusion. Consultation with a pediatric cardiologist is recommended before providing supplemental oxygen to increase saturations by approximately 80%. In many instances, even subambient oxygen is used to prevent saturations of greater than 90% and resultant closure of the ductus.

- Initiate monitoring of the heart rate and before and after ductal oxygen saturation, as previously described.

- Obtain vascular access for maintenance fluids and medication administration. If intravenous access is difficult, the umbilical vein and/or arteries can be cannulated by a practitioner (physician or advanced practice nurse) trained in their placement.

- Obtain appropriate laboratory data and other diagnostic study results: arterial blood gases; blood culture results; blood glucose, electrolyte, calcium, blood urea nitrogen, and creatinine levels; a chest radiograph; an electrocardiogram; and an echocardiogram.

- Give the patient nothing by mouth.

- Administer alprostadil via continuous intravenous infusion to reestablish patent ductus arteriosus. Alprostadil also causes vasodilation of all arterioles, inhibits platelet aggregation, and stimulates intestinal smooth muscle.

  ° Because the medication is extremely short acting, it must be administered as a continuous infusion.

  ° It may be administered via a peripheral intravenous or an umbilical line but must be given directly into the hub of the neonate's vascular access; the medication cannot be piggybacked several inches up the intravenous tubing.

  ° The maximal medication effect is usually seen within 30 minutes; however, immediate effects, such as increased oxygen saturation and decreased cyanosis, may be noted within minutes.

  ° Apnea is a common adverse effect of PGE_1 administration, and endotracheal intubation may be required. Other adverse effects include flushing, fever, brady-

Table 12-16 Signs and Symptoms of Congenital Heart Disease*

Signs and Symptoms	Description
General appearance and behavior	Easily fatigued
	Does not cry much or for a long time
	Irritability
	Mottling
	Edema (especially peripheral)
	Diaphoresis
Respiratory	Cyanosis during crying or feeding
	Dyspnea during crying or feeding
	Respiratory distress
	Clear breath sounds in a tachypneic and cyanotic infant (highly suspicious of congenital heart disease)
	Cyanosis
	Dyspnea
	Increased work of breathing
	Rales on auscultation
Cardiovascular	Prolonged capillary refill
	Diminished lower-extremity pulses (e.g., coarctation of the aorta)
	Lower blood pressure reading in lower extremities (significant if $\geq$ 20 mm Hg below the BP in upper extremities)
	Murmur may or may not be present
	Tachycardia
	Visible precordial impulse (active precordium)
	Gallop rhythm
	Hypertension or hypotension
Central nervous system	Decreased level of consciousness
	Poor muscle tone
	Poor sucking response
Gastrointestinal/urinary	Does not feed well or for as long as would be expected; falls asleep early in feeding
	Poor weight gain
	Distended abdomen (hepatomegaly)
	Decreased urine output
Hematopoietic	Profound pallor
	Polycythemia

*Data are taken from Verklan et al.[13]

cardia, and hypotension.[33] The smallest dose needed to maintain the patent DA should be given to decrease the risk of apnea.

Discharge Education

The first few weeks of life after the birth of a neonate require major adjustments for both the newborn and caregivers. A new mother is experiencing hormonal changes, body image changes, and sleep deprivation. Although the caregivers may have attended prenatal classes and received educational information after the birth of the child, the overwhelming responsibilities of the neonate may cause frustration and exhaustion. Information previously learned may be forgotten. The following information is a sample of what can be shared both verbally and via written materials.

Health Promotion and Illness Prevention

- Educate caregivers concerning immunizations and the immunization schedule. Provide referral to community immunization resources as needed. Be sure that adults are up to date on pertussis immunization.[34]

- Review with caregivers the importance of well-baby checks, immunizations, and establishing a relationship with a primary care provider (PCP) for the infant. Provide PCP referral or resources for obtaining or selecting a primary care provider.

- Teach caregivers the early signs of illness in the neonate and infant: low temperature or fever, poor feeding, vomiting, diarrhea, decreased urination, unusual irritability, decreased activity, decreased responsiveness, or extended posture.

- Review with caregivers what to do in case of an emergency, including when to call the PCP and when to go to the emergency department.

- Review the importance of hand washing, especially after using the bathroom, changing a diaper, and before handling infant formula or feeding an infant.

- Review feeding information as appropriate. Stress the need for a good maternal diet when breastfeeding. Refer to a lactation consultant if experiencing difficulties with breastfeeding.

- Review safe bottle feeding practices. For example, always hold your baby when feeding him or her; do not prop the bottle or place the infant to bed with a bottle, do not microwave infant bottles to heat them, and never feed leftover formula from a bottle at a later time.

- Review types of formulas and the preparation process. Ensure caregivers understand the need to read the label on infant formulas. Mark the date and time when a can or bottle is opened.

- Review the risk of infant botulism associated with giving honey to an infant.

- Infants should only be given breast milk or infant formula for the first four to six months of life.

- Teach the caregiver to never give the baby water, sugar water, tea, or anything else without first calling the baby's primary care physician.

- Advise the caregiver to keep the infant's environments (home and car) cigarette smoke free.

- Discuss the importance of minimizing exposure to sick individuals, including family, siblings, and nurseries.

- Encourage caregivers to learn infant cardiopulmonary resuscitation. Provide information on hospital or community-based classes.

- Keep the Poison Control Center telephone number handy: 1-800-222-1222.

Injury and Abuse Prevention[35, 36]

- Review use of infant car seats. Stress the importance of using a rear-facing car seat, properly secured in the backseat, with the infant strapped into the car seat at all times as long as possible or until he or she reaches the upper limit recommended by the manufacturer of the convertible car seat. Emphasize the danger of placing an infant car seat in the front seat with a passenger airbag. Provide information on where to have a car seat installation inspected for safety. Teach that infants should be removed from the car seat when they are brought in the house and not left to sleep in them.

- Caution caregivers about leaving the infant in a car unattended, even for brief periods, and especially to never leave an infant or child in a car during the summer months.

- Discuss the infant's sleeping position with caregivers. An infant should always be positioned on the back ONLY, not side lying nor prone. All toys, loose bedding, and stuffed animals should be removed from the crib for sleeping. Keep the room temperature comfortable, not hot or cold.

- Ensure that crib slats are no more than two and three-eighths inches apart with a snug-fitting mattress. Keep the sides of the crib and playpen raised to their highest point at all times.

- Consider allowing the infant to use a pacifier for sleeping because it may reduce the risk of sudden infant death syndrome.

- Do not place the infant on soft surfaces, such as a water bed, bean bag, couch, or pillow. Infants should only sleep in their crib or bassinette.

- Discuss cobedding, in which parents and infants sleep in the same bed. Although this is a common practice in some cultures, recent studies have shown that is associated with an increased incidence of sleep-related deaths, most likely from suffocation.

- Set the hot water heater thermostat to lower than 120°F (49.2°C). Always test the water temperature with a bath thermometer or at your wrist to make sure it is not too hot before bathing the infant. A safe temperature is approximately 100°F (67.4°C). Never leave the baby alone in a tub of water. Use a small basin filled with approximately five inches of warm water, enough to allow the baby's shoulders to be covered.

- Make sure smoke detectors are in every room of the house and working. Install smoke detectors if not already in place.

- Supervise your baby at all times around water. Immediately empty tubs, buckets, and small pools after use.

- Do not leave the infant on high places, such as changing tables, beds, sofas, or chairs. Always keep one hand on the infant.

- Never leave the baby alone or with a young sibling or pet.

- Do not carry or drink hot liquids while holding the infant or pour hot liquids while reaching over the infant. If your baby is burned, place the burn in cold water, then cover loosely with a dry bandage or clean cloth, then call your primary care physician.

- Never, never, never shake an infant. This can cause irreversible brain damage or death.

- Provide information on prevention of foreign body aspiration, both from improperly prepared foods and from objects in the environment.

Summary

Neonates are our smallest and most vulnerable patients. Their signs and symptoms of illness are often subtle. Our knowledge of their unique physiology, the ability to obtain a thorough medical history, and the ability to perform an appropriate physical examination will increase the possibility of identifying disease. Neonates are dependent on us and their caregivers to advocate for them because they cannot speak for themselves. We are challenged to educate, support, encourage, and empower their families, ultimately making a difference in the lives of children.

References

1. Heron, M., Hoyert, D. L., Murphy, S. L., Xu, J., Kochanek, K. D., & Tejada-Vera, B. (2009). Deaths: Final data for 2006. *National Vital Statistics Report, 57,* 1–134.

2. *Infant deaths by age at death.* (2006). Retrieved from http://www.marchofdimes.com/peristats/level1.aspx?dv=ls&reg=99&top=6&stop=199&lev=1&slev=1&obj=3

3. Kim, U. O., Brousseau, D. C., & Konduri, G. G. (2008). Evaluation and management of the critically ill neonate in the emergency department. *Clinical Pediatric Emergency Medicine, 9,* 140–148.

4. Kattwinkel, J., Perlman, J. M., Aziz, K., Colby, C., Fairchild, K., Gallagher, J., . . . Zaichkin, J. (2010). Neonatal resuscitation: 2010 American Heart Association Guidelines for Cardiopulmonary Resuscitation and Emergency Cardiovascular Care. *Pediatrics, 126,* e1400–e1413.

5. Merenstein, G. B., & Gardner, S. L. (2006). *Handbook of neonatal intensive care* (6th ed.). Edinburgh, Scotland: Elsevier Mosby.

6. Gomella, T. L., Cunningham, M. D., & Eyal, F. G. (2009). *Neonatology: Management, procedures, on-call problems, diseases and drugs* (6th ed.). New York, NY: McGraw-Hill Medical.

7. Silvestri, J. M. (2008). Apparent life-threatening events in the young infant and neonate. *Clinical Pediatric Emergency Medicine, 9,* 184–190.

8. Blackburn, S. T. (2007). *Maternal, fetal, and neonatal physiology: A clinical perspective* (3rd ed.). Philadelphia, PA: Saunders.

9. American Academy of Pediatrics. (2004). The fourth report on the diagnosis, evaluation, and treatment of high blood pressure in children and adolescents. *Pediatrics, 114* (suppl), 555–576.

10. Tappero, E. P., & Honeyfield, M. E. (2009). *Physical assessment of the newborn: A comprehensive approach to the art of physical examination* (4th ed.). Santa Rosa, CA: NICU Ink Book Publishers.

11. Lund, C. H., Kuller, J., Raines, D. A., Ecklund, S., Archambault, M. E., & O'Flaherty, P. (2007). *Neonatal skin care: Evidence-based clinical practice guideline* (2nd ed.). Washington, DC: Association of Women's Health, Obstetric and Neonatal Nurses.

12. Ferry, R. J. (2008). *Circumcision.* Retrieved from http://www.emedicinehealth.com/circumcision/article_em.htm

13. Verklan, M. T., Walden, M., Association of Women's Health Obstetric and Neonatal Nurses, American Association of Critical-Care Nurses, & National Association of Neonatal Nurses. (2010). *Core curriculum for neonatal intensive care nursing* (4th ed.). St. Louis, MO: Saunders.

14. Karlsen, K. A. (2006). *The S.T.A.B.L.E. resuscitation/pre-transport stabilization care of sick infants* (5th ed.). Park City, UT: The S.T.A.B.L.E. Program.

15. Cowett, R. M., & Farrag, H. M. (2004). Selected principles of perinatal-neonatal glucose metabolism. *Seminars in Neonatology, 9,* 37–47.

16. Krechel, S. W., & Bildner, J. (1995). CRIES: A new neonatal postoperative pain measurement score: Initial testing of validity and reliability. *Pediatric Anaesthesia, 5,* 53–61.

17. Stevens, B., Johnston, C., Petryshen, P., & Taddio, A. (1996). Premature infant pain profile: Development and initial validation. The *Clinical Journal of Pain, 12,* 13–22.

18. Lawrence, J., Alcock, D., McGrath, P., Kay, J., MacMurray, S. B., & Dulberg, C. (1993). The development of a tool to assess neonatal pain. *Neonatal Network, 12,* 59–66.

19. Hummel, P., Puchalski, M., Creech, S. D., & Weiss, M. G. (2008). Clinical reliability and validity of the N-PASS: Neonatal pain, agitation and sedation scale with prolonged pain. *Journal of Perinatology: Official Journal of the California Perinatal Association, 28,* 55–60.

20. *CDC growth charts.* (2009). Retrieved from http://www.cdc.gov/GrowthCharts

21. Perinatal HIV Guidelines Working Group. (2009). *Public Health Service Task Force recommendations for use of antiretroviral drugs in pregnant HIV-infected women for maternal health and interventions to reduce perinatal HIV transmission in the United States: April 29, 2009.* Retrieved from http://aidsinfo.nih.gov/ContentFiles/PerinatalGL.pdf

22. American Academy of Pediatrics. (2008). Hospital discharge of the high-risk neonate. *Pediatrics, 122,* 1119–1126.

23. Bull, M., Agran, P., Laraque, D., Pollack, S. H., Smith, G. A., Spivak, H. R., ... Katcher, M. L. (1999). American Academy of Pediatrics: Committee on Injury and Poison Prevention: Safe transportation of newborns at hospital discharge. *Pediatrics, 104* (pt 1), 986–987.

24. Berkowitz, C. D. (2008). *Pediatrics: A primary care approach* (3rd ed.). Elk Grove Village, IL: American Academy of Pediatrics.

25. Tomashek, K. M., Shapiro-Mendoza, C. K., Davidoff, M. J., & Petrini, J. R. (2007). Differences in mortality between late-preterm and term singleton infants in the United States, 1995-2002. *The Journal of Pediatrics, 151,* 450–456.

26. Brierley, J., Carcillo, J. A., Choong, K., Cornell, T., Decaen, A., Deymann, A., ... Zuckerberg, A. (2009). Clinical practice parameters for hemodynamic support of pediatric and neonatal septic shock: 2007 update from the American College of Critical Care Medicine. *Critical Care Medicine, 37,* 666–688.

27. Robinson, D. T., Kumar, P., & Cadichon, S. B. (2008). Neonatal sepsis in the emergency department. *Clinical Pediatric Emergency Medicine, 9,* 160–168.

References *continued*

28. Bhutani, V. K., & Johnson, L. (2008). The jaundiced newborn in the emergency department: Prevention of kernicterus. *Clinical Pediatric Emergency Medicine, 9,* 149–159.

29. Kenner, C., & Lott, J. W. (2007). *Comprehensive neonatal care: An interdisciplinary approach* (4th ed.). St. Louis, MO: Saunders Elsevier.

30. American Academy of Pediatrics Subcommittee on Hyperbilirubinemia. (2004). Management of hyperbilirubinemia in the newborn infant 35 or more weeks of gestation. *Pediatrics, 114,* 297–316.

31. National Heart, Lung, and Blood Institute. Diseases and Conditions Index. (n.d.) *Congenital heart defects.* Retrieved from http://www.nhlbi.nih.gov/health/dci/Diseases/chd/chd_what.html

32. Steinhorn, R. H. (2008). Evaluation and management of the cyanotic neonate. *Clinical Pediatric Emergency Medicine, 9,* 169–175.

33. Taketomo, C. K., Hodding, J. H., & Kraus, D. M. (2009). *Pediatric dosage handbook* (16th ed.). Hudson, OH: Lexi-Comp.

34. Centers for Disease Control and Prevention. (n.d.) *2010 Child and adolescent immunization schedule.* Retrieved from http://www.cdc.gov/vaccines/recs/schedules/child-schedule.htm

35. *Tips and tools: safety for your child: birth to 6 months.* (n.d.) Retrieved from http://www.healthychildren.org/English/tips-tools/Pages/Safety-for-Your-Child-Birth-to-6-Months.aspx

36. *Anticipatory guidance: Infancy.* (n.d.) Retrieved from http://www.brightfutures.org/wellchildcare/06_education/resources/infancy.html

Chapter 13 | The Adolescent

Julie L. Gerberick, MS, RN, CEN
Janelle Glasgow, RNC, CPEN

Objectives

On completion of this chapter, the learner should be able to do the following:

- Determine anatomical, physiological, and developmental characteristics of adolescent patients as a basis for assessment.
- Describe common emergent conditions associated with the adolescent population.
- Plan appropriate interventions for adolescents with emergent conditions.
- Indicate health promotion strategies related to adolescent care and illness prevention.

Introduction

Challenges to Treating Adolescents

Adolescents present unique challenges for healthcare professionals because of the developmental, ethical, and legal issues that arise in adolescent healthcare. They may use the emergency department (ED) as a means of gaining access to healthcare without the knowledge or presence of a parent. For example, an adolescent may come to the ED with a basic complaint, such as abdominal pain, but may actually be concerned about a sexually transmitted infection (STI), pregnancy, or another complaint that he or she finds embarrassing and frightening and does not want to discuss with his or her caregivers.[1] An issue that frequently arises is balancing the adolescent's need and right for privacy with the caregivers' need for information to provide continued care for the adolescent's complaint. When caregivers are present, the adolescent may refrain from asking or answering questions honestly in fear of divulging personal information or feeling embarrassed. All adolescents should be allowed an opportunity to be interviewed and examined without caregivers present to allow them to talk confidentially.[1]

Each adolescent is unique in terms of his or her level of cognitive development, healthcare beliefs, cultural beliefs,

and previous healthcare experiences. All adolescents deserve honest, straightforward, and clear explanations about treatments and procedures. Most adolescents are able to understand verbal explanations, but some will require the use of pictures, diagrams, and anatomical models to grasp the meaning of what a procedure entails. Adolescents learn much of what they know from peers; thus, some may have misconceptions about medical care or body functions. Time should be taken to determine what the adolescent believes to be true and to clarify any misconceptions without making the adolescent feel inferior.[1] Because adolescents develop at vastly different rates, approaching each adolescent must be based on his or her individual developmental level, not necessarily chronological age. The HEEADSSS mnemonic (**Box 13-1**) can be used to guide and organize questions regarding the adolescent's psychosocial history. Some techniques that may be useful in interviewing adolescents can be found in **Box 13-2**.[2]

For successful treatment and management, care providers must gain the trust of their adolescent patients and work with families and guardians to facilitate open communication regarding the specific needs of the adolescent while respecting the caregivers' rights and family interests. Parents and healthcare professionals may disagree about what to tell the adolescent and who should authorize testing

Box 13-1 HEEADSSS Mnemonic*

Letter (Description)	Examples of Questions to Ask (Not an Exhaustive List)
H (home environment)	Who lives with you? Where do you live? What are relationships like at home? To whom can you talk at home? Have you ever run away? What made you need to run away? Is there any physical violence at home?
E (education/employment)	What are your favorite subjects at school? How are your grades? Have you changed schools in the past few years? What are your future education/employment plans/goals? Tell me about your friends at school. Is your school a safe place?
E (eating)	What do you like and not like about your body? Have there been any recent changes in your weight? Have you dieted in the last year? How often? How much exercise do you get in an average day? Week? Do you eat in front of the TV?
A (activities)	What do you and your friends do for fun? Do you participate in any sports or other activities? Do you have any hobbies?
D (drugs)	Do any of your friends use tobacco? Alcohol? Other drugs? Does anyone in your family use tobacco? Alcohol? Other drugs? Do you use tobacco? Alcohol? Other drugs? Do you ever drink or use drugs when you are alone?
S (sexuality)	Have you ever been in a romantic relationship? Have any of your relationships ever been sexual relationships? What does the term *safer sex* mean? Tell me about the people you have dated.
S (suicide/depression)	Do you feel sad or down more than usual? Are you "bored" all the time? Are you having trouble getting to sleep? Have you thought about hurting yourself or someone else? Does it seem that you've lost interest in things that you used to really enjoy?
S (safety)	Have you ever been seriously injured? Do you always wear a seat belt in the car? Is there violence in your home? Have you ever ridden with a driver who was drunk or high? Do you use safety equipment for sports and/or other physical activities? Have you ever been picked on or bullied?

*Data are taken from Goldenring, J. M., & Rosen, D. S. (2004). Getting into adolescent heads: An essential update. *Contemporary Pediatrics, 21*(1), 64–90.

and treatments. Each case must be addressed individually. Caregiver decision-making can be motivated by fear, uncertainty, previous experience, and intuition. An adolescent may disagree with parents about the plan of care and who should know about the diagnosis. Communication among family members is critical, and decisions should be made based on the best interest of the patient.[1] The healthcare provider may need to help find an acceptable compromise when faced with conflicts between parental expectations and adolescent preferences.[3]

Adolescent Legal Issues

Consent/Confidentiality

In addition to knowledge of the physical and psychosocial development of teenagers, a clinician must be familiar with the complex legal and ethical considerations when adolescents receive medical care. Adolescents are considered minors (< 18 years) and are not able to consent or have decision-making authority regarding their healthcare.[4] Understanding the relevant state and federal laws on consent and confidentiality is imperative.[4]

In most instances, parents/guardians will give legal consent for medical care for their minor children. A minor patient is able to consent for his or her own healthcare under specific circumstances, including the following:

- *Emancipated minor*: defined as an individual who is married, enlisted in the military, financially independent from parents, living independently from parents, the parent of their own child or pregnant, or otherwise declared emancipated by a court of law.[5] Each state identifies the criteria for an emancipated minor in its jurisdiction.[5]

- *Mature minor:* a court determines that the minor living under the supervision of a parent or guardian has the maturity to make independent decisions; providers can determine if the minor understands the risks and benefits of treatment or if parental involvement may be problematic or may discourage the adolescent from seeking necessary medical care.[5] (This decision is made with each individual situation.)

- When specific services are sought, including the following:[6, 7]

  ○ Reproductive healthcare, including family planning and contraception

Box 13-2 Adolescent Interview Techniques*

Focus on the adolescent patient, rather than on the caregiver or guardian

Encourage questions

Be sympathetic, supportive, and reassuring

Be yourself: adolescents can sense when an adult is putting up a front

Ask direct questions about psychosocial issues

Try to keep a neutral facial expression

Start with neutral topics

Avoid lecturing and being judgmental

Do not rush through assessment

Do not talk about the adolescent with others as if the adolescent is not present

Be aware of, acknowledge, and explore nonverbal cues (i.e., facial expressions, body gestures, and tone of voice)

Use active listening: encourage adolescents by asking "And then what happened?"

Provide education as an active part of care throughout the emergency department visit, not just at discharge

*Data are taken from Holland-Hall and Brown.[2]

- Pregnancy-related care, including prenatal care and care during labor and delivery
- Sexually transmitted infection screening and treatment
- Drug/alcohol treatment
- Mental health services

Adolescents have the right to consent to confidential treatment for family planning services mandated by the federal Title X of the Public Health Services Act without parent/guardian knowledge of the services.[8] Several major medical organizations have historically supported the need for confidential care based on the concern that adolescents will not seek necessary services if confidentiality is not ensured. This lack of care can have potentially harmful personal and public health implications. Adolescents should be encouraged to talk with caregivers/guardians or another trusted adult regarding healthcare needs. Providers must inform patients that results may be disclosed to caregivers or guardians if the practitioner decides it is medically necessary, such as in cases of child abuse/neglect, statutory rape, a suicide attempt, homicidal ideations, and violent injuries.[7]

Noncompliance

Caring for adolescents includes an evaluation for patterns of noncompliance, such as failure to take medications, failure to follow a dietary regimen, failure to adjust lifestyle, and risk-taking behaviors. The importance of peer approval during midadolescence may predispose an adolescent to choose a noncompliant posture rather than to appear different from his or her peers. Body image takes precedence in adolescence; medications that cause weight gain, such as steroids, may not be taken as directed, and diseases, such as asthma, may become poorly controlled. Other chronic illnesses (e.g., type I diabetes) are more likely to become poorly controlled during adolescence. Erratic eating patterns and consumption of fast foods are common, and the need to follow fairly inflexible dietary patterns can make the teenager with diabetes feel different and isolated.[9]

The developmental and cognitive level of the adolescent determines the best education techniques to be used for discharge. An older adolescent can appreciate the consequences of noncompliance and explanations of potential long-term health effects, but an adolescent who is still governed by egocentric and concrete thought processes lives in the here and now and is unable to understand this concept.[9]

Risk-Taking Behaviors

Adolescents are more likely to participate in activities that carry a high risk for injury and loss of life than any other age group. Peer groups are more important than parents to the adolescent; to fit in, adolescents are more likely to engage in behaviors that are risky.[1] Some degree of risk taking in adolescence is normal. Most adolescents are able to cope with the stresses of adolescence and are able to avoid and resolve situations that may threaten their well-being. Indicators of a more serious psychological problem include repeatedly engaging in high-risk activities, showing persistent disregard for attempts at limit setting by authority figures, and aggressive behavior.

Unintentional Injuries and Violence

Injuries may be unintentional, such as those caused by motor vehicle crashes, or intentional, such as those caused by violence and suicide. The mortality rate has been decreasing during the past 25 years, from 97.9 to 64.4 deaths per 100,000 adolescents.[10] However, injuries continue to be the leading cause of death and disability for people aged one to 34 years in the United States.[11] Injuries requiring medical attention affect more than 20 million children and adolescents (250 per 1,000 persons) and cost $17 billion annually for medical treatment.[11] **Figure 13-1** and **Figure 13-2** illustrate the five leading causes of death and injury, respectively, for those aged 11 to 18 years.

Teenaged Driving

Motor vehicle crashes are the leading cause of death for US teenagers, accounting for one in three deaths in this age group. Injuries sustained in motor vehicle crashes range from minor to severe. The risk of motor vehicle crashes is higher among those aged 16 to 19 years than any other age group, and teenaged drivers are four times more likely to crash than older more experienced drivers. Male adolescents are 1 to 1.5 times more likely to crash than female adolescents, with excess speed and alcohol consumption being contributing factors.[12] The crash risk is particularly high during the first year of licensure regardless of the age at which the new teenaged driver begins driving.[12]

In a study performed by Students Against Destructive Decisions in 2007, of 900 teenagers with driver's licenses, the behaviors in **Box 13-3** were rated by teenagers as extremely distracting while driving.[13] Although teenagers are aware that they find texting distracting while driving, they persist in this behavior because "the desire to stay connected is so strong for teens and their parents that safety sometimes takes a backseat to staying in touch with friends and family."[14] In addition, this group has the lowest compliance of seat belt use, with 9.7% of high school students reporting that they rarely or never wear a seat belt; it becomes apparent why motor vehicle crashes are the primary killer of teens in this age group.[15] Many injury prevention measures have been enacted throughout the United States in response to the many fatalities and significant injuries resulting from motor vehicle crashes. These include the following:

- Limiting the number of passengers in the vehicle with the teenaged driver to prevent distraction.

- Laws regarding use of cellular telephones for talking or texting while driving.

- Limiting the hours of the day and night that a teenager is permitted to drive.

- Graduated driver's licensing.

- Documented hours driven with parent/adult supervision.

- Documented hours of night driving.

- Documented driver's education courses.

- Stiffer penalties for moving violations, including loss of licensure.

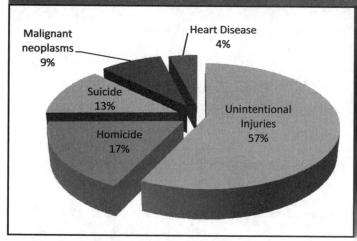

Figure 13-1 Five Leading Causes of Death From 1999–2007 in Children Aged 11 to 18 years*

*Data are taken from the Centers for Disease Control and Prevention.[36]

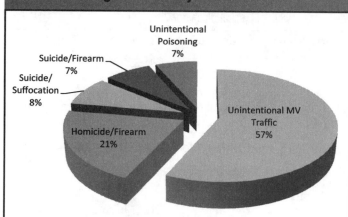

Figure 13-2 Five Leading Causes of Injury-Related Death From 1999–2007 in Children Aged 11 to 18 years*

Note: MV indicates motor vehicle.
*Data are taken from the Centers for Disease Control and Prevention.[36]

Box 13-3 Distracting Behaviors Among Teenage Drivers*

Behavior	% of Drivers Distracted
Instant or text messaging while driving	37
The teenaged driver's emotional state	20
Having several friends in the car	19
Talking on a cellular telephone	14
Eating or drinking	7
Having a friend in the car	5
Listening to music	4

*Data are taken from Bayliss.[13]

- Zero tolerance laws in every state that make it illegal for those under 21 years of age to drive after drinking any alcohol.

Car Surfing

Car surfing is an extremely dangerous thrill-seeking activity that involves a person riding on the exterior of a moving vehicle, such as on the roof or hood, while someone else is driving.[16] Since 1990, at least 99 people have died as a result of car surfing, most commonly because of head injuries when the person who is surfing falls from the moving vehicle. This can occur at any speed and usually happens when the vehicle makes an unanticipated maneuver, such as swerving or braking. The average age range of persons who car surf is between 15 and 19 years, and the average age of injured persons is 17.6 years; however, children as young as age 10 years have been injured when participating in this activity. Males are more likely to car surf than females.[16]

The Choking Game

The choking game is an activity primarily seen in children aged nine through 16 years, but deaths have been reported in those as young as aged six years and as old as aged 30 years. This activity consists of having someone press on the chest or neck of another person to cut off oxygen and blood flow to the brain, resulting in a near or a complete loss of consciousness as the brain starves for oxygen. When the person who has been choked begins to have blood flow return to the brain, he or she experiences a rush sensation that is similar to what is felt with the use of an illicit drug. This rush sensation is as addictive as any illegal substance.[17] Participants say that it feels like a vivid dream that lasts for approximately 30 minutes. Adolescents tend to participate in this game to relieve stress, with the stress relief perception coming from a lack of oxygen to the stress areas of the brain.

Deaths most commonly occur when a person attempts to achieve this sensation alone by tying a rope or belt around his or her neck to cut off oxygen and blood flow, with the intent to release the ligature before actually losing consciousness. However, loss of consciousness cannot be predicted, and if the person loses consciousness with a ligature around the neck, the ligature can continue to tighten and the person is asphyxiated.[17] Deaths may be mistakenly attributed to suicide by hanging or suffocation but may, in fact, be unintentional because of the choking game.

Thousands of video recordings are posted on the Internet on sites such as YouTube showing young people engaging in this activity. More females participate in this activity, but males are more likely to die. All economic or sociological groups are at risk. The achievement of a rush is free, not illegal; and caregivers are usually unaware that this activity even exists, so adolescents have not been told that they should not do it. Physical signs and symptoms include the following:

- Headaches
- Bloodshot eyes or visual changes
- Marks on the neck
- Behavior changes
- Disorientation after being alone

Environmental signs include knots tied in items in the adolescent's bedroom, wear marks on bedposts or doorknobs, and locked doors.[17] There is also a chance of seizures, a cerebrovascular accident, and cumulative brain damage each and every time someone performs this activity.[17]

Youth Violence

Violence has become increasingly prominent in the lives of children in the United States. The child homicide rate of 2.6 per 100,000 for children younger than 15 years is five times higher than the combined rate of 25 other industrialized countries.[18] Children and adolescents face serious long-term physical and emotional consequences as victims, perpetrators, and witnesses to violence and homicide.[18] It is estimated that for every homicide in the adolescent age group, as many as 100 ED visits take place for other injuries related to assault and violence.[18]

For most adolescents, hanging out with friends is an important part of growing up and forming attachments outside the family. Youth street gangs are unsupervised groups of adolescents that meet together with some regularity and are self-determining with respect to membership criteria, organizational structure, and the types of behavior that are considered acceptable and necessary for belonging. These groups develop from interactions and decisions among adolescents on their own terms.[19] Gangs become problematic when they engage in criminal activity or delinquency, conflict with each other, or otherwise disrupt families, schools, communities, and institutions.[19] For many gangs, membership initiation may include homicide, gang rape, theft, or assault. Continued membership may include theft, the sale of illegal drugs, or a variety of other illegal acts. Adolescents may join gangs for perceived safety in their neighborhood, where crime may be rampant.[19]

Screening for at-risk adolescents should be part of the assessment and care of adolescents in the emergency department. Referral for additional resources from child welfare agencies may be necessary for patients who exhibit the following:[19]

- Signs of intentional injury
- Exposure to violence in the home
- Inappropriate supervision
- Gang involvement or exposure
- Substance abuse in the patient or caregiver
- Frequent loss of temper
- Frequent physical fighting
- Enjoying hurting animals and other people
- History of aggressive behavior
- Fascination with weapons
- History of discipline problems

Legal and Illegal Substance Use and Abuse

Adolescence is a critical time of life when the body and brain are still developing and use of alcohol, tobacco, or drugs can have profound effects physically, mentally, and socially. Although reports have shown decreases in alcohol and cigarette use among adolescents, marijuana and ecstasy use has increased in recent years.[15] The number of new female users of alcohol, cigarettes, and marijuana has continued to increase since 2004.[20] Adolescent females display a unique set of vulnerabilities that places them at higher risk for substance abuse. These risk factors include the following:

- Depression/anxiety
- Concerns about weight and appearance
- Risky sexual behavior
- Early puberty
- Conduct disorders
- Physical/sexual abuse

Peer pressure, low self-esteem, or low self-worth place the adolescent female, more than her male counterpart, at high risk to turn to alcohol or other drugs as coping mechanisms when dealing with the stressors of adolescence. Female adolescents tend to drink alcohol to fit in, whereas male adolescents will drink and then join a group who also drinks.[20]

Alcohol Abuse

Alcohol is the most commonly abused substance by teenagers in the United States. Of high school students,

72.5% report having consumed alcohol, with 41.8% currently drinking and 24.2% binge drinking (i.e., consuming more than five alcoholic drinks in a short period). The students reveal that they drink for the physical effects they experience from alcohol consumption (**Table 13-1**). They are usually unaware that exposing the adolescent brain to alcohol may interrupt key cognitive development, such as short-term memory skills, which may result in difficulty with academic achievement.

In 2005, more than 1,800 college students died from alcohol poisoning as the result of binge drinking,[21] with 20% of male college freshmen reporting that they partake in binge drinking. The same report notes that it is not uncommon to find that college students drink 10 to 20 alcoholic drinks in a short period. Also, it is estimated that girls who binge drink alcohol are up to 63% more likely to become teenaged mothers.[20]

Tobacco Use

Increased stress in an adolescent's life and trying to fit in are just two reasons that adolescents use cigarettes and smokeless tobacco. In the United States, 46.3% of teenagers disclosed having tried smoking cigarettes, 19.5% currently smoke cigarettes, and 11.2% smoke cigarettes every day. Of the teenagers who smoke daily, 50.8% report having tried to stop smoking in the previous 12 months.[15] Although the number of adolescents who smoke is high, it has decreased since the 1990s, reaching an all-time low in 2008.[22]

Adolescents who smoke report beginning between the ages of 11 and 14 years. This is a time when thought processes are egocentric and concrete: adolescents believe that they are invincible and that nothing can happen to them. Many lack the ability to understand long-term health consequences or appreciate that their actions can have a significant impact on their lives later on. Coupled with an immature and still physically developing brain, the likelihood of addiction is high.[22]

Huffing

A variety of chemical substances may be inhaled to produce euphoric effects, thus altering moods, feelings, and perceptions. Inhalants are easily accessible, legal, and everyday products, making them attractive to the adolescent. Inhalants are addictive and are considered gateway drugs. Often, the adolescent progresses from inhalants to illegal drugs and alcohol abuse.[23] The products used for huffing are not intended for human consumption and include adhesives (glues and cements), aerosols (spray paint and hair spray), or solvents (nail polish). The signs and symptoms of huffing are listed in **Table 13-2.**

Table 13-1 Progressive Effects of Alcohol*

Blood Alcohol Concentration (%)	Changes in Feelings and Personality	Physical and Mental Impairments
0.01–0.06	Relaxation	Thought
	Sense of well-being	Judgment
	Loss of inhibitions	Coordination
	Lowered alertness	Concentration
	Joyous	
0.07–0.10	Blunted feelings	Impaired reflexes
	Disinhibition	Reasoning
	Extroversion	Depth perception
	Impaired sexual pleasure	Distance acuity
		Peripheral vision
		Glare recovery
0.11–0.20	Overexpression	Reaction time
	Emotional swings	Gross motor control
	Angry or sad	Staggering
	Boisterous	Slurred speech
0.21–0.29	Stupor	Severe gross motor control
	Lose understanding	Loss of consciousness
	Impaired sensations	Memory blackout
0.30–0.39	Severe depression	Bladder function
	Unconsciousness	Breathing
	Death possible	Heart rate
≥ 0.40	Unconsciousness	Breathing
	Death	Heart rate

*Data are taken from Virginia Tech Alcohol Abuse Prevention. (n.d.). *Progressive effects of alcohol.* Retrieved from http://www.alcohol.vt.edu/Students/alcoholEffects/index.htm

Table 13-2 Signs and Symptoms of Huffing*

Tell-tale Signs	Signs of a Long-term User	Short-term Effects	Long-term Effects
Painting fingernails with magic markers or correction fluid	Hallucinations	Rapid heart rate	Central nervous system damage
Sitting with a pen or marker by the nose	Anxiety	Headache	Brain damage
Constantly smelling clothing sleeves	Excitability/irritability	Muscle weakness	Heart damage
Showing paint or stain marks on face, fingers, or clothing	Restlessness/anger	Mood swings/violent behavior/ disinhibition	Kidney damage
		Abdominal pain	Desaturation/death
		Slurred speech	
		Tingling of hands and feet	

*Treatment consists of counseling patients about the risk of huffing and its long-term effects, along with treating the symptoms.

Drugs of Abuse

Risky behaviors, in combination with substance abuse, commonly bring adolescents to the ED for treatment. Common reasons for these visits include the following:[24]

- Trauma (motor vehicle crashes, falls, and near drowning)
- Overdose
- Intoxication
- Drug-seeking behavior
- Inappropriate behavior
- Caregivers wanting their child tested for drug use

Illicit drugs are known by many different names or slang terms. An adolescent may not be aware of the proper name of an illicit drug; therefore, healthcare providers must be aware of both the street names and the proper names of illicit drugs. **Table 13-3** lists different names that street drugs may be commonly referred to by the adolescent, and **Table 13-4** lists common terms indicating use of illicit/licit drugs. **Chapter 17, "Toxicological Emergencies,"** provides additional information.

Marijuana/Cocaine

Marijuana is the most commonly used illegal drug by adolescents in the United States, with 36.8% of US teenagers having tried marijuana and 20.8% currently using it. Marijuana use is followed by the abuse of cocaine, with 6.4% of US teenagers reporting having tried cocaine in some form and 2.8% being current users.[15]

Table 13-3 Common Terms for Illicit/Licit Drug Use: Street Names*

Marijuana	Cocaine	Heroin	DXM	MDMA (Ecstasy)	Methamphetamine	Prescription Medications	Inhalants
Shake	Base	Raw	Dex	Adam	Ice	Trail Mix	Laughing gas
Joint	Big C	Sweet stuff	Vitamin D	Clarity	Crank	Oxy	Buzz bomb
Bong	Bernie	Brown sugar	Poor man's PCP	Ecstasy	Purple haze	OC	Poppers
Blunt	Booger Sugar	Dope	Robo	Eve	Chalk	Killer	Snappers
Dope	Candy sugar	H	Triple C	Lover's speed	Fire	Vike	Quicksilver
Ganga	Coke	Junk	CCC	X	Crystal	Goodfella	
Mary Jane	Flake	Skag	Skittles	XTC	Glass	Loads	
Reefer	Glad stuff	Smack	Red hots	STP	Go fast	Jackpot	
Skunk	Gold dust	White horse	Red devils	E-tards	Meth	TNT	
Weed	Icing		Candy	Scooby snacks	Speed	Smart drugs	
Herb						Vitamins	
Pot							

Note: DXM indicates dextromethorphan; MDMA, 3,4-methylenedioxymethamphetamine; PCP, phencyclidine.
*Data are taken from the National Institutes of Drug Abuse.[29]

Table 13-4 Terms of Use*

Marijuana	Cocaine	Heroin	DXM	MDMA (Ecstasy)	Methamphetamine	Prescription Medications	Inhalants
Toke	Blow	Slamming	Sheeting	Roll	Tweaking	Pharming	Shoot the breeze
Toot	Freebase	Speedballing	Roboing	Rolling	Get geeked up		Bolt
	Sniff		Robocopping	Candy flipping	Go to the moon		Thrust
	Snort						Climax
	Speedballing						Locker room
	Toke						
	Toot						

Note: DXM indicates dextromethorphan; MDMA, 3,4-methylenedioxymethamphetamine.
*Data are taken from the National Institutes of Drug Abuse.[29]

Marijuana is a mixture of dried and shredded leaves and flowers of the *Cannabis sativa* plant and is most commonly smoked, but it can also be ingested in food or drinks.[25] Smoking marijuana has increased the number of adolescents presenting to the ED with a chief complaint of wheezing, with no underlying history of asthma. Marijuana smokers are becoming more susceptible to developing asthma, with early chronic obstructive pulmonary disease changes being seen on a chest radiograph.

Marijuana may also be dipped with phencyclidine (PCP), formaldehyde, or formalin. Occasionally after smoking marijuana laced with formaldehyde, male adolescents complain of genitourinary symptoms similar to those of a sexually transmitted infection, such as burning with urination or bumps at the head of the penis. When they are tested for an STI, the results are usually negative. Treatment consists of discontinuing smoking for a few days, with all symptoms subsiding.

Cocaine is derived from the coca plant and can be inhaled (snorted), ingested, injected, or smoked. Cocaine is a strong central nervous system stimulant that increases levels of dopamine in the brain's reward circuit; it is commonly associated with pleasure and movement. However, cocaine may not be the only substance that is being abused. Commonly, substance abusers will indulge in polysubstances, with alcohol being the substance of choice that may alter the normal drugs of abuse screen completed in the emergency department. If a healthcare provider suspects that cocaine has been abused, a comprehensive drug screen should be ordered. If the screen result is positive for benzoylecgonine, the individual truly has cocaine in his or her system.

Heroin

Heroin is an opiate synthesized from morphine. Nationwide, 2.5% of US teenagers report having used heroin.[15] Heroin usually appears as a white or brown powder or a black and sticky substance called *black tar heroin*; typically, it is injected, snorted, or smoked.

Heroin abuse is associated with many serious health conditions, especially among intravenous users, with the most serious being human immunodeficiency virus/acquired immunodeficiency syndrome and hepatitis from sharing needles. Pneumonia is commonly related to the depressive action that this substance has on the respiratory centers in the brain. In addition to the effects of the drug itself, street heroin contains many contaminants or additives that can cause damage to blood vessels as it is injected and damage to the heart and other organs during circulation.[26]

Methamphetamine

Methamphetamine is a central nervous system stimulant similar to amphetamines. Nationwide, 4.1% of US teenagers report having used methamphetamines.[15] Although these numbers appear small, methamphetamine use is epidemic. Methamphetamine is a bitter white crystalline powder that dissolves easily and can be ingested, snorted, smoked, or injected.[27]

Signs of long-term methamphetamine use include the following:

- Methamphetamine mouth (i.e., poor dental hygiene)
- Agitation
- Continuous picking at imaginary bugs with numerous "bug bites" to the face and arms
- Decreased appetite

Treatment for methamphetamine use includes the following:

- There is no reversal agent or antidote to counteract the effects of methamphetamine. Treatment of symptoms is all that can be done.
- Benzodiazepines may assist with the agitation type of symptoms seen.

Ecstasy

3,4-Methylenedioxymethamphetamine or Ecstasy is a synthetic psychoactive drug that is chemically similar to the stimulant methamphetamine and the hallucinogen mescaline. In the United States, 6.7% of teenagers report having used Ecstasy.[15] Ecstasy is available as a tablet or capsule and is most commonly seen in dance clubs or raves. 3,4-Methylenedioxymethamphetamine may be used in combination with marijuana, cocaine, methamphetamine, ketamine, and alcohol.[28]

Prescription and Over-the-Counter Drug Misuse

Prescription and over-the-counter cough and cold medication abuse is rapidly becoming a national health concern for adolescents. Pharming, the more commonly known term for this practice, is a growing phenomenon among adolescents and is a clean way for them to get high. This avoids the concern of additives and toxins that may be added to street drugs. It can be done either individually or with other teenagers at parties and has become an alternative to illicit drug use because prescription drugs are inexpensive, easily accessible, and wave fewer red flags to caregivers. According to the National Institute for Drug

Abuse, the most widely used prescription drugs among adolescents are as follows:

- Opioids
  - Oxycodone (OxyContin), hydrocodone (Vicodin), propoxyphene (Darvon), and hydromorphone (Dilaudid)
- Central nervous system depressants
  - Diazepam (Valium) and alprazolam (Xanax)
- Stimulants
  - Dextroamphetamine sulfate (Adderall), methylphenidate (Ritalin), and dextroamphetamine sulfate (Dexedrine)[29]

Dextromethorphan (Coricidin HBP) is another commonly abused over-the-counter medication found in a wide variety of cough and cold preparations.[30] Adolescents can place five to 10 dextromethorphan tablets in a water bottle and drink it throughout the day to stay high while in school.

Energy Drinks

Today in the United States, there is increased use of various energy drinks among children as young as aged 12 years, with approximately a third of 12- to 24-year-old persons saying that they consume energy drinks regularly. These drinks have become the fastest-growing slice of the beverage market, making them synonymous with exercise and improved cognitive abilities. In 2010, more than 4.2 billion cans of Red Bull were sold worldwide.[31] This excessive consumption of the caffeine-and-sugar–loaded energy drink can take its toll on the body.

Studies have shown improved cognitive abilities with the use of energy drinks because of the high amounts of caffeine contained in these drinks, but the high amounts of caffeine are not all good for the human body. Consuming high amounts of caffeine can cause abnormal heart rhythms and even death. If an adolescent who may have a minor cardiovascular issue and does not know about it begins to consume numerous energy drinks, and then begins to exercise, he or she may be at risk, with just mild exercise, for lethal cardiac arrhythmias and death. The caffeine content of these drinks varies and exceeds many common beverages. Consider the following:

- An average 12-ounce serving of Coca-Cola or Pepsi has between 29.5 and 31.7 mg of caffeine.[32]
- An average 8.3-ounce serving of Red Bull contains between 64.7 and 66.7 mg of caffeine.[32]

- An average 8.4-ounce serving of Amp contains 69.6 mg of caffeine.[32]
- A 9.5-ounce Starbucks Frappuccino Mocha contains 71.8 mg of caffeine.[32]

In addition to containing caffeine, these drinks are high in sugar (many contain up to 18 teaspoons), which may increase a young person's risk of rapid atrial fibrillation and type II diabetes.

When talking with an adolescent who may present with complaints of palpitations, hyperglycemia, light-headedness, insomnia, high blood pressure, gastroesophageal reflux disease, or even problems with menses, the nurse should discuss the adolescent's intake of energy drinks. Also, adolescents should be asked if they add any alcohol to these drinks. Many consumers mix energy drinks, such as Red Bull, with vodka or other liquor to keep the party going.

Intentional Injuries and Violence

Self-Injury/Self-Harm Behaviors

Self-injury can be defined as "deliberate attempts to harm or damage oneself without suicidal intent."[33] Self-injury is also known as self-mutilation, self-abuse, and deliberate self-harm. Some common behaviors associated with self-injury include cutting and burning of the skin, swallowing sharp objects, and inserting sharp objects into the skin.[33] Self-injury can occur in many different populations and age groups but is becoming an increasing problem for adolescents who use it as a means for coping with extreme psychological distress. These teenagers may have difficulty verbalizing their feelings, and the physical pain provides a calming effect to counter the distress, frustrations, anger, or anxiety being felt.[33] The reasons teenagers engage in self-injury behaviors are complex, and research has just begun to identify characteristics of those who self-injure and the causes for their behaviors. Self-injury may begin with experimentation but may become a habitual way of coping with stress. The intent of the self-injury can be to release tension, establish control, vent anger, or gain a sense of security and uniqueness.

Skin cutting is the most prevalent type of behavior, but most adolescents use multiple methods of self-injury. These stress-relieving measures are rarely life threatening but can result in dangerous infections or scarring. The adolescent often feels relief, shame, guilt, and disappointment and may hide the behaviors from others. Approximately 2 million Americans engage in superficial or moderate self-injury each year, and girls may be more likely to engage in self-injurious behaviors than boys.[33] Adolescents who self-injure often feel powerless, have difficulty trusting others with emotions, feel isolated or alienated, feel afraid, and have low self-esteem. They may be experiencing family situations that prompt this behavior, such as family conflict, parental neglect, parental separation, parental alcoholism and depression, and loss or disruption of an important interpersonal relationship. Self-injury may also be associated with depression, drug and alcohol use, negative body image, physical and sexual abuse, eating disorders, and obsessive-compulsive disorder. Evidence also suggests that adolescents with a childhood illness, such as diabetes, asthma, epilepsy, and cardiac disease, may be more prone to self-injury.[33]

Adolescents who self-injure do not necessarily have suicidal intentions; however, it does place them at increased risk. Those who are suicidal may use self-injurious behaviors as a means for suicide. Self-injury and suicide are different in important ways, such as intent, method, lethality, aftermath, demographics, and number of acts. Self-injurious behaviors are used to bring temporary relief while suicide brings permanent relief through death.[34] The methods are similar in that they cause physical harm, are often the result of psychological needs and poor coping mechanisms, and are concerning to friends, parents, teachers, and mental health professionals; however, they have different intended outcomes.[33]

Treatments are as varied and complex as the methods of self-injury. Most therapies focus on teaching specific skills and behavioral interventions, such as problem solving, the development of self-image and self-esteem, and building on personal strengths. Medications prescribed for depression and anxiety may help to reduce the symptoms of mental disorders, which may include self-injurious behaviors.[35]

Suicide

Suicide is a complex problem encompassing all cultural, social, religious, and economic dimensions.[36] In the United States and worldwide, suicide and self-inflicted injuries are the third leading cause of death in adolescents aged 11 to 18 years.[36,37] For female adolescents ages 15 to 24 years in the United States, suicide is the second leading cause of death, second only to unintentional injury. Male adolescents ages 15–19 years, are three and a half times more likely to complete suicide than female adolescents in the same age group.

Hanging is the most common method of suicide among children and young male adolescents. Female adolescents of all ages consistently choose poisoning as a means of suicide. Males in late adolescence prefer shooting as their primary means of suicide. Stabbing is the second most common mechanism in both sexes.[37] White males and females account for greater than 90% of all suicides.[38] The 2007 National Youth Risk Behavior Survey found that 14.5% of high school students had seriously considered attempting suicide and that 6.9% of students had attempted suicide one or more times during the 12 months before the survey.[15]

There are several risk factors to observe for in an adolescent that may be an indicator of potential suicide risk. These risk factors include the following:[38]

- Prior suicide attempt
- History of abuse
- Co-occurring mental and substance abuse disorders
- History of family suicide or mental disorders and substance abuse
- Stressful life event or loss
- History of broken family or family discord
- Gay or bisexual adolescents
- Poor school performance and learning disabilities

Clinicians must be comfortable when screening for suicide and mood disorders. Assessing for emotional difficulties, identifying lack of developmental progress, and estimating the level of distress, the impairment of functioning, and the level of danger to self and others are important parts of that screen. The best way to assess for suicidal ideation is by directly asking the individual. Also, clinicians, family, and friends should be alerted for certain behavior patterns and signs of suicidal ideation/behaviors. These behaviors and signs include the following:[38]

- Sadness, hopelessness, and emptiness
- Lack of energy and insomnia
- Loss of interest in social life and school or boredom
- Substance abuse or change in social behavior
- Giving away prized possessions

Suicide prevention is the key. Prevention measures include the following:[38]

- General suicide education
- Screening programs to identify high-risk adolescents
- School gatekeeper training to identify and refer students
- Community gatekeeper training to train staff and healthcare providers to identify teenagers at high risk
- Peer support programs

- Crisis centers and hotlines
- Restriction of access to handguns, drugs, and other common means of suicide
- Intervention after a suicide attempt

Cybersuicide

There is a growing suicide trend referred to as Internet suicide or cybersuicide. It is rapidly spreading across the world's generations, cultures, and races. The Internet provides a media outlet for vulnerable adolescents who may be at high risk for suicide from other factors. With increasing technological knowledge, the adolescent population has access to new and creative methods of dying. There are three main types of Internet suicide: suicide pacts, death casting, and fake suicide. *Death casting* refers to the live broadcasting of one's death on the Internet. Fake suicide refers to the false simulation of suicide on the Internet.[36]

Suicide pacts are the most common form of cybersuicide. The first reported case occurred in Japan in 2000; since then, more than 400 similar deaths have occurred worldwide. Individuals with suicidal ideations find support and encouragement with others like themselves. The participants in the pact support the suicidal behavior, and the dread of dying alone is no longer a concern.[39] Cybersuicide is a serious worldwide public health concern and a major challenge for the future. Education, screening, and intervention techniques for this widespread phenomenon must be developed and explored.[39]

Bullying and Suicide

Bullying has become a serious public health problem, with victims reporting unhappiness at school along with signs of low self-esteem, loneliness, isolation, and somatic complaints. Studies show that children who have been bullied and those who bully are at greater risk for suicidal thoughts and suicidal acts because of the strong association with major depression, substance use, and emotional/psychological distress.[40] Reports show that adolescents who perpetrate bullying behaviors have more signs of depression, are more likely to be involved in antisocial behaviors, and have legal problems as adults.[41]

Several studies conclude that the amount of bullying plays a significant role in the level of suicidal risk in an adolescent. Those who are victimized frequently are associated with higher risks of suicidal ideations or actions. Some studies show that females involved in bullying (both those who are bullied and those who bully) are at greater risk for suicidal ideations.[40]

Adolescent Sexuality

Dating

Dating is a positive experience for most teenagers. It is considered a healthy forum for developing and refining communication skills, interpersonal relations, and conflict management abilities. Dating is considered a training ground for the development of psychological and sexual intimacy and sharing, which are key building blocks for forming mature, satisfying, and enduring romantic relationships in adulthood.[42] As part of this process, teenagers are gradually moving toward committed exclusive dating relationships that are characterized by intense positive emotion, excitement, preoccupation and fantasizing, beliefs that the relationship can weather any challenge, and love. Dating is part of the larger process through which teenagers negotiate increasing autonomy and independence from family while developing closer ties with peers and opposite- or same-sex partners.[42]

Dating Violence

Dating violence is a problem that exists across all classes, communities, and ethnic groups, with females being the primary victims of dating violence. Dating relationships are rehearsals for eventual marriage; many times, adolescents act out their parts as they perceive they should be in a committed relationship. They are beginning to explore their roles in relationships at this stage in their development, and many times these roles are based on sex role stereotypes of the dominant male and the submissive female.[42] Adolescents who are exposed to domestic violence in the home may assume that this is normal male-female relationship behavior.

Dating violence during adolescence is more hidden than violence in adult relationships. Several reasons are associated with nonreport of episodes of dating violence:[40, 41]

- Isolation: the teenager has given up friends and activities at the insistence of his or her partner and feels that there is no one to talk to about the problem.
- Shame: it may be difficult for the teenager to admit that a mistake has been made in his or her choice of a partner.
- Fear: the teenager may attempt to hide the problem from parents for fear they will restrict activities or confront the issue openly in a way that may be embarrassing.
  - Fear of retaliation or revenge and escalation of the violence.
- Ongoing emotional ties with the perpetrator.
- Hope that the situation will improve on its own.

- Feelings of helplessness.
- Confusion: violence may be a new experience for a young person who may not know where to turn.

Arguments and lack of communication within relationships seem to precipitate many incidents. The pattern of abuse is similar to adult abuse: control is enforced by verbal or physical abuse. Attitudes and emotions most often cited as the cause of abusive incidents include jealousy, guilt, fear, insecurity, and confusion. As with adult domestic violence, substance abuse and dating violence often occur together. Alcohol or other drugs may increase the likelihood of violent outbursts and anger if a person is already prone to these behaviors. Using alcohol or drugs also impairs the ability for self-protection from assault.[43]

Primary preventative education should occur in early adolescence, before dating typically begins.

Secondary prevention begins with identifying adolescents at risk and ensuring that they are connected with the resources that they need to stay safe. According to the 2007 Youth Risk Behavior Survey, 9.9% of teenagers in the United States reported having been victims of violence in a dating relationship.[15] Teenagers who participate in high-risk behaviors, live in poverty, or are from a disadvantaged home are at increased risk for dating violence. It is believed that 33% of males and 68% of females are victims of dating violence in this group.[44] Suspicious signs to assess for include the following:

- Unexplained injuries
- Injuries that appear to be from questionable sources
- Wounds in various stages of healing
- Delays in seeking healthcare
- Strained partner relationships
- Conflicting reports from patients

Adolescents are not likely to disclose events of domestic violence unless specifically asked. It is important for healthcare providers to establish rapport with the individual, listen intently, and convey a sense of belief about the incident. A combination of directive and probing questions (**Box 13-4**) may be raised to discover violence in the dating relationship.[44] Adolescents may have a false sense of what is expected in a relationship with the opposite sex and may believe common dating myths that potentially lead to dating violence (**Box 13-5**).[44]

Date Rape

Rape, or forced sexual intercourse, can happen in different situations, including dating, incest, rape in marriage, and rape by a stranger. The most common form of rape is date or acquaintance rape. The topic of rape is relevant to adolescents because they represent a high-risk group. According to the US Department of Justice, one in two rape victims is younger than 18 years and one in six is younger than 12 years.[45]

Box 13-4 Dating Violence Interview Questions*

Directive Questions

During the past year, did your boyfriend or girlfriend do anything physically to you that made you feel uneasy or uncomfortable?

Do you feel safe at home?

Do you feel safe in your relationship?

Have threats of violence ever been made by your boyfriend or girlfriend?

Does your partner seem jealous, controlling, or possessive?

Have you ever been forced to have sex?

Have weapons ever been used against you?

Probing Questions

Tell me about a time when you have felt unsafe in your home.

Tell me about a time when you have felt unsafe in your relationship.

To what types of violent behaviors have you been subject?

Tell me about your partner's behaviors related to jealousy, control, or possessiveness.

Tell me about your experiences when forced to have sex.

Tell me about your experience when weapons were used against you.

*Data are taken from Herman.[44]

Box 13-5 Dating Violence Myths*

"I deserved it."

Some hitting, "getting even," or anger is justified after sexual betrayal.

Partners like others who are strong and "take charge."

"If I tell someone, he or she will think it was my fault."

"I bought dinner, so my partner owes me sex."

"When a date says no, he or she really means yes."

"If I try harder, my partner will treat me better."

"Even if I get hit, I'm nothing without my partner."

*Data are taken from Herman.[44]

Although there are no guarantees against rape, there are steps a person can take to reduce his or her risk of becoming a victim. Adolescents need information about self-protection, defense, and the best ways to cope with the aftermath of a rape. Simple preventive skills for adolescents to be educated about include the following:[45,46]

- Abstaining from alcohol or other drug use: drinking or taking other drugs increases the chances of being raped considerably because of impairment of mental and physical functioning and lowered inhibitions.

- Learning to trust one's own instincts (i.e., getting away when a social setting feels uncomfortable).

- Taking self-defense courses to learn how to fend off an attacker.

- Never leaving a drink unattended.

- Never accepting a drink from anyone.

Date rape drugs are used to assist in the execution of a sexual assault.[46] Commonly, these drugs are slipped into a drink without the victim's knowledge. The three most common date rape drugs are γ-hydroxybutyric acid (GHB), flunitrazepam (Rohypnol), and ketamine (Ketalar). All three drugs are odorless and tasteless when added to a flavored drink. They are quickly metabolized (having a half-life of approximately four hours), leaving little physical evidence. The effects of date rape drugs include memory loss (≤ 48 hours), confusion, dizziness, sleepiness, visual disturbances, and loss of muscle control.[46] Memory loss induced by these drugs can last up to 48 hours after ingestion, rendering a victim unaware of the attack even after the 48 hours have passed; this makes collecting sufficient evidence to prosecute the offense difficult.[46] In the ED, it is essential that any individual who reports amnesic symptoms of how they may have arrived there–even if fully clothed–or having memories of going in and out of consciousness, should be screened for sexual assault. Adolescents must be taught the importance of seeking medical care in the event of sexual assault or any suspicion of having a date rape drug used in his or her presence.

Collection of physical evidence for criminal investigation must be performed within 72 hours of the incident. Baseline diagnostic procedures for pregnancy and STIs are usually performed along with dispensing prophylactic antibiotics. The patient may also be offered pregnancy prophylaxis.[47] However, going to the ED can be difficult for an adolescent for many reasons, such as the following:[45]

- Victims often experience shame, and this makes reporting rape difficult.

- The physical examination process can feel like a second rape and an invasion of privacy.

- The female victim may be afraid to have a male health-care provider.

Attending to the physical injuries of rape is only the first step for recovery. Rape victims may develop symptoms of posttraumatic stress disorder and a spectrum of negative emotions. Professional psychological counseling is recommended to aid survivors of rape in dealing with the emotional damage that occurs.

Sexual Behaviors

Becoming sexually active is a normal part of human development during the transition to adulthood. Regardless of personal beliefs and views, medical professionals must offer reproductive services to all patients of child-bearing age. Adolescents need education and guidance in making decisions regarding sexuality, with abstinence or use of contraceptives being two of the predominant forms of education. Many adolescents turn to friends for information and advice because parents may feel uncomfortable and uncertain when discussing sexuality and contraception with their children. Misconceptions regarding causes of pregnancy, what is considered sexual activity, STIs, and contraception are common and should be clarified for the adolescent's safety. In 2007, 48% of all high school students reported having had sexual intercourse,[48] with 7.1% reporting that their first sexual encounter occurred before the age of 13 years.[15]

Sexting

Cellular telephone use by adolescents has dramatically increased in the past several years. In 2009, 58% of 12-year-old and 83% of 17-year-old individuals owned cellular telephones. Of these individuals, 66% use text messaging for communication. Sexting (i.e., the creating, sending, or forwarding of sexually suggestive, nude, or seminude images) is a practice that many teenagers are using as a part of their sexual interactions and explorations.[49] In several surveys completed in 2009,[49] up to 19% of teenagers say they have sent a sexually suggestive, nude, or seminude image of themselves to someone else; up to 31% of teenagers say they have received such an image. These studies showed no difference between males and females in sending or receiving images. Teenagers may not realize that what they are doing is actually illegal and that the legal ramifications may be quite severe. In many states, sexting is considered pornography and adolescents who possess these images or are known to have taken, sent, or forwarded images can be charged with the production and distribution of child pornography. Teenagers have been charged with "disorderly conduct," "illegal use of a minor in nudity oriented material," and felony "sexual abuse of children … criminal [use] of a communications facility, or open lewdness."[49] Sentencing can include required registration as a sexual offender.[49]

According to the National Center for Missing and Exploited Children, 2,100 juveniles have been identified as victims of Internet pornography. Of these juveniles, one-fourth initially sent the image themselves.[50] However, because they cannot control where these photographs are subsequently sent, they run the risk of contact with a sexual predator or with someone else who could potentially harm them.[51]

Emotional distress after a sexting incident can be quite severe. Unfortunately, adolescents do not think about what kind of message they may be sending to others when sending explicit pictures. Because cellular telephones make it easy for adolescents to act on impulse, one moment of questionable behavior and bad judgment may result in multiple peers seeing these images. In teenaged culture, one incident can ruin an adolescent's reputation for what feels like forever to the teenager.[51] Adolescents must be educated on these risks in an effort to reduce this potentially dangerous and embarrassing behavior.[51]

Contraception

The use of contraceptives has greatly increased since the mid-1980s. Contraceptive failure rates can vary significantly, depending on correct and consistent use of the chosen method.[52] For adolescents, there are several barriers to accessing contraceptive services: financial resources, reluctance to discuss with practitioners, access to confidential services, access to age-appropriate services, and access to community-based programs.[53] Box 13-6 lists the various methods of contraception. In the event of contraceptive failure or unprotected intercourse within the previous 12 hours, an adolescent has the option to request emergency contraception (i.e., the morning after pill). This medication gives the body a short and high burst of synthetic hormones, thus disrupting hormone patterns needed for pregnancy. Progestin-only emergency contraceptive pills (e.g., Plan B and Next Choice) have fewer adverse effects than combined emergency contraception. One large study by the World Health Organization looked at the adverse effects from the two types of emergency contraceptive pills. Approximately one in four (23%) women who use progestin-only emergency contraception feels sick to her stomach. Nausea and vomiting are more common

after taking combined emergency contraceptive pills. To prevent nausea and vomiting, meclizine (i.e., Dramamine or Bonine) is recommended. Taking two (25 mg) tablets one hour before taking emergency contraception reduces the risk of nausea and vomiting. This medication causes drowsiness; therefore, the individual must be educated not to drive while taking this medication.

Pregnancy

Approximately 410,000 children were born in 2009 in the United States to mothers between the age of 15 and 19 years. This birth rate to adolescents is higher than in other developed countries, but lower than previous years.[54] Of these teen mothers, only half used any method of birth control.[55] These teenagers may present to the ED unaware that they are pregnant and may have various complaints, including the following:

- A missed or abnormal menstrual period
- Abdominal pain/cramping
- Fatigue
- Breast tenderness/fullness
- Urinary frequency
- Appetite changes
- Vaginal bleeding/spotting
- Presumptive symptoms of pregnancy
- Request for a pregnancy test
- In labor with no prenatal care, not knowing she is pregnant

Any female of potentially child-bearing age with these complaints must be assessed for the possibility of pregnancy in a private setting, away from caregivers. Use the date of the last menstrual period to determine the gestation of the adolescent's pregnancy. Results of the pregnancy test must be given in a private and confidential manner, and the female adolescent must be encouraged to involve her caregivers, partner, or another trusted adult in decision making and planning for care. Providing nonjudgmental support and

Box 13-6 Contraceptive Methods*	
Condoms	Vaginal rings
Oral contraceptives	Intrauterine devices
Hormonal injections	Cervical caps
Spermicides/sponges	Implantations
Diaphragms	Transdermal patches
	Emergency contraceptives

*Data are taken from Neinstein and Nelson.[53]

counseling, with referral for follow-up care, whether this be a continuation or a termination of pregnancy, is extremely important.[2]

One of the most challenging issues to sort out is bleeding/spotting. If there is vaginal bleeding/spotting, ectopic pregnancy, threatened abortion, or spontaneous abortion must be considered. A pelvic examination must be completed in conjunction with the following:

- Complete blood cell count
- Blood type with Rh factor
- Beta- (β) human chorionic gonadotropin (HCG) pregnancy test
- Screen for STI and human papillomavirus
- Pelvic ultrasonography

The adolescent may even elect to terminate her pregnancy and may present to the ED with complications of the abortion, as described in **Box 13-7**. Regardless of the practitioner's personal beliefs about the termination of pregnancy, the adolescent will require physical and emotional support in a nonjudgmental manner. Healthcare providers also need to be aware of "Newborn Safe Haven" or other protection laws in their state for voluntary relinquishment of newborns.

Sexually Transmitted Infections

Sexually active adolescents aged 15 to 19 years are at a higher risk for acquiring sexually transmitted infections (STIs) because of risky sexual behavior, biological susceptibility, lack of sexual health knowledge, concern for confidentiality in obtaining healthcare, and limited access to healthcare.[56] **Table 13-5** lists common STIs, signs and symptoms, complications and risks, and treatments. According to the National Youth Risk Behavior Survey 2007, 14.9% of students surveyed had sexual intercourse

Box 13-7 Complications of Elective Abortion*	
Heavy vaginal bleeding	Chills
Severe abdominal or pelvic pain	Fever
Passage of large clots	Foul-smelling vaginal discharge
Continuing symptoms of pregnancy	

*Data are taken from Holland-Hall and Brown.[2] Data are also taken from Scott-Jones, D. (2001). Teenage parenting: Childbearing. In J. Lerner (Ed.), *Adolescence in America: An encyclopedia* (pp. 746–750). Santa Barbara, CA: ABC-CLIO.

with four or more persons during their lives, and among the 35% of sexually active students, 61.5% had used a condom during last sexual intercourse.[15] Many cases of STIs and some viral infections, such as human papillomavirus and herpes, go undiagnosed. Socioeconomic barriers to quality healthcare and STI prevention, screening, and treatment services have likely contributed to the higher STI rates among racial and ethnic minorities, with African Americans having significantly higher rates of STIs.[56]

An assessment of the adolescent's understanding of how STIs are transmitted (orally, vaginally, or through anal intercourse), along with the susceptibility to further STIs with another concurrent STI, should be completed.[56] Adolescents represent nearly half of the sexually active population with steadily increasing STI rates.[56] A sexual health history is an important assessment tool. This history should include the following:

- Sexual development
- Sexual activity
- Contraception
- Pregnancy
- STI history

Treatment of STIs should follow the most up-to-date information from the Center for Disease Control and Prevention's STI treatment guidelines. A comprehensive approach to STI prevention must include increased awareness, screening, treatment, treatment of infected partners, and behavioral interventions.

Adolescent Nutrition

Eating Disorders

The term *eating disorder* refers to a pattern of abnormal attitudes and behaviors relating to food. Eating disturbances exist along a continuum of severity, often beginning with dieting as a means of controlling weight, and continue to one of the three main eating disorders: anorexia nervosa, bulimia nervosa, or binge eating. Females are bombarded by media images of unrealistically thin females whose message implies that success and thinness go hand in hand. This obsession with fitness and thinness in Western cultures is the key reason that adolescent females develop eating disorders.

In the United States, an estimated 3% of young women have one of the three main eating disorders.[57] Overwhelmingly, adolescent females are the majority of individuals affected by eating disorders, although males can be af-

Table 13-5 Sexually Transmitted Infections*

Sexually Transmitted Infection	Signs and Symptoms	Complications/Risks	Treatment
Chlamydia Causative agent: *Chlamydia trachomatis*	May be asymptomatic Women: abnormal vaginal discharge, burning with urination, lower abdominal pain, lower back pain, nausea, fever, and pain with intercourse Men: discharge from penis	Can cause irreversible damage to reproductive organs, including infertility; can be passed from infected mom to neonate during delivery; increased risk of preterm delivery; bleeding between menstrual periods; PID; and epididymitis or urethritis and possible sterility in males	Azithromycin or doxycycline
Lymphogranuloma venereum Causative agent: *C. trachomatis*	Genital papules and/or ulcers in the urethra, vagina, or rectum; swelling of lymph glands in the genital area; and rectal bleeding, pain, and discharge	Enlargement and ulcerations of external genitalia and lymphatic obstruction, which may lead to elephantiasis of genitalia; and increased incidence in men having anal sex with men	Doxycycline, erythromycin, or azithromycin
Gonorrhea Causative agent: *Neisseria gonorrhoeae*	May be asymptomatic Women: pain or burning with urination; increased vaginal discharge; vaginal bleeding between periods Men: some burning with urination; white, yellow, or green discharge; anal infection; and anal itching, soreness, or bleeding	Can be spread from mom to neonate during delivery, PID with damage to the fallopian tubes, epididymitis and possible sterility in men, can spread to blood or joints, and can be life threatening	Cephalosporins
Syphilis Causative agent: *Treponema pallidum* ("the great imitator")	Primary: single sore (chancre) is firm, round, small, and painless; can be multiple sores; can last three to six weeks and heals with or without treatment; and if not treated, will progress Secondary: skin rash and mucous membrane lesions; rough, red, or reddish brown spots on the palms of hands and soles of feet; rash does not itch; possible fever, swollen lymph glands, sore throat, patchy hair loss, headaches, weight loss, muscle aches, and fatigue; will resolve with or without treatment; and without treatment, will progress Latent (hidden): infection remains in body, but without signs or symptoms; and can last for years Late: 15% of people with untreated syphilis will experience development of the disease into the late stages; can develop 10–20 years after the infection is acquired; difficulty coordinating muscle movements, paralysis, numbness, gradual blindness, and dementia	Can be passed from mother to neonate during pregnancy; increased risk for stillbirth; if not treated, may cause developmental delay, seizures, or death of an infant; in late stage, the disease can damage internal organs, including brain, nerves, eyes, heart, blood vessels, liver, bones, and joints; and can cause death	Penicillin; can treat disease but cannot repair damage done before treatment
Trichomoniasis Causative agent: *Trichomonas vaginalis* Spreads to the vagina in women and the urethra in men	Women: frothy yellow-green vaginal discharge with strong odor; irritation, itching, and discomfort during urination and intercourse; and rarely, lower abdominal pain Men: may be asymptomatic, irritation inside penis, mild discharge, or slight burning after urination or ejaculation	Increased risk for early- or low-birth-weight neonate	Metronidazole or tinidazole
PID Causative agents: Many different bacteria but increased risk with chlamydia or gonorrhea	General term referring to infection of uterus, fallopian tubes, and other reproductive organs; symptoms range from asymptomatic to severe; two-thirds of the time, goes unrecognized; lower abdominal pain; fever; unusual vaginal discharge with foul odor; painful intercourse; irregular menstrual bleeding; and pain in the upper right abdomen (rare)	Causes damage to reproductive organs without treatment and increased risk for infertility, ectopic pregnancy, abscess formation, and scarring of fallopian tubes and other pelvic structures, causing chronic pelvic pain	Various antibiotics: usually given two antibiotics to cover a broad range and can treat the disease but cannot repair the damage done before treatment

Table 13-5 Sexually Transmitted Infections* *continued*

Sexually Transmitted Infection	Signs and Symptoms	Complications/Risks	Treatment
HPV (40 different types)	Some types are asymptomatic; genital warts	Rarely passed from mom to neonate or passed as RRP and some types cause genital warts, others cause cervical cancer, and still others cause cancer of the vulva, vagina, penis, anus, tongue, tonsils, or throat	HPV vaccine: protects against four key strains of HPV that account for 70% of cervical cancers and 90% of genital warts; three-dose vaccine recommended for girls aged 11–12 years; and in 90% of cases, the body's immune system clears the virus within two years
Herpes simplex virus Causative agents: type 1 or 2	Type 1: usually mouth and lips ("fever blisters") and can spread to genitals Type 2: usually genital; blisters on or around genitals or rectum becoming sores and lasting 2–4 weeks; possible flulike symptoms, fever, and swollen glands with subsequent outbreaks	Painful genital sores, psychological distress, potentially fatal in neonates, and neonate delivered by cesarean section during an active herpes outbreak	No cure and antiviral medications shorten or prevent outbreaks
Viral hepatitis Causative agents: HAV, HBV, and HCV	Fatigue, low-grade fever, anorexia, malaise, nausea, vomiting, abdominal pain, and jaundice; skin rashes, arthralgias, and arthritis can also occur with HBV	Chronic hepatitis, cirrhosis, hepatocellular carcinoma, hepatic failure, and death from HBV and HCV and infectious long-term carriers; may be completely asymptomatic	Vaccine to prevent HBV and HCV and no cure
Human immunodeficiency virus Covered in depth in Chapter 11, "Childhood Illnesses"	NA	NA	NA

Note: HAV indicates hepatitis A virus; HBV, hepatitis B virus; HCV, hepatitis C virus; HPV, human papillomavirus; NA, not applicable; PID, pelvic inflammatory disease; RRP, recurrent respiratory papillomatosis.
*Data are adapted from the Centers for Disease Control and Prevention.[56]

fected as well. Eating disorders are most prevalent among men and boys who engage in activities that involve weight restrictions, such as body building, wrestling, dance, gymnastics, and jockeying.[58]

Bulimia nervosa is the practice of compulsive overeating/bingeing, almost always followed by purging through vomiting, starvation, excessive exercise, and laxatives. *Anorexia nervosa*, the extreme restriction of food, is associated with a higher annual mortality rate than any other psychiatric disorder. Deaths typically result from starvation, body chemistry imbalances, and suicide.[55] *Binge eating* is referred to as compulsive overeating, without the inappropriate compensatory behaviors seen in bulimia nervosa.[57]

Signs and symptoms for eating disorders consist of the following:

- Significant weight loss (25% of total body weight when not on a diet)

- Irregular periods in females

- Scrapes/lesions on the knuckles of the adolescents' hands as a result of using fingers to induce vomiting

- Symptoms of dehydration

- Electrolyte imbalance

- Depression

- Palpitations

- Gastroesophageal reflux disease symptoms

Adolescents with eating disorders have a high risk of medical complications and sequelae of events, requiring aggressive medical treatment because of a general breakdown of organ size and function as the body becomes more compromised. Changes that may occur that require immediate treatment include the following:

- Hypokalemia

- Hypotension

- Electrocardiographic changes with a prolonged QTc interval

- Hyponatremia (from water loading)

- Hypomagnesemia

- Dehydration

- Sinus bradycardia (with heart rates as low 20 or 30 beats per minute at rest)
- Hepatic and/or renal compromise
- Hemodynamic instability/hypotension
- Hypophosphatemia if refeeding has been initiated

Recovery from eating disorders usually requires the support of several treatment modalities. Disturbed eating patterns are treatable, but the best prognosis is for individuals who seek treatment early, including therapy, medications, and counseling.[57]

Obesity

The promotion of healthful eating in children and adolescents is becoming an increasingly important public health and research priority because the prevalence of obesity among children and adolescents continues to increase.[59] Preventing or modifying dietary behaviors at an early age is likely to contribute to the prevention of obesity in adults. The World Health Organization identifies a body mass index of greater than 25 (calculated as weight in kilograms divided by height in meters squared) as overweight. The number of US teenagers who are overweight is 15.8%, with an additional 13% meeting the criteria for obesity; worldwide rates have tripled compared with 25 years ago. Children who are overweight and obese have an increased risk for the following complications:[60]

- Bone and joint problems
- Cardiovascular disease
- Type II diabetes
- Dyslipidemia
- Asthma
- Academic and social discrimination

Children and adolescents who are overweight or obese are more likely to become overweight or obese adults. The prevention and treatment of obesity begins at an early age. Children and adolescents must be taught good eating habits, encouraged to participate in physical activity, and limited in the amount of screen time, or time in front of the television, video games, or computer. By adolescence, the dietary and physical activity lifestyle that a child has been exposed to is well established. As adolescents mature, they are cognitively able to appreciate that their actions will affect their future health. Education should include information on the long-term effects of obesity and realistic goals and expectations for achieving and maintaining a healthy body weight.[59]

At-Risk Adolescents

Body Modification

Piercing and tattooing have been used as forms of body art or as ways to identify oneself as a part of a group for thousands of years and are becoming more popular with adolescents and young adults. Most often, body art is used as a form of decoration rather than as a form of destruction and mutilation. Adolescents also may use body art to enhance self-identity and to obtain peer acceptance and group membership. Body piercings are more common than tattoos, but it is estimated that 3% to 5% of Western society and 13% of the population in the United States has a tattoo.[61,62]

Body modification is not without complications, and clinicians must be aware of the potential problems with these procedures. Infectious complications with tattooing may include local skin infection (bacterial, fungal, or viral) and a theoretical risk of blood-borne infections (e.g., hepatitis B or C and human immunodeficiency virus), although the needles are solid bore and make transmission less likely.[62] Problems can occur depending on the specific site of the piercing. Healing times vary with each site, and complete healing may take up to one year (**Table 13-6**).[63]

Homeless Teenagers

It is estimated that up to 1.3 million adolescents (aged 13–17 years) in the United States are on their own, with no family support or resources.[64] Some homeless adolescents are throwaway teenagers, forced out of their homes by their parents, and others are runaway teenagers who left home of their own volition. Both groups of teenagers report that their family and home environments were far from ideal and describe them as unstable, neglectful, and abusive, often with parental substance abuse and alcoholism. Up to 40% report physical abuse and up to 25% report sexual abuse in the home.[64] Throwaway teenagers report being forced to leave home because of extremely high levels of conflict with parents, family lack of money or room, pregnancy, sexuality, or substance abuse.[64]

Approximately half of homeless teenagers are street teens, not accepting help from any social services organization, with the other half being shelter teens who do accept assistance from shelters or drop-in centers for teenagers.[64] Street teenagers do not accept help from shelters or social services because social agencies are often mandated, by the state in which they are located, to notify parents or civil authorities when they provide assistance for more than a period of a few hours. Despite the harshness of the conditions of living on the street, almost no street teenager is willing to go home or enter placement. In contrast, approximately half of shelter teenagers are willing to return home eventually.[64] Homeless teenagers are exposed to a life for which they were not prepared and report that their greatest needs are finding a place to sleep, a job or job training, food, a place to shower, medical and dental care, and counseling.[64] It is common for these adolescents to be exposed to the death of friends and suicide attempts and to have severe health problems, such as malnutrition, STIs, anemia, ulcers, hepatitis, and scabies.[64]

To obtain money, food, or a place to stay, many homeless adolescents are forced to extreme measures for survival, including panhandling, selling drugs, theft, or prostitution. Most street teenagers regularly use alcohol and illicit drugs, and most homeless youths are sexually active. They are knowledgeable about acquired immunodeficiency syndrome and other STIs but routinely engage in unprotected sex.[64]

Human Trafficking and Prostitution

Millions of people, especially women and young children, become victims of human trafficking each year. Sex trafficking involves the recruitment, harboring, transportation, provision, or attainment of a person for the purposes of a commercial sex act, during which the act is induced by force, fraud, or coercion or during which the person to perform such an act is younger than 18 years. Sex trafficking usually involves women, adolescent females, and young children.[65] In the United States, prostitution is the most common form of trafficking, followed by agricultural work. Although human trafficking is generally a transnational crime, the US Department of State believes that thousands of children and adolescents in the United States are trafficked within the borders of the country.[65]

Adolescents who are homeless are at high risk for domestic sex trafficking. These adolescents usually come from homes that already have abuse (60%). Victims are manipulated by a pimp, in the beginning, with an initial period of false love and feigned affection to obtain long-term control of the victim. Adolescents are targeted because of their naïveté, virginity, youthful appearance, and vulnerability.[65]

Victims do not often seek help on their own or identify themselves as victims of domestic sex trafficking. They are usually under confinement and accompanied by a pimp or another member of the sex ring who will report back to the pimp; have been threatened with violence to themselves, friends, or family; and believe they will be arrested for prostitution. Potential indicators of a victim of sex trafficking are similar to those exhibited by a person who has been physically, emotionally, or sexually abused. In addition to these signs, the adolescent victim may claim to be an adult, although appearance suggests adolescent features.[66]

Attempting to build trust with the patient is the first priority after ensuring that physical injuries and complaints are addressed. The most common health complaints of these victims include the following:

- STIs
- Gynecological complaints/pain
- Stress-related complaints (e.g., chest pain, dyspnea, syncope, headaches, anxiety, or gastrointestinal complaints)

The victim may be unaware that what has been done to him or her is a crime and may have an inherent distrust of police and medical establishments. It is important to examine the patient alone, reassuring the patient that he or she will be safe. Consultation with social services and the local jurisdiction of police is necessary to ultimately help a victim free himself or herself of this crime.[66]

Health Promotion

- Yearly comprehensive health assessment, including a physical examination, a psychosocial history, and immunizations (to include the human papillomavirus vaccine).
- Ongoing general healthcare, including dental examinations.
- Nutrition and exercise, including a healthy diet, appropriate weight management, and exercise.
- Routine screening, including hemoglobin level and urinalysis once during the adolescent years; scoliosis; and annual screening for sexually active adolescents, including a pelvic examination, a Papanicolaou smear, and STIs.
- Sexuality education, including abstinence education; use of contraception; STI prevention, routine screening, treatment of infected partners, and behavioral interventions; and sexual exploitation awareness and education.
- Referrals for pregnancy-related care.
- Mental health services as needed.
- Substance use assessment and counseling for alcohol, smoking, and other drugs, including recreational use of prescription medications.
- Injury prevention, including safe driving, water safety, bicycle/motorcycle helmets, and athletic protective equipment.
- Chronic illness care specific to the adolescent.
- Violence awareness, education, intervention, and prevention.

Table 13-6 Complications from Body Modification

Local Signs/Symptoms	Systemic Signs/Symptoms

• Cellulitis
  – Common organisms
    (*Streptococcus aureus* and *Staphylococcus aureus*)
• Allergy to metal
• Embedded jewelry
	• Minor complications
	  – Fever, fatigue, and loss of appetite
	• Major complications
	  – Mental status changes
	  – Muscle spasms
	  – Tachycardia
	  – Endocarditis
	  – Dyspnea
	  – Human immunodeficiency virus infection
	  – Glomerulonephritis

Specific Body Part Complications

Ear	• Perichondrial auricular abscesses – Common organisms: *Pseudomonas aeurginosa, Staphylococcus aureus*, and group A β-hemolytic streptococci	• Tearing and splitting of the earlobe
Oropharyngeal	• Increased salivary flow and gingival injury • Loss of sensory and oral function	• Infections – Common organisms: *Haemophilus aphrophilus, Neisseria mucosa, S. aureus*, and *P. aeruginosa*
Genitalia	• Urethral tear • Testicular tear • Prostatitis • Priapism	• Genital mucosa tear • Infections – Common organisms: *Escherichia coli, Klebsiella pneumonia, Proteus mirabilis, P aeruginosa, S aureus, Enterococcus faecium*, and *Staphylococcus saprophyticus*
Nipple	• Mastitis – Common organism: *S. aureus*	

Interventions

• Cleanse pierced site at least twice a day
  – Avoid using hydrogen peroxide or alcohol for cleaning
• Rinse oral piercings with antimicrobial mouth rinse at least three times a day
  – Avoid oral sex during healing process
  – Avoid cigarettes or chewing tobacco
• Administer appropriate antimicrobial therapy
	• Treat contact dermatitis by replacing brass and/or nickel with surgical-grade steel or titanium
	• Use antihistamine to treat pruritus or 0.1% triamcinolone acetonide to treat inflammation
	• Tetanus prophylaxis
	• Hepatitis B vaccination

Summary

As with all patients, when the adolescent patient arrives at the ED, the clinician must complete an immediate assessment of the primary and secondary survey and provide interventions as appropriate for the findings. Once the adolescent has been stabilized as necessary, the teenager's psychosocial history and the information surrounding the events will guide continued evaluation and ongoing care. Adolescence can be a difficult and confusing time for many teenagers. They are not just *big kids*, yet they are not *small adults* either. They are working to synthesize their own identity from cultural, religious, societal, and familial roots. Clinicians must be knowledgeable of the physical, social/emotional, and cognitive changes occurring in the adolescent. For some teenagers, their psychosocial history may be as important, or even more important, than their physical assessment. The clinician must not hesitate to ask the hard questions regarding the behaviors of adolescents, which places them at significant risk for serious illness, injury, violence, or poor outcome. The clinician must have strong communication and assessment skills to help gather information, educate, and provide guidance for the adolescent and family.

References

1. Kelly, S. (1998). *Pediatric emergency nursing* (2nd ed., pp. 47–48). Norwalk, CT: Appleton & Lange.

2. Holland-Hall, C., & Brown, R. (2002). *Adolescent medicine secrets* (pp. 5–12, 18, 29–34, 44, 214–215, 220–223). Philadelphia, PA: Hanley & Belfus.

3. Summers, D., Alpert, I., Rousseau-Pierre, T., Minguez, M., Manigault, S., Edwards, S., ... Diaz, A. (2006). An exploration of the ethical, legal and developmental issues in the care of an adolescent patient. *The Mount Sinai Journal of Medicine, 73,* 592–595.

4. Guttmacher Institute. (2010, January). *State policies in brief: An overview of minor's consent law.* Retrieved from http://www.guttmacher.org/statecenter/spibs/spib_OMCL.pdf

5. Emergency Nurses Association. (2010). *Sheehy's emergency nursing: Principles and practice* (6th ed.). St. Louis, MO: Mosby Elsevier.

6. Diaz, A., Neal, W. P., Nucci, A. T., Ludmer, P., Bitterman, J., & Edwards, S. (2004). Legal and ethical issues facing adolescent health-care professionals. *The Mount Sinai Journal of Medicine, 71,* 181–185.

7. Lerand, S. J. (2007). Teach the teacher: Adolescent confidentiality and minor's consent. *Journal of Pediatric Adolescent Gynecology, 20,* 377–380.

8. *Title X family planning regulations.* (2000, October). Retrieved from http://www.hhs.gov/opa/about/legislation/ofp_regs_42cfr59_10-1-2000.html

9. Ludwig, S., & Jay, M. (1993). Emergency care of adolescents. *State of the Art Reviews, Adolescent Medicine, 4,* 1–10, 149–181.

10. Federal Interagency Forum on Child and Family Statistics. 2009.

11. Danseco, E. R., Miller, T. R., Spicer, R. S. (2000). Incidence and costs of 1987–1994 childhood injuries: Demographic breakdowns. *Pediatrics, 105,* E27.

12. Centers for Disease Control and Prevention. (2009). *Teen drivers: Fact sheet.* Retrieved from http://www.cdc.gov/MotorVehicleSafety/Teen_Drivers/teendrivers_factsheet.html

13. Bayliss, J. (2007). *Teens admit text messaging most distracting while driving: Students against destructive decisions.* Retrieved from http://www.sadd.org/press/textingadvisory.htm

14. Madden, M., & Lenhart, A. (2009). *Teens and distracted driving: Texting, talking, and other uses of the cell phone behind the wheel.* Washington, DC: Pew Research Center, Pew Internet, and American Life Project.

15. Centers for Disease Control and Prevention. (2010, June 4). Youth risk behavior surveillance—United States, 2009. *Morbidity and Mortality Weekly Report, 59* (SS-5). Retrieved from http://www.cdc.gov/mmwr/PDF/ss/ss5704.pdf

16. Centers for Disease Control and Prevention. (2008). Car surfing and its consequences: CDC's findings on a dangerous thrill-seeking activity. *Morbidity and Mortality Weekly Report, 57,* 1121–1124.

17. McClave, J., Russell, P., Lyren, A., O'Riordan, M., & Bass, N. (2010). The choking game: Physicians' perspectives. *Pediatrics, 125,* 82–87. doi:10.1542/peds.2009-1287

18. American Academy of Pediatrics. (2009). *Policy statement: The role of the pediatrician in youth violence prevention.* Retrieved from http://aappolicy.aappublications.org/cigi/reprint/pediatrics:65/3/649.pdf

19. Youth gangs. (2009). In J. Miller (Ed.), *21st century criminology: A reference handbook* (pp. 694–696). Thousand Oaks, CA: Sage Publications.

20. Office of National Drug Control Policy, Executive Office of the President. (2006). *Girls and drugs.* Retrieved from http://www.theanti-drug.com/pdfs/girls_and_drugs.pdf

21. *Journal of studies on alcohol and drugs: College drinking problems, deaths on the rise.* (2009). Retrieved from http://www.science-daily.com/releases/2009/06/090615093919.htm

22. National Institute on Drug Abuse, National Institutes of Health, US Department of Health and Human Services. (2009). *Cigarettes and other tobacco products. NIDA Info Facts.* Retrieved from http://www.drugabuse.gov/pdf/infofacts/Tobacco09.pdf

23. Loukas, A. (2001). Inhalants. In J. Lerner (Ed.), *Adolescence in America: An encyclopedia* (pp. 365–368). Santa Barbara, CA: ABC-CLIO.

24. Hertz, J., Knight, J. (2006). Prescription drug misuse: A growing national problem. *Adolescent Medicine Clinics, 17,* 751–769.

25. National Institute on Drug Abuse, National Institutes of Health, US Department of Health and Human Services. (2009). *Marijuana. NIDA Info Facts.* Retrieved from http://www.drugabuse.gov/PDF/InfoFacts/Marijuana09.pdf

26. National Institute on Drug Abuse, National Institutes of Health, US Department of Health and Human Services. (2009). *Heroin. NIDA Info Facts.* Retrieved from http://www.drugabuse.gov/PDF/Infofacts/Heroin09.pdf

27. National Institute on Drug Abuse, National Institutes of Health, US Department of Health and Human Services. (2009). *Methamphetamine. NIDA Info Facts.* Retrieved from http://www.drugabuse.gov/pdf/infofacts/Methamphetamine09.pdf

28. National Institute on Drug Abuse, National Institutes of Health, US Department of Health and Human Services. (2009). *MDMA (Ecstasy). NIDA Info Facts.* Retrieved from http://www.drugabuse.gov/PDF/Infofacts/MDMA09.pdf

References *continued*

29. *National Institutes of Drug Abuse.* (2007). Retrieved from www.drugabuse.gov/DrugPages/DrugsofAbuse.html

30. Williams, J., & Kokotailo, P. (2006). Abuse of proprietary (over-the-counter) drugs. *Adolescent Medicine Clinics, 17,* 733–750.

31. Red Bull USA. (n.d.). *Company figures.* Retrieved from http://www.redbullusa.com/cs/Satellite/en_US/company-figures/001242989767460?pcs_c=PCS_Product&pcs_cid=1242989293775

32. McCusker, R., R., Goldberger, B. A., & Cone, E. J. (2006). Technical note: Caffeine content of energy drinks, carbonated sodas, and beverages. *Journal of Analytical Toxicology, 30*(2), 112–114.

33. Sherer, S., Radzik, M., & Neinstein, L. (2002). Suicide. In L. S. Neinstein (Ed.), *Adolescent healthcare: A practical guide* (4th ed., pp.1443–1453). Philadelphia, PA: Lippincott Williams & Wilkins.

34. Klonsky, E. D., & Muehlenkamp, J. J. (2007). Self-injury: A research review for the practitioner. *Journal of Clinical Psychology, 63,* 1045–1056.

35. Gallagher, L. A. (2001). Self-injury. In J. Lerner (Ed.), *Adolescence in America: An encyclopedia* (pp. 638–640). Santa Barbara, CA: ABC-CLIO.

36. Naito, A. (2007). Internet suicide in Japan: Implications for child and adolescent mental health. *Journal of Child Psychology and Psychiatry, 12,* 583–597.

37. Branco, B. C., Inaba, K., Barmparas, G., Talving, P., David, J., Plurad, D., ... Demetriades, D.(2010). Sex-related differences in child-hood and adolescent self-inflicted injuries: A national trauma data bank review. *Journal of Pediatric Surgery, 45,* 796–800.

38. Centers for Disease Control and Prevention, National Center for Injury Prevention and Control. (2010). *Web-based Injury Statistics Query and Reporting System (WISQARS). (1999-2007). Leading causes of death reports.* Retrieved from http://webappa.cdc.gov/sasweb/ncipc/leadcaus10.html

39. Birbal, R., Maharajh, H. D., Birbal, R., Clapperton, M., Jarvis, J., Ragoonath, A., & Uppalapati, K. (2009). Cybersuicide and the adolescent population: Challenges of the future? *International Journal of Adolescent Medicine and Health, 21,* 151–159.

40. Kim, Y. S., & Leventhal, B. (2008). Bullying and suicide: A review. *International Journal of Adolescent Medicine and Health, 20,* 133–154.

41. Olweus, D. (1994). Bullying at school: Basic facts and an effective intervention programme. *Promot Education, 1,* 27–31, 48.

42. Davies, P. (2001). Dating. In J. Lerner (Ed.), *Adolescence in America: An encyclopedia* (pp. 183–187). Santa Barbara, CA: ABC-CLIO.

43. Dating violence. (2007). In *Domestic violence: A reference handbook* (pp. 90–91). Santa Barbara, CA: ABC-CLIO.

44. Herman, J. (2009). There's a fine line ... adolescent dating violence and prevention. *Pediatric Nursing, 35,* 164–170.

45. Rogers-Siren, L. (2001). Rape. In J. Lerner (Ed.), *Adolescence in America: An encyclopedia* (pp. 571–574). Santa Barbara, CA: ABC-CLIO.

46. Date rape drugs. (2007). In F. Malti-Douglas (Ed.), *Encyclopedia of sex and gender: Culture, society, history* (p. 376). New York, NY: Macmillan Reference USA.

47. Mahowald, M. (2006). Violence and discrimination toward women and children. In *Bioethics and women: Across the lifespan* (pp. 179–180). New York, NY: Oxford University Press.

48. Centers for Disease Control and Prevention. (2009). *National surveillance data for chlamydia, gonorrhea, and syphilis sexually transmitted diseases in the United States,* 2008. Retrieved from http://www.cdc.gov/mmwr/pdf/ss/ss5905.pdf

49. Lenhart, A. (2009). Teens and sexting. In *Millennials, a portrait of generation next.* Washington, DC: Pew Research Center, Pew Internet, and American Life Project. Retrieved from http://www.pewinternet.org/Reports/2009/Teens-and-Sexting/Overview/Findings.aspx

50. Koch, W. (2009). Teens caught "sexting" face porn charges. *USA Today.* Retrieved from http://www.usatoday.com/tech/wireless/2009-03-11-sexting_N.htm

51. Carney, S. (2009). Sexting and teens: The risks of sending sexual material by cell phone. In *Youth Development, Suite 101.* Retrieved from http://youthdevelopment.suite101.com/article.cfm/sexting_and_teens.

52. Neinstein, L.S. & Farmer, M. (2002). Teenage pregnancy. In L.S. Neinstein (Ed.), *Adolescent healthcare: A practical guide* (4th ed., pp. 810–833). Philadelphia, PA: Lippincott Williams & Wilkins.

53. Neinstein, L.S. & Nelson, A. L. (2002). Contraception. In L.S. Neinstein (Ed.), *Adolescent healthcare: A practical guide* (4th ed., pp. 834–856). Philadelphia, PA: Lippincott Williams & Wilkins.

54. Centers for Disease Control and Prevention, Division of Adolescent and School Health, National Center for Chronic Disease Prevention and Health Promotion. (2011). Vital signs: Teen pregnancy – United States, 1991–2009. *Morbidity and Mortality Weekly, 60*(13), 414–420.

55. Centers for Disease Control and Prevention, Division of Adolescent and School Health, National Center for Chronic Disease Prevention and Health Promotion. (2012). Prepregnancy contraceptive use among teens with unintended pregnancies resulting in live births-Pregnancy Risk Assessment Monitoring System (PRAMS), 2004–2008. *Morbidity and Mortality Weekly, 61*(2), 25–29.

56. Centers for Disease Control and Prevention. (2010). *Sexually transmitted diseases.* Retrieved from http://www.cdc.gov/STD/default.htm

References *continued*

57. Chaves, A. (2001). Eating problems. In J. Lerner (Ed.), *Adolescence in America: An encyclopedia* (pp. 247–251). Santa Barbara, CA: ABC-CLIO.

58. Eating disorders. (2007). In F. Malti-Douglas (Ed.), *Encyclopedia of sex and gender: Culture, society, history* (pp. 427–430). New York, NY: Macmillan Reference USA.

59. Van der Horst, K., Oenema, A., Ferreira, I., Wendel-Vos, W., Giskes, K., van Lenthe, F., & Brug, J. (2006). A systematic review of environmental correlates of obesity-related dietary behaviors in youth. *Health Education Research, 22,* 203–226.

60. Physical development crises in US public education. (2008). In N. Salkind (Ed.), *Encyclopedia of educational psychology* (pp. 796–798). Thousand Oaks, CA: Sage Publications.

61. Muehlenkamp, J. J. (2005). Self-injurious behavior as a separate clinical syndrome. *American Journal of Orthopsychiatry, 75,* 324–333.

62. Stewart, C. (2000). Body piercing: Dangerous decoration? *Emergency Medicine, 32,* 92–98.

63. Carroll, L., & Anderson, R. (2002). Body piercing, tattooing, self-esteem, and body investment in adolescent girls. *Adolescence, 37,* 627–637.

64. Dornbusch, S. (2001). Homeless youth. In J. Lerner (Ed.), *Adolescence in America: An encyclopedia* (pp. 355–358). Santa Barbara, CA: ABC-CLIO.

65. San Miguel, C. (2009). Human trafficking. In J. Miller (Ed.), *21st century criminology: A reference handbook* (pp. 599–609). Thousand Oaks, CA: Sage Publications.

66. *Domestic sex trafficking: The criminal operations of the American pimp: A condensed guide for service providers and law enforcement.* (2006). Washington, DC: The Polaris Project.

Chapter 14 | Shock

Cam Brandt, MS, RN, CEN, CPEN, CPN

Objectives

On completion of this chapter, the learner should be able to do the following:

- Determine anatomical, physiological, and development characteristics of pediatric patients as a basis for assessment of shock.
- Describe common causes and characteristics of shock.
- Plan appropriate interventions for the pediatric patient in shock.
- Indicate health promotion strategies related to shock morbidity and mortality.

Introduction

In contrast to cardiopulmonary arrest in adults, cardiopulmonary arrest in infants and children is rarely a sudden event. In the pediatric patient, the most common causes of cardiopulmonary arrest are conditions that represent a terminal event of progressive shock or respiratory failure. Although cardiopulmonary arrest in pediatric patients is relatively uncommon, advances in prearrest, intra-arrest, and postresuscitative therapies are improving survival rates. More than 25% of children treated for in-hospital cardiopulmonary arrests and more than 10% of children older than one year treated for out-of-hospital cardiopulmonary arrests survive to hospital discharge.[1] Knowing that pediatric patients with shock have an increased mortality rate compared with pediatric patients without shock, and that outcomes are improved with early recognition and treatment,[2] it follows that assessment, recognition, and prompt treatment are fundamental in caring for pediatric patients.[3]

Anatomical, Physiological, and Developmental Characteristics as a Basis for Signs and Symptoms

There are specific characteristics in the cardiovascular system of the pediatric patient with important clinical significance. These specific characteristics are summarized in **Table 14-1**.

Definition of Shock

In 1872, Dr. Samuel David Gross described shock as the "rude unhinging" of the machinery of life.[4] Shock is the manifestation of cellular metabolic insufficiency. There are multiple causes of shock. However, the common denominator of shock, no matter what its cause, is inadequate delivery of oxygen and nutrients necessary for normal tissue and cellular function; or an imbalance between supply and demand at the cellular level.[4] The final common pathway in all types of shock is impair-

Table 14-1 Anatomical, Physiological, and Developmental Differences*

Characteristics	Clinical Significance
Stroke volume is dependent on the amount of blood able to be ejected by the left ventricle (preload), myocardial contractility, and resistance against blood flow into the peripheral vasculature (afterload). With smaller contractile mass and shorter myocardial fibers, stroke volume cannot be increased (1.5 mL per beat per minute in a child versus 75–90 mL per beat per minute in an adult.)	Heart rate rather than stroke volume increases to maintain cardiac output, which decreases precipitously with bradycardia (heart rate < 60 beats per minute) or tachycardia (heart rate > 200 beats per minute). A fast heart rate can decrease ventricular filling time decreasing preload and cardiac output. Vasoconstriction, with resultant increased systemic vascular resistance, can increase afterload. All of these factors affect cardiac output.
Infants have a higher cardiac output (200 mL/kg per minute versus 100 mL/kg per minute in the adult).	Cardiac output provides for increased oxygen needs but leaves little output in reserve.
Pediatric patients have a higher oxygen demand per kilogram of body weight because the child's metabolic rate is high. Oxygen consumption in infants is 6 to 8 mL/kg per minute versus 3 to 4 mL/kg per minute in adults.	Any stressors, such as hypothermia or sepsis, can lead to acute deterioration. Apnea, inadequate alveolar ventilation, hypoxemia, and potential tissue hypoxia can develop more rapidly. A slow or irregular respiratory rate in an acutely ill infant or child is an ominous clinical sign.
Children require an increased circulating blood volume to meet tissue perfusion needs as the result of the greater percentage of total water body weight. Infant, 90 mL/kg; child, 80 mL/kg; adult, 70 mL/kg.	There is a greater potential for dehydration. Increased insensible water losses with even small blood or fluid volume losses can cause circulatory compromise.
A child can maintain adequate cardiac output for long periods because of strong compensatory mechanisms. Blood pressure will remain normal or will even increase. Rapid deterioration can occur when compensatory mechanisms are exhausted.	Systemic vascular resistance increases to maintain perfusion. A narrowed pulse pressure (difference between systolic and diastolic readings) with an elevated diastolic reading is indicative of increased systemic vascular resistance. Hypotension is a late sign of circulatory decompensation. Children may remain normotensive until 25%–30% of their blood volume is lost.
Even in compensated shock, automated blood pressure readings may be difficult to obtain.	Automated blood pressure devices are accurate only when distal perfusion is adequate. Increased peripheral vascular resistance may give false high or low readings. Treat patients based on clinical examination results: Assess capillary refill as an indicator of peripheral perfusion (capillary refill should be less than two seconds in a warm ambient environment) and radial/brachial or femoral pulses. Preferable sites for assessment of capillary refill are those located at the level of the heart. In the smaller pediatric patient, a finger or toe is often not the most appropriate site. A prolonged capillary refill and weak or absent peripheral pulse are indicative of hypotension.

*Data are adapted from Feliciano et al[4] and Fleisher et al.[5] Data are also adapted from the following sources: (1) Bell, L. M. (2006). Shock. In G. H. Fleisher, S. Ludwig, & F. M. Henretig (Eds.), *Textbook of pediatric emergency medicine* (5th ed., pp. 51–62). Philadelphia, PA: Lippincott Williams & Wilkins. (2) Brierley, J., Carcillo, J. A., Choong, K., Cornell, T., DeCaen, A., Deymann, A., ... Zuckerberg, A. (2009). Clinical practice parameters for hemodynamic support of pediatric and neonatal septic shock: 2007 update from the American College of Critical Care Medicine. *Critical Care Medicine, 37,* 666–688. (3) Ralston, M., Hazinski, M. F., Zaritsky, A. L., Schxnader, S. M., & Kleinman, M. E. (2006). *Pediatric advanced life support.* Dallas, TX: American Heart Association. (4) Thomas, D. O., & Bernardo, L. M. (2009). *Core curriculum for pediatric emergency nursing* (2nd ed.). Des Plaines, IL: Emergency Nurses Association.

Table 14-2 Conditions That May Contribute to Shock by Increasing Demand or Decreasing Supply for Oxygen and Nutrients*

Pathophysiology	Potential Cause	Treatment Priorities
Increase demand	Hyperthermia/hypothermia, tachycardia, tachypnea, respiratory distress, fear, and pain	Treat underlying causes.
Decrease supply	Decreased blood supply (hemorrhage or anemia), vomiting/diarrhea, osmotic diuresis (diabetic ketoacidosis), and burns	Give fluids: up to 60 mL/kg of normal saline or lactated Ringer's solution. Consider blood or colloid replacement if these losses are the underlying cause (trauma, anemia, or burns). Infuse 10 mL/kg of warmed packed red blood cells. Monitor for coagulopathies, acidosis, and hypothermia, which can worsen the condition.

*Data are adapted from Feliciano et al.[4] Data are also adapted from the following source: Ralston, M., Hazinski, M. F., Zaritsky, A. L., Schxnader, S. M., & Kleinman, M. E. (2006). *Pediatric advanced life support.* Dallas, TX: American Heart Association.

ment of cellular metabolism, leading to cellular death, the end result is cardiopulmonary arrest if the process is uninterrupted (**Table 14-2**).

Compensated Shock

The etiology of shock can be dissimilar, but the body's response is uniform, allowing the caregiver to identify signs and symptoms of shock. In early shock, the body will attempt to compensate for the alterations in perfusion that have occurred. Stimulation of the sympathetic nervous system initiates an increase in stroke volume and increased vasoconstriction and systemic vascular resistance. Stroke volume, or the blood that is ejected by the left ventricle, depends on the filling volume of the ventricle (preload), myocardial contractility, and the resistance caused by pumping blood into the peripheral system (afterload). Cardiac output (CO) is a product of stroke volume (SV) and heart rate (HR) (CO = HR × SV). The small size of the ventricle, short myocardial fibers, and natural systemic resistance in pediatric patients results in a limited ability to alter their stroke volume; the heart rate must increase to affect cardiac output.[5] Tachycardia will be an early sign of compensated shock in a pediatric patient. Additional signs and symptoms will include tachypnea, mild irritability or lethargy, and decreased peripheral perfusion. The pediatric patient's body will attempt to compensate during early shock by increasing cardiac output to maintain perfusion to the brain and heart. There are systemic and cellular responses that are initiated to meet the body's oxygen demands. The results of the compensatory mechanisms are increased workload and increased myocardial oxygen consumption. Interventions must stop the shock process before compensatory mechanisms fail.

Decompensated Shock

The faster the heart rate, the less time is available to fill the ventricle or increase the stroke volume. As shock progresses and early compensatory mechanisms fail, the body's response becomes more complex, leading to lethal consequences. The pathophysiological sequelae may be the result of direct effects of inadequate tissue perfusion or the body's adaptive responses.

Decompensated shock, sometimes referred to as hypovolemic shock, is present when signs of shock are associated with systolic hypotension. The body's responses to decompensated shock and its physiological complications are summarized in **Table 14-3**.

The consequences of decompensated shock include the following:

- Fluid shifts from plasma into the interstitial space are caused by damage to cellular membranes. Generalized edema is found first in dependent areas, then in soft tissues, including the face, sclera, fingers, and genitalia.

- Disseminated intravascular coagulopathy (DIC) is caused by stimulation of the coagulation cascade. Petechiae begin to appear under areas of pressure and then become prominent over the trunk and extremities. Petechiae may coalesce into purpuric lesions on the skin, particularly over areas of movement or pressure (joints). Bleeding begins at all puncture sites of the skin and in the retina, kidneys, and digestive tract. Urine and feces will test positive for blood. Eventually, gross hematuria and bloody stools will be present.

- The continued release of vasoactive and inflammatory mediators allows the inflammatory response to go unchecked. Increased respiratory effort with tachypnea may be difficult to relieve with oxygen administration alone. Airway swelling and closure may also occur, requiring rapid endotracheal intubation.

  ○ Intracellular acidosis, hypoperfusion, and hypoxia result in cell death. The dying cells release mediators that compound the inflammatory response.

- Pulmonary tissue hypoxia may lead to acute respiratory distress syndrome (ARDS). This noncardiac pulmonary edema causes severe hypoxia. Positive-pressure ventilation with peak expiratory pressure support (PEEP) is necessary to maintain oxygen, carbon dioxide, and pH levels within normal limits.

- Multiple organ dysfunction syndrome (MODS) and eventually multiple organ failure and death may result if the progress of the decompensated shock state cannot be controlled.

  ○ Kidney and liver functions are altered as the result of decreased perfusion, oxygenation, and microemboli formation.

  ○ Small-bowel and pancreatic functions are decreased as the result of these same conditions.

    - Digestive enzymes and *Escherichia coli* can permeate via diffusion from the small intestine into nearby tissues as the result of changes in tissue permeability.

    - Bowel necrosis and sepsis can ensue. Fever, abdominal pain with rigidity, hypotension, increasing liver function procedure results, and altered blood glucose levels are signs of this process. The unique attributes of septic shock are given in **Table 14-4**.

Causes of Shock

An overview of the different causes of shock, focused assessments, and focused treatments are described in **Table 14-5**.

Table 14-3 The Body Systems' Responses to Shock*

Body System	Description
Cellular level	Impairment of cellular metabolism
	Decreased production of adenosine triphosphate
	Failure of the sodium-potassium pump
	Development of anaerobic metabolism
	Vascular to interstitial compartment fluid shifts
	Destruction of cellular membranes as the result of cellular edema
	Impaired glucose delivery and uptake
	Lysosomal enzyme release
	Sluggish capillary flow
	Activation of the clotting cascade
Immune system (anaphylactic and septic shock)	Activation of the complement cascade system
	Phagocytic cells initiate activity (macrophages, monocytes, and neutrophils)
	Primary mediator release (cytokines, tumor necrosis factor, interleukin 1, and anaphylatoxin-C5A)
	Intense cellular response occurs with release of secondary mediators (cytokines, prostaglandins, tumor necrosis factor, platelet-activating factor, and oxygen-free radicals)
	Inflammatory cascade results in continued activation of the previous processes, leading to cellular destruction
Cardiac system	Myocardial depressant factor
	Decrease in cardiac output and systemic vascular resistance
	Development of ischemia and dysrhythmias
Pulmonary system	Increased permeability (to fluid shift)
	Decreased oxygen transport/diffusion
	Hypoxia and acidosis
Neurological system	Decreased brain perfusion leads to alteration in consciousness
	Blood-brain barrier and autoregulation may fail
Renal system	Decrease in glomerular perfusion
	Decrease in urinary output
	Decrease in detoxification
	Activation of the renin-angiotensin I to angiotensin II feedback loop system for increased vasoconstriction in the periphery
Adrenal system	Aldosterone is released to stimulate sodium reabsorption in the kidney
	Stress hormones are released, including epinephrine, norepinephrine, and cortisol
Gastrointestinal system	Microcirculatory failure
	Loss of gut barrier with systemic spread of bacteria
Hepatic system	Glycogenolysis is activated by epinephrine, resulting in breakdown of glycogen to glucose
	Glycogen stores may be used up rapidly in a child
	Hepatic vessels constrict to redirect flow to vital areas
	The body shifts from using glucose to protein for energy, resulting in increased ammonia production. Ammonia is toxic to cells.
Integumentary system	Blood is shunted away from skin, causing sluggish and delayed capillary refill
	The skin will be prone to injury and breakdown
	Hypothermia
	Bleeding and edema may be difficult to control

*Data are taken from Feliciano et al.[4] and Fleisher et al.[5] Data are also taken from the following sources: (1) Brierley, J., Carcillo, J. A., Choong, K., Cornell, T., DeCaen, A., Deymann, A., ... Zuckerberg, A. (2009). Clinical practice parameters for hemodynamic support of pediatric and neonatal septic shock: 2007 update from the American College of Critical Care Medicine. *Critical Care Medicine, 37*, 666–688. (2) Ralston, M., Hazinski, M. F., Zaritsky, A. L., Schxnader, S. M., & Kleinman, M. E. (2006). *Pediatric advanced life support.* Dallas, TX: American Heart Association. (3) Thomas, D. O., & Bernardo, L. M. (2009). *Core curriculum for pediatric emergency nursing* (2nd ed.). Des Plaines, IL: Emergency Nurses Association.

Nursing Care of the Pediatric Patient with Shock

Assessment

The pediatric patient who presents in a shock state requires a rapid assessment simultaneously with the initiation of critical interventions. Conditions or medical history that may seem non–life threatening can contribute to the shock response by increasing tissue demand for oxygen and nutrients. For example, a pediatric patient who presents to the emergency department with complaints of fever may actually be compromised because of concomitant vomiting, diarrhea, tachypnea/tachycardia, and decreased oral intake. A careful medical history and physical examination are imperative when treating pediatric patients.

Additional History

Chapter 5, "Initial Assessment," lists general questions to ask during a history interview. Additional or specific history data important in the evaluation of shock include the following:

- Any obvious bleeding sites or history of blood loss
- Vomiting or diarrhea
- Decreased fluid intake
- Any obvious sites of fluid loss, such as a burn injury
- Congenital heart disease
  - History of myocardial infarction
- Massive pulmonary embolism
- Potential source of infection (e.g., tracheostomy, urinary catheter, G-tube, asplenia, or meningitis)
- History of recent trauma
- History of recent surgery

Signs and Symptoms

- An altered level of consciousness (LOC) may result from several factors, such as injury to the brain, drugs, or hypoxia; any alteration in LOC should be considered the result of decreased cerebral perfusion until proven otherwise. In a pediatric patient, an altered LOC may be assessed as follows:
  - Confusion
  - Inability to recognize caregivers
  - Decreased response to environment
  - Anxiety, restlessness, or irritability
  - Agitation alternating with lethargy
- Alteration in vital signs
  - Increased or decreased temperature
  - Increased or decreased heart and respiratory rates
- Hypotension: In the early stages of shock, the pediatric patient may be normotensive or may have a slightly increased blood pressure, with a narrowed pulse pressure (difference between systolic and diastolic reading).
  - The increase in the diastolic reading is indicative of the increased systemic vascular resistance needed to maintain perfusion. As shock progresses and systemic vascular resistance decreases, a widened pulse pressure will be noted. Hypotension and bradycardia are late ominous signs in the pediatric patient in shock.
- Changes in skin color and temperature are caused by the body's compensatory mechanisms that shunt blood away from the skin to vital organs to maintain a blood pressure compatible with life.
  - Vasoconstriction of the skin causes it to appear pale, ashen, mottled, or cyanotic; also, it may feel cool and/or clammy.

Table 14-4 Comparison of Septic Shock Presentations*

Variable	Warm Shock	Cold Shock
Capillary refill	Flash (< 2 seconds)	Delayed (> 2 seconds)
Pulses	Bounding	Diminished
Skin color/temperature	Flushed/hot	Pale and mottled/cool
Urine output	Normal or slightly decreased	Decreased (< 1 mL/kg per hour)
Blood pressure	Normal or slightly elevated	Early, normotensive with narrowed pulse pressure; late, hypotensive with widened pulse pressure
Pathophysiology	Body's attempt to eradicate pathogens releases macrophages and neutrophils, then dilates the microvascular flow to increase delivery of the killing forces. A systemic response causes vasodilatation.	Body's attempt to maintain vascular flow and oxygen delivery is aimed at vasoconstriction and increased systemic vascular resistance. As blood is shunted away from the periphery, decreased perfusion ensues. The narrowing of the pulse pressure occurs with an elevated diastolic pressure, indicative of vasoconstriction. Hypotension and widened pulse pressure indicate a loss of compensatory mechanisms, such as vasoconstriction.

*Data are taken from Feliciano et al[4] and Fleisher et al.[5]

Table 14-5 Differential Focus on Causes of Shock*

Hypovolemic Shock

Etiology	Inadequate circulating intravascular volume as a result of dehydration or hemorrhage

	Trauma:
	  Burn injuries
	  Hemorrhage (both obvious and occult)

	Possible causes of dehydration:
	  Vomiting
	  Diarrhea
	  Osmotic diuresis (e.g., DKA)
	  Increased insensible water losses (i.e., tachycardia, tachypnea, fever, and inability to concentrate urine)

Pathophysiology	Circulating blood volume is inadequate to meet organ and cellular needs. Vasoconstriction and increased cardiac output are required to maintain circulation.
	In case of burns, fluid shifts outside the vascular bed because of increased tissue permeability, resulting in decreased circulating blood volume. Fluid is also lost because of the loss of the protective skin barrier.
	The sensation of pain from injured tissue and baroreceptors activates the autonomic nervous system and adrenal medulla to release catecholamines.

Frequent physical findings	General:
	  Prolonged capillary refill
	  Tachycardia
	  Tachypnea
	  Cool, pale, and mottled skin
	  Weak pulses
	  Altered mental status
	  Normal or decreased blood pressure

	Signs of dehydration: Dry mucous membranes, sunken eyes, and sunken fontanel

	Hemorrhage:
	  Active bleeding
	  Occult bleeding (swelling/bruising)
	  Surface trauma/burns

Frequent history findings	Gastroenteritis symptoms (vomiting and diarrhea)
	Fever
	Decreased appetite
	Decreased urine output
	Burn injury
	Trauma (focus on mechanism of injury)

Treatment in early shock	Blood loss:
	  Apply pressure to stop the bleeding and provide comfort measures to decrease oxygen demands. Offer fluids, if tolerated.
	  Assess for increased comfort and absence of ongoing blood loss.

	Fluid loss: Offer small frequent amounts of fluids, such as Pedialyte or diluted electrolyte solution.
	Reassess for tolerance of fluids and increased activity. Inability to tolerate fluids might be indicative of need for antiemetics and/or intravenous or SQ fluid replacement therapy.

Treatment focus
(assuming airway patency and cardiopulmonary function)
	Fluid boluses of 20 mL/kg:
	  Normal saline or lactated Ringer's solution administered rapidly (typically over five minutes, with signs of moderate to severe shock).
	  Expect up to 60 mL/kg: If no improvement, consider ongoing fluid loss versus different cause of shock state. In cases of hemorrhage, repeat bolus up to 60 mL/kg, then consider a 10 mL/kg transfusion of packed red blood cells.

Table 14-5 Differential Focus on Causes of Shock* *continued*

Cardiogenic Shock

Etiology	Myocardial dysfunction, with possible causes including the following:
	  Rhythm abnormality (most common is supraventricular tachycardia; asystole and ventricular fibrillation are uncommon without significant history)
	  Drug toxicity
	  Congenital heart defect
	  Myocarditis
	  Cardiomyopathy
	  Metabolic abnormalities (i.e., hypoglycemia or hypokalemia/hyperkalemia)

Pathophysiology	Fluid volume is generally normal or slightly increased, but myocardial dysfunction leads to diminished cardiac output and subsequent tissue hypoxia. In the case of supraventricular tachycardia, the elevated heart rate results in the inability of the left ventricle to fill, with resultant decreased cardiac output. Heart rate, time in the arrhythmia, age, and general health of the child are factors that lead to stable versus unstable findings.
Frequent physical findings	Torso scar from previous surgery Murmur (or gallop) Extremely high heart rate Can often be differentiated from other forms of shock because of associated signs of congestive heart failure, including rales and/or enlarged liver
Frequent history findings	Previous cardiac surgery Congenital heart defect SVT: decreased feeding, tires easily, sweating when feeding or crying, decreased crying, and acrocyanosis Viral illness followed by decreased activity Ingestion of cardiac medications Hypotension Syncope
Focused diagnostics	Ultrasonography Echocardiography Electrocardiography
Treatment in early shock	Cardiology consult Supportive care aimed at decreasing oxygen and metabolism needs
Treatment focus (assuming airway patency and cardiopulmonary function)	Fluid bolus of 5–10 mL/kg of normal saline or lactated Ringer's solution, administered slowly (over 10–30 minutes), then reassess for improvement of perfusion status Assess for signs of fluid overload Defibrillate or provide synchronized cardioversion based on cardiac rhythm Consider the use of levosimendan (Simdax) or enoximone (Perfan) SVT: Consider adenosine (Adenocard) or vagal maneuvers

Table 14-5 Differential Focus on Causes of Shock* *continued*

Obstructive Shock

Etiology	Mechanical obstruction of the circulation
	Possible causes include the following:
	Ductal-dependent lesion, such as hypoplasia, or stenosis
	Cardiac tamponade
	Tension pneumothorax
	Pulmonary embolism
Pathophysiology	Fluid volume is generally normal, but obstruction to flow results in impeded venous return to the heart or problems with cardiac filling or emptying.
	With tension pneumothorax or cardiac tamponade, there is decreased cardiac output associated with increased central venous pressure.
Frequent physical findings	Cardiac tamponade:
	Muffled heart sounds, widened pulse pressure, distended neck veins (may not be visible in younger children or in shock states)
	Tension pneumothorax:
	Asymmetrical chest rise and fall, signs of injury on affected side, decreased breath sounds on affected side (breath sounds are hyperresonant in smaller pediatric patients and may be heard throughout, despite the presence of a pneumothorax)
	Pulmonary embolism
Frequent history findings	Blunt force trauma to the chest, neck, or trunk
	Recent long bone fracture
	Neonate with little or no prenatal care or home birth
	Pulmonary embolism: sickle cell disease, central venous catheter, or coagulation disorder
Treatment in early shock	Treat underlying cause
	Supportive care aimed at decreasing oxygen and metabolism needs
Treatment focus (assuming airway patency and cardiopulmonary function)	Medication or treatments related to cause of obstruction:
	Ductal-dependent lesion: Alprostadil (Prostaglandin E_1) infusion
	Cardiac tamponade: Possible pericardiocentesis
	Tension pneumothorax: Needle decompression and chest tube placement
	Pulmonary embolism: Possible anticoagulants

Table 14-5 Differential Focus on Causes of Shock* *continued*

Distributive Shock

Etiology	Inability of the brain/central nervous system to communicate to the peripheral vascular system
	Possible causes include the following: Anaphylactic: allergen exposure Neurogenic: spinal cord injury, spinal anesthesia, and nervous system damage Septic: infectious organisms
Pathophysiology	Anaphylactic: Hypersensitivity reaction causing angioedema, a condition characterized by vasodilatation and capillary leakage.
	Neurogenic: Vasodilatation and loss of vascular tone because of the inability to receive central nervous system impulses to vasoconstrict, resulting in decreased return and decreased cardiac output
	Septic: Result of body's response to invasion of an infectious organism, leading to serious neuroendocrine, immunological, inflammatory, and cellular reactions and the resultant release of inflammatory mediators and an associated redistribution of intravascular volume, together with depression of myocardial function
Frequent physical findings	Anaphylactic: Angioedema, respiratory distress Hives, swelling of lips, tongue, or uvula Hypotension/syncope Vomiting/diarrhea
	Neurogenic: Bradycardia Hypotension Warm extremities (if adequate circulating volume) or cool extremities (if hypovolemic) Widened pulse pressure
	Spinal: Bradycardia Decreased deep tendon reflexes, decreased sensory level, and flaccid sphincter Hypotonia
	Sepsis: Tachycardia Altered mental status Blood pressure normal (compensated) or hypotensive (decompensated) Hyperthermia or hypothermia
Frequent history findings	Anaphylactic: Exposure to known allergen Sudden onset of symptoms
	Neurogenic: History of trauma or access to neuromuscular-blocking agents
	Septic: History of fever, exposure to communicable disease, or other symptoms of infectious disease History of immunosuppression

Table 14-5 Differential Focus on Causes of Shock* *continued*

Distributive Shock *continued*

Focused diagnostics	Anaphylactic: Laboratory and radiological studies as indicated by presentation and focused interventions
	Neurogenic: Radiological studies

	Sepsis:
	  Laboratory studies
	    Cultures
	      Blood
	      Body fluids, including cerebrospinal fluid
	      Wounds
	      Indwelling devices
	    Lumbar puncture (if patient is stable enough)

Treatment in early shock	Anaphylactic:
	  Keep calm
	  Supportive respiratory care
	  Epinephrine, given intramuscularly, via manual syringe or autoinjector

	Neurogenic:
	  Keep calm (especially if alteration is in the presence of neuromuscular blocking agents)
	  Minimize movement that may aggravate injury

	Septic:
	  Supportive care to stabilize temperature and vital signs
	  Antibiotics
	  Oral fluids as tolerated

Treatment focus (assuming airway patency and cardiopulmonary function)	Anaphylactic:
	  Intravenous access and 20 mL/kg normal saline or lactated Ringer's solution bolus
	  Diphenhydramine (Benadryl) and/or ranitidine (Zantac) and corticosteroids

	Neurogenic:
	  Fluid bolus of 20 mL/kg of normal saline or lactated Ringer's solution, to exclude hypovolemia, then maintenance fluids
	  Vasopressor therapy
	  Assess need for warming/cooling measures

	Septic:
	  Intravenous access and 20 mL/kg normal saline bolus, prepare to repeat up to 60 mL/kg in the first hour
	  Reassess

Note: DKA indicates diabetic ketoacidosis; SQ, subcutaneous; SVT, supraventricular tachycardia.

*Data are adapted from Feliciano et al[4] and Fleisher et al.[5] Data are also adapted from the following sources: (1) Brierley, J., Carcillo, J. A., Choong, K., Cornell, T., DeCaen, A., Deymann, A., ... Zuckerberg, A. (2009). Clinical practice parameters for hemodynamic support of pediatric and neonatal septic shock: 2007 update from the American College of Critical Care Medicine. *Critical Care Medicine, 37*, 666–688. (2) Brierley, J., & Peters, M. J. (2008). Distinct hemodynamic patterns of septic shock at presentation to pediatric intensive care. *Pediatrics, 122*, 752–759. (3) Gausche-Hill, M., Fuchs, S., & Yamamoto, L. (2007). *The pediatric emergency medicine resource* (Rev. 4th ed.). Sudbury, MA: Jones & Bartlett. (4) Jones, J. G., & Smith, S. L. (2009). Shock in the critically ill neonate. *Journal of Perinatal and Neonatal Nursing, 23*, 346–354. (5) Ralston, M., Hazinski, M. F., Zaritsky, A. L., Schxnader, S. M., & Kleinman, M. E. (2006). *Pediatric advanced life support.* Dallas, TX: American Heart Association. (6) Thomas, D. O., & Bernardo, L. M. (2009). *Core curriculum for pediatric emergency nursing* (2nd ed.). Des Plaines, IL: Emergency Nurses Association.

Table 14-4 provides a comparison between warm and cold shock.

- The exception to this is warm septic shock, when vasodilatation results in warm flushed skin and bounding pulses.
- Changes in the quality of peripheral and central pulses are the result of decreased vascular volume. When assessed, they will be weak, thready, unequal, or absent.
  - Difficulty in obtaining a blood pressure is the result of vasoconstriction and decreased cardiac output.
  - Mechanical noninvasive blood pressure (NIBP) devices are accurate only when there is adequate distal perfusion.
    - The initial blood pressure should be obtained manually by auscultation, palpation, or ultrasonic Doppler techniques. The noninvasive blood pressure reading should be correlated with manual measurements. If pulses are weak or absent, the pediatric patient should be considered hypotensive. Hypotension in decompensated shock is a brief phase before cardiopulmonary collapse and arrest.
- Decreased or absent bowel sounds are the result of increased sympathetic tone and lowered vascular perfusion.
- Decreased or absent urinary output occurs. The pediatric patient should have urine output of greater than 1 mL/kg per hour. Decreases are because of severe changes in glomerular filtration rate, which result from insufficient perfusion.

Diagnostic Procedures

A variety of radiographic and laboratory studies may be indicated based on the suspected etiology of the pediatric patient's condition. Definitive diagnostic procedures are performed as the resuscitation effort is in progress or after the pediatric patient is stabilized. The following procedures and studies may be indicated for the pediatric patient with shock.

Monitoring

- Cardiac monitor
- Pulse oximeter. Poor perfusion may impede the monitor's ability to obtain an accurate reading. A normal reading does not negate the pediatric patient's need for supplemental oxygen.
- Capnography
- 12-lead electrocardiogram (ECG)
- Echocardiography

Radiographic Studies

A chest radiograph is completed to determine the presence of an enlarged heart, a congenital heart defect, a pulmo-

nary infection, or hemothorax or pneumothorax. Other radiographic studies might be indicated in cases of known or suspected trauma and other suspicious findings.

Other Diagnostic Procedures

- Laboratory studies
  - Complete blood cell count and coagulation studies
  - Serum or whole blood glucose test
  - Electrolytes, including calcium
  - Blood sample for typing
  - Lactate level
    - Many sources state that lactate levels are indicative of anaerobic metabolism and are an indirect marker of oxygen debt after shock. Factors such as alcohol and recreational drugs, ketoacidosis, and hepatic dysfunction can falsely elevate lactate levels.[4]
  - Arterial blood gas
    - Decreasing pH indicates a worsening of the cellular oxygen debt as acidosis develops as the result of anaerobic metabolism, lactic acid production, and/or respiratory insufficiency.
    - An elevated partial pressure of carbon dioxide, arterial, may indicate respiratory acidosis and impaired ventilation of the alveoli.
    - A low partial pressure of oxygen in the alveoli indicates hypoxia.
    - Base excess
      » Evaluates resuscitative efforts and resolving or worsening acidosis.
      » There is great variability in these readings because of compensation and respiratory interventions, but increases in arterial base deficit can be indicative of a worsening condition.
  - Urinalysis

Planning/Implementation/ General Interventions

The outcome or goal of treatment strategies is to maintain or restore tissue perfusion by expanding plasma volume, reestablishing normal cellular function, preventing damage to end organs by improving tissue oxygen delivery, and reestablishing homeostasis. Evaluation and ongoing assessments are aimed at identifying expected findings to adapt intervention strategies. General interventions are listed later; cause-specific interventions are listed in **Table 14-5**.

General Interventions

Airway

- Anticipate intubation in a child who is unable to maintain an airway because of decreased mental status, tiredness from prolonged distress, or the need for improved ventilation and oxygenation.

- Simultaneous cervical spine immobilization is indicated in the pediatric patient suspected of high cervical trauma, especially with signs of neurogenic shock.

Breathing and Oxygenation

- The underlying pathophysiology of shock includes inadequate tissue oxygenation; breathing and oxygenation are imperative. Administer 100% oxygen via high-flow delivery or bag-mask, if indicated.

- Hypoxia is the most common cause of bradycardia in infants and young children; they generally respond to assisted ventilation with 100% oxygen at an age-appropriate rate with an adequate tidal volume.

- Capnography and oxygen saturation level must be continuously monitored.

Circulation

- For an absent or ineffective pulse, initiate cardiopulmonary resuscitation when indicated by the pediatric patient's condition.

- Initiate chest compressions in all pediatric patients with heart rates too low to adequately perfuse their vital organs. Chest compressions are initiated if the infant or child's heart rate is less than 60 beats per minute and accompanied by signs of poor systemic perfusion.

  - Effective chest compressions should produce a central pulse. The optimal rate is 100 compressions per minute. The technique for compressions is based on the age and size of the child. Children younger than one year are considered infants, and chest compressions are performed with two fingers over the sternum just below the nipple line or by using the encircling two-hand method. This method uses both thumbs to compress the sternum with the fingers placed around the back of the infant. Chest compressions are performed with one hand for children aged one to eight years. Chest compressions for children older than eight years are performed in the same fashion as for adults.[6]

- Control any obvious bleeding.

- Obtain vascular access using the most expedient site possible. Peripheral venous access can be difficult and time-consuming in the child with circulatory collapse. An intraosseous line should be inserted if access is

needed emergently and cannot be obtained by conventional means. (**Chapter 9, "Vascular Access,"** provides more information.)

- Initiate volume replacement.

  - Administer a 20 mL/kg bolus of warmed isotonic crystalloid solution. A bolus of fluid is given in its entirety over five to 20 minutes based on the patient's clinical condition and can be repeated based on the pediatric patient's response. Immediately after each bolus, reevaluate airway, breathing, and circulation/perfusion, assessing for any changes. Additional fluid boluses may be required for persistent signs of shock.

  - Because approximately one-fourth of the crystalloid solution remains in the plasma compartment, infusion of four to five times the fluid lost may be required to restore plasma volume.

  - Colloids are more efficient volume expanders than crystalloids because they remain in the intravascular compartment longer than crystalloid solutions. However, colloids may not be as readily available as crystalloid solutions, and they may cause sensitivity reactions. Certain types of shock may respond better to the administration of colloid solutions, whereas blood products may be indicated for replacement of blood loss or treatment of coagulopathies.

Thermoregulation

- Administer antipyretics as indicated for fever. Hyperthermia results in increased metabolic needs, further depleting reserves.

- Provide supplemental warmth (i.e., overbed warmers, warm blankets, warm intravenous fluids, and warm humidified oxygen).

  - In children, the combination of body exposure to the environment, high body surface area to volume ratio, and rapid administration of unwarmed blood products, crystalloids, or colloids may contribute to the development of hypothermia.

  - Hypothermia causes shunting of blood away from the periphery, resulting in poor peripheral perfusion and further complicating assessment of the pediatric patient.

  - Hypothermia may adversely affect myocardial and metabolic functions, further depleting compensatory reserves and resulting in a poor response to resuscitative efforts.

Metabolic and Electrolyte Considerations

- Correct hypoglycemia

  - Infants have limited glycogen stores that are rapidly depleted during periods of stress. A whole blood glucose (bedside glucose) or serum glucose level is required for any pediatric patient who is critically ill. Glucose monitoring should be performed during resuscitation and in the postresuscitation phase. Documented hypoglycemia is treated with intravenous dextrose solution.

- Administer 2 to 4 mL/kg of 25% dextrose solution (D_{25}) slowly, either intravenously or intraosseously. If a prepared D_{25} solution is unavailable, mix equal amounts of 50% glucose solution and sterile water. For example, if 20 mL of D_{25} is ordered, mix 10 mL of 50% glucose solution with 10 mL of sterile water. The administration of D_{25} through small peripheral veins can cause vascular and tissue injury; therefore, further dilution to a 12.5% solution may be necessary in smaller pediatric patients with only peripheral access.

- In neonates, administer 2 mL/kg of $D_{10}W$ intravenously over one minute for documented and symptomatic hypoglycemia.

- Reassess the serum glucose level 15 to 20 minutes after the dextrose bolus and hourly until the glucose level is stable.

- Correct electrolyte imbalances

  - Buffers (i.e., sodium bicarbonate) may be administered to the pediatric patient with documented severe acidosis but only after the provision of adequate oxygenation and ventilation because most acidosis is caused by respiratory failure in children.

  - In infants younger than three months, a 4.2% solution is used.

  - The initial dosage for children in shock is 1 mEq/kg of 8.4% solution.

  - Sodium bicarbonate is recommended in the treatment of symptomatic patients with hyperkalemia, hypermagnesemia, and poisonings.

Treat the Underlying Cause of Shock

- Inotropes, vasopressors, and vasodilators are classes of medications that may be used to support circulatory function.

  - Because pediatric patients rarely present to the emergency department with primary cardiac dysrhythmia, epinephrine is the preferred medication in the treatment of bradydysrhythmias or asystole (after initiation of a patent airway, ventilation, and oxygenation) because of the prominent α-adrenergic effects in the vascular bed and β-adrenergic effects on the heart.

  - Atropine is used to diminish vagally mediated bradycardia associated with intubation, and atrioventricular block.

  - In the unstable pediatric patient, continuous infusions of vasoactive agents may be used to improve cardiac output and treat postresuscitation myocardial dysfunction.

Serial Assessments

- Continually monitor and document the results of the primary assessment, vital signs, urinary output, and the pediatric patient's response to specific interventions.

- Assessment of cardiac output is imperative in identifying responses to interventions. Echocardiography may be indicated in the absence of invasive central monitoring.

- Apply expected outcomes to assessment findings to anticipate future interventions.

- Anticipate that initial responses to interventions may be temporary, requiring further resuscitative efforts.

Family Involvement

- Promote and support the family's involvement in the pediatric patient's care.

  - Assign a healthcare professional to provide explanations of procedures and treatment plans to the caregivers and give emotional support during the time in the emergency department.

  - Involve the pediatric patient's family as soon as possible in the resuscitation process. A poor response to resuscitative efforts may necessitate making decisions about the termination of resuscitative efforts and organ donation. Involve the caregivers in this decision-making process.

Evaluation and Ongoing Assessment

The pediatric patient who is in shock requires meticulous and frequent reassessment of airway patency, breathing effectiveness, perfusion, and mental status. The etiologies of shock and cardiovascular compromise encompass a broad range of disorders. Initial improvements may not be sustained, and additional interventions may be required. The pediatric patient's response to interventions and trending of the pediatric patient's condition must be closely monitored. To evaluate the pediatric patient's progress, monitor the following:

- Airway patency, including the adequacy and patency of airway adjuncts

- Effectiveness of breathing; ventilation, and oxygenation
- Perfusion
  - Pulse rate and quality (central versus peripheral)
  - Skin color and temperature
  - Capillary refill
  - Blood pressure
  - Cardiac rhythm
- Level of consciousness and pupillary reaction
- Urinary output
- Oxygen saturation and capnography readings
- Arterial pH; partial pressure of oxygen in the alveoli; partial pressure of carbon dioxide, arterial; and base deficit
- Laboratory values, including serum lactate levels[7]

Discharge Education and Health Promotion

Health promotion and discharge education principles affecting shock-related morbidity and mortality are focused on prevention and early recognition of change in condition. Depending on the pediatric patient's condition, the caregivers' readiness to learn, and underlying cause of shock, components of **Table 14-6** may be used.

Table 14-6 Health Promotion and Discharge Teaching Principles

Type of Strategy	Description
General strategies (identify opportunities to educate caregivers, children, and communities)	Importance of well-child checkups
	Importance of vaccinations to prevent illness
	Trauma prevention
	Importance of basic life support classes
Medical	Signs and symptoms of infection
	Signs of dehydration (including change in activity and decrease in urinary output)
	Basic oral rehydration strategies (including appropriate rehydration fluids, small and frequent feedings, and diet advancement)
Special needs	Signs of supraventricular tachycardia (including irritability or decreased activity, decreased appetite, sweating with irritability, changes in color, feeling of fast or "fluttery" heart beat when hand is placed on chest, or older child's description of heart beating fast)
	Strategies to decrease the risk of infection and early recognition of fever and infection in children with long-term healthcare needs, indwelling devices, and immunocompromised situations

Summary

Evaluation of the pediatric patient in shock requires astute assessment of peripheral perfusion, vital signs, LOC, and urinary output. Shock and respiratory failure are common pathways to cardiovascular collapse and subsequent cardio-pulmonary arrest in the pediatric patient. Early recognition of the signs of shock is critical to the initiation of prompt intervention and the prevention of adverse outcomes. The central piece of the puzzle in the care for the pediatric patient in shock is the interlocking relationship between early recognition of life-threatening illnesses and injuries that cause shock and the initiation of the rapid interventions to achieve the desired outcomes of adequate oxygen delivery to the tissues without long-term mortality or morbidity.

Selected Emergency: Case Study of a Child in Septic Shock SCCM Algorithm*

Emergency Department

0 min — Recognize decreased mental status and perfusion. Begin high flow O_2. Establish IV/IO access.

5 min — **Initial resuscitation:** Push boluses of 20 mL/kg isotonic saline or colloid up to and over 60 mL/kg until perfusion improves or unless rales or hepatomegaly develop. Correct hypoglycemia & hypocalcemia. Begin antibiotics.

(If 2nd PIV start inotrope.)

shock not reversed?

15 min — **Fluid refractory shock:** Begin inotrope IV/IO. use atropine/ketamine IV/IO/IM to obtain central access & airway if needed. *Reverse cold shock* by titrating central dopamine or, if resistant, titrate central epinephrine *Reverse warm shock* by titrating central norepinephrine.

shock not reversed?

60 min — **Catecholamine resistant shock:** Begin hydrocortisone if at risk for absolute adrenal insufficiency

Pediatric Intensive care unit

Monitor CVP in PICU, attain normal MAP-CVP & $ScvO_2 > 70\%$

Cold shock with normal blood pressure:	Cold shock with low blood pressure:	Warm shock with low blood pressure:
1. Titrate fluid & epinephrine, $ScvO_2 > 70\%$, Hgb > 10g/dL	1. Titrate fluid and epinephrine, $ScvO_2 > 70\%$, Hgb > 10g/dL	1. Titrate fluid and norepinephrine, $ScvO_2 > 70\%$,
2. If $ScvO_2$ is still < 70% add vasodilator with volume loading (nitrosovasodilators, milrininone, imrinone, & others) Consider levosimendan	2. If still hyposensitve consider norepinephrine 3. If $ScvO_2$ is still < 70% consider dobutamine, milrininone, enoximone or levosimendan	2. If still hyposensitve consider vasopressin, terlipressin, or angiotensin 3. If $ScvO_2$ still < 70% consider low dose epinephrine

shock not reversed?

Persistent catecholamine resistant shock: Rule out and correct pericardial effusion, pneumothorax, & intra-abdominal pressure > 12 mm/Hg. Consider pulmonary artery, PICCO, or FATD catheter, &/or doppler ultrasound to guide fluid, intrope, vasopressor, vasodilator and hormonal therapies. Goal C.I. > 3.3 & < 6.0 $L/min/m^2$

shock not reversed?

Refractory shock: ECMO

*Algorithm for time sensitive, goal-directed, stepwise management of hemodynamic support, in infants and children. Proceed to next step, if shock persists. 1) First-hour goals: Restore and maintain heart rate thresholds, capillary refill ≤ 2 seconds, and normal blood pressure, in the first hour/emergency department. Support oxygenation and ventilation as appropriate. 2) Subsequent intensive care unit goals: If shock is not reversed, intervene to restore and maintain normal perfusion pressure (mean arterial pressure [MAP]-central venous pressure [CVP]) for age, central venous O_2 saturation > 70% and CI > 3.3 < 6.0 $L/min/m^2$, in pediatric intensive care unit (PICU), Hgb, hemoglobin; PICCO, pulse contour cardiac output; FATD, femoral arterial thermodilution, ECMO, extra-corporeal membrane oxygenation; CI, cardiac index; CRRT, continuous renal replacement therapy; IV, intravenous; IO, interosseous; IM, intramuscular; ScvO2, central venous oxygen saturation.

Reprinted with permission from Brierley, J., Carcillo, J. A., Choong, K., Cornell, T., Decaen, A., Deymann, A., … Zuckerberg, A. (2009). Clinical practice parameters for hemodynamic support of pediatric and neonatal septic shock: 2007 update from the American College of Critical Care Medicine. *Critical Care Medicine, 37,* 666–688.

Background

The American College of Critical Care Medicine (ACCM) updated their 2002 "Clinical Guidelines for Hemodynamic Support of Neonates and Children with Septic Shock" in 2007 with further review in 2009. The emphasis is on early recognition of sepsis and severe sepsis and early age-specific therapies. The diagnosis of septic shock is suspected when the triad of fever, tachycardia and vasodilatation common in children is coupled with a change in mental status and clinical signs of inadequate tissue perfusion.

ACCM guidelines emphasize early and aggressive use of resuscitation fluids. It has been noted in studies in both North America and internationally that mortality increases dramatically with delay in fluid resuscitation and inotrope therapy. Recognition of symptoms of shock and rapid fluid resuscitation of 40–60 mL/kg, up to 200 mL/kg, should be accomplished in the first hour of admission to the ED, with careful assessment to avoid fluid overload. If the symptoms of shock are not reversed (fluid refractory shock); inotropes including dopamine and epinephrine should be considered, with the goal of attaining normal perfusion and blood pressure. Antibiotics should be begun within one hour of the identification of severe sepsis. Hypoglycemia and hypocalcemia should be corrected. Normothermia is encouraged. Close monitoring of circulation and blood pressure is indicated.

*Data are taken from Brierley, J., Carcillo, J. A., Choong, K., Cornell, T., Decaen, A., Deymann, A., … Zuckerberg, A. (2009). Clinical practice parameters for hemodynamic support of pediatric and neonatal septic shock: 2007 update from the American College of Critical Care Medicine. *Critical Care Medicine, 37,* 666–688.

Application

A five-year-old girl presents to the emergency department with a chief complaint of fever. When asked for her medical history, the mother discloses that the child was diagnosed as having acute monocytic leukemia and underwent chemotherapy last week. The pediatric assessment triangle reveals that she is alert but quiet, has no increased work of breathing, and is slightly pale. Further assessment reveals that she is tachycardic, with a slightly prolonged capillary refill. Her vital signs are as follows: temperature, 38.4°C (101°F); heart rate, 132 beats per minute; respiratory rate, 30 breaths per minute; and blood pressure, 90/50 mm Hg.

Is this an emergency? Why or why not? What type of shock would pertain? What are assessment and treatment priorities? (Refer to **Table 14-4.**)

Thirty minutes later, the girl is much sleepier than earlier, and her hands are cool to touch.

While being suspicious of septic shock, priorities of care do not change: Maintain or restore airway, breathing, and circulation. The child is administered oxygen, with the knowledge that the healthcare team should be prepared to intubate at the first sign of increased or decreased respiratory effort. Vascular access should be rapidly obtained for fluid resuscitation and medications. Fluid boluses of 20 mL/kg of an isotonic crystalloid solution are anticipated while baseline laboratory specimens are obtained, including blood gases, complete blood cell count with differential, bedside glucose level, electrolyte panels (watching especially for the glucose and calcium levels), lactate level, and cultures as appropriate. Early antibiotic administration is also recommended, followed by close assessment for hypotension.

Despite infusion totals of 60 mL/kg of normal saline, the child continues to have an altered mental status, tachypnea, increased work of breathing, tachycardia, prolonged capillary refill, and low blood pressure. Elective intubation was achieved; and dopamine, 5 mcg/kg per minute, was administered, with improvement noted to the respiratory and circulatory systems. The child was transferred to the Pediatric Intensive Care Unit.

References

1. Topjian, A. A., Nadkarni, V. M., & Berg, R. A. (2009). Cardiopulmonary resuscitation in children. *Current Opinion in Critical Care, 15,* 203–208.

2. Carcillo, J. A., Kuch, B. A., Han, Y. Y., Day, S., Greenwald, B. M., McCloskey, K. A., … Orr, R. A. (2009). Mortality and functional morbidity after use of PALS/APLS by community physicians. *Pediatrics, 124,* 500–508.

3. Oliveira, C. F., Nogueira de Sá, F. R., Oliveira, D. S., Gottschald, A. F., Moura, J. D., Shibata, A. R., … Carcilla, J. A. (2008). Time- and fluid-sensitive resuscitation for hemodynamic support of children in septic shock: barriers to the implementation of the American College of Critical Care Medicine/Pediatric Advanced Life Support Guidelines in a pediatric intensive care unit in a developing world. *Pediatric Emergency Care, 24,* 810–815.

4. Feliciano, D. V., Mattox, K. L., & Moore, E. E. (2007). *Trauma* (6th ed.). New York, NY: McGraw-Hill Medical.

5. Fleisher, G. R., Ludwig, S., Henretig, F. M., Ruddy, R. M., & Silverman, B. K. (2005). *Textbook of pediatric emergency medicine* (5th ed.). Philadelphia, PA: Lippincott Williams & Wilkins.

6. Ralston, M., Hazinski, M. F., Zaritsky, A. L., Schxnader, S. M., & Kleinman, M. E. (2006). *Pediatric advanced life support.* Dallas, TX: American Heart Assocation.

7. Glatter, R. D., & Winters, M. E. (2009). *What is the clinical utility of obtaining serum lactate and arterial base deficit values in patients with early signs of sepsis and septic shock?* Retrieved from http://www.medscape.com/viewarticle/585490

Chapter 15 | Rhythm Disturbances

Darleen A. Williams, MSN, RN, CEN, CCNS, EMT-P

Objectives

On completion of this chapter, the learner should be able to do the following:

- Determine anatomical, physiological, and developmental characteristics of pediatric patients as a basis for assessment of cardiac dysrhythmias.
- Describe the common causes and characteristics associated with pediatric patients with dysrhythmias.
- Plan appropriate interventions for pediatric patients experiencing dysrhythmias.
- Indicate strategies for early recognition of cardiac dysrhythmias.

Introduction

Despite the fact that cardiopulmonary arrest from cardiac causes in pediatric patients is not a frequent event, it is important to be able to recognize the common dysrhythmias seen in pediatric patients and understand the necessary treatments. The purpose of this chapter is to identify some key cardiac anatomical and physiological characteristics unique to pediatric patients and to identify dysrhythmias seen in children and their treatment. For some brief basic electrocardiographic information, see **Appendix 15-A**. A review of congenital cardiovascular abnormalities can be found in **Table 15-1**. Additional causes of sudden cardiopulmonary arrest (SCA) in children, including long QT and Marfan syndromes, will also be briefly reviewed.

Most pediatric arrest situations are secondary to respiratory or metabolic compromise that has not been recognized or corrected. Rates of survival from documented asystole are dismal in infants and children. It is imperative to identify the patient's subtle signs and symptoms of distress early and initiate interventions to prevent an arrest situation. This is done using an organized, systematic approach to assessment, as taught in the Emergency Nursing Pediatric Course.

Key Cardiac Characteristics

A pediatric patient's cardiac output (CO) is twice that of an adult's cardiac output. This increased output is necessary to support the pediatric patients's higher oxygenation needs. Because the actual stroke volume (SV) of children is relatively fixed as the result of less compliant cardiac muscle fibers, the only way to increase their CO is to increase their heart rate (HR): $CO = HR \times SV$. This compensatory mechanism is capable of maintaining the necessary CO for a long time; however, when the mechanism is exhausted, rapid deterioration will occur. Bradycardia in pediatric patients is a sign that they are decompensating and may soon experience cardiopulmonary arrest. Even while tachycardic, the filling time decreases, resulting in a decreased cardiac output. Pediatric patients have higher metabolic rates, contributing to increased oxygen demands and the need for increased cardiac output.

There are numerous cardiac changes that occur in infants during the first few weeks after birth. Sympathetic innervation of the heart is incomplete, making the neonate more easily affected by parasympathetic stimulation from activities such as sucking and defecating.[1] These necessary

Table 15-1 Common Cardiac Lesions Seen in the Emergency Department*

Lesion	Brief Description	ED Considerations
Atrial septal defect	Abnormal opening between the atria	Patients are usually asymptomatic Grade 2/4 or 3/6 systolic murmur (upper left sternal border) Heart failure and pulmonary hypertension can occur
Ventricular septal defect	Abnormal opening between the ventricles	May see signs of heart failure, including fatigue and shortness of breath Pulmonary hypertension may be present Grade 2/6 to 5/6 systolic murmur may be audible (left lower sternal border)
Patent ductus arteriosus	Patency of fetal connection between the pulmonary artery and aorta	Continuous "machinery murmur" heard Normally heard in the neonatal period and closes early in the first week of life May see signs and symptoms of heart failure (lethargy and poor feeding) if the ductus remains patent without underlying CHD or if it closes with an underlying ductal-dependent lesion Needs aggressive intervention if it closes with a ductal-dependent lesion, including intravenous access and infusion of PGE$_1$
Coarctation of the aorta	Narrowing or kinking of the aorta	Hallmark is discordant blood pressures between upper and lower extremities Severe lesions may present with sudden signs of heart failure (often after patent ductus arteriosus closes naturally) Needs aggressive intervention, including intravenous access and PGE$_1$ infusion Patient may need emergent surgery
Truncus arteriosus	Failure of normal septation of the embryonic bulbar trunk into the pulmonary artery and aorta, resulting in a single vessel overriding both ventricles*	Cyanosis with signs of heart failure May hear systolic/diastolic murmur May have bounding peripheral pulses with wide pulse pressure Heart failure starts when pulmonary vascular resistance begins to decrease (at the age of 4–6 weeks)*

Note: CHD indicates congenital heart disease; ED, emergency department; PGE$_1$, prostaglandin E$_1$.

*Data are adapted from the following sources: (1) O'Brien, P. A. (2005). The child with cardiovascular dysfunction. In M. J. Hockenberry, D. Wilson, & M. L. Winkelstein (Eds.), *Wong's essentials of pediatric nursing* (7th ed., pp. 890–937). St. Louis, MO: Mosby. (2) Ojanen-Thomas, D., & Bernado, L. (2009). Cardiovascular emergencies. In *Core curriculum for pediatric emergency nursing* (2nd ed., p. 180). Des Plaines, IL: Emergency Nurses Association.

activities commonly cause transient bradycardia in the neonate. Common nursing activities, such as suctioning and nasogastric or orogastric tube placement, can also cause transient bradycardia. However, as children grow, they experience less sensitivity to these vagal stimulations.

Selected Emergencies

Sudden Cardiac Arrest in Children

Sudden cardiopulmonary arrest (SCA) occurs when the heart's electrical system malfunctions suddenly, and the heart abruptly stops beating normally. It is often confused with a heart attack, which occurs when blocked arteries prevent blood from reaching the heart's muscle. It is estimated that approximately 2,000 patients younger than

25 years will die annually from an SCA,[2] although specific data regarding incidence are difficult to determine because there is no centralized or mandatory registry for pediatric SCA.[3] Older reports estimate the frequency of SCA in children and adolescents as between 0.8 and 6.2 per 100,000 per year.[4] Although SCA can occur at rest and at a young age, athletic participation enhances the likelihood of SCA in the child and young adult.[5] In fact, it is estimated that one in 200,000 athletes dies of cardiovascular disease on the field every year.[6, 7]

Causes of sudden cardiac death (SCD) in pediatric patients are many, including several completely different inherited and congenital conditions and some less commonly acquired conditions. Many causes of SCD in pediatric patients can be grouped into two main categories.[3, 8] The first category includes disorders that predominantly affect the structure of the heart. This category includes the following:

- Cardiomyopathies, especially hypertrophic cardiomyopathy
  - This condition is the most common, representing approximately one third of cases
- Arrhythmogenic right ventricular cardiomyopathy
- Myocarditis
- Congenital coronary artery anomalies
- Marfan syndrome with aortic aneurysm and congenital heart disease, including repaired congenital heart disease

The second category involves arrhythmogenic disorders, including channelopathies such as congenital long QT syndrome (LQTS), the incidence of which is estimated to be greater than one in 5,000.[9] Some cases of sudden infant death syndrome (SIDS) and sudden death in older children and young adults may be associated with channelopathies, which are dysfunctional myocyte ion channels that result in abnormal movement of electrolytes into and/or out of the cell, predisposing the heart to arrhythmias.[10]

Prevention Strategies

Several primary and secondary strategies may be used to prevent the tragedy of SCD in pediatric patients.[11] The goal of primary prevention strategies is to prevent SCD in a patient prone to SCD *before* an adverse event. These strategies involve the following:

- Screening programs
  - Especially a sports preparticipation history and physical examination is a useful and cost-effective tool for screening (the only widely adopted screening in the United States)
- Public education
- Physician awareness

Indications for further cardiac evaluation include the following:

- Exertional symptoms
- History of hypertension or heart murmur
- Family history of sudden death (most concerning if before the age of 50 years) and heart murmur or other auscultatory findings (be sure to listen to the murmur while the child is both supine and standing; with hypertrophic cardiomyopathy, the murmur will be louder while standing)

- Abnormal blood pressure, abnormal pulses, tachycardia, or the features of Marfan syndrome
- Variable results are reported with electrocardiographic screening of athletes

Marfan Syndrome

Marfan syndrome is an inherited genetic mutation that interferes with how the body makes the protein fibrillin-1, an important part of connective tissue. Marfan syndrome features can appear at any age, including in infants and young children, and may worsen as the child grows. It is possible that symptoms or features of this disorder may not be identified as Marfan syndrome until later in life (even though children are born with this syndrome). Specifically, the heart and blood vessels are subject to aneurysms and the development of mitral valve prolapse.[12] Treatment of patients with Marfan syndrome after diagnosis includes close medical supervision and prompt attention to any changes in the patient's symptoms or condition.

Long QT Syndrome

Long QT syndrome, like Marfan syndrome, is also an inherited disorder. Long QT syndrome affects the heart's electrical conduction system and commonly affects children and young adults. Studies have shown that, although many patients with this syndrome have no symptoms, children with LQTS may have at least one fainting episode by age 10.[13]

These patients may have an abnormal HR/rhythm and a prolonged QT interval while exercising, experiencing severe emotions, such as anger, fear, and pain, or when startled by sudden or loud noises. Some dysrhythmias associated with LQTS can cause sudden death. One type of inherited LQTS can cause the patient to become deaf. Despite the presence of this disorder, the results of the electrocardiogram may be normal.

Treatment begins with first identifying the disorder. Medications commonly used for LQTS include β-blockers, antidysrhythmic agents, calcium channel blockers, anticoagulants, and, in severe cases, the insertion of implantable cardioverter defibrillators.

Red Flags

- Chest Pain
  - If you believe it may be cardiac in origin, look for pathological Q waves, ST abnormalities, arrhythmias, or hypertrophy.

- Syncope
  - Look for T-wave abnormalities, QT interval abnormalities, or arrhythmias.
- Palpitations
  - Look for conduction disturbances, blocks, or preexcitation problems.

Common Dysrhythmias

Normal variances in a healthy pediatric patient's sinus rhythm occur more often than we know; if caught on an electrocardiogram, these variances may be thought of as abnormal. Many of these rhythm changes are relatively common and are, therefore, likely to be entirely benign. The frequency with which these changes occur calls attention to the importance of understanding the correlation of symptoms with a rhythm change when investigating any unusual events. This is especially true when these changes occur secondary to a respiratory or metabolic alteration or compromise. Both the rhythm and the cause of the dysrhythmia should be treated.

Pediatric dysrhythmias are divided into three basic categories: too fast, too slow, and absent. In addition to identifying the rhythm, it is important to note if the patient is stable or unstable. **Table 15-2** provides information on rhythm disturbances in children.

Table 15-2 Rhythm Disturbances in Children*

	Rhythm	Cause	Characteristics	Treatment
Fast Rhythms	**Sinus tachycardia**	Fever, anxiety, pain, and hypovolemia	Rapid sinus rhythm; rate, 140–220 beats per minute	Treat underlying cause.
	Supraventricular tachycardia	Reentry mechanism	Paroxysmal sinus rhythm; P waves are often undetectable; and rate, > 220 beats per minute (infant) and > 180 beats per minute (child)	Stable: Vagal maneuvers. Consider adenosine if no response. If no response, consider the following: alternative medications (e.g., amiodarone and procainamide) or cardioversion, 0.5–1 J/kg. Unstable: Cardioversion, 0.5–1 J/kg; if not effective, increase to 2 J/kg. Sedate if possible, but do not delay cardioversion.
	Ventricular tachycardia	Structural disease, hypoxia, acidosis, electrolyte imbalance, and toxic ingestion (e.g., tricyclic antidepressants)	Rate of 120 beats per minute or greater, wide QRS, and no P waves	Pulse and stable: Amiodarone or procainamide. Consider sedation and cardioversion with 0.5–1 J/kg. Pulse but unstable: Cardioversion, 0.5–1 J/kg; if not effective, increase to 2 J/kg. Sedate if possible, but do not delay cardioversion. Pulseless: Defibrillation with 2 J/kg, high-quality BLS for 2 minutes; if no response, repeat defibrillation using 4 J/kg, followed by high-quality BLS for 2 minutes; repeat as needed. Epinephrine intravenously or IO: 0.01 mg/kg (1:10,000: 0.1 mL/kg) as soon as vascular access is obtained, or via ETT if no access is available. ETT: 0.1 mg/kg (1:1,000: 0.1 mL/kg). Repeat the dose every 3–5 minutes. Consider antidysrhythmic agents: Amiodarone, lidocaine, and magnesium, if indication of torsades de pointes.
Slow Rhythms	**Sinus bradycardia**	Hypoxemia, hypotension, and acidosis	Sinus rhythm; slow rate (< 80 beats per minute in infants and < 60 beats per minute in children)	Ventilation, oxygenation, cardiac compressions for a heart rate of < 60 beats per minute (with signs of poor perfusion); epinephrine (1:10,000), 0.01 mg/kg intravenously or IO; repeat every 3–5 minutes. If increased vagal tone or primary AV block: Atropine. Consider cardiac pacing.
	Junctional rhythm and heart blocks	Hypoxemia, hypotension, and acidosis	Rare in children, slow rate, and P waves may or may not be present	Ventilation, oxygenation, cardiac compressions for a heart rate of < 60 beats per minute with signs of poor perfusion. Atropine Epinephrine, 0.01 mg/kg of 1:10,000 or 0.1 mL/kg intravenously. Consider cardiac pacing.
Absent Rhythms	**Asystole/ Pulseless electrical activity (PEA)**	Acidosis, hypoxia, hypovolemia, hypoglycemia, hypothermia, electrolyte imbalance, traumatic cardiothoracic injury, ingestion	Asystole: No electrical activity PEA: Electrical activity with monitoring, usually slow and disorganized. No palpable pulse Usually the end result of respiratory failure and cardiac collapse.	Ventilation, oxygenation, cardiac compressions Epinephrine intravenously 0.01 mg/kg (1:10,000 or 0.1 mL/kg) every 3–5 minutes Assess for and reverse possible causes
	Ventricular fibrillation	Traumatic injury, congenital cardiac malformations or ingestion, hypoxia, hypovolemia, electrolyte imbalance	Can be sudden cardiac collapse with injury, congenital malformations or ingestion. It is more commonly the end result of respiratory failure and degeneration of other dysrhythmias.	Ventilation, oxygenation, cardiac compressions Defibrillation with 2 J/kg, high-quality BLS for 2 minutes; if no response, repeat defibrillation using 4 J/kg, followed by high-quality BLS for 2 minutes; repeat as needed. Epinephrine intravenously 0.01 mg/kg (1:10,000 or 0.1 mL/kg)

A basic electrocardiographic interpretation review can be found in **Figure 15-1**. Common indications for performing an electrocardiogram can be found in **Table 15-3**.

The most important concept with any of these dysrhythmias is to determine if the pediatric patient is stable or unstable. Those individuals with cardiovascular instability will display signs of shock (e.g., altered level of consciousness; respiratory distress; poor peripheral and/or end-organ perfusion; delayed capillary refill; pale, cool, and clammy skin; and hypotension). Hypotension is a late sign, and these other signs and symptoms will become more profound before it is evident. If any of these rhythms are unstable, quickly determine the cause and provide treatment before total collapse and cardiopulmonary arrest occurs.

Note: The following sections related to specific dysrhythmias include the most current treatment recommendations from the American Heart Association's *Pediatric Advanced Life Support (PALS) Guidelines* at publication. Because of the continual evolution of treatment modalities and medication therapies, these recommendations may be revised before the next revision of the Emergency Nursing Pediatric Course. It is the responsibility of the healthcare provider to check with the healthcare institution regarding updated policies and procedures relating to medications and nursing practice. See **Appendix 15-B** for more information regarding PALS resuscitation medications and specific electrical therapy options.

Case Presentations

Too Slow (Bradydysrhythmias)

A mother presents to triage with her 6-month-old child. The mother states, "My baby has had a fever for the last two days, and just in the last hour, she has started acting strangely. I cannot get her to eat, she is breathing very fast, and her color just isn't right."

Figure 15-1 Relationship of the Electrocardiogram (ECG) to the Heart and Waveform*

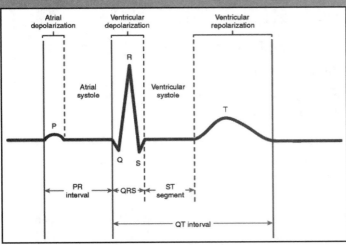

*Reprinted from Urden, L. D., Stacy, K. M., & Lough, M. E. (2009). *Critical care nursing: Diagnosis and management* (6th ed.). St. Louis, MO: Mosby/Elsevier.

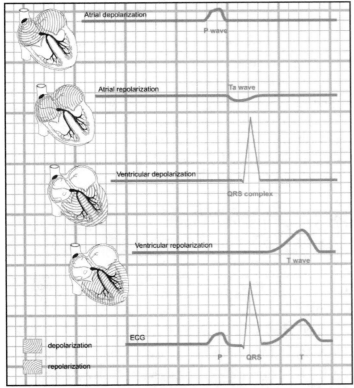

*Reprinted with permission from Huszar, R. J. (2002). *Basic dysrhythmias: Interpretation & management* (3rd ed.). St. Louis, MO: Mosby/Elsevier.

Table 15-3 Common Indications for Pediatric Electrocardiography*

Diagnosis and management of congenital heart disease

Diagnosis and management of arrhythmia

Diagnosis and management of rheumatic fever, Kawasaki disease, pericarditis, and myocarditis

Syncope, seizures, and "funny turns"

Cyanotic episodes

Chest pain or other symptoms related to exertion

Family history of sudden death or life-threatening event, especially prior to age 50

Electrolyte abnormalities

Toxic drug ingestion

*Data are taken from: Dickinson, D. F. (2005). The normal ECG in childhood and adolescence. *Heart, 91,* 1626–1630.

This child should be quickly triaged to the treatment area in order to perform a rapid focused assessment and obtain a brief medical history. The child is placed on the cardiac monitor with the rhythm seen in **Figure 15-2**.

In a pediatric patient, bradycardia is any HR less than the normal HR for that child's age. However, a HR that is less than 60 beats per minute in any pediatric patient should be considered too slow. (You must also remember that an adolescent who is a highly trained athlete may have a HR in the 50s, which can be a normal variation for that adolescent.)

Clinically significant bradycardia occurs when a patient has a HR of less than the normal rate for the child's age and is associated with poor systemic perfusion.[14] A HR less than 60 beats per minute with poor perfusion, despite adequate oxygenation and ventilation, is an indication to begin chest compressions.[10] Once this dysrhythmia is recognized, rapid interventions include providing adequate oxygenation and ventilation immediately.

Hypoxemia is the most frequent cause of slow or bradydysrhythmias in the pediatric patient. Assess the symptomatic patient using an organized and systematic approach starting with the ABCs. First, ensure that the patient's airway is patent and maintain patency. Second, assess breathing, including rate, depth, and quality of respirations. Third, assess circulation, including comparison of both central and peripheral pulses and capillary refill. Appropriate interventions are initiated at each step (i.e., administration of oxygen, circulatory support) if the assessment reveals that actions are necessary. Frequently, adequate ventilation and oxygenation will result in the return of a normal sinus rhythm.

Additional Patient History

- Excessive suctioning secondary to increased secretions in the mouth or nose
- Hypothermia
- Recent or multiple intubation attempts

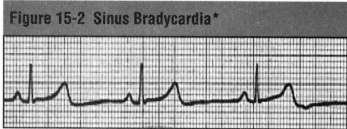

Figure 15-2 Sinus Bradycardia*

Sinus bradycardia of 39 beats/min. The pacemaker is the sinus node, and conduction is normal.

*Reprinted from Conover, M. B. (1996) *Understanding electrocardiography* (7th ed.). St. Louis, MO: Mosby.

- Suspected overdose or ingestion (especially calcium channel blockers, β-blockers, or digoxin)
- Congenital heart disease
- Recent trauma (i.e., head or chest)

Signs and Symptoms of Bradycardia

- Heart rate less than normal for age or less than 60 beats per minute
- Signs of poor perfusion: hypotension, diminished pulses, delayed capillary refill (longer than two seconds), cool/pale skin, and decreased urinary output
- Increased work of breathing
- Altered level of consciousness and listlessness
- May be asymptomatic
- Electrocardiogram shows both atrial and ventricular rates that are slow

Look for potential causes for this dysrhythmia and treat after considering the reversible causes (**Table 15-4**).

Interventions for Bradycardia

- If there are no signs of decreased CO, then no treatment is necessary.
- Administer oxygen at 100% by either a nonrebreather (NRB) mask or a bag-mask device because the most common cause is the result of hypoxia in pediatric patients. If these devices are not providing adequate ventilation, then intubation should be considered.
- Establish vascular access with either a peripheral intravenous or an intraosseous (IO) device.
- If adequate ventilation does not improve or increase the HR, initiate chest compressions for heart rates below 60, even though there is a pulse. (Heart rates of < 60 beats per minute are too low to support an adequate CO in infants and young children.)

Table 15-4 Common Causes for Cardiopulmonary Arrest*

Hs	Ts
Hypovolemia	Toxins
Hypoxia	Tamponade (cardiac)
Hydrogen ion (acidosis)	Tension pneumothorax
Hypokalemia/hyperkalemia	Thrombosis (coronary or pulmonary)
Hypoglycemia	Trauma (hypovolemia and increased intracranial pressure)
Hypothermia	

*Data are taken from the American Heart Association.[15]

- Consider pharmacological agents.[14]
  - Epinephrine
    - This agent has α-adrenergic–stimulating properties that cause vasoconstriction by increasing peripheral vascular resistance, which increases blood flow to vital organs.
    - Epinephrine also has positive chronotropic properties (increases the HR) along with inotropic properties (increases myocardial contractility), leading to increased oxygen consumption by the heart.
  - Atropine
    - This agent is considered in the pediatric patient only when vagal stimulation or cholinergic drug toxicity is suspected.
    - **Remember that the first-line interventions for bradycardia with poor perfusion in pediatric patients are oxygenation and ventilation, followed by treatment with epinephrine.**
  - Cardiac pacing
    - This treatment may be considered in patients with symptomatic bradycardia. Pacing may be lifesaving in selected cases of bradycardia caused by complete heart block or abnormal sinus node function, especially if associated with congential or acquired heart disease.[10]
    - Transcutaneous pacing can be painful in the conscious patient; this procedure may be reserved only for those pediatric patients experiencing life-threatening bradycardia.
    - If transcutaneous pacing is considered, sedation before implementation should be initiated.
    - Use pediatric-sized electrodes based on manufacturer's recommendation.
    - Use adult-sized electrodes for children weighing more than 10 kg. Following the manufacturer's guidelines for all specific equipment and supplies is always recommended.[14]
    - Pacing electrodes can be placed using either the anterior-anterior or posterior-anterior position, with the latter being the recommended position (**Figure 15-3**).
    - The initiation of transcutaneous pacing for pediatric patients with symptomatic bradycardia includes setting the demand rate to 100 beats per minute and then adjusting the output (in milliamps) to the maximum output that achieves capture. This setting may be adjusted as needed to maintain capture.

Too Fast (Tachydysrhythmias)

Tachydysrhythmias are defined as a HR that is faster than the normal HR for the child's age. These rapid rhythms need immediate treatment to prevent the patient from decompensating into a shock state and resulting in life-threatening dysrhythmias. There are two categories of tachydysrhythmias: atrial and ventricular. These dysrhythmias will be addressed individually; however, all dysrhythmias require the organized and systematic assessment and interventions that begin with the ABCs, as previously discussed.

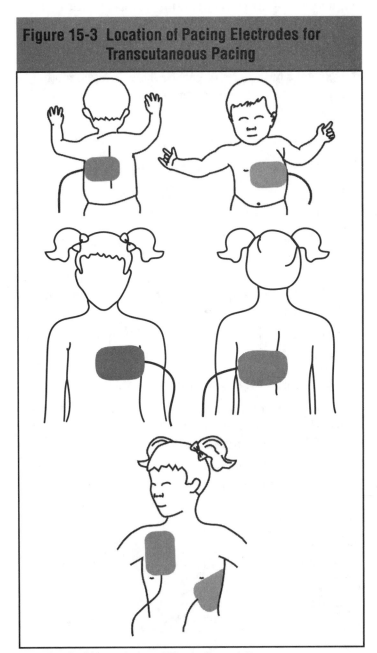

Figure 15-3 Location of Pacing Electrodes for Transcutaneous Pacing

Reprinted with permission of Physio-Control, Inc.

Sinus Tachycardia

Figure 15-4 provides an example of sinus tachycardia (ST).

Additional Patient History

- Fever
- Pain
- Recent volume loss (trauma or illness)
- Intake of caffeinated/energy beverages
- Congenital heart disease (CHD)
- Excessive crying or agitation

Signs and Symptoms of Sinus Tachycardia

- Rapid and possible thready peripheral pulses
- Possible increased work of breathing/crying
- Delayed capillary refill, pale/cool extremities, mottled skin, and decreased blood pressure
- Dry mucous membranes
- Decreased number of wet diapers
- Increased stool/diarrhea or vomiting
- Rapid HR (with beat-to-beat variability)
  - Does NOT have an abrupt onset.
  - Rate is normally less than 220 beats per minute in infants and less than 180 beats per minute in children.
  - If the rate exceeds these values, consider supraventricular tachycardia (SVT), especially if there is no beat-to-beat variability.
  - The QRS complex is narrow with P waves that are present.

Interventions for Sinus Tachycardia

- Support the ABCs as needed. If there are signs of poor perfusion and pulses are not palpable, proceed with the PALS Pulseless Arrest Algorithm.[10]
- Search for and treat reversible causes (e.g., antipyretic for fever, pain relief measures for pain, fluids for shock).[10] Refer to **Chapter 14, "Shock,"** for further guidance.

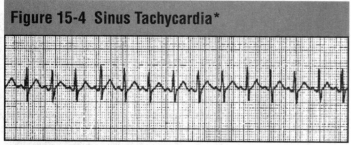

Figure 15-4 Sinus Tachycardia*

*Reprinted from Andreoli, K. G. (1971). *Comprehensive cardiac care* (2nd ed.). St. Louis, MO: Mosby.

- Obtain blood for laboratory studies, as indicated by the patient's medical history and condition.
- Obtain a urine specimen; if infection is suspected, consider obtaining a specimen via catheter and sending for culture and sensitivity analysis.
- Offer fluids by mouth ONLY if appropriate and the child is not obtunded.
- Monitor and maintain a normal body temperature.

Supraventricular Tachydysrhythmias

Figure 15-5 provides an example of supraventricular tachycardia (SVT).

Supraventricular tachycardia is one of the most common tachydysrhythmias that produces cardiovascular compromise during infancy.[14] Supraventricular tachycardia is characterized by the following features:

- A rate greater than 220 beats per minute in infants and greater than 180 beats per minute in children.
- Regularity (i.e., does not vary with the child's agitation or crying).
- P waves, which are difficult to distinguish, as they may be hidden in the QRS complex.

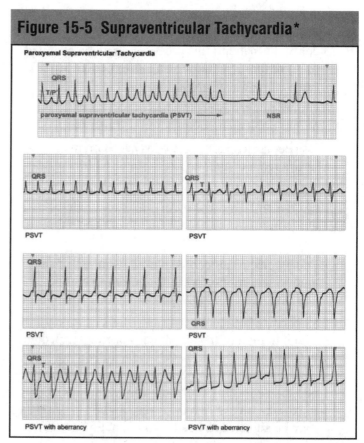

Figure 15-5 Supraventricular Tachycardia*

*Reprinted from Huszar, R. J. (2002). *Basic dysrhythmias: Interpretation & management* (3rd ed.). St. Louis, MO: Mosby/Elsevier.

- QRS complexes, which are narrow and regular, with no beat-to-beat variability.
- It is common for this rhythm to be so rapid that the patient will become symptomatic. These symptoms are the result of decreases in diastolic filling time, resulting in a marked decrease in cardiac output.

Additional Patient History

- History of previous episodes of SVT or Wolff-Parkinson-White syndrome
- History of congenital heart disease
- Poor feeding
- History is important in discriminating SVT from sinus tachycardia (the origin of SVT is usually vague)

Signs and Symptoms of SVT

- Pale (may be cyanotic or may have mottled skin)
- Hypotension
- Signs of poor perfusion (faint or absent peripheral pulses or delayed capillary refill)
- Altered level of consciousness
- Irritability
- Heart rate too fast to count (usually > 220 beats per minute in infants and > 180 beats per minute in older children)
- May have signs of congestive heart failure (crackles or enlarged liver)

Interventions for SVT

The choice of therapy is determined by the degree of hemodynamic instability.[10]

- Attempt vagal stimulation:
  - In infants and small children apply ice to the face for 10 to 15 seconds. Caution should be taken to not obstruct the mouth and nose.[10]
    - Alternatively the insertion of a rectal thermometer may stimulate the vagal response.
  - In older pediatric patients, consider vagal maneuvers such as:
    - Coughing
    - Bearing down as if they are having a bowel movement
    - Trying to blow through an obstructed straw
    - Carotid sinus massage[10]
- The ABCs: Provide adequate oxygenation and ventilation and obtain intravenous access (the antecubital site is preferred because of its proximity to the heart).

- If asymptomatic, closely monitor and consult a pediatric cardiologist.
- If the pediatric patient is showing signs of poor perfusion, the rhythm must be promptly treated with adenosine (Adenocard), if intravenous access is readily available.
- Adenosine (Adenocard) is the medication of choice for SVT in stable patients.
  - Before administration, ensure that a continuous electrocardiogram is being run to document the patient's rhythm changes.
  - Adenosine (Adenocard) must be given rapidly at the port closest to the infusion site and followed immediately by a rapid normal saline flush of at least 5 mL. (Use a two-syringe technique.) Adenosine may also be given IO, if that is the only route available.[10]
  - Adenosine (Adenocard) MUST be used with caution in children with heart transplants.
  - Higher doses of adenosine (Adenocard) may be required in patients receiving theophylline or caffeine because both of these medications can decrease the effects of adenosine.
- Verapamil may be used in older pediatric patients, but should NOT be used in infants without expert consultation as it may cause myocardial depression, hypotension and cardiac arrest.[10]
- If the pediatric patient is unstable, with poor perfusion and hypotension, or if adenosine is ineffective, synchronized cardioversion must be initiated. The procedure for synchronized cardioversion is similar to defibrillation, with the following important differences:
  - The defibrillator/cardiac monitor must be set on the synchronized mode. This is to avoid delivery of energy during the relative refractory portion of the cardiac electrical cycle.
  - The initial dose is delivered with 0.5 to 1 Joules/kg (J/kg), and repeat doses are delivered with 2 Joules/kg.[10]
  - Paddle/pad discharge buttons must be held down until the electrical current has been delivered.
  - Consider sedation before synchronized cardioversion.
  - If the second shock is unsuccessful or tachycardia recurs quickly, amiodarone or procainamide may be considered prior to a third shock. Expert consultation is strongly recommended in this instance.[10]

Ventricular Tachycardia

Ventricular tachycardia (VT) is uncommon in pediatric patients and, in this population, may be secondary to underlying congenital heart disease, prolonged QT syndrome, or myocarditis/cardiomyopathy. Ventricular tachycardia has a regular rate greater than 120 beats per minute, with a wide QRS complex, a tombstone-like appearance, and no P waves identified.

Figure 15-6 provides an example of ventricular tachycardia.

Additional Patient History

- Structural/congenital heart disease
- Myocarditis/cardiomyopathy
- Prolonged QT syndrome
- Suspected overdose (e.g., tricyclic antidepressants and cocaine)
- Electrolyte imbalance (e.g., hyperkalemia, hypocalcemia, and hypomagnesemia)

Signs and Symptoms of Ventricular Tachycardia

- Symptoms of poor perfusion (delayed capillary refill, cool/clammy skin, decreased or absent peripheral pulses, and change in level of consciousness)
- Ventricular rate of at least 120 beats per minute and regular[14]
- Wide QRS complex (> 0.09 seconds), tombstone-like appearance, and no atrial activity
- May or may not have palpable pulses
- Palpitations
- Increased work of breathing
- Hypotension secondary to the ventricles not filling adequately and pumping blood normally
- Sustained VT can worsen until it deteriorates into ventricular fibrillation

Treatment of VT with a Pulse

- If VT is present in an awake pediatric patient with a pulse and adequate perfusion, an immediate consultation with an expert in pediatric arrhythmias is strongly recommended before treating children who are hemodynamically stable.[10]
- Support the airway and provide adequate oxygenation/ventilation; the method chosen, either a nasal cannula or nonrebreather mask, can be determined by the patient's condition.
- Obtain an electrocardiogram.
- Establish venous access.

- Consider synchronized cardioversion with a biphasic (preferred) or monophasic defibrillator with 0.5–1 Joules/kg. Sedate the patient prior to cardioversion.
- Consider the use of the following agents:
  - Adenosine (Adenocard) IV if rhythm is regular and QRS is monomorphic
  - Amiodarone (Cordarone) intravenously
  - Procainamide (Pronestyl) intravenously

Treatment of VT Without a Pulse

Treat the patient the same as you would for a diagnosis of ventricular fibrillation. The treatment can be found in the following section on "Ventricular Fibrillation." If torsades de pointes is identified, treat with a rapid (over several minutes) IV infusion of magnesium sulfate.[10]

Ventricular Fibrillation

Ventricular fibrillation (**Figure 15-7**) and pulseless VT are not common dysrhythmias in the pediatric population; however, they do occur. Management is different from the adult patient in that defibrillation is administered at a lower setting using appropriately sized paddles/pads. As previously mentioned, it is important to follow all manufacturers' guidelines when using equipment and supplies.

Additional Patient History

- Electrocution
- Recent viral illness

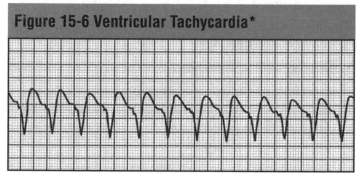

Figure 15-6 Ventricular Tachycardia*

*Reprinted from Urden, L. D., Stacy, K. M., & Lough, M. E. (2009). *Critical care nursing: Diagnosis and management* (6th ed.). St. Louis, MO: Mosby/Elsevier.

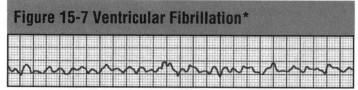

Figure 15-7 Ventricular Fibrillation*

*Reprinted from Urden, L. D., Stacy, K. M., & Lough, M. E. (2009). *Critical care nursing: Diagnosis and management* (6th ed.). St. Louis, MO: Mosby/Elsevier.

- History of cardiac surgery or heart transplantation
- Ingestion of a toxic substance
- Blunt impact to the chest, especially in sports

Signs and Symptoms of Ventricular Fibrillation

- Unresponsive, gray-colored pediatric patient with a prolonged capillary refill
- Because the ventricles are not pumping, there is an absence of palpable pulses
- Chaotic and wavy lines, with no discernable P or T waves or QRS.

Interventions for Ventricular Fibrillation/ Pulseless Ventricular Tachycardia[14]

If ventricular fibrillation or pulseless VT is present in a pediatric patient, the following interventions must be immediately initiated along with prompt defibrillation:

- Whenever a pediatric patient is noted to be unresponsive and not breathing, begin compressions. Kleinman et al., state, "Throughout resuscitation, emphasis should be placed on provision of high quality CPR (Providing chest compressions of adequate rate and depth, allowing complete chest recoil after each compression, minimizing interruptions in compressions and avoiding excessive ventilation)."[10]
- Begin cardiac compressions: high-quality CPR is critical. Follow current American Heart Association guidelines for CPR in infants and children.
- Provide adequate oxygenation/ventilation.
- Defibrillate with a biphasic or monophasic defibrillator with 2 to 4 Joules/kg.
- Immediately resume compressions.
  ○ Provide high-quality CPR for two minutes.
- Recheck rhythm: if continuous VF or pulseless VT, defibrillate with 4 Joules/kg.
- Immediately resume compressions.
  ○ Provide high-quality CPR for two minutes.
- Give epinephrine 1:10,000 intravenous or utilize epinephrine 1:1,000 via the endotracheal tube only **IF** the intravenous or IO route is not available. Repeat epinephrine every three to five minutes.
- If there is no change, defibrillate with 4 Joules/kg.
  ○ Immediately resume compressions.
  ○ Provide high-quality CPR for two minutes.

- ○ Consider an advanced airway. Do not delay compressions for placement of the airway.
- If there is still no change, consider amiodarone (Cordarone) given via intravenous or intraosseous routes at 5mg/kg or Lidocaine @ 1mg/kg. May be repeated up to two times. Amiodarone cannot be given endotracheally.
- Subsequent shocks should be administered at minimum of 4 Joules/kg. A maximum of 10 Joules/kg or the adult dose may be administered.[10]
- Consider family presence during the resuscitation, with an assigned staff member present at all times to stay with the family.
- Consider termination after extended CPR, with no response.

Pulseless Electrical Activity

Pulseless electrical activity (PEA) is a display of organized electrical activity on the cardiac monitor (most commonly slow, wide QRS complexes) that does not produce a palpable pulse. The electrical activity that can be seen on the monitor is too weak to produce an arterial pressure that can be detected by manually palpating peripheral or central pulses. It is critical that this dysrhythmia be identified early and treated before it degenerates to asystole.

Signs and Symptoms of Pulseless Electrical Activity

- Electrical activity on the cardiac monitor (usually bradycardia) with no palpable central or peripheral pulses
- Change in the pediatric patient's level of consciousness
- Respiratory distress progressing to failure
- Profound signs of shock: pale/cool skin, delayed capillary refill, and decreased/absent blood pressure

Interventions for Pulseless Electrical Activity[10]

- Begin cardiac compressions, support the airway and provide adequate ventilations.
  ○ High-quality CPR is critical.
- Monitor continuously with defibrillation or pacer pads.
- Initiate intravenous or IO access.
- Administer epinephrine 1:10,000 intravenously or IO (preferred route) or epinephrine 1:1,000 via the endotracheal tube. Repeat every three to five minutes.
- Consider advanced airway. Once airway in place, continue compressions at a rate of at least 100 per minute and deliver ventilations at a rate of one breath every six to eight seconds.

- Consider the reversible causes and treatments (Hs and Ts) (**Table 15-4, page 250**).
  - Hypoxia*: provide adequate ventilation.
  - Hypothermia*: consider warmed fluids, warmed humidified oxygen, blankets, a Bair Hugger, or overhead lights.
  - Hypovolemia*: administer a 20 mL/kg bolus of crystalloid solution, such as normal saline or lactated Ringer's solution.
  - Hypoglycemia*: replace with $D_{10}W$ or $D_{25}W$ (whichever is age/weight appropriate).
  - Hydrogen ion (acidosis)
  - Electrolyte imbalances (especially hypercalcemia/hypocalcemia, hyperkalemia/hypokalemia, and hypermagnesemia/hypomagnesemia).
  - Cardiac tamponade secondary to trauma: assist with pericardiocentesis. (**Chapter 16, "Trauma,"** has more information.)
  - Tension pneumothorax: assist with needle thoracentesis.
  - Toxins/poisons: treat the patient, then the toxin, if known.
  - Thromboembolism.

Note: These are the most common contributing factors in pediatric patients.

Asystole

Pediatric cardiopulmonary arrest is uncommon. However, when it does occur, the patient generally has poor outcomes. Asystole usually occurs secondary to prolonged hypoxia and acidosis. Therefore, it is important to recognize and attempt to resolve a pediatric patient's medical problems before the patient reaches this state. Rapid treatment of bradycardia is essential.

Additional Patient History

- Time patient was found pulseless.
- Description of activity before the pulseless event. Time last seen by the caregiver, last feeding, position in crib, and objects in the crib (i.e., blanket, pillows, or stuffed toys).
- Name of the primary caregiver at the time of the event.
- Time basic life support (BLS) was initiated and by whom (i.e., bystanders, law enforcement, or emergency medical services).
- Time advanced life support (ACLS) was initiated.

Signs and Symptoms of Asystole

- Absent electrical activity on the cardiac monitor (flat line) (**Figure 15-8**)
- Apnea
- Signs of profound shock/poor peripheral perfusion
- Absent heart sounds
- No palpable pulses (central and peripheral)

Treatment of Asystole

- Sequence of treatment is the same as that outlined above for pulseless electrical activity.[10]
- The best intervention is prevention!
- Confirm asystole on a cardiac monitor in two leads.
- Consider family presence with an assigned staff member.
- Look for causes and initiate treatment (Hs and Ts) as discussed for pulseless electrical activity.
- The entire team must determine the amount of time they will continue the resuscitative efforts. The total time without a pulse and resuscitative efforts that have occurred must be determined.

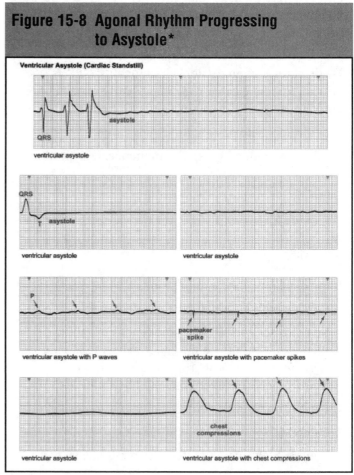

Figure 15-8 Agonal Rhythm Progressing to Asystole*

*Reprinted from Huszar, R. J. (2002). *Basic dysrhythmias: Interpretation & management* (3rd ed.). St. Louis, MO: Mosby/Elsevier.

After Arrest

The 2010 American Heart Association Guidelines state that "The goals of post-resuscitation care are to preserve neurologic function, prevent secondary organ injury, diagnose and treat the cause of illness and enable the patient to arrive at a pediatric tertiary care facility in an optimal physiologic state."[10] Key points include avoiding hyperoxemia, as well as monitoring exhaled CO_2. The reader is referred to these guidelines for an in depth discussion of post–resuscitation care.

Therapeutic hypothermia of 32°C to 34°C may be of benefit to comatose patients after arrest.[10] The European and Australian clinical trials excluded children and cardiopulmonary arrests of noncardiac etiology (e.g., respiratory failure or shock), which are typical in pediatric patients. While there are no randomized studies in the pediatric population regarding the effect of hypothermia, it is known to be of benefit in adults following witnessed out-of-hospital VF arrest and in asphyxiated newborns.[10] The National Heart and Lung Institute is funding a large multicenter study entitled "Therapeutic Hypothermia After Pediatric Cardiac Arrest." This study will evaluate whether regulating body temperature will improve outcomes for children after cardiopulmonary arrest. There is also another study evaluating arrests that occur in pediatric patients in and out of the hospital; the goal of this study is "to determine if therapeutic hypothermia improves survival with good neurobehavioral outcomes in children who have had a cardiac arrest."[15]

Children with Special Healthcare Needs

A pediatric patient with special healthcare needs may require emergency care for such things as obstruction of a tracheostomy, failure of ventilator or disease progression, and events and illnesses that may occur in the lives of all children. Any individual caring for a child with special needs must know how to assess patency of the airway, clear the airway, and replace the tracheostomy tube. In addition, they need to be able to perform CPR using the tracheostomy. If the chest does not rise during ventilation, the tracheostomy tube needs to be suctioned and may need to be replaced. If a clean tube is not available, mouth to stoma or mask to stoma ventilations may be necessary. In children with a patent upper airway, the tracheal stoma may be occluded and ventilation provided via the normal route.[10]

Summary

The evaluation and treatment of pediatric patients with cardiac dysrhythmias require that healthcare providers be skilled in all the basic assessment components. Pediatric patients are able to compensate for decreased CO while exhibiting only subtle signs and symptoms. Shock and respiratory failure are the most common causes of cardiovascular collapse and subsequent cardiopulmonary arrest in the pediatric population. The outcome of cardiopulmonary arrest in the pediatric patient is most frequently death or recovery with poor neurological functioning. Early recognition of the subtle signs and symptoms of cardiac dysrhythmias is essential, along with immediate implementation of appropriate interventions to minimize adverse outcomes.

Appendix 15-A
The Electrocardiogram

Electrocardiogram Basics Reviewed

Before a dysrhythmia can be identified, the learner must first understand the basics of electrocardiograms (ECGs). This technology demonstrates on paper the electrical conduction of the heart. Although the use of technology is an important aspect of patient care, it must not be forgotten that nothing replaces the actual physical assessment/evaluation of the patient in conjunction with the use of any technology.

The three basic complexes of the ECG are the P wave, a QRS complex, and the T wave. The P wave represents actual atrial depolarization; QRS complex, depolarization of the ventricles; and T wave, repolarization of the ventricles (**Figure 15-1**).

Analyzing the Rhythm Strip

The first step is to determine the rate: Is it normal for the child's age, too fast, or too slow? Looking at the distance between the R waves will help in deciding if it is regular or irregular. The next step is to look for the P waves: Are they regular and is there one before each QRS complex? Calculate the PR and QRS intervals: Is this rhythm conducive to life? Is it perfusing adequately for the patient? With this information and the patient assessment data, determine if the patient is stable or in need of immediate resuscitation interventions.

Developmental Changes in the ECG

Changes that occur over childhood account for the differences in ECG interpretation in the pediatric patient. The developmental differences can be seen as follows: gradual decrease in heart rate, gradual lengthening of the PR interval, gradual lengthening of the QRS interval, and shift from right to left ventricle dominance. See Table for normal pediatric ECG intervals.

Normal Pediatric Electrocardiogram Values*

Age	Heart Rate (bpm)	QRS Axis (degrees)	PR Interval (seconds)	QRS Interval (seconds)	R in V1 (mm)	S in V1 (mm)	R in V6 (mm)	S in V6 (mm)
1 week	90–160	60–180	0.08–0.15	0.03–0.08	5–26	0–23	0–12	0–10
1–3 weeks	100–180	45–160	0.08–0.15	0.03–0.08	3–21	0–16	2–16	0–10
1–2 months	120–180	30–135	0.08–0.15	0.03–0.08	3–18	0–15	5–21	0–10
3–5 months	105–185	0–135	0.08–0.15	0.03–0.08	3–20	0–15	6–22	0–10
6–11 months	110–170	0–135	0.07–0.16	0.03–0.08	2–20	0.5–20	6–23	0–7
1–2 years	90–165	0–110	0.08–0.16	0.03–0.08	2–18	0.5–21	6–23	0–7
3–4 years	70–140	0–110	0.09–0.17	0.04–0.08	1–18	0.5–27	4–24	0–5
5–7 years	65–140	0–110	0.09–0.17	0.04–0.08	0.5–14	0.5–24	4–26	0–4
8–11 years	60–130	-15–110	0.09–0.17	0.04–0.09	0–14	0.5–25	4–25	0–4
12–15 years	65–130	-15–110	0.09–0.18	0.04–0.09	0–14	0.5–21	4–25	0–4
> 16 years	50–120	-15–110	0.12–0.20	0.05–0.10	0–14	0.5–23	4–21	0–4

*Courtesy of Ra-id Abdulla, MD

Appendix 15-B Medications and Electrical Therapy Used in PALS for Rhythm Disturbances

Medication	Indications	Precautions
Adenosine (Adenocard)	Medication of choice for treatment of symptomatic SVT in stable patients.	Short half-life (use rapid injection techniques).
Amiodarone (Cordarone)	Wide range of atrial and ventricular arrhythmias and shock-refractory VF/VT.	May cause bradycardia and hypotension, may prolong QT interval and increase risk for polymorphic VT: cannot be given endotracheally and do not routinely combine with other medications that prolong the QT interval (e.g., procainamide).
Atropine sulfate	Vagally induced symptomatic bradycardia; and symptomatic bradycardia, refractory to oxygenation, ventilation, and epinephrine.	Low dose may cause paradoxical bradycardia, and tracheal absorption may be unreliable.
Calcium chloride (10% solution = 27.2 mg/mL of elemental calcium)	Symptomatic hypocalcemia, hyperkalemia, and calcium channel blocker overdose.	Rapid intravenous push may result in bradycardia or asystole, do not mix with buffer, and infiltration may cause skin to slough.
Calcium gluconate (10% solution = 9 mg/mL of elemental calcium)	Symptomatic hypocalcemia, hyperkalemia, and calcium channel blocker overdose.	Rapid intravenous push may result in bradycardia or asystole; do not mix with buffer (infiltration may cause skin to slough).
Synchronized cardioversion attempt	Tachyarrhythmias (SVT, VT, atrial fibrillation, and atrial flutter) with symptoms of cardiovascular compromise.	Activate sync mode and provide sedation with analgesia when possible.
Defibrillation attempt	VF/pulseless VT.	Do not delay and use largest paddle size with good skin contact and no bridging.
Epinephrine for bradycardia	Symptomatic bradycardia refractory to oxygenation and ventilation.	May produce profound vasoconstriction, tachyarrhythmias, and hypertension; do not mix with buffer.
Epinephrine for asystolic or pulseless arrest*	Pulseless arrest (aystole, PEA, shock-refractory VF/VT).	May produce profound vasoconstriction, tachyarrhythmias, and hypertension; do not mix with buffer; and avoid use in cocaine-related VT.
Epinephrine infusion	Refractory hypotension or persistent bradycardia.	May produce profound vasoconstriction, tachyarrhythmias, and hypertension; do not mix with buffer; and avoid use in cocaine-related VT.
Lidocaine bolus*	Alternative treatment for wide-complex tachycardias or VF/pulseless VT.	High dose may cause myocardial depression and seizures; do not use if rhythm is wide-complex bradycardia (ventricular escape beats).
Lidocaine infusion	Alternative for recurrent VT/VF or ventricular ectopy, especially if associated with ischemic heart disease.	High doses may cause myocardial depression and seizures and do not use if rhythm is wide-complex bradycardia (ventricular escape beats).
Magnesium sulfate	Torsades de pointes VT or symptomatic hypomagnesemia.	May cause hypotension with rapid bolus.
Procainamide	Alternative treatment for recurrent or refractory VT and SVT.	Hypotension, bradycardia, and ST prolongation; do not routinely administer with amiodarone.
Sodium bicarbonate	Hyperkalemia, sodium channel blocker toxicity, and severe metabolic acidosis (documented or suspected after prolonged arrest) with adequate ventilation.	Infuse slowly; may produce CO_2; therefore, ventilation must be adequate; do not mix with catecholamines or calcium.

Note: CO_2 indicates carbon dioxide; ECG, electrocardiogram; ETT, endotracheal tube; IO, intraosseous; PALS, pediatric advanced life support; PEA, pulseless electrical activity; ST, sinus tachycardia; SVT, supraventricular tachycardia; VF, ventricular fibrillation; VT, ventricular tachycardia.
*For endotracheal administration, dilute with normal saline to a volume of 3–5 mL and follow up with several positive-pressure ventilations.

References

1. Ojanen, T. D., & Bernado, L. (2009). Cardiovascular emergencies. In *Core curriculum for pediatric emergency nursing* (2nd ed.). Des Plaines, IL: Emergency Nurses Association.

2. Kung, H. C., Hoyert, D. L., Xu, J., & Murphy, S. L. (2008). Deaths: Final data for 2005. *National Vital Statistics Report, 56,* 1–120.

3. Shephard, R., & Semsarian, C. (2009). Advances in the prevention of sudden cardiac death in the young. *Therapeutic Advances in Cardiovascular Disease, 3,* 145–155.

4. Shen, W. K., Edwards, W. D., Hammill, S. C., Bailey, K. R., Ballard, D. J., & Gersh, B. J. (1995). Sudden unexpected nontraumatic death in 54 young adults: a 30-year population-based study. *American Journal of Cardiology, 76,* 148–152.

5. Maron, B. J., Doerer, J. J., Has, T. S., Tierney, D. M., & Mueller, F. O. (2006). Profile and frequency of sudden death in 1463 young competitive athletes: From a 25 year US national registry: 1980-2005. *Circulation, 114,* 830.

6. Maron, B. J., Shirani, J., Poliac, L. C., Mathenge, R., Roberts, W. C., & Mueller, F. O. (1996). Sudden death in young competitive athletes: Clinical, demographic and pathological profiles. *JAMA: The Journal of the American Medical Association, 276,* 199–204.

7. Maron, B. J., Thompson, P. D., Ackerman, M. J., Balady, G., Berger, S., Cohen, D., ... Puffer, J. C.; American Heart Association Council on Nutrition, Physical Activity, and Metabolism. (2007). Recommendations and considerations related to preparticipation screening for cardiovascular abnormalities in competitive athletes: 2007 update: A scientific statement from the American Heart Association Council on Nutrition, Physical Activity, and Metabolism: Endorsed by the American College of Cardiology Foundation. *Circulation, 115,* 1643–1655.

8. Maron, B. J. (2003). Sudden death in young athletes. *New England Journal of Medicine, 349,* 1064–1075.

9. Berger, S., Kugler, J. D., Thomas, J. A., Friedberg, D. Z. (2004). Sudden cardiac death in children and adolescents: Introduction and overview. Pediatric Clinics of North America, 51, 1201–1209.

10. Kleinman, M.E., Chameides, L., Schexnayder, S.M., Samson, R.A., Hazinski, M.F., Atkins, D.L., ... Zaritsky, A.L. (2010) Part 14: pediatric advanced life support: 2010 American Heart Association Guidelines for Cardiopulmonary Resuscitation and Emergency Cardiovascular Care. *Circulation, 122* (Suppl 3), S876–S908.

11. Siddiqui, S., & Patel, D. (2010). Cardiovascular screening of adolescent athletes. *Pediatric Clinics of North America, 57*(3), 635–647.

12. *National Marfan Organization.* (n.d.). Retrieved from http://www.marfan.org/marfan/2493/Children-and-Teens/.

13. American Heart Association. (n.d.). *Long QT.* Retrieved from http://www.americanheart.org/presenter.jhtml?identifier=993.

14. American Heart Association. (2011). *Pediatric advanced life support (provider manual).* Dallas TX: Author.

15. University of Utah School of Medicine. (n.d.). *Therapeutic hypothermia after pediatric cardiac arrest.* Retrieved from http://clinicaltrials.gov/ct2/show/NCT00880087?term=Therapeutic+Hypothermia+after+Pediatric+Cardiac+arrest&rank=1

Chapter 16 | Trauma

Nancy Denke, MSN, RN, FNP-C, ACNP-BC, FAEN

Objectives

On completion of this chapter, the learner should be able to do the following:

- Determine anatomical, physiological, and developmental characteristics of pediatric patients as a basis for assessment of trauma.
- Describe common mechanisms of injury associated with pediatric trauma patients.
- Plan appropriate interventions for pediatric trauma patients.
- Indicate health promotion strategies related to trauma care and injury prevention.

Introduction

Trauma has a greater impact on morbidity and mortality than all other complaints in the pediatric population. Of all injury-related deaths in children younger than 19 years, 65 % are unintentional. Unintentional injury is the number one killer of people aged one to 24 years.[1] Approximately 20,000 deaths of those children who are killed each year are the result of preventable injuries, such as drownings, fires and burns, and motor vehicle crashes.[2] There are several factors that influence who is injured, with age, time of day, and sex being the most important factors for patterns of injury.[1] According to the CDC, "[d]uring 2008 in the United States, 968 children ages 14 years and younger died as occupants in motor vehicle crashes, and approximately 168,000 were injured … In 2008, about 3,500 teens in the United States aged 15–19 were killed and more than 350,000 were treated in emergency departments for injuries suffered in motor-vehicle crashes."[1] In Europe, unintentional injury is the leading cause of death among children and adolescents aged five to 19 years.[3] In Europe, traffic incidents are the major cause of fatalities (approximately 47%), whereas falls are the leading cause of the burden of injuries in children younger than 15 years and the most common cause of mortality and morbidity among young children.[4]

Fires and burns are the fifth leading cause of unintentional injury–related death among children aged 14 and younger.[1] Most burn-related injuries occur at home and are considered preventable. Young children have less perception of danger and less ability to escape a burning situation on their own. Even though the number of deaths because of fire and burn injuries has declined during the past decade, many of these deaths are preventable. Approximately four of 10 home fire–related deaths occur in homes without smoke alarms.[5] Children with special healthcare needs and mobility impairments, slow or awkward movements, muscle weakness or fatigue, or slower reflexes increase the risk of spills while moving hot liquids and the ability to escape a fire.[6]

Timely access to a pediatric trauma center is essential to halt the anatomical and physiological cascade of events associated with severe trauma. In a study performed by Nance et al. in 2009,[7] a total of 170 unique pediatric trauma centers were found in the United States. This access to care did increase when the child involved in trauma had access to air transportation; however, there were still an estimated 17.4 million children who did not reach a pediatric trauma center within 60 minutes.[7] The Institute of Medicine has strongly advocated for coordination, regionalization, and accountability in its vision of pediatric emergency and trauma care.[8]

Anatomical, Physiological, and Developmental Characteristics as a Basis for Signs and Symptoms

The mechanisms of injury are influenced by developmental milestones in a pediatric patient's development, thus practical knowledge of pediatric anatomy, physiology, and the patient's response to injury is of utmost importance in treating the traumatized child. Inherent in this process is the recognition of the distinct anatomical and physiological characteristics of the pediatric patient.[9]

Cardiovascular Characteristics

- Pediatric patients have a healthy cardiovascular system and the physiological ability to initially compensate for hypovolemia by vasoconstriction and tachycardia. By increasing their heart rate, pediatric patients can increase their cardiac output. They have little ability to increase their stroke volume.

- Hypotension related to hypovolemia in pediatric trauma patients is a late sign and may indicate a loss of at least 20% to 25% of their circulating blood volume.

- Pediatric patients have a greater body surface area in proportion to their body weight and a higher extracellular to intracellular fluid volume ratio; they will require proportionally more fluid during resuscitation.

- Young children also require maintenance fluids, which are not usually accounted for in most burn resuscitation formulas.

Respiratory Characteristics

- The faster respiratory rate in pediatric patients contributes to greater insensible pulmonary fluid loss.

  ○ In closed-space fires, this increased respiratory rate may lead to increased uptake of toxic gases. Most pediatric victims of closed-space fires (70%) die as a result of inhalation of toxic gases, such as carbon monoxide and cyanide, rather than burns.[10]

- Pediatric patients have smaller airways. The inhalation of irritants and heated air may cause edema, resulting in a decreased airway diameter. This leads to a greater resistance to airflow and more pronounced signs of respiratory distress. Interstitial fluid shifts occurring with major burns may also result in airway edema without inhalation injury.

Temperature Regulation

- Pediatric patients have a less mature thermal regulatory mechanism.

- Pediatric patients are susceptible to heat loss as the result of a high ratio of body surface area to body mass, a large head in proportion to the rest of the body, and a small amount of subcutaneous tissue.

- Hypothermia can impede the child's response to resuscitative measures.

- Factors that can lead to hypothermia in the pediatric trauma patient include the following:

  ○ Prehospital environmental exposures

  ○ Uncovering the patient for even a short period

  ○ Cool ambient temperature of emergency vehicles and trauma rooms

  ○ Wet or moist dressings

  ○ Clothing saturated with blood, secretions, vomitus, perspiration, or other causes

- Young children have thinner skin, resulting in deeper burns than adults for the same temperature and exposure time to a scalding substance.[6]

  ○ Young children can sustain significant burn injuries from exposure to less heat.

Other Anatomical and Physiological Characteristics

- The head is large and heavy, and the neck muscles are weak, predisposing the pediatric patient to head and neck trauma. (Remember that the head is proportionally larger than the rest of the body until the child is aged six to eight years).

- The cranium is thinner and more pliable in young children, with the scalp being vascular.

- In a child, a round protuberant abdomen, immature abdominal muscles, a rib cage sitting higher in the abdominal cavity, and a small pelvis offer little protection to the underlying solid and hollow abdominal organs. The solid organs and the kidneys are also larger and less protected. Therefore, abdominal organs are prone to injury.

- The sigmoid and ascending colon are not fully attached in the peritoneal cavity and, therefore, are more prone to deceleration injuries.

- The rib cage is flexible, with a softer and thinner chest wall, allowing for an increase in compliance; this makes children less effective at energy dissipation. The ribs are also oriented horizontally, and therefore are less effective at protecting the upper abdominal structures and lungs.

- Disruption of the integumentary system as a protective barrier predisposes the child to infection or sepsis.

- Hypoglycemia is common in children; therefore, it is important to monitor blood glucose routinely, especially in the burn and trauma patient.

Developmental Characteristics

- Pediatric patients are easily distracted and impulsive, have little concept of cause and effect, and lack experience with similar situations.

- Pediatric patients have difficulty determining the speed or distance of an oncoming vehicle.

- It is often difficult for pediatric patients to localize sound, and their visual field tends to focus on a single object similar to their own height.

- They often believe that because they see the car, the driver must see them.

- Young children have little understanding of cause and effect and do not always realize the consequences of their actions.

Causes, Types, Mechanisms, and Patterns of Injury in Children

Blunt Injuries

Most pediatric trauma occurs as a result of blunt trauma. Injury occurs by blunt trauma first to the outer skin and soft tissue and then to the underlying structures. This is generally caused by motor vehicle collisions, falls, or direct blows. A cautious evaluation with a high index of suspicion for intra-abdominal injury is required for all children with blunt trauma. There is a 1% delay of diagnosis as the result of blunt trauma, and the more severely injured patients are at greatest risk for missed injuries.[11]

Motor Vehicle Crashes

The most trauma-related deaths in pediatric patients are the result of motor vehicle crashes. During a motor vehicle crash, three separate collisions occur: (1) the vehicle strikes another object, (2) the body collides with something in the vehicle, and (3) the organs strike other organs, muscle, bone, or supporting structures. A fourth collision can occur if there are loose objects in the vehicle that become projectile forces.

Head trauma is a common injury for unrestrained children involved in a motor vehicle crash. Until the age of six or eight years, the head is significantly larger in proportion to

the remainder of the child's body. When involved in a motor vehicle crash, the unrestrained child's large head acts like a missile, leading the torso throughout the vehicle cabin. In a front-end crash with a speed of 30 miles per hour, an unrestrained child will hit the dashboard with the same force as the impact received after falling three stories to a solid surface. Although mechanisms of pediatric injury vary, the most common part of the child's body that comes in contact with an unyielding object is the head.

All states within the United States have mandated the use of car seats for young children. Regardless of geographic region, compliance and proper use of pediatric safety restraint devices continues to be a problem. Participation in safety restraint education programs is important for all healthcare workers who care for children. Improper use of restraint systems can also lead to injury. These patterns of injury vary by the child's size, location in the vehicle, and type and method of restraint used. The infant has a higher center of gravity. During a motor vehicle crash, infants have a greater risk of cervical fracture at the level of C-1 to C-3 when in a safety restraint seat that is positioned facing forward or in the front seat of the vehicle. Placing the infant in a rear-facing restraint seat, secured in the backseat of the vehicle, can potentially prevent this type of injury by minimizing the fulcrum effect of the infant's head whipping forward.

The use of lap belts in children has been associated with a triad of injuries that include severe flexion-distraction injuries of the lumbar spine, abdominal wall bruising, and hollow viscous injury. Children are prone to lap belt injuries because they often slouch with the belt loose and across the abdomen (rather than the hips). Most abdominal organ injuries sustained by children wearing a lap belt are generated by direct compression of the organ under the belt.[12] The presence of a seat belt sign may have greater usefulness for ruling in potential abdominal injuries rather than excluding them.[13] A booster seat corrects improper restraint position by lifting the child up and forward, allowing better fit of both the lap and the shoulder belts. Recommendations for booster seat use extend to 36 kg or eight years in Canada and to 36 kg or 12 years in the United States and the United Kingdom.[14] However, actual use is low in most countries, and preventable lap belt injuries continue to occur.

Air Bag Injuries

Air bags are standard equipment in all new cars and are designed to supplement the protection provided by safety belts in frontal crashes. Although air bags have a good overall safety record and have saved an estimated 1,200 lives as of the end of 1995, they pose several risks for children. In 2001, the National Highway Traffic Safety Association demonstrated that passenger-side airbags may cause serious injuries and deaths to children seated in the right front seat. The child's height and/or weight did not affect his or her risk of serious injury or death when seated in front of an airbag.[15] Children from birth through the age of 14 years who were seated in the front seat when the airbags did not deploy during crashes were more than six times as likely to sustain serious injury or death than when airbags did deploy.[15] Then, it is reasonable to encourage parents to keep their children in the back seat at least through age 12 years. We must also remember that children in the zone of air bag deployment can sustain facial trauma, upper extremity fracture, intra-abdominal injury, abrasions and chemical irritation of the skin, cervical spine injury, and partial to complete decapitation.

Side air bags in the rear seat are available in a variety of vehicles; advise caregivers to check their vehicle's owner's manual for specific information regarding children and air bags. There is little crash experience of their effect on child occupants. Transport Canada found that rear seat air bags could cause injury (sometimes serious) to out-of-position three- and six-year-old child dummies.[16] Because most children are out of position for portions of any journey, it is wise to avoid rear seat air bags in cars in which children are the intended passengers. US policy is that cars with rear air bags be sold with the bags deactivated, to avoid injury to children.[14] Consult the National Highway Traffic Safety Administration car seat recommendations (**Figure 16-1**).

Pedestrian Injuries

Common injuries in pediatric pedestrians are to the head, face, torso, and long bones.

Figure 16-1 Car Seat Recommendations

Car Seat Recommendations for Children

○ Select a car seat based on your child's age and size, and choose a seat that fits in your vehicle and use it every time.

○ Always refer to your specific car seat manufacturer's instructions; read the vehicle owner's manual on how to install the car seat using the seat belt or LATCH system; and check height and weight limits.

○ To maximize safety, keep your child in the car seat for as long as possible, as long as the child fits within the manufacturer's height and weight requirements.

○ Keep your child in the back seat at least through age 12.

AGE

 Birth – 12 months
Your child under age 1 should always ride in a rear-facing car seat.
There are different types of rear-facing car seats: Infant-only seats can only be used rear-facing. Convertible and 3-in-1 car seats typically have higher height and weight limits for the rear-facing position, allowing you to keep your child rear-facing for a longer period of time.

 1 – 3 years
Keep your child rear-facing as long as possible. It's the best way to keep him or her safe. Your child should remain in a rear-facing car seat until he or she reaches the top height or weight limit allowed by your car seat's manufacturer. Once your child outgrows the rear-facing car seat, your child is ready to travel in a forward-facing car seat with a harness.

 4 – 7 years
Keep your child in a forward-facing car seat with a harness until he or she reaches the top height or weight limit allowed by your car seat's manufacturer. Once your child outgrows the forward-facing car seat with a harness, it's time to travel in a booster seat, but still in the back seat.

 8 – 12 years
Keep your child in a booster seat until he or she is big enough to fit in a seat belt properly. For a seat belt to fit properly the lap belt must lie snugly across the upper thighs, not the stomach. The shoulder belt should lie snug across the shoulder and chest and not cross the neck or face. Remember: your child should still ride in the back seat because it's safer there.

DESCRIPTION (RESTRAINT TYPE)

A **REAR-FACING CAR SEAT** is the best seat for your young child to use. It has a harness and in a crash, cradles and moves with your child to reduce the stress to the child's fragile neck and spinal cord.

A **FORWARD-FACING CAR SEAT** has a harness and tether that limits your child's forward movement during a crash.

A **BOOSTER SEAT** positions the seat belt so that it fits properly over the stronger parts of your child's body.

A **SEAT BELT** should lie across the upper thighs and be snug across the shoulder and chest to restrain the child safely in a crash. It should not rest on the stomach area or across the neck.

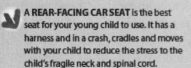 www.facebook.com/childpassengersafety

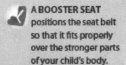 http://twitter.com/childseatsafety

March 21, 2011

Preschool-aged children may be injured when they play around parked cars and run across the street. Pedestrians who are struck by automobiles often have one or more injuries.[17] The biomechanics of the child pedestrian who is struck by a vehicle include the following:[18]

- Classically, an injury occurs as the child hits the vehicle and is thrown away from the vehicle.

- The child's physical size and the type of vehicle involved are the two factors that most affect the pattern of injuries sustained.

- Waddell's triad, a commonly taught pattern of injury, has been studied and found that in pediatric pedestrian versus automobile collisions, the pattern of injuries including the head, chest or abdomen and lower extremities is not common in pediatric patients, although these injuries are common separately.[19]

- Toddlers and preschoolers may be knocked down and dragged under the vehicle. The vehicle's front bumper may cause chest, abdomen, pelvic, or femur injuries.

- Older preschool and school-aged children may sustain femur fractures from the bumper and chest injuries from the hood.

- If the child is thrown onto the hood of the vehicle and strikes the windshield, head and facial injuries may occur. When the car decelerates or stops, the child slides or rolls to the street, usually striking his or her head on the pavement.

Children struck by motor vehicles are at high risk for multi-system injury. The pattern of injury sustained is dependent on the relationship among variables, such as the speed of the vehicle, the point of initial impact, additional points of impact, the child's height and weight, and landing surfaces. A thorough trauma assessment is essential to identify all injuries.

Falls

Falls account for greater than one-third of childhood injuries requiring medical evaluation. The factors that contribute to the injuries sustained from a fall include the following: (1) the velocity of the fall, (2) the child's body orientation at impact, (3) the type of impact surface, and (4) the time that the force is applied to the body on impact. In early childhood, children are prone to falls because of their higher center of gravity, increased mobility, and a limited perception of danger.

- Infants more commonly sustain falls from low objects, such as high chairs, baby walkers, shopping carts, countertops, changing tables, beds, and tables.

- Toddlers and preschoolers sustain falls from low objects and falls from heights, such as windows, balconies, and stairs.

- The school-aged child is often involved in a fall related to sports or recreational activities, such as tree climbing, bicycling, playground equipment, skating, and organized sporting activities.

Recreational Injuries

Injuries related to sports are responsible for a significant number of emergency department (ED) visits. Those sports responsible for the highest number of emergency visits are basketball, biking, football, baseball, skating (ice, roller, and skateboarding), softball, and soccer. The injuries that occur from these sports include extremity injuries, fractures, sprains and strains, head trauma, abdominal injury as the result of collision (particularly in football and soccer), and spinal cord or vertebral column injury; they require a high index of suspicion by the clinician.

Biking has become a popular sport among children and adults. The most common injury related to bicycle incidents is head injury. An estimated 140,000 children are treated each year in EDs for head injuries sustained while bicycling. This includes skull fractures, concussions, and subdural hematomas. The use of bicycle helmets has reduced the mortality related to bicycle incidents; however, compliance with wearing a helmet is reported at only 5%.[20] Not only is compliance important in helmet use, but the condition and fit of the helmet are just as important. Although the use of helmets during well visits was high, most patients did not have helmets that were in reasonable condition or that fit properly.[21] Abdomen to handlebar trauma is associated with pancreatic injury, small-bowel injury, and solid organ injury.[22] Although they are seemingly harmless incidents, direct impact on the handlebars may result in more severe injuries than flipping over them. Skateboard injuries account for approximately 50,000 ED visits each year, and they have been linked to an increase in extremity and head injuries.[23] Of these injuries, 74% involved injuries to an extremity (ankle or wrist) and 21% were injuries to the head (face) or neck.[23] Younger children more commonly sustain head trauma because of their higher center of gravity and limited ability to break the fall. Older children usually sustain extremity trauma as they try to break their fall. Deaths from skateboarding injuries are rare but most often result from the child colliding with a motor vehicle or "skitching a ride" (holding onto the side or rear of a moving vehicle while riding a skateboard). Nonpowered lightweight scooters have become popular and result in similar injuries to those sustained by skateboards.

Snowboarding and skiing are popular in many areas of the world. The injuries associated with these sports are brain injuries (most common) and chest, spine, and extremity injuries. Most of these injuries were sustained because of falls or collisions with natural objects.[24]

Trampolines have become popular and are a source of traumatic injuries in children. The injury rate was continuously growing from 2005 to 2007 (10.6%–58.1%).[25] Most trampoline-related injuries occur on home trampolines when children land incorrectly while jumping or performing stunts. Other injuries occur when children fall from the trampoline to the surface below or collide with another person on the equipment.

The use of all-terrain vehicles (and utility vehicles) and golf carts are other recreational activities with a growing number of injuries annually. This is generally because users do not follow manufacturer's recommendations (i.e., operator should be aged ≥ 16 years) and lack of helmet laws.

Sports and Minor Traumatic Brain Injury

The growing concern of concussions sustained by adolescent athletes and how they are underestimated, misdiagnosed, and managed has gained national media attention.[26] According to the Centers for Disease Control and Prevention, there are "as many as 3.8 million sports-recreation-related concussions estimated to occur in the United States each year."[27] Sports injuries occur most frequently during activities such as basketball, football, wrestling, ice hockey, lacrosse, volleyball, soccer, and baseball/softball because of the high incidence of collisions and vigorous body contact. Many of these injuries are preventable by just being aware of the common causes, including the following:[28]

- Inferior protective equipment
- Inexperienced or ill-advised coaching
- Infractions of rules
- Incompetent officiating
- Insufficient physical conditioning

Regardless of the preventative measures taken, some injuries are inevitable because of the nature of some sports. Optimum safeguards for young athletes must include attention to the recognition, assessment, and treatment of any injury or illness.[28]

Adolescents are particularly at high risk for mild traumatic brain (mTBI) injury while playing sports for a variety of reasons, including the following:[28]

- Young athletes develop at varied rates and physical strength.
- Young athletes are impatient about restrictions on activities, even when restrictions are necessary for healing injuries.
- Many young athletes are disinterested and indifferent about the fitting, adjustment, and care of their protective equipment and may not wear it appropriately.

- Most young athletes participate in sports sponsored by schools or community recreational programs and may not have the benefit of supervision and advice from an athletic trainer who is educated about the physical and cognitive abilities of adolescents across all levels.

Concussions or mild traumatic brain injuries may not be reported for numerous reasons: fear of letting down parents/ coaches, the adolescent "did not think the injury was serious enough to warrant reporting it," not wanting to be withheld from competition, and even not aware that the symptoms that he or she is having were because of a concussion. Many athletes do not understand the consequences of failing to report these injuries and the long-term and even catastrophic consequences that may occur.[26]

The consequences of concussions can be immediate, leaving the athlete with cognitive impairments, including slowed reaction times and attention and memory difficulties. An athlete who returns to play before symptoms of a concussion are completely resolved is at risk for the life-threatening condition known as second impact syndrome. A second blow to the head, even a minor one, can result in sudden loss of autoregulation of the brain's blood supply, leading to hemorrhage and herniation of the brain, which is usually fatal.[29]

An adolescent's brain is sensitive. Education of athletes, coaches, and parents to better understand the signs and symptoms of a concussion is the key to prevention of further injury. Athletes should NEVER be able to return to the playing field on the same day that they are injured. An athlete must be symptom free of the effects of a concussion or traumatic brain injury while at rest before resuming any type of exercise or sports activity. The resumption of sports activities must be done incrementally, as outlined in the Centers for Disease Control and Prevention's *Heads Up* program.[27]

What to do if you suspect the player has sustained a concussion:[26]

- Remove the athlete from play.
- Ask if the player has had a previous concussion.
- Ensure that the athlete is evaluated by a healthcare provider that is knowledgeable about mTBI.
- Educate the player, teammates, coaches, parents, and trainers about the signs and symptoms of a concussion.
- Remind the athlete that it is better to miss one game than the entire season.
- Return to play must be gradual and incremental, monitoring for symptoms and stopping to rest if symptoms re-emerge.

- Allow the athlete to only return to play when he or she has been cleared by a medical professional.

Asphyxiation and Submersion Injuries

Asphyxiation

Asphyxiation and suffocation are among the leading causes of death in children because of inhalation injuries during a fire, mechanical suffocation, foreign body obstruction or inhalation, or hangings. In addition to the hypoxia sustained during a hanging injury, the child may also sustain a spinal cord injury, a cerebral injury, laryngeal edema, and pulmonary edema. Vertebral injury is uncommon in hanging incidents.

Submersion

More than 1,500 children die in the United States each year from submersion injuries.[30] Submersion injury is a common cause of death in the pediatric patient. Drowning occurs when a pediatric patient is submerged and then attempts to breathe and either aspirates water or has a laryngospasm, leading to hypoxemia and neuronal death. Submersion injury is not isolated to pools and ponds (commonly seen in those aged one to five years), but it may include bathtubs, buckets, or water that is greater than one to two inches in depth, especially in young toddlers.[31] In young adults aged 15 to 19 years, submersion injuries occur in ponds, lakes, and rivers and are frequently associated with alcohol. Males experience submersion four times more often than females.[32]

Near drowning is defined as survival or temporary survival after asphyxia as the result of a submersion episode.[32] The major reason for death in a near drowning is because of hypoxemia and the decrease in oxygen delivery to vital tissues. Immersion in water with ice is associated with a better outcome than prolonged immersion in warm or cold (without ice) water. The length of time the pediatric patient is submerged and the water quality will affect the length of resuscitation and the outcome.

One of the most important signs seen in these victims is hypovolemia, which is the result of a decrease in capillary permeability from hypoxia and loss of fluid in the intravascular space. Other signs and symptoms may be delayed in onset and are associated with cerebral hypoxia and pulmonary injury. These may vary in severity from minimal or no symptoms to cardiopulmonary arrest.

Penetrating Injury

Firearm injuries represent the fifth leading cause of death in the United States for children younger than 14 years and 22.5% of all injury-related deaths in children and adolescents aged one to 19 years.[32] Penetrating trauma caused by stabbings, firearms, and blast injuries represents approximately 12% to 13% of the trauma-related mortality in children.[33]

The injuries sustained from a penetrating force will depend on the location of the impact and the type of penetrating object. With firearms, the amount of tissue damage is related to the projectile, mass, shape, fragmentation, type of tissue struck, and striking velocity. The injury sustained from a stabbing is dependent on the length of the instrument, the velocity at which the force was applied, and the angle of entry. Regardless of how one classifies an injury these two mechanisms can be inter-related and your assessment must be thorough with attention to detail.

Initial Assessment of the Pediatric Trauma Patient

Primary Assessment

The primary assessment consists of assessment of the airway with simultaneous stabilization of the cervical spine, breathing, circulation, neurological status, and exposure to environmental control. Interventions to correct any life-threatening conditions are performed before continuing the assessment. **Chapter 5, "Initial Assessment,"** provides a review of a comprehensive primary assessment. Assessment and intervention components unique to the primary assessment of the pediatric trauma patient are delineated in the following section.

Airway with Cervical Spine Stabilization

- Inspect and open/clear the pediatric patient's airway while maintaining cervical spine stabilization. (The jaw thrust or chin lift may be done to manually open the airway and avoid manipulation of the neck.)

  - If the pediatric trauma patient presents to your facility without cervical spinal stabilization and you are unable to perform clearance of the spine before transporting the patient, complete stabilization must be done. Cervical spine stabilization includes holding the head in a neutral position, placing bilateral support devices, and using tape to secure the head and the devices. Do not hyperextend, flex, or rotate the neck during these maneuvers. If immediately available, apply a rigid cervical collar before applying the head supports and tape. The pediatric patient's body movement must be controlled before the head is secured; therefore, begin taping at the feet and maintain manual stabilization of the cervical spine until the head is secured. The tape must extend to the rigid surface beneath the pediatric patient.

- Because infants and young children have a large occiput, positioning them supine on a backboard causes their cervical vertebrae to flex and move anteriorly. Flexion may contribute to airway compromise and/or decreased effectiveness of the jaw thrust or the chin lift maneuvers. To provide neutral alignment of the cervical spine, place padding under the patient's shoulders to bring the shoulders into horizontal alignment with the external auditory meatus.[34]

- If the patient is awake and breathing, he or she may have assumed a position that maximizes the ability to breathe. Before proceeding with cervical spine stabilization, be sure that interventions do NOT compromise the pediatric patient's breathing status.

- The mucous membranes lining the narrow passages are delicate and thereby easily traumatized. In a burn victim, look for singed nasal hair, facial hair, or eyebrows; soot around the nose or mouth; burns to the face and neck; stridor; drooling; the presence of increased secretions; a decreased or absent cough reflex; changes in voice; or a hoarse cough.

- An oropharyngeal airway may be inserted if the pediatric patient is unconscious.

- Be sure to have suction available, but use it sparingly to reduce the risk of gagging that may result in vomiting/aspiration or bradycardia.

- Consider endotracheal intubation for definitive airway control for patients who require manual positioning to maintain a patent airway or who meet other intubation criteria (GCS < 8).

  - Because of the differences in pediatric anatomy, maintaining the airway of the pediatric patient who is immobilized on a backboard is more difficult. Intubation must be performed without manipulation of the cervical spine.

  - A rapid-sequence intubation technique may be indicated.

- Use the oral route if any facial trauma indicates the presence of a basilar fracture. All intubated children should have a gastric tube.

Breathing

- Pediatric patients have thin chest walls, and breath sounds may be hard to assess; therefore, listen over the lateral portions and axillary regions.

- Administer oxygen via a nonrebreather mask to all multiple trauma patients. A flow rate of 12 to 15 L/minute is required to keep the reservoir bag of the nonrebreather mask inflated. All multiple trauma patients must receive supplemental oxygen until a complete assessment of the oxygenation and perfusion status is completed.

- If the Glasgow Coma Scale (GCS) score is 8 or less, be prepared to intubate while maintaining the pediatric patient's head in a neutral position.

  - The following must be performed when assessing for endotracheal tube positioning: observe for symmetrical rise and fall of the chest, auscultate bilateral breath sounds over the axilla, listen over the epigastrium for gurgling that may indicate an esophageal intubation, and observe the exhaled carbon dioxide (CO_2) detector for correct color change (after six manual ventilations). The mnemonic, *Yellow is Mellow* or *Gold is Good,* confirms correct tracheal placement. However, if the patient is in cardiopulmonary arrest, the color may not change on the exhaled CO_2 detector.

- Prepare for and assist with needle thoracentesis if a tension pneumothorax is present or evident, based on respiratory distress, markedly diminished or absent breath sounds, and/or asymmetrical chest wall movement.

- Apply a nonporous occlusive dressing taped on three sides if an open (sucking) pneumothorax is present.

- Consider a gastric tube to decrease diaphragmatic compromise. Children swallow air when crying, which may impair diaphragmatic movement as the result of gastric distention, making it hard to ventilate the patient.

- Anticipate escharotomy of the chest when a circumferential (full-thickness) burn of the chest is evident because it has the potential to impair respiratory function.

Circulation

- Identify, prevent, and treat shock (**Chapter 14, "Shock"**) during this portion of the primary assessment.

- Control any uncontrolled external bleeding by doing the following:

  - Applying direct pressure over the bleeding site

  - Elevating the extremity

  - Applying pressure over arterial pressure points

- Establish two peripheral intravenous access sites in critically injured pediatric patients.

  - Obtain peripheral vascular access using the largest caliber needle that the vessel can accommodate.

  - Initiate fluid resuscitation with two to three *warm* isotonic solution boluses of 20 mL/kg.

  - If the pediatric patient shows any evidence of hypovolemic shock and fails to respond to the initial fluid resuscitation, (2 to 3 boluses of isotonic crystalloid) he or she should receive blood at 10 mL/kg and an evaluation by a pediatric surgeon for possible operative intervention.

○ During pediatric resuscitation or with severe shock, pursue intraosseous (IO) and peripheral access simultaneously, or IO as a first line intervention. The establishment of IO access must be initiated if peripheral vascular access cannot rapidly be achieved.[35]

○ Any fluid or medication can be infused into the IO needle that can be infused into a peripheral intravenous catheter. Be sure that the fluid flushes easily and that the IO needle is in the correct position by observing the posterior tibia/fibula area for extravasation of fluid.

○ If available, use a rapid infuser device as indicated. The patient must weigh more than 20 kg (requiring a fluid bolus of approximately 500 mL), and a 20-gauge or larger intravenous catheter must be in place.

○ Use tubing with Y sites and normal saline when blood administration is anticipated.

• When venous or intraosseous access is secured, obtain blood samples for laboratory studies per your institution's policy.

• Prepare for and assist with an emergency thoracotomy as indicated by the injuries. Emergency thoracotomies are rarely performed for children and are associated with a dismal outcome. Patient history, patient presentation, and trauma protocol determine the indications for emergency thoracotomy.

Disability

• Closed head injuries are common in pediatric trauma because of a larger head in proportion to the rest of the body until children are aged eight years.

• If the disability assessment indicates a decreased level of consciousness, conduct further investigation during the secondary assessment.

• Check the response to the external environment using the AVPU (Alert, Verbal, Pain, Unresponsive) mnemonic. The patient is either Alert, responds only to Verbal stimuli, responds only to Painful stimuli or is Unresponsive.

• Check pupils for size, symmetry, and response to light. Observe motor function.

• Initiate pharmacological therapy as ordered (dextrose, or naloxone).

Exposure

• Any clothing that remains on the pediatric patient should be cut away or removed to allow a complete assessment of all body areas. All clothing should be saved for forensic evidence, to identify the mechanism of injury or suspected injuries, or for the family. If the pediatric patient is a victim of a penetrating injury, be sure not to cut through the hole created by the device used for the penetrating injury.

• Warming methods must be initiated to maintain a normothermic state (radiant warmer, warmed blankets, overbed warmer, warmed oxygen, or warmed intravenous fluids). Infants and younger children are predisposed to hypothermia and are influenced by the environmental temperature. Even raising the temperature in the trauma room can make a difference.

Secondary Assessment

Chapter 5, "Initial Assessment," provides a review of a comprehensive secondary assessment. Assessment and intervention components unique to pediatric trauma patients are delineated in the following section.

Full Set of Vital Signs and Focused Adjuncts

• Palpate central and peripheral pulses and auscultate an apical pulse; if at all possible for a full minute, as a baseline rate. Compare bilateral peripheral pulses for strength and equality. There may be neurovascular compromise in an injured extremity; therefore, it is important to palpate pulses on an uninjured extremity when evaluating peripheral perfusion.

• Auscultate an initial blood pressure. Remember that blood pressure in a pediatric patient may be normal despite significant blood loss. A noninvasive automated blood pressure monitor must be used with caution on critically injured children because of the pitfalls with measurements using different monitors and the size/arm circumference of the infant.[36]

• Obtain a temperature to monitor for hypothermia. The rectal route should be used in critically injured pediatric patients unless otherwise contraindicated.

• Obtain a bedside glucose or serum glucose level for all infants and children with serious illness or injury because of their increased risk for hypoglycemia when physiologically stressed.

• Consider insertion of a gastric tube to decrease gastric distention if abdominal injury is suspected, gastric distention is present, or the pediatric patient has been intubated.

• If there are no contraindications, consider insertion of a urinary catheter to monitor fluid status and the effectiveness of fluid resuscitation.

• Initiate ongoing cardiac monitoring, pulse oximetry, and exhaled CO_2 monitoring as appropriate for the pediatric patient's condition. (Remember: The pulse oximeter probe cannot differentiate between carboxyhemoglobin and oxyhemoglobin; therefore, it must be used with caution if carbon monoxide poisoning is suspected.)

• Facilitate laboratory studies if not done when initiating peripheral intravenous lines. Blood typing is a priority in the critically injured patient.

Family Presence

- Facilitate and support the family's involvement in the pediatric patient's care. Assign a staff member to remain with the family to provide explanations about procedures and to support the family while in the emergency department.

Give Comfort Measures

- Initiate pain control measures as soon as possible, including the following:

  ○ Cover burns (with a clean or sterile sheet) as quickly as possible to decrease air currents flowing across the burn area, which can cause pain.

  ○ Immobilize possible fractures.

  ○ Apply ice to injuries and elevate injured extremities.

  ○ Give medications as indicated.

  ○ Provide nonpharmacologic measures as appropriate.

Head-to-Toe Assessment

Chapter 5, "Initial Assessment," provides a description of the head-to-toe assessment.

History

- Obtain information from prehospital personnel as indicated by the injury event, using the Mechanism, Injuries, Vitals, Treatment (MIVT) mnemonic. This information often serves as a predictor of type and severity of injuries sustained.

- *Mechanism* and pattern of injury.

  ○ Obtain information regarding the use of restraints, position in the vehicle, site of impact on the vehicle, vehicle speed, ejection, rollover, air bag deployment, and any fatalities in the vehicle.

  ○ The type and the velocity of penetrating object should be identified.

  ○ If the patient sustained a fall, inquire about the height from which the patient fell. Falls two to three times the patient's height and the surface onto which the patient fell are significant indicators of the type and severity of sustained injuries.

  ○ If the injury was sustained in an incident with a pedestrian versus a motor vehicle, obtain information regarding the speed the vehicle was traveling, whether the child was run over or caught under the vehicle, what type of surface the incident occurred on, and where the patient was struck on the body.

  ○ Additional history for burn victims: when, where, and how the burn injury occurred; the place where the patient was found (bedroom or closet); type of burn; duration of exposure; and pattern of injury suggestive of child maltreatment.

- *Injuries* suspected. Ask prehospital personnel to describe the patient's general condition and apparent injuries.

- *Vital signs* on scene or en route, including levels of consciousness.

- *Treatment* initiated and patient responses to treatment.

- Obtain any additional history from the caregiver, if available. **Chapter 5, "Initial Assessment,"** provides additional tips on how to collect the patient history.

- Listen carefully to the history. It may reveal discrepancies or unlikely events to suggest intentional trauma.

Planning/Implementation

Chapter 5, "Initial Assessment," provides a list of general interventions. Indications for laboratory and radiographic studies are determined by the pediatric patient's clinical presentation, pattern of injury, history, and specific institution protocols. Additional interventions specific to the pediatric trauma patient include the following.

Diagnostic Procedures and Additional Interventions

- A computed tomography (CT) scan of the cervical spine should be the basis for cervical spinal clearance.

- Consider a CT scan of the entire spine if the pediatric patient is involved in a trauma, so that clearance can be formally documented. Routine use of magnetic resonance imaging (MRI) remains controversial.[37] MRI may be considered as a secondary diagnostic tool if CT is negative in the face of ongoing signs and symptoms of injury. (e.g., SCIWORA)

- Concern for radiation exposure in relation to CT scan should never be a consideration if the patient exhibits clinical manifestations of brain or spinal cord injury. It is unnecessary to perform additional or redundant radiographs. Nurses should advocate for the use of CT scanners that deliver weight-based dosing, reducing exposure to pediatric patients.[37]

- Perform a CT scan of the brain; identification of patients should be based on the Pediatric Emergency Care Applied Research Network (PECARN) criteria for the need for CT scanning:

  ○ Altered mental status

  ○ High energy mechanism

  ○ Clinical signs of basilar skull fracture

  ○ Any loss of consciousness

- History of persistent vomiting

- Severe headache[38]

  - However, clinical decision making is still key!

- Unstable or open-book pelvic fractures can lead to severe hypovolemic shock from blood loss. Use a pelvic binder or sheet to stablize the fracture and decrease the bleeding.

- Anticipate antidote therapy for toxic inhalants. This may include the administration of 100% oxygen, hyperbaric therapy, and sodium thiosulfate for cyanide inhalation.

- If not done so already, laboratory results should be obtained for the following variables:

  - Complete blood cell count with differential

  - Electrolytes

  - Blood type and cross match

  - Blood urea nitrogen and creatinine

  - Prothrombin and partial thromboplastin times

  - Arterial blood gases (ABGs)

- Consider an alcohol or toxicology screen. Current ACS Level I verification requires alcohol screening and follow-up for all pediatric patients over the age of 12 years.

- Perform a urinalysis and urine screen for pregnancy (for all female patients of childbearing age) as per institutional policy.

- Administer antibiotics as indicated, especially if open fractures are noted.

- Apply topical antibiotics to decrease the risk of infection from small or superficial burns (e.g., bacitracin).

- Consider obtaining carboxyhemoglobin and cyanide levels in burn patients.

- Administer a tetanus vaccine, as indicated.

- Provide psychosocial support to assist the patient in coping with changes in body image and fear of treatment procedures.

- Evaluate for indicators of child maltreatment.

- Calculate a pediatric GCS score (or FOUR [Full Outline of UnResponsiveness] score), for rapid assessment of level of consciousness in the injured child (See **Table 5-7** in **Chapter 5, "Initial Assessment,"** for further guidance). A Pediatric Trauma Score should be calculated on admission to and discharge from the ED (**Table 16-1**).

- Early surgical evaluation for high-risk patients may be necessary.

- Prepare for escharotomies if a full-thickness circumferential burn of the extremity is accompanied by inadequate neurovascular function.

- Contact the regional burn center for transfer, per policy or procedure (**Table 16-2**).

Evaluation and Ongoing Assessment

Children involved in trauma require meticulous and frequent reassessment of airway patency, breathing effectiveness, perfusion, and mental status. Initial improvements may not be sustained, and additional interventions may be needed. The pediatric patient's response to interventions and trending of the pediatric patient's condition must be closely monitored for achievement of desired outcomes. The following parameters must be monitored in the pediatric trauma patient:

- Airway patency

- Breathing effectiveness and signs of respiratory distress

- Endotracheal tube placement, as appropriate

- Circulation (perfusion)

Table 16-1 Pediatric Trauma Score*			
Category Component	**Score 2**	**Score 1**	**Score -1**
Size (kg)	>20	10–20	<10
Airway	Normal	Maintainable	Unmaintainable
Systolic BP (mm Hg)†	>90	50–90	<50
CNS	Awake	Obtunded/LOC	Coma/decerebrate
Skeletal	None	Closed fracture	Open/multiple fractures
Cutaneous/wounds	None	Minor	Major/penetrating

Note: BP indicates blood pressure; CNS, central nervous system; LOC, loss of consciousness.
*Reprinted with permission from Tepas III, J. J., Mollitt, D. L., Talbert, J. L., & Bryant, M. (1987). The pediatric trauma score is a predictor of injury severity in the injured child. *Journal of Pediatric Surgery, 22,* 14–18. If the score is less than 8, refer to a Pediatric Trauma Center.
†If proper size BP cuff is not available: 2 indicates palpable pulse at wrist; 1, palpable pulse at groin; and −1, no palpable pulse.

- Vital signs, including temperature and pain reassessments

- Cardiac rhythm, oxygen saturation, and exhaled CO_2, as appropriate

- Pediatric coma scale, GCS, or FOUR Score, as appropriate for age

- Volume of intravenous fluids and blood infused

- Output: urine, gastric tube, and chest tube

- Ongoing blood and blood product replacement and blood loss

- Follow-up for any completed interventions

Selected Injuries

Assessment data and interventions specific to the pediatric patient with the particular injury being discussed are delineated in the following sections. **Chapter 14, "Shock,"** provides specific shock management information.

Burns

An estimated two million patients younger than 20 years are treated annually in US EDs for burn-related injuries.[10] Each year, 2,500 children die in the United States and 10,000 sustain permanent disfiguring disability as the result of burns.[39] Burn injury can occur through five mechanisms: inhalation, thermal, electrical, chemical, and radiation.

When burns occur, the integument of the body is disrupted. Capillaries become permeable and, as a result, proteins and electrolytes shift from the intravascular space pulling fluid into the interstitial space. This results in edema of the burned area and loss of circulating volume.

At the burn site, the vessels supplying the area are occluded, decreasing blood flow to the burn. The injured cells release vasoactive substances, causing vasoconstriction and the development of peripheral vessel thrombosis. Tissue necrosis can develop as a consequence of decreased skin perfusion.

Electrolytes shift after a burn and can produce significant changes in serum potassium, sodium, calcium, and base bicarbonate levels. For example, the loss of cell wall integrity allows the extrusion of potassium from the cell into the extracellular fluid. The serum potassium concentration will reflect hyperkalemia, although the intracellular potassium level is depleted.

Approximately 24 to 36 hours after the initial burn trauma, the capillaries are repaired and fluid remobilization begins. Fluid then returns to the intravascular space, the kidneys excrete sodium, and potassium returns to the cells. The pediatric patient may develop hypernatremia, hypokalemia, and anemia from hemodilution and red blood cell destruction.

Pediatric patients must be assessed for progressive edema of the soft tissue and mucosa, leading to airway obstruction. More soft tissue in the child's airway predisposes pediatric patients to the development of mucosal edema. Approximately 48 to 72 hours after a burn injury, the damaged mucosal layer may slough, producing acute airway obstruction.

Assessment

- Airway
  - Assess for airway compromise (e.g., stridor or hoarseness)

Table 16-2 American Burn Association Transfer Criteria*

1. Partial-thickness burns of greater than 10% of the total body surface area.
2. Burns that involve the face, hands, feet, genitalia, perineum, or major joints.
3. Third-degree burns in any age group.
4. Electrical burns, including lightning injury, and chemical burns.
5. Inhalation injury.
6. Burn injury in patients with preexisting medical disorders that could complicate management.
7. Any patients with burns and concomitant trauma (such as fractures) in which the burn injury poses the greatest risk of morbidity or mortality.
8. Burned children in hospitals without qualified personnel or equipment for the care of children.
9. Burn injury in patients who will require special social, emotional, or rehabilitative intervention.

*Data are adapted from the American Burn Association.[6]

- Inspect the mouth of persons with burns/wounds
  - Note any carbonaceous sputum, drooling, and edema/blisters of the face or lips or singed nasal hairs, eyebrows or lashes
- Breathing
  - Assess for burns to the chest that may limit chest excursion.
  - Assess for possibility of inhaled toxins or aspiration.
- Circulation
  - With small circulating volumes in the pediatric patient, delays in resuscitation can result in profound shock.[40]
  - Consider pediatric maintenance fluid containing dextrose to prevent hypoglycemia because glycogen stores are limited.[40]
  - For burn victims, a number of fluid administration formulas (i.e., Parkland, Galveston Shriners, or modified Brooke) are available to guide fluid resuscitation.[39]
  - Use warmed lactated Ringer's when using the Parkland formula for resuscitation.
  - The prescribed rate must be based on the patient's physiological response. The adequacy of fluid administration is assessed by urine output, which is the most important indicator.[39] Urine output should be greater than 1 to 2 mL/kg per hour. In addition, serum electrolyte, osmolarity, and albumin levels should be normal.[41]
- The timing of fluid resuscitation within the first 24 hours after the burn is critical to prevent shock and maintain organ function. The Parkland formula suggests that half of the first 24-hour fluid requirement be given in the first eight hours. It is started from the time of injury.
- Determine the depth and extent of the burn injury.
  - The depth of the burn injury may not be completely determined in the emergency department. Burns that initially appear to be partial-thickness burns may be identified as full-thickness burns days after the initial injury. **Table 16-3** summarizes the characteristics of burns.[39]
  - The extent of burn injury is expressed by the percentage of area burned in relation to total body surface area. Several methods are available to calculate the percentage of total body surface area burned. Only partial- and full-thickness burns are included in the calculations.
    - The *Rule of Nines* is the most common method for calculating burns but is not accurate when calculating the percentage of burns in infants and children (**Figure 16-2**).
    - The Lund and Browder Chart is the most accurate calculation for infants and children (**Table 16-4**).

- Rule of Palm (including fingers): *The Advanced Burn Life Support Course Instructors Manual* states: "The size of the patient's hand-including the fingers (from the wrist crease to the finger tips) represents approximately 1% of his/her total body surface area."[42] Adding the number of times the child's palm would fit into the affected area will provide an estimation of the extent of the burn surface area.[41] This technique of estimating percentage of body burned has no age guideline, is useful when calculating scattered burns, and is one of the most efficient methods of estimating total body surface area.

Interventions

- STOP the burning process: never put ice on the burn!
  - Remove all clothing, including diaper, jewelry, and any other constrictive articles on the patient's body
  - Cover with a sterile sheet or a clean, dry sheet

Table 16-3 Depth of Burn and Parkland Fluid Resuscitation*

Superficial Partial-Thickness (First-degree burn)
- Epidermis
- Local redness and pain
- Minimal or no edema or blistering
- Heals within 7 days

Deep Partial-Thickness (Second-degree burn)
- Epidermis and part of dermis
- Mottled with pink, red, white and tan areas
- Moist wound with large wet blisters
- Intense pain
- Heals in 5 to 35 days

Full-Thickness (Third-degree burn)
- Epidermis, dermis, subcutaneous tissues
- May involve muscle, tendons, vasculature, bones
- May appear white, brown, charred, or leathery
- Dry, with no blistering
- Insensate, but surrounded by painful partial-thickness
- Requires excision and grafting

Parkland Formula for Fluid Resuscitation

Percent of TBSA (total body surface area) burned × child's weight in kilograms × 4 mL = number of mL to be infused in the first 24 hours following the burn injury.

- Administer ½ total amount in first 8 hours
- Administer ½ total amount over the next 16 hours
- When administering over the first 8 hours, begin timing at the hour of injury, not when the patient arrives in the emergency department or when the fluids begin.
- Add maintenance fluids with glucose for children under age 5 years.

*Adapted from Ribbens, K. A., & DeVries, M. (2012). Burns. In Hammond, B. B., & Zimmermann, P. G. (Eds.), Sheehy's manual of emergency care (7th ed., pp. 453–462). St. Louis, MO: Elsevier; and Cerepani, M. J. (2009). Burn trauma. In Emergency Nurses Association, Core curriculum for pediatric emergency nursing (2nd ed., pp. 441–460). Des Plaines, IL: Author.

Figure 16-2 Rule of Nines

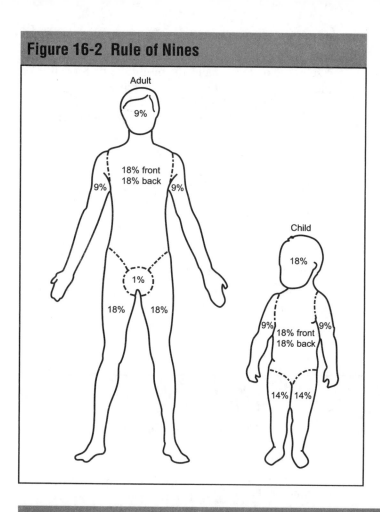

- ° To prevent hypothermia, cool with room temperature water for no more than 10 to 20 minutes for burns that are less than 10% of the total body surface area

- With a chemical burn, you will need to eliminate the offending agent. (If it is in a powder form, be sure to brush most of the agent off the skin before coming in contact with water.)

- For a minor burn, wash the area with a mild soap.

- Debride loose skin and large blisters (greater than two centimeters). (You may leave blisters intact to promote wound healing in minor burns.) Blister fluid contains high levels of inflammatory mediators, which can increase burn wound ischemia.[40] Follow recommendations from the burn center with which you have a transfer agreement. They may wish the blisters to remain intact and debridement deferred until they are able to evaluate the burn. Additionally, any ointment applied will need to be removed upon arrival to the burn center. Dry dressings may be indicated.

- Dress the wound using the antibiotic ointment of choice and gauze pads with stockinette.

- Consider the carboxyhemoglobin level in all burns with smoke or fumes. Carboxyhemoglobin levels greater than 25% in children will cause lethargy.[39]

Table 16-4 Modified Lund and Browder Chart*

Burned Area	Age in Years					
	1	1–4	5–9	10–14	15	Adult
Head	19	17	13	11	9	7
Neck	2	2	2	2	2	3
Anterior trunk	13	13	13	13	13	13
Posterior trunk	13	13	13	13	13	13
Right buttock	2.5	2.5	2.5	2.5	2.5	2.5
Left buttock	2.5	2.5	2.5	2.5	2.5	2.5
Genitalia	1	11	11	1	1	1
Right upper arm	4	4	4	4	4	4
Left upper arm	4	4	4	4	4	44
Right lower arm	3	3	3	3	3	3
Left lower arm	3	3	3	3	3	3
Right hand	2.5	2.5	2.5	2.5	2.5	2.5
Left hand	2.5	2.5	2.5	2.5	2.5	2.5
Right thigh	5.5	6.5	8	8.5	9	9.5
Left thigh	5.5	6.5	8	8.5	9	9.5
Right leg	5	5	5.5	6	6.5	7
Left leg	5	5	5.5	6	6.5	7
Right foot	3.5	3.5	3.5	3.5	3.5	3.5
Left foot	3.5	3.5	3.5	3.5	3.5	3.5

*Data are taken from the Emergency Nurses Association.[9]

- Early intubation should be considered if a long transport is expected or if the patient has a large burn that you, as the provider, anticipate will lead to airway edema.[40] The provider should anticipate this airway to be difficult and obtain the necessary equipment for a difficult intubation.

- Insert a gastric tube: paralytic ileus is an early complication of burns.

- If an electrical burn occurs, be sure to obtain blood for a creatine phosphokinase level and monitor for dark (tea-colored) urine that is suggestive of myoglobinuria.

- Administer opioids intravenously because of the fluid shifts noted with burns leading to unpredictable absorption.

Prepare for admission or transfer to a burn center by following the transfer criteria in **Table 16-2**.

Head Trauma

Head injury is estimated to occur in approximately 200 per 100,000 individuals per year, from birth to the age of 19 years.[43] Data reported by trauma centers show that head injury represents 75% to 97% of pediatric trauma deaths.[43] Severe head injuries are a global challenge with local (country) differences.[44] Standards are being sought in the treatment of head trauma because of varying therapeutic concepts in neurosurgery worldwide. The first assessment in the field is essential in the management of the child with a head injury, and children younger than one year with a GCS score of 8 or less had poorer outcomes.[44]

There are anatomical and physiological differences in children that increase the susceptibility to brain injury. These differences include the following:

- The head is proportionally larger and heavier regarding both body surface area and weight. This, along with the lack of strength in their neck muscles, places pediatric patients at higher risk for head injury.

- In young children, the cranium is undergoing changes in thickness and elasticity. The child's brain may receive a greater insult as the result of a thinner and more pliable cranium.

- The pediatric brain has a higher water content than the adult brain (88% vs. 77%), which makes it softer and more prone to acceleration-deceleration injury.[43]

- In young children, small changes in cerebral blood volume and/or cerebral tissue volume can result in significant insult to the brain and rapid decompensation.

- The brain is less myelinated in the infant and young child and, thus, more prone to shear injury.

- Children are at greater risk for secondary brain injury as the result of intracranial hypertension and cerebral

hyperemia (excess blood in the brain). The initial increase in intracranial pressure (ICP) is a result of the cerebral hyperemia, not brain edema.

- Young children can accumulate a significant percentage of their blood volume in their cranial vault and can lose relatively large amounts of blood from scalp lacerations and subgaleal hematomas; they may present in hypovolemic shock.

Specific brain injuries in pediatric patients differ by age. Infants younger than 12 months with head trauma often sustain tears in the subcortical white matter of the temporal and frontal lobes. The white matter is not well myelinated and is more susceptible to shearing injury and tears. In children younger than two years, there is a higher incidence of diffuse brain swelling and a lower incidence of subdural and epidural hematoma formation after head trauma because of the compliant skull. They are also able to tolerate an increase in ICP because of open sutures. Because the head is larger in proportion to the body surface area, stability is dependent on the ligamentous rather than bony structure leading to an increase in the amount of cervical spine ligamentous injuries.[43] Other manifestations of head injury in pediatric patients include impact seizures and diastatic fractures. With this in mind, the management of pediatric patients brought to the ED with head trauma must include specific triage guidelines to provide a rapid and safe method of screening for the presence of risk of intracranial injury and prioritization according to the severity of the injury.

Nursing Care of the Pediatric Patient with Head Trauma

Obtaining a good medical history and performing a physical examination are invaluable tools that will determine the severity of the intracranial injury and identify those at risk for secondary injury. These tools can also be useful in identifying injuries to other regions that may contribute to illness and death.

History

- Blood dyscrasias (i.e., hemorrhaging).

- Loss of consciousness (reports may be inconsistent and, thus, unreliable).

- If comatose, find out if the onset is sudden (e.g., vascular catastrophe) or acute (e.g., ingestion of a toxin).

- Temporary amnesia.

- Amount of blood at the scene (this may be underestimated by professionals and overestimated by caregivers).[45]

- Agitation, irritability, listlessness, or inability to recognize caregivers.

- Nausea or vomiting since the injury. Many children will vomit two to three times after even a minor head injury. However, persistent vomiting and retching may be associated with other symptoms that may indicate a more severe head injury and intracranial pressure (ICF).

- Abnormal behavior for age.

- Prolonged seizure after injury. A brief seizure at the time of injury may not be clinically significant. Infants may not exhibit the normal tonic-clonic movements that are noted in the older population. They may exhibit abnormal eye movements, lip smacking, or bicycling movements.

Assessment

- Cushing triad (bradycardia, hypertension, and alteration of respiration). This is a late manifestation indicative of herniation. (Hypotension associated with bradycardia in a trauma patient should be highly suggestive of spinal cord injury.)

- Breathing patterns may be altered. Observe for hyperventilation, Cheyne-Stokes respiration, and apnea.

- Neurological assessment.

  ○ The GCS or Pediatric GCS score (refer to page 75).

  ○ Check pupillary response. Unilateral (ipsilateral) dilation may indicate herniation and compression of cranial nerve (CN) III. Bilateral dilated pupils may result from bilateral compression of (CN) III or global cerebral anoxia. Pinpoint pupils might indicate a pontine lesion. Nystagmus may indicate a cerebellar injury.

- Assess for deformity, lacerations, abrasions, step off, depressions, or edema of the head/skull. Note presence and size of a hematoma.

- Evaluate for signs of basilar skull fracture, such as hemotympanum (disruption of CNs VII and VIII), periorbital ecchymosis (raccoon eyes), and postauricular ecchymosis (Battle sign).

- Assess otorrhea and rhinorrhea for the presence of cerebrospinal fluid (CSF).

  ○ CSF will produce a halo sign when on linen or gauze where a dark inner ring is surrounded by a lighter outer ring.

  ○ CSF contains approximately 60% to 70% of the level of glucose found in serum. Use a glucometer to test for glucose. Wound drainage, tears, and mucus contain no glucose.

- A bulging anterior fontanel indicative of increased intracranial pressure.

- Horner syndrome or ipsilateral pupillary constriction, ptosis, and anhydrosis accompany damage of the hypothalamus and disruption of the sympathetic pathways.[43]

- Assess the gait, including the width of the base, stability, the Romberg test, and heel-to-toe tandem walking for a more alert and cooperative patient.

- A neurological assessment in the secondary assessment should focus on sensorimotor deficits to assess the integrity of the spinal cord.

- Test the grip strength and equality in older children. In younger children and infants, test the strength of extremity movement, withdrawal to touch, and tone assessment (resistance to passive movements).

- If the pediatric patient is comatose, additional assessment of reflexes associated with select CNs may indicate the integrity of brainstem function (**Appendix 16-A**). Remember, a Babinski sign is a normal reflex in an infant.

- Signs of increased intracranial pressure.

  ○ Monro-Kellie doctrine states that the intracranial compartment is a fixed container inside a rigid skull and consists of three components: blood, brain, and cerebrospinal fluid. An increase in the volume of one intracranial compartment (blood, brain, or CSF) must be accompanied by a decrease in one or more of the other compartments if the ICP is to remain unchanged. The CSF and cerebral blood volume are the two compartments best able to be manipulated to buffer changes in increased intracranial volume.

Cerebral perfusion pressure (CPP) is the difference between the pressure of blood going to the brain (the mean arterial pressure [MAP]) and the back pressure to this flow (the ICP), and is determined as follows: CPP = MAP − ICP. Pediatric blood pressure levels are normally lower, but there are few data on normal levels of ICP in children; thus, a normal level of CPP must be derived.[46] A CPP of 40 to 65 mm Hg is associated with a favorable outcome, and a CPP lower than 40 mm Hg is associated with a poor outcome.[47] However, there is no consensus on the level at which CPP should be maintained to optimize outcome in children with a head injury. Maintaining an adequate CPP, by preventing hypotension, is probably more important than normalizing the intracranial pressure.

- A normal ICP in adults or older children is lower than 10 to 15 mm Hg. In pediatric patients, it is as follows: newborn, 0.7–1.5 mm Hg, infant, 2 to 6 mm Hg and young children, 3 to 7 mm Hg.[48]

  ○ The ICP will increase with agitation and coughing but should rapidly return to baseline.

  ○ Patients with sustained increases in ICP should be treated in a stepwise fashion to try to decrease their ICP, with the least invasive means possible being used first.

Other signs and symptoms of increased ICP:

- Mental status changes
- Slurred speech
- Posturing
- Seizures
- Inability to track objects
- Ataxia while sitting, crawling, standing, or walking

Additional Interventions Specific to Brain Injuries

- Elevation of the head of the bed (HOB) to 30°; keeping the head midline may enhance venous drainage or at least prevent venous congestion.

  ○ Maintain spinal immobilization until all radiographs are obtained and cleared.

- Trend neurological status and vital signs for indications of increases in intracranial pressure.

- Ensure adequate oxygenation and ventilation to maintain a partial pressure of $PaCO_2$ between 30 and 35 mm Hg.

- Prepare for intubation and ventilation with 100% oxygen if the GCS score is 8 or less.

  ○ Pediatric patients who are unconscious or have signs of increased ICP must be intubated. Both hypoxia and hypercarbia have potent vasodilatory effects on the cerebral vasculature, resulting in an increased cerebral blood flow and, therefore, an increased intracranial pressure. Hyperventilation causes cerebral vasoconstriction and decreases the intracranial pressure. Ventilate the pediatric patient to keep the partial pressure of CO_2, arterial, at approximately 30 to 35 mm Hg.[44] Care must be taken to avoid prolonged or profound hyperventilation as the associated vasoconstriction will lead to decreased cerebral perfusion.

  ○ Rapid-sequence intubation (RSI) must be considered, and the medications used for rapid-sequence intubation must be selected based on potential effects on ICP (avoid medications known to increase intracranial pressure).[49]

    - Etomidate (Amidate) intravenously or IO. This medication will lower the ICP and does not usually lower the blood pressure.

    - Rocuronium (Zemuron) intravenously.

    - Succinylcholine intravenously. Because of multiple side effects, extreme caution should be used for any pediatric trauma patient receiving succinylcholine.

    - Vecuronium (Norcuron) intravenously.

    - The above medications have no sedative or analgesic qualities. Sedation and pain medication must also be administered.

○ Routine hyperventilation is no longer recommended, even in the case of head injury. However, intentional, brief hyperventilation used as a temporizing rescue therapy may be indicated if there are signs of impending brain herniation, including sudden increased intracranial pressure, dilation and nonreaction of one or both pupils, bradycardia or hypotension.

- Pediatric patients who are agitated or are possibly in pain should be sedated. Sedation can be accomplished by using sublimize (Fentanyl) as needed and by using midazolam (Versed), intravenously. Giving Lidocaine IV before suctioning may blunt the increased ICP associated with this intervention. Additional sedation and/or analgesia should be considered before suctioning, patient transfer, or diagnostic procedures that may increase agitation. **Chapter 7, "Common Procedures and Sedation,"** provides additional information.

- Ensure judicious fluid resuscitation to prevent cerebral edema.

- Administer osmotic and/or loop diuretics (e.g., mannitol or furosemide) as ordered to deplete water from the intracellular and interstitial compartments, ultimately resulting in a decrease in cerebral fluid volume and a decrease in intracranial pressure.

  ○ Mannitol (Osmitrol) intravenously. (Larger doses may be appropriate in an acute intracranial hypertensive crisis. In conjunction with mannitol, other measures may be used to control intracranial pressure.)[49]

  ○ Furosemide (Lasix) intravenously.[49]

- Maintain a normal body temperature. Hyperthermia and seizures cause elevations in ICP and should be anticipated, prevented if possible, and treated aggressively.

- Although anticonvulsants are not routine prophylaxis for all pediatric patients with a traumatic brain injury, they are indicated to decrease the incidence of early posttraumatic seizures (within seven days of injury).[50]

- Avoid hyperglycemia (increases osmolality) or hypoglycemia (hinders resuscitation).

- Corticosteroids are not indicated in the management of traumatic brain injury; however, they may have a role in the management of edema surrounding a brain tumor.

Skull Fractures

Linear, Basilar, and Depressed Skull Fractures

A linear skull fracture results from low-energy blunt trauma over a wide surface area of the skull. It is nondisplaced and not depressed. Most children are asymptomatic, except for swelling and tenderness over the site. This type of fracture usually heals spontaneously within two to three months and requires few interventions. Linear fractures associated with serious sequelae include those that run through a vascular channel, venous sinus groove, or a suture (i.e., basilar skull fracture).[51]

A basilar skull fracture is a fracture of any bone that comprises the base of the skull: frontal, ethmoid, sphenoid, temporal, or occipital. A fracture of these bones creates a potential for infection and a CSF leak, resulting in the potential for tears in the dura. The patient may present with all the signs of an increased ICP along with otorrhea, rhinorrhea, hemotympanum, unilateral hearing loss, Battle sign, and raccoon eyes. If CSF drainage occurs, do not pack the ears or nose. Apply a nonocclusive, sterile, dry dressing below the draining nose and/or ear.

A depressed skull fracture is often associated with a significant direct force from a solid heavy object, causing bony fragments to be displaced inward and toward the brain. Depressed skull fracture fragments may require surgical elevation if the depression depth is significant or if fragments pose a threat to underlying cerebral tissue and vasculature.

Cerebral Tissue Injuries

Concussion/Contusion or Mild Traumatic Brain Injury

A concussion is a closed head injury usually associated with a blow to the head or rapid deceleration, resulting in transient neurological changes. Although symptoms are usually minor, permanent neurological sequelae, often related to cognitive ability, may occur. A contusion is a bruising of the brain tissue characterized by areas of hemorrhage and edema, commonly caused by a direct blow to the head. Areas of hemorrhage at the site of impact are referred to as a coup injury; contusions at sites opposite or distant from the site of impact are referred to as contrecoup injuries. Signs and symptoms may include nausea or vomiting, headache, dizziness, and a brief loss of consciousness. If this injury is associated with a sporting injury, prevention, timely identification and careful management regarding when to return to play is of utmost importance. The Centers for Disease Control and Prevention offers a tool kit entitled *Heads Up*, which provides a straightforward and practical method to prevent the disabling effects of mild traumatic brain injury.[52]

Diffuse Axonal Injury

Damage to the nerve axon can result from acceleration or deceleration forces that shear or stress the axon. This results in diffuse, microscopic, hemorrhagic lesions. A prolonged coma may result because of involvement of the brainstem and reticular activating system. The diagnosis of diffuse axonal injury (DIA) may be delayed for several days. A magnetic resonance imaging scan is used to confirm the diagnosis. The outcome varies and ranges from minimal sequelae to permanent lifelong disability or death.

Intracranial Hemorrhage

Intracranial hemorrhages may occur as a result of a fall, a direct blow to the head, or violent shaking. **Table 16-5** and **Figure 16-3** compare the various types of intracranial hemorrhages. **Figure 16-4** shows coup/contrecoup injury.

Brain Injuries with Sports

A concussion or a mild traumatic brain injury is caused by a coup/contrecoup type of injury. Most individuals recover quickly, but older adults, young children, and teenagers may have a slower recovery. Those who have had a concussion in the past are also at risk of having another one and may find that it takes longer to recover if

Table 16-5 Types of Intracranial Hemorrhages

Variable	Epidural Hematoma	Subdural Hematoma	Subarachnoid Hemorrhage
Definition	Disruption of the middle meningeal artery Blood collects between the skull and dura mater Blunt trauma	Venous bleeding Blood collects between the dura mater and arachnoid mater May be caused by violent shaking Consider child maltreatment or abusive head trauma	Arterial disruption Blood collects between the arachnoid mater and pia mater Frequently a result of child maltreatment
Signs and symptoms	Initial loss of consciousness, followed by transient consciousness, leading to unconsciousness Ipsilateral pupil dilation Contralateral paresis or paralysis	With acute subdural hematoma; irritability, vomiting, lethargy, coma There may be a large amount of blood loss before signs of increased intracranial pressure	Stiff neck Headache Seizures Irritability

they have another concussion. Symptoms of a concussion can be divided into the following four categories (from mild to severe): thinking/remembering, physical, sleeping, and mood/emotional. The Centers for Disease Control and Prevention's *Heads Up* tool kit has criteria for returning to work, school, and sports to allow the brain to fully rest.

If the individual is allowed to go back to playing before the brain is fully recovered, a condition called second impact syndrome may occur which is often fatal. Adolescents are at a higher risk of severe increased ICP with subsequent concussion in a short period. Teach the athlete and family that after all physical and cognitive symptoms have resolved and a medical provider has released the athlete to return to play, a gradual increase in activity is recommended with continual monitoring for return of symptoms.

Figure 16-3 Types of Intracranial Hemorrhages*

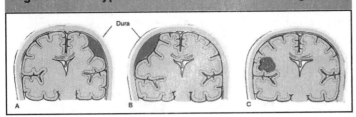

A, subdural hematomal. B, epidural hematoma. C, intracerebral hematoma.

*Reprinted from Urden, L. D., Stacy, K. M., & Lough, M. E. (2009). *Critical care nursing: Diagnosis and management* (6th ed.). St. Louis, MO: Mosby/Elsevier.

Figure 16-4 Coup/Contrecoup Injury*

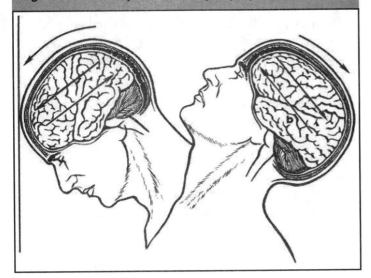

*Reprinted from Tucker, S. M., Canobbio, M. M., Paguette, E. V., & Wells, M. F. (2000). *Patient care standards: Collaborative planning & nursing interventions* (7th ed.). St. Louis, MO: Mosby/Elsevier.

Dental Trauma

Fracture or Avulsion of a Tooth

Pediatric patients may present with fractured or missing teeth as the result of a fall, a sports injury, a bicycle crash, or a motor vehicle crash. The tooth may be in place but broken or it may be avulsed from the socket. In certain situations, a permanent tooth may be replanted. Primary teeth are not replanted because of the risk of damage to the permanent tooth bud. To ensure optimal results, treatment of the avulsed tooth should begin within 30 minutes of the avulsion. This patient will need follow-up with his or her dentist.

Additional Interventions

The following is the procedure for handling an avulsed tooth:

- Find the permanent tooth.
- Gently rinse the tooth with water or saline and do not scrub the crown or root.
- Insert the tooth into the socket or place the tooth in milk until replantation. Placing the tooth in the socket may place the patient at risk for foreign body aspiration. Evaluate the child's neurological status and developmental level before using this option.
- Refer to or contact a dentist or oral surgeon. If the consulting physician is coming to the ED, obtain the necessary supplies to replant the tooth.

Vertebral or Spinal Cord Trauma

Spinal injuries in a child present uniquely and occur most often in motor vehicle crashes, followed by sports injuries.

Cervical spine injury must be presumed to be present in the pediatric trauma patient until proved otherwise. The cervical spine of a child is less protected than the cervical spine of an adult for a variety of reasons. These differences include the following:

- Pediatric patients have relatively weak muscles of the neck, and larger heads cause greater forces to the neck when the head is jerked.
- Craniocervical disruption (atlanto axial dislocation) is almost unique to children and is difficult to diagnose without a high index of suspicion.[53]
- Vertebral bodies are wedged anteriorly; they also have a tendency to slide forward with flexion. Neck ligaments are more lax, which leads to spinal cord injury without radiographic abnormality (SCIWORA).
- Facets of the upper cervical spine are flatter.
- Growth plates are active so injury to the bone can cause damage. Growth and development are cephalocaudal,

or head to tail, so that development in the upper cervical spine differs from development in the lower cervical spine.[53] The level at which spinal injuries occur varies with age. In children who are younger than eight years, injuries are more common to the upper cervical region (C-1 to C-3); in older children and adults, injuries of the lower cervical region are more common.

Frontal impact motor vehicle crashes accompanied by rapid deceleration forces can cause midlumbar (flexion-distraction or Chance) vertebral fractures in children who wear lap safety restraints improperly. Children tend to wear the safety restraint around the abdomen versus the pelvis. Injuries usually occur between the second and fourth lumbar vertebrae. External abrasions across the lower abdomen are important clues to the injury.

Spinal cord injury without radiographic abnormality (SCIWORA) is unique to the pediatric population due to the incompletely calcified vertebral column of the pediatric patient. Traumatic forces of hyperextension, flexion, and traction may cause spinal cord injury without radiographic abnormality. Neurological deficits, neck pain or spinal tenderness may be noted despite lack of any anatomical evidence of injury. MRI evaluation is important to determine stability of the vertebral column. A CT scan of the cervical spine should be performed based on cervical spinal clearance, in combination with the interpretation of films by an expert radiologist. All spinal regions should be imaged, and clearance should be formally documented.[37]

Additional Signs and Symptoms of Spinal Cord Injury

- Spinal deformity
- Neck pain or tenderness to palpation
- Injuries to the neck, face, head, and/or back
- Flaccid extremities or unequal strength
- Altered sensation in the extremities and/or trunk
- Incontinence or absence of sphincter tone
- Priapism

Interventions Specific for Spinal Cord Injury

- Maintain full spinal immobilization
- Obtain an immediate neurosurgical consultation

Use of methylprednisolone is indicated in the acutely injured pediatric patient with a spinal cord injury and is most effective if started within eight hours of injury.

Cardiothoracic Trauma

Significant cardiothoracic trauma rarely occurs alone and is often a component of major multisystem injury. Cardio-thoracic trauma in children can be caused by either blunt or penetrating mechanisms. Blunt trauma is commonly seen as a result of a motor vehicle crash. The ribs remain cartilaginous and pliable, along with mediastinal mobility in children until approximately the age of eight years; therefore, the presence of rib fractures may indicate a significant underlying injury. Pulmonary contusions and rib fractures are common and can be seen in 50% and 25%, respectively, of pediatric blunt thoracic trauma victims.[54] A high degree of suspicion must be maintained in any individual who sustains a blunt thoracic injury. Penetrating injuries are not as common in children, but are increasing in general both nationally and internationally.[51]

Pneumothorax/Hemothorax

A simple pneumothorax is one of the most common forms of pediatric chest trauma and may result from a blunt or penetrating injury. The severity of the signs and symptoms is dependent on the percentage of lung collapsed. Pediatric patients with a small pneumothorax may be asymptomatic and need no treatment. A large pneumothorax may require a chest tube.

An open pneumothorax occurs when there is a loss in chest wall integrity and air enters the pleural space through both the wound and the trachea. An open pneumothorax is easily recognized by the sucking heard with inspiration and the bubbling sound heard with expiration.

A tension pneumothorax develops when air enters the pleural space on inspiration but cannot escape on expiration. The intrathoracic pressure increases, causing collapse of the lung on the side of the injury and a mediastinal shift of the heart, great vessels, and trachea. When enough air accumulates, the unaffected lung collapses. Venous return is impeded, cardiac output decreases, and hypotension results. Needle decompression followed by chest tube placement, is the treatment of choice.

A hemothorax occurs when blood accumulates in the pleural space, eventually leading to collapse of the affected lung. In the adult patient, only 25% of hemothoraces are large enough to produce shock. Pediatric patients have a smaller circulating blood volume, and the accumulation of smaller amounts of blood may be significant enough to produce signs of hypovolemic shock and respiratory distress. In addition, pediatric patients can lose up to 40% of their circulating blood volume into the pleural space. Exploration of the thorax is indicated when a chest tube is inserted and an immediate return of 20% of the pediatric patient's circulating volume is noted.

Pulmonary Contusion

A pulmonary contusion is a bruise of the lung tissue, resulting in alveolar capillary damage. Interstitial and alveolar edema and hemorrhage decrease lung compliance and impair transport of oxygen and carbon dioxide. A pulmonary contusion is identified on a chest radiograph by consolidation and pulmonary infiltrates. Treatment may include rest and restriction of IV fluids as overhydration can extend the area of contusion.

Cardiac Contusion

A myocardial contusion is a bruise of the myocardium caused by blunt trauma. Damage may range from mild muscular ecchymosis to infarction. The diagnosis is often difficult because of concurrent injury to the respiratory system and/or the presence of shock. Consider the restriction of IV fluids to avoid overhydration. Cardiac contusions are sometimes associated with commotio cordis, or the development of ventricular fibrillation after a blow to the chest.

Pericardial Tamponade

Pericardial tamponade is a collection of blood in the pericardial sac. This life-threatening cardiac injury most frequently occurs with penetrating injury but can occur with blunt trauma as well. As blood accumulates in the noncompliant sac, it exerts pressure on the heart and inhibits ventricular filling. The impairment of cardiac function is related to the rate and amount of fluid accumulation in the pericardial sac. Hallmark signs include muffled heart tones and jugular vein distention (JVD).

Assessment Specific to Cardiothoracic Trauma

- Presence of respiratory distress, increased work of breathing, or tachypnea.
- Diminished or absent breath sounds on the injured side. Auscultate the axillary areas along with the anterior and posterior lung fields.
- Localized rales, wheezes, or decreased breath sounds and hemoptysis are seen with a pulmonary contusion.
- Physical signs of trauma, such as tire marks, bruising, or open wounds (i.e., open pneumothorax).
- Paradoxical chest wall movement with breathing, decreased breath sounds, or decreases in oxygen saturation.
- Distended neck veins (i.e., tension pneumothorax or pericardial tamponade). This may be difficult to evaluate in infants and young children because of their short fat necks.
- Deviation of the trachea (assess for tracheal deviation by palpating the trachea just above the suprasternal notch). It may be difficult to appreciate in infants and young children. In young children, a tension pneumothorax may be present without tracheal deviation.
- Percuss for hyperresonance or dullness; hyperresonance indicates air in the pleural space (e.g., pneumothorax), and dullness indicates blood in the pleural space (e.g., hemothorax).
- Signs of decreased cardiac output (faint peripheral pulses may be seen with a tension pneumothorax or a cardiac contusion).
- Electrocardiographic abnormalities ranging from dysrhythmias (e.g., premature ventricular contractions) to ST and T-wave changes. Dysrhythmias may be transient with cardiac contusion.
- Bradycardia, pulseless electrical activity, and asystole may be seen with pericardial tamponade.
- Pale or cyanotic skin.

Additional Interventions Specific to Cardiothoracic Trauma

- A CT scan of the chest can identify injuries that may not be identified on the normal chest radiograph. If a tension pneumothorax is suspected, immediately prepare for or perform a needle decompression. This pediatric patient will require insertion of a chest tube as soon as possible after needle decompression.
- Prepare for chest tube insertion to evacuate the air or blood from the pleural space.
- If an open pneumothorax is present, apply a nonporous dressing taped on three sides and monitor for the development of a tension pneumothorax.
- Restrict intravenous fluids.
- If there is no cervical spine injury, elevate the head of the bed to a level of comfort.
- Perform cardiac monitoring for dysrhythmias.
- Perform a 12-lead electrocardiogram.
- Administer antidysrhythmic medications as ordered.
- Prepare for pericardiocentesis if tamponade is suspected. Obtain a large spinal needle and attach a 30 mL syringe. The physician will insert this needle into the left subxiphoid area. Be sure to have the cardiac monitor running, and observe for any ventricular dysrhythmias. Blood obtained from the pericardial sac should not coagulate.
  ○ Prepare for a possible ED pericardial window or a thoracotomy.
  ○ Prepare for an operative intervention to identify the source of bleeding.

Abdominal Trauma

Abdominal trauma in pediatric patients is related to a variety of causes, including sports, recreational activities, motor vehicle crashes, and bicycle crashes. Pediatric patients who sustain any blunt trauma to the abdomen shortly after eating are at a greater risk for injury because of distention and the risk for aspiration. There are many physiological characteristics that increase the patient's risk for developing injuries related to abdominal trauma, including the following:

- The abdominal muscles are thinner, weaker, and less developed than those of an adult.
- The chest wall is more pliable and the ribs are more horizontal and therefore do not provide as much protection to abdominal organs.
- The duodenum has an increased vascular blood supply, resulting in more blood loss when traumatized.
- The liver, spleen, and kidneys are less protected by the ribs and overlying muscle and fat, which makes them more easily injured.

Specific Assessment Associated with Abdominal Trauma

- Location, quality, and radiation of abdominal pain
- Respiratory pattern and depth
  - Children are abdominal breathers. Therefore, abdominal pain, such as that caused by peritoneal irritation, may alter the breathing pattern.
  - Children with intra-abdominal bleeding often exhibit an expiratory grunt.
- Rigidity, guarding, and abdominal distention (peritoneal signs)
- Evidence of external soft tissue injury (e.g., safety restraint marks); consider vertebral injury
- Bloody urinary drainage: consider bladder or renal injury
- Consider pancreatic injury with blunt trauma due to bicycle handlebars.

Interventions Specific to Abdominal Trauma

- If open abdominal wounds are present, cover with a sterile dressing moistened with sterile saline. Do not attempt to push abdominal contents back into the abdominal cavity.
- Consider use of focused assessment with sonography for trauma (FAST). FAST has a modest sensitivity for the detection of pediatric patients with hemoperitoneum; however, a negative FAST result has questionable utility as the sole diagnostic procedure to rule out the presence of an intra-abdominal injury.[55]
- Prepare the pediatric patient for surgery. Pediatric patients with solid organ injury, resulting in hemodynamic instability and unresponsiveness to fluid resuscitation, may require operative intervention.

Splenic Injuries

Trauma of the spleen is often caused by a blunt impact sustained from a sports activity or a fall from a bicycle. Splenic injuries are associated with trauma to the left upper quadrant of the abdomen or left lower chest. Conservative preservation management of splenic injuries in children has indicated full recovery in 90% to 98% of patients because a child's spleen stops bleeding spontaneously. The only absolute indication for performing a splenectomy in children is massive disruption and hemodynamic instability.[22]

Liver Laceration

Laceration of the liver is a major cause of morbidity and mortality in children with abdominal trauma.[22] Management varies and is dependent on the hemodynamic status of a pediatric patient. As long as the pediatric patient remains hemodynamically stable, nonoperative treatment is recommended. The CT scan provides information for the grading of liver injuries. Liver trauma must be considered when the patient sustains abrasions or contusions to the right upper quadrant of the abdomen or the right lower chest, abdominal distention, right-sided rib fractures, guarding, tenderness or rigidity to palpation, or signs of shock.

Musculoskeletal Trauma

Pediatric patients often sustain musculoskeletal injuries without multisystem injuries. These injuries are frequently related to sports and recreational activities, and they occur more often as a child's environment expands to include bicycles, skateboards, snowboards, or high-energy devices, such as all-terrain vehicles, trampolines, or automobiles. Musculoskeletal injuries may be categorized as a fracture, sprain, subluxation, or dislocation of a joint. One of the most common injuries is a radial head subluxation, or annular ligament displacement that occurs as a result of a sudden, forceful, longitudinal pull on an extremity, commonly referred to as a nursemaid's elbow or subluxation of the radial head. The history is consistent with a sudden pulling injury, such as a young child being pulled up by an extended arm. Simple manipulation is usually all that is needed to correct this.

Fractures

A fracture or break in the bone may be complete, incomplete, spiral, or open (with bone extended through the skin or closed). Fractures are common in pediatric patients, and the prognosis for healing is usually excellent. One of the more common types of fractures in children is the greenstick fracture, which is an incomplete fracture through the bone with a portion of the cortex and periosteum remaining intact. This type of fracture is common in young children because their bones can sustain more buckling and bending. Fractures are not always readily seen in the younger population, making it more difficult to diagnose the fracture. Problems with healing and future bone growth can occur if the fracture extends through or involves the epiphyseal (growth) plate (**Figure 16-5**).

Assessment Specific for Musculoskeletal Trauma

- Deformity, shortening, or rotation of the affected extremity
- Edema or soft tissue injury (i.e., lacerations, abrasions, or contusions)
- Tenderness on palpation
- Reluctance or refusal to move or use an affected extremity
- Neurovascular status (assess for the presence of the **Six Ps**):
  - **Pallor:** Is the extremity a different color than the uninjured one?
  - **Pain:** Is there pain? Where? How severe?
  - **Pulselessness:** Are the peripheral pulses distal to the injury present, strong, and equal?
  - **Paresthesia:** What is the sensory status of the affected area and the area distal to the injury?
  - **Paralysis:** Can the child spontaneously move the injured extremity?
  - **Poikilothermia:** cool to touch

Interventions Specific to Musculoskeletal Injuries

- Always compare the peripheral circulation of the affected extremity with that of the unaffected extremity.
- Evaluate the peripheral circulation, and implement measures to provide optimal tissue perfusion. If impaired, check the alignment of the extremity, assess the patient's hemodynamic status, and notify the physician. Proper alignment may be needed to restore adequate circulation to the affected extremity.

Figure 16-5 Types of Epiphyseal Injuries*

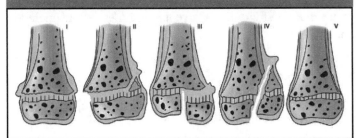

I, fracture through the growth plate. **II,** fracture through the growth plate and metaphysis. **III,** fracture through the growth plate and epiphysis. **IV,** fracture through growth plate, metaphysis, and epiphysis. **V,** compression fracture through growth plate.
*Reprinted from Burns, C. (2008). *Pediatric primary care* (4th ed.). Philadelphia, PA: Saunders, an imprint of Elsevier.

- Prepare for possible closed reduction using procedural sedation.
- Immobilize the injured extremity, including the joints above and below the site of injury, to avoid further injury or pain. This can be accomplished by using the following items:
  - Rigid intravenous boards
  - Metal or plastic splints
  - Plaster or fiberglass splints
- Assess and document the neurovascular status of the affected extremity before and after immobilization.
- Obtain comparison view radiographs as warranted.
- Provide fluid replacement if the femur or hip is involved.

Discharge teaching:

- If crutches are given, instruct the child on walking techniques and assess the return demonstration for correct use. Include safety teaching regarding stairs or slick surfaces.
- If splints are applied, instruct the caregiver on the signs and symptoms of neurovascular compromise.
- If appropriate, teach the caregiver how to loosen and reapply the bandages or splints.
- Instruct the caregivers and pediatric patients to avoid placing sharp objects inside the cast or splint to relieve itching. Also, instruct patients and caregivers to keep the cast or splint dry.
- If pain continues or increases beyond 48 hours after the injury, the pediatric patient must be reexamined.

Compartment Syndrome

Compartment syndrome occurs when pressures within the fascial compartment exceed the pressures exerted by the arterioles and capillaries providing oxygen and nutrients to the muscles and other intracompartment structures. Causes of compartment syndrome include extremity fracture, crush injuries, snakebites, circumferential burns, bandages or casts. Any injury that causes swelling of the extremity including significant soft tissue injury should result in assessment for signs of compartment syndrome.

Assessment Specific to Compartment Syndrome

The **Seven Ps** are similar to those for musculoskeletal trauma, but with an added P. They are listed in order of severity.

- **Pain:** Pain is the first sign, and for those providers who know when to expect, it may be the only sign needed. Pain in compartment syndrome is disproportional to the injury and worsens rather than improves over time.

- **Paresthesia:** Look for paresthesia in areas where specific nerves may be identified. As compartment pressures increase, paresthesia becomes anesthesia and the pain may diminish. This is ominous as ischemia and necrosis occur at this point.

- **Pallor:** Pallor is indicative of lack of arterial circulation. It may start with cyanosis as the flow becomes compromised, but as it occludes, pallor results.

- **Paralysis:** Loss of intentional movement will often coincide with paresthesia.

- **Poikilothermia:** Cool skin will coincide with pallor.

- **Pulselessness:** Once the pulse cannot be located, even with ultrasound, circulation is compromised. However, the presence of a pulse may be misleading as collateral circulation may maintain pulses in larger vessels while the arterioles and capillary beds are completely collapsed.

- **Pressure:** Intracompartmental pressure may be measured with a handheld device in which a probe is inserted. Pressures in adults are normally 5 to 10 mm Hg. Children have a slightly higher normal between 13.3 and 16.6 mm Hg.[56] Loss of tissue and limb-threat occurs at 30 mm Hg.[57]

In the pediatric trauma patient, being aware of the mechanism of injury and the risk of compartment syndrome, the nurse should constantly reassess any injuries at risk. This is especially true for the preverbal infant, the unconscious patient, or the delayed child. Patients transferred in for care of an extremity fracture should be assessed immediately on arrival to the receiving facility for signs of compartment syndrome.

Additional Interventions Specific to Compartment Syndrome

The only treatment for compartment syndrome is fasciotomy of the affected limb. Incision into the rigid fascia relieves the pressure and allows blood flow until swelling can be relieved.

If the cause is a bandage or cast that is too tight, it should be removed.

Discharge Instructions

- Teach caregivers to assess the casted or bandaged extremity distal to the injury for signs of diminished blood flow.

- Instruct caregivers to track improvement of pain status and be aware of worsening pain and report it for re-evaluation.

- Splint injuries initially until swelling can go down before casting will lessen the risk.

- If the patient must be discharged with an elastic bandage, strong emphasis on the importance of regular removal and assessment of the injured extremity must be included in the discharge teaching.

Amputations

Fingertip amputations are often caused by a closing door and are one of the most common amputations in children. Many amputated extremities can be successfully reimplanted if the elapsed time from injury to surgery is minimal. Most successful reattachments are guillotine-type amputations (i.e., a clean and complete severing of the tissue). Amputations caused by a crushing force are more difficult to reimplant. Amputation injuries occur because of children's curiosity, lack of coordination, and inherent lack of understanding of danger.

Additional Interventions Specific for Amputations

- If profuse active bleeding is present, elevate the extremity and apply a pressure dressing.

- When bleeding is controlled, apply a sterile nonadhering dressing to the stump and wrap with sterile gauze. Once the area is covered, the anxiety of the pediatric patient and parent should decrease.

- Care of the amputated part:[58]

  ○ Gently rinse (avoid scrubbing) the part with sterile saline to remove gross dirt.

  ○ Wrap the part in gauze slightly moistened with sterile saline, and place the part in a sealable plastic bag.

  ○ After sealing the bag, place the bag on ice water for transport to surgery or the closest replantation center. Remember to label the container.

  ○ If radiographs are performed, include the part(s) and the stump.

Health Promotion

Prevention measures have an impact on trauma-related morbidity and mortality. Current recommendations include the following:

- Promote no extra seat or no extra rider on farm equipment ("Farm Safety for Kids").

- Promote installation of four-sided fencing around pools, along with pool alarms and automatic pool covers.

- Stress the use of personal flotation devices or life jackets while boating. Children should never be left unsupervised when they are in or around water.

- Develop community-based education and legislation to promote the use of bicycle helmets by all children and adults, educate caregivers and children on the importance of wearing bicycle helmets, and encourage state and local governments to pass legislation requiring helmet use by all bicyclists and mandating bicycle rental agencies to include helmets as part of the rental contract.

- Develop programs that support decreased availability of alcohol and drugs to young people.

- Increase enforcement of existing alcohol and drug use laws.

- Advocate for the passing and enforcing of child passenger safety laws. Instruct caregivers that all occupants of motor vehicles should use appropriate safety devices. Encourage caregivers to check the seat's temperature before placing a child younger than one year in a car seat. Hot straps or buckles can cause second-degree burns!

- Educate caregivers on firearm safety.

- Educate caregivers and children on the importance of wearing helmets when skiing or snowboarding. Encourage resorts and rental agencies to include helmets as part of the rental contract.

- Encourage state governments to ban the manufacturing and sale of mobile baby walkers and support efforts to redesign them. Educate caregivers on the hazards of mobile baby walkers. Develop liaisons with other organizations (e.g., National Safe Kids Campaign[59] and American Academy of Pediatrics) to discourage the manufacture and sale of mobile baby walkers.

- Encourage caregivers to install gates at the top and bottom of stairs until children can climb up and down safely.

- Encourage the use of helmets, lightweight balls, and proper instruction for soccer players.

- Keep hot liquids and appliances (e.g., pans with hot substances, coffee pots, or a curling iron) away from the edge of a table, counter, or stove and use the back burners.

- Educate caregivers on the importance of installing smoke and carbon monoxide detectors in the home and setting water heaters at a safe temperature of 120°F (49°C) or the low setting. Water heated at higher settings can cause burns in two or three seconds.

- Always test the temperature of bath water before your child gets into the tub. Supervise young children in the bathtub. Consider temperature restrictions or thermostat changes on the hot water heater (e.g., tempering/antiscald valve).

- Educate caregivers and children about fire safety and what to do in case of a fire (i.e., stop, drop, and roll).

- Identify appropriate prevention strategies for children with special needs (e.g., evaluating the status of the cervical spine of the child with Down syndrome before sports activities).

- Promote the installation of protective window guards in second story bedrooms. Keep windows locked and all furniture away from windows. Permanent bars are not recommended as they prohibit escape in case of fire.

- Secure or cut cords for blinds and drapes to prevent strangulation injuries.

- Encourage caregivers to always stay close to shopping cart to monitor child. Do not allow children to stand up in the cart. Use of shopping cart seat belts should also be encouraged and is now required in most states.

Injury prevention must include education, enforcement, and environmental interventions. Other suggested areas for injury prevention are listed in **Table 16-6.**

Summary

Care of the pediatric trauma patient requires a coordinated effort from the trauma team and the family. Collaboration by the multidisciplinary team facilitates optimal patient care and integrates the resources that are needed to care for the pediatric trauma patient. This is especially true when caring for pediatric burn patients who will need specialized acute and long-term care. Knowledge of normal growth and development, anatomy, mechanisms of injury, and responses to injury (physiological and psychosocial) is the foundation for providing trauma nursing care to the pediatric patient. Following a systematic approach to assessment and intervention contributes to positive patient outcomes through early identification of injuries and recognition of life-threatening conditions. Incorporating the family throughout the care process is important for meeting the psychosocial and emotional needs of the patient and his or her family.

Table 16-6

Prevention Strategies by Developmental Stage (Infancy through Adolescence) and Ecological Context Children's Safety Network (CSN) National Injury and Violence Prevention Resource Center National Child Death Review Resource Center					
Ecological Context	**Infants (age < 1)**	**Toddlers and Preschoolers (ages 1–4)**	**School-Aged Children (ages 5–9)**	**Tweens (10–14)**	**Adolescents (ages 15–19)**
Individual		Participate in fire safety education programs (i.e. "I Spot Something Hot") Tell a parent or an adult if touched inappropriately by another person	Learn fire safety (i.e. stop, drop, and roll) Learn respect for others and self	Stranger danger awareness Online safety awareness Learn not to bully others and be a good bystander	Learn CPR Mentor younger kids Negotiate safe driving agreements with parents Take a safe babysitting class
		Learn pedestrian safety—hold hands when crossing a street, look both ways, don't play behind cars Use child restraints (i.e., safety seats and booster seats) Learn what to do in an emergency (9-1-1, get parent, follow instructions from teachers/parents)		Use seat belts Wear properly fitted safety gear (i.e., motorcycle helmets, bicycle helmets, ATV helmets, gloves, leather, boots, etc.) Participate in alcohol and other illegal and prescription drug education.	
		Wear appropriate, properly fitted exercise and sports gear including Use properly fitted bicycle helmets Use personal floatation devices when boating Bullying prevention—learn respect for others			
Family	Prevent choking (i.e., no toy or items small enough to fit through toilet paper tube) Water safety (i.e., supervise bathing, Ensure safe sleep (i.e., safe cribs, back to sleep, separate sleep environment) Do not shake babies Parenting classes Learn infant CPR	Teach safe pedestrian safety— hold hands when crossing a street, look both ways, not to play behind cars) Teach what to do in an emergency (9-1-1, get parent, follow instructions from teachers/parents)	Use booster seats Provide safe routes to school	Mandate seat belt use Monitor computer use (reduce cyber-bullying)	Support home-school partnership programs to promote parental involvement Enforce zero tolerance alcohol policies Support GDL programs with parent support provisions Implement GDL laws in your community
		Use approved, correctly installed child restraints (i.e., safety seats and booster seats) Provide a safe home environment (lower water temperatures, remove poisonous plants, install smoke and carbon monoxide alarms, padded furniture corners, cabinet locks, decrease fall hazards; use window guards, remove access to firearms, and fire safe clothing, poisons/prescriptions/alcohol) Become familiar with the CPSC Playground Safety Guidelines Develop and practice fire safety and disaster plans Do not leave children in cars alone			Learn about GDL and how to implement it
		Create safe home and community play areas that are age appropriate Educate for dog bite prevention—do not approach unknown dogs Train children to dial 9-1-1 in an emergency and know what to tell the operator		Learn about signs of suicidal ideation and where to get help Provide information about teen dating violence prevention Teach dangers of prescription medications and keep out of reach	

Table 16-6 *continued*

Ecological Context	Infants (age <1)	Toddlers and Preschoolers (ages 1-4)	School-Aged Children (ages 5-9)	Tweens (10-14)	Adolescents (ages 15-19)
Family (cont)			Provide and use properly fitting safety gear (i.e. helmets, knee pads, wrist and shin guards, etc.) Be involved with the school in creating a safe school environment Maintain oversight of computer use to reduce cyber-bullying and other forms of harassment Advocate for training on cyber-bullying and its prevention Know the signs of concussion and who to contact for assessment Limit exposure to media violence and sexting		
		Provide properly fitted bicycle helmets/require use whenever riding Require use of personal floatation devices when boating Do not bully others and be a good bystander			
	Reduce access to poisons and prescription medications and clearly post the 1-800-222-1222 poison control center number. Install four-sided fencing on pools (house is not considered one side) Install working smoke alarms and carbon monoxide detectors (check monthly) Keep all guns unloaded and locked and away from access from all family members in the home Contact policymakers to help with safety measures				
Community	Increase access to prenatal and postnatal services Increase access to parenting skills training Provide home visit services to high risk families	Provide early childhood enrichment programs	Develop school policies to prevent injuries, violence Teach bystander interventions Require use of protective gear in sports including mouth guards, eye protection, and joint protectors	Train health care professionals in identification and referral of high-risk youth	Provide mentoring for high-risk youth Provide education to promote healthy relationships and decrease dating violence Provide safe babysitting courses Provide young worker safety training to students and businesses. Enforce GDL laws
	Conduct home hazard assessment and recommend safety changes Require childcare to follow safety standards and guidelines Provide infant and booster seat installation sites. Provide grandparent training in new safety issues such as poisoning, drowning, car seat use, etc.		Participate in "Safe Routes to School" programs Provide after-school and recreational programs to extend adult supervision Create safe havens for children on high-risk routes to and from school Conduct school-based education to increase use of passenger restraints, seats, and non-use of cell phones for talking and texting Create a bully free environment in schools and community Train school nurses, administrators, and other school personnel about injury prevention, violence prevention, and substance use prevention Require training for coaches, teachers and school health personnel related to concussions Provide social development training in anger management, social skills, and problem solving		
				Provide information about teen dating violence prevention programs Provide gatekeeper training in suicide prevention Teach conflict resolution/mediation Include youth in planning and implementing safety interventions	
	Support Smart Growth initiatives Institute traffic calming measures Provide safe pedestrian and bike paths separate from motorized traffic Provide safe playground and sports facilities. Comply with CPSC Guidelines Encourage all families to have safety plans Support Poison Control Center Provide suicide prevention education for health professionals Work with policy makers to develop safety measures				

Table 16-6 *continued*

Ecological Context	Infants (age <1)	Toddlers and Preschoolers (ages 1-4)	School-Aged Children (ages 5-9)	Tweens (10-14)	Adolescents (ages 15-19)
Social-Cultural	Adopt recommendations for safe sleep Require new parents take parenting classes				Enforce laws prohibiting illegal transfers of guns to youth Support restrictions on access to alcohol Support GDL laws and their enforcement Support enforcement of DWI laws
	Adopt and enforce child safety seat laws Enforce product safety standards Upgrade older playground equipment to ensure safe design		Support passage and enforcement of bicycle and motorcycle helmet laws Restrict use of ATVs Enforce speed limits in vicinity of schools and play areas Reduce levels of media violence		
	Support increased use of passenger restraints, seats and non-use of cell phones for texting and talking Required four-sided pool fencing. Post life guards at public swimming areas Enforce community spa and pool safety standards Assure that all education materials and programs are culturally, ethnically and linguistically appropriate to the community Learn and respect community differences Require emergency departments to collect injury data in an aggregate form Mandate use of sprinklers in new or remodeled homes and businesses, and multilevel housing Become aware of the economic costs of injuries and the savings of implementing prevention measures. Support Poison Control Centers Make cars "no phone" zones Require suicide prevention education for health providers Determine methods for agencies to share data for the purpose of prevention (protecting confidentiality)				

Note: ATV indicates all-terrain vehicle; CPR, cardiopulmonary resuscitation; CPSC, Consumer Product Safety Commission; DWI, driving while intoxicated; GDL, graduated driver's licensing.

*Modified and reprinted with permission from the Children's Safety Network, National Injury and Violence Prevention Resource Center, and National Child Death Review Resource Center.

Appendix 16-A
Cranial Nerve Assessment

A gross evaluation of cranial nerve function can be completed relatively quickly. However, the pediatric patient's condition and developmental level may preclude evaluation of all cranial nerves. A basic cranial nerve evaluation should include eye movement and function, a gag reflex, and facial symmetry.

Evaluation of Eye Movement and Function (Cranial Nerves II, III, IV, and VI)

- In the conscious pediatric patient, an evaluation of eye movement and function includes an assessment of extraocular movements and gross visual acuity. However, a complete evaluation of all extraocular movements may not be possible in children younger than two to three years of age. The assessment includes evaluation for the presence of the following:
  - Equal rise of eyelids
  - Equality of pupil size and reactivity to light and accommodation
  - Ability to see and track an object
  - Ability to identify color
  - Ability to follow an object through the six fields of gaze
- In conscious infants younger than three months, the assessment includes an evaluation for the presence of the following:
  - Equal rise of eyelids
  - Equality of pupil size and reactivity to light and accommodation
  - Blinking in response to a bright light
  - Ability to follow or track a dangling object or moving the head to follow an object
- In infants and children with an altered level of consciousness, the position of the eyes at rest and the presence of abnormal spontaneous eye movement should also be noted. The assessment includes an evaluation for the presence of the following:
  - Equal rise of eyelids (if an eye opening response is present)
  - Equality of pupil size and reactivity to light and accommodation

- Abnormal eye position:
    - Deviation of the eyes toward one field of gaze
    - Dysconjugate gaze
  - Abnormal movement (nystagmus)

Evaluation of Reflex Responses (Cranial Nerves IX and X; Cranial Nerves V and VII; and Cranial Nerves III, VI, and VIII)

- The assessment of reflex response includes evaluation for the function of the following:
  - Cranial nerves IX and X (gag, cough, and swallowing):
    - Ability to swallow
    - Ability to cough
    - Presence of gag reflex
    - Presence of clear speech or alterations in speech pattern
  - Cranial nerves V and VII (corneal reflex):
    - Spontaneous blinking
    - Blinking in response to a corneal stimulus
  - Cranial nerves III, VI, and VIII: Oculocephalic and oculovestibular responses are only tested for the evaluation of severe brainstem dysfunction in the unresponsive infant or child. This assessment includes evaluation for the presence of:
    - Doll's-eyes reflex (i.e., when the head is turned but the eyes move in the opposite direction). If the eyes move in the same direction when the head is turned, the doll's-eyes reflex is considered absent; this is an abnormal finding.
    - Nystagmus in response to an ice water caloric test. No eye movement or asymmetric eye movement in response to the ice water caloric test is considered an abnormal response.

Evaluation of Facial Movement and Expression (Cranial Nerves V and VII)

- The assessment of facial movement and expression includes evaluation for the presence of the following:
  - Facial symmetry with movement or during crying and sucking in infants
  - Ability to raise eyebrows, smile, clench teeth, and chew
  - Tears with crying
  - Sucking reflex and strength of reflex in infants

Evaluation of Motor and Muscular Function (Cranial Nerves XI and XII)

- The assessment of motor and muscular function related to the cranial nerves includes observing for the presence of the pediatric patient's ability to do the following:

  ○ Shrug shoulders

  ○ Turn head and move the upper extremities

  ○ Stick out the tongue. In infants, the position of the tongue when crying is observed; the midline position is the norm.

Basic Evaluation of Hearing (Cranial Nerve VIII)

- The assessment of hearing function includes observing for the patient's ability to do the following:

  ○ Respond to verbal commands and answer questions

  ○ Repeat words

- In infants younger than three months, the following behaviors are observed:

  ○ Spontaneous movements and/or sucking stop in response to voice or sounds. The infant should then resume the activity.

  ○ Quieting to the sound of a voice or soothing sounds.

  ○ Turning of the head or eyes toward the sound.

  ○ Vocalization in response to sounds or a voice.

References

1. Centers for Disease Control and Prevention, National Center for Injury Prevention and Control. (2010). *Web-based Injury Statistics Query and Reporting System.* Retrieved from http://www.cdc.gov/ncipc/wisqars

2. Salomone, J. A., & Salomone, J. P. (2003). *Abdominal trauma, blunt.* Retrieved from http://www.emedicine.com/emerg/topic1.htm

3. Sluys, K., Lannge, M., Iselius, L., & Eriksson, L. E. (2009). Outcomes in pediatric trauma care in the Stockholm region. *European Journal of Trauma and Emergency Surgery* [published online September 5, 2009]. doi 10.1007/s00068-009-9080-6

4. World Health Organization Europe. (2008). *European report on child injury prevention.* Retrieved from http://www.euro.who.int/Document/E92049.pdf

5. Ahrens, M. (2009). *Smoke alarms in U.S. home fires.* Quincy, MA: National Fire Protection Association.

6. American Burn Association. (n.d.). *Scald injury prevention educator's guide: A community fire and burn prevention program supported by the United States Fire Administration Federal Emergency Management Agency.* Retrieved from http://www.ameriburn.org/

7. Nance, M. L., Carr, B. G., & Branas, C. C. (2009). Access to pediatric trauma care in the United States. *Archives of Pediatric and Adolescent Medicine, 163,* 512–518.

8. Committee on the Future of Emergency Care in the US Health System. (2006). *Future of emergency care: Emergency care for children: Growing pains.* Washington, DC: National Academy Press.

9. Emergency Nurses Association. (2007). Special populations: pregnant, pediatric, and older adult trauma patients. In *Trauma nursing core course (provider manual)* (6th ed., pp. 225–249). Des Plaines, IL: Author.

10. D'Souza, A. L., Nelson, N. G., & McKenzie, L. B. (2009). Pediatric burn injuries treated in US emergency departments between 1990 and 2006. *Pediatrics, 124,* 1424–1430.

11. Connors, M. J., Ruddy, R. M., McCall, J., & Garcia, V. F. (2001). Delayed diagnosis in pediatric blunt trauma. *Pediatric Emergency Care, 17,* 1–4.

12. Arbogast, K. B., Kent, R. W., Menon, R. A., Ghati, Y., Durbin, D. R., & Rouhana, S. W. (2007). Mechanisms of abdominal organ injury in seat belt-restrained children. *Journal of Trauma, 62,* 1473–1480.

13. Stacey, S., Foreman, J., Woods, W., Arbogast, K., & Kent, R. (2009). Pediatric abdominal injury patterns generated by lap belt loading. *Journal of Trauma, 67,* 1278–1283.

14. National Highway Traffic Safety Administration. (2010). *Child safety.* Retrieved from http://www.nhtsa.gov/portal/site/nhtsa/menuitem.dcee64704e76eeabbf30811060008a0c

15. Newgard, C. D., & Lewis, R. J. (2005). Airbags may increase risk of serious injury in children age 14 and younger. *Pediatrics, 115,* 1579–1585.

16. Howard, A. W. (2002). Automobile restraints for children: A review for clinicians. *Canadian Medical Association Journal, 167,* 769–773.

17. Ivarsson, B. J., & Crandall, J. R. (2006). Influence of age-related stature on the frequency of body region injury and overall injury severity in child pedestrian casualties. *Traffic Injury Prevention, 7,* 290–296.

18. Waddell, J. P., & Drucker, W. R. (1971). Occult injuries in pedestrian accidents. *Journal of Trauma, 11,* 844–852.

19. Orsborn, R., Haley, K., Hammond, S., & Falcone, R. E. (1999). Pediatric pedestrian versus motor vehicle patterns of injury: Debunking the myth. Air Medical Journal, 18(3), 107–110.

20. American Academy of Pediatrics, Committee on Injury and Poison Prevention. (2008). AAP Policy Statement for Bicycle Helmets. *Pediatrics, 122,* 450. doi:10.1542/peds 2008-1427

21. Parkinson, G. W., & Hike, K. E. (2003). Bicycle helmet assessment during well visits reveals severe shortcomings in condition and fit. *Pediatrics, 112,* 320–323.

22. Wegner, S., Colletti, J. E., & Van Wie, D. (2006). Pediatric blunt abdominal trauma. *Pediatric Clinics of North America, 53,* 243–256.

23. American Academy of Pediatrics, Committee on Injury and Poison Prevention. (2002). Skateboard and scooter injuries. *Pediatrics, 109,* S42–S43.

24. McBeth, P. B., Ball, C. G., Mulloy, R. H., & Kirkpatrick, A. W. (2009). Alpine ski and snowboarding traumatic injuries: incidence, injury patterns, and risk factors for 10 years. *The American Journal of Surgery, 197,* 560–564.

25. Eberl, R., Schalamon, J., Singer, G., Huber, S. S., Spitzer, P., & Höllwarth, M. E. (2009). Trampoline-related injuries in childhood. *European Journal of Pediatrics, 168,* 1171–1174.

26. Denke, N. J. (2008). Brain injury in sports. *Journal of Emergency Nursing, 34,* 363–364.

References *continued*

27. Centers for Disease Control and Prevention. (n.d.). *Facts for physicians about mild traumatic brain injury.* Retrieved from http://www.cdc.gov/concussion/headsup/pdf/Facts_for_Physicians_booklet-a.pdf

28. Injuries to young athletes: Committee on pediatric aspects of physical fitness, recreation, and sports. (1980). *Pediatrics, 65*(2). A53–54. Retrieved from http://aappolicy.aappublications.org/cgi/reprint/pediatrics;65/3/649.pdf

29. Harmon, K. (1999). Assessment and management of concussion in sports. *American Family Physician.* Retrieved from http://www.aafp.org/afp/990901ap/887.html

30. Committee on Injury, Violence, and Poison Prevention. (2010). Policy statement: Prevention of drowning. *Pediatrics, 126,* 1–8.

31. Hansen, S. (2009). Submersion injuries. In D. O. Thomas & L. M. Bernardo (Eds.), *Core curriculum for pediatric emergency nursing* (2nd ed., pp. 431–434). Des Plaines, IL: Emergency Nurses Association.

32. Verive, M. J. (2009). *Near-drowning.* Retrieved from http://emedicine.medscape.com/article/908677-overview

33. Amick, L. F. (2001). Penetrating trauma in the pediatric patient. *Clinical Pediatric Emergency Medicine, 2,* 63–70.

34. Kadish, H. A. (2001). Cervical spine evaluation in the pediatric trauma patient. *Clinical Pediatric Emergency Medicine, 2,* 41–47.

35. Ralston, M., Hazinski, M. F., Zaritsky, A. L., Schexnayder, S. M., & Kleinman, M. E. (Eds.). (2007). *Pediatric advanced life support course guide and PALS provider manual.* Dallas, TX: American Heart Association.

36. Dannevig, I., Dale, H. C., Liest, K., & Lindemann, R. (2005). Blood pressure in the neonate: Three non-invasive oscillometric pressure monitors compared with invasively measured blood pressure. *Acta Paediatrica, 96,* 191–196.

37. Hutchings, L., Atijosan, O., Burgess, C., & Willett, K. (2009). Developing a spinal clearance protocol for unconscious pediatric trauma patients. *Journal of Trauma, 67,* 681–686.

38. Kuppermann, N., Holmes, J. F., Dayan, P. S., Hoyle Jr., J. D., Atabaki, S. M., Holubkov, R., ... Pediatric Emergency Care Applied Research Network (PECARN). (2009). Identification of children at very low risk of clinically-important brain injuries after head trauma: a prospective cohort study. *Lancet, 374,* 1160–1170.

39. Joffe, M. D. (2010). Burns. In G. R. Fleisher & S. Ludwig (Eds.), *Textbook of pediatric emergency medicine* (6th ed., pp. 1281–1288). Philadelphia, PA: Lippincott Williams & Wilkins.

40. Herndon, D. N. (2007). *Total burn care* (3rd ed.). St. Louis, MO: Elsevier.

41. Perry, C. (2003). Thermal injuries. In P. A. Moloney-Harmon & S. J. Czerwinski (Eds.), *Nursing care of the pediatric trauma patient* (pp. 277–294). Philadelphia, PA: Saunders.

42. American Burn Association. (2001). *Advanced burn life support course instructors manual.* Chicago, IL: Author.

43. Stock, A., & Singer, L. (2009). *Head trauma.* Retrieved from http://emedicine.medscape.com/article/907273-overview

44. Kapapa, T., König, K., Pfister, U., Sasse, M., Woischneck, D., Heissler, H., & Rickels, E. (2010). Head trauma in children, part 1: Admission, diagnostics, and findings. *Journal of Child Neurology, 25,* 146–156.

45. Tebruegge, M., Misra, I., Pantazidou, A., Padhye, A., Maity, A., Dwarakanathan, B., ... Nerminathan, V. (2009). Estimating blood loss: comparative study of the accuracy of parents and healthcare professionals. *Pediatrics, 124,* e729–e736.

46. Jones, P. A., Andrews, P. J., Easton, V. J., & Minns, R. A. (2003). Traumatic brain injury in childhood: Intensive care time series data and outcome. *British Journal of Neurosurgery, 17,* 29–39.

47. Huh, J. W., & Raghupathi, R. (2009). New concepts in treatment of pediatric traumatic brain injury. *Anesthesiology Clinics, 27,* 213–240.

48. Marcoux, K. K. (2005). Management of increased intracranial pressure in the critically ill child with an acute neurological injury. *AACN Clinical Issues, 16*(2), 212–231.

49. Hegenbarth, M. (2008). Preparing for pediatric emergencies: Drugs to consider. *Pediatrics, 121,* 433–443.

50. National Guideline Clearinghouse. (2007). *Guidelines for the management of severe traumatic brain injury: Antiseizure prophylaxis.* Retrieved from http://www.guideline.gov/

51. Sanford, R. A. (2010). Prevention of growing skull fractures. *Journal of Neurosurgery, 5,* 213–218.

52. Centers for Disease Control and Prevention, National Center for Injury Prevention and Control. *Heads up.* Retrieved from http://www.cdc.gov/concussion/HeadsUp/youth.html

53. Hayes, J. S., & Arriola, T. (2005). Pediatric spinal injuries. *Pediatric Nursing, 31,* 464–467.

54. Roddy, M. G., Lange, P. A., & Klein, B. L. (2005). Cardiac trauma in children. *Clinical Pediatric Emergency Medicine, 6,* 234–243.

References *continued*

55. Holmes, J. F., Gladman, A., & Chang, C. H. (2007). Performance of abdominal ultrasonography in pediatric blunt trauma patients: a meta-analysis. *Journal of Pediatric Surgery, 42,* 1588–1594.

56. Staudt, J. M, Smeulders, M. J, & van der Horst, C. M. (2009). Normal compartment pressures of the lower leg in children. *The Journal of Bone and Joint Surgery,* British edition, 90(2), 215-219.

57. Fleisher, G. R., & Ludwig, S. (Eds.). (2010). Textbook of pediatric emergency medicine (6th ed.). Philadelphia, PA: Lippincott Williams & Wilkins.

58. Cerepani, M. J. (2010). Orthopedic and neurovascular trauma. In P. K. Howard & R. A. Steinmann (Eds.), *Sheehy's emergency nursing: Principles and practice* (6th ed., p. 316). St. Louis, MO: Mosby/Elsevier.

59. Safe Kids Canada. (2010). *Skiing/snowboarding.* Retrieved from http://www.safekidscanada.ca/parents/safety-information/winter-safety/snowboarding-winter/snowboarding.aspx

Internet Resources

American Academy of Pediatrics (http://www.aap.org/)

American Trauma Society (http://www.amtrauma.org)

Centers for Disease Control and Prevention (http://www.cdc.gov)

National Guideline Clearinghouse (http://www.guideline.gov/)

National Highway Traffic Safety Administration (http://www.nhtsa.dot.gov)

National Youth Sports Safety Foundation (http://www.nyssf.org)

Transport Canada Road Safety (http://www.tc.gc.ca/roadsafety/rsindx_e.htm)

Chapter 17 | Toxicological Emergencies

Rose Ann Gould Soloway, MSEd, BSN, RN, DABAT

Objectives

On completion of this chapter, the learner should be able to do the following:

- Determine anatomical, physiological, and developmental characteristics of pediatric patients as a basis for assessment of poisoning.

- Describe common causes and characteristics of poisoning in the pediatric patient.

- Plan appropriate interventions for suspected or actual poisonings in a pediatric patient.

- Indicate health promotion strategies to reduce the incidence and severity of poisoning in the pediatric population.

Introduction

The US Centers for Disease Control and Prevention (CDC) defines poison as "any substance that is harmful to your body when ingested, inhaled, injected, or absorbed through the skin. Any substance can be poisonous if enough is taken. This definition does not include adverse reactions to medications taken correctly."[1] A poison exposure is contact with such a substance, whereas a poisoning indicates that harm has actually occurred.

Poison exposures are common in the pediatric population.

- In 2008, US poison centers managed more than 1.6 million emergency calls regarding pediatric patients (through the age of 19 years). Most were for children younger than six years, and most children were treated at home, with poison center guidance. Older pediatric patients were more likely to require emergency department care and were more likely to die as a result of poisoning (**Table 17-1**).[2]

- In a two-year period, the US CDC reported an estimated 71,224 pediatric emergency department visits for medication overdoses and an additional 32,217 for unintentional exposures to nonpharmacological substances. Unsupervised ingestions were the cause of most visits. Emergency department treatment for a medication overdose was needed for one of every 180 two-year-old children.[3]

Poisonings may be either unintentional or intentional. Most poisonings in pediatric patients are unintentional,

Table 17-1 Age, Management Site, and Serious/Fatal Outcomes of Pediatric Poison Exposures*				
Age in Years	No. of Cases†	% Managed in a Healthcare Facility	Medical Outcome	
			Life Threatening or Permanent	Fatal
≤5	1,292,754	9.9	832	32
6–12	153,121	11.1	228	9
13–19	168,094	42.8	2,054	77

*Data are taken from Bronstein et al.[2]
†The entire database contains 2,491,049 poison exposures in persons of all ages.

often associated with children being left unattended around open products, improper storage of poisons, and therapeutic error.[3] Children from the ages of one to five years are at risk for toxic exposure, particularly through ingestion, because of differences in developmental characteristics and environmental influences. Most often, these are single-substance ingestions, nontoxic or minimally toxic, and discovered soon after they occur.

Intentional poisonings are more common in the adolescent population. These may be suicide attempts, often related to academic, social, romantic, and family difficulties; and abuse of drugs and other substances, such as inhalants. Adolescents are also subject to therapeutic errors,[3] misuse of household products, and exposure to chemicals in the workplace.[4] After medical stability has been achieved, the exploration of psychosocial issues is a vital part of the intervention for pediatric patients presenting with intentional poisoning.

Causes of Poisonings

Most poison exposures in children five years and younger are because of common substances found in a home: cosmetics and personal care products, analgesics, household cleaning substances, foreign bodies/toys/miscellaneous products, topical preparations, cough and cold preparations, vitamins, antihistamines, pesticides, and plants.[2]

Common exposures were not necessarily the most dangerous.

- Children five years and younger most often died from carbon monoxide/smoke inhalation, oxycodone, sodium bicarbonate, and an array of other pharmaceutical and nonpharmaceutical substances.

- In children aged six to 12 years, fatalities were associated with carbon monoxide/smoke inhalation, bupropion, methadone, tramadol, hair spray, and paraquat.

- Fatalities in teenagers were reportedly because of methadone, oxycodone, bupropion, quetiapine, acetaminophen/oxycodone, 3,4-methylenedioxymethamphetamine (or Ecstasy [a hallucinogenic amphetamine]), opioid, salicylate, amphetamine, lithium, and a variety of other substances, most of them pharmaceuticals.[2]

A number of adult medications can be especially dangerous for young children. **Table 17-2** provides a list of medications identified as toxic to toddlers who swallow the equivalent of only one or two adult doses.

Table 17-2 Medications Dangerous or Fatal to Toddlers with a Single Adult Dose*

Antiarrhythmics (e.g., quinidine and procainamide)

Antipsychotics (e.g., loxapine and chlorpromazine)

Calcium channel blockers (e.g., verapamil and nifedipine)

Camphor

Methyl salicylate

Opioids

Oral hypoglycemics (e.g., chlorpropamide and glipizide)

Podophyllin

Quinine-based antimalarials (e.g., chloroquine and quinine)

Theophylline

Tricyclic antidepressants (e.g., amitriptyline and imipramine)

*Data are taken from Rosenbaum and Kou,[20] Bar-Oz et al.,[21] Sachdeva and Stadnyk,[44] and Little and Boniface.[46]

Anatomical, Physiological, and Developmental Characteristics as a Basis for Key Findings

Anatomical and Physiological Characteristics

The properties of a substance affect its rate of absorption, metabolism, distribution, and excretion from the body. Anatomical differences and physiological maturity also influence these factors in infants and young children.

The absorption of a substance occurs through one of five routes: oral, dermal, ocular, inhalation, and parenteral.

Most poison exposures are through the oral route.[2] Although absorption can occur anywhere along the gastrointestinal (GI) tract, most ingested substances are absorbed in the small intestine. Variability in gastric emptying, blood flow, rapid peristalsis, and changes in gastric pH also influence the absorption of medications and other substances from the GI tract.[5]

Substances absorbed by a lactating mother may be excreted in breast milk and consequently ingested by the breastfed infant. A variety of over-the-counter, illicit, and therapeutic medications and environmental and occupational chemicals may be excreted in breast milk at varying levels.[6]

Pediatric patients' skin is thinner and more porous than the skin of adults. The proportion of body surface area to weight is greater. Pediatric patients are more likely to absorb substances and are more prone to caustic injuries. The site of the exposure also determines the likelihood of significant absorption of substances. For example, the palm is relatively resistant, whereas the groin and armpits are more permeable.[7]

The rate of absorption of inhaled gases and fumes is determined by metabolic rate, ventilation, and pulmonary blood flow. Because infants and young children have higher metabolic rates, their respiratory rates are normally faster. This contributes to increased inhalation and absorption of toxic substances when exposed.

Pediatric patients have a smaller airway diameter than adults. Small amounts of airway edema can quickly lead to increased airway resistance and airway obstruction. Support and management of airway, ventilation, and oxygenation must always be considered in poisonings that may affect airway and breathing in infants and children, such as hydrocarbons and caustics.

Immature organ systems predispose infants and young children to enhanced absorption and decreased metabolism and excretion of many substances.[8]

- The absorption of medications from the GI tract is slower in young children, delaying time to peak blood levels.

- The glomerular filtration rate is lower than adult values until approximately the age of 12 months, making it harder to metabolize medication.

- Hepatic enzymes develop at variable rates, making it harder to metabolize medication.

- Infants have lower serum albumin concentrations; thus, they have fewer binding sites for medications.

- The percentages of body water and body fat differ from neonates to older children to adults, thus altering the distribution of medications into physiological compartments.

Developmental Characteristics

Young children are naturally curious. Challenges such as closed cupboards and high shelves present an opportunity to further explore their environment. Brightly colored packages and candy-coated pills are attractive to unknowing toddlers, particularly when they are hungry. Increased oral gratification, hand-to-mouth activity, and increased mobility in young children make them particularly susceptible to ingestion of medicines, household products, foreign bodies, tobacco products, alcoholic beverages, and any number of other substances on or near the floor or within reach.

School-aged children continue to be curious. Their expanding world leads to encounters with unfamiliar products, medicines, and outdoor wildlife. They may need therapeutic medications but not understand safe medication-taking practices or label instructions. Depending on their emotional and developmental maturity, they may engage in magical thinking (if one is good, three are better) and/or respond to the dares of playmates.

Teenagers are at risk from intentional overdoses and drug abuse for the reasons previously noted. Also, they may be in charge of taking their own therapeutic medications without fully understanding how to do so safely. Like adults, they may ignore instructions for the proper use of household products. Also, they may not understand the need to protect themselves from workplace chemicals, especially if their supervisors do not encourage safe use of these products.

Focused Assessment

Assessment

Chapter 5, "Initial Assessment," provides a review of the primary assessment. Once airway, breathing, and circulation have been established, a secondary survey is performed, including a complete neurological assessment. Additional assessment data related to specific poisonings are listed in the following sections.

Additional History

When obtaining a history of toxic exposure, include the following questions specific to the exposure or substance (the five Ws):

- Who?
  - Other family members exposed
  - Other children exposed
- What and how much?
  - Route(s) of exposure
  - Open bottles or containers found near the patient
  - Evidence of exposure: pills found in the immediate vicinity, pill fragments in the mouth, product spilled on clothing, plant pieces, or leaves
  - Estimated amount of exposure: count remaining pills or liquid and compare with original amount in the container minus the amount used; always assume that the maximum amount available was consumed
  - Treatment administered before arrival in the emergency department

- When?
  - Time exposure occurred/time it was discovered
  - Estimated duration of exposure
- Where?
  - Where did the exposure occur (e.g., home, other relative's home, child-care provider, indoors, or outdoors)
  - Availability of other products or substances in the general area where the exposure occurred
- Why?
  - Intent: unintentional, self-harm, abuse, malicious, or criminal
  - Circumstances of exposure (error in medication administration or curiosity)

Key Findings

The symptoms, severity, and time of onset will vary depending on the type and quantity of poison involved and the route of exposure. Signs and symptoms of each particular exposure are listed with each poison.

Planning and Implementation

Diagnostic Procedures

Laboratory studies may be indicated based on the suspected etiology of the patient's poisoning. Definitive diagnostic procedures are performed while the resuscitation is in progress or after the patient is stabilized. Specific diagnostic procedures are listed in the "Specific Interventions" sections of the selected poisonings. The following general procedures/studies may be indicated for the patient with a suspected or actual poisoning.

Monitoring

- Noninvasive blood pressure and cardiorespiratory status
- Pulse oximetry

Radiographic Studies

- Chest radiograph (to evaluate for evidence of infiltrates from aspiration and the presence of a foreign body)
- Abdominal film (for foreign bodies, ingestion of iron and other radiopaque medications and medication bezoars)

Laboratory Studies

Laboratory studies may be ordered based on the suspected or known poison. The following should be considered:

- Initial patient management proceeds before a toxicology screen is available. Toxicology screens may confirm a suspected poison exposure or provide information when a poisoning is suspected but not known for sure. A toxicology screen can complement but NOT replace the need for taking an accurate history, identifying the possible poison, and treating clinical symptoms.
- The components of a toxicology screen vary among laboratories and may not include the patient's suspected or actual exposure. A negative toxicology screen result does not necessarily indicate the absence of exposure.
- Specific quantitative levels, such as acetaminophen, iron, salicylates, lithium, digitalis, certain anticonvulsants, methanol, ethylene glycol, and carbon monoxide, may be necessary to determine appropriate ongoing management.
- Other laboratory procedures may be ordered based on the potential actions of the medication, or poison and signs and symptoms exhibited by the patient. Examples may include arterial blood gas, electrolytes, blood glucose, liver and renal function, and coagulation.

Interventions

Chapter 5, "Initial Assessment," provides a description of the general nursing interventions for pediatric patients with an alteration in airway, breathing, or circulation. After ensuring a patent airway, effective ventilation, and adequate circulation, interventions may include decontamination, the administration of available antidotes, and the elimination of medications, drugs, or poisons.

Consult the Poison Center

After stabilizing a patient's vital functions, consult the poison center (1-800-222-1222, nationwide number for all US poison centers) for up-to-date patient-specific treatment recommendations. Calls are automatically routed to the local poison center and are answered by specialists in poison information. These local experts are nurses and pharmacists with additional training and national certification in recognizing and treating poisons. There is 24-hour backup by medical toxicologists for especially serious or unusual cases.

In addition to recommending treatment, poison center staff can recommend necessary laboratory studies, assist with obtaining unusual antidotes, and provide continuity if a patient is admitted to an inpatient unit for ongoing medical care. If the patient is discharged home, the poison center will follow up with the parents to be sure that recovery is complete, to refer the patient back for additional care if needed, to answer questions that the caregivers may have about the poison, and to provide poison prevention materials.

The Health Insurance Portability and Accountability Act's Privacy Rule permits poison centers to receive protected health information for treatment and follow-up, as follows: "poison control centers are healthcare providers for purposes of th[e] rule"; "counseling and follow-up consultations provided by poison control centers with individual providers regarding patient outcomes are considered to be treatment."[9]

Therefore, nurses caring for poisoned patients should freely consult the poison center for treatment recommendations and provide follow-up, just as they would for other consulting clinical services.

Another advantage to consulting the poison center is that cases then become (anonymous) entries into the major, near-real-time, US surveillance system for evidence of public health emergencies, including chemical and biological warfare attacks.[2, 10]

Additional Interventions
External Decontamination

Initiate external dermal decontamination for the pediatric patients with exposure to toxic or hazardous materials, as indicated by institutional policies and procedures. Prompt decontamination will lessen exposure for the pediatric patient, healthcare providers, and treatment areas.

Dermal exposures should be irrigated with running water for 15 to 20 minutes. Any clothing left on the pediatric patient should be removed. Follow institutional procedure for bagging/containing clothing and other items that could pose a risk to healthcare professionals.

Ocular exposures should be flushed with normal saline or lactated Ringer's solution for a minimum of 20 to 30 minutes. (If these solutions are not immediately available, tap water should be used until the solutions are available.) The goal is an ocular pH of seven, checked with a pH strip gently touched to the cul-de-sac inside the lower eyelid. If this pH is not achieved with the initial 20 to 30 minutes of irrigation, continue irrigation until the pH is seven. Follow this with a complete ocular examination.

Gastric Decontamination

The aim of gastric decontamination, when indicated, is to prevent absorption of the poison.[11] If GI decontamination is needed, the recommended method usually is the administration of activated charcoal. Gastric lavage is useful in limited circumstances only. The benefit from decontamination decreases as the duration from ingestion increases;

as a rule, decontamination should be initiated within one hour. Exceptions might be medications that slow gastric motility (e.g., opioids and anticholinergic medications).

- The benefit of gastric lavage for gastric decontamination in poisoned patients is unproved and in many cases, dangerous. The amount of toxin reduced with gastric lavage is limited and diminishes rapidly. In addition, orogastric/nasogastric tubes are not often large enough to be able to retrieve pills or pill particles in the pediatric patient. The American Academy of Clinical Toxicology/European Association of Poisons Centres and Clinical Toxicologists position statement concludes that gastric lavage "should not be considered unless a patient has ingested a potentially life-threatening amount of a poison and the procedure can be undertaken within 60 minutes of ingestion." Gastric lavage is associated with a higher prevalence of aspiration pneumonia, esophageal and gastric injury, dysrhythmias, changes in oxygenation, and laryngospasm.[12]

- Activated charcoal reduces the absorption of a substance by binding with it in the GI tract (adsorption). It is derived from organic material and exposed to agents that make it extremely porous and adsorbent. It can bind with up to 37% of a charcoal-adsorbent substance if given within 60 minutes of the ingestion. As with all methods of gastric decontamination, its efficacy diminishes with time and it is of most value if given within one hour of ingestion.[13]

  ○ Because of its poor palatability and gritty texture, activated charcoal is often given via nasogastric tube to young children. The recommended dose of charcoal is 1 g/kg. Cathartic agents, such as sorbitol, are not recommended.[14] Charcoal does not adsorb alcohols, hydrocarbons, caustics, or heavy metals (e.g., iron, lead, mercury, lithium, and arsenic).

- Whole-bowel irrigation is indicated for ingestions of potentially dangerous amounts and types of substances that are not adsorbed by activated charcoal (e.g., iron) and/or are formulated as sustained-release preparations (e.g., calcium channel blockers). It may also be indicated for body packers or body stuffers, who swallow packets of cocaine, heroin, or other illegal drugs.

  ○ Whole-bowel irrigation is accomplished by the administration of polyethylene glycol electrolyte solution (GoLYTELY, NuLYTELY, or Colyte) through a gastric tube, at a rate of 25 mL/kg or up to 2 L/hour for adolescents. It is continued until the rectal effluent is clear or until radiographs show that foreign bodies have been eliminated. Because the solution is not absorbed, fluid and electrolyte imbalance is unlikely.

If vomiting occurs, temporarily decrease the rate of administration and, if necessary, give intravenous metoclopramide (Reglan). Whole-bowel irrigation is contraindicated in patients with suspected paralytic ileus, bowel obstruction, or perforation.[15]

Antidotes

There are few antidotes. However, in some cases, the administration of an antidote can be lifesaving or, at minimum, can decrease the severity of toxic effects. The use of antidotes is reviewed with the specific poisonings, where appropriate. **Table 17-3** lists selected antidotes and the substances for which they are used.

Elimination of Toxic Substances

Once a substance has been absorbed, it is free to act on receptors. Certain properties of a drug can make it more amenable to enhanced elimination from the system. Some of these methods include forced diuresis, urine alkalization, hemodialysis, charcoal hemoperfusion, and exchange transfusion.[16] Methods appropriate to the poison are mentioned as part of specific poison management.

Evaluation and Ongoing Assessment

Pediatric patients who have been exposed to a toxic substance require meticulous and frequent reassessment of airway patency, breathing effectiveness, perfusion, and mental status. Initial improvements may not be sustained, and additional interventions may be needed. Monitoring of drug levels may be needed to achieve the desired outcomes.

Table 17-3 Selected Antidotes*

Antidote	Indication(s)
N-acetylcysteine (Acetadote, Mucomyst)	Acetaminophen
Crotalidae polyvalent immune digoxin-specific antibody fragments, ovine	North American crotaline snake envenomation
Antivenin (*Latrodectus mactans*)	Black widow spider envenomation
Antivenin (*Micrurus fulvius*)	Eastern and Texas coral snake envenomation
Atropine sulfate	Organophosphorous and N-methyl carbamate insecticides
Botulism antitoxin, equine (A, B)	Botulism
Botulism immune globulin (BabyBIG)	Infant botulism
Calcium chloride or calcium gluconate	Fluoride and calcium channel blockers
Calcium disodium EDTA	Lead
Cyanide antidote kit or hydroxocobalamin hydrochloride	Cyanide poisoning
Deferoxamine mesylate (Desferal)	Acute iron poisoning
Digoxin-immune antibody fragments	Cardiac glycosides
Dimercaprol	Heavy metal toxicity (arsenic, mercury, and lead)
Ethanol	Methanol and ethylene glycol poisoning
Fomepizole (Antizol)	Methanol and ethylene glycol poisoning
Flumazenil (Romazicon)	Benzodiazepine toxicity
Glucagon hydrochloride	ß-Blockers and calcium channel blockers
Methylene blue	Methemoglobinemia
Naloxone (Narcan)	Opioid and opiate medications
Octreotide acetate (Sandostatin)	Sulfonylurea-induced hypoglycemia
Physostigmine salicylate	Anticholinergic syndrome
Pralidoxime (Protopam)	Organophosphorous insecticides

*Data are adapted from Dart, R. C., Borron, S. W., Caravati, E. M., Cobaugh, D. J., Curry, S. C, Falk, J. L. ... Zosel, A. (2009). Expert consensus guidelines for stocking of antidotes in hospitals that provide emergency care. *Annals of Emergency Medicine, 54,* 386–394.

Selected Poisonings

Typical pediatric poison emergencies are presented later. Consultation with the poison center experts to identify appropriate and current treatment modalities is an essential component of emergency care, planning, and interventions.

Each of the following assumes that:

- Patient assessment has been initiated and is ongoing.
- Symptomatic and supportive care is being rendered.
- Decontamination has been or is being performed, if indicated.
- Discharge instructions will include poison prevention teaching, as indicated.

Additional history, signs and symptoms, interventions, and discharge instructions specific to selected poisonings are listed.

Unknown Poison or Overdose

Occasionally, a pediatric patient who is unconscious or nonverbal will be seen in the emergency department for an exposure to an unknown poison. Consider possible poisoning in a patient who presents with the following:

- Altered level of consciousness
- Seizures
- Abnormal vital signs
- Cardiac dysrhythmias
- Multiple symptoms with no known cause

In these cases, the patient's clinical presentation may provide clues toward identifying the responsible agent. **Table 17-4** summarizes the clinical features associated with common types of poisons, or toxidromes. Consult the regional poison center for assistance in determining if poisoning could be the cause of unusual presentations.

While a diagnosis of poisoning is being considered, assessment and treatment proceed as for any critically ill patient.

Table 17-4 Toxidromes: Signs and Symptoms Associated With Specific Poisons*

Toxidrome	Signs and Symptoms	Possible Poison
Anticholinergic	Flushing, hallucinations, dry mouth, dry skin, tachycardia, urinary retention, mydriasis, decreased bowel sounds, seizures, coma, and cardiac dysrhythmias	Cyclic antidepressants, antihistamines, over-the-counter sleep preparations with antihistamines, Jimson weed *(Datura stramonium)*, and some wild mushrooms
Cholinergic	Salivation, lacrimation, urination, defecation, emesis (SLUDGE), bronchoconstriction, muscle fasciculations, and seizures	Organophosphates and carbamate insecticides, some wild mushrooms, and severe black widow spider bites
Opiate/opioid	Altered mental status, unresponsiveness, miosis, respiratory depression, bradycardia, hypothermia, hypotension, and decreased bowel sounds	Opioids, heroin, and clonidine
Salicylates	Hyperthermia, tachypnea, altered mental status, tinnitus, vomiting, acidosis, and shock	Aspirin, methyl salicylate, and gastrointestinal preparations with bismuth subsalicylate
Sedative hypnotics	Sedation, confusion, hallucinations, coma, diplopia, blurred vision, slurred speech, ataxia, nystagmus, respiratory depression, and hypotension	Benzodiazepines and barbiturates
Serotonin syndrome	Altered mental status, tachycardia, hypertension, hyperreflexia, clonus, and hyperthermia	Any combination of serotonergic agents (e.g., citalopram, fluoxetine, fluvoxamine, paroxetine, and sertraline); rarely occurs after a single overdose
Sympathomimetic	Tachycardia, hypertension, hyperthermia, mydriasis, restlessness, agitation, hyperactivity, diaphoresis, tremors, and cardiac dysrhythmias	Amphetamines, including methamphetamine, hallucinogenic amphetamines (e.g., Ecstasy), and methylphenidate; related medications used to treat attention-deficit/hyperactivity disorder; cocaine; and phencyclidine

*Data are taken from Liebelt[22] and the following additional sources: (1) Holstege, C. P., Dobmeier, S. G., & Bechtel, L. K. (2008). Critical care toxicology. *Emergency Medicine Clinics of North America, 25,* 715–739. (2) Haynes, J. F. (2006). Medical management of adolescent drug overdoses. *Adolescent Medicine, 17,* 353–379.

Acetaminophen

Acetaminophen is an analgesic and antipyretic agent found in many over-the-counter and prescription preparations. It is one of the most common medications ingested by children, and it is also one of the most common causes of poisoning-related death in adolescents and adults.[2] There are several commercially available concentrations of acetaminophen-containing products (e.g., infant drops, pediatric elixir, children's chewable tablets, and junior tablets). Also, there are numerous products that contain acetaminophen plus other ingredients, such as cough and cold preparations, allergy medications, and sleep aids. The risk of improper dosing is increased because of confusion about various concentrations and packaging.

Ingestion of acetaminophen may lead to hepatic failure and death; kidney failure may occur but is less common. Toxicity can occur with a single large exposure or multiple exposures over time (hours or days). The onset of symptoms is dependent on the total amount ingested per kilogram of body weight. Those who ingest greater than 150 mg/kg are at risk for hepatotoxicity. Even though young children tend to develop less hepatic toxicity than adolescents and adults because of differences in metabolic pathways, they are still vulnerable to the effects of overdose.

Acetaminophen levels assist in assessing the treatment needs of a patient with potential toxicity from a single acute ingestion. Toxicity may develop after an acute ingestion of 150 mg/kg or more.[17] Blood levels drawn four hours or longer after an acute ingestion, interpreted on the Rumack-Matthew nomogram,[17] are used to determine potential toxicity and the need for treatment with N-acetylcysteine (NAC). To prevent hepatocellular damage, NAC is ideally administered within eight hours of ingestion but may still be effective up to 24 hours or more after ingestion. If the nomogram is not posted in the emergency department, consult the poison center for blood level interpretation.

For chronic ingestions, do NOT use the nomogram. Whether the antidote is indicated depends on the total dose ingested, the time over which the medication was taken, and the result of liver function procedures. (The acetaminophen level is no longer useful because, as the medication is metabolized, the level will decrease automatically. However, toxicity is the result of metabolites that are not measured and could still be active.)

Each case should be considered individually. Consult the poison center to determine if treatment is needed and, if so, to promote continuity of care when the patient is admitted.

Key Findings

Acetaminophen-induced injury occurs in stages, with the first stage beginning shortly after ingestion. Symptoms progress at a variable rate depending on the dose and time of ingestion. **Table 17-5** describes the phases of acetaminophen poisoning.[18]

Specific Interventions

- Perform appropriate laboratory procedures
  - Acetaminophen level at least four hours after ingestion for acute ingestions
  - Acetaminophen level plus liver and renal function procedures if ingestion is chronic or presentation was delayed
- Administer activated charcoal if given within one to two hours of ingestion

Table 17-5 Four Phases of Acetaminophen Poisoning*

Phase	Time Frame (Approximate)	Symptoms/Effects
1	24 Hours after ingestion	Asymptomatic or signs of GI irritation, including anorexia, nausea and vomiting, decreased appetite, and/or general malaise
2	24–48 Hours after ingestion	Signs of hepatic damage, including elevation in liver enzymes (AST, ALT, and bilirubin), PT, PTT, and oliguria
3	72–96 Hours after ingestion	Signs of hepatic failure, hepatic necrosis, and encephalopathy, including right upper quadrant pain, altered mental status, and jaundice; renal failure; coagulation defects; death as the result of hepatic failure may occur during this phase
4	Four days to two weeks	Death OR full recovery

Note: ALT indicates alanine aminotransferase; AST, aspartate aminotransferase; GI, gastrointestinal; PT, prothrombin time; PTT, partial thromboplastin time.
*Data are taken from Marzullo.[18]

- Anticipate and prepare for the administration of the antidote, NAC.

  ◦ NAC may be administered intravenously or orally. In each case, a loading dose is followed by a series of maintenance doses. Dosing is determined by a patient's body weight. Consult the poison center for intravenous and oral doses.

  ◦ If intravenous NAC is given to infants or young children, the amount of intravenous fluid may need to be adjusted from standard recommendations to avoid fluid overload.

  ◦ If oral NAC is given, mask the unpleasant odor and smell by serving the medication over ice, in a covered cup, through a straw.

  ◦ Vomiting may occur with oral NAC. Antiemetics may be used, or the route may be switched to the intravenous route.

Alcohols

Alcohols include methanol, ethylene glycol, isopropyl alcohol, and ethanol. For pediatric patients, some alcohol ingestions can be life threatening. Isopropyl alcohol and ethanol will cause toxic effects quickly, generally within one hour or less. Methanol and ethylene glycol are potentially toxic in any amount more than a taste. Toxicity from methanol and ethylene glycol is delayed because it is their metabolites that cause poisoning. **Table 17-6** outlines alcohol types and sources.

Key Findings

Methanol

Methanol produces a triad of clinical symptoms, including GI, central nervous system (CNS), and ocular symptoms. There is a latent period of several hours before a poisoned patient develops significant symptoms. Metabolites cause acidosis and CNS depression. The metabolite formic acid damages the optic nerve, potentially causing permanent blindness in survivors. Effects include the following:

- Symptoms of intoxication without an ethanol odor to the breath
- Visual disturbances
- Anion gap metabolic acidosis
- CNS depression and coma

Ethylene Glycol

Ethylene glycol ingestion causes GI, CNS, and renal effects. There is a latent period of several hours before a poisoned patient develops significant symptoms. Metabolites cause acidosis and renal failure as the result, at least in part, of the deposit of calcium oxalate crystals in the kidneys. Effects include the following:

- Symptoms of intoxication without an ethanol odor to the breath
- Anion gap metabolic acidosis
- CNS depression and coma
- Calcium oxalate crystals in the urine
- Renal failure

Isopropyl Alcohol

Isopropyl alcohol is rapidly absorbed by the GI tract and excreted via the kidney. The remainder is metabolized by the liver, producing acetone. Effects include the following:

- Symptoms of intoxication without an ethanol odor to the breath
- "Fruity" acetone odor to the breath
- GI irritation
- CNS depression

Ethanol

Ethanol is rapidly absorbed by the GI tract; 90% is metabolized by the liver. The remainder is excreted by the kidney.

- Signs of intoxication include cognitive impairment; slurred speech and ataxia, progressing to lethargy; stupor; depression; and coma.
- Ethanol may cause hypoglycemia in young children because of their limited glycogen stores and limited capacity for gluconeogenesis. This can result in seizures, coma, and death.

Table 17-6 Types and Examples of Alcohols

Type of Alcohol	Examples of Products
Ethanol	Alcoholic beverages, perfumes, mouthwash, and hand sanitizer
Isopropyl	Rubbing alcohol, hand sanitizer, and solvents
Ethylene glycol	Radiator antifreeze and deicer
Methanol	Windshield washer fluid, solvents, and gasoline

Specific Interventions

- Support airway and breathing through positioning, insertion of an oral airway (if protective reflexes are absent), suctioning, monitoring, supplemental oxygen, and possible intubation/ventilation.

- Obtain laboratory specimens:

  ° Specific alcohol levels: ethanol, isopropanol/acetone, methanol, and ethylene glycol

  ° Electrolytes

  ° Glucose

  ° Renal function

  ° Arterial blood gases

  ° Osmolar gap

Symptomatic and supportive care, including respiratory support and management of hypoglycemia, may be sufficient for poisoning with ethanol and isopropyl alcohol, although dialysis may be indicated for severe poisoning.

Methanol and ethylene glycol poisonings require aggressive treatment measures in addition to symptomatic and supportive care.[19] Administer sodium bicarbonate for acidosis. Block metabolism by administering fomepizole (preferred) or ethanol. If ethanol blocking is used, frequent monitoring for hypoglycemia is needed. Prepare for hemodialysis and intensive care unit (ICU) admission.

Antidepressants: Tricyclic Antidepressants and Selective Serotonin Reuptake Inhibitors

Tricyclic Antidepressants

Despite the increased use of newer medications to treat depression, tricyclic antidepressant toxicity continues to be a cause of both morbidity and mortality in pediatric patients and adults. Amitriptyline (Elavil), imipramine (Tofranil), and desipramine (Norpramin) are commonly ingested tricyclic antidepressants. In addition to their use to treat depression, tricyclics are often prescribed as adjuvant therapy for neuropathic pain, nocturnal enuresis, migraine headaches, and sleep disorders.[20] Almost any amount can be toxic to a toddler.[21]

Toxicity is manifested by a variety of neurological and cardiovascular signs and symptoms. These are related to anticholinergic activity, blockade of norepinephrine reuptake, and quinidinelike effects of the medication. Significant complications, including wide complex dysrhythmias, hypotension, seizures, and coma, typically occur within one to six hours after the ingestion of a toxic amount. Serum levels are not well correlated with toxicity; in any case, they are not available quickly enough to influence emergency care.

The lethal cardiac effects of tricyclic antidepressant overdose are related to the quinidinelike effects of the medication: myocardial depression, prolongation of the PR and QRS intervals, conduction delays, ventricular dysrhythmias, decreased cardiac output, and hypotension. The widened QRS interval is an indication of toxicity in overdose cases.[22]

Signs and Symptoms

- Altered level of consciousness (drowsiness or sedation, confusion, agitation, hallucinations, and coma)

- Seizures

- Decreased respirations

- Cardiovascular effects

  ° Dysrhythmias (widened QRS and ventricular dysrhythmias)

  ° Hypotension secondary to myocardial depression and norepinephrine depletion

  ° Tachycardia

- Peripheral anticholinergic symptoms

  ° Flushing, dry mouth, and dilated pupils

- Urinary retention

- Decreased bowel sounds

- Hyperthermia

Specific Interventions

- Arterial blood gases and electrolytes

- 12-lead electrocardiogram

- Continuous cardiac monitoring

- Treat hypotension with fluid bolus initially, and use norepinephrine if blood pressure remains low after fluid administration

- Intravenous sodium bicarbonate and hypertonic saline for signs of cardiac toxicity (e.g., widened QRS and ventricular dysrhythmias), hypotension, and seizures

- Benzodiazepines for seizures

- Treat urinary retention

- Monitor electrolytes

Selective Serotonin Reuptake Inhibitors

Selective serotonin reuptake inhibitors have a much wider margin of safety than tricyclic antidepressants in therapeutic use and in overdose. Among those available are citalopram (Celexa), escitalopram (Lexapro), fluoxetine (Prozac), fluvoxamine (Luvox), paroxetine (Paxil), and sertraline (Zoloft). They are widely used to treat depression, obsessive-compulsive disorder, migraine headache, and several other conditions. Toxicity usually is minimal in overdose cases.

Key Findings

- Nausea and vomiting
- Tachycardia
- CNS depression
- Certain medication may cause seizures and electrocardiogram abnormalities

Specific Interventions

Symptomatic treatment and supportive care are usually enough to treat patients with these overdoses.

Benzodiazepines

Diazepam (Valium), lorazepam (Ativan), clonazepam (Klonopin), and alprazolam (Xanax) are among the common benzodiazepines prescribed to adults and, often, available to anyone in the home. In 2008, 6,569 children younger than six years were reported to have exposures to a benzodiazepine; none of those children died.[2] In the first reported series of benzodiazepine ingestions in children 1 to 10 years of age who required hospitalization, most patients recovered with activated charcoal and supportive care alone.[23]

Key Findings

- Ataxia
- Lethargy
- Coma
- Respiratory depression

Specific Interventions

Symptomatic treatment and supportive care are sufficient in most cases. Flumazenil (Romazicon) is a specific antidote for benzodiazepine overdose.

- It is rarely indicated because most patients recover with symptomatic and supportive care alone.

- It is contraindicated in patients with mixed overdoses and/or seizure disorders because it lowers the seizure threshold.
- It is contraindicated in those receiving chronic therapy with benzodiazepines or those abusing benzodiazepines because it can precipitate withdrawal.

Cardiovascular Medications

Common cardiac medication poisonings seen in the emergency department include β-adrenergic blockers and calcium channel blockers, which are primarily, although not exclusively, used as antihypertensive agents in adults. Digoxin (Lanoxin), a cardiac inotrope, is prescribed for infants with congenital cardiac anomalies and for pediatric patients with heart failure. Digoxin toxicity may be either acute or chronic. Small amounts of any of these medications may cause toxicity; a single tablet of a calcium channel blocker was associated with death in a toddler.

A variety of cardiac arrhythmias may be seen with ingestion of these agents. They also can cause significant hypotension and CNS deterioration.[24] Aggressive GI decontamination is critical if the patient is seen early enough. Intensive supportive care is indicated for all of these medications. Digoxin-specific antibody fragments are an antidote available for digitalis poisoning.

Key Findings

Symptoms associated with calcium channel blocker toxicity include bradycardia, hypotension, AV conduction abnormalities, complete heart block, altered mental status, coma, and death.[25]

Symptoms associated with β-blocker toxicity include seizures, hypotension, bradycardia, prolonged QRS and QT intervals, asystole, respiratory depression, and death.[26]

Symptoms associated with digitalis toxicity include nausea, vomiting, lethargy, confusion, weakness, delirium, visual disturbances, significant hyperkalemia, and almost any dysrhythmia.[27]

Diagnostic Procedures
Monitoring

- All patients require continuous monitoring of cardiovascular and respiratory functions, arterial blood gases, and electrolytes.

Laboratory Studies

- Digitalis levels are available and can help determine the need for an antidote. Levels of calcium channel and β-blockers are generally not available and do not determine therapy.

- Serial arterial blood gases, electrolytes (especially potassium and calcium), and glucose are determined.

Specific Interventions

- Airway protection and aggressive respiratory support; patients can deteriorate quickly.

- Fluid resuscitation.

- Cardiac ultrasonography if available for calcium channel and β-blockers.

- Whole-bowel irrigation is indicated for many of these ingestions, especially calcium channel blockers, many β-blockers, and sustained-release forms of these medications.

- Therapies for β-blocker toxicity may include glucagon, norepinephrine, sodium bicarbonate, and insulin/glucose.[28]

- Therapies for calcium channel blocker toxicity may include calcium, glucagon, norepinephrine, sodium bicarbonate, and insulin/glucose.[28]

- Therapies for digitalis toxicity may include multiple doses of activated charcoal, potassium, digoxin-specific antibody fragments, phenytoin, lidocaine, atropine, pacemaker, and cardioversion.[27]

Caustic Substances

Caustic agents include strong acids and strong alkaline substances. Substances with a pH of two or less or 12 or greater are most likely to cause injury. The mechanism of injury is different for acids and alkaline substances, but the outcome is essentially the same. An injury, substantially the equivalent of a burn, occurs to any tissue touched by these substances: skin, eyes, GI tract, or respiratory tract. Many caustic substances are found at home. Acids include toilet bowl cleaners and swimming pool chemicals. Alkaline substances include drain opener, oven cleaner, and automatic dishwasher detergent. Industrial strength cleaning products brought from the workplace are sometimes found at home.

- Solid and granular products tend to produce their greatest injury in the mouth and upper GI tract, although serious gastric injury can also occur. Liquid products tend to produce their greatest injury in the stomach, although serious injury to the mouth and upper GI tract

can also occur. The absence of visible injury does not necessarily mean the absence of any injury.

- Hydrofluoric acid causes systemic and local toxicity (not discussed herein). For a patient with hydrofluoric acid exposure, consult the poison center immediately for treatment recommendations.

Key Findings[29]

- Ocular, facial, and other dermal injury and pain
- Oral and pharyngeal edema
- Drooling and dysphasia
- Vomiting
- Chest and abdominal pain
- Respiratory distress

Assessment

- Chest and abdominal radiographs to assess for perforation
- Electrolytes
- Arterial blood gases in patients in respiratory distress

Specific Interventions

- Ocular irrigation for at least 20 to 30 minutes, until the pH is at least 7; check by touching a pH strip into the tear well.

- Dermal irrigation for 20 to 30 minutes. Remove and bag contaminated clothing. Do NOT attempt to "neutralize" the substance because the chemical reaction will generate heat and cause a thermal burn.

- Give patients nothing by mouth unless there are absolutely no symptoms. In that case, give a small amount of water to wash material down to the stomach.

- Consult gastroenterology about the need for endoscopy in symptomatic patients or patients with a history of intentional ingestions (which tend to be larger).

- Consult ophthalmology for ocular exposures; outpatient follow-up is likely to be needed.

Cough and Cold Preparations

In 2008, more than 47,000 cases of exposure to cough and cold preparations were reported in children younger than six years. An additional 14,000 cases were reported in children aged six to 19 years.[2] These numbers occur despite the following facts:

- Since 2007, the US Food and Drug Administration has recommended that these preparations not be given at all to children younger than two years of age.[30]

- There is evidence that they are ineffective[31] and potentially harmful or fatal.[32]
- Abuse of dextromethorphan (Pertussin) by adolescents is increasing and can cause severe intoxication.[33]

Cough and cold preparations may be single- or multiple-ingredient products containing antihistamines (diphenhydramine, chlorpheniramine, or brompheniramine), decongestants (phenylephrine or pseudoephedrine), cough suppressants (dextromethorphan), expectorants (guaifenesin), and/or analgesics (acetaminophen or ibuprofen).

Key Findings

- Antihistamines cause anticholinergic effects. The patient may be hot, dry, flushed, agitated, or tachycardic; and may have CNS depression or urinary retention. Seizures are possible.
- Decongestants cause sympathomimetic effects. The patient may be flushed, diaphoretic, and agitated, with enlarged pupils and elevation in heart rate, respiratory rate, and blood pressure. Seizures are possible (see the "Sympathomimetic Medications" section for further details.)
- Dextromethorphan (Pertussin) may have mild symptoms in low doses: tachycardia, hypertension, vomiting, mydriasis, diaphoresis, nystagmus, and euphoria. In larger doses, agitation, hyperthermia, hallucinations, and metabolic acidosis may occur.[33] Dextromethorphan may cross-react with phencyclidine on some toxicology screens.
- Guaifenesin is not expected to produce toxicity.

Specific Interventions

- Acetaminophen poisoning must be considered in all cases of combination or unknown cough/cold preparations, unless the ingestion is definitively known to exclude acetaminophen.
- Activated charcoal is indicated if the patient presents within one hour after ingestion of a liquid or one to two hours after ingestion of a solid preparation.
- Treatment is symptomatic and supportive. Naloxone (Narcan) is sometimes effective in treating dextromethorphan intoxication.

Foreign Bodies

Any foreign body can present a choking hazard if ingested. Some present mechanical or physical hazards if swallowed or inserted into the nostril, ear, or other body opening. Some have toxic implications. These include the following:

- Button batteries, found in toys, remote controls, hearing aids, medical devices, flashlights, flashing jewelry, watches, cameras, and numerous other consumer objects.
- Small magnets, found especially in toys.
- Small lead objects, such as children's jewelry, charms, toy figurines, and fishing and drapery weights.

Table 17-7 lists signs, symptoms, and additional interventions for these dissimilar foreign bodies.

Hydrocarbons

Hydrocarbons comprise a large group of substances that are generally thought of as fuels, oils, polishes and waxes, solvents, aerosol propellants, and refrigerants. Many are inert, but some, especially those considered solvents, may cause systemic toxicity. There are numerous ways of categorizing hydrocarbons (by chemistry, functionality, or physical properties). For the emergency nurse treating an acutely exposed child, it is more important to recognize potential toxicity by route of exposure.

Ingested hydrocarbons:

- Gasoline, kerosene, furniture polish, lamp oil, and fuel oil are among the most commonly ingested hydrocarbons. They can irritate the GI tract but are not expected to cause systemic toxicity.
  - Gastrointestinal decontamination is not indicated unless the hydrocarbon is mixed with a toxic substance (e.g., a pesticide). In fact, it usually is contraindicated to minimize the chance of vomiting and aspiration.
  - A patient who swallows one of these substances and does not cough or choke can be observed for respiratory symptoms at home for 24 hours.
- Aspiration is the primary danger.
  - If there is a history of coughing or choking, the patient must be seen in the emergency department for a respiratory evaluation and a chest radiograph. If the patient is asymptomatic, with a negative radiograph, at six hours after exposure, the patient can be discharged, with poison center follow-up.[34]
  - If the patient continues to have any respiratory symptoms, or if there are any pulmonary changes, the patient must be admitted for close observation.
  - Pine oil, turpentine, and toluene are among the hydrocarbons that can cause systemic toxicity. Initial symptoms can include CNS depression. Treatment is symptomatic and supportive.

Table 17-7 Signs, Symptoms, Treatment, and Additional Interventions or Selected Foreign Bodies

Object	Signs and Symptoms
Button battery*	If battery was swallowed, patient may be asymptomatic or may have nonspecific respiratory or abdominal symptoms.
	If battery was inserted into an orifice, patient may be asymptomatic or may have localized pain, drainage, or evidence of injury.
	Treatment/Additional Interventions
	For all cases of battery exposure, consult the poison center or the National Button Battery Hotline (202-625-3333, 24 hours a day) for treatment recommendations AND so patients can be observed by battery experts.
	Immediately obtain a radiograph, to include throat to lower abdomen, if child is known or thought to have swallowed a battery.
	Batteries in the esophagus must be removed immediately. Potentially fatal tissue injury, leading to exsanguination, can begin within two hours of ingestion.
	If battery has passed to stomach or beyond, patient can be discharged with follow-up by poison center or National Button Battery Hotline.
	Physical examination of nares, ear canal, or other orifice where battery may have been inserted.
	Immediate removal of impacted battery because permanent tissue injury can occur within two hours.[†]
Object	**Signs and Symptoms**
Small magnets	Patient may be asymptomatic, especially if a single magnet was ingested.
	If more than one magnet was ingested, patient may present with gastrointestinal complaints secondary to tissue necrosis, perforation, fistula formation, or intestinal obstruction.[‡]
	Treatment/Additional Interventions
	Single magnets typically pass uneventfully.
	Patients who ingest multiple magnets must be evaluated immediately by gastroenterology.
	If multiple magnets adhere to each other, trapping tissue between them, prompt surgery to remove the magnets is required.
Object	**Signs and Symptoms**
Lead objects	Patient may be asymptomatic.
	Patient may have symptoms suggestive of lead poisoning.[§]
	Treatment/Additional Interventions
	Lead objects can be visualized on a radiograph.
	Objects that are moving quickly through the gastrointestinal tract may be allowed to pass, if the patient is asymptomatic and has a low lead level.
	Multiple objects may need to be removed to prevent lead poisoning.[§]

*Data are taken from Litovitz, T., & Schmitz, B. F. (1992). Ingestion of cylindrical and button batteries: An analysis of 2382 cases. *Pediatrics, 89,* 747–757.

[†]Data are taken from Bhisitkul, D. M., & Dunham, M. (1992). An unsuspected alkaline battery foreign body presenting as malignant otitis externa. *Pediatric Emergency Care, 8,* 141–142.

[‡]Data are taken from Abdulrahman, M. A., Soundappan, S. S., Jefferies, H., & Cass, D. T. (2007). Ingested magnets and gastrointestinal complications. *Journal of Pediatrics and Child Health, 43,* 497–498.

[§]The "Lead" section of the text contains additional information.

Inhaled hydrocarbons:

- Adolescents may abuse hydrocarbons by huffing or sniffing. The primary risk is sudden death as the result of ventricular fibrillation or *sudden sniffing death syndrome*. The patient who is seeking a high becomes hypoxic; a catecholamine surge causes myocardial irritability.[35]

  - This can occur with so-called simple asphyxiants, including gasoline, butane, nitrous oxide, computer keyboard cleaner, aerosol propellants, and hundreds of household products. These products generally are not inherently toxic but displace oxygen. Butane, propane, and air fresheners are associated with the highest fatality rates.[36]

  - Solvent inhalation (e.g., toluene in glue and nail polish) can cause systemic toxicity over time. Solvents also can cause sudden sniffing death.

  - Inhaling refrigerants (e.g., from air conditioners) can literally freeze the mouth and upper airway, causing death.

  - Fatalities can occur from mechanical or behavioral effects (e.g., asphyxiation from a solvent-soaked rag or plastic bag over the face, drowning, or crashing a car while high).

- Substances other than hydrocarbons can be abused by inhalation. For example, abusing nitrates by inhalation can cause methemoglobinemia, requiring treatment with methylene blue.

- Anyone who is in enclosed spaces with solvents (e.g., glue for a hobby project or on the job) may inadvertently inhale concentrated hydrocarbon fumes, with similar effects.

- Treatment of hydrocarbon inhalation is symptomatic and supportive. Because the patient is already experiencing catecholamine excess, epinephrine should be avoided in resuscitation or treatment.

Dermal and ocular exposure:

- Hydrocarbons have a defatting action on cells. A short exposure may cause irritation; a longer duration of contact may cause significant injury, equivalent to a burn.

- Irrigation and removal of contaminated clothing are essential.

- Treatment of injury is symptomatic and supportive. Significant injuries are treated as burns.

Iron

In 2008, more than 46,000 children younger than six years were reported to have unintentional exposure to vitamins, some of which contained iron.[2] Prenatal vitamins and other adult-strength iron preparations have been associated with significant toxicity and fatalities in children younger than six years.[37]

The severity of iron poisoning is directly related to the amount of elemental iron ingested compared to a person's body weight. If the number and type of ingested tablets are known, the poison center can quickly determine if toxicity is likely. Serum iron levels and the patient's condition will determine the need for antidotal treatment and whether ICU admission will be required. A serum iron concentration of greater than 350 mg/dL is likely to be associated with systemic toxicity.[38]

Key Findings

Symptoms of iron toxicity can occur as early as 30 minutes after ingestion. Symptoms of iron toxicity are divided into five stages, which can overlap:

Stage 1: Approximately one half to six hours after ingestion, GI symptoms occur. These include vomiting, diarrhea, hematemesis, and abdominal pain.

Stage 2: Six to 12 hours after ingestion, the patient may experience temporary improvement of symptoms. However, hypoperfusion and metabolic acidosis may be developing.

Stage 3: Approximately 12 hours after ingestion, metabolic acidosis, circulatory failure, and CNS depression, leading to coma and multisystem organ failure, may occur.

Stage 4: At 72 to 96 hours after ingestion, hepatic necrosis, with coma, coagulopathy, and jaundice, may occur.

Stage 5: Two to four weeks after ingestion, bowel obstruction may occur.[39]

Specific Interventions

- Laboratory studies, including iron levels, complete blood cell count, liver function and coagulation studies, electrolyte and glucose measurement, and type and cross match.

- Abdominal radiographs to determine the presence and number of iron tablets in the GI tract.

- Anticipate whole-bowel irrigation if iron tablets are seen on abdominal film.

- Prepare for intravenous administration of the antidote deferoxamine in patients with systemic iron poisoning. Deferoxamine binds free iron; this complex is excreted renally. After its administration, the child's urine may turn a pink salmon or rose color, indicating that the iron is binding with the antidote. Urine will appear clear after detoxification.

- Anticipate admission to the intensive care unit. Not only can iron cause life-threatening toxicity, the administration of deferoxamine is associated with hypotension.[40]

- Surgery may be indicated to prevent intestinal perforation and peritonitis.

Lead

Lead poisoning is usually chronic, resulting from environmental exposures and causing nonspecific low-grade symptoms. Typically, lead-poisoned patients do not present to the emergency department for treatment. Exceptions would be those who have recently swallowed a lead object, such as a toy, charm, jewelry item, lead fishing or drapery weight, or other small item; those with such high lead levels that they are experiencing lethargy, seizures, and coma; and those who are frankly encephalopathic.

The ingestion of small lead objects can lead to acute lead poisoning if the object remains in the GI tract for any length of time.[41] If a patient is known or suspected to have swallowed an object made from lead, an abdominal radiograph is needed. Gastrointestinal evacuation may be indicated. Referral for follow-up to the patient's pediatrician or the local health department is essential so that lead levels can be determined, treated if necessary, and followed up.

Children who are acutely ill will require symptomatic and supportive care until they are admitted to the intensive care unit. Lead levels may not be available on an emergency basis. Even though these children will require chelation therapy, this is unlikely to be instituted in the emergency department.

Additional History[42]

- Known or suspected ingestion of a foreign body

- Exposure to lead paint

  ○ Living in a home painted before 1978; afterward, the lead content was limited in residential paint

  ○ Recent renovation of an older home

  ○ Caregiver with a job involving lead (e.g., automobile battery manufacturing)

  ○ Caregiver with a hobby involving lead (e.g., pottery glaze, lead fishing sinkers, and exposure to caregivers' clothing after using indoor firing ranges)

- Use of traditional or folk medicines or cosmetics containing lead

- Exposure to drinking water with high lead levels (e.g., cisterns with lead liners, water systems with lead-soldered joints, and water systems standing on lead surfaces)

- Use of improperly fired pottery (usually imported)

Key Findings

Acute lead encephalopathy is uncommon. It may cause the following symptoms:

- Altered level of consciousness, apathy, bizarre behavior, seizures, and coma

- Ataxia, incoordination, myalgia, and muscular exhaustion

- Vomiting, severe abdominal pain, and colic

- Loss of recently acquired skills

Symptomatic lead poisoning without encephalopathy may include the following symptoms:

- Lethargy, decrease in play activity, irritability, fatigue, and difficulty concentrating

- Anorexia, sporadic vomiting, abdominal pain, weight loss, and constipation

- Headache and anemia

Specific Interventions

- Consider an abdominal radiograph, which may show radiopaque foreign materials that were ingested during the preceding 24 to 36 hours.

- Obtain the blood lead level.

- Prepare for ICU admission of severely poisoned children.

- Arrange referral (pediatrician, local health department, or social services) for patients who require chelation but whose lead levels do not require inpatient admission.

- Children with elevated lead levels may NOT return to their usual environment until the source of lead has been identified and remediated. Lack of a safe environment for the child may necessitate hospital admission.

Methadone

Methadone (Methadose/Dolophine) is an opioid used by adults as a detoxification and maintenance medication for heroin users and as an analgesic, sedative, and recreational drug.[43] Like other opioids, it can cause CNS depression, respiratory depression, and constricted pupils. It is different from other opioids in that its half-life is as long as 40 hours, much longer than the duration of action of naloxone. It is also among the most toxic opioids for children younger than 6 years, who can die after swallowing a single tablet.[44]

Key Findings

- Respiratory depression
- CNS depression
- Pinpoint pupils

Additional Considerations

- Naloxone (Narcan) will reverse the symptoms of methadone ingestion. Start with an intravenous bolus dose. Then, prepare for a continuous intravenous infusion and ICU admission.

- Close observation of respiratory rate is essential for at least two hours after naloxone is discontinued to ensure that respiratory depression does not recur.

- Methadone poisoning in children is likely to be from the careless storage of the medication or even parental administration in an attempt to quiet or calm a child.[43] Follow-up may range from poison prevention information to social services and a Child Protective Services referral.[45]

Oral Hypoglycemics

A single tablet of such oral hypoglycemics as chlorpropamide (Diabinese) and glipizide (Glucotrol) is potentially fatal to a toddler.[21] Sulfonylureas and related medications, which stimulate the secretion of insulin from pancreatic beta cells, are widely used to treat type II diabetes mellitus and, thus, are widely available in homes. Children who swallow these medications can experience delayed, profound, and prolonged hypoglycemia.

Key Findings

- The symptoms are consistent with those of hypoglycemia: dizziness, pallor, diaphoresis, tachycardia, restlessness, agitation, lethargy, seizures, and coma.

Specific Interventions

- Monitor the glucose level by finger stick every hour.
- Allow free access to food and drink.
- Administer glucose by intravenous bolus, followed by continuous intravenous infusion, titrated to the patient's glucose readings.

- Octreotide (Sandostatin) suppresses insulin release and is indicated if the blood glucose level cannot be maintained by intravenous glucose.

- Glucagon usually is not indicated for the following reasons:
  - Children have a limited capacity for gluconeogenesis.
  - The increase in serum glucose can be accompanied by an increase in insulin secretion, thus worsening rather than improving hypoglycemia.[46]

- A period of observation including inpatient admission may be necessary.

Sympathomimetic Drugs

Although they are used and abused for a variety of purposes, from a toxicology aspect these drugs are stimulants. Sources vary, but the "fight-or-flight" physiological effects are similar from drug to drug. This section will present signs, symptoms, and treatments for the drugs as a category. Additional considerations are noted for cocaine; illicit amphetamines; legal stimulants used to treat hyperactivity, attention-deficit disorder, and obesity; decongestants; caffeine; and energy drinks. Children who are exposed to illegal substances may require referral to Child Protective Services.[45]

Key Findings

- Tachycardia and dysrhythmias
- Hypertension, followed by hypotension and shock
- Rapid respiratory rate, followed by respiratory arrest and respiratory failure
- Hyperthermia
- Agitation, psychosis, seizures, and coma
- Effects related to vasoconstriction: chest pain, abdominal pain, headache, myocardial infarction, and stroke
- Mydriasis
- Diaphoresis
- *Crack lung,* a syndrome usually occurring one to 48 hours after cocaine smoking; it consists of a grouping of symptoms:
  - Chest pain
  - Cough with hemoptysis
  - Dyspnea
  - Bronchospasm
  - Pruritus
  - Fever

○ Diffuse alveolar infiltrates without effusions

○ Pulmonary and systemic eosinophilia

Specific Interventions

- Aggressive control of temperature

- Fluids for hypotension

- Benzodiazepines for seizures and agitation

- Hypertonic sodium bicarbonate and lidocaine for wide complex dysrhythmias associated with cocaine toxicity

- Never give β-blockers to a patient with tachycardia as the result of cocaine abuse. β-Blockers should not be administered to patients with an ST-elevated myocardial infarction precipitated by cocaine use because of the risk of exacerbating a coronary spasm as the result of its unopposed α stimulation.[47]

  ○ Nitroglycerin is appropriate in managing cocaine-associated infarction or ischemia because it reduces cocaine-induced vasoconstriction in healthy and atherosclerotic segments of the coronary arteries.

- For a cardiopulmonary arrest, vasopressin may offer considerable advantage over epinephrine.[47]

- Monitor for hypoglycemia.

Additional Considerations

Cocaine

- Cocaine is used therapeutically as a potent vasoconstrictor and illicitly as a CNS stimulant.

- Cocaine may be taken intranasally, intravenously, or topically; or may be smoked and inhaled as freebase or crack cocaine.

- Infants and toddlers have been poisoned by swallowing cocaine powder or rocks, inhaling crack cocaine smoked by adults,[48] or being breastfed by a woman abusing cocaine.[49]

- Preparation of crack cocaine involves the use of caustic chemicals, presenting yet another hazard to young children.[50]

- Adolescents (and adults) attempting to avoid arrest may swallow cocaine or cocaine packets. Cocaine packets may also be swallowed or inserted into the rectum or vagina in an attempt to smuggle them. Packet rupture can cause rapid devastating toxicity. If packet ingestion is suspected, an abdominal radiograph is indicated. Whole-bowel irrigation and intensive monitoring for the effects of leaking or ruptured packets are indicated.

Illicit Amphetamines/Methamphetamines/Hallucinogenic Amphetamines

- Young children are at risk of exposure to illicit amphetamines by ingestion, if the drug is within their reach, and by inhalation, if in the presence of others smoking ice, a smokeable form of methamphetamine.

- Pediatric patients most commonly present with agitation. Seizures, tachycardia, and hypertension also occur.[51]

- Methamphetamine is often made in home laboratories, exposing family members not just to the drug but also to the caustic chemicals used in drug manufacturing.[52]

- The half-life may be longer than 24 hours; symptomatic patients are likely to require admission for monitoring and possible ongoing treatment.

- Hallucinogenic amphetamines (e.g., Ecstasy) are often used by adolescents as party drugs. In addition to hallucinations, sympathomimetic effects may be exaggerated by dehydration, caused by diaphoresis while dancing.

Licit Amphetamines Used for Obesity and Attention-Deficit/Hyperactivity Disorder

- Toddlers may find and swallow these medications, just as they might other substances at home.

- Adolescents may abuse methylphenidate and other medications used for attention-deficit/hyperactivity disorder. Also, they may share medications with other adolescents.

Decongestants

- Phenylephrine and pseudoephedrine are commonly found in cough and cold preparations. Pediatric patients who swallow overdoses of pediatric or adult preparations may experience typical symptoms of a sympathomimetic overdose.

- Adolescents who abuse cough and cold medicines in an attempt to get high may experience significant toxicity from decongestants, including hypertension and hallucinations.

- Large quantities of these medications may be available in homes used as methamphetamine laboratories because diverted medications are used in the synthesis of methamphetamine.

Caffeine and energy drinks

- Caffeine is found in coffee, tea, soft drinks, chocolate, over-the-counter medications intended to promote wakefulness, and increasingly in energy drinks. The amount of caffeine in an energy drink may or may not exceed the amount of caffeine in coffee, in terms of milligrams per milliliter, but energy drinks typically contain more liquid than a typical cup of coffee.

- Other caffeine-containing ingredients in energy drinks may include Guarana, kola nut, cocoa, yerba mate, and tea.

- Nausea, palpitations, and jitteriness typically precede significant caffeine poisoning, thus an individual may limit further consumption. Hallucinations, chest pain, seizures, rhabdomyolysis, and death are possible.[53]

Discharge Education

Caregivers should be provided with specific information related to the treatment just rendered to the patient, along with poison prevention information to prevent future poisoning episodes.

- If the patient received activated charcoal, advise the parents to expect black stools.

- Provide instructions about what signs and symptoms should prompt a call or return visit.

- If you consulted the poison center as advised, tell the parents to expect a follow-up call from the poison center.

- Provide materials with the poison center's 24-hour telephone number. (The emergency department may obtain these materials from the local poison center. Call 1-800-222-1222 and ask to speak to the educator or visit http://www.aapcc.org to find the website of the local poison center.)

Health Promotion/Poison Prevention Education

Pediatric patients of all ages depend on caregivers to provide a safe environment, although elements of safety will change with a child's age and development. There are age-specific poison prevention messages and resources available to nurses and parents. Information for caregivers of pediatric patients with special needs should be tailored to that patient's needs and abilities, which may differ from other children of the same chronological age.

Poison prevention messages appropriate for all ages:

- Teach or remind caregivers about the relationship between injury risk and child development.[54]

- Adults should model safe use of products and medicines: use them for their intended purpose only, and follow label instructions for selection, use, and disposal.

- Store medicines and household products in their original containers. Do not transfer to food or beverage containers.

- Store medicines and foods in a different place from household products and chemicals.

- Use measuring devices intended for medicines, not household spoons.

- Call the poison center at 1-800-222-1222 immediately if a possible poisoning is suspected.

Poison prevention messages appropriate for children younger than six years:

- Child proof every home where a child spends time.

- Use child-resistant closures on medicines and household products. Resecure closures after each use.

- Lock medicines and household products out of sight and reach of children.

- Take medicines where children cannot watch; children learn by imitating adults.

- Call medicine by its proper name; do not refer to medicine as "candy."

- As children grow old enough to understand, teach them to ask an adult before eating or drinking anything; children cannot tell the difference between safe items and look-alike poisons.

- Be sure that each adult knows who is administering medicine to each child. Develop a method to be sure that children are not inadvertently given overdoses.

- At well-child visits, ask the pediatrician about the need for lead screening in the local area.

Poison prevention messages appropriate for parents and caregivers of school-aged children and adolescents:

- Before allowing children to self-medicate or have access to over-the-counter and prescription medicines, be certain that they understand exactly how to take medicines safely.

- Before allowing children to use household products, be certain that they understand label instructions for safe use.

- Observe for sign/symptoms/evidence of substance abuse, including abuse of legal medications, illegal drugs, inhalants, alcohol, and tobacco.

- Keep track of, and consider locking, prescription medications and alcoholic beverages kept at home.

Table 17-8 lists resources for poison prevention and substance abuse awareness and prevention.

Table 17-8 Selected Resources for Poison Prevention Education and Substance Abuse Awareness and Prevention

Resource	Description
Local poison center: 1-800-222-1222 (calls from anywhere in the United States are automatically answered by expert health professionals at the local poison center)	24-hour telephone service for poison treatment and poison-related questions Magnets and telephone stickers with the poison center 24-hour number Written poison prevention materials with locally relevant information (e.g., local snakes and spiders) Most poison centers have websites with additional information
American Association of Poison Control Centers (http://www.aapcc.org)	Names and websites of local poison centers Poison prevention materials and national data about poison exposures
Health Resources and Services Administration, US Department of Health and Human Services (http://poisonhelp.hrsa.gov)	Downloadable poison prevention materials for health professionals and the general public, written and electronic Fact sheets and additional types of resources, including public service announcements
Poison Prevention Week Council (http://poisonprevention.org)	Posters for National Poison Prevention Week List of materials that can be ordered from government, not-for-profit, and private organizations
White House Office of National Drug Control Policy (http://www.ondcp.gov/publications/pdf/prescrip_disposal.pdf)	Updated guidelines for proper disposal of prescription medications
Partnership for a Drug-Free America (http://www.drugfree.org)	Information for parents about a wide variety of abused substances, with tips for talking to children about substance abuse prevention
National Inhalant Prevention Coalition (http://inhalants.org/)	Information for parents and health professionals about inhalant abuse and inhalant abuse prevention Inhalant prevention resource guide for teachers

Summary

Almost anything can be poisonous if used in the wrong way, taken by the wrong person, or taken in the wrong amount. Children younger than six years are at special risk of poisoning because of their immature organ systems, natural curiosity, and inability to distinguish safe from unsafe substances and behaviors. All caregivers should be taught about injury prevention, including poison prevention.

Pediatric patients present to the emergency department when prevention fails. The patient's chance of a successful outcome is increased by the attentions of an astute emergency nurse, who obtains a careful medical history, assesses the patient thoroughly, and consults with the poison center to determine the best next steps.

References

1. US Centers for Disease Control and Prevention. (2010). *Poisoning in the United States: Fact sheet.* Retrieved from http://www.cdc.gov/HomeandRecreationalSafety/Poisoning/

2. Bronstein, A., Spyker, D., Cantilena, J. L., Green, J., Rumack, B., & Giffin, S. (2009). 2008 annual report of the American Association of Poison Control Centers' National Poison Data System (NPDS): 26th annual report. *Clinical Toxicology, 47,* 911–1084.

3. Schillie, S., Shehab, N., Thomas, K., & Budnitz, D. (2009). Medication overdoses leading to emergency department visits among children. *American Journal of Preventive Medicine, 37,* 181–187.

4. Woolf, A., Alpert, H., Garg, A., & Lesko, S. (2001). Adolescent occupational toxic exposures: A national study. *Archives of Pediatric and Adolescent Medicine, 155,* 704–710.

5. Howland, M. (2006). Pharmacokinetic and toxicokinetic principles. In N. Flomenbaum, L. Goldfrank, R. Hoffman, M. Howland, N. Lewin, & L. Nelson (Eds.), *Goldfrank's toxicologic emergencies* (8th ed., pp. 140–159). New York, NY: McGraw-Hill.

6. Fine, J. (2006). Reproductive and perinatal principles. In N. Flomenbaum, L. Goldfrank, R. Hoffman, M. Howland, N. Lewin, & L. Nelson (Eds.), *Goldfrank's toxicologic emergencies* (8th ed., pp. 465–486). New York, NY: McGraw-Hill.

7. Lee, D. C., & Korzun, T. (2008). Skin decontamination. In C. King & F. M. Henretig (Eds.), *Textbook of pediatric emergency procedures* (2nd ed., pp. 1179–1184). Philadelphia, PA: Wolters Kluwer/Lippincott Williams & Wilkins.

8. Zuppa, A. F., & Barrett, J. S. (2008). Pharmacokinetics and pharmacodynamics in the critically ill child. *Pediatric Clinics of North America, 55,* 735–755.

9. Standards for Privacy of Individually Identifiable Health Information. 65 Fed. Reg. 82,626 (Dec. 28, 2000).

10. Wolkin, A. F., Patel, M., Watson, W., Belson, M., Rubin, C., Schier, J. ... Litovitz, T. (2006). Early detection of illness associated with poisonings of public health significance. *Annals of Emergency Medicine, 47,* 170–176.

11. Bailey, B. (2008). To decontaminate or not to decontaminate? The balance between potential risks and forseeable benefits. *Clinical Pediatric Emergency Medicine, 9,* 17–23.

12. American Academy of Clinical Toxicology and European Association of Poisons Centres and Clinical Toxicologists. (2004). Position paper: gastric lavage. *Journal of Toxicology Clinical Toxicology, 42,* 933–943.

13. American Academy of Clinical Toxicology and European Association of Poisons Centres and Clinical Toxicologists. (2005). Position paper: single-dose activated charcoal. *Clinical Toxicology, 43,* 61–87.

14. Shannon, M. (2008). Activated charcoal administration. In C. King & F. Henretig (Eds.), *Textbook of pediatric emergency procedures* (2nd ed., pp. 1172–1174). Philadelphia, PA: Wolters Kluwer, Lippincott Williams & Wilkins.

15. Tenenbein, M. (2008). Whole bowel irrigation. In C. King & F. Henretig (Eds.), *Textbook of pediatric emergency procedures* (2nd ed., pp. 1175–1178). Philadelphia, PA: Wolters Kluwer, Lippincott Williams & Wilkins.

16. Goldfarb, D., & Matalon, D. (2006). Principles and techniques applied to enhance elimination. In N. Flomenbaum, L. Goldfrank, R. Hoffman, M. A. Howland, N. Lewin, & L. Nelson (Eds.), *Goldfrank's toxicologic emergencies* (8th ed., pp. 160–172). New York, NY: McGraw-Hill.

17. Rumack, B. H., Peterson, R. C., Koch, G. G., & Amara, I. A. (1981). Acetaminophen overdose: 662 cases with evaluation of oral acetylcysteine treatment. *Archives of Internal Medicine, 141*(3), 380–385.

18. Marzullo, L. (2005). An update of *N*-acetylcysteine treatment for acute acetaminophen toxicity in children. *Current Opinion in Pediatrics, 17,* 239–245.

19. McMahon, D. M., Winstead, S., & Weant, K. A. (2009). Toxic alcohol ingestions: focus on ethylene glycol and methanol. *Advanced Emergency Nursing Journal, 31,* 206–213.

20. Rosenbaum, T. G., & Kou, M. (2005). Are one or two dangerous? Tricyclic antidepressant exposure in toddlers. *Journal of Emergency Medicine, 28,* 169–174.

21. Bar-Oz, B., Levichek, L., & Koren, G. (2004). Medications that can be fatal for a toddler with one tablet or teaspoonful. *Pediatric Drugs, 6,* 123–126.

22. Liebelt, E. (2008). An update on antidepressant toxicity: An evolution of unique toxicities to master. *Clinical Pediatric Emergency Medicine, 9,* 24–34.

23. Wiley, C. C., & Wiley II, J. F. (1998). Pediatric benzodiazepine ingestion resulting in hospitalization. *Clinical Toxicology, 36,* 227–231.

24. Lee, D. C., Greene, T., Dougherty, T., & Pearigen, P. (2000). Fatal nifedipine ingestions in children. *Journal of Emergency Medicine, 19,* 359–361.

25. DeRoos, F. (2006). Calcium channel blockers. In N. E. Flomenbaum, L. R. Goldfrank, R. S. Hoffman, M. A. Howland, N. A. Lewin, & L. S. Nelson (Eds.), *Goldfrank's toxicologic emergencies* (8th ed., pp. 911–923). New York, NY: McGraw-Hill.

26. Brubacher, J. (2006). Beta-adrenergic antagonists. In N. E. Flomenbaum, L. R. Goldfrank, R. S. Hoffman, M. A. Howland, N. A. Lewin, & L. S. Nelson (Eds.), *Goldfrank's toxicologic emergencies* (8th ed., pp. 924-941). New York, NY: McGraw-Hill.

References *continued*

27. Hack, J. B., & Lewin, N. A. (2006). Cardioactive steroids. In N. D. Flomenbaum, L. R. Goldfrank, R. S. Hoffman, M. A. Howland, N. A. Lewin, & L. S. Nelson (Eds.), *Goldfrank's toxicologic emergencies* (8th ed., pp. 971–988). New York, NY: McGraw-Hill.

28. Kerns II, W. (2007). Management of beta-adrenergic blocker and calcium channel antagonist toxicity. *Emergency Medicine Clinics of North America, 25,* 309–331.

29. Camp, N. E. (2005). Understanding the assessment and treatment of caustic ingestions and the resulting burns. *Journal of Emergency Nursing, 31,* 594–596.

30. US Food and Drug Administration. (2008). *FDA released recommendations regarding use of over-the-counter cough and cold products.* Retrieved from http://www.fda.gov/NewsEvents/Newsroom/PressAnnouncements/2008/ucm116839.htm

31. Scharfstein, J. M., North, M., & Serwint, J. R. (2007). Over the counter but no longer under the radar: Pediatric cough and cold medications. *New England Journal of Medicine, 357,* 2321–2324.

32. Dart, R. C., Paul, I. M., Bond, G. R., Winston, D. C., Manoguerra, A. S., Palmer, R. B., ... Rumack, B. H. (2009). Pediatric fatalities associated with over the counter (nonprescription) cough and cold medications. *Annals of Emergency Medicine, 53,* 411–417.

33. Boyer, E. W. (2004). Dextromethorphan abuse. *Pediatric Emergency Care, 20,* 858–863.

34. Lewander, W. J., & Aleguas Jr, A. (2007). Petroleum distillates and plant hydrocarbons. In M. W. Shannon, S. W. Borron, & M. J. Burns (Eds.), *Haddad and Winchester's clinical management of poisoning and drug overdose* (4th ed., pp. 1343–1346). Philadelpha, PA: Saunders Elsevier.

35. Williams, J. F., & Storck, M. (2007). Inhalant abuse. *Pediatrics, 119,* 1009–1017.

36. Marsolek, M. R., White, N. C., & Litovitz, T. L. (2010). Inhalant abuse: Monitoring trends by using poison control data, 1993-2008. *Pediatrics, 125,* 906–913.

37. Litovitz, T. L., & Manoguerra, A. (1992). Comparison of pediatric poisoning hazards: An analysis of 3.8 million exposure incidents. *Pediatrics, 89,* 999–1006.

38. Aldridge, M. D. (2007). Acute iron poisoning: What every pediatric intensive care unit nurse should know. *Dimensions of Critical Care Nursing, 26,* 43–48.

39. Tenenbein, M. (2001). Iron. In M. D. Ford, K. A. Delaney, L. J. Ling, & T. Erickson (Eds.), *Clinical toxicology* (pp. 305–309). Philadelphia, PA: WB Saunders Co.

40. Valentine, K., Mastropietro, C., & Sarnaik, A. P. (2009). Infantile iron poisoning: Challenges in diagnosis and management. *Pediatric Critical Care Medicine, 10,* e31–e33.

41. US Centers for Disease Control and Prevention. (2006). Death of a child after ingestion of a metallic charm: Minnesota, 2006. *Morbidity and Mortality Weekly Review, 55,* 340–341.

42. Woolf, A. D., Goldman, R., & Bellinger, D. C. (2007). Update on the clinical management of childhood lead poisoning. *Pediatric Clinics of North America, 54,* 271–294.

43. Riascos, R., Kumfa, P., Rojas, R., Cuellar, H., & Descartes, F. (2008). Fatal methadone intoxication in a child. *Emergency Radiology, 15,* 67–70.

44. Sachdeva, D. K., & Stadnyk, J. (2005). Are one or two dangerous? Opioid exposure in toddlers. *Journal of Emergency Medicine, 29,* 77–84.

45. Wells, K. (2009). Substance abuse and child maltreatment. *Pediatric Clinics of North America, 56,* 345–362.

46. Little, G. L., & Boniface, K. S. (2005). Are one or two dangerous? Sulfonylurea exposure in toddlers. *Journal of Emergency Medicine, 28,* 305–310.

47. McCord, J., Jneid, H., Hollander, J. E., de Lemos, J. A., Cercek, B., Hsue, P., ... Newby, L. K.; American Heart Association Acute Cardiac Care Committee of the Council on Clinical Cardiology. (2008). Management of cocaine-associated chest pain and myocardial infarction: a scientific statement from the American Heart Association Acute Cardiac Care Committee of the Council on Clinical Cardiology. *Circulation, 117,* 1897–1907.

48. Bateman, D. A., & Heagerty, M. C. (1989). Passive freebase cocaine ("crack") inhalation by infants and toddlers. *American Journal of Diseases of Children, 143,* 25–27.

49. Chaney, N. E., Franke, J., & Wadlington, W. B. (1988). Cocaine convulsions in a breast-feeding baby. *Journal of Pediatrics, 112,* 134–135.

50. Massa, N., & Ludemann, J. P. (2004). Pediatric caustic ingestion and parental cocaine abuse. *International Journal of Pediatric Otorhynolaryngology, 68,* 1513–1517.

51. Matteucci, M. J., Auten, J. D., Crowley, B., Combs, D., & Clark, R. F. (2007). Methamphetamine exposures in young children. *Pediatric Emergency Care, 23,* 638–640.

52. Farst, K., Duncan, J. M., Moss, M., Ray, R. M., Kokoska, E., & James, L. P. (2007). Methamphetamine exposure presenting as caustic ingestions in children. *Annals of Emergency Medicine, 49,* 341–343.

53. Babu, K. M., Church, R. J., & Lewander, W. (2008). Energy drinks: The new eye-opener for adolescents. *Clinical Pediatric Emergency Medicine, 9,* 35–42.

54. James, S. R., & Ashwill, J. W. (2007). *Nursing care of children: Principles and practice* (3rd ed.). St. Louis, MO: Saunders Elsevier.

Chapter 18 | Behavioral Emergencies

Beverly G. Hart, PhD, RN, PMHNP-BC

Objectives

On completion of this chapter, the learner should be able to do the following:

- Determine anatomical, physiological, and developmental characteristics of pediatric patients as a basis for assessment of behavioral health emergencies.
- Describe common causes and characteristics of behavioral health emergencies encountered when caring for the pediatric patient.
- Plan appropriate interventions for the pediatric patient with behavioral health emergencies.
- Indicate health promotion strategies related to behavioral health conditions.

Introduction

Emergency departments (EDs) have become the safety net for a fragmented and overtaxed mental healthcare system.[1] Psychiatric disorders occur as a result of complex interactions between personality, behavior, genetics, and the environment.[2] Specifically, pediatric and adolescent patients who present to the ED in crisis as the result of mental health problems often prove to be both challenging and frightening for many emergency nurses.[3] In addition to behavioral health issues, these patients present with high medical acuity, requiring prompt assessment, treatment, and possible admission. Unfortunately, one recent survey found that only 6% of EDs have the recommended and necessary pediatric equipment and supplies to adequately treat pediatric patients.[4] Approximately 20% of all children and adolescents in the United States have a diagnosable behavioral health disorder that is serious enough to cause significant distress and to interfere with the activities of daily living.[5] Obtaining pertinent clinical information and accurately assessing young people, especially children younger than 12 years, requires the following specific considerations:

- Most importantly, the ED should provide an environment that is safe for pediatric and adolescent patients, their caregivers and families, and staff and visitors. This

environment should promote the support of family-centered care.[6]

- Caregivers will often bring children to the ED for behavioral problems when the real problem involves the whole family. For example, marital problems, poor parenting skills, and/or inadequate communication skills can all contribute to pediatric behavioral emergencies and crisis situations.[5]
- Varying stages of human development add to the complexity of caring for pediatric and adolescent patients; therefore, both pertinent information about the situation and necessary communication can be limited.[5]
- Fundamental knowledge of the various stages of growth and development is essential for the emergency nurse to assess, plan, implement, and evaluate effective care for behavioral health emergencies.[5]

Suicide/Homicidal Ideation and Crisis Intervention

Suicide is rare among pediatric patients younger than 10 years but is the third leading cause of death in the United States in those aged 10 through 19 years.[7, 8] Among all ethnic groups, Caucasian males ages 15–19 years are at the greatest risk for suicide, followed by African American and Native American males. Hispanic/Latina teenage girls have the highest number of suicide attempts.[8]

Contrary to popular belief, even young children are involved in various acts of violence against themselves, other children, animals, and even adults.[8] Several psychological and sociological factors, when present, can be triggers for suicidal ideation and behaviors. These include major depressive disorders and any underlying psychiatric disorder, history of sexual and/or physical abuse, poor self-esteem, hopelessness, helplessness, poverty, alcohol and drug use and abuse, poor social skills, and poor academic performance.[5, 8, 9] Any child or adolescent with suicidal ideations must be hospitalized if a trained professional has any doubt about a family's ability to safely supervise the minor or if the child is unwilling to cooperate with outpatient treatment regimens.[10]

Approaching the Patient with Suicidal/Homicidal Ideations

The most effective way to assess the pediatric patient for suicidal/homicidal ideations is to ask the following questions in simple terms: "Do you have any thoughts of hurting yourself? Do you have any thoughts of hurting someone else? Have you ever done anything to hurt yourself in the past?" In addition, pediatric patients will relate to simple questions, such as "Are you feeling sad or unhappy?," instead of asking if they are depressed or having depressive symptoms. Also consider asking a pediatric patient, "Has something monumental or important (stressful) happened in your life lately?" Assessing for and correctly identifying suicidal/homicidal ideations is paramount to suicide intervention and prevention.

Denial of rights is generally a concern for those caring for adult psychiatric patients; however, this must be accomplished for those pediatric patients who are 18 years of age or older or those who have an emancipated minor status who present involuntarily or rescind consent. This includes a medical screening examination to determine if they present a danger to themselves or others. If they are deemed dangerous, denial of rights is necessary to legally hold and treat them.

During the pediatric triage and assessment process, the main concern of the emergency nurse is to maintain a safe environment for the patient and to encourage and foster hopefulness until the patient can be further assessed by a psychiatric professional for possible admission to the hospital. The patient should be housed in a room free from any environmental hazards that can be used to harm self and others and should be located away from all exits. In addition, the patient's clothing and shoes should be removed (some hospitals have discontinued this practice, so follow your organization's policy) and the patient should be placed in a hospital gown, being constantly monitored via video and/or face-to-face ED personnel. Suicidal patients may be carrying a weapon or medications on their person or in their belongings; by removing them, the nurse can limit the risk of self-harm in the ED. Explaining to the patient the need for the providers to listen to their heart and lungs may assist the patient in being more willing to change into a hospital gown. If the parent is calm and supportive, the child may want to sit with him or her. In adolescents, the nurse should assess for risky sexual behavior and substance use, both found to correlate positively with psychological distress.[11] A pediatric patient can request help for behavioral health issues, such as suicide and substance abuse, without parental permission and may talk more freely without his or her parents in the examination room. Always know what pertinent state's laws and hospital policies pertain to mental healthcare for minors.

Focused Assessment

The appearance of psychiatric symptoms may present secondary to other primary causes (e.g., hypoglycemia, fever, seizure, substance abuse). The physical assessment should be completed prior to the behavioral health assessment to rule out physical or neurological etiology as the source of the psychiatric symptoms.

Behavioral Health Assessment

- Assess eye contact.
- Assess speech rate, rhythm, volume, and tone of speech.
- Assess thought content for presence or absence of hallucinations or delusions.
- Compare developmental level against chronological age.
- Assess integumentary system for burns, brandings, or superficial cutting. Note stages of healing and acuity of scars as well as the number and location of cuts.

Depressive Disorders

The same *Diagnostic and Statistical Manual of Mental Disorders* (4th ed.) (DSM-IV), criteria are used for diagnosing depression in children and adolescents.[12] The one difference is that adults must feel depressed or express a loss of pleasure, whereas pediatric patients may describe or demonstrate a mood that is depressed or irritable, with a loss of interest in previously pleasurable activities.[5]

Signs and symptoms of depression that the ED staff can assess for are as follows:

- Weight gain or loss
- Sleeping too much or too little
- Increased or decreased psychomotor activity
- Low energy and feelings of guilt or worthlessness
- Trouble concentrating or thinking, poor performance in school, and thoughts of death or suicide[5]

Pediatric depression and other mood disorders commonly manifest themselves through physical symptoms, such as stomach pain and headaches.

There are several psychiatric disorders that may be comorbid with depressive disorders. These include anxiety disorders that are found in approximately 40% of children with depression. Conduct disorders also coincide with 23% of depressed children, as well as substance use and abuse, attention-deficit hyperactivity disorder (ADHD), and learning disorders.[5]

Bipolar Disorder

Many children, especially adolescents, experience mood swings as a normal part of growing up. When these feelings persist and interfere with a child's ability to function in daily life, bipolar disorder may be the cause. Bipolar disorder is a specific psychiatric illness that includes symptoms of problems with mood and encompasses both depressive episodes as well as periods of abnormal mood, or manic episodes. Younger children may experience mixed manic and depressive episodes.[13] In general, about 5% of children and adolescents nationally could fit the diagnosis of bipolar disorder at any time. Further studies show that this number changes as children age; about 1% of preschoolers, 2% of school-aged children, and 5% of adolescents are affected.[13] Although the core symptoms of bipolar disorder are the same for children as they are for adults, the specific behaviors are different and vary according to the age and developmental level of the child.

Pediatric patients are often unable to say they are depressed, sad, out of control, or irritable. They may say they are bored, angry, short-tempered, or "just don't want to," when it comes to expected chores or responsibilities such as school, extracurricular activities, or friends. In pediatric patients, bipolar disorder appears more frequently as a chronic and persistent alteration in mood and behavior with some periods of time being worse than others. Studies show that the most common depressive phase symptoms in pediatric patients are sadness, inability to feel pleasure, irritability, fatigue, insomnia, lack of self-esteem, and social withdrawal.[13]

Younger children are more likely to suffer from physical symptoms than are adolescents. Physical symptoms include stomachaches, headaches, hallucinations, agitation, and extreme fears. Adolescents show more despairing thoughts, weight changes, and excessive daytime sleepiness.[13]

Younger children typically show a mixed picture consisting of both depression and mania during a manic phase: a distraught type of mood, combined with a lack of energy, lack of sleep, disorganized behavior, and extreme irritability. Adolescents tend to exhibit more classic manic behavior: elevated mood and self esteem, racing thoughts, rapid speech, impulsive and intrusive behaviors, and decreased need for sleep.

Safety is the first priority when caring for pediatric patients with bipolar disorder in the emergency department. Additional nursing interventions generally focus on a thorough and accurate diagnostic evaluation of the patient, evaluation of the effectiveness and appropriate use of medication, and the need to support and educate parents. Providing comfort measures, distraction, and a low stimulus environment are also helpful interventions when caring for these patients. Individual and family therapy is often beneficial as is evaluation of the school and home environments.

Psychosis

Psychosis is an altered mental state in which the patient experiences a variety of disturbances in his or her perception of reality. These patients suffer from hallucinations, delusions, and disorganized behavior and speech patterns. This is not a developmental issue but a change in previously established thought and behavior patterns. Because of this altered view of reality, hostility and aggression can be seen in these pediatric patients; care must be taken to ensure the safety of all involved. New-onset psychosis in pediatric patients is uncommon. Symptoms generally develop in relation to another psychiatric disorder—such as severe anxiety, posttraumatic stress disorder or depression—or an organic cause, such as hypoglycemia, cerebral hypoxia, meningitis, encephalitis, or drug toxicity.[14] Pediatric patients with symptoms suggestive of a primary psychiatric diagnosis should undergo a medical evaluation to exclude possible reversible causes. The clinical presentation dictates the extent and type of medical testing that is needed.[14]

Once the determination of the underlying cause of the psychotic symptoms has been found, interventions are similar to other behavioral disorders. The highest priority is the safety of the patient, the family, and the healthcare staff. Screening for all psychiatric manifestations, thorough medical and psychiatric history, medical evaluation, recent events, social support, and family functioning are all important assessments for the pediatric patient. Interventions will be based on the severity of the symptomatology and the safety of the patient and family. Treatment may include medications, outpatient therapy, and inpatient hospitalization. It is vital to include any current therapists, the family and the patient, as possible, in the pediatric patient's plan of care.[14]

Anxiety Disorders

Panic Attacks

According to the literature, anxiety disorders are the most common of all mental health disorders, but their prevalence in children is not clearly documented.[5] Children often have difficulty describing their feelings and may express feelings of anxiety through crying or clinging to a parent. Anxiety in adolescents is often manifested through panic attacks, and 25% of adults with anxiety disorders recall having their first panic attack in their middle teenaged years. These panic attacks often lead to an ED visit. Common signs and symptoms of anxiety/panic attacks include the following:

- Chest pain or discomfort
- A choking sensation
- Sweating, dizziness, or lightheadedness
- Fear of dying
- Racing pulse
- Nausea and abdominal discomfort
- Numbness and tingling in the extremities
- Shortness of breath and hyperventilation
- Trembling[5, 8]

The physical symptoms of panic attacks are similar to cardiac emergencies and are frightening to patients. Nursing care should focus on calming and reassuring patients that they are safe. Stay with patients and instruct them to try and slow their breathing down if they are hyperventilating. Once the panic attack has resolved, encourage the patient to talk about his or her feelings and try and ascertain what triggered the panic episode. The patient may need a referral to outpatient behavioral services for therapy, medication, and self-exploration to prevent future panic attacks.

Eating Disorders

Anorexia Nervosa and Bulimia Nervosa

The onset of anorexia nervosa usually begins in early adolescence and is characterized by a refusal to maintain normal body weight. Eating disorders are associated with significant morbidity and mortality. With bulimia nervosa, the patient experiences repeated episodes of binge eating, followed by self-induced vomiting, misuse of laxatives and/or diuretics, excessive exercise, and fasting. A disturbance in the perception of weight and body shape, or body dysmorphic disorder, is an essential feature of both disorders (*DSM-IV-TR*). Patients with anorexia typically lack insight into, or have significant denial regarding, their condition and are extremely difficult to treat (*DSM-IV-TR*). In a meta-analysis of 119 outcome studies, approximately half of all patients diagnosed as having anorexia never recover and approximately 10% to 25% of those eventually battle bulimia.[15,16] In the United States, eating disorders are more commonly found in Caucasian and Hispanic population groups and less commonly found among African Americans and Asians.[17,18] Unfortunately, the incidence and prevalence of anorexia have remained the same during the past decade, despite prevention efforts. This supports the theory that eating disorders have a strong genetic or biological predisposition.[19]

Early assessment and intervention are key to recovery and relapse prevention. Emergency nurses must be aware of the following signs and symptoms of eating disorders:

- Low body weight or a body mass index of 17.5 kg/m^2 or less
- Irritability
- Depression
- Preoccupation with food
- Inflexible thinking
- Complaints of constipation and cold intolerance
- Lethargy
- Emaciation and amenorrhea
- Hypotension, skin dryness, bradycardia, or other arrhythmias
- Dental enamel erosion and scarring or calluses on the dorsum of the hand related to induced vomiting

Diagnostic laboratory findings include the following:

- Electrolyte imbalances
- Alkalosis or metabolic acidosis

- Elevated liver function and blood urea nitrogen (BUN) levels
- Leukopenia and mild anemia

In addition, the nurse should be attentive to cardiac implications, such as electrocardiographic changes, prolonged QT intervals, ventricular tachycardia, cardiomyopathy, and possible sudden death. Most important, these individuals can present as medically emergent.[8]

Relevant triage and assessment should include the following: questions about depression, suicidal ideations, history of eating disorders, family history of any eating disorders, and a physical assessment for signs and symptoms of cutting. Self-mutilation or cutting is often associated with eating disorders and borderline personality disorders. In other words, patients will superficially cut themselves, usually on the arms and thighs, as a mechanism to relieve uncomfortable feelings they are unable to control and to self-regulate.[20] Once the patient is medically cleared, the emergency nurse should arrange for possible admission to the hospital and/or referral to an outpatient behavioral health agency that specializes in treating eating disorders. Discharge to outpatient follow-up should only occur if the caregivers agree and are capable of following through with the discharge or transfer plan.

Attention-Deficit Hyperactivity Disorder

Many children misbehave and do not end up in the emergency department. However, children diagnosed as having ADHD will often present to the ED as a result of behavior problems at home or in school and/or medication management issues. Some data suggest that between 5% and 35% of children younger than 17 years have ADHD, or approximately two students per classroom.[21] In addition, children with ADHD are more injury-prone than their peers without ADHD, suggesting that, although they are taught accident prevention, they may have more difficulty with behavioral inhibition and impulsivity and, therefore, present more often to the emergency department.[21]

This disorder is characterized by symptoms of inattention, hyperactivity, and impulsiveness. The ED should assess and observe for signs of the patient having trouble paying attention and following commands or completing tasks, being easily distractible or forgetful, inappropriately leaving his or her seat, inappropriately climbing or running, talking excessively, and commonly interrupting or intruding on others.[5] In adolescence, the hyperactivity may present as restlessness, causing impairment at home,

school, or work.[22] Adolescents with ADHD have a higher risk for motor vehicle crashes and license revocation and are four to five times more likely to be arrested for a serious offense.[21,23]

Nursing intervention in the ED will generally focus on the evaluation of the effectiveness of medication management for the patient and the need to support and educate parents of children with ADHD. This diagnosis can be devastatingly stressful for parents and the family system as a whole. The emergency nurse can encourage parents, identify strengths and support systems, and refer them to outpatient facilities/resources that provide more ongoing psychiatric services. Psychostimulant or central nervous system stimulant medications, such as methylphenidate (Concerta), dextroamphetamine (Adderall), and dexmethylphenidate (Foculin), are typically used to treat ADHD and can have several negative adverse effects. The emergency nurse should assess the patient for insomnia, tachycardia, hypertension, weight loss, rebound agitation, an increase in tics or other compulsive behaviors, anxiety, and psychotic reactions.[8] Baseline temperature, pulse, blood pressure, respiratory rate, and weight are essential for successful assessment and intervention. If psychotic symptoms are present or if the patient is experiencing hallucinations, delusions, or other cognitive abnormalities, then baseline laboratory procedure results, such as complete blood cell count, blood glucose level, serum toxicology screen, and head computed tomography, may be necessary to exclude any medical issues.

Conduct Disorders/ Oppositional Defiant Disorder

In behavioral health, conduct disorders are found in as high as 6% to 16% of all boys; unfortunately, 50% of these boys will eventually be diagnosed as having antisocial personality disorder as adults.[5] Patients with true conduct disorders will present to the ED with a history of some type of aggression toward people or animals and maybe even a sexual attack of some sort, property destruction, lying or theft, and/or a serious rule violation. The emergency nurse should also consider various brain disorders that can cause antisocial behavior, such as a brain tumor, an infection, or a seizure disorder.[5] If this destructive behavior is new or historically unusual, the patient will need a comprehensive physical and neurological examination, along with baseline laboratory diagnostic procedures, a serum toxicology screen, head computed tomography, and possibly an electroencephalogram, to exclude potential medical issues.

Oppositional defiant disorder (ODD), sometimes considered a precursor to more serious conduct disorders, affects both sexes equally during adolescence. Overall, approximately one in 20 children is diagnosed as having oppositional defiant disorder.[5] Many of the clinical symptoms mimic normal adolescent responses to authority figures and only emerge as problematic when the patient's behavior causes significant distress in school, work, and/or social functioning. Symptoms of ODD include frequently losing one's temper, being argumentative with adults, deliberately doing things to annoy others, and being angry, resentful, spiteful, and vindictive.[5]

Oppositional defiant disorder can occur as a result of poor or inconsistent parenting; therefore, it is essential for the emergency nurse to assess the family situation and dynamics in an effort to plan successful intervention strategies. In essence, the parent may be the precipitating factor for triggering negative behaviors. Safety is paramount, so the emergency nurse must ascertain whether the patient is living in a safe home environment. If not, the emergency nurse must enlist the help of the medical social worker or social services to arrange alternative placement for the patient and/or possible hospitalization. Eventually, either in an outpatient or an inpatient setting, the child or adolescent should be evaluated for any learning disabilities that can contribute to frustration and difficult behaviors. Without regular behavioral therapy, many children with ODD and other conduct disorders will become victims of drug and/or alcohol use and abuse as a coping mechanism.[5]

Autism Spectrum Disorders

When caring for children who have been diagnosed with autism spectrum disorders (ASD), the healthcare provider needs special assessment techniques and knowledge. Autism spectrum disorder is a complex developmental disorder, represented by varying degrees of problems with communication and social interaction. Using the National Institute of Health's definitions, autistic disorder (classic autism), Asperger's syndrome, and pervasive development disorder not otherwise specified (atypical autism) are categories of ASD.[24]

Generally observed by 18 months of age, primary signs and symptoms of ASDs involve problems in communication, both verbal and non-verbal, social interaction such as sharing emotions and understanding how others think and feel, and the use of routines or repetitive behaviors such as repetitive actions and obsessively following routines or schedules.[24] These last symptoms were highlighted in the 1988 movie *Rain Man*, a movie about a highly intelligent man with autism.

General Assessment Principles

ASDs are not diagnosed in the ED, and caregivers do not generally bring their children in with symptoms of autistic behavior. The pediatric emergency nurse is likely to encounter patients within the autism spectrum presenting with other complaints. While varying from child to child, common challenges in caring for these special children involve a delay in processing communication, difficulty in expressing feelings, and difficulty in acceptance of physical contact. As with other chronic conditions, the primary caregiver is the best person to assist in optimizing care. Primary caregivers will know the best way to approach the child with ASD and provide a connection to normalcy and routine. By allowing extra time during assessment, completing the more stressful components, including physical contact, of the exam last, and by allowing the child to use their usual coping mechanisms, optimum care can be achieved. **Table 18-1** provides additional tips for caring for a child with autistic spectrum disorder.

Pediatric Psychotropic Medications and Adverse Effects

When prescribing specific classes of psychotropic medications for pediatric patients, healthcare professionals must be cognizant of the many detrimental adverse effects that these powerful medications can produce. In particular, one class of medications is the psychostimulants or agents for attention-deficit hyperactivity disorder. These central nervous stimulants can cause insomnia, restlessness, tremor, palpitations, tachycardia, hypertension, and anorexia.[25] With pediatric and adolescent patients, the emergency nurse should specifically assess blood pressure, pulse, weight, height, appetite, and any personal or family history of cardiac abnormalities. In addition, the nurse should inquire about medication-free holidays (weekends, school breaks, and summers) when the patient does not take the medication and the higher potential of these medications to be abused.[25]

Selective serotonin reuptake inhibitors (SSRIs) are frequently used to treat anxiety, depression, and obsessive compulsive disorders in young patients.[26] The acute stimulation of certain serotonin receptors can trigger acute mental agitation, anxiety, or panic attacks. Other potential adverse effects of SSRIs include akathisia, psychomotor retardation, and even some mild parkinsonism and dystonic movements.[27] In addition, other common adverse effects include nausea, vomiting, gastrointestinal cramping, and diarrhea.[27] Serotonin syndrome is the most

Table 18-1 Tips for Caring for a Child with Autistic Spectrum Disorder*

Classification of ASD	General Assessment Differences
Autistic disorder	Will not like to be touched
	May not look you in the eye when you talk to them
	May be non-verbal, or with minimal verbal skills
	May demonstrate flapping or repetitive activity
	May be aggressive
	Sensitive to overstimulation or inability to revert to routines

	Possible Interventions
	Have caregiver remain with child if possible; avoid physical contact if possible; otherwise move slowly and use a distal to proximal approach.
	As possible, do not necessitate eye contact.
	Use primary caregiver in developing a mode of communication, including use of pictures or common words. Allow extra time to process verbal input; use short, concrete sentences.
	If possible, allow for activity
	State expectations at the child's developmental level; assess and be prepared to intervene if self-injurious
	Have only one person talk at a time; decrease stimulation; allow extra time; allow routines as possible (e.g., the need to put toys in a row before responding to healthcare provider); assure child that he is safe and provide a safe environment, ensuring there is no medical equipment that can be ingested.

Classification of ASD	General Assessment Differences
Asperger's syndrome (milder than autism, but shares some of its symptoms. Children have been described as "odd" and "little professors")	High level of vocabulary, formal speech patterns, and obsessive interest in single subject.
	Rigid, literal thinkers
	Lack understanding of social cues and recognizing others' feelings; rigid and inflexible
	Problems with motor skills, physical clumsiness
	Abnormal eye contact or aloofness

	Possible Interventions
	Communication is vital and is best accomplished by following the child's cues, including their interests.
	May need pictures to understand what is expected of them.
	Clearly explain what is expected of them. If possible, allow the activities that will decrease stress. Decrease stimulation.
	Assess for injuries
	As possible, do not necessitate eye contact

Classification of ASD	General Assessment Differences
Pervasive development disorder not otherwise specified (atypical autism, includes childhood disintegrative disorder, and Rett's syndrome)	Assessment is child-dependent. Atypical presentations of autism or loss of verbal or motor skills that were once mastered are possible.
	Rett syndrome has associated physical symptoms including scoliosis, cardiac arrhythmias, and gastrointestinal problems.

	Possible Interventions
	Interventions are dependent on assessment, variations as listed under autistic disorders and Asperger's.
	Ensure definitive assessment and diagnostics as clinically relevant.

*Data adapted from National Library of Medicine. (2010, April 26). *Asperger syndrome*. Retrieved from http://www.nlm.nih.gov/medlineplus/ency/article/001549.htm; and National Institutes of Health. (2010, August 10). *Rett syndrome*. Retrieved from http://www.nichd.nigh.gov/health/topics/rett_syndrome.cfm.

serious adverse effect of the SSRIs and is characterized by a change in mental status, agitation, confusion, flushing, diaphoresis, diarrhea, nausea, vomiting, myoclonus, tremors, hyperthermia, and tachycardia. If serotonergic medication is not discontinued, symptoms can progress to hypertension, rigor, acidosis, respiratory failure, and rhabdomyolysis. Emergency department treatment would include immediate medication discontinuation, supportive cardiac and respiratory care, evaluation of metabolic acidosis, and eminent hospitalization.[25]

Pediatric and adolescent schizophrenia, bipolar mania, autism, and some developmental disorders are usually treated with atypical antipsychotic medications, such as quetiapine (Seroquel), risperidone (Risperdal), olanzapine (Zyprexa), and aripiprazole (Abilify).[25,27] Occasionally, two older medications, lithium (Eskalith) and valproate (Depakote), are also used as mood stabilizers. These two medications are relatively inexpensive and can be monitored through therapeutic blood levels; often, they produce frequent and severe adverse effects in younger children.[27] Extrapyramidal symptoms are caused by antipsychotic treatment, and the nurse must evaluate patients for signs and symptoms to ensure early intervention and rapid treatment. Extrapyramidal symptoms are characterized by akinesia; akathisia; dystonia; oculogyric crisis (denoting an emergency situation), during which the eyes roll back toward the head; pseudoparkinsonism or shuffling gait; drooling; muscle rigidity; and tremor. The patient may also exhibit rabbit syndrome, or rapid movement of the lips, which simulates a rabbit's mouth movements.[25] Tardive dyskinesia (TD) can also present as a serious adverse effect of antipsychotic medication use. Symptoms of TD include tongue protrusion, smacking of lips, and involuntary movements of the mouth, fingers, and extremities. Unfortunately, these movements can become permanent over time.[25] Last, neuroleptic malignant syndrome, a potentially fatal syndrome caused by antipsychotics and other drugs that affect dopamine receptors, is often precipitated by dehydration; therefore, children and adolescents in warm climates and/or in summer are more prone to developing neuroleptic malignant syndrome.[25] Neuroleptic malignant syndrome occurs in approximately 0.02% to 2.4% of patients, and mortality rates are as high as 10% to 20%.[10] The nurse should be alert for the following signs and symptoms:

- Fever of 103°F (39.7°C) or higher

- Blood pressure fluctuations (both hypertension and hypotension)

- Tachycardia, tachypnea, and respiratory distress

- Agitation and tremor

- Diaphoresis and pallor

- Muscle rigidity

- Elevated creatine phosphokinase level, leucocytosis, myoglobinuria, and elevated liver enzymes

- Progressive changes in mental status from stupor to comatose[25,27]

Emergency personnel should immediately discontinue the antipsychotic medication, monitor vital signs frequently, and anticipate hospital admission. Treating the high temperature with acetaminophen is a high priority, and the use of a cooling blanket may be necessary. Accurate fluid intake and output are essential because dehydration can exacerbate this condition. Patient safety is also extremely important because of the rigidity and/or spastic movements of the joints and extremities.[28] The medications most commonly used to treat neuroleptic malignant syndrome are dantrolene (Dantrium) and bromocriptine (Parlodel); supportive measures are also used to stabilize the patient's blood pressure and pulse rates.

Support and education of the family is also important. Explaining the care can help alleviate fear and reduce anxiety. Finally, both the SSRIs and the atypical antipsychotics carry black box warnings by the US Food and Drug Administration, alerting the emergency nurse to the fact that these medications have been associated with an increased risk of suicidality (suicidal thinking and behavior) in children, adolescents, and young adults. Thus, suicidal risk assessment is extremely important in this population group.[25]

Discharge Planning for Patients with Behavioral Health Problems

The most effective discharge planning begins on admission to the emergency department. Effective communication with parents or caregivers of pediatric and adolescent behavioral health patients is essential for thorough assessment and treatment planning. The emergency nurse can answer questions, reassure the patient and family, and provide necessary information through printed materials (e.g., maps, essential telephone numbers, crisis line telephone numbers, and follow-up appointment and contact information). Cloutier et al.[29] found that both parents and patients came to the ED for concerns related to basic safety, such as suicidal ideation or a suicide attempt. In contrast, it was more difficult for caregivers and youth to recognize more subtle disorders, such as depression or anxiety. This study also revealed that most caregivers are unaware of what community behavioral health services are available and how they can access these services for their child or adolescent.[29] Historically, the most successful treatment regimens combine medication management with psychotherapy, and education for both the patient and family is central to this process. Cronholm et al.[30] found that most providers in the ED suggested the need

for follow-up procedures, similar to those used to address abnormal laboratory results after the patients have left the ED, for behavioral health patients and mental health referral. If your facility does not have the resources to care for pediatric psychiatric patients in an inpatient setting, transfer must be arranged to meet the patient's needs. Establishing transfer agreements with hospitals that offer these services will expedite their care. See **Chapter 23, "Stabilization and Transport,"** for more information.

Summary

Pediatric and adolescent behavioral health patients who present to the ED often require many ED and mental health resources. Creating a safe ED environment is essential because security incidents are frequent and potentially put the patient and ED staff at risk for injury.[31] Several psychotropic medications can produce dangerous and life-threatening adverse effects, so emergency nurses must assess and recognize these untoward signs and symptoms and provide the appropriate nursing care. All pediatric and adolescent patients who present to the ED with any behavioral health issues must undergo thorough screening for suicidal ideations and/or behaviors. Finally, research also suggests that other paramount considerations for best practices in the ED include an evaluation of the physical layout of the ED for the safe accommodation of behavioral health emergency patients, pertinent ED staff education and development for this age-specific patient group, increased and more seamless access to mental health records and information, individualized crisis intervention plans, increased patient- and family-centered care strategies, availability of equipment and supplies specifically for pediatric patients, and increased communication and collaboration with mental health professionals and services.[6, 31]

References

1. American Academy of Pediatrics, American College of Emergency Physicians. (2006). Pediatric mental health emergencies in the emergency medical services system. *Annals of Emergency Medicine, 48,* 484–486.

2. American Psychiatric Nurses Association and International Society of Psychiatric–Mental Health Nurses. (2007). *Psychiatric–mental health nursing: Scope and standards of practice.* Silver Spring, MD: American Nurses Association.

3. Hart, B. G. (2008). ENA: Advocating care for psychiatric emergency patients. *Journal of Emergency Nursing, 34,* 359–360.

4. Gausche-Hill, M., Schmitz, C., & Lewis, R. J. (2007). Pediatric preparedness of the United States emergency departments: A 2003 survey. *Pediatrics, 120,* 1229–1237.

5. Morrison, J., & Anders, T. F. (2006). *Interviewing children and adolescents: Skills and strategies for effective DSM-IV diagnosis.* New York, NY: Guilford Press.

6. American Academy of Pediatrics, Committee on Pediatric Emergency Medicine, American College of Emergency Physicians, Pediatric Committee, and Emergency Nurses Association Pediatric Committee. (2009). Joint policy statement: Guidelines for care of children in the emergency department. *Pediatrics, 124,* 1233–1243.

7. Anderson, R. N. (2002). Deaths: Leading causes. *National Vital Statistics Reports, 50,* 1–86.

8. Boyd, M. A. (2008). *Psychiatric nursing: Contemporary practice* (4th ed.). Philadelphia, PA: Wolters Kluwer/Lippincott Williams & Wilkins.

9. Woo, S. M., & Keatinge, C. (2008). *Diagnosis and treatment of mental disorders across the lifespan.* Hoboken, NJ: John Wiley & Sons.

10. Sadock, B. J., & Sadock, V. A. (2003). *Kaplan & Sadock's synopsis of psychiatry: Behavioral sciences/clinical psychiatry* (9th ed.). Philadelphia, PA: Lippincott Williams & Wilkens.

11. Dorfman, D. H., Trokel, M., Lincoln, A. K., & Mehta, S. D. (2010). Increased prevalence of behavioral risks among adolescent and young adult women with psychological distress in the emergency department. *Pediatric Emergency Care, 26,* 93–98.

12. American Psychiatric Association. (2005). *Diagnostic and statistical manual of mental disorders* (4th ed.). Arlington, VA: Author.

13. Goldman, W. T. (2000, September 9). *Bipolar disorder.* Retrieved from http://www.keepkidshealthy.com/welcome/conditions/bipolar_disorder.html

14. Fleisher, G. R., & Ludwig, S. (2010). *Textbook of pediatric emergency medicine* (6th ed.). Philadelphia, PA: Lippincott Williams & Wilkins.

15. Steinhausen, H. C. (2002). The outcome of anorexia nervosa in the 20th century. *The American Journal of Psychiatry, 159,* 1284–1293.

16. White, J. H. (2000). Symptom development in bulimia nervosa: A comparison of women with and without a history of anorexia nervosa. *Archives of Psychiatric Nursing, 14,* 81–92.

17. Bisaga, K., Whitaker, A., Davies, M., Chuang, S., Feldman, J., & Welsh, B. T. (2005). Eating disorder and depressive symptoms in urban highschool girls from different ethnic backgrounds. *Journal of Developmental and Behavioral Pediatrics, 26,* 257–266.

18. Stegal-Moore, R. H., Dohn, F. A., Kraemer, H. C., Taylor, C. B., Daniel, S., Crawford, P. B., & Schreiber, G. B. (2003). Eating disorders in black and white women. *American Journal of Psychiatry, 160,* 1326–1331.

19. Currin, L., Schmidt, U., Treasure, J., & Jick, H. (2005). Time trends in eating disorder incidence. *British Journal of Psychiatry, 186,* 132–135.

20. Hart, B. G. (2007). Cutting: Unraveling the mystery behind the marks. *AAOHN Journal, 55,* 161–166; quiz, 167–168.

21. Barkley, R. A. (2005). *ADHD: A handbook for diagnosis and treatment* (3rd ed.). New York, NY: Guilford Press.

22. Owens, J., & Hoza, B. (2003). Diagnostic utility of the *DSM-IV-TR* symptoms in the prediction of *DSM-IV-TR* ADHD subtypes and ODD. *Journal of Attention Disorders, 7,* 11–27.

23. Young, S. (2000). ADHD children group up: An empirical review. *Counseling Psychology Review Quarterly, 13,* 191–200.

24. National Institutes of Health. (2010, July 28). *Autism spectrum disorders.* Retrieved from http://www.nichd.nih.gov/health/topics/asd.cfm.

25. Pedersen, D. D., & Leahy, L. G. (2010). *Pocket psych drugs: Point of care clinical guide.* Philadelphia, PA: F. A. Davis.

26. Hirsch, A. J., & Carlson, J. S. (2007). Prescription practices and empirical efficacy of psychopharmacologic treatments for pediatric major depressive disorder. *Journal of Child and Adolescent Psychiatric Nursing, 20,* 222–233.

27. Stahl, S. M. (2005). *Essential psychopharmacology: Neuroscientific basis and practical applications* (2nd ed.). Cambridge, NY: Cambridge University Press.

References *continued*

28. Bostrom, A. C., & Boyd, M. A. (2008). Schizophrenia: Management of thought disorders. In M. A. Boyd (Ed.), *Psychiatric nursing: Contemporary practice* (4th ed.) (pp. 276–324). Philadelphia, PA: Wolters Kluwer/Lippincott Williams & Wilkins.

29. Cloutier, P., Kennedy, A., Maysenhoelder, H., Glennie, E. J., Cappelli, M., & Gray, C. (2010). Pediatric mental health concerns in the emergency department. *Pediatric Emergency Care, 26,* 99–106.

30. Cronholm, P. F., Barg, F. K., Pailler, M. E., Wintersteen, M. B., Diamond, G. S., & Fein, J. A. (2010). Adolescent depression: Views of healthcare providers in a pediatric emergency department. *Pediatric Emergency Care, 26,* 111–117.

31. Stewart, C., Spicer, M., & Babl, F. E. (2006). Caring for adolescents with mental health problems: Challenges in the emergency department. *Journal of Pediatrics and Child Health, 42,* 726–730.

Chapter 19 | Environmental Emergencies

Kathleen Flarity, PhD, ARNP, CEN, CFRN, FAEN

Objectives

On completion of this chapter, the learner should be able to do the following:

- Determine anatomical, physiological, and developmental characteristics of pediatric patients as a basis for assessment of environmental emergencies.
- Describe the common causes and characteristics of environmental emergencies associated with the pediatric patient.
- Plan appropriate interventions for the pediatric patient experiencing environmental emergencies.
- Indicate health promotion strategies for prevention of pediatric environmental emergencies.

Case Scenario

An 11-year-old boy collapses on the field while playing soccer. His parent runs to him and finds him confused but breathing and calls 9-1-1. On arrival to the emergency department, the boy is drowsy and complains of nausea; he vomited once en route. His temporal artery temperature is 103.1°F (39.5°C); respiratory rate, 18 breaths per minute; heart rate, 116 beats per minute; and blood pressure, 90/60 mm Hg.

What heat emergency is this boy experiencing?

Introduction

Outdoor activities are extremely popular with individuals of all ages. Environmental emergencies are common because children participate in outdoor activities, such as competitive sports, biking, hiking, camping, skiing/snowboarding, and swimming. However, some of these activities may place the pediatric population at risk for illness and injury secondary to the weather, the activity, and various animals, including envenomations from snakes or spiders. Specific environmental emergencies discussed in this chapter are related to heat and cold stress, water immersion, bites, and stings.

Anatomy and Physiology and Developmental Review

Infants and small children are at increased risk of heat-related illness as the result of poorly developed thermoregulatory mechanisms. Children produce more heat during exercise than adults; also, children sweat less than adults. In addition, the temperature at which children begin to sweat is higher than the temperature for adults. The body surface area per weight of children and infants is higher, they have less subcutaneous tissue, and they have a larger head in proportion to the rest of the body, thus making them more susceptible to the extremes of temperature. In addition, children acclimatize slower than adults; in the cold environment, neonates lack the ability to shiver.[1-3]

Selected Emergencies

Heat-Related Emergencies

Many cases of heat-related illness are reported annually in the United States and are implicated in an average of 688 deaths annually.[4] Approximately 4% of the annual deaths occur in children younger than 14 years.[5] Pediatric patients are extremely vulnerable to heat-related emergencies and rely on others to regulate their intake of fluids and their environment. Children do not often think to rest when having fun and may not drink enough fluids when playing or participating in sports. Children with chronic health problems may be more susceptible to heat-related illness. In addition, children who are overweight or wear heavy clothing during exercise, such as football uniforms, are also more susceptible. Only head injury, spinal cord injury, and heart failure are responsible for more deaths in athletes than heat illness.[6] The effects of environmental heat stress can be mild or severe, depending on the degree of heat and the length of exposure. Emergencies related to heat stress range in severity from heat cramps to heat exhaustion to potentially life-threatening heat stroke. Prevention is key in heat-related emergencies. Some good ideas that help prevent injury from heat exposure include the following: drinking enough water, avoiding long exposure to heat/sun, using hats to shade heads and faces, and using an umbrella when planning to be out in the sun for prolonged periods.

Heat Cramps

Heat cramps are the mildest form of heat injury and consist of painful muscle cramps and spasms that occur during or after intense exercise and sweating in high heat or high humidity. Associated symptoms may include weakness, nausea, tachycardia, flushed skin or pallor, profuse diaphoresis, and cool moist skin. The pediatric patient's core temperature may be normal or slightly elevated. The salt depletion from excessive perspiration in combination with excessive water consumption leads to muscle cramping. Increased water intake alone does not replace sodium losses caused by perspiration. Instead, water dilutes serum sodium, causing hyponatremia, the key factor in the development of heat cramps.[1, 7, 8] Management for heat cramps includes the following: removal from heat, rest, and electrolyte replacement with oral or parenteral fluids. Strenuous activity should be avoided for at least 12 hours after discharge.[1, 9]

Heat Exhaustion

Heat exhaustion is more severe than heat cramps and results from a loss of water and salt in the body. It occurs in conditions of extreme heat and excessive sweating, without adequate fluid and salt replacement. Heat exhaustion occurs when the body is unable to cool itself properly and, if left untreated, can progress to heat stroke.[1, 6, 10, 11] The symptoms may be vague and may include rapid onset (within minutes) of extreme thirst, general malaise, muscle cramping, headache, nausea, vomiting, irritability, anxiety, and tachycardia. Associated dehydration may cause orthostatic hypotension, syncope, and mild to severe

temperature elevation (98.6°F–105.0°F [37.0°C–40.6°C]). Diaphoresis may or may not be present. Initial management consists of moving the child to a cool and quiet environment and removing constrictive clothing. When significant hyperthermia is present, moist cloths placed on the patient reduce temperature by evaporation. Fluid and electrolyte replacement should be initiated. Oral replacement with a balanced commercial electrolyte preparation can be used if the patient is not nauseated. Intravenous 0.9% saline solution should be used if the patient is nauseated or vomiting. Salt tablets should not be used in the pediatric patient because of hypernatremia and potential gastric irritation. The patient's temperature should be monitored carefully during treatment. Admission should be considered for any pediatric patient who does not improve significantly with three to four hours of emergency treatment.[1, 10–13]

Heat Stroke

Heat stroke is the most severe form of heat illness and occurs when the body's heat-regulating system is overwhelmed by excessive heat. It is a life-threatening emergency and requires immediate medical attention. Mortality is as high as 70% and is directly related to the speed and effectiveness of diagnosis and treatment.[1] Heat stroke is defined as an abnormal form of hyperthermia, resulting from a failure of the body's physiological systems to dissipate heat and cool down. Heat stroke is characterized by an elevated core temperature of 104.9°F (40.5°C) or greater with central nervous system dysfunction.[8]

There are two types of heat stroke: nonexertional (classic form) and exertional. Classic heat stroke occurs during prolonged exposure to sustained high ambient temperatures and humidity. Children locked in cars on hot days are extremely vulnerable and are at great risk for heat stroke. Vehicles warm up extremely rapidly: within 15 to 30 minutes, internal temperatures reach 117.0°F (47.6°C) in that period. Slightly opening the window did not even reduce the rate of temperature elevation.[14]

Poor dissipation of environmental heat is the underlying cause of classic heat stroke. In contrast, those patients with exertional heat stroke are usually young and healthy, often competitive athletes. In these individuals, heat production overcomes the internal heat dissipation mechanisms. The onset of heat stroke is usually sudden and may present with changes in neurological function, such as anxiety, confusion, hallucinations, loss of muscle coordination, combativeness, and coma. In those with heat stroke, all temperature regulation is lost. A precipitous increase in core body temperature occurs, leading to pathological changes in every organ. Direct thermal damage to the brain, combined with decreased cerebral blood flow, can lead to cerebral edema and hemorrhage. The brain, particularly the cerebellum, is extremely sensitive to thermal injury; therefore, the range of neurological symptoms is broad.[1, 10–13]

The management of heat stroke is directed at reducing core temperature as rapidly as possible and treating subsequent complications. Heat stroke is often fatal despite rapid treatment. The maintenance of airway, breathing, and circulation is crucial for patient recovery. After airway, breathing, and circulation are secured, rapid and aggressive cooling is the cornerstone of therapy. An airway should be established, and supplemental oxygen should be administered by the method most appropriate for the pediatric patient's level of consciousness. Fluid volume is not depleted in most victims of hyperthermia.

Lactated Ringer's (LR) solution is not recommended because the liver may not be able to metabolize lactate. Remove the patient's clothing and provide air conditioning. Spray the patient with tepid water while fanning the entire body to promote cooling by evaporation. Ice packs can be applied in vascular areas, such as the groin, axilla, and neck. Cooling blankets may be used; however, cooling from wet skin is 25 times more effective than cooling from dry skin. Immersion in an ice water bath is contraindicated. Ice water immersion can also cause shivering, which dramatically increases oxygen consumption and can increase body temperature.[1, 10–12, 15]

Cooling (0.4°F [0.2°C] per minute) should be continued until the rectal temperature is 102°F (39°C). The core temperature should be monitored continuously during the cooling phase to prevent inadvertent hypothermia. Careful hemodynamic monitoring is indicated until normal vital signs are restored. A urinary catheter should be placed for monitoring urinary output and core temperature. Hypoglycemia in the pediatric patient should be treated.[1, 10–13]

Heat Injury Prevention

- Encourage children to drink plenty of fluids during vigorous or outdoor activities, especially on hot days.

- Dress children in light-colored, lightweight, tightly woven, loose-fitting clothing on hot days.

- Schedule vigorous activity and sports for cooler times of the day. Encourage rest periods in shady or cool areas.

- Protect children from the sun by having them wear a hat and sunglasses and by using an umbrella. Use a sunscreen that is at least a sun protection factor of 15.

- Increase time spent outdoors gradually to get the child's body used to the heat.

- Teach children to take frequent drink breaks and wet down or mist themselves with a spray bottle to avoid becoming overheated.

- Do not leave children unattended in a hot automobile.

- Teach children to warm up and cool down before and after exercising.

Case Scenario

An eight-year-old girl is brought into the emergency department after falling out of her father's kayak while kayaking on the Columbia River. She had a life jacket on but floated downstream before she could be rescued, with a total of 30 minutes of immersion in the cold water. On arrival, she is awake and shivering and feels weak. Her speech seems slow. Her temperature is 94°F (34.5°C); heart rate, 84 beats per minute; and blood pressure, 92/50 mm Hg.

What type of cold emergency is this girl experiencing?

Cold-Related Emergencies

Approximately 700 fatalities occur annually in the United States from cold exposure.[16] Infants and young children can develop cold-related emergencies from a simple exposure to cold while wearing inadequate clothing for the environmental conditions. Most cases of unintentional hypothermia in children are associated with near drowning in cold or icy water environments.

Injuries related to cold exposure are classified as localized or generalized. Localized cold emergencies include chilblains, frostbite, and injuries to limited or focal areas; a generalized cold emergency involves the entire body. Cold-related emergencies occur with prolonged exposure to cold ambient temperatures, immersion in cold water, or as a result of factors such as inadequate clothing or alcohol. An ambient temperature is a product of air temperature and wind speed; the greater the wind speed, the lower the ambient temperature. Heat loss occurs 24 times more quickly with immersion in cold water.[1, 10–12, 17, 18]

Chilblains

Chilblains are localized areas of itching and redness accompanied by recurrent edema on exposed or poorly insulated body parts, such as the ears, fingers, and toes. Typically, this injury occurs in pediatric patients because they play outside in the cold and are not dressed appropriately. Chilblains are the result of inflammation of small blood vessels of these body parts that are exposed to cold when they are suddenly rewarmed. There is generally no pain; however, the patient may experience transient numbness and tingling. Prevention of this injury is the best management strategy by ensuring that children wear the correct clothing when going out in the cold. If chilblain is suspected, the child should be moved to a warm area in conjunction with covering the affected area with a warm hand or placing fingers under the axilla. Avoid direct heat application, and never massage or rub injured tissue. Tissue damage is rarely seen with chilblains; however, the patient should be instructed to protect the area from injury and further environmental exposure.[1, 19] Symptoms usually resolve in 10 to 14 days.

Frostbite

Frostbite is damage to the skin from freezing and is the result of prolonged exposure to cold temperatures, usually less than 32°F (0°C). It occurs when ice crystals form in the skin or deeper tissue. The most susceptible sites for frostbite are the fingers, hands, toes, feet, ears, nose, and cheeks. Frostbite can be superficial or deep, depending on several factors, including temperature, length of exposure, windchill factor, dampness, and type of clothing worn. Children are more prone to frostbite than adults because they lose heat from their skin faster and do not want to come inside when having fun playing outdoors. If feet are affected, do not allow the child to walk.[1, 10, 11, 20]

Superficial Frostbite

Superficial frostbite involves skin and subcutaneous tissue and is similar to a superficial burn. Symptoms include tingling, numbness, burning sensation, and a white waxy color. Frozen skin feels cold and stiff. After the tissue thaws, the patient may feel a hot stinging sensation, and the area may be edematous. Within a few hours, the affected areas become mottled and blisters develop. Frostbitten tissue is extremely sensitive to subsequent exposure to cold and heat and, therefore, susceptible to repeated frostbite injury.

Injured tissue is friable, so recovery depends on gentle handling. Do not rewarm if there is a chance of refreezing. Do not massage or rub the affected area. Apply warm soaks or circulating water (104°F–110°F [40°C–43°C]) and elevate the extremity. Rewarming may take 20 to 40 minutes. The nurse should constantly monitor the temperature of the water to ensure that it does not get too hot. Place the patient on bed rest for several days until the full extent of the injury has been evaluated and normal circulation has returned. The patient's room should be warm; however, avoid heavy blankets because friction and weight on the affected area can lead to sloughing.[10, 11] Consult a wound care specialist as needed.

Deep Frostbite

Deep frostbite occurs when the temperature of a limb is lowered. Deep frostbite usually involves muscles, bones, and tendons. The degree of frostbite depends on ambient temperature, windchill factor, duration of exposure, whether the patient was wet or in direct contact with metal objects while exposed, and the type of clothing worn. Deep frostbite appears white or yellow-white and is hard, cool, and insensitive to touch. The patient has a burning sensation, followed by a feeling of warmth and then numbness. Blisters typically appear one to seven days after injury. Edema of the entire extremity occurs and may persist for months.[1]

Management includes gentle handling and moderate elevation of the affected part. Rapid rewarming under controlled conditions is the ideal treatment for maintaining tissue viability. Rewarming the pediatric patient with hypothermia and severe frostbite should occur under strict medical control. A baseline core temperature should be obtained, and then the affected area should be immersed in warm water (104°F–110°F [40°C–43°C]). Thawing frozen tissue is extremely painful, thus liberal administration of parenteral narcotics is needed in severe cases. Warmed intravenous fluids need to be provided, tetanus immunization status must be assessed, and antibiotic therapy for deep infections should be considered. If hypothermia is not present, warm oral liquids must be administered. Cover the patient with warm blankets but avoid friction and pressure on the affected area. After thawing, meticulously protect the area from injury. Elevate the extremity, and place cotton or gauze between toes/fingers to limit maceration. A final determination of the depth of injury may not be possible for several weeks; therefore, amputation is not considered in the emergency department.[21, 22]

Hypothermia

Hypothermia can occur in the pediatric patient in many different situations, including cold ambient air, cold water immersion, or cold water submersion. Hypothermia presents in three different categories of severity:

- Mild hypothermia: A core temperature of 89.6°F to 95°F (32°C to 35.1°C)
- Moderate hypothermia: A core temperature of 82.4°F to 89.6°F (28°C to 32°C)
- Severe or profound hypothermia: A core temperature of less than 82.4°F (< 28°C)

The body's metabolic responses depend on a normal temperature. As the core temperature decreases, cellular activity and organ function experience a progressive decline. When the temperature decreases by 18°F (10°C), the basal metabolic rate decreases by two to three times the normal rate. The most obvious response is seen in the central nervous system. The patient becomes apathetic, weak, and easily fatigued, with impaired reasoning, coordination, and gait. The patient's speech is slow or slurred. Renal blood flow decreases; therefore, the glomerular filtration rate declines. Impaired water reabsorption leads to dehydration. Decreased respiratory rate and effort lead to carbon dioxide retention, hypoxia, and acidosis. Shivering consumes glucose stores, thus the patient becomes hypoglycemic. Insulin levels decline, decreasing usable glucose forcing the body to metabolize fat for energy. Metabolism in the liver is sluggish, so medications may last longer.[23, 24]

The cardiovascular system is also dramatically affected. Cold heart muscle is irritable and prone to dysrhythmias. The Osborne or J wave is a striking electrocardiographic feature seen in approximately one-third of hypothermic patients.[25] The J wave is described as a "humplike" deflection between the QRS complex and the early part of the ST segment. The most common dysrhythmias are atrial and ventricular fibrillation. The cold patient is in great danger of ventricular fibrillation when core temperature decreases below 82°F (28°C). Ventricular fibrillation at these extremely cold temperatures does not respond to conventional treatment without prior rewarming. A defibrillation attempt is appropriate if ventricular fibrillation or tachycardia is present. If the patient fails to respond to the initial defibrillation attempt or drug therapy, defer subsequent defibrillation attempts or additional boluses of medication until the core temperature increases to greater than 86°F (30°C).[1,17] Intravenous medications are also limited until the core temperature is greater than 86°F (30°C). Careful handling of hypothermic patients, especially when their temperatures reach the vulnerable mid-80s range, is imperative because even turning may cause ventricular fibrillation. Rewarming procedures are active or passive, and external or internal warming.[23]

The clinical finding of hypothermia in children and adolescents depends on the degree of hypothermia, which can be categorized as mild, moderate, or severe. The goal in mild hypothermia, in which the patient is still shivering, alert, and oriented, is to prevent further heat loss and rewarm the patient as rapidly as possible.[1, 23] Passive external rewarming techniques, such as moving the patient to a warm environment, replacing wet clothing with dry material, and wrapping with warm blankets, may be effective. Giving the patient warmed oral fluids that contain glucose or other sugars provides more heat through calories. Passive rewarming increases the temperature at a rate of 1°F to 4°F (0.5°C to 2°C) per hour. However, many patients require active external rewarming using warmed humidified oxygen or warmed intravenous fluids.

In moderate hypothermia, gradually rewarm truncal areas at 1°F (0.5°C) per hour to prevent rewarming shock or afterdrop, in which the cold peripheral blood circulates back to the core as the periphery vasodilates. Use active external warming techniques including heating blankets, force hot air devices, such as Bair Hugger Therapy, radiant heating lamps, warmed oxygen, warmed intravenous fluids, and hot water bottles. Monitor closely for marked vasodilatation and subsequent hypotension.

In cases of severe hypothermia, active internal (invasive) rewarming techniques are used in conjunction with active external rewarming procedures. Peritoneal, gastric, and bladder lavage, esophageal rewarming tubes, extracorporeal cardiac life support, and hemodialysis are examples of active internal warming measures. Active internal warming can be essential in preventing rewarming shock that can occur when the core temperature continues to decrease after rewarming is initiated as cold peripheral blood returns to the central circulation. The circulation of cold blood through the heart also increases ventricular irritability and leads to fibrillation. Rewarming may also cause peripheral vasodilatation, which can precipitate hypotension and cardiovascular collapse. Successful rewarming depends on the patient's age, general condition before the hypothermic event, length of exposure, and careful handling by the emergency department team. To prevent hyperthermia secondary to aggressive rewarming, discontinue active rewarming when the core temperature reaches 89.6°F to 93°F (32°C to 34°C).

Bites, Stings, and Envenomations

Because of children's curiosity, they are prone to exposure to bites, stings, and envenomations that may lead to the need for emergency department treatment. Injuries can range from inconspicuous surface wounds, with or without infection, to anaphylaxis, major puncture wounds, crush injuries, and severely envenomated snakebites.

There are some common elements of care for essentially all bites and stings, including:

- Reassurance of the child and caregivers. Keeping the child calm may decrease the spread of toxins throughout the body.

- Physical assessment must include a search for all bites and stings, not just one that is evident when the pediatric patient presents for treatment.

- Cleanse the wound by irrigating with saline to remove possible foreign bodies and decrease the risk of infection.

- Determine the status of the pediatric patient's tetanus immunizations, and administer tetanus immune globulin and/or tetanus toxoid as appropriate.

Animal Bites

Most animal bites are caused by dogs or cats that are family pets. Animal bites can produce lacerations and deep puncture wounds. Some animals, particularly dogs, can also produce crush injuries as a result of the powerful jaws closing onto an extremity or other exposed body part. In addition, animal bites have the potential for infection and the transmission of diseases, such as rabies. Animal bite injuries may also result in damage to the scalp, face, hands, and feet and may cause long-term scarring and loss of function. Children are at greatest risk of being bitten by animals, particularly dogs; because of the small size, it is not uncommon to sustain dog bites to the neck. Dog bites in children may also require psychological support in addition to treatment of their physical injuries. Dog bites account for 90% of the bite injuries that are treated in the emergency department. Cat bites are usually deep puncture wounds that cannot be completely cleaned. As a result, cat bites have a higher risk of infection and cellulitis from the organism *Pasteurella*, which is carried in the cat's mouth.[10–12, 26]

Interventions

- After physical assessment, irrigate the wound with normal saline. Inspect for the presence of foreign bodies. Whether the wound should be sutured or remain open depends on the characteristics of the bite, location, how long since the bite occurred, and whether there is evidence or likelihood of infection. Antibiotic treatment depends on many of the same factors.

- Determine if the dog is known to the child's family and if the status of the dog's rabies immunization is known. Animal control may need to be contacted to provide assistance in accordance with local requirements and laws.

- If the animal was not captured, or if the status of the rabies vaccination is unknown, the child will need rabies prophylaxis. Contact the local health department or poison center for current treatment recommendations.

- Other animals that can transmit rabies include cats, bats, foxes, skunks, and raccoons. Contact the local health department about the need to capture an animal. Begin rabies prophylaxis as indicated.

- If you find a bat in a room with an unattended child, seek immediate medical attention. Contact the local or state health department for assistance with and testing for the bat. When it cannot be ruled out that the bat is free from rabies, rabies prophylaxis is indicated.

- Teach caregivers to care for the wound, observe for signs of infection, and make an appointment with a healthcare provider for follow-up care.

Hymenoptera Stings

Hymenopterans are an insect family found in temperate regions and include the honeybee, wasp, hornet, and fire ant. Stings are more common in the summer months when children are outside playing. The venom of hymenopterans varies among species and may be cytotoxic, hemolytic, allergenic, or vasoactive. Hymenopteran stings cause 40 to 150 deaths annually in the United States.[1] Stings are cumulative: the greater the number of stings, the more severe the reaction, with the exception of the honeybee. Fire ants have a painful sting that causes a wheal that expands to a large vesicle. The area then reddens, and a pustule forms. When the pustule is reabsorbed, crusting and scar formation occur.

Signs and Symptoms

- Reactions can occur at the time of the sting and up to 48 hours later.

- Local reactions may appear dramatic to frightened parents. Local reactions include pain, itching, erythema, and swelling at and around the bite site. Infection is a possibility, but these stings are not otherwise expected to be dangerous.

  ○ The pediatric patient may also have severe systemic reactions, including urticaria, pruritus, edema, bronchospasm, laryngeal edema, and hypotension.

- Systemic reactions indicating hypersensitivity/allergy will begin within 30 minutes, if not sooner. Symptoms includes hives, redness, and generalized edema which is a sign of angioedema, a condition characterized by vasodilatation and capillary leak. Antihistamines should be administered, and the child should be observed until the symptoms resolve.

- Anaphylaxis from a hymenoptera sting is treated the same as any other allergic reaction from any other cause: cardiovascular and respiratory support, epinephrine, steroids, and antihistamines, and fluid resuscitation.

Otherwise, treatment for hymenoptera stings includes the following:

- Inspection of the site for a retained stinger. If one is present, scrape it out with the dull side of a knife or credit card to prevent absorption of the venom.
  - The stinger actively injects venom into the wound for one minute after the sting.[1, 12, 19]
- Symptomatic and supportive care for local effects, including cold packs, analgesics, and topical antihistamine or steroid creams.
- Assuring the caregivers that a delayed hypersensitivity reaction is not expected.
- If the child experienced his or her first hypersensitivity reaction to a hymenoptera sting, even if anaphylaxis did not develop, advising the caregivers to follow up with the pediatrician for a possible prescription for an epinephrine autoinjector.

Spider Bites

All spiders inject venom when they bite. Most venom causes itching, stinging, swelling, or a combination of symptoms in a local area. Despite the many arthropod bites and stings occurring on a daily basis, systemic reactions occur in only 4% of the population, with anaphylaxis in only 0.4% of the population. In the United States, approximately four deaths per year are reported as a result of spider bites.[1, 12, 19] Although most spiders are venomous, most do not have strong enough venom or strong enough fangs to cause human poisoning. If examined closely, two tiny fang marks may be visible. Cleansing the area and observing for infection are indicated.

Tarantula bites usually cause only local reactions (i.e., slight pain and stinging). Two spiders in the United States associated with human poisoning are the black widow spider (*Latrodectus*) and the brown recluse spider (*Loxosceles*).[27] Black widow and brown recluse spider venom may cause systemic reactions and anaphylaxis.

Black Widow Spider

The black widow or hourglass spider is the most dangerous species in the United States because of its potent venom. Spiders of the genus *Latrodectus* are worldwide in distribution. In the United States, they are found in every state except Alaska. They are predominantly observed in Southern and Western states. Spiders of the *Latrodectus* genus are not aggressive, biting only when disturbed. Black widow spiders spin webs and await their prey. They can usually be found in their webs, which are often located near protected places, such as the undersides of stones and logs; in the angles of doors, windows, and shutters; and in littered areas, such as city dumps, garages, barns, outhouses, and sheds. Often, these webs are found around outdoor toilet seats, resulting in bites on or near the genitalia. Adult females are recognizable by their shiny black body and the bright red hourglass marking on their abdomen. In the United States, the incidence of envenomation from black widow spiders is unknown. In Texas, 760 black widow spider bites were documented from 1998 to 2002, with an increased prevalence in western Texas. In 1997, more than 13,000 spider bites were reported to the American Association of Poison Control Centers, with no deaths. More than 1,300 of the bites were described as moderate or severe. The reported death rate from documented bites occurs in less than 1% of reported cases.[1] Young children are at greatest risk for a lethal bite. The black widow spider's venom is neurotoxic. Initially, severe pain in local muscle groups occurs, which then spreads to regional muscle groups. Severe cramps and contraction of musculature may extend throughout the body. The abdominal pains are frequently most severe, mimicking appendicitis, colic, or food poisoning. Other symptoms include headache, restlessness, anxiety, fatigue, and insomnia.[1, 12, 19, 28] Symptoms from envenomation peak two to three hours after onset, but they can last several days.[1, 12, 19]

Reactions may be minor and require only local wound care; however, severe systemic responses may also occur. The outcome, even in untreated cases of black widow bites, generally is favorable with supportive care. Most patients do not require hospitalization, and symptoms subside in approximately two days; however, the very young and the very old, and patients with cardiovascular disease, are at increased risk for complications.[1, 19]

Signs and Symptoms

- Bites are locally painful, but the bite site may appear insignificant.
- Local pain begins quickly, within about 30 minutes after the bite.
- Systemic symptoms are primarily neurological and can include muscle spasm, muscle rigidity, hyperreflexia, hypertension, and ptosis, among other effects. Abdominal rebound pain may lead to a suspicion of appendicitis.

Interventions

- Stabilize the airway, breathing, and circulation.
- Apply ice to the bite area to slow the action of the neurotoxin.

- Contact a poison control center for further consultation.

- Treatment may include intravenous benzodiazepines (diazepam [Valium], or lorazepam [Ativan], for muscle spasms/rigidity; and opiates [morphine], for pain).

- Antivenin is available and is indicated for hypertension not controlled by other means, seizures, and respiratory arrest, which are possible but uncommon effects.

  ○ It is produced in horses (the animal is given a small dose of venom, and an antibody to it is created); it is available for *Latrodectus* venom and is efficacious regardless of which *Latrodectus* species. Patients appropriately treated with antivenin recover rapidly in one to two days, but fatigue, weakness, and other nonspecific symptoms may persist for seven to 10 days. Because the possibility of anaphylaxis or serum sickness always exists, use antivenin only in those who are at high risk for severe complications. Premedication with diphenhydramine (Benadryl), methylprednisolone (Solu-medrol), ranitidine (Zantac), and acetaminophen (Tylenol) may help to decrease the possible allergic reaction to antivenin infusion.

- With aggressive supportive therapy, symptoms usually subside within 48 hours; however, hypertension and muscle spasms may recur for 12 to 24 hours.

Brown Recluse Spider

The brown recluse spider, also known as the fiddleback or violin-back spider, is the most prevalent of the *Loxosceles* species in the United States. All *Loxosceles* species have the potential to inflict injury to varying degrees. Brown recluse spiders have a light brown color with a dark brown fiddle-shaped mark that extends from the six white eyes down the back. These spiders are seen predominantly in the south central part of the United States; however, the brown recluse spider has been discovered as far north as Illinois and on both coasts. They prefer dark, dry, and undisturbed locations, such as the undersides of logs, boards, and rocks and inside barns and garages. Genital bites have been seen on patients using outhouses. Within homes, they are found in attics, closets, and storage areas for bedding, clothing. and furniture. Both the male and female spider can envenomate. They are most active at night, from spring to fall. However, bites are rare, even in houses heavily infested with brown recluse spiders.[1, 12, 19, 29, 30]

The venom of the brown recluse spider is cytotoxic and hemolytic. Bites of the recluse spider can cause a condition termed *necrotic arachnidism*, which begins with the development of an eschar at the bite site, followed by tissue necrosis and skin sloughing. Several groups of spiders have been linked to necrotic skin lesions, but recluse spiders cause most of these lesions. Although most recluse bites heal uneventfully, 10% have a protracted course, with the wound taking months to resolve completely.

Signs and Symptoms

- The bite typically is painless, and findings of a central papule and associated erythema may not be seen for six to 12 hours.

  ○ Wounds destined for necrosis usually show signs of progression within 48 to 72 hours of the bite.

- Central blistering with a surrounding gray-to-purple discoloration of the skin may be seen at the bite site.

  ○ A surrounding ring of blanched skin is itself surrounded by a large area of asymmetric erythema, leading to the typical red, white, and blue sign of a brown recluse bite.

  ○ At this stage of evolution, these bites may be associated with significant pain related to developing necrosis of skin and subcutaneous tissues. The resultant eschar and ulceration may take months to resolve.

  ○ Patients who are destined for a severe reaction usually develop key signs within six to 12 hours, such as bullae formation, cyanosis, and hyperesthesia.

  ○ Areas with increased adipose tissue, such as the thighs, buttocks, and abdomen, are more likely to undergo severe necrosis than other sites of the body.

    - Methicillin-resistant *Staphylococcus aureus* and cutaneous anthrax should also be considered in patients with these symptoms.[1, 12, 19, 29, 30]

- Systemic effects are uncommon and may be delayed for up to a week after the bite. Patients may present with joint pains, fever, chills, seizures, myoglobinuria, and renal failure. Treatment is symptomatic and supportive because no specific measures have been shown to be effective.

Interventions

Treatments for the bite of the brown recluse spider have been varied and controversial. Almost all brown recluse spider bites heal in two to three months, without medical treatment. The long-term medical outcome is excellent without treatment. Surgery should be avoided. When treatment is deemed appropriate, it should be conservative, using cold compresses, simple analgesics, elevation of an affected extremity, and cleansing of the bite site.[1, 12, 19]

If tissue breakdown occurs and/or the bite appears in an anatomical site that is difficult to keep clean, a prophylactic antibiotic may be added to prevent the occurrence of a superimposed cellulitis; tetanus prophylaxis also is indicated. Necrotic skin lesions occur in 10% of patients with envenomization; in most patients, no systemic agent can be recommended to prevent necrosis. Excision of a necrotic skin site may be advisable (especially for the rare large lesion) but only after six to eight weeks of wound care, when an eschar has formed, adjacent tissues seem to have recovered, and normal healing is possible.[1, 12, 19, 29, 30]

Scorpion Stings

There are approximately 90 different species of scorpions found in the United States. Typically, a scorpion sting only causes minor symptoms when the patient is stung. Scorpions are most active in spring and summer and frequently hide in bed linens and shoes. The only species in the United States that causes severe symptoms is the bark scorpion, which can be life threatening to young children. Symptoms are mainly neurological; scorpion stings do not always require intensive treatment.

Signs and Symptoms

- Intense pain with numbness and tingling but usually little edema
- Muscle twitching and abnormal eye movements
- Drooling and sweating
- Restlessness
- Respiratory distress

Interventions

Mild envenomation does not usually require any treatment other than ice to relieve any swelling and pain medication for the mild pain that occurs. Symptoms tend to resolve in a couple of hours or within two to three days. Until recently, there has been no antivenin; and supportive care was the only treatment for the management of the violent neuromotor hyperactivity and respiratory compromise. In a randomized, double-blind, placebo-controlled study performed by Boyer et al.[31] the researchers showed that "treatment with a specific F(ab′)2 antivenin can effectively resolve the clinical neurotoxic syndrome associated with envenomation by the centruroides scorpion." These findings were similar to those found in uncontrolled studies in Mexico using the same

antivenin. Anascorp is the antivenom that is produced in Mexico and has just been approved by the Food and Drug Administration (FDA) for use in the U.S.

Case Scenario

A five-year-old girl is brought into the emergency department after being bitten by a snake. The parents report that while they were scrambling on rocks the child was bitten on the forearm by a western rattlesnake. On examination, the patient's respiratory rate is 26 breaths per minute; heart rate, 128 beats per minute; and blood pressure, 104/58 mm Hg. Her forearm is swollen and erythematous, with two fang marks. Her hand is pink, with strong pulses, and capillary refill is less than two seconds.

What are the priorities of care for this girl?

Snakebites

In the pediatric population, most snakebites occurred in adolescents and school-aged children around the perimeter of the home during summer months in the afternoon.[32] There are two families of venomous snakes that are native to the United States and Croatia: pit vipers (rattlesnakes, copperheads, and cottonmouths) and Elapidae (coral snakes). It is estimated that as many as 2.5 million venomous snakebites occur internationally per year, and estimates of annual deaths from snakebites are as high as 125,000 worldwide.[1] Annually, more than 45,000 snakebites occur in the United States, but envenomation occurs in only 8000 cases. Venomous snakebites account for 10 to 15 deaths each year in the United States.[1] Virtually all of the venomous bites in this country (95%) are from pit vipers.[1, 10–12, 19, 29, 30] When a pediatric patient presents with a snakebite, ask the parent if the species of snake that bit the child is known. If the snake is reported as a nonpoisonous species, treatment consists of inspecting the wound for foreign objects (e.g., retained teeth), wound care, tetanus update as indicated, and instructions to the parent to observe for infection. If the snake is reported as a poisonous species, or if the type of snake is unknown, be certain to consult the poison center for guidance. Definitive treatment for an envenomated snakebite is antivenin, but not all bites of poisonous snakes require antivenin.

Pit Vipers

Pit vipers get their common name from a small pit between the eye and nostril that detects heat and allows the snake to sense prey at night. These snakes deliver venom through hypodermic-like fangs that the snake can retract at rest, but that spring into biting position rapidly. Snakebite venom is a complex substance containing enzymes, glycoproteins, peptides, and other substances capable of causing tissue destruction (cardiotoxic, neurotoxic, hemotoxic, or any combination of these). Pit viper venom is primarily hemotoxic, whereas coral snake venom is primarily neurotoxic. In venomous creatures, all venom is designed to do the same thing: immobilize or kill the prey and begin the digestive process. Clinical presentations associated with envenomation are the result of digestive proteins, which break down muscles, break down cell barriers, destroy cell integrity, and trigger the coagulation cascade.

The amount of venom actually delivered by a pit viper bite varies. It is estimated that 20% to 30% of patients seen who have been bitten by a snake with fang marks have not received any venom at all, also known as dry bites. The reason for this may be poor timing by the snake. Pit vipers have a sophisticated mechanism that allows them to deliver venom at the exact instant the teeth are sunk into the flesh. Thus, it has to be precise timing. A *dry bite* is defined as the absence of local, systemic, or coagulopathic effects. Typically, if there are no effects noted in 8 to 12 hours, the patient may be cleared for discharge.[1, 10–12, 19, 29, 30]

Signs and Symptoms

Signs and symptoms of snakebites depend on the circumstance of the bite, including the type and size of the snake, size and age of the patient, location and depth of the bite, number of bites, and amount of venom injected. Most snakebites occur in the lower extremities, around dawn or dusk, during warm weather months. Major signs and symptoms are divided into local and systemic reactions.

Local Reactions

- One or two fang or teeth marks
- Edema around the bite site one to 36 hours after the bite
- Pain at the site, petechiae, ecchymosis, loss of function of the limb, and necrosis 16 to 36 hours after the bite

Systemic Reactions

- Nausea, vomiting, diaphoresis, syncope, and a metallic or rubber taste
- The patient may develop paralysis, excessive salivation, difficulty speaking, visual disturbances, muscle twitching, paresthesia, epistaxis, blood in the stool, vomitus or sputum, and ptosis
- Neurological symptoms include constricted pupils and seizures

- Life-threatening systemic reactions include severe hemorrhage, renal failure, and hypovolemic shock[1, 10, 11, 19, 29, 30]

Interventions

The initial assessment includes a history of the snakebite (i.e., the size of the snake, location and depth of the injury, number of bites, and amount of venom injected, if known). Document the time of injury and all interventions before emergency department arrival. The initial management of hypotension or shock should include aggressive intravenous infusion of crystalloids at 20 mL/kg. If organ perfusion remains inadequate after vigorous fluid infusion (two to three 20 mL/kg boluses), evidence supports a trial infusion of albumin because of the rapid onset of increased vascular permeability after significant pit viper envenomation. Clean the wound, and clearly mark and time the leading edges of envenomation every 15 minutes. Administer analgesics or titrated doses of opiates (e.g., intravenous morphine sulfate) for pain. Avoid aspirin and nonsteroidal anti-inflammatory medications because they may exacerbate coagulopathy. Administer tetanus prophylaxis if the patient's immunization history is incomplete or outdated. Crotaline polyvalent immune Fab (antivenin) should be considered in all patients based on the severity of signs and symptoms of envenomation.

Suspect compartment syndrome if the extremity becomes increasingly tense secondary to edema and third-space fluid accumulation. Compartment pressures should be measured in this situation, and an orthopedist should be consulted for possible fasciotomy to relieve pressure.[1, 10–12, 19, 29, 30]

Specific Interventions

- Keep the patient calm and supine to minimize exertion
- Immobilize the limb at or below the level of the heart to reduce blood flow
- Remove all jewelry or tight-fitting clothing
- Using a surgical skin marker, indicate the borders of the affected area to show the extent of swelling at recommended intervals (typically hourly for the initial 6–12 hours) and documenting hourly measurements of affected limb circumference (at the same location).
- Consider a venom sequestration technique, such as applying a lymphatic or superficial venous constriction band, or pressure immobilization if a delay to transport to the emergency department is possible. This technique involves immediately wrapping the entire snakebitten extremity with an elastic ace wrap. If used, it should

not be removed until antivenin is available because of a potential bolus of venom release after removal.[1, 12]

- Coagulopathy commonly occurs with rattlesnake envenomation. Consider the following laboratory procedures:
  - ○ Complete blood cell count with differential
  - ○ Platelets
  - ○ Prothrombin time
  - ○ Activated partial thromboplastin time
  - ○ Fibrinogen
  - ○ Type and screen
  - ○ Urinalysis
- Provide antivenin as indicated.
  - ○ Crotaline polyvalent immune Fab (antivenin) should be considered in all patients based on the severity of signs and symptoms of envenomation. The dosage of this antivenin is calculated according to the venom load rather than patient size.[33] There are data showing efficacy and safety for patients as young as 14 months of age with the antivenin. Antivenin is most therapeutic when given within four to six hours of the bite and has limited value after 12 hours. Two antivenins for pit viper bites are available in the United States: crotaline polyvalent immune Fab and antivenin crotalidae polyvalent. It appears that crotaline polyvalent immune Fab causes fewer acute anaphylactic reactions than antivenin crotalidae polyvalent.

Do not use the following measures:

- Incision, suction, tourniquets, electric shock, ice, or alcohol
- Until recently, the Sawyer extraction pump was recommended, but various studies concluded that it does not work for venomous snakebites and could potentiate the bite effects.[1, 12]

Discharge Education

- Provide referral or information on obtaining a primary care provider if one is not already established.
- For heat-related prevention, exertion should be avoided between 10 a.m. and 4 p.m.; ensure adequate intake of an electrolyte-containing solution before and during heavy exercise.
- Aftercare instructions for wound care should be given to the patient and family with a careful explanation of the signs and symptoms of infection.
- Infants younger than one year should never sleep in a cold room because they lose body heat more easily than adults; unlike adults, infants cannot make enough body heat by shivering.
- An excellent resource entitled "Extreme Cold: A Prevention Guide to Promote Your Personal Health and Safety" is available from the Centers for Disease Control and Prevention (http://www.bt.cdc.gov/disasters/winter/pdf/cold_guide.pdf).

Summary

Pediatric environmental emergencies cover a broad spectrum of injuries arising from a variety of environmental factors. Recognition of symptoms and consideration of environmental etiology may result in early diagnosis and appropriate management. Morbidity and mortality are directly related to the magnitude and duration of the exposure, regardless of the source.

References

1. Auerbach, P. A. (2007). *Wilderness and environmental emergencies* (5th ed.). St. Louis, MO: Mosby.

2. Denke, N. J. (2009). Cold emergencies. In D. O. Thomas & L. M. Bernardo (Eds.), *Core curriculum for pediatric emergency nursing* (2nd ed.). Des Plaines, IL: Emergency Nurses Association.

3. ECC Committee, Subcommittees and Task Forces of the American Heart Association. (2005). 2005 American Heart Association Guidelines for Cardiopulmonary Resuscitation and Emergency Cardiovascular Care. *Circulation, 112,* IV-1–IV-203.

4. Centers for Disease Control and Prevention. (2006). Heat-related deaths: United States, 1999–2003. *MMWR: Morbidity and Mortality Weekly Report, 55,* 796–798.

5. Centers for Disease Control and Prevention. (2004). Nonfatal and fatal drowning in recreational water settings: United States, 2001-2002. *MMWR: Morbidity and Mortality Weekly Report, 53,* 447.

6. National Center for Injury Prevention and Control. (2007). *Water-related injuries.* Atlanta, GA: Centers for Disease Control and Prevention.

7. Howe, A. S., & Boden, B. P. (2007). Heat-related illness in athletes. *American Journal of Sports Medicine, 35,* 1384.

8. Denke, N. J. (2009). Heat emergencies. In D. O. Thomas & L. M. Bernardo (Eds.), *Core curriculum for pediatric emergency nursing* (2nd ed.). Des Plaines, IL: Emergency Nurses Association.

9. Lugo-Amador, N. M., Rothenhaus, T., & Moyer, P. (2004). Heat related illness. *Emergency Medicine Clinics of North America, 22,* 315.

10. Flarity, K. M. (2007). Environmental emergencies. In *Emergency nursing core curriculum* (6th ed., pp. 310–348). St. Louis, MO: Saunders, Elsevier.

11. Flarity, K. M. (2007). Environmental emergencies. In K. Oman, J. Koziol McLain, & L. Scheetz, *Emergency nursing secrets.* Philadelphia, PA: Hanley & Belfus.

12. Flarity, K. M. (2010). Environmental emergencies. In *Sheehy's emergency nursing: Principles and practice* (6th ed.). St. Louis, MO: Saunders.

13. Jardine, D. S. (2007). Heat illness and heat stroke. *Pediatrics in Review, 28,* 249–258.

14. McLaren, C., Null, J., & Quinn, J. (2005). Heat stress from enclosed vehicles: Moderate ambient temperatures cause significant temperature rise in enclosed vehicles. *Pediatrics, 116,* e109–e112.

15. Platt, M., & Vicarios, S. Heat illness. (2009). In P. Rosen, R. J. Marx, R. S. Hockberger, & R. Walls (Eds.), *Rosen's emergency medicine* (7th ed., pp. 1882–1892). St. Louis, MO: Mosby.

16. Centers for Disease Control and Prevention. (2004). Hypothermia-related deaths: United States, 2003. *MMWR: Morbidity and Mortality Weekly Report, 53,* 172–173.

17. Tisherman, S. A. (2010). When it comes to hypothermia and trauma: Kids are really little adults. *Pediatric Critical Care Medicine, 11,* 301–302.

18. Ulrich, A. S., & Rathlev, N. K. (2004). Hypothermia and localized injuries. *Emergency Medicine Clinics of North America, 22,* 281.

19. Greenberg, M. I., Hendrickson, R. G., Silverberg, M., Campbell, C., Morocco, A., Salvaggio, C., & Spencer, M. T. (2005). *Greenberg's text: Atlas of emergency medicine.* Philadelphia, PA: Lippincott Williams and Wilkins.

20. Prendergast, H. M., & Erickson, T. B. (2010). Procedures pertinent to hypothermia and hyperthermia. In R. R. Roberts & J. R. Hedges (Eds.), *Clinical procedures in emergency medicine* (5th ed., pp. 1235–1258). St. Louis, MO: Saunders/Elsevier.

21. Biem, J., Koehncke, N., Classen, D., & Dosman, J. (2003). Out of cold: Management of hypothermia and frostbite. *Canadian Medical Association Journal, 168,* 305.

22. Danzel, D. F. (2009). Frostbite. In P. Rosen, J. Marx, R. S. Hockberger, & R. Walls (Eds.), *Rosen's emergency medicine* (7th ed., pp. 1868–1881). St. Louis, MO: Mosby.

23. Hazinski, M. F., Cummins, R. O., & Field, J. M. (Eds.). (2005). *2005 Handbook of emergency cardiovascular care for healthcare providers.* Dallas, TX: American Heart Association.

24. Wissler, E. H. (2003). Probability of survival during accidental immersion in cold water. *Aviation, Space, and Environmental Medicine, 74,* 47–55.

25. Van Mieghem, C., Sabbe, M., & Knockaert, D. (2004). The clinical values of the EKG in non-cardiac conditions. *Chest, 125,* 1561.

26. Mullins, J., & Harrahill, M. (2008). Dog bites: A brief case review. *Journal of Emergency Nursing, 34,* 490–491.

27. Diaz, J. H., & Leblanc, K. E. (2007). Common spider bites. *American Family Physician, 75,* 869–873.

28. Goddard J. (1999). *Physician's guide to arthropods of medical importance* (3rd ed.). Boca Raton, FL: CRC Press.

29. Norris, R. (2005). *Snake envenomations, coral.* Retrieved from http://www.emedicine.com/emerg/topic542.htm

References *continued*

30. Otten, E. J. (2009). Venomous animal injuries. In P. Rosen, J. Marx, R. S. Hockberger, & R. Walls (Eds.), *Rosen's emergency medicine* (7th ed., pp. 743–757). St. Louis, MO: Mosby.

31. Boyer, L. V., Theodorou, A. A., Berg, R. A., Mallie, J., Chávez-Méndez, A., García-Ubbelohde, W., … Alagón, A. (2009). Antivenom for critically ill children with neurotoxicity from scorpion stings. *The New England Journal of Medicine, 360,* 2090–2098.

32. Sotelo, N. (2008). Review of treatment and complications in 79 children with rattlesnake bite. *Clinical Pediatrics, 47,* 483–489.

33. Offerman, S., Bush, S. P., Moynihan, J. A., & Clark, R. F. (2002). Crotaline Fab antivenom for the treatment of children with rattlesnake envenomation. *Pediatrics, 110,* 968–971.

Chapter 20 | Child Maltreatment

Angela Black, MSN, RN, CPN

Objectives

On completion of this chapter, the learner should be able to do the following:

- Define the five forms of child maltreatment.
- Determine cultural, physical, medical, and predisposing factors that influence the assessment for child maltreatment.
- Describe common causes and characteristics associated with child maltreatment.
- Plan appropriate interventions for the effective management of the maltreated pediatric patient.
- Indicate health promotion strategies related to prevention of child maltreatment.

Introduction

The following devastating stories reveal the multiple forms of child maltreatment.

- A seven-year-old girl is starved and kept in a dirty spare room, duct taped to a chair for hours each night. She is routinely beaten and raped by her stepfather while her mother turns a blind eye.
- A 53-year-old man is convicted of impregnating a 12-year-old girl.
- A 43-year-old junior high teacher is charged with drugging and having sexual relations with a 12-year-old student in his home.
- A mother finds her 19-month-old son unresponsive and vomiting after leaving him with her boyfriend for 15 minutes. The child also has bruises all over his body, and his bowel is eviscerated and requires surgery. The boyfriend admits to punching the boy because he was crying.
- A 45-year-old man faces charges of luring children for sex over the Internet at his business and at his home.
- The parents of a nine-month-old boy who sustained severe head injuries and retinal hemorrhages are charged.

Child maltreatment is a serious threat to the health and well-being of children of all ages. The recognition of child maltreatment can be difficult and requires careful assessment by healthcare providers. In the United States, approximately 3.3 million referrals for child maltreatment were made to child protective service agencies in 2008, resulting in 1,740 deaths.[1] The number of fatalities from child maltreatment has been increasing during the past five years. In addition, many researchers believe that child fatalities as the result of maltreatment are grossly underreported, by as much as 60%.[2] Children younger than one year accounted for more than 42% of child fatalities, and 75% were younger than four years. Younger children are most vulnerable because of their dependency, small size, and inability to effectively communicate or defend themselves.

Mandated reporters are required by law to report child maltreatment if there is reasonable suspicion that abuse or neglect has occurred. State statutes define who mandated reporters are and the conditions for reporting maltreatment; therefore, it is important to be knowledgeable of child abuse laws in the jurisdiction in which one practices. Failure to report a case of suspected child maltreatment could result in civil or criminal charges.[3] In most states, standard mandated reporters include, but are not limited to, physicians, nurses, paramedics, psychologists, social workers, teachers, child-care providers, and law enforcement personnel.

More times than not, maltreated children present to the healthcare system without declaration of abuse or neglect. This, along with a caregiver's false presentation of the child's medical history or intentional withholding of information, contributes to the difficulty in identifying child maltreatment. A thorough physical examination and a detailed medical history are the diagnostic tools needed most in identifying maltreatment. Nurses play a unique role in caring for these patients because they may be the first to see the child and caregiver and are the consistent healthcare provider if the child is hospitalized.

Definitions of Different Types of Maltreatment

Definitions of child maltreatment differ by community, culture, and country. The broad term *child maltreatment* includes, at a minimum, any recent act or failure to act on the part of a parent or caregiver that results in death, serious physical or emotional harm, or sexual abuse or exploitation; or an act or failure to act that presents an imminent risk of serious harm.[2] The prevalence of each type of maltreatment is given in **Figure 20-1**.

Neglect

Neglect is characterized by a failure to provide for a child's basic needs. Neglect may be physical, emotional, or educational.[1]

- *Physical neglect* includes refusal of, or delay in, seeking healthcare, abandonment, expulsion from the home, and inadequate supervision.

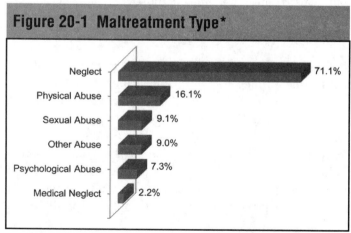

Figure 20-1 Maltreatment Type*

Neglect	71.1%
Physical Abuse	16.1%
Sexual Abuse	9.1%
Other Abuse	9.0%
Psychological Abuse	7.3%
Medical Neglect	2.2%

*Data are adapted from Administration for Children and Families, US Dept of Health and Human Services.[1] Percentages total more than 100 because of rounding.

- *Emotional neglect* includes inattention to the child's needs for affection, refusal or failure to provide needed psychological care, and spousal abuse in the child's presence.
- *Educational neglect* includes the allowance of long-term absenteeism, failure to enroll a child of mandatory school age in school, and failure to attend to a special educational need.

Emotional Abuse

The deliberate attempt to destroy or impair a child's self-esteem or competence constitutes emotional abuse. Psychological maltreatment occurs when a person conveys to a child that he or she is worthless, flawed, unloved, or unwanted.[4] All forms of child maltreatment involve some level of emotional or psychological abuse.

Physical Abuse

Physical abuse is the deliberate infliction of physical injury on a child, usually by the child's caregiver. One or more body systems may be involved. Because the abuse is often ongoing, there is usually evidence of both acute and chronic injuries.

Sexual Abuse

Sexual abuse is the engagement of a child in sexual activities that the child cannot comprehend, for which the child is developmentally unprepared and cannot give informed consent; and/or that violate the social and legal taboos of society.[5] Types of sexual abuse include, but are not limited to, digital manipulation; fondling; actual or attempted oral, vaginal, or anal intercourse; exhibitionism; and pornography.

Munchausen Syndrome by Proxy

Munchausen syndrome by proxy (MSBP) is a rare form of child maltreatment in which the caregivers/perpetrators exaggerate, feign, or induce symptoms and/or illnesses in children and are motivated by the need to assume the sick role by proxy or to gain another form of attention.[6] It is often the mother who has exposure to the healthcare environment and is highly involved in the child's care.

Conditions Mistaken for Child Maltreatment

There are a number of circumstances or conditions that can be confused for child maltreatment, including cultural, physical, and medical conditions. Because the diagnosis of child maltreatment has serious consequences for the child, the family, and the suspected perpetrator, it is important not to arrive at the diagnosis of child maltreatment hastily. It is essential to obtain a careful medical history, perform a thorough physical examination, and conduct necessary diagnostic procedures to rule out conditions other than abuse.

The healthcare team must maintain an awareness of cultural and religious health practices in the evaluation of potential maltreatment. This complex issue requires balancing the parent's rights with keeping the child healthy and safe. Certain cultural practices or remedies can be misdiagnosed as child maltreatment by uninformed professionals.[7]

- **Cupping:** this practice is used in Asia, Europe, Russia, and the Middle East. A heated cup containing steam is applied to specific points on the body to draw out the poison or evil elements causing illness. When the heated air within the container cools, a vacuum is created, producing circular ecchymotic areas on the skin. Cupping is often used for headaches and respiratory ailments.

- **Coining:** this is a Vietnamese practice that may produce weltlike lesions on the child's back when a coin is repeatedly rubbed lengthwise on the oiled skin to rid the body of disease. The intent is to promote the release of toxins that may be causing illness. This practice is often used for respiratory ailments.

- **Burning:** this is a Southwest Asian practice in which small areas of the skin are burned to treat pain, cough, diarrhea, failure to thrive, enuresis, and temper tantrums.

- **Moxibustion:** this is a Southeast Asian practice in which a stick of burning mugwort, incense, or yarn is placed over an affected area of the body. This may produce lesions that resemble cigarette burns, usually in a pattern of four, six, or eight marks, in a pyramid formation.

- **Topical garlic application:** this is a practice of the Yemenite Jews in which crushed garlic is applied to the wrists to treat infectious diseases. This can result in blisters or garlic burns.

- **Traditional remedies that contain lead:** greta and azarcon are used in the Mexican culture to treat digestive problems, paylooah is used in the Southeast Asian culture to treat rash or fever, and surma is used in Indian culture to improve eyesight.

These practices are those of well-intentioned caring parents who are attempting to relieve pain and suffering for their children in the way their culture has taught them. It is important to explain to the caregivers why some of these types of remedies may be considered harmful (e.g., those containing lead). This may require collaboration with a folk healer to explore different options of modifica-tion to these practices that would cause less injury to the child, such as not rubbing so hard during the practice of coining. Some medical conditions may also be mistaken for child maltreatment. **Table 20-1** provides a summary of these medical conditions.

Predisposing Factors

Multiple dynamics lead to situations that may result in the maltreatment of children. There are factors that place the child at risk for maltreatment and the caregiver at increased risk for becoming abusive. Younger children, children with an irritable temperament, excessively demanding children, and children with chronic illness or developmental disabilities are more often victims of physical abuse than older children and children without these characteristics.[8] Children with developmental disabilities may have behavioral, physical, and emotional challenges that place the child at greater risk for maltreatment. **Table 20-2** lists the risk factors for child maltreatment.

The number of children surviving disabling medical conditions is increasing because of technological advances. The rates of child maltreatment are high in children who are blind, deaf, chronically ill, developmentally delayed, and have behavioral or emotional disorders. In addition, child maltreatment may result in a disability, which, in turn, can precipitate further abuse. Several elements increase the risk of maltreatment for children with disabilities. Children with chronic illnesses or disabilities often place higher emotional, physical, economic, and social demands on their families. Caregivers with limited social and community support may be at especially higher risk for maltreating children with disabilities. Lack of respite or breaks in child-care responsibilities can contribute to an increased risk of abuse and neglect.[9]

Focused Assessment

Indicators of Maltreatment

When a pediatric patient presents to the emergency department (ED) with an injury, the historical data and physical findings must be compared and evaluated in terms of congruency. The interactions among the pediatric patient, caregivers, and staff are also important to evaluate. Pediatric patients or caregivers may exhibit some of the behaviors listed in **Table 20-3,** which could indicate that the pediatric patient has sustained a form of child maltreatment. In a study performed by Pierce et al. in 2010,[10] compelling evidence is provided "that bruising without a clear confirmatory history for any infant who is not

Table 20-1 Medical Conditions Mistaken for Child Maltreatment

Medical Condition	Clinical Features
Congenital dermal melanocytosis (Mongolian spots)	Benign bluish gray areas of pigmentation commonly seen in African American, Asian, Latino, and Native American infants Usually found over the sacral area and buttocks Seen at birth and fades during childhood
Erythema multiforme	Symmetrical red blotchy lesions in a circular pattern on the skin
Epidermolysis bullosa	Blistering after minimal pressure to the skin Often appears in infancy from simple handling of the infant
Impetigo	Small vesicle surrounded by a circle of reddened skin Appears first on the face and legs
Phytophotodermatitis	Streaky eruptions of the skin after contact with a plant and then exposure to the sun
Henoch-Schönlein purpura	Pain in the knees and ankles Purpuric skin lesions that appear predominantly on the lower abdomen, buttocks, and legs Gastrointestinal bleeding
Idiopathic thrombocytopenia purpura	Purpura and petechiae Bleeding from the nose, mouth, digestive tract, or urinary tract
Leukemia	Lethargy, paleness, and easy bruising
Hemophilia	Unusually heavy bleeding and bruising from a minor injury
Glutaricaciduria type 1	Rare disorder of amino acid metabolism that can result in subdural and retinal hemorrhages with minimal trauma
Osteogenesis imperfecta	Abnormal collagen synthesis characterized as brittle bone disease Sclera have a blue tint Bones fracture easily and can be deformed

Table 20-2 Risk Factors of Child Maltreatment

Child	Caregiver	Environmental
Crying	Childhood history of abuse	Domestic violence
Prematurity	Unmet emotional needs	Poverty
Prenatal drug exposure	Belief in use of corporal punishment	Unemployment
Developmental or physical disability	Rigid or unrealistic expectations of the child	Poor housing
Chronic illness	Negative perceptions of the child	Homelessness
Recent illness	Lack of parenting knowledge	Frequent relocations
Hyperactivity (attention-deficit/hyperactivity disorder)	Single parent	Violence in the community
Product of multiple births	Social isolation	
Product of unwanted pregnancy	Alcohol or other substance abuse	
Toilet training or difficulty with developmental milestones	Poor impulse control	
High-risk infants	Psychological distress	
	Low self-esteem	
	Short- or long-term stressors	

cruising and bruising to the torso, ears, or neck of a child four years of age or younger should be considered red flags and should serve as signs of possible physical child abuse." The torso, ears, neck, age ≤ 4 (TEN4) mneumonic can help you remember this.

Obtaining a Comprehensive Medical History

It is essential to obtain a comprehensive medical history when maltreatment is suspected. It is also important to coordinate the collection of the complete history with all healthcare professionals who will be involved in the patient's care. This may include nurses, physicians, and social workers. Ideally, this conversation should be led by a healthcare professional who has been specifically trained in forensic interviewing. The following are general guidelines to assist in obtaining a comprehensive history when child maltreatment is suspected.

- Use a nonjudgmental and nonaccusatory approach, even when it is apparent that the caregiver has injured the pediatric patient. Convey a genuine concern for the pediatric patient.

Table 20-3 Indicators of Child Maltreatment

Child

Extremes of behavior (excessive compliance and passivity or overaggression)
Wary of physical contact with a caregiver
Clingy and indiscriminate in his or her attachment
Shows no expectation of being comforted and flat affect
Does not cry during painful procedures
Sexualized behavior toward adults or other children and has specific knowledge beyond the developmental level
Sudden and severe decline in school performance
Delinquency
Regressive behaviors
Child appears malnourished, inappropriately dressed, or unkempt

Caregiver

Inappropriate response to the seriousness of the child's condition
No explanation or a changing explanation for the injury
Explanation does not match clinical findings
Concealment of past injuries
Delay in seeking medical attention
Bypass hospitals closer to home
Caregiver exhibits psychologically destructive behaviors toward child
Hostility toward hospital staff
Uncooperative
Tension between caregivers

- Conduct the interviews in a private setting.
- Interview the verbal pediatric patient alone, if possible. If separating the pediatric patient and caregiver is too distressing for the patient, allow the caregiver to remain in the room while cautioning him or her that he or she is to observe and support the patient without answering questions.
- Interview the caregivers separately.
- Use open-ended and nonleading questions. Begin with "What happened?" and follow with more specific questions.
- Do not promise not to tell anyone.
- Document what the pediatric patient says as direct quotes whenever possible.
- If a language barrier is present, use professional interpreters in the correct language.
- Complete a cultural assessment, as appropriate.
- Obtain a pertinent history for the current problem using the CIAMPEDS format. Elicit other pertinent information, as follows:
  - Developmental milestones the pediatric patient has achieved.
  - Social history, including who cares for the pediatric patient routinely, who lives in the home, and who cared for the pediatric patient during the past several days.
  - Family history of chronic disorders.
  - Medical history, including previous illnesses or injuries, hospitalizations, and ED visits.

Along with a comprehensive medical history, it is imperative to complete a thorough physical examination to ensure that no injuries are missed. The physical examination should include a complete head-to-toe examination with the pediatric patient unclothed. Height and weight should also be measured and plotted on a standard growth chart. Finally, all injuries, old and new, should be identified and documented; historical information should be compared with clinical evidence.

Planning and Implementation

General Nursing Interventions for the Maltreated Child

Chapter 5, "Initial Assessment," provides a description of the general nursing interventions for the pediatric patient. After the primary assessment has been completed, the following interventions are initiated, as appropriate, for the pediatric patient's condition.

- Provide a safe environment.
- Provide appropriate treatment for injuries or identified medical needs.
- Provide emotional support to the pediatric patient and family. Assign one staff member to care for the family.
- Explain and prepare the pediatric patient and caregiver for all procedures and interventions.
- Provide information to caregivers regarding normal growth and development and alternatives to corporal punishment as appropriate.
- Refer caregivers to the appropriate social and community agencies for support and therapy.
- Report suspected child maltreatment in accordance with state and local guidelines.

Documentation and Evidence Collection

The medical records of evaluation for child maltreatment frequently become legal documents with important implications. Careful documentation of the reported medical history and physical findings can determine legal outcomes. Statements made by the pediatric patient to a healthcare provider may be admissible as evidence, depending on jurisdiction.

The following should be documented when child maltreatment is suspected.

- The date and time of the interview. The information gathered during the interview, including the names of those present.
- The questions asked, the responses (verbatim), and nonverbal or emotional reactions observed during the interview.
- All relevant verbal statements made by the pediatric patient and caregivers should be documented verbatim, using quotations whenever possible.
- Date, time, and place of occurrence. Presence of witnesses.
- Sequence of events with recorded times.
- Description of the interactions between caregiver and child and the interactions between caregivers.
- The physical examination should be documented with great detail. All injuries must be documented carefully and consistently on the pediatric patient's medical record.
  - Location, size, shape, and color of all cutaneous injuries, including a drawing of a body outline.
  - Distinguishing characteristics indicating a pattern injury.
  - Symmetry or asymmetry of the injury.
  - Evidence of past injuries, general state of health, and hygiene.

Table 20-4 is one example of a child maltreatment documentation template.

Proper evidence collection is an essential component of the care of the maltreated child. The evidence collected during the examination may be used in court and can drastically affect the outcome of such proceedings and the future safety of the pediatric patient.

- All visible external injuries, such as bruises and burns, should be photographed in color. Forensic photography should be performed by local law enforcement specialists or specially trained forensic nurse examiners, if available. Forensic photographs must include a ruler, standard color chart in the field (if available), and patient data (e.g., name, date of birth, and medical record number).
- In cases of sexual abuse, specific medical and forensic evidence may be collected. Protocols and equipment used for collecting and preparing medical evidence may vary from setting to setting; therefore, it is important to know what is used by your state and local jurisdiction.
- Psychosocial preparation for the examination is essential and increases the likelihood of cooperation.
- Pediatric patients who are unable to cooperate must never be physically restrained for an examination. Forced restraint for the examination could further traumatize the pediatric patient. In such cases, the pediatric patient may be examined under sedation in the ED or under general anesthesia later in the operating room.
- The specimens and other evidence collected are determined based on whether the suspected sexual assault occurred within the last 72 hours and the nature of the sexual acts committed. The primary goal is to not only collect the offender's deoxyribonucleic acid (DNA) but also to corroborate the pediatric patient's story linking the offender to the scene. The offender's DNA can be found in blood, semen, saliva, and hair. Types of specimens or items that may be collected for evidence include the following:
  - Clothing to look for hair, fibers, semen, and other DNA that may be detected. If not laundered, DNA may be detectable for years. The integrity of the clothing may also be evaluated (e.g., torn areas, dirt, and fibers). Individual pieces of clothing must be placed in separate brown paper, not plastic, bags to maintain integrity of the DNA.
  - Hair samples to look for any loose hairs from the offender.

- Oral, vaginal, or penile and rectal swabs to look for the presence of semen and to perform DNA typing of the offender.
- Fingernail scrapings: If the victim scratched his or her offender or scraped his or her fingernails on the offender's clothing or items at the scene, valuable evidence might be found under the nails.
- Miscellaneous stains or bite marks may be swabbed in an attempt to collect the offender's DNA. Examination under a Wood lamp may be helpful in finding semen on the pediatric patient's body.
- Blood from the victim to accompany the preceding evidence to provide a DNA standard for comparison.

Table 20-4 Child Maltreatment Documentation Template*

Variable	Description
Consistency of injury with developmental stage	Is the incident as described plausible for the age and development of the child? Refer to the "Developmental Milestones" section* "Noncruisers are nonbruisers!"
History inconsistent with injury	Does the medical history of the child, or the incident history, change from person to person? Is there a previous history of fractures, ingestions, or injuries? Is the injury consistent with the presenting history?

Inappropriate caregiver concerns	Do caregivers:
	    Ask pertinent questions?
	    Seem concerned about outcomes?
	    Offer comfort measures to the child?

Lack of supervision	Question family member/caregiver regarding the following:
	    What happened? When did it happen?
	    How did it happen? Where did it happen?
	    Who was present?

Delay in seeking care	Is the time frame between when the injury occurred and when medical care was sought reasonable? Note unusual delays.
Affect	Document the reaction of the child to all family members/caregivers present. Document the response and behavior of family members/caregivers present.

Bruises of varying ages	Document findings/absence of findings of the head-to-toe examination with patient unclothed. In documenting bruises, note the following:
	    Location
	    Size
	    Number
	    Pattern
	    Color

Unusual injury patterns	Describe injury characteristics and diagnostic procedures performed. Try to differentiate between nonintentional and inflicted patterns (e.g., belt loops, bites, iron burns, and hand imprints).
Suspicions	Remember that a report to Child Protective Services is just for a suspicion of abuse or neglect. You do not have to prove it. Photograph suspicious areas.
Environmental cues	If a run report from EMS is present, does it contain any contributing information about the environment in which the injury occurred? Gather information from EMTs before their departure from the emergency department.

Note: EMS indicates emergency medical services; EMT, emergency medical technician.
*Data are taken from Illinois Emergency Medical Services for Children. (2002). *Illinois emergency medical services for children child abuse and neglect policy and procedure guidelines*. Retrieved from http://www.luhs.org/depts/emsc/Child%20Abuse.Neglect%20Guideline.doc

All items must be sealed and stored securely to maintain the integrity of the evidence until released to law enforcement personnel. Chain of custody should be maintained and completely documented in the nursing record.

Assessment and Interventions for Specific Types of Child Maltreatment

Neglect and Emotional Abuse

Neglect is the most common form of child maltreatment and accounts for approximately 71% of all reported child maltreatment cases in the United States.[1] Failure to thrive is a condition in children younger than five years whose growth persistently and significantly deviates from norms for age and sex, based on national growth charts.[11] Generally, these children are below average in height, weight, and head circumference when plotted against normal childhood growth patterns. An actual weight of less than 70% of the predicted weight for length requires urgent attention.[11] The cause of failure to thrive may be organic, which is caused by a medical condition (e.g., celiac disease, lead poisoning, or malabsorption) or inorganic (i.e., psychosocial issues). Psychosocial causes are often linked to and reported as child neglect.[11]

Emotional abuse is often suspected, but it is difficult to substantiate. Physical signs are often absent or nonspecific, and healthcare providers must rely on behavioral indicators (e.g., depression or acting-out behaviors) to help identify a possible abusive situation. Any persistent and unexplained change in the child's behavior is an important clue to possible emotional abuse.

History

The medical history of a pediatric patient who has been neglected may include the following:

- Delay in seeking healthcare for an injury, illness, or poor health status, such as no immunizations
- History of injuries, ingestions, or exposure to toxic substances
- Self-stimulating behaviors, such as finger sucking, biting, or rocking
- Excessive absenteeism from school
- Substance abuse
- Delinquency
- History of being left alone, abandoned, or inadequately supervised

Signs and Symptoms

- Malnourishment or nonorganic failure to thrive (weight below the fifth percentile)
- Inactivity or extreme passiveness
- Poor hygiene and/or inappropriate attire
- Untreated dental caries and periodontal disease that can lead to pain, infection, and loss of function. This can adversely affect learning, communication, nutrition, and other activities necessary for normal growth and development.[12]
- Lags in emotional and intellectual development, especially language

Diagnostic Procedures

- Consider a toxicology screen if ingestion or exposure to toxic substances is suspected.
- Evaluate appropriate growth charts, with past and present growth parameters, including head circumference, to assist in identifying failure to thrive.

Physical Abuse

Physical abuse may result in injuries from a single or multiple episodes and can range from minor bruising to death. Inflicted injuries may involve the skin and soft tissues, bone, and/or all major organ systems.

History

The history of a pediatric patient who has been physically abused may include the following:[13]

- History inconsistent with developmental milestone achievements or abilities
- No explanation for the injury
- Vague, unclear, or changing account of how the injury occurred
- Discrepancy between the caregiver's and the pediatric patient's accounts
- Inappropriate reaction to the injury, such as failure to cry with pain
- Unreasonable delay in seeking medical attention
- Unrealistic expectations of the pediatric patient
- History of previous ED visits or hospitalizations for an injury

Signs and Symptoms

Bruises

Characteristics and locations for noninflicted bruises:

- On extensor and bony surfaces, such as the elbows, knees, and shins
- Forehead and chin of toddlers

Characteristics and locations for potentially inflicted bruises. Abusive trauma often involves multiple bruises.[10]

- Unexplained bruises or welts
- Multiple or symmetrical bruises or marks
- Bruises and welts to the face, mouth, neck, chest, abdomen, back, flank, thighs, or genitalia
- Bruises and welts with patterns descriptive of an object, such as a looped cord, belt buckle, shoe or boot pattern, wire hanger, chain, wooden spoon, hand, or pinch marks (crescent-shaped bruise)
- Bruises in various stages of healing

Burns

Chapter 16, "Trauma," includes the assessment and treatment of burn injuries. Correlation of the severity and pattern of the burn injury with the history provides a basis for the identification of inflicted burns.

Characteristics of noninflicted burns include the following:

- Asymmetrical and/or splash pattern congruent with history
- Contact burn that is not uniform
- Treatment sought immediately

Characteristics of potentially inflicted burns include the following:

- Immersion burns
  - Circumferential and often symmetrical stocking pattern burns on the feet, glovelike pattern burns to the hands, or doughnut pattern burns to the buttocks
- Burns with sharply demarcated edges without a splash pattern and/or symmetrical burns
- Patterns descriptive of an object used, such as cigar or cigarette burns; rope burns on wrists, ankles, torso, or neck from being bound; or uniform burns in the shape of an iron, radiator, or electric stove burner
- Burns to the dorsum of the hand
- Splash patterns indicative of hot liquid being thrown on the pediatric patient
- Delay in seeking medical attention
- Multiple bruises proximal to limb burns, indicating that the limb was forcefully held to heat source (e.g., in boiling water).

Bite Marks

Bite marks are lesions that may indicate abuse. Bite marks should be suspected when ecchymosis, abrasions, or lacerations are found in an ovoid pattern. The normal distance between the canine teeth in adult humans is two and a half to four centimeters. The canine marks in a bite will be the most prominent or deepest parts of the bite. If the distance is greater than three centimeters, the bite was likely from an adult.[12] Forensic dentists can make impressions from the bite mark to help identify the offender. DNA may also be obtained from the bite mark before cleaning the wound.

Abusive Head Trauma

Head trauma is the leading cause of death in child abuse victims.[13] *Shaken baby syndrome* is well-known terminology used by healthcare providers and the public to describe abusive head trauma inflicted on infants and children. Although this terminology has been used for decades, the American Academy of Pediatrics recommends adoption of the term *abusive head trauma* as a diagnosis used in medical records to describe the constellation of cerebral, spinal, and cranial injuries resulting from inflicted head injury to infants and young children.[14]

Injuries from shaking and blunt trauma have the potential to result in death or permanent neurological disability, including static encephalopathy, cognitive and developmental delays, cerebral palsy, cortical blindness, seizure disorder, and learning disabilities.[14] Signs and symptoms of abusive head trauma may vary from mild and nonspecific to severe. Signs and symptoms include the following:

- History of poor feeding, vomiting, lethargy, and/or irritability
- Respiratory depression or apnea
- Altered level of consciousness or coma
- Seizure, abnormal posturing, hypotonia, or full fontanel
- Subdural hematoma, subarachnoid hemorrhage, and/or depressed skull fracture from an impact
- Bruising or fractures of the upper extremities or ribs (grip marks/injuries)

The following head injuries are suggestive of physical abuse:

- Skull fractures: Multiple fractures, depressed occipital fractures, or any skull fracture in an infant. All skull fractures should have a history of appropriate severity.
- Subdural hematomas or subarachnoid hemorrhages are the most common types of inflicted head injury

in children. If associated with a retinal hemorrhage, abusive head trauma should be suspected.

- Scalp bruises and traumatic alopecia.
- Dislocated lens, hyphema, corneal or conjuctival abrasion, laceration, or ulceration.
- Bruising to the eyelid or periorbital tissue or an orbital fracture.
- Low-velocity or short vertical falls rarely result in serious head injuries (e.g., fall from a sofa).

Skeletal Fractures

Any fracture can be caused by abuse. A child may sustain a single or multiple fractures from an incident of abuse. During the radiographic examination, a practitioner may find recent or old fractures or a combination and the fractures may be found at one or more sites. The healthcare provider may choose to perform a total body radiological film study when appropriate in cases of suspected abuse. The humerus is one of the most frequently injured bones in abuse situations as a result of being violently grabbed by the arm, pulled, swung, or jerked.[15] Suspicious fractures include the following:

- Multiple fractures in various bones, with different stages of healing
- Metaphyseal-epiphyseal fractures at the end of long bones
- Rib, scapular, or sternal fractures usually resulting from a direct blow
- Transverse, oblique, and spiral shaft fractures
- Bilateral or symmetrical fractures

Abdominal Injuries

Abdominal injuries may be caused by a kick or punch, resulting in injury to hollow and solid organs. Abdominal injuries are difficult to identify because they may have no signs of external injury, although the patient's condition may be poor and shock may be present.[15] Abdominal injuries may have occurred several days before presentation because signs and symptoms are subtle; therefore, it is important to extend the history to days before presentation.

Types of abdominal injuries seen in abuse cases include the following:

- Perforation of the gut
- Hemorrhaging
- Laceration, contusion, or hematoma of the liver, spleen, duodenum, pancreas, mesentery, or kidney

Symptoms associated with abdominal injury may include the following:

- Abdominal distention or rigidity
- Vomiting and abdominal pain
- Bruising to the abdomen
- Fever and septic shock
- Hypovolemic shock
- Hematuria

Diagnostic Procedures for Child Maltreatment

The differential diagnosis of child abuse includes nonabusive injuries and medical conditions that may mimic abuse. Ancillary procedures may provide additional evidence of abuse or may uncover further injury. These diagnostic procedures may also provide important medicolegal information.

Laboratory Studies

- Consider obtaining a complete blood cell count, a platelet count, and bleeding, prothrombin, and partial thromboplastin times when contusions or hematomas are found to rule out bleeding disorders.
- Consider obtaining a urine sample for glutaric aciduria, a spinal tap, and blood cultures to rule out central nervous system dysfunction.
- Consider obtaining liver enzyme and amylase levels, blood cultures, a complete blood cell count, and a urine sample to check for blood (with abdominal injuries).

Radiographic Studies

Full-body radiographic screening is indicated in children younger than two years with evidence of abuse and in infants with evidence of abuse and/or neglect. This screening may detect multiple and/or old fractures and should include multiple views of the skull, thorax, long bones, hands, feet, pelvis, and spine. However, fractures in children can be difficult to visualize, and serial radiographs are often advised. Radiographs should be obtained in radiology versus portable because the quality of the film is much better.

Some types of radiographic studies that may be obtained in suspected maltreatment include the following:

- Radiographs of any suspected injury. Fractures should be documented with at least two views.

- Computed tomography for children with abusive head injuries to detect intracranial hematomas and cerebral edema. Computed tomography of the abdomen to uncover damage to the abdominal organs.
- Magnetic resonance imaging or ultrasonography.

Selected Abuse Emergencies

Sexual Abuse

Sexual abuse presents in many ways; and because children who are sexually victimized generally are coerced into secrecy, a high level of suspicion may be required to recognize the problem.[5] The primary portal of entry into the healthcare system for many children who have been sexually abused is the emergency department.

Sexual Development in Children

Sexual abuse can be differentiated from sexual play by determining whether there is developmental asymmetry among the participants and by assessing the coercive nature of the behavior.[5] Sexual play can be characterized as follows:[16]

- Children of the same developmental age and/or stage looking at or touching genitalia
- No coercion or force
- No intrusion into the body or orifices
- Nonabusive

An understanding of the normal development of sexual behavior is helpful for distinguishing between normal and abnormal sexual activities. Genital self-stimulation is evident by the age of 18 months in both sexes. Children learn to identify themselves as boys or girls by the age of two to three years and enjoy displaying their nude bodies. Between the ages of three and six years, children understand the differences between boys and girls, and masturbation is common. By the age of six to seven years, children become more modest, although they remain curious about sex, dirty words, and pornography. As children enter adolescence, interest turns more toward the opposite sex. Up to one-fourth of adolescents initiate sexual intercourse by the age of 12 years.[16]

A behavioral history may reveal events or behaviors relevant to sexual abuse, even without a clear history of abuse in the child. An appropriate history should be obtained before performing the physical examination.[5]

The history may reveal the following characteristic behaviors:

- Sexualized activity with peers, adults, animals, or objects; and seductive behaviors.
- Age-inappropriate sexual knowledge or curiosity and excessive masturbation.
- Regressive behavior (e.g., wetting the bed or sucking a thumb) and/or aggressive behavior.
- Sudden onset of phobias or fears.
- Sleep disorders or nightmares.
- Depression, withdrawn behaviors, and/or suicidal gestures.
- Poor school performance, running away, and/or substance abuse.
- Self-mutilation and/or eating disorders.

In addition to the interview guidelines for child maltreatment stated earlier in this chapter, the following techniques may also be used with a pediatric patient who has been sexually abused, preferably by a trained forensic interviewer.

- Use clear and simple language. Determine and use the pediatric patient's own terminology for describing body parts.
- Use age-appropriate media, such as anatomical drawings and anatomically correct dolls, to facilitate verbal communication.
- Avoid multiple interviews, and limit the interview to one hour or less.

The following information should be gathered when obtaining the history of the sexual abuse incident(s):

- Date, time, and location of the incident(s).
- Description and/or name of the offender(s), if known by the pediatric patient. Nondisclosure is more common if the victim knows the offender.[17]
- The number of offenders and statements made by the offender(s), including threats, bribes, or intimidation.
- Physical force or other violent activity and involvement of other children or adults.
- Loss of consciousness and/or amnesia of the incident, which may indicate use of drugs (e.g., date-rape drugs).

Physical findings are often absent, even when the perpetrator admits to penetration of the pediatric patient's genitalia. Many types of abuse leave no physical evidence, and mucosal injuries often heal rapidly.[5]

Examples of potential signs or symptoms indicating sexual abuse include the following:

- Vaginal, penile, or rectal pain, discharge, or bleeding.

- Bruises, lacerations, or irritation of external genitalia, the anus, the mouth, or the throat.

- Chronic dysuria, enuresis, constipation, or encopresis.

- Sexually transmitted infections (STIs), nonspecific vaginitis, or genital warts.

- Difficulty sitting or walking.

- Pregnancy in adolescents.

Diagnostic Procedures

- Cultures obtained from the mouth, anus, and genitals for *Neisseria gonorrhoeae*, *Chlamydia trachomatis*, and herpes simplex virus.

- Wet preparation for *Trichomonas vaginalis* and the presence of sperm.

- Blood for the Venereal Disease Research Laboratory, which tests for syphilis.

- Blood for hepatitis B and human immunodeficiency virus testing. Hepatitis A, B, C, and D can all be transmitted sexually; however, the most significant pathogen in sexual abuse is hepatitis B.[17]

- Pregnancy testing.

Additional Interventions

The risk of a child acquiring an STI as a result of sexual abuse has not been well studied. According to the Centers for Disease Control and Prevention,[18] presumptive treatment for children who have been sexually abused is not recommended for the following reasons: (1) the incidence of most STIs in children is low after abuse/assault, (2) prepubertal girls are at lower risk for ascending infection when compared with adolescent girls or adult women, and (3) regular follow-up of children usually cannot be ensured. However, if there is concern about the possibility of infection with an STI, even if the risk is perceived to be low by the healthcare provider, presumptive treatment in some settings may be considered after all specimens for diagnostic procedures relevant to the investigation have been collected.

Drug-Facilitated Rape

Alcohol or other drug use immediately before a sexual assault has been reported by more than 40% of adolescent victims and offenders.[19] Adolescent acquaintance rape has been associated with the illegal availability of date-rape drugs, such as flunitrazepam (Rohypnol) and γ-hydroxy-

butyrate (GHB).[19, 20] These drugs can go undetected if added to any drink. Date-rape drugs cause sedation and amnesia to the extent that victims cannot resist or may not be aware of a sexual assault. Any substance that is administered to lower sexual inhibition and enhance the possibility of unwanted sexual intercourse is potentially a date-rape drug.[20, 21]

Signs that a date-rape drug was administered:

- Patient awakens in strange surroundings with disheveled clothing and/or the feeling of being sexually violated.

- If some memory of the event remains, the victim may describe feeling paralyzed or powerless and may experience a disassociation between the mind and body.

- Symptoms may be similar to alcohol intoxication, although the severity may not match the amount consumed.

- Sudden onset of symptoms after consuming a drink (15–20 minutes after ingestion). Symptoms can range from drowsiness, confusion, and impaired memory to coma.

Evidence Collection

The sooner a urine specimen is collected after the event, the more likely that rapidly excreted drugs will be detected. Most hospital laboratories will not detect date-rape drugs; therefore, a urine specimen should be sent to the local crime laboratory while maintaining the chain of evidence.

Methamphetamine Exposure

With the growing prevalence of methamphetamine use and production in home laboratories, children are at risk for injuries resulting from living in a drug-endangered environment.[22] Child welfare has not yet addressed the needs of the children living in homes in which methamphetamines are manufactured. These children are endangered not only from the chemicals involved but also from parental abuse and neglect. Pediatric patients with methamphetamine poisoning commonly present with signs and symptoms, such as tachycardia, agitation, inconsolable crying and irritability, and vomiting.[23] Consider the need for decontamination in these children.

Munchausen Syndrome by Proxy

Munchausen syndrome by proxy (MSBP) occurs when a parent, usually the mother, simulates or inflicts disease in her child for the gratification or attention she receives from having a child undergo medical diagnosis and treatment. This form of abuse includes both falsifying the medical history to make it appear as if the child has an illness and actually producing illness in the child. The history provided is often elaborate and sophisticated and may also include a falsified family history. The mother often demands an extensive medical evaluation and appears to be very concerned for the child.

History

Indicators for a potential case of MSBP include the following:

- Unexplained, prolonged, recurrent, or extremely rare illness.
- Discrepancies between clinical findings and medical history.
- Discrepancy between the child's apparent good health and a history of grave symptoms.
- Illness is unresponsive to treatment.
- Signs and symptoms occur only in the parent's presence.
- Parent is knowledgeable about illness, procedures, and treatments.
- Parent is interested in interacting with the healthcare team.
- Parent is attentive toward child and does not want to leave his or her side.
- Signs and symptoms subside once the child is separated from the parent.

The most common chief complaints or presentations of MSBP include the following:

- Apnea and seizures: May be falsified or created by partial suffocation.
- Vomiting or diarrhea: May be created by administering syrup of ipecac or laxatives.
- Simulated or actual hemorrhage, bacteremia, rash, and fever.

Additional Interventions

Hospitalized children should be under constant surveillance.[24] This may include hidden video monitoring in coordination with law enforcement. All cases should be reported promptly and with careful documentation to child protective service agencies. The consequences of MSBP include persistence of abuse, emotional problems, chronic disability, and death. Other siblings may also be at risk of this form of abuse. There is an association of this syndrome with unexplained infant deaths.

Evaluation and Ongoing Assessment

Children who have been maltreated require careful and frequent reassessment of airway patency, breathing effec-

tiveness, perfusion, and mental status. Appropriate medical, surgical, and psychiatric treatment should be promptly initiated. Hospital admission is indicated for children whose medical or surgical condition requires inpatient management, in whom the diagnosis is unclear, and when no alternative safe place for custody is immediately available. If the safety of the child is in doubt, healthcare professionals should always err on the side of protecting the child. No matter how severe the abuse, children will usually grieve the separation from their caregivers. They need help to understand why they cannot return home and that it is in no way their fault or a punishment.

The caregiver should be told by the healthcare team that an inflicted injury is suspected, that the team is legally obligated to report the circumstances, that the referral is being made to protect the child, that the family will be provided with services, and that child protective services and law enforcement will be involved. Consider informing the family after security or law enforcement personnel are available to prevent possible removal of the child before further evaluation, or possible violent reaction towards ED staff. Siblings and children cared for by the suspected abuser should undergo full examinations within 24 hours because they are also at risk of child maltreatment.

Health Promotion

Prevention

It is essential that healthcare providers are able to recognize children and families at risk for abuse. The prevention of child maltreatment has been an extremely difficult task. Some interventions that may assist in prevention include the following:

- Having educational and informational materials on positive parenting techniques, child abuse prevention, and domestic violence readily available in the ED waiting and treatment rooms.
- Providing information on normal child growth and development and routine healthcare needs.
- Making referrals to appropriate services when the need for assistance is identified. Nurses need to know what kinds of community services are available, including self-healing groups.
- Unlike preventive efforts for physical abuse and neglect, the prevention of sexual abuse focuses on educating children to protect themselves. Sexual abuse prevention is more than teaching a child to say "no" or to recognize his or her rights not to be touched in "private places." It is just as important to teach safety in terms of potential risk situations and to notify a trusted adult no matter what the other person says or does.

Summary

Child maltreatment is a serious threat to the health and well-being of children of all ages and all socioeconomic backgrounds. Recognizing and reporting child maltreatment are essential in preventing subsequent injury. Most fatalities resulting from child abuse occur in children who have already experienced some form of maltreatment before the severe or fatal injury occurs. Nurses play a key role in prevention through early identification of children and caregivers at risk and initiation of appropriate referrals. Nursing care for the maltreated child includes providing a safe environment for the child, appropriate treatment of injuries, and emotional support to the child and family. Reporting all suspected child maltreatment cases to the appropriate child protective agency and law enforcement is critical in preventing further maltreatment.

A thorough physical examination and a comprehensive medical history are essential in diagnosing child maltreatment and should be documented in great detail. The physical examination should include a complete head-to-toe assessment, paying special attention to any injuries noted. These injuries should be carefully and consistently documented, including location, size, color, distinguishing patterns, symmetry, and evidence of past injuries. Ideally, the child and caregiver should be interviewed by a healthcare professional trained in forensic interviewing. The child should be interviewed alone, and the caregivers should be interviewed separately. Careful documentation of both the medical history and physical examination can determine legal outcomes. All evidence that is gathered by healthcare professionals must be sealed and stored securely along with a written record of the chain of evidence.

The healthcare team must be knowledgeable about the variety of conditions that may be mistaken for child maltreatment, including cultural, physical, and medical conditions. The diagnosis of child maltreatment requires obtaining a thorough medical history, physical examination results, and ancillary diagnostic procedures to rule out medical conditions that may mimic abuse.

References

1. Administration for Children and Families, US Dept of Health and Human Services. (2008). *Child maltreatment 2007.* Retrieved from http://www.acf.hhs.gov/programs/cb/pubs/cm07/

2. Child Welfare Information Gateway. (2009). *Child abuse and neglect fatalities: Statistics and interventions.* Retrieved from http://www.childwelfare.gov/pubs/facesheets/fatality.cfm

3. Myers, J. E. B. (1998). *Legal issues in child abuse and neglect practice* (2nd ed.). Newbury Park, CA: Sage.

4. Kairys, S. W., Johnson, C. F., & Committee on Child Abuse and Neglect. (2002). The psychological maltreatment of children: Technical report. *Pediatrics, 109,* e68.

5. Kellogg, N., & Committee on Child Abuse and Neglect. (2005). The evaluation of sexual abuse in children. *Pediatrics, 116,* 506–512.

6. Hettler, J. (2002). Munchausen syndrome by proxy. *Pediatric Emergency Care, 18,* 371–374.

7. Ratliff, S. S., & Nguyen, H. (1989). *Southeast Asian healing practices, birthmarks, and amulets* [Poster]. Columbus, OH: Children's Hospital.

8. Giardino, A. P., & Giardino, E. R. (2002). *Recognition of child abuse for the mandated reporter* (3rd ed.). St. Louis, MO: G. W. Medical Publishing.

9. Hibbard, R.A., Desch, L.W., Committee on Child Abuse and Neglect, & Committee on Children With Disabilities. (2007). Assessment of maltreatment of children with disabilities. *Pediatrics, 119,* 1018–1025.

10. Pierce, M. C., Kaczor, K., Aldridge, S., O'Flynn, J., & Lorenz, D. J. (2010). Bruising characteristics discriminating physical child abuse from accidental trauma. *Pediatrics, 125,* 67–74.

11. Block, R. W., Krebs, N. F., Committee on Child Abuse and Neglect, & Committee on Nutrition. (2005). Failure to thrive as a manifestation of child neglect. *Pediatrics, 116,* 1234–1237.

12. Kellogg, N., & Committee on Child Abuse and Neglect. (2005). Oral and dental aspects of child abuse and neglect. *Pediatrics, 116,* 1565–1568.

13. Kellogg, N., & Committee on Child Abuse and Neglect. (2007). Evaluation of suspected child physical abuse. *Pediatrics, 119,* 1232–1241.

14. Christian, C. W., Block, R., & Committee on Child Abuse and Neglect. (2009). Abusive head trauma in infants and children. *Pediatrics, 123,* 1409–1411.

15. Hobbs, C. J., Hanks, H. G. I., & Wynne, J. M. (1999). *Child abuse and neglect: A clinician's handbook* (2nd ed.). London, England: Harcourt Brace & Co.

16. Reece, R. M., & Ludwig, S. (2001). *Child abuse: Medical diagnosis and management* (2nd ed.). Philadelphia, PA: Lippincott Williams & Wilkins.

17. Olshaker, J. S., Jackson, M. C., & Smock, W. S. (2001). *Forensic emergency medicine.* Philadelphia, PA: Lippincott Williams & Wilkins.

18. Centers for Disease Control and Prevention. (2006). *Sexually transmitted diseases treatment guidelines 2006.* Retrieved from http://www.cdc.gov/std/treatment/2006/sexual-assault.htm#children

19. Kaufman, M., & Committee on Adolescence. (2008). Care of the adolescent sexual assault victim. *Pediatrics, 122,* 462–470.

20. Weir, E. (2001). Drug-facilitated date rape. *Canadian Medical Association Journal, 165,* 80.

21. Schwartz, R. H., Milteer, R., & LeBeau, M. A. (2000). Drug-facilitated sexual assault ("date rape"). *Southern Medical Journal, 93,* 558–561.

22. Farst, K., Duncan, J., Moss, M., Ray, R., Kokoska, E., & James, L. (2007). Methamphetamine exposure presenting as caustic ingestions in children. *Annals of Emergency Medicine, 49,* 341–343.

23. Kolecki, P. (1998). Inadvertent methamphetamine poisoning in pediatric patients. *Pediatric Emergency Care, 14,* 385–387.

24. Hall, D. E., Eubanks, L., Meyyazhagan, S., Kenney, R. D., & Johnson, S. C. (2000). Evaluation of covert video surveillance in the diagnosis of Munchausen syndrome by proxy: Lessons from 41 cases. *Pediatrics, 105,* 1476–1479.

Chapter 21 | Crisis

Justin J. Milici, MSN, RN, CCRN, CEN, CFRN, TNS

Objectives

On completion of this chapter, the learner should be able to do the following:

• Summarize factors that may precipitate, exacerbate, and mitigate the severity of response to crisis in the pediatric patient.

• Assess families and family members for behavioral or physical indicators of crisis.

• Indicate prevention strategies for vicarious traumatization in healthcare team members.

• Discuss strategies to recognize and alleviate pediatric healthcare team stress in the workplace.

Introduction

The occurrence of injury and illness is always stressful for children and families and may, in fact, precipitate crisis in coping or functioning for the pediatric patient or family. Children may become injured or ill during a traumatic experience. Events that may provoke a psychological response include severe motor vehicle crashes, natural disasters (i.e., tornadoes and floods), man-made disasters (i.e., explosions and war), violence in the community, and child maltreatment. The experience of traumatic stress or trauma is distinct from the experience of stress and is often associated with long-term adverse consequences and neurobiological changes. Adults may not realize the extent to which children are distressed and may underestimate their problems.

Definitions

Stress is tension, strain, or pressure, such as feelings that occur after a family has waited for extended periods in the emergency department (ED) or when the ED staff is overwhelmed by conflicting demands and stimuli.[1] Crisis refers to an acute emotional upset arising from situational, developmental, or social sources, resulting in the temporary inability to cope using one's usual problem-solving devices. Examples include sudden illness, injury, or death.

Although it is well recognized that many situations in the ED can cause a crisis for the family, the involved staff may also experience a crisis.[1]

Crisis management is the entire process of working through the crisis to the end point of resolution. *Crisis intervention* is a short-term process that focuses on the resolution of the immediate problem through the use of personal, social, and environmental resources. The positive or negative resolution of the crisis often depends on crisis intervention.

Whether a stressful event precipitates a crisis depends on the following factors:

• Interpretation of the events

  ◦ The meaning that the family attaches to the event. Families may feel responsible for causing or not preventing the event.

• Coping abilities and previous experience

• Physical and behavioral attitudes and beliefs

• Social and personal resources

Several characteristics of an event may increase the level of stress experienced by a child's family or the staff member:

• Sudden onset of the event

• Unusual event

- Unanticipated event, especially one not previously experienced
- Lack of control over the event
- Other stressful events occurring in the family dynamic or in the emergency department

Emergency department staff members' ability to respond to a crisis and lend empathy and support depends on their own beliefs, experiences, and support systems.[1]

Focused Assessment

During interaction with family members, the emergency nurse should assess for and note family behavior, especially behavioral or physical signs of crisis. Specific signs and symptoms of crisis may include the following:

- Behavioral
  - Withdrawal or isolation
  - Demanding behavior
  - Talking fast, loudly, and profanely
  - Self-destructive behavior
  - Aggressive or assaultive behavior (toward family members or the healthcare team)
  - Anger
    - Anger is a coping mechanism that can be allowed as long as it does not cause or result in violent behavior that may cause injury to staff members or others.[1]
- Fight-or-flight response
  - Tachycardia
  - Sweaty palms
  - Dry mouth
  - Hyperventilation
  - Chest pain
  - Syncope
- Freeze-and-withdraw response
  - Shallow breathing
  - Pale/clammy skin
  - Fearfulness
  - Decreased responsiveness

Planning and Implementation

The approach the nurse takes with the family can positively influence the family's ability to cope with the crisis. Emergency department staff have the potential to provoke or escalate a potentially angry family member who is on the verge of losing control. In sudden unexpected situations, family members will often take cues from the demeanor and behavior of the ED staff. It is essential that families are provided with timely information concerning care being provided to their child/loved one, allowing them to participate in decisions/care of their child while receiving realistic hope and compassionate support. Approaches to meet the family's needs include the following:

- Create a supportive environment.
- Maintaining privacy (i.e., showing them to a private area where open discussion can take place).
- Assigning one staff member (emergency nurse, nursing supervisor, or chaplain) to communicate information about the child's condition.
- Explaining that the ED physician will talk with them as soon as he or she is able to leave the child's care to do so.
- Never delivering news concerning the patient alone.
- Allowing the family to ask questions and expect expressions of emotions, such as anger, guilt, and remorse, depending on the situation.

Communicate with the family. Talking with a family whose child is injured or critically ill is not an easy task, but family members will appreciate the contact of someone who is involved or knowledgeable about their child's care. Suggestions for talking with the family include the following:

- Introduce yourself: use "Mr." or Mrs." and the name of the child (ask if the child has a nickname that can be used). Do not refer to the caregiver as Mom or Dad.
- Maintain a calm and deliberate manner because this will significantly ease a family's fears.
- Provide clear and concise information but not more than the family seems be able to handle or process at the time.
- Meet the family's physical needs (bathroom, water, or tissues). Extras, such as a warm blanket, are often greatly appreciated.
- Provide accurate and realistic information without taking away hope.
- Inquire if the family has a desire to speak with a member of the clergy or the chaplain; most hospitals have a chaplain or spiritual counselor available for support.
- Provide brief and frequent updates on the child's condition.

Communicate with the child.

- Provide an environment that is safe, where the surroundings are predictable.

- Maintain a calm and deliberate manner because this will significantly ease a child's fears.

- Explain what you are doing using age-appropriate terms.

- Assume that the child can hear everything that is being said, even if he or she is intubated and sedated.

- Assign a staff member to talk to the child during the resuscitation, touching and holding his or her hand and letting him or her know what is being done.

  ◦ If calm family members are present, allow them to talk softly to the child to provide comfort.

Care of the Family Experiencing Grief From the Death of a Child

The sudden death of a child is among the most profoundly traumatic events a family can experience. Like other traumatic exposures, the ability to resolve grief is affected by what families experience during the recoil phase, which immediately follows the event. When a child has died or death is imminent, the family, including surviving siblings, benefits from the following:

- **Timely, accurate, and clear information.** Explain to the family the medical status of their child and what to expect, what they will see, hear, and smell when in the resuscitation room. Use concrete words such as "dead" and "dying," rather than "passed away" or "expired." Children should be provided with information in developmentally appropriate but accurate language.

- **The time and space to say good-bye.** Facilitate family presence in the resuscitation area while the child is alive if at all possible. Provide family members the opportunity to view, hold, and touch the child. Explain the nature of what they will see regarding the child's present condition. If there are jurisdictional requirements to leave in tubes and lines, review these with the family. Facilitate baptism or other religious rites if the caregivers request them. Families differ in how much time they need, and space outside the ED may need to be arranged. A family member as well as a staff member should be present with the sibling who is saying good-bye.

- **Validation and support during a time of overwhelming feelings.** Avoid statements minimizing or negating thoughts or feelings. For example, do not say things such as "It's all for the best" or "She is your little angel." Let your concern and caring show by saying "I'm sorry." Provide support and decision-making assistance with issues such as organ donation, autopsy, and disposition of the body. Help the family contact other family members and community resources. Mobilize hospital resources such as pastoral care and social work, if available.

- **Support after leaving the hospital.** Provide families with contact numbers for questions about the child's death. Provide written bereavement information including community resources for caregivers and surviving siblings. These should also be provided to family support persons because caregivers may understandably not be processing the information provided. Provide bereavement follow-up over the next weeks or months through phone calls or written communication if possible. Encourage families to include children in family rituals related to death and to avoid hiding their own grief with the mistaken belief that this will protect the siblings from pain.

- **Additional interventions in support of surviving siblings.** Reassure siblings that the adults are not mad at them but are sad and may be acting in a confusing manner because of the death. Reassure them that the death was not the result of anything they said, did, or thought. Support age-appropriate responses to death, which may include playing, talking openly about the deceased, and not crying. Let families know that this is to be expected and does not mean that the child is not sad.

Care of the Team

Healthcare providers caring for children witness critical incidents that harm children because of acts of violence or natural disasters. Caring for these children may place stress on providers who believe these incidents may have been preventable. Professionals respond to constant exposure to unbearable and unspeakable tragedies in identifiable ways, such as absenteeism, sleep disorders, health problems, and burnout. Similar to patients whom they treat, professionals benefit from simple environmental interventions to decrease the impact of exposure to traumatic stress in the workplace.

Situations such as the death of a child, overwhelming numbers of critically ill patients in the department, or an act of violence against staff and families are referred to as critical incidents. A *critical incident* is any situation experienced by healthcare team members that causes them to feel unusually strong emotional reactions that have the potential to interfere with their ability to function.[2] Examples include the following:

- Any event with significant emotional power to overwhelm usual coping mechanisms.

- Death of a child or a child injured by abuse or neglect.
- Patients who are relatives or friends of the healthcare team.
- Events that threaten the safety or life of the healthcare team members.
  - Events that attract excessive media attention.
  - Patients or visitors assaulting staff verbally or physically.
- Incidents with unusual circumstances and/or distressing sights, sounds, or smells.
  - Mass casualty situations.
  - Patients with extensively burnt flesh.

Emergency department staff members are exposed to critical incidents fairly routinely. Emergency departments should have written policies and procedures to support staff members coping with critical incidents. The consequences of untreated stress related to critical incidents can lead to physical, cognitive, emotional, and behavioral problems (Table 21-1).[2]

Repeated exposure to critical incidents can, over time, contribute to the phenomenon of *vicarious traumatization*. Vicarious traumatization is a transformation that occurs within the healthcare team member as a result of his or her empathetic engagement with the patient who is critically ill or injured.[3] Vicarious traumatization can lead to changes in cognitive and emotional functioning that affect both personal well-being and the quality of nursing care. It has been associated with burnout, substance misuse,

health problems related to stress, and poor sleep and family problems. Nurses may experience flashbacks of patient care episodes or vivid images of scenes described to them. More subtle signs include a gradual numbing of emotional responses and a pervasive cynical attitude toward others.

Critical Incident Stress Debriefing

Critical incident stress debriefing (CISD) is a structured intervention for professionals that is used in some settings. There is disagreement about whether the use of CISD is helpful for all individuals or whether it can make symptoms worse. The effectiveness of CISD has received scrutiny during the past decade and participation must be voluntary. Although debriefing does not necessarily prevent psychiatric disorders or mitigate the effects of traumatic stress, it may help defuse and resolve feelings of grief, without causing pathological reactions. Staff members may be given the opportunity to describe their part of the event, what they saw and heard, what was most difficult for them, and, most important, what happened that is of some comfort in reviewing the incident (e.g., good team work, better appreciation of the work of a particular staff member, or good care of the child's family). A debriefing can be a conversation among colleagues that begins with a simple question from a leader to all participants, such as "What stands out for you when you look back at [the incident]?"[1] Some other strategies to help staff cope with death or other critical incidents in the ED include the following:

- Protocols that describe the treatment of patients or families after death.
- Education on the grieving process.

Table 21-1 Signs and Symptoms of Stress Caused by Critical Incidents*

Physical	Cognitive	Emotional	Behavioral
Fatigue	Confusion	Anxiety	Withdrawal
Nausea	Intrusive images	Guilt	Emotional outbursts
Muscle tremors	Nightmares	Grief	Suspiciousness
Chest pain	Deficits in:	Denial	Alcohol consumption
Dyspnea	Decision making	Fear	Inability to rest
High blood pressure	Concentration	Uncertainty	Pacing
Tachycardia	Memory	Loss of emotional control	Nonspecific somatic complaints
Thirst	Problem solving	Depression	Change in sexual function
Headaches	Abstract thinking	Apprehension	Changes in activity and speech
Visual disturbances		Intense anger	Family problems
Dizziness		Irritability	
		Agitation	

*Data are taken from the Emergency Nurses Association.[2]

- Evaluation of one's own feelings concerning death and available support systems.

- Support from the hospital chaplain.

- Recovery time after a death, or an especially traumatic incident, even if only for a short time.

- Support of each other from ED staff, the ED nurse manager, or the ED nursing director.

- A sympathy card signed by the staff members who directly cared for the child, which was sent to family members.

- Encouragement of ED staff to take care of themselves physically, mentally, and spiritually.

- A focus on the positive: most children do get better and go home.

Posttraumatic Stress Disorder

For the past 20 years, posttraumatic stress disorder (PTSD) has been recognized as a major health problem following physical or emotional trauma.[4] However, recognizing that children experience posttraumatic stress reactions to stressful and traumatic events is a relatively recent finding.[5] Today, children are exposed to various types of traumatic events and violence. Natural disasters, such as tornadoes or earthquakes, have little potential for being personalized; therefore, they lie on one end of this spectrum. In contrast, victims of rape or torture usually face their assailants. Evidence suggests that the more personal the trauma, the more likely it is that long-term psychological problems are to arise from it.[6] After a traumatic event, children may initially exhibit agitated or confused behavior, as well as intense fear, helplessness, anger, sadness, horror, or denial. Children who experi-ence repeated trauma may develop a kind of emotional numbing to deaden or block the pain and trauma. This is called *dissociation*. Children with PTSD avoid situations or places that remind them of the trauma. They may also become less responsive emotionally, depressed, with-drawn, and more detached from their feelings. A child with PTSD may also exhibit the following symptoms:

- Worry about dying at an early age

- Loss of interest in activities

- Physical symptoms, such as headaches and stomachaches

- More sudden and extreme emotional reactions

- Problems falling or staying asleep

- Irritability or angry outbursts

- Problems concentrating

- Reverting to childhood behaviors (e.g., clingy or whiny behavior or thumb sucking)

- Increased alertness to the environment

- Behavior that reminds them of the trauma

The symptoms of PTSD may last from several months to many years; therefore, early intervention is essential. Support from parents, school, and peers is important. Emphasis needs to be placed on establishing a feeling of safety. Psychotherapy (individual, group, or family) that allows the child to speak, draw, play, or write about the event is helpful. Behavior modification techniques and cognitive therapy may help reduce fears and worries. Medication may also be useful in dealing with agitation, anxiety, or depression.

Summary

The psychosocial aspects of injury and illness include, but are not limited to, stress, crisis, and grief. Sustaining an injury or having a critical illness is a source of stress not only to the patient but also to family and significant others related to the patient. Caring for critically ill or injured children and their families in the ED can be a difficult challenge physically and emotionally. The treatment of families by nurses is crucial and may affect the family members' lasting memories of the trauma or death of their child. Although caring for the physiological needs of the ill or injured child is the primary focus of the emergency care team, attention to the trauma-related emotional needs of the child and family may mitigate long-term traumatic responses. The emergency care team may also experience vicarious traumatization; although the feelings of the staff are often addressed last, they should not be neglected. Staff members often provide the best support for each other. Giving staff members a break and a time to regroup and, most important, recognizing difficult situations and jobs well done promotes a healthy work environment.

References

1. Lenehan, G. P., & Turner, A. C. (2009). Crisis intervention and management. In D. O. Thomas & L. M. Bernardo (Eds.), *Core curriculum for pediatric emergency nursing* (2nd ed., pp. 361–372). Des Plaines, IL: Emergency Nurses Association.

2. Emergency Nurses Association. (2007). *Trauma nursing core course (TNCC) provider manual* (6th ed.). Des Plaines, IL: Author.

3. Emergency Nurses Association. (2004). *Emergency nursing pediatric course (ENPC) provider manual* (3rd ed.). Des Plaines, IL: Author.

4. Farrar, J. A. (2002). Psychosocial impact of trauma. In K. A. McQuillan, K. T. Von Rueden, R. L. Hartsock, M. B. Flynn, & E. Whalen (Eds.), *Trauma nursing: from resuscitation through rehabilitation* (3rd ed., pp. 366–392). Philadelphia, PA: Saunders Elsevier.

5. Lewandowski, L. A., & Frosch, E. (2003). Psychosocial aspects of pediatric trauma. In P. A. Maloney-Harmon & S. J. Czerwinski (Eds.), *Nursing care of the pediatric trauma patient* (pp. 340–358). St Louis, MO: Saunders Elsevier.

6. E-Medicine Health. *Post traumatic stress disorder (PTSD).* Retrieved from http://www.emedicinehealth.com/post-traumatic_stress_disorder_ptsd?page5_em.htm

Chapter 22 | Disaster

Lori A. Upton, MS, BSN, RN, CEM

Objectives

On completion of this chapter, the learner should be able to do the following:

- Describe the four phases of emergency management.
- Identify the anatomical, physiological, and developmental characteristics that affect vulnerability of the pediatric patient to effects of disasters.
- Discuss pediatric assessment parameters and treatment modalities associated with selected chemical, explosive, and biological exposure agents.
- Plan disaster-specific psychosocial interventions for the pediatric population.

Introduction

Emergency management is the discipline of assessing and lessening risk. It involves identifying risks, preparing for a disaster before it happens, responding to a disaster (e.g., emergency evacuation, quarantine, or mass casualty incident), and supporting and rebuilding society after a natural or human-made disaster has occurred.[1, 2]

The four phases of emergency management are a continuous cycle of improvement. These phases are known as mitigation, preparedness, response, and recovery.

Mitigation

Mitigation is the cornerstone of emergency management. It is the continuing effort to lessen the impact that disasters have on people and property. *Mitigation* is defined as "sustained actions that reduce or eliminate long-term risk to people and property from natural and manmade hazards and their effects."[1, 2]

Mitigation can take many forms. It can involve the following actions:

- Buying flood insurance to protect one's belongings
- Relocating or elevating structures out of the floodplain
- Securing shelves and hot water heaters to walls
- Developing, adopting, and enforcing building codes and standards
- Engineering roads and bridges to withstand earthquakes
- Using fire-retardant materials in new construction
- Providing immunizations

Preparedness

Unlike mitigation activities, which are aimed at preventing a disaster from occurring or decreasing the effects of a disaster, preparedness focuses on preparing equipment, personnel, and procedures for use when a disaster occurs.[1, 2]

Preparedness measures can take many forms, including the following:

- Constructing shelters
- Securing appropriate supplies and equipment
- Educating individuals
- Installing warning devices
- Creating backup services (e.g., generators, water, and heating, ventilation, and air conditioning)
- Rehearsing evacuation plans
- Conducting exercises and drills

Response

Response is defined as the actions taken to save lives and prevent further damage in a disaster or emergency situation. Response is putting preparedness plans into action.[1, 2]

Response activities may include the following:

- Damage assessment
- Search-and-rescue operations
- Fire fighting
- Sheltering victims
- Triaging, transporting, receiving, and treating victims at healthcare facilities
- Allocation of resources

Recovery

Recovery is defined as the actions taken to return the community to normal after a disaster. Short-term recovery involves returning vital life support systems to minimum operating standards, and long-term recovery such as electricity, water, shelter, and basic healthcare may take years and could involve total redevelopment of the affected area(s).[1, 2]

Recovery actions may include the following:

- Repairing damaged infrastructure
- Replacing damaged structures/property
- Rebuilding property damaged or lost
- Reopening societal venues, such as schools, churches, and healthcare facilities
- Psychological support for victims/families/responders
- Rehabilitation and long-term physical and psychological care of survivors

Risk Assessment

Rapid response to a naturally occurring agent, chemical release, or a bioterrorism-related outbreak requires prompt identification of its onset. Because of the rapid progression to illness and potential for dissemination of some of these agents, it may not be practical to await diagnostic laboratory confirmation. Instead, it may be necessary to initiate a response based on the recognition of high-risk syndromes.

Epidemiological principles must be used to assess whether a patient's presentation is typical of an endemic disease or is an unusual event that should raise concern. Features that should alert healthcare providers to the possibility of an incident or outbreak include:

- A rapidly increasing disease incidence (e.g., within hours or days) in a normally healthy population.
- An epidemic curve that rises and falls during a short period of time.
- An unusual increase in the number of people seeking care with same or similar symptoms, especially with fever, respiratory, or gastrointestinal complaints.
- An endemic disease rapidly emerging at an uncharacteristic time or in an unusual pattern.
- Lower incidence of symptoms among people who had been indoors, especially in areas with filtered air or closed ventilation systems, compared with people who had been outdoors.
- Clusters of patients arriving from a single locale.
- Large numbers of cases rapidly deteriorating to fatality.
- Any patient presenting with a disease that is relatively uncommon and has bioterrorism potential (e.g., pulmonary anthrax, smallpox, or plague).

According to the US Department of Health and Human Services, 25% of the US population is children, with more than 20 million of those younger than six years.[3] It is essential that the unique needs of children be included in emergency planning and response. Unfortunately, most disaster plans do not account for the needs of the pediatric patient nor do they address the unique needs of the family with a child with special healthcare needs.[4] Many of these medically fragile children are technologically dependent, relying on electricity for feeding pumps, suction machines, portable ventilators, and intravenous fluid pumps.

Prior emergency preparedness methods mirrored themselves with military responses. Most of these plans were adult focused and did not address children as possible victims. According to the National Advisory Committee on Children and Terrorism, "On the morning of September 11, 2001, approximately 1.2 million children were enrolled in the New York City public schools. In the immediate vicinity of Ground Zero, more than 6,000 children were in 7 schools (elementary, middle, and high), 28 licensed day-care facilities, 58 family child care or group homes, and 14 child care sites, including one childcare center in the Twin Towers."[4] As evidenced by the attack on the Russian school in Beslan, children may become the focus and be identified as the intentional targets. The Beslan school attack resulted in the taking of 1,200 hostages and the death of nearly 340 people. More than half the deaths from this incident were children.[5, 6] The 2005 Gulf Coast hurricane disaster itself affected more than one million children in four states in the United States. More than 4,500 children were reported to the National Center for Missing and Exploited Children after the incident, and one month later only half had been located.[7]

When discussing terrorist attacks, vulnerable child-related arenas include schools and day-care facilities, churches and other religious institutions, and child-focused events, such as sporting events, camps, and parks. Natural disasters include all of those previously described, plus the place children feel safest (i.e., their homes).

A historical look at disaster incidents in recent years involving children includes the following:[8–12]

- 1984: Bhopal, India, chemical gas, 20,000-plus dead and affecting a population of 520,000 (200,000 were < 15 years)
- 1993: London, England, bus incident, 56 children injured and two dead
- 1995: Oklahoma City Bombing, 19 children dead
- 1997-2006: school shootings, eight separate incidents with more than five children dead/wounded at each incident
- 2001: World Trade Center, 1.2 million children in the vicinity
- 2004: Chechen Terrorist School Attack in Beslan, 156 dead
- 2005: Hurricane Katrina, over 5,000 children were separated from their parents and caregivers. It took over five months, in some cases, to reunite family groups
- 2008: Sichuan Province, China, earthquake, poorly constructed school buildings resulted in the death of many children. Many families lost their only child, resulting in a psychosocial disaster
- 2009: H1N1 influenza outbreak, 262 confirmed pediatric deaths

Every healthcare facility has the legal and moral obligation to provide appropriate emergency planning to ensure continued care of its patients. There is not enough surge capacity in existing pediatric hospitals in communities to accommodate the number of children potentially needing hospital care during a disaster. A relatively large proportion of the adult population uses hospital facilities compared with the relatively small percentage of the total pediatric population (< 5%) that uses inpatient care. As a result, pediatric inpatient capacity and resources are more limited relative to the baseline population of children.[13]

Anatomy and Physiology/ Developmental Review

The unique characteristics of pediatric patients make them more vulnerable to the effects of a chemical or biological agent release or the aftermath of a natural disaster.

- Infants, toddlers, and young children may not have the motor skills to escape from the area of a chemical, biological, or other terrorist incident.
- Pediatric patients lack cognitive decision-making skills that would help them to figure out how to flee danger or to follow directions from others.
- Pediatric patients have smaller circulating blood volumes than adults, so if treatment is not immediate, relatively small amounts of blood/fluid loss can lead to irreversible shock or death.
- Pediatric patients are more sensitive to changes in body temperature, have a faster metabolism, and have less blood and fluid reserves; a child's condition can shift from stable to life threatening rapidly.[13–16]

Respiratory System

Pediatric patients have an increased respiratory rate compared with adults, which may make them more vulnerable to large quantities of inhaled chemicals or biological agents.[13] In addition, their shorter stature lowers their *breathing zone,* making them more susceptible to inhalation injuries from chemicals, fire, or biological agents. Their increased respiratory rate also lends to an increase in insensible fluid loss, further placing them at risk for dehydration.[17] The unique characteristics of the airway in the pediatric patient make it more susceptible to compromise or further worsening of the patient status. The trachea is more anterior, with a smaller diameter that can easily become blocked with mucus, edema, or secretions. The relatively large tongue (in relation to the jaw) increases the chances for obstruction if the child is unconscious or unable to effectively keep the tongue anterior.

Cardiac System

Pediatric patients have less fluid reserve and smaller circulating blood and fluid volumes, which makes them more prone to dehydration.[13, 17] The causes of dehydration may include the following: injury related to heat exposure, burns, vomiting, and/or diarrhea, leaving these children more susceptible to chemical exposure at smaller amounts than adults in chemical disasters. Children who experience burns as a result of a disaster incident have a greater likelihood of poor outcomes because of decreased fluid reserves. The smaller circulating blood volume makes the traumatically injured child more susceptible to developing irreversible hemodynamic shock and subsequent death.[15]

Integumentary System

The skin of children is thinner, and they possess a larger surface to mass ratio than adults, which could lead to increased absorption of a chemical agent.[15, 17] They can also have a greater depth of a burn in less time.

Skeletal System

Significant underlying injury to tissues and organs may be present in the absence of bony deformity.

Endocrine System

An increased metabolism compared with adults may cause children to metabolize drugs differently, requiring different drugs and dosages when initiating antidotes.[13, 15, 17] Their limited glycogen stores put them at greater risk during stress.

Planning and Implementation

The essential elements of pediatric disaster planning should include the following:

1. Surge capacity

   Preparedness plans should include assessment and planning for a surge in the pediatric population after an event. A report by the National Advisory Committee on Children and Terrorism revealed that only approximately 20% of hospitals have access to pediatric emergency physicians and most emergency practitioners have little pediatric experience or training. All hospitals must prepare themselves to provide care for the pediatric population in the event of a disaster or terror incident, even if that facility does not normally provide care to children. Each facility may find itself performing as a primary treatment site if it is the closest facility to the incident or if the pediatric specialty hospitals are overwhelmed.[4]

   It is essential for emergency planners to identify their internal capabilities in respect to pediatric patients and develop surge plans for increases in pediatric volume; mutual aid agreements to share staff and/or resources; and memoranda of understanding to quickly transfer pediatric patients to facilities with the capability and capacity to provide the necessary level of care.

   In planning for pediatric surge capacity, consider the following:

   - Have you identified cribs/beds and space availability beyond the average daily census?

   - Is there rapid access to additional pediatric-specific supplies and equipment?

   - Are these supplies stored in a cache or stockpile, or is there a memorandum of understanding with vendors or other healthcare facilities?

   - Plans should also include a *safe area* designated for children arriving to the hospital who do not need treatment or are unescorted. Ensure that these plans include available and appropriate staff for the area.

2. Pediatric supplies and equipment

   Plans should include appropriately sized pediatric equipment readily available and personnel trained in the use of it. One adjunct to assist in meeting this recommendation is the use of the Broselow Resuscitation Tape. The Broselow Resuscitation Tape has been commercially available and in use for more than 10 years and is relatively easy to use. The tape assigns children a *color zone* based on a single length or weight measurement. This enables the practitioner to choose appropriate precalculated medication dosages and size-appropriate equipment to facilitate care during an emergency. Weight-based medication dosages for the more commonly used medications during resuscitation are included on the measuring tape. The Broselow System has recently developed a chemical resuscitation tape for use in chemical antidote treatment of the pediatric population. These adjuncts can assist the practitioner not familiar with caring for the pediatric population, a handy guide to proper equipment needs, sizes, and appropriate weight-based medication calculations.

3. Weight-based medications

   Ensure antibiotics and antidotes are readily available and in appropriate weight-based doses. Current strategic national stockpiles and state-based stockpiles are appropriate for use in adults but have limited pediatric content. Pediatric dosages are determined most often by milligram per kilogram. Again, practitioners not familiar with calculating pediatric doses outside of an emergency situation will find this stressful and more prone to calculation errors.

4. Nutritional support

   Formula, glucose water, and electrolyte solutions will be essential in caring for the younger pediatric population. Infants have little glucose reserve to draw from. With the additional stress of a disaster situation, these small reserves will quickly be used up and the child will become hypoglycemic. Fluid replacement is required to prevent the onset of dehydration, which, stated earlier, could occur more quickly in the pediatric population because of fewer fluid reserves.

5. Maintaining the family unit

Caregivers and children alike will not be willing to be separated. Pediatric facilities must be prepared to provide care for the adult population, just as adult facilities must be ready to care for the pediatric patient.[17] Separation of the child from the parent may occur either before or during the event; therefore, precise tracking mechanisms must be in place. Developmentally delayed or preschool-aged children may not be able to provide any information other than their name to rescue or hospital workers. A large influx of pediatric patients without parents presenting to a facility may overwhelm available staff. Community volunteers may need to be enlisted to assist in the support and care of the children until they can be reunited with their parents. Connect with and utilize your community's reunification center planning agents. Consider establishing a reunification center in your facility to ensure that caregivers and their children are reunited.

6. Mental health and psychological support

Plan for and elicit assistance with the psychological effects of disaster and/or terrorism. Many emergency preparedness plans for a city or region include the use of schools and churches as temporary treatment centers, shelters, and morgues. Consider the after effects on children when designating these safe havens as part of the disaster plans. Planning should include age-appropriate counseling, the use of communication adjuncts (e.g., art and/or play therapy), and early return to normalcy for children and their families.

Responding to a mass pediatric disaster is also overwhelming for the healthcare providers. Critical incident stress debriefing teams or other trained psychological support for the responders and healthcare providers is essential to maintain productivity and decrease the incidence or effects of posttraumatic stress disorder (PTSD) syndrome.

Response

Triage

The difference in caring for pediatric patients in a disaster situation begins at triage. Most emergency responders and emergency department personnel are familiar with the process of triage. Conventional triage categorizes the presenting patient on an acuity-based system, with the most severely injured or ill patients being seen first. Those with less urgent complaints or symptoms are seen and treated after those deemed emergent. This process works well in a traditional nondisaster situation. However, in a disaster situation, with multitudes of patients, conventional triage will quickly diminish the available resources by using them first on the patients who are in the worst shape or who are not expected to survive.

The most widely used form of disaster triage is START triage. START triage stands for Simple Triage and Rapid Treatment. Developed in the early 1980s in California by Hoag Hospital and the Newport Beach Fire and Marine, it allows the provider to triage many victims and has the benefit of being easy to remember. Using the START method makes moving through a mass casualty scene or triaging many patients at a healthcare facility quick and reliable. Unfortunately, START triage does not account for the unique physiological responses of the pediatric patient.

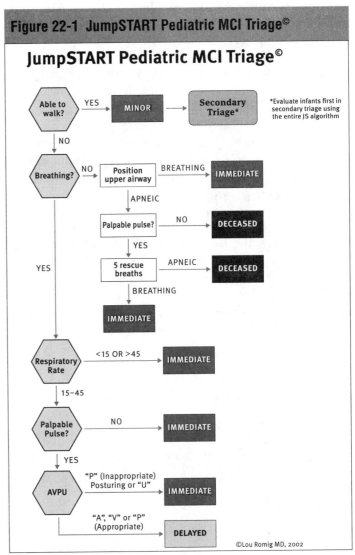

Figure 22-1 JumpSTART Pediatric MCI Triage©

Courtesy of Lou Romig, MD

JumpSTART triage was developed by Dr. Lou Romig in 1995 and modified in 2001 (**Figure 22-1**). Dr. Romig, a board-certified pediatric emergency physician at Miami Children's Hospital in Miami, Florida, recognized that no published or commonly used mass casualty triage system adequately addressed the unique anatomy and physiology of children. JumpSTART parallels the START system but uses decision points appropriate to the wide variations of normal physiology within the pediatric age group.[18]

JumpSTART triage uses the principles of rapid triage based on ambulation, respiration, pulse, and mental status, with trials of ventilatory support for the pediatric patient. JumpSTART triage is indicated for children aged one to eight years because it considers the physiological causes of apnea and arrest in children as opposed to adults.

In a mass casualty incident, unless there is clear airway obstruction or compression, traumatic respiratory failure in adults usually follows circulatory failure or catastrophic head injury. An apneic adult usually has already had enough internal injury to make his or her condition relatively unsalvageable.

In children, the opposite is more often true; circulatory failure usually follows respiratory failure, and apnea may occur relatively rapidly, rather than after a prolonged period of hypoxia. There may be a brief period in which the child is apneic but not yet pulseless because the heart has not experienced prolonged hypoxia. It is in this period that airway clearance and a brief trial of ventilation may stimulate spontaneous breathing.

The JumpSTART triage process permits a limited number of rescuers to rapidly triage many pediatric patients younger than eight years, without specialized training. Patients are systematically transferred to treatment areas where more detailed assessment and treatment are conducted.[18] Patients are rapidly assessed using four criteria and then assigned one of the following color categories of acuity:

- *Black* (dead or unsalvageable)
- *Red* (immediate care)
- *Yellow* (delayed care)
- *Green* (minor or ambulatory)

The components of the assessment include the following:

- The ability to ambulate and these three factors or RPMs:
  - Respirations-R
  - Perfusion-P
  - Mental status-M

Ambulatory

The rescue worker starts at the first victim/patient he or she encounters. If the patient is able to ambulate on his or her own, he or she is designated minor or *green* and directed to a secondary triage site for further assessment. Infants younger than 12 months are directed to the secondary triage site for evaluation using the JumpSTART algorithm.

Children who are ambulatory, possess acceptable respiratory rates, and have a palpable pulse, but are inappropriate in their response are triaged *red*/immediate.

Nonambulatory with Spontaneous Respirations

- If the child has spontaneous respirations of less than 15 or more than 45 per minute (or irregular), he or she is triaged as *red*/immediate.
- If the child has a respiratory rate between 15 and 45 breaths per minute, perfusion is checked.
  - If the peripheral pulse is absent, triage the child as *red*/immediate.
  - If the peripheral pulse is present, mental status is assessed using the AVPU method (Alert, Verbal, Pain, and Unresponsive [used to assess the level of consciousness]).
    - If the child is unresponsive, unable to follow simple commands, or has an inappropriate response to pain, he or she is triaged *red*/immediate.
    - If the child is responsive, or can follow simple commands, he or she is triaged as *yellow*/delayed.

Nonambulatory with NO Spontaneous Respirations

- If there are no spontaneous respirations, the airway is repositioned and status is checked again.
  - If the child resumes spontaneous respirations after repositioning of his or her airway, he or she is tagged *red*/immediate and transported for definitive care.
  - If spontaneous respiration does not occur after repositioning, the peripheral pulse is assessed.
    - If a peripheral pulse is absent, he or she is tagged *black*/deceased.
    - If a peripheral pulse is present, the rescuer will deliver five rescue breaths (using a barrier method).
      » If the child resumes spontaneous respirations, after the rescue breathing, he or she is triaged as *red*.
      » Failure to respond to the rescue breathing is a triage designation of *black*/deceased.

The benefit of JumpSTART triage is that it provides a rapid triage system specifically designed for children while accounting for their unique anatomy and physiology. The system has been modified from a widely accepted system for adults, thereby making it easier to incorporate into practice. The use of objective triage criteria for children will help to eliminate the role of emotions in the triage process, provide emotional support for triage personnel, and help "ensure the best for the most with the least."[18]

Decontamination

When planning and deploying decontamination units, ensure that they fulfill the needs of the adult and pediatric populations. Special pediatric considerations to address during the planning phase of decontamination units should include the needs of the following groups:

- Infants/nonambulatory children: Additional staff will be required to process this group through the decontamination lines.

- Preschool-aged children: Children in this age group may have difficulty following directions. Again, additional staff will be necessary to assist these children in the process. This age group understands that something bad has happened, and they may fear the rescue workers in their decontamination gear.

- School-aged children: Although this age group can follow directions, they will be reluctant to remove their clothing in the presence of strangers. They have an understanding that something bad has happened and may even be able to describe in detail their recollection of the events. They understand death and may fear they are dying as well.

- Pediatric patients with special needs and those who are developmentally delayed present unique challenges. With advances in pediatric and neonatal medicine, more and more technologically dependent children are in the mainstream of society and, therefore, just as at risk. Planning and practicing how to safely decontaminate a ventilator-dependent child in a wheelchair is just as important as practicing how to decontaminate a nonambulatory adult.[19]

Additional areas to address during planning for decontamination include the following:

- Water temperature and pressure: Water temperature should be maintained at approximately 110°F (43.6°C), and pressure does not need to be any stronger than the pressure of a home shower. Air temperature should also be warm.

- Facilitation of the process, as described previously, will require additional staff support.

- Children and infants have a disproportionate ratio of body surface area to body surface mass and less subcutaneous tissue, thereby making them more susceptible to the effects of hypothermia. It is essential that a warm air and water temperature be maintained, and children are dried and wrapped in warm blankets or towels immediately following the decontamination process. Adjunct engineering devices such as radiant heat sources or lamps may be considered.

When setting up zones of decontamination, the principle most commonly used incorporates three zones—hot, warm, and cold. The hot zone is at the site of the disaster. Patients are quickly triaged in the hot zone to determine the priorities for decontamination. Full personal protective equipment for any healthcare provider is indicated in the hot zone. The warm zone is the site of decontamination. It can be set apart from the disaster site or just outside the emergency department. Proximity to the resuscitation area of the emergency department minimizes heat loss after removal of clothing and shower decontamination. The cold zone is within the emergency department after complete decontamination. The triage process is repeated to reassess priorities of care.[19]

The D-I-S-A-S-T-E-R Paradigm

The Emergency Nurses Association recognizes the importance of a commonality in management of the disaster scene and supports the utilization of the D-I-S-A-S-T-E-R paradigm (**Table 22-1**). The D-I-S-A-S-T-E-R paradigm organizes the responders' preparation, response and recovery to disaster management. It is adaptable to natural or man-made disasters and facilitates ongoing assessment of an incident.[20]

Table 22-1 The D-I-S-A-S-T-E-R Paradigm

D	Detect
I	Incident Command
S	Scene Safety and Security
A	Assess Hazards
S	Support
T	Triage and Treatment
E	Evacuation
R	Recovery

Selected Emergencies

Chemical

Chemical terrorism is the deliberate release of toxic chemicals to inflict mass casualties on a population. Chemical terrorism often refers to the release of military-grade chemicals on a population; however, chemical terrorism may also take the form of the intentional explosion of a chemical factory or transport vehicle. Although the heightened awareness of the possibility of a chemical attack has increased since the September 11, 2001 terror attack in the United States, there have been several examples of intentional chemical releases.

Brief history:[21–24]

- 1962–1971: U.S. military released agent orange during the Vietnam war
- 1987: sulfur mustard release on a civilian village by Iraqi military
- 1988: release of nerve agents in civilian villages in Iran by Iraqi military
- 1995: release of sarin gas in the Tokyo, Japan, subway
- 1995: chlorine bomb scare at Disneyland
- 2004: identified ricin in US Senate office buildings

Chemical weapons are categorized based on the predominant symptoms they cause. The Centers for Disease Control and Prevention (CDC) has identified certain agents as having a higher potential of use during an intentional release. These include the following agents:

- Nerve Agents: the most toxic and rapidly acting of the known chemical warfare agents. They are similar in composition to organophosphates found in certain kinds of pesticides. However, nerve agents are much more potent than organophosphate pesticides.

  ◦ VX: an oily, odorless, and tasteless liquid that is amber and slow to evaporate. Originally developed in the United Kingdom in the 1950s, VX is the most potent of the nerve agents.[22,25]

  ◦ Tabun: a clear, colorless, and tasteless liquid with a faint fruity odor. Originally developed in Germany as a pesticide, Tabun can become a vapor if heated. Tabun is also known as GA.[22,25]

  ◦ Sarin: a clear, colorless, and tasteless liquid that has no odor in its pure form. Originally developed in Germany as a pesticide, sarin can evaporate into a vapor (gas) and spread into the environment. Sarin is also known as GB.[22,25]

  ◦ Soman: a clear, colorless, and tasteless liquid with a slight camphor or rotting fruit odor. Originally developed in Germany as a pesticide, it can become a vapor if heated. Soman is also known as GD.[22,25]

- Blister Agents: the most commonly used chemical warfare agents during World War I. The most likely routes of exposure are inhalation and dermal and ocular contact. Because of the high reactivity of these chemicals, blistering agents bind with proteins and other cellular components, including DNA, to cause changes in the cellular structures immediately after exposure.[26]

  ◦ Mustard: can be found as a vapor, an oily liquid, or a solid. It usually has the smell of garlic, onions, or mustard. Occasionally, mustard will have no smell. Until recently, sulfur mustard was used in the treatment of psoriasis. Currently, it has no medical use.[22,25]

  ◦ Lewisite: an oily colorless liquid in its pure form, it can appear amber to black in its impure form. Lewisite has an odor like geraniums. Lewisite contains the poison arsenic and has been used only as a chemical warfare agent. It has no medical or other practical use.[22,25]

- Blood Agents

  ◦ Hydrogen cyanide: developed in 1782 by a Swedish chemist, hydrogen cyanide is a colorless gas with what has been described as a bitter almond smell. Cyanide prevents cell oxygenation at all organ levels. Historically used by the Germans in Nazi concentration camps during World War II, US prison death chambers, and reportedly during the Iran-Iraq War, hydrogen cyanide is used commercially for fumigation and electroplating.[22]

  ◦ Cyanogen chloride: developed in 1802 by a French chemist, cyanogen chloride is a colorless vapor at normal temperatures and a clear liquid at low temperatures. It has a pungent pepper-like odor similar to tear gas. The effects of chemical asphyxia are similar to those seen with hydrogen cyanide, but exposure to cyanogen chloride also includes symptoms of lacrimation, bronchorrhea, and rhinorrhea. Originally used by the French during World War I, cyanogen chloride is still used commercially in the development of herbicides, in ore refinement, and as a metal cleaner.[22]

- Pulmonary Agents

  ◦ Phosgene: developed by a British physician in 1812, phosgene gas may appear colorless or as a white to pale yellow cloud. Phosgene gas and liquid are irritants that can damage the skin, eyes, nose, throat, and lungs. Phosgene gas is heavier than air and, therefore, larger concentrations of the toxic substance will be found closer to ground level. It has a pleasant odor of newly mown hay or green corn. It was used extensively during World War I as a chemical weapon and remains an industrial chemical used in the manufacturing of plastics and pesticides.[22,25]

○ Chlorine: a natural element that was first liquefied in 1822 by an English chemist. When liquid chlorine is released, it quickly turns into a gas that stays close to the ground and spreads rapidly. Chlorine gas is yellow-green and is easily recognized by its "bleach-like" irritating odor. It was used during World War I as a chemical warfare weapon and remains one of the most commonly manufactured chemicals in the United States.[22,25]

Presentation and Treatment Modalities

The following treatment modalities are recognized as recommendations only, and practitioners are encouraged to consult with experts in pharmacy and emergency medicine in their area. Unless otherwise stated, treatment always includes assessment and support of airway, breathing, and circulation.

Nerve Agents

The symptoms of nerve agent exposure include salivation, lacrimation, urination, defecation, and gastric emptying. The onset of symptoms occurs within seconds of exposure, and symptoms become progressively worse relative to the extent of exposure. Decontamination requirements include removal of clothing and copious amounts of soap and water.

Recommended antidotes for children:

- Atropine: 0.05 to 0.1 mg/kg intravenously (IV) or intramuscularly (IM) (minimum, 0.1 mg; maximum, 5 mg), may repeat every two to five minutes, as needed, for marked secretions or bronchospasms.

- Pralidoxime (Protopam): 25 to 50 mg/kg IM or IV (maximum, 1 g IV or 2 g IM), may repeat in 30 to 60 minutes, as needed, then again every one hour for one or two more doses, as needed, for persistent weakness.

- Diazepam (Valium): 0.3 mg/kg (maximum, 10 mg) IV, as needed, for severe exposure or persistent seizure activity. Substitutes may include lorazepam (Ativan), 0.1 mg/kg IV or IM (maximum, 4 mg); or midazolam (Versed), 0.2 mg/kg (maximum, 10 mg) intramuscularly.[17,22]

Mark I kits with pediatric doses are not available in the United States. However, pediatric autoinjectors of atropine (0.25, 0.5, and 1 mg) have recently been approved by the US Food and Drug Administration. The Pediatric Expert Advisory Panel recommends "the Mark I kit to be used in children 3 years of age and older. The Mark I represents

acceptable dosage ranges for the first 60 minutes of treatment. Benefits of use in children under the age of 3 with a true nerve agent exposure should outweigh the risks associated."[17] A pediatric AtroPen, under consideration for the treatment of children exposed to nerve agents, is not indicated for children who weigh less than 15 kg nor is it equivalent to the Mark I because it does not contain pralidoxime.[17]

Blister Agents

Symptoms of blistering agents include skin reddening, blistering, coughing, eye irritation, and dyspnea. The onset of symptoms with mustard may not be evident for hours after exposure. The onset of symptoms after exposure to Lewisite will be immediate. Decontamination requirements include removal of clothing/blistering agent and copious amounts of soap and water.

- Recommendations for mustard exposure in the pediatric patient are symptomatic and include maintaining airway and adequate respiratory support, fluid replacement, and pain control.

- Treatment for Lewisite exposure is symptom focused and may include the use of bronchodilators and steroids for pulmonary involvement. British Anti-Lewisite is recommended as a possibility in children only in severe systemic cases and should be used only after weighing the risks and benefits. The normal recommended dosage for British Anti-Lewisite is 3 mg/kg IM every four to six hours.[22]

Blood Agents

Cyanide binds with hemoglobin in the blood, thereby blocking cellular oxygenation. Victims of exposure to blood agents, such as hydrogen cyanide and cyanogen chloride, may display signs and symptoms of anxiety, hyperventilation, respiratory distress, lactic acidosis, and increased venous oxygen. The onset of symptoms usually occurs within seconds, and there is no need for decontamination.

Treatment in children includes the following:

- An amyl nitrite ampoule, 0.3 mL, crushed and inhaled through a mask may be used initially until intravenous access is established.

- Once an intravenous line is established, a modified adult cyanide kit should be used.

  ○ 3% Sodium nitrite, 0.33 mL/kg, followed by:

  ○ 25% Sodium thiosulfate, 1.65 mL/kg (maximum, 50 mL)

  ○ Sodium bicarbonate, as needed, to correct acidosis[22]

Pulmonary Agents

Persons exposed to pulmonary agents, such as phosgene or chlorine, may display symptoms of eye and airway irritation, dyspnea, chest tightness, and delayed pulmonary edema and acute respiratory distress syndrome (ARDS). The onset of symptoms occurs within seconds to hours. There is no need for decontamination related to vapor exposure. Gross liquid exposure may necessitate decontamination with copious amounts of soap and water. There are no pharmacological antidotes for exposure to pulmonary agents; treatment is symptomatic.[22]

Treatment modalities are the same for adults and children:

- Terminate exposure to the substance
- Oxygen administration and other supportive therapy, as indicated
- Provide symptomatic care, including:
  ○ ABCs of resuscitation
  ○ Rest and observation

Biological

Biological terrorism is the deliberate use of any biological agent against people, animals, or agriculture to cause disease, death, destruction, or panic for political or social gains. Biological warfare has been recorded as far back as the twelfth century, when Emperor Barbarossa attempted to poison his enemies in Italy by throwing deceased human remains into water wells.[22,23]

Brief History:[22–24,27]

- 1346: Mongols catapult deceased plague victims over the city walls of Crimea
- 1763: British trade smallpox-laden blankets with Native Americans
- 1915: Germans attempt to infect Allied forces with glanders
- 1937: Japanese use various microorganisms, including anthrax, on prisoners of war
- 1940: Japanese planes drop plague-infested fleas in China and Manchuria
- 1942: British military drop bombs loaded with anthrax over Scottish Island of Gruinard
- 1979: Russia unintentionally releases airborne anthrax spores
- 1984: Rajneeshee cult contaminates salad bars in Oregon with salmonella
- 2001: Letters containing anthrax spores are mailed to US news agencies, governor's offices, and the US Capitol building.

The CDC has identified the most likely biological agents that could be used in an intentional attack on a population as follows: anthrax, botulism, plague, and smallpox.

Anthrax

Anthrax is an acute infectious disease caused by the spore-forming bacterium *Bacillus anthracis*. Anthrax is indigenous to the agricultural regions of South and Central America, Southern and Eastern Europe, Asia, Africa, the Caribbean, and the Middle East, where it occurs in animals. Anthrax spores can live in the soil for many years, and people can become infected by handling infected animals and infected animal products or ingesting undercooked infected meat. Because of strict control of livestock, it is rare to find anthrax in the United States.[22,25]

An anthrax infection can occur in three forms: cutaneous, inhalation, and gastrointestinal.

Symptoms

- Cutaneous: Usually caused by introduction of the anthrax bacterium into open wounds or abrasions. The skin infection begins as a raised itchy bump that resembles an insect bite. Within one to two days, the lesion develops into a vesicle and then into a painless ulcer, with a characteristic black necrotic area in the center. Lymph glands in the adjacent area may also swell. Approximately 20% of untreated cases of cutaneous anthrax will result in death.[22,25,26,28]
- Inhalation: caused by inhaling the anthrax bacterium, the initial symptoms of inhalation anthrax may resemble a common cold and include sore throat, mild fever, muscle aches, and malaise. After several days, the symptoms may progress to severe breathing problems, shock, and respiratory failure. Inhalation anthrax is usually fatal.[22,25,26,28]
- Gastrointestinal: The intestinal disease form of anthrax may follow the consumption of contaminated meat and is characterized by an acute inflammation of the intestinal tract. Initial symptoms include nausea, loss of appetite, vomiting, and fever; these symptoms are followed by abdominal pain, vomiting of blood, and severe diarrhea. Intestinal anthrax results in death in 25% to 60% of cases.[22,25,26,28]

Recommendations for the prophylactic treatment of anthrax include the following:

- First choice: Ciprofloxacin, 10 to 15 mg/kg twice a day
- Second choice: Doxycycline, 2.2 mg/kg twice a day

Pediatric use of fluoroquinolones and tetracycline is associated with adverse effects that must be weighed against the risk of developing a lethal disease. If anthrax exposure is confirmed, the organism must be tested for penicillin susceptibility. If susceptible, exposed children may be treated with oral amoxicillin, 40 mg/kg body mass per day, divided every eight hours (not to exceed 500 mg three times a day).

Prophylaxis should continue until anthrax exposure has been excluded. If exposure is confirmed, prophylaxis should continue for eight weeks. In addition to prophylaxis, postexposure immunization with an inactivated cell-free anthrax vaccine is also indicated after anthrax exposure. If available, postexposure vaccination consists of three doses of vaccine at zero, two, and four weeks after exposure. With vaccination, postexposure antimicrobial prophylaxis can be reduced to four weeks.[25,28]

Botulism

Botulism is a serious paralytic disease caused by a nerve toxin that is produced by the bacterium *Clostridium botulinum*. There are three main kinds of botulism: (1) Food-borne botulism is caused by eating foods that contain the botulism toxin. (2) Wound botulism is caused from a wound infected with *C. botulinum*. (3) Infant botulism is caused by consuming the spores of the botulinum bacteria, which then grow in the intestines and release toxin. According to the CDC, approximately 145 cases of botulism are reported annually, with 15% being food borne; 20%, wound; and 65%, infant. Food-borne botulism is usually caused by eating contaminated home-canned foods. Wound botulism is increasing, especially in California, because of the increased use of contaminated black tar heroin. Infant botulism is most often associated with the ingestion of honey in children younger than 12 months. [28–30]

Symptoms

- Food-borne botulism: Botulism causes a classic symmetrical pattern in nerve pathways affected. Frequently, early signs may include diplopia, bilateral drooping eyelids, difficulty swallowing/speaking, altered voice, and dry mouth. As the disease progresses, symmetrical descending flaccid paralysis forms in a central to distal pattern. Associated symptoms may include abdominal pain, nausea, vomiting, and diarrhea. If left untreated, the disease may progress to respiratory failure and death as the result of respiratory muscle paralysis. Botulism is not contagious and is not transmitted from human to human.[25]

- Wound botulism: Neurological symptoms are identical to food-borne botulism, with the exception of the associated gastrointestinal symptoms. Wounds usually contain necrotic dead areas and are usually deep. They may not appear to be obviously infected.[25]

- Infant botulism: The action of disease on the nervous system is identical to food-borne botulism, causing symmetrical nerve paralysis in a central to peripheral pattern. These early paralysis symptoms may be displayed by poor feeding, diminished sucking or crying ability, neck and limb weakness, constipation, and respiratory distress/failure.[29]

There are no pharmaceutical treatments for botulism. Supportive treatment and care (i.e., respiratory sufficiency; airway, circulatory, and nutritional support; treatment of secondary infections; and skin care) are essential.[25,28]

Plague

An infectious disease of animals and humans is caused by the bacterium *Yersinia pestis*. The vector for plague transmission is usually an infected rodent flea. Plague was responsible for the death of millions of people in England during the Middle Ages and is still found today in regions of the United States, primarily the Southwest (New Mexico, Arizona, Nevada, and California).[25]

Symptoms

- The most common symptom of plague is a swollen and tender lymph gland, accompanied by pain. The swollen gland is called a bubo. Bubonic plague should be suspected when a person develops a swollen gland, fever, chills, headache, and extreme exhaustion; and has a history of possible exposure to infected rodents, rabbits, or fleas. If left untreated, plague bacteria invade the bloodstream and rapidly spread throughout the body.[25]

- Once the lungs become affected, the bacterium causes the pneumonic form of plague. Pneumonic plague is a severe, often fatal, illness associated with high fever, chills, cough, hemoptysis, and respiratory distress/failure. If left untreated, the disease can progress rapidly to death. The respiratory form (pneumonic plague) is contagious and can be transmitted from human to human through respiratory and droplet transmission. Respiratory and contact isolation is required.[25,31,32]

The recommended prophylactic treatment for plague includes the following:

- First choice: Doxycycline, 2.5 mg/kg twice a day

- Second choice: Ciprofloxacin, 10 to 15 mg/kg twice a day

Prophylaxis should continue for seven days after the last known or suspected plague exposure or until exposure has been excluded.[25,28]

Smallpox

Smallpox, which is caused by the variola virus, is a highly contagious and sometimes fatal disease. Except for laboratory stockpiles, the virus that causes smallpox has been eliminated in the United States for years. Any confirmed case of smallpox in the United States is considered a public health emergency. During the early phases of the disease, the person will experience a high fever (101°F–104°F [38.6°C–40.3°C]), malaise, and head and body aches. As the rash begins to form around day four, the first blisters begin in the mouth and tongue. The rash quickly spreads to the face and arms and then to the legs, hands, and feet; finally, the rash will cover the entire body within 24 hours. These blisters are filled with a thick opaque fluid and have the characteristic dimple in the center. Around day nine, the blisters form into hard pustules, which scab over around day 15. These scabs will begin falling off and continue for about three weeks. The person is highly contagious until all scabs have fallen off.[25,33]

The rash associated with smallpox is distinguishable from chickenpox in that the rash associated with chickenpox is more centrally located (face and trunk) and the infected person will display various stages of the rash. The rash associated with smallpox is more distally located (face and extremities) and it is in one stage at a time.

Smallpox is spread by direct contact with infected body fluids or infected linens, bedding, or clothing. Contact isolation is required. Respiratory transmission is rare.

There are no pharmaceutical treatments for smallpox. Supportive treatment and care (i.e., respiratory sufficiency; airway, circulatory, and nutritional support; fever; and pain control), treatment of secondary infections, and skin care are essential. There is a smallpox vaccine that is available but offers no protection or therapeutic benefits to individuals four to seven days after exposure.[25,28]

Bombings/Explosives

The extent and pattern of injuries produced by an explosion are a direct result of several factors, including the amount and composition of the explosive material (i.e., shrapnel, loose materials, and radiological or biological contamination), the surrounding environment (e.g., enclosed space vs. open area), the distance between the victim and the blast, and any other environmental hazards.

No two events are identical, and the spectrum and extent of injuries produced vary widely. After an explosion in a confined space, such as a subway train, more casualties with primary blast injuries and lung damage would be expected, in addition to penetrating injuries from environmental projectiles. Explosions in confined spaces and structural collapse are associated with greater morbidity and mortality.[34]

Brief History:

- India, May 13, 2008: nine synchronized bombs, 63 dead and more than 200 injured.
- India, July 26, 2008: 21 bombs, 56 dead and 200 injured.
- Pakistan, September 2008: 40 dead and 200 wounded.
- Israel, April 2006: suicide bomber in a restaurant, nine dead and dozens injured.
- United Kingdom, July 7, 2005: four bombs, involving three trains and a bus, 52 dead and more than 700 injured.
- Spain, 2004: 10 detonations on four trains, 191 dead and more than 2000 injured.
- United States, 1995: Oklahoma City Bombing, 169 dead and more than 800 injured.
- United States, 1993: World Trade Center, six dead and 1042 injured.

There are four distinct categories of injury associated with bombing/explosions. The primary blast injury is the result of the blast wave or overpressure in the atmosphere. The secondary blast injury is caused by blunt or penetrating trauma associated with flying debris or structural collapse. Tertiary blast injuries are the result of blunt or penetrating trauma associated with the individual being thrown around, and quaternary blast injuries are associated with miscellaneous causes, such as heat, fire, crushing forces, asphyxia, or contamination. **Table 22-2** provides a brief overview of injuries associated with each blast injury category.

Primary Blast Injury

The most common injuries seen by a primary blast are the result of barotrauma.

- Pulmonary injuries (second most susceptible organ)
  - Pneumothorax
  - Hemothorax
  - Air embolism as the result of pulmonary disruption or edema
- Auditory injuries (the most susceptible organ)
  - Tympanic membrane rupture

- Abdominal injuries to gas-filled organs, resulting in perforation or hemorrhage
- Traumatic brain injury (concussions/contrecoup injuries) as the result of a pressure wave

Secondary Blast Injury

These injuries may be more common than the primary blast injury because the victim does not have to be in the immediate blast zone. The most common injuries associated with a secondary blast are the result of flying debris.[33] These injuries include the following: penetrating injuries as the result of explosive debris; imbedded shrapnel, such as nails or screws; amputated and projected human body parts; and surrounding structural or environmental debris (e.g., wood, steel, and glass).

Tertiary Blast Injury

These injuries are caused by the individual being thrown about the scene; the most common injuries are blunt trauma injuries, axial loading, fractures, impalement, and traumatic amputations.[34]

Quaternary Blast Injury

These injuries are caused by the destruction of the environment; the most common types of injuries are burns, crush injury, eye irritation/injury, and exacerbation of underlying health conditions, such as asthma or chronic obstructive pulmonary disease.[35]

General Laboratory Studies

Most patients injured by significant explosions should undergo urinalysis to check for occult blood. If the explosion occurred in an enclosed space or was accompanied by fire, carboxyhemoglobin and electrolytes should be tested to assess acid/base status. Pulse oximetry readings may be misleading in cases of carbon monoxide poisoning. When in doubt, apply 100% oxygen by a tight-fitting face mask until carbon monoxide levels can be measured.[35]

Victims of major trauma should undergo baseline hemoglobin determinations, cross matching for potential blood transfusion, and screening for disseminated intravascular coagulation (including prothrombin time/partial thromboplastin time, thrombin time, fibrogen and fibrogen split products, D-dimer, and serial complete blood cell count with platelets).

If the patient presents with significant crush injury, compartment syndrome, or severe burns, emergency nurses should be attentive to the possibility of rhabdomyolysis with resulting hyperkalemia and renal failure.[35]

General Imaging Studies

Chest radiographs should be performed on all patients who exhibit respiratory symptoms, have abnormal findings on auscultation, or have visible external signs of thoracic trauma. If significant abdominal pain is present, consider

Table 22-2 Mechanism of Blast Injury*

Category	Characteristics	Body Part Affected	Types of Injuries
Primary	Results from the impact of the overpressurization wave with body surfaces.	Gas filled structures are most susceptible (i.e., lungs, GI tract, and middle ear).	Blast lung (pulmonary barotrauma), TM rupture and middle ear damage, abdominal hemorrhage and perforation, globe (eye) rupture, and concussion (TBI without physical signs of head injury)
Secondary	Results from flying debris and bomb fragments.	Any body part may be affected.	Penetrating ballistic (fragmentation) or blunt injuries and eye penetration (can be occult)
Tertiary	Results from individuals being thrown by the blast wind.	Any body part may be affected.	Fracture and traumatic amputation and closed and open brain injury
Quaternary	All explosion-related injuries, illnesses, or diseases not the result of primary, secondary, or tertiary mechanisms (i.e., exacerbation or complications of existing conditions).	Any body part may be affected.	Burns (flash, partial, and full thickness); crush injuries; closed and open brain injuries; asthma; COPD; other breathing problems from dust, smoke, or toxic fumes; angina; hyperglycemia; and hypertension

Note: COPD indicates chronic obstructive pulmonary disease; GI, gastrointestinal; TBI, traumatic brain injury; TM, tympanic membrane.
*Data are taken from National Center for Injury Prevention and Control, Office of Noncommunicable Diseases, Injury and Environmental Health. (2006). *Explosions and blast injuries: A primer for clinicians*. Retrieved from http://www.bt.cdc.gov/masscasualties/explosions.asp

an immediate abdominal series (flat and upright films) or abdominal computed tomography (CT) to detect pneumoperitoneum from enteric rupture. Focused abdominal ultrasonography for trauma is a potentially useful tool for rapidly screening patients, especially in the setting of multiple seriously injured victims. A negative finding on a focused ultrasonographic examination for trauma is unreliable in the setting of penetrating trauma to the abdomen, flank, buttocks, or back; it should be followed up with a CT examination of the abdomen and pelvis.[34,35]

Specific Injuries

Blast Lung Injury

The term *blast lung* is typically used to describe a severe pulmonary contusion, hemorrhage, and/or edema, with direct alveolar and vascular complaints from primary blast injuries. It may be complicated by pneumothorax, hemothorax, or pulmonary emboli. Blast lung injury is present in less than 10% of all casualties seen at the scene but represents 30% to 60% of all admitted casualties. The incidence of blast lung injury increases in enclosed spaces as opposed to an open area explosion.[34,35]

Pulmonary contusion is one of the most common injuries from blunt thoracic trauma in pediatric patients. The injury may not be clinically apparent initially and should be suspected when abrasions, contusions, or rib fractures are present. A chest radiograph and CT are essential in diagnosis, especially when blast lung is suspected.[34]

Treatment

Treatment is focused on ventilatory support and restoration of lung function. High-flow oxygen and balanced fluid resuscitation should be initiated. Chest decompression may be necessary for hemothorax or pneumothorax. In severe cases, intubation and ventilatory support in an intensive care unit setting will be required.[34,35]

Recovery and Mental Health Challenges

The basic principles of disaster mental health begin with the central premise that the target population primarily consists of normal people who have been through an abnormally stressful disaster or emergency situation. Victims of disasters generally will not stop functioning, but they will react in fairly predictable ways based on factors such as age, maturity, degree of established coping mechanisms, and previous life experiences. By incorporating mental health professionals on response teams, various crisis intervention techniques, and outreach services can be instituted to quickly triage affected persons and provide brief counseling or referral for formal services, in an effort to return them to pre-disaster levels of functioning as quickly as possible.[36]

Young children's reactions are strongly influenced by caregiver reactions to the event. After a disaster or traumatic event, children may display age-specific reactions and coping mechanisms.[15] Caregivers should be educated about the possible behavioral changes and encouraged to seek professional advice or treatment for children affected by a disaster, especially those who have witnessed destruction, injury, or death.

A key action in mental health and recovery should be return to normalcy for the child and family. In alignment with *Maslow's Hierarchy of Needs: Psychology: The Search for Understanding*, after meeting the basic needs of food, water, and health, the child needs a safe and secure environment in the form of housing.[35] Routines, such as set meal, sleep, and productive times, should be established in congregate shelters or temporary housing locations. Returning to a sense of normalcy should continue by integration and reunion with family, friends, loved ones, and pets.[37] The resumption of school and school activities helps children reclaim their sense of confidence and self-esteem, allowing them to move on in their development. **Table 22-3** lists age-specific reactions commonly identified in children after a traumatic or disaster-related event.

Table 22-3 Reactions to Disaster/Traumatic Events by Age Groups*

Age Group of Children in Years		
< 5	**6–11**	**12–17**
May become immobile; may return to previous behaviors, such as thumb sucking, bedwetting, or fear of the dark; may cling to a parent or caregiver; crying or screaming; whimpering or trembling; and wandering about aimlessly	May isolate themselves or become quiet around friends, family, and teachers; may develop nightmares or other sleep problems; may become irritable or disruptive (i.e., outbursts of anger or fighting); may develop difficulty concentrating; may refuse to go to school or participate in previous activities; may develop somatic physical complaints or fears; and may become depressed or overwhelmed, with feelings of guilt	May experience flashbacks to the event; may avoid reminders of the event; may begin experimenting or abusing drugs, alcohol, or tobacco; may develop antisocial or risk-taking behaviors; may display disruptive, disrespectful, or destructive behavior; may develop somatic physical complaints or fears; may experience nightmares or other sleep problems; may experience feelings of isolation or confusion; and may exhibit signs of depression or suicidal thoughts

*Data are taken from Markenson and Reynolds.[17] Data are also taken from the following sources: (1) Hagan, J. (2005). Psychosocial implications of disaster or terrorism on children: A guide for the pediatrician: Clinical report. *Pediatrics, 116,* 787–795. (2) Norwood, A., Ursano, R., & Fullerton, C. (2000). Disaster psychiatry: Principles and practice. *Psychiatric Quarterly, 71,* 207–226. (3) US Department of Health and Human Services, Substance Abuse and Mental Health Services Administration, Center for Mental Health Services. (2010). *After a disaster: A guide for parents and teachers.* Retrieved from http://www.samhsa.gov (4) The Child Advocate. (2003). *Disaster help for parents and children.* Retrieved from http://childadvocate.net/disaster (5) Ursano, R., Fullerton, C., & McGaughey, B. (1994). *Trauma and disaster: Individual and community responses to trauma and disaster: The structure of human chaos* (pp. 3–27). Cambridge, England: Cambridge University Press. (6) World Health Organization. (1992). *Psychosocial consequences of disasters: Prevention and management.* Geneva, Switzerland: Division of Mental Health, World Health Organization.

Summary

In summary, in the event of a wide-scale disaster or mass casualty incident, practitioners with little or no pediatric experience may be called on to assume the role of primary or support treatment facilities. Future considerations in planning for pediatric disaster or mass casualty incidents should include properly sized equipment and the rapid availability of weight-based pharmaceuticals. Decontamination facilities should be designed to accommodate ambulatory and nonambulatory children. Additional support staff may be necessary to facilitate the flow of the pediatric patient through the decontamination line. Water temperature and pressure must have the ability to be regulated to prevent hypothermia and/or subsequent high-pressure injuries.

Specialty-trained response teams, well versed in the physical and psychological care of the pediatric patient, should be formed, trained, and drilled regularly. Mental health teams and family reunification teams are essential components in mitigating the psychological effects. Children's reactions to events outside the normal experience vary greatly based on age, experience, and social and developmental status. Children are also influenced by the reactions of caregivers around them. Providing psychological support to families and healthcare providers may help mitigate any long-term emotional or psychological effects.

Assistance with emergency response education and planning with schools, day-care centers, and after-school facilities should be included in any response plan. Minimal requirements should include guidelines for evacuation, "sheltering in place," notification of parents, and family reunification.

Case Studies

Case Study 1

It is the annual Children's Festival in the City Park. Attendance is expected to exceed 1,000 children and adults. It was noticed by attendees that some type of aerial spray was released at the scene. Attendees assumed it was mosquito spraying and paid no attention. Within minutes, victims begin arriving to your facility. You are assigned as the triage officer. How would you assign the following patients?

1. A 3-year-old with burning eyes, runny nose, and a dry cough. He is ambulatory and crying. Respirations are 26 breaths/minute. Pulse is 110 beats/minutes. He is inconsolable.

   ○ Red (Immediate)
   ○ Yellow (Delayed)
   ○ Green (Minor)
   ○ Black (Deceased or unsalvageable)

2. A 6-year-old, lying limp and quiet in her father's arms. Respirations are 40 breaths/minute. Pulse is 100 beats/minute. She is non-responsive.

   ○ Red (Immediate)
   ○ Yellow (Delayed)
   ○ Green (Minor)
   ○ Black (Deceased or unsalvageable)

3. A 2-year-old, with no spontaneous respirations. You open the airway and spontaneous respirations do not begin. The patient has a pulse rate of 70. You provide five rescue breaths and breathing does not return.

   ○ Red (Immediate)
   ○ Yellow (Delayed)
   ○ Green (Minor)
   ○ Black (Deceased or unsalvageable)

Answers to Case Study 1

1.   Green (Minor)
2.   Red (Immediate)
3.   Black (Deceased or unsalvageable)

Case Study 2

Forty children of various ages and their chaperones are riding in a bus on a field trip. The bus loses control, slams into a median, and then rolls over. How would you categorize the following patients?

1. A preschool-aged boy is found lying on the roadway 10 feet from the bus. Respiratory rate is 10 breaths/min. He has good distal pulses and groans and pulls away from painful stimuli.

   ○ Red (Immediate)
   ○ Yellow (Delayed)
   ○ Green (Minor)
   ○ Black (Deceased or unsalvageable)

2. A school-aged girl crawls out of the wreckage. She is able to stand and walk towards you, crying. Her jacket and shirt are torn, and she has no obvious signs of bleeding.

   ○ Red (Immediate)
   ○ Yellow (Delayed)
   ○ Green (Minor)
   ○ Black (Deceased or unsalvageable)

3. A toddler lies among the wreckage. His lower body is trapped under a seat inside the bus. Respiratory rate is 50 breaths/minute. He has a palpable distal pulse and withdraws from painful stimuli.

   ○ Red (Immediate)
   ○ Yellow (Delayed)
   ○ Green (Minor)
   ○ Black (Deceased or unsalvageable)

4. A toddler is found outside the bus, lying on the ground. She is apneic and remains apneic despite a jaw thrust to open her airway. A faint distal pulse is palpated.

   ○ Red (Immediate)
   ○ Yellow (Delayed)
   ○ Green (Minor)
   ○ Black (Deceased or unsalvageable)

Answers to Case Study 2

1.   Red (Immediate)
2.   Green (Minor)
3.   Red (Immediate)
4.   Black (Deceased or unsalvageable)

References

1. Lindell, M., Prater, C., & Perry, R. (2006). *Fundamentals of emergency management.* Retrieved from http://training.fema.gov/EMIWeb/edu/fem.asp

2. Alexander, D. (2002). *Principles of emergency planning and management.* Harpenden, England: Terra Publishing.

3. US Department of Health and Human Services. (2009). *Federal interagency forum on child and family statistics: ChildStats.* Retrieved from http://childstats.gov

4. National Advisory Committee on Children and Terrorism. (2003). *Recommendations to the Secretary.* Washington, DC: US Department of Health and Human Services.

5. O'Brien, J. (2006). *Remembering Beslan school two years on: UNICEF–Russian Federation.* Retrieved from http://UNICEF.org/infobycountry/Russia_35565.html

6. Chivers, C. J., & Myers, S. (2004, September 2). Insurgents seize school in Russia and hold scores. *The New York Times.*

7. Abramson, D., Redlener, I., Stehling-Ariza, T., & Fuller, E. (2007). *The legacy of Katrina's children: Estimating the numbers of at-risk children in the Gulf Coast states of Louisiana and Mississippi.* New York, NY: Columbia University Mailman School of Public Health National Center for Disaster Preparedness.

8. Broughton, E. (2005). The Bhopal disaster and its aftermath: A review. *Environmental Health, 4,* 6.

9. Kurzman, D. (1987). *A killing wind: Inside Union Carbide and the Bhopal catastrophe.* New York, NY: McGraw-Hill.

10. Michel, L., & Herbeck, D. (2001). *American terrorist* (p. 220). New York, NY: Harper Collins Publishers.

11. Centers for Disease Control and Prevention. (2010). *2009 H1N1 flu: Situation update.* Retrieved from http://www.cdc.gov/h1n1/flu/

12. Stamell, E. F., Foltin, G. L., & Nadler, E. P. (2009). Lessons learned for pediatric disaster preparedness from September 11, 2001: New York City trauma centers. *Journal of Trauma, 67* (suppl.), S84–S87.

13. Ginter, P. M., Wingate, M. S., Rucks, A. C., Vásconez, R. D., McCormick, L. C., Baldwin, S., & Fargason, C. A. (2006). Creating a regional pediatric medical disaster preparedness network: imperative and issues. *Maternal Child Health Journal, 10,* 391–396.

14. Markenson, D., & Redlener, I. (2003). *Executive summary: Pediatric preparedness for disasters and terrorism—A national consensus conference.* Retrieved from http://www.hhs.gov/od/documents/cshcn%5B1%5D.colconf.emprep.2003.pdf

15. American Academy of Pediatrics. (2004, July). *The youngest victims: Disaster preparedness to meet children's needs.* Retrieved from http://www.aap.org/terrorism

16. Gausche-Hill, M. (2009). Pediatric disaster preparedness: Are we really prepared? *Journal of Trauma, 67* (suppl.), S73–S76.

17. Markenson, D., Reynolds, S., American Academy of Pediatrics Committee on Pediatric Emergency Medicine; & Task Force on Terrorism. (2006). The pediatrician and disaster preparedness. *Pediatrics, 117,* e340–e362.

18. Romig, L. (2009). *JumpSTART pediatric MCI triage tools.* Retrieved from http://www.jumpstarttriage.com

19. Freyberg, C. W., Arquilla, B., Fertel, B. S., Tunik, M. G., Cooper, A., Heon, D., ... Foltin, G. (2008). Disaster preparedness: Hospital decontamination and the pediatric patient—Guidelines for hospitals and emergency planners. *Prehospital and Disaster Medicine, 23,* 166–173.

20. Emergency Nurses Association. (2007). *Trauma nursing core course provider manual* (6th ed.). Des Plaines, IL: Author.

21. Haber, L. F. (1986). *The poisonous cloud: Chemical warfare in the first world war.* Oxford, England: Oxford University Press.

22. CBWinfo. (2010). *Factsheets on chemical and biological warfare agents.* Retrieved from http://www.cbwinfo.com

23. Rega, P. (2001). *History of bioterrorism: A chronological history of bioterrorism and biowarfare throughout the ages: The biological terrorism response manual.* Maumee, OH: MASCAP.

24. Croddy, E. (2002). *Chemical and biological warfare: A comprehensive survey for the concerned citizen.* New York, NY: Springer.

25. Centers for Disease Control and Prevention. (2009). *Emergency preparedness and response: Bioterrorism.* Retrieved from http://emergency.cdc.gov/agent/botulism/

26. U.S. Army Medical Research Institute of Chemical Defense. (1999). *Medical management of chemical casualties handbook* (3rd ed.) Aberdeen Proving Ground, MD: International Medical Publishing.

27. Phillips, M. (2005). Bioterrorism: A brief history. *Northeast Florida Medicine Journal, 56,* 32–35.

28. World Health Organization. (2010). *Botulism* [fact sheet No. 270]. Retrieved from http://www.who.int/mediacentre/factsheets/fs270/en/

29. Feigin, R. D., Cherry, J. D., Demmler, G. J., & Kaplan, S. L. (2004). *Infant botulism: Textbook of pediatric infectious diseases* (5th ed., pp. 1758–1766). Philadelphia, PA: WB Saunders.

30. Passaro, D. J., Werner, S. B., McGee, J., Mac Kenzie, W. R., & Vugia, D. J. (1998). Wound botulism associated with black tar heroin among injecting drug users. *JAMA: The Journal of the American Medical Association, 279,* 859–863.

31. Pickering, L. K., Baker, C. J., Long, S. S., & McMillan, J. A. (2006). *Plague: Report of the Committee on Infectious Diseases* (27th ed., pp. 523–525). Elk Grove Village, IL: American Academy of Pediatrics.

References *continued*

32. World Health Organization. (2000). *Plague: WHO report on global surveillance of epidemic-prone infectious diseases.* Retrieved from http://www.who.int/csr/resources/publications/surveillance/plague/pdf

33. Henderson, D. A., Inglesby, T. V., Bartlett, J. G., Ascher, M. S., Eitzen, E., Jahrling, P. B., ... Tonat, K. (1999). Smallpox as a biological weapon: medical and public health management Working Group on Civilian Biodefense. *JAMA: The Journal of the American Medical Association, 281,* 2127–2137.

34. Centers for Disease Control and Prevention. (2006). *Bombings: Injury patterns and care.* Retrieved from http://www.bt.cdc.gov/masscasualties/bombings_injurycare.asp

35. Avidan, V., Hersch, M., & Armon, Y. (2005). Blast lung injury: Clinical manifestations, treatment, and outcome. *American Journal of Surgery, 190,* 927–931.

36. Weaver, J. D. (1999). *Innovations in clinical practice: A source book* (vol. 17). Sarasota, FL: Professional Resource Press.

37. Simons, J. A., Irwin, D. B., & Drinnien, B. A. (1987). *Maslow's hierarchy of needs: Psychology: The search for understanding.* New York, NY: West Publishing Co.

Chapter 23 | Stabilization and Transport

Paul C. Boackle, BSN, RN, CCRN, CEN, CFRN, CPEN, CTRN

Objectives

On completion of this chapter, the learner should be able to do the following:

- Identify pediatric conditions that may require specialized or a higher level of care.

- Recognize national, state, and/or provincial laws and regulations in place to protect patients and to facilitate improvement of outcomes and transport for pediatric patients with complex illnesses and injuries.

- Examine the risks and benefits of pediatric patient transport.

- List characteristics of transport modes and qualifications of transport team members.

Introduction

Patients in the pediatric population require a specialized skill set and, in many cases, a facility that specializes in pediatric care (many facilities worldwide do not possess these features). Adolescents and children compose 21% of all emergency department visits annually.[1] Management of the critically ill pediatric patient is best performed by facilities with comprehensive knowledge and experience with pediatric patients.[2] When the components for the safe management of the pediatric patient are unavailable, the patient must be transferred to an appropriate facility. This was the reason for regionalization of pediatric and critical care. With the regionalization of care, there has been a growth in interfacility transport programs, allowing for greater access to tertiary medical care.[3]

In 2007, the Institute of Medicine conducted a study on trends and problems in emergency care. The focus of the study *Growing Pains* was pediatric emergency care. The findings of this study reinforced the need for improvement in transfers, training, and evidence-based pediatric care.[4]

Laws and Regulations

Consolidated Omnibus Budget Reconciliation Act

Before 1986, many emergency departments in the United States refused to care for indigent patients. In 1986, the Consolidated Omnibus Budget Reconciliation Act was passed; this act addressed the responsibility of any emergency department that participated in Medicare to provide a medical screening examination. If any patient presents with an emergency condition, the facility must provide treatment and stabilization within its capabilities. When the facility has used its skill and resources, that facility may then transfer the patient to another facility with additional capabilities and resources. This transfer must be requested by the sending care provider, the patient, or the patient's guardian. Medical necessity documentation is originated by the sending medical provider (physician or nurse practitioner). This documentation outlines the risks and benefits associated with a transfer to another facility; also, the fact that the patient received and understood these risks and benefits is verified.

In 1994, a section of the Consolidated Omnibus Budget Reconciliation Act entitled the Emergency Medical Treatment and Active Labor Act (EMTALA) was updated.[5-7] The Emergency Medical Treatment and Active Labor Act clarified two additional circumstances that were also appropriate for patient transfer: (1) the physician or referring provider determines that the benefits of the transfer outweigh the risks of not transferring the patient and (2) the patient or guardian requests the transfer.

Indications for Transport

Despite the progress that has been made in the care of the pediatric patient, the transport of these critically ill patients remains a challenge because of the limited resources available. In a study by Orr et al.,[3] 1,085 patients were transported to a children's hospital after a request for a specialized team was made: 94% were transferred by the specialized transport team, and 6% were transported by nonspecialized teams. Among the patients transported by the nonspecialized teams, "there were significantly more major interventions, unplanned events, and deaths."[3] This study noted that when interfacility transport was performed with the specialized team there were "improved survival rates and fewer unplanned events."[3] Gausche et al.[2] noted that "paramedics were less confident in assessing vital signs in children less than two years of age." In this same study, children younger than 14 years were undertreated when compared with their adult counterparts.[3]

Why do nonspecialized teams have worse outcomes? Numerous studies have shown that increased familiarity with specialized populations improves the ability of the care provider to provide appropriate care, with improved outcomes. Babl et al.[8] reported that even in a busy advanced life support service, there was a lack of familiarity with pediatric procedures and equipment, leading to errors in both assessment and treatment. That is why teams that only transport children have a greater familiarity with this population and, therefore, better outcomes.

Teams performing transports for multiple age groups have proved to provide exceptional care, provided they received pediatric-specific training on equipment and care.

When treating a pediatric patient who potentially needs to be transferred to another facility, it is helpful to follow guidelines to confirm the benefit of transfer.

- Is this patient's condition likely to deteriorate and require emergent transport?
- Does this facility possess the resources to provide the standard of care for this pediatric patient?

- ° Nurse: skill level and resources (i.e., Emergency Nursing Pediatric Course and Pediatric Advanced Life Support)
- ° Physician, nurse practitioner, or physician assistant: skill level and resource specialists
  - Pediatrician
  - Pediatric Intensivist
  - Surgeon (trauma or pediatric)
  - Orthopedist
  - Neurosurgeon or neurologist
- ° Ancillary staff, such as the following:
  - Radiology
  - Respiratory therapy
- ° Appropriate pediatric-specific equipment

Transfer Requirements

Once the transfer decision has been made and the provisions regarding consent have been met, it is necessary to meet some additional requirements. These additional requirements include the following:

- The receiving facility must have adequate bed space/staff to care for patients
- The receiving physician has agreed to accept the patient being transferred
- Pertinent medical records related to this episode of care and previous history must accompany patient to the receiving facility
- Personnel with appropriate training, equipment, and an appropriate vehicle to safely transfer the patient
  - ° The type of equipment and level of training will depend on the acuity of the patient

In addition to the previous requirements involved with transport, other questions need to be addressed before transfer:

- Does our facility have a transfer agreement with the facility we are transferring to?
- Are the personnel transferring the patient adequately trained to transport this patient?
- What is the capability of the mode of transport?
- Weather or road conditions? Either of these can affect the choice of transport.

Table 23-1 provides a comparison of the personnel and modes of transport.

Table 23-1 Comparison of Types of Personnel and Modes of Transport

Personnel Variable	Advantage	Disadvantage
Local EMS	Readily available	Limited training experience with pediatrics
BLS crew	Direct transport to another facility	Minimal medical care capabilities and basic measures only
ALS crew	Direct transport to another facility	Increased medical training, limited pediatric expertise, and limited resources
Adult critical care team	Critical care experience	Limited or no pediatric experience
Pediatric critical care team	Pediatric intensive care experience and initiate pediatric critical care while en route	May not be readily available (may take one hour to get to a transferring facility)

Mode of Transport Variable	Advantage	Disadvantage
Ground transport	Availability Space in the vehicle Can travel in any weather conditions Ability to carry several prehospital personnel Ability to carry more equipment Family may accompany child in vehicle	Transport can take up to three times longer by ground than by air Traffic and road conditions can interfere with transport Loss of vehicle to community
Air transport	Saves time Improved communication ability Heightened emergency response at receiving facility because of experience with helicopter transport patients Continued availability of ground EMS resources within the referral area	Weather restrictions Lack of availability Cost Physiological impact Noise Vibrations Temperature changes Gas expansion with altitude Fear of flying Space and weight restrictions

Note: ALS indicates advanced life support; BLS, basic life support; EMS, emergency medical services.

Stabilization Before Transfer

Before transport, the sending caregivers should ensure that the patient has been prepared and stabilized as much as possible with the resources available. This process should involve the systematic completion of a primary assessment with the correction of any and all life-threatening conditions. Examples include the intubation of patients who are unable to protect their airway. Those patients with compromised breathing might need a chest tube placed before the transport team's arrival. Trauma patients should receive two large-caliber appropriate intravenous catheters. Basic intravenous fluid resuscitation with isotonic fluids should also be initiated before transport. A baseline neurological assessment is needed, including pupil assessment and best score on the AVPU scale (alert, voice, pain, unresponsive). Trauma patients who need immobilization or splinting should be properly immobilized and secured before the arrival of the transport team. Medical conditions requiring infusions should be initiated whenever possible. Medications should be administered for management of pain and anxiety during transport.

On arrival, the transport team will also assess the patient to ensure that all immediate needs are addressed, along with anticipation of any changes in condition that may occur during transport. These priorities may involve the following: inserting a gastric tube to decompress the stomach, preparing for additional interventions based on air physiology (i.e., chest tube for a small pneumothorax), securing intravenous lines, splinting suspected fractures, and facilitating family presence. These priorities ensure the safe transport of all patients.

Summary

The transfer of the pediatric patient is a complex and cooperative effort. It requires integrated communication between sending and receiving staff members, as well as transport team members. From the laws and regulations, to the mode of transportation, to the type of injury or illness, many details play a role in the process that becomes stabilization and transport.

References

1. Centers for Disease Control and Prevention. (2010). *Emergency department visits*. Retrieved from http://www.cdc.gov/nchs/FASTATS/ervisits.htm

2. Gausche, M., Henderson, D. P., & Seidel, J. S. (1990). Vital signs as part of the prehospital assessment of the pediatric patient: a survey of paramedics. *Annals of Emergency Medicine, 19,* 173–178.

3. Orr, R. A., Felmet, K. A., Han, Y., McCloskey, A., Dragotta, M. A., Bills, D. M., … Watson, R. S. (2009). Pediatric specialized transport teams are associated with improved outcomes. *Pediatrics, 124,* 40–48.

4. Thomas, D. O., & Bernardo, L. M. (Eds.). (2009) *Core curriculum for pediatric emergency nursing* (2nd ed., pp. 3–4). Des Plaines, IL: Emergency Nurses Association.

5. *Emergency medical treatment and active labor act.* (n.d.). Retrieved from http://library.findlaw.com/2001/Jan/1/126650.html

6. *Emergency medical treatment and active labor act.* (n.d.). Retrieved from http://www.medlaw.com/healthlaw/EMTALA/statute/emergency-medical-treatme.shtml

7. *Emergency medical treatment and active labor act.* (n.d.). Retrieved from http://www.cms.gov/EMTALA

8. Babl, F. E., Vinci, R. J., Baucherner, H., & Mottley, L. (2001). Pediatric pre-hospital advanced life support care in a urban setting. *Pediatric Emergency Care, 17,* 5–9.

Management of the Ill or Injured Pediatric Patient Skill Station

Principles of Pediatric Initial Assessment and Interventions

The care of the ill or injured pediatric patient is based on performance of systematic assessment and initiation of the appropriate interventions. The management priorities are based on the life-threatening compromises found in the primary assessment, other abnormalities found during the secondary assessment, the pediatric patient's age, and the resources available for providing care.

The primary assessment consists of assessment of the airway with cervical spine stabilization or maintenance of spinal stabilization when trauma is suspected, breathing, circulation, disability or neurological status, and exposure with environmental control. Life-threatening conditions are identified and treated before the assessment continues. The secondary assessment is a systematic approach to identifying additional problems and determining priorities of care.

Simultaneous assessment, diagnosis, and intervention may be required for the pediatric patient who is critically ill or injured. The priorities of intervention will depend on the complexity of the pediatric patient's condition and the availability and qualification of the emergency care providers. Those conditions that have the greatest potential to compromise the airway, breathing, circulation, and/ or disability are given the highest priority.

The pediatric patient must be re-evaluated after any interventions that have an immediate effect on him or her to determine their effectiveness. The evaluation and ongoing assessment begin at the completion of the secondary assessment. These include primary reassessment and a re-evaluation of vital signs.

The systematic assessment can be remembered as follows:

A = Airway with simultaneous cervical spine stabilization

B = Breathing

C = Circulation

D = Disability—brief neurological assessment

E = Exposure and environmental control

F = Full set of vital signs, focused adjuncts, and family presence

G = Give comfort measures

H = Head-to-toe assessment and history

I = Inspect posterior surfaces

The template for Management of the Ill or Injured Pediatric Patient provides guidelines for conducting the primary and secondary assessments and identifying the appropriate interventions.

Summary

During evaluation, the learner must demonstrate all critical steps designated with one (*) or two (**) asterisks and 70% of the total number of points. Each learner will be evaluated using a different scenario. Therefore, concentrate on understanding the principles of the station and not memorizing the specific case scenarios. Learners will not be evaluated on the ability to perform spinal stabilization during this station.

Certain critical steps must be demonstrated or described in order during the primary assessment. These are designated with ** on the evaluation form. The total number of critical steps (**) in any scenario is 6 to 8. Critical steps designated with ** may include:

• Assessing airway patency.

- Identifying one appropriate airway intervention.
- Assessing breathing effectiveness.
- Identifying one appropriate intervention for ineffective breathing.
- Assess perfusion status.
- Stating one appropriate intervention for ineffective circulation.
- Assessing the level of consciousness (AVPU).

Additional critical steps that must be demonstrated or described during the remainder of the station are designated with an asterisk (*) on the evaluation form. All of these steps must also be performed to successfully complete the station:

- States one measure to prevent heat loss.
- Identifies appropriate diagnostic studies and interventions.
- Identifies appropriate evaluation and ongoing assessment.

At the end of the primary and secondary assessments, the learner will be asked the following three questions:

- What additional diagnostic studies or interventions may be completed? If the learner has identified any appropriate diagnostic studies or interventions as he or she progressed through the primary and secondary assessments these will be counted toward the total of five that is necessary to complete this step.

- What is the evaluation and ongoing assessment of this patient? At a minimum, the learner should identify the need to reassess the components of the primary assessment and vital signs. In addition, the learner should identify the need to reassess the additional problems/injuries found during the secondary assessment.

- Is there anything that the learner would like to add or revise related to the assessment of this patient? Although the learner may not add to or revise any of the ** steps, it does allow the learner to identify additional components of the secondary assessment criteria or interventions that may have been overlooked.

Management of the Ill or Injured Pediatric Patient Template

Primary Assessment

Assessment	Potential Interventions
Determines patient's level of consciousness	Positions the patient **AND** demonstrates manually opening the airway while considering spinal stabilization

A = Airway

Assess at least three of the following (**): • Vocalization • Tongue obstruction • Loose teeth or foreign objects • Vomitus, blood, or secretions • Edema • Preferred posture • Drooling • Dysphagia • Abnormal airway sounds	Must identify at least one of the following interventions based on needs identified by the assessment (**): • Open the airway with jaw thrust or chin lift • Repositions head to neutral position • Suction • Remove foreign objects • An oropharyngeal/nasopharyngeal airway • Prepare for endotracheal intubation/rapid sequence intubation • Prepare for needle or surgical cricothyroidotomy

B = Breathing

Assess at least three of the following (**):
• Level of consciousness
• Spontaneous respirations
• Rate and depth of respirations
• Symmetric chest rise and fall
• Presence and quality of breath sounds
• Skin color
• Work of breathing (Assess at least three of the following)
  ◦ Nasal flaring
  ◦ Retractions
  ◦ Head bobbing
  ◦ Expiratory grunting
  ◦ Accessory muscle use
	Must identify at least one of the following interventions based on needs identified by the assessment (**):
	• Maintain position of comfort
	• Provide supplemental oxygen
	• Provide bag-mask ventilation
	  ◦ Reassessment of breathing effectiveness should occur prior to proceeding with primary assessment (**)
	• Prepare for endotracheal intubation/rapid sequence intubation
	  ◦ Assessment of tube placement should be done prior to proceeding with primary assessment (**)
	  ◦ Insert gastric tube to reduce abdominal distention

C = Circulation

Assess at least two of the following (**): • Central **AND** peripheral pulse rate and quality • Skin color **AND** temperature • Capillary refill • Jugular vein distention and tracheal position in the trauma patient	Must identify at least one of the following interventions based on needs identified by the assessment (**): • Perform cardiopulmonary resuscitation and advanced life-support measures • Control any obvious bleeding • Prepare for defibrillation/synchronized cardioversion • Obtain intravenous or intraosseous access • Administer 20 mL/kg fluid bolus of isotonic crystalloid solution • Administer medications • Administer blood or blood products • Correct electrolyte and acid-base imbalance • Prepare for needle thoracentesis

D = Disability

• Level of consciousness (AVPU)(**) • Pupils	• Perform further investigation during secondary assessment • Administer pharmacological therapy

Primary Assessment

E = Exposure and Environmental Control

- Obvious skin abnormalities
- Sources of heat loss

Must identify at least one of the following (*):
- Apply warm blankets
- Provide overhead warming light
- Provide radiant warmer or approved warning device
- Maintain warm ambient environment
- Increase room temperature as needed
- Administer warm intravenous fluids
- Administer warm humidified oxygen

Secondary Assessment

F = Full Set of Vital Signs

- Heart rate
- Respiratory rate
- Blood pressure
- Oxygen saturation (SpO2)
- Temperature
- Weight (kg)

- Obtain a weight
  - Use a scale for a measured weight
  - Estimate a weight using a length-based resuscitation tape (e.g., Broselow tape)

F = Family Presence

- Identification of family members and their relationship to the child
- Needs of the family
- Need for additional support and desire to be in resuscitation room

- Facilitate and support family involvement
- Assign healthcare professional to liaison with family and provide explanation of procedures, plan of treatment
- Assign a staff member to provide family support

F = Focused Adjuncts

- Place on dynamic cardiopulmonary monitor
- Obtain a bedside glucose reading or serum blood glucose
- Insert a gastric tube if indicated, if there are no contraindications and if not already done with endotracheal intubation
- Insert a urinary catheter if indicated and if not contraindicated
- Obtain blood samples to send to the laboratory for analysis

G = Give Comfort Measures

- Presence and level of pain

- Facility family presence for support of the child
- Initiate pain management measures
  - Use age-appropriate nonpharmacological methods to facilitate coping
  - Administer analgesics and other appropriate medications
  - Initiate physical measures (splints, dressing, ice)

H = Head-to-Toe Assessment

- Head-to-toe assessment using inspection, palpation, and auscultation techniques for signs and symptoms of illness or injury such as rashes, lesions, petechiae, edema, ecchymosis, or tenderness
- Reassessment of airway, breathing, and circulation status once head-to-toe assessment is completed

- Initiate appropriate interventions based on findings

Primary Assessment

H = History

- MIVT
- Complete history (CIAMPEDS)
- Focused history
- Social history
- Family history

- Initiate social service consult as needed

I = Inspect Posterior Surfaces

- Inspect and palpate posterior surfaces for signs and symptoms of illness or injury such as rashes, lesions, petechiae, edema, ecchymosis, or tenderness

- Logroll patient to maintain airway patency and spinal alignment

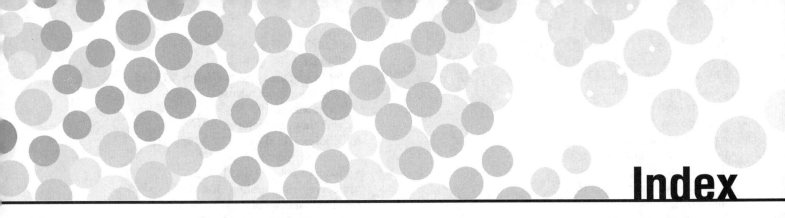

Note: Page numbers followed by t indicate information in tables or boxes.

G

Gag reflex, 134
Gamma-hydroxybutyrate, 354
Gamma-hydroxybutyric acid, 216
Gang violence, 13, 207
Garlic application, 345
Gastric decontamination, 299–300
Gastric lavage, 299
Gastric tubes
    assessing need for, 71
    positioning children for insertion, 102–3, 104
    with respiratory distress, 135
    with traumatic injuries, 268, 269
Gastroenteritis, 151
Gastroesophageal reflux, 167
Gastrointestinal anthrax infection, 374
Gastrointestinal system
    common disorders, 154–56
    decontamination procedures, 299–300, 312
    in neonates, 174–75
    shock effects, 229, 230t
Gastronomy tube placement, 103
General appearance, assessing, 74
General hospitals, 11
Generalized cold emergencies, 331
Genitalia
    abuse signs, 351, 353, 354
    acute scrotal pain, 163–66
    initial assessments, 76
    in neonates, 175
    self-awareness of, 353
    sexually transmitted infections, 218, 219t–20t
Genital warts, 220t
Genitourinary disorders, 161–63
Genitourinary system in neonates, 175
Gentamicin, 193
Georgetown University National Center for Cultural Competence, 27t
German measles, 150t
Glasgow Coma Scale, 74, 75t, 268, 271
Glipizide, 311
Glucagon, 311
Glucagon hydrochloride, 300t
Glucose-6-phosphate dehydrogenase deficiency, 193
Glucose levels in neonates, 176–77, 183. *See also* Laboratory studies
Glucose testing, 157
Glucose therapy, 238–39, 311
Glucotrol, 311
Glutaricaciduria type 1, 346t
Glycogen stores, 176–77
Glycosuria, 157
Gonorrhea, 219t
Grasping reflex, 34, 176t
Greata, 345
Greater saphenous veins, 124
Greenstick fractures, 282
Grief care for families, 361

Groshong catheters, 128
Gross, Samuel David, 227
Ground transport, 385t
Growing Pains study, 383
Growth defined, 30
Growth in neonates, 177–78
Growth plates, 279, 282, 283
Grunting, 134
Gulf Coast hurricane (2005), 367

H

H1N1 deaths, 367
H1N1 immunization, 16
Hallucinogenic amphetamines, 312
Hallucinogenic drug use, 17. *See also* Substance abuse
Halo sign, 276
Hand, veins of, 125
Hand-foot-and-mouth disease, 150t
Hand-foot syndrome, 160
Hand washing, 33
Hanging, suicide by, 213
Hanging injuries, 267
Head and brain trauma
    assessment and interventions, 275–79
    from bicycle crashes, 265
    from explosions, 377
    mechanisms of injury, 275
    in motor vehicle crashes, 263
    pediatric risks, 32t, 262, 275
    in sports, 266–67
    in suspected abuse cases, 351
Head bobbing, 134
Head size
    injury risk and, 32t, 262, 275
    in neonates, 176
Heads Up tool kit, 278
Head-to-toe assessment, 74–77
Health care services, 11–12, 14
Health promotion instructions
    about obesity, 42, 42t
    for adolescents, 40, 222
    following traumatic injuries, 284–85
    general considerations, 33
    for neonates and infants, 35, 198–99
    for preschoolers, 37
    for respiratory problems, 145
    for school-aged children, 39
    for toddlers, 36
Health promotion resources, 44t
Health Resources and Services Administration, 314t
Healthy Children, 44t
Hearing assessment, 290
Heart blocks, 248t
Heart disease in neonates, 195–96, 197t
Heart rate
    in children, 31t
    factors affecting, 71t

Oxygen challenge test, 195
Oxygen saturation monitoring, 65. *See also* Pulse oximetry

P

Pacifiers, 199
Pain
    age-related perceptions of, 46t–47t
    factors affecting, 83
    fallacies and facts, 84t
    impact on acuity rating decisions, 57
    physiology of, 84–85
    types, 84
    typical responses, 85–86
Pain assessment
    during initial assessments, 71–72
    in neonates, 177
    pediatric scales, 86–87, 88t
    suggested general approach, 33
    typical responses, 85–86
Pain management. *See also* Sedation
    common interventions, 87–91
    common procedures requiring, 106, 107t
    discharge education, 91
Pallor in neonates, 174, 181t, 189
Palmar water loss, 85
Pancreas, 229
Panic attacks, 320
Papoose Boards, 100
Papules, 150t
Paradoxical respirations, 65, 134
Parenting resources, 33
Parents, 16, 26–27. *See also* Caregivers; Families
Paresthesias, 283
Parkland formula, 273
Parlodel, 324
Paroxetine, 305
Partial seizures, 153t
Partnership for a Drug-Free America, 314t
Passy-Muir speaking valves, 143, 144
Patent ductus arteriosus, 246t
Paxil, 305
Paylooah, 345
Peak expiratory flow metering, 138, 140
Pedestrian injuries, 264–65
Pediatric Advanced Life Support (PALS) course, 1
Pediatric assessment triangle (PAT), 52, 54, 74
Pediatric Coma Scale, 74, 75t
Pediatric critical care team transport, 385t
Pediatric emergency care
    CDC data, 11
    current shortcomings, 1
    general approach guidelines, 30–33
    guidelines, 6–9
    history, 1–2
    nurses' role, 3
Pediatric nurse coordinators, 2, 6

Pediatric patients
    age group characteristics, 33–40
    defining, 13, 19–20
    emergency department guidelines, 6–9
    general approach guidelines, 6–9, 30–33
Pediatric physician coordinators, 6
Pediatrics in Practice, 44t
Pediatric trauma centers, 261
Pediatric Trauma Score, 271
Pediatric trays, 9
Pelvic inflammatory disorder, 219t
Pelvis, initial assessments, 76
Penetrating injuries, 267, 377. *See also* Impaled objects
Penis, in neonates, 175
Pentobarbital sodium, 93t, 111t
Pericardial tamponade, 281
Pericardiocentesis, 281
Periodic breathing in neonates, 173
Periorbital ecchymosis, 74
Peripherally inserted central catheters, 128–29
Peripheral vascular access, 124–26
Persistent pulmonary hypertension of the newborn, 172
Pertussis, 13, 142
Petechiae, 150t, 229
Pharmacokinetics, 115–16
Pharmacological interventions for pain management, 90–91, 105–10
Pharming, 211
Phencyclidine, 211
Phenylephrine, 312
Phobias, 353
Phosgene, 372–73
Phototherapy, 194, 195
Physical abuse
    conditions mistaken for, 344–45, 346t
    from dating partners, 214–16
    focused assessment, 345–50
    ongoing assessment and health promotion, 355
    overview, 343–44
    recent New Zealand statistics, 19
    recent Portuguese statistics, 21
    risk factors, 345, 346t
    selected types, 350–55
    triage assessment, 57–58
Physical assault, 12, 16
Physical comfort measures. *See* Comfort measures
Physical neglect, 344
Physical signs of stress, 362t
Physician coordinators for pediatric emergency care, 6
Physicians, 6
Physiological monitoring, during initial assessments, 71
Physostigmine salicylate, 300t
Phytophotodermatitis, 346t
PID, 219t
Piercings, 221
Pirbuterol, 139t
Pit vipers, 337–38
Plague, 375–76

Work of breathing
    initial assessments, 65
    respiratory distress symptoms, 134
    respiratory failure and, 133
    triage assessment, 54
World Trade Center attacks, 366, 367
Wound botulism, 375

X

Xanax, 212, 305

Y

Yersinia pestis, 375
Youth violence, 207–8

Z

Zidovudine, 185
Zoloft, 305
Zones of decontamination, 371
Zyprexa, 324